Blood

Pig-crowds in successive, screaming pens
We still to greedy drinking, trough by trough
Tusk-heavy boars, fat mud-beslabbered sows:
Gahn, let him drink you slut, you've had enough
~~Laughing~~ and grave by turns, in milky boots
We stand and yarn, and whet our butcher's knife,
Sling cobs of corn — hey, careful of his nuts!
It's made you cruel, all that gay city life...

In paper spills, we roll coarse, sweet tobacco
That's him down there, the one we'll have to catch
That little Berkshire with the pointy ears.
I call him Georgie. Here, you got a match?

The shadow of a cloud moves down the ridge,
On summer hills, a patch of autumn light
My cousin sheathes in dirt his priestly knife.
They say pigs see the wind. You think that's right?

I couldn't say. It sounds like a good motto.
I know some poets — Yah! get back, you sods.
Let him drink his fill: it's his last feed
He'll get some peaches after. Hell, what odds?

I'm sentimental — 'course, I know you're not.
~~Beyond~~ the circle of my jabbing stick
Excited mobbing pigs ~~old~~ mindless eyes
Peer at our favourite munching, and the thick

LES MURRAY

LES MURRAY
A LIFE IN PROGRESS

PETER F. ALEXANDER

OXFORD
UNIVERSITY PRESS
253 Normanby Road, South Melbourne, Victoria, Australia 3205

Oxford University Press is a department of the University of Oxford.
It furthers the University's objective of excellence in research,
scholarship and education by publishing.

Oxford New York

Athens Auckland Bangkok Bogotá Buenos Aires Calcutta
Cape Town Chennai Dar es Salaam Delhi Florence Hong Kong Istanbul
Karachi Kuala Lumpur Madrid Melbourne Mexico City Mumbai Nairobi Paris
Port Moresby São Paulo Singapore Shanghai Taipei Tokyo Toronto Warsaw

with associated companies in Berlin Ibadan

OXFORD is a registered trade mark of Oxford University Press
in the UK and certain other countries

© Peter F. Alexander 2000
First published 2000

This book is copyright. Apart from any fair dealing for the purposes of private
study, research, criticism or review as permitted under the Copyright Act, no part
may be reproduced, stored in a retrieval system, or transmitted, in any form or by
any means, electronic, mechanical, photocopying, recording or otherwise without
prior written permission. Enquiries to be made to Oxford University Press.

Copying for educational purposes
Where copies of part or the whole of the book are made under Part VB of the
Copyright Act, the law requires that prescribed procedures be followed.
For information, contact the Copyright Agency Limited.

National Library of Australia
Cataloguing-in-Publication data:

Alexander, Peter (Peter F.)
　Les Murray: a life in progress.

　Bibliography.
　Includes index.
　ISBN 0 19 553501 4.

　1. Murray, Les A. (Les Allan), 1938– . 2. Poets,
　Australian—Biography. I. Title.

A821.3

Edited by Sally Nicholls
Text designed by Derrick I. Stone Design
Cover designed by Derrick I. Stone Design
Typeset by Solo Typesetting, South Australia
Printed by Australian Print Group

Dedicated to the memory of my daughter
Rebecca Mary Alexander
born 20 October 1981
died 7 October 1999
who looked forward to reading this book.

Poetry is what I do in real life.

Les Murray, *Independent Monthly*, May 1996

CONTENTS

	Acknowledgments	viii
	Les Murray's Family Tree	xiii
	Map: Les Murray's country	xiv
1	Prelude	1
2	The Beginning, 1848–1938	5
3	Childhood, 1938–51	18
4	Death of the Family, 1951–54	34
5	Taree High, 1955–56	47
6	Sydney University, 1957–58	61
7	Trying Again, 1958–60	71
8	In the Pit, 1960–62	84
9	Halt and Turn, 1962	100
10	Thyrsis and Corydon, 1962–65	110
11	The Antipodes, 1965–68	125
12	The Vernacular Republic, 1968–71	141
13	The Test of Faith, 1971–74	153
14	The Battle of the Books, 1974–76	161
15	Public and Private, 1977–81	179
16	Anguish & Robbery, 1978–92	197
17	Stealing the Funeral, 1979–81	206
18	Autism and Isolation, 1981–87	215
19	The Power of the Dog, 1987–89	227
20	Fighting the Black Dog, 1989–92	236
21	Becoming a Name, 1992–94	249
22	Killing the Black Dog, 1994–96	262
23	Forgiving the Victim, 1996–98	276
24	Fredy Murray, 1993–	287
	Epilogue	295
	Notes	296
	Select Bibliography	346
	Index	380

ACKNOWLEDGMENTS

Writing the biography of a subject still alive is a risky enterprise. Sir Walter Raleigh, in the introduction to his *History of the World*, remarked sagely, 'Whosoever in writing a modern History shall follow truth too near the heels, it may haply strike out his teeth', and the warning is as applicable now as then. A subject who, by the mere fact of being still alive, denies the biography closure is problem enough: how do you finish a book the subject of which is turning out a book of poems a year, travelling ceaselessly, winning major prizes at a rapid rate, involving himself in constant controversy and generally living faster than the most dedicated biographer can write? The situation appears like that in *Alice Through the Looking-Glass*: run as quick as you will, the finishing line recedes rapidly into the distance.

If this is the biographer's problem even with a willing subject, an unwilling one has a range of defences at hand: destruction of correspondence, denial of cooperation, refusal to let libraries allow access to copyright material, the urging of friends not to cooperate, and (above all) denial of copyright permission. If the pertinacious biographer persists in writing and publishing in spite of all these obstacles, there are yet other recourses: a living subject may flatly deny facts, contradict opinions, prove shrewd deductions wrong, or (worst coming to worst) bring a suit for libel.

With these fears in mind, I have never before essayed the biography of a living writer, and I had the gravest doubts when Peter Rose of Oxford University Press approached me with the proposal that I write the life of Les Murray. My initial impulse was to refuse. I knew that several other books on the poet, biographical and critical, had been started and later abandoned; Murray had the reputation of being a prickly subject who would not hesitate to stop a book he disapproved of, and he had done so at least once.

More than that, there was a stigma attached to working on him. He espoused unpopular causes, he attacked Australia's elites (including academics and universities), he defended the right of outcasts like Helen Darville, Pauline Hanson and Lindy Chamberlain to be heard, he was said to be anti-feminist, he proudly proclaimed himself a redneck. The response was one I understood well from having seen something of his persecution by academics while he was Writer in Residence at my university in 1983: the poster attacking him by name on a colleague's door, the furious, sneering questions after his public talks, the messages in lipstick on the walls of the staff toilet he used, the packet of excrement he received through the university mail.

He was Australia's most important poet, but he was emphatically not a safe subject. There was a clear and present danger in contact with such a lightning-rod; biographical research is very expensive, and in Australia the grants that make it possible are allocated by peer review. If Murray had as many enemies in academe as I believed, my career would suffer a severe check. You have a family and a mortgage, said a cautious little voice. In the event my fears were to prove amply justified, when publication of this book was delayed for a year by repeated threats of legal action.

Two things drew me to Peter Rose's proposal. The first was that I liked and admired Murray as a human being, and relished the thought of working with him; the second was that I thought him the best poet writing in English. Do it, said my daemon.

I agreed to try to write the work, on condition that I could secure both Murrays' complete cooperation. The biography of a married subject is always a joint exercise, and the Murrays' marriage is particularly close: I needed Valerie Murray's permission too. I knew them both well enough to ask, and drove out to Bunyah to see them. As I covered the last few kilometres, following the swooping gravel road through Murray's green ancestral valley, and came in sight of the Habsburg-yellow posts and the milk-churn letterbox that mark the poet's drive, I anticipated a refusal. A biographer is a most uncomfortable visitor for a living author and his family. Skeletons clatter in all our closets, everyone's life has black patches, shames, sorrows: no one, you would think, would willingly submit to Judgement Day come early.

To my surprise, both Murray and Valerie seemed not just willing, but positively enthusiastic about the idea. I thought it only fair to let them know what they were letting themselves in for. I explained that I wanted complete access to everything—manuscripts, letters, diaries, accounts—that I would be interviewing them repeatedly over months, and that I would also be talking to family members, friends, ex-friends, enemies and literary rivals. 'Read what you like, talk to anyone you like, and whatever you can find you can print', Murray said expansively. 'Ex-girlfriends?' I warned. 'Boyfriends? Illegitimate children?' He laughed at the idea: 'You can publish anything you can find', he repeated. It was, I later came to realise, the quality of sprawl.

As for Valerie: 'Hear that noise?' she asked. 'It's the sound of hands rubbing.' What confidence, what courage! And in the years the project has taken, the Murrays' tolerance of my probings and their courage in facing what I uncovered have never abandoned them. I started this biography liking and admiring them: I finish it thinking them among the most remarkable human beings I have met. I owe them a debt this book only begins to repay.

There are many other debts, too. I give particular thanks to Ruth Hutchison, most thorough and patient of research assistants, who kept the work on this book going even when I was inundated with administrative tasks in running my school, and who did everything from finding articles in obscure journals to travelling to distant libraries to photocopy them for me. Without her unstinting and meticulous help this book would have taken at least another year to complete. I also thank Annette Nelson, who transcribed many of the interviews and provided expert opinions on subjects as diverse as theology and Latin grammar.

I am grateful to Peter Rose of Oxford University Press for commissioning the book and for keeping my nose to the grindstone during the years of labour. He shared with me his own memories of Murray, and suggested many useful contacts.

Les Murray's circle of friends is extraordinarily wide, and spread across four continents. Only a handful declined to be interviewed, and many not only talked freely to me, but supplied me with copies of their correspondence, photographs and other material. I am deeply grateful to all those who generously helped me by sharing their memories, or supplying me with copied letters, manuscripts or other biographical matter. They include Mr Anthony Akerman, Mrs Ann Barden, Mr Peter Barden, Mr John Barnie, Mr Ken Bolton, Dr Peter Braude, Mr Bill Burrell, Mr Mick Byrne, Professor Bruce Clunies Ross, Professor Tony Coady, Mrs Elisabeth Davis, Mr Walter Davis, Mr Bruce Dawe, Mr Michael Duffy, Mr Bob Ellis, Dr Jon Gani, Mr Lionel Gilbert, Mrs Margaret Gilbert, Dr Peter Goldsworthy, Mr Alan Gould, Mr Jamie Grant, Mr Robert Gray, Dr Stephen Gray, Ms Judith Green, Mrs Leila Griffis, Professor Gareth Griffiths, Mrs Ellen Harris, Mr Colin Hogan, Mr Clive James, Mrs Libby Jones (née Sweet), Professor Clive Kessler, Mr Christopher Koch, Mrs Naomi Kronenberg, Mrs Shirley Lantry, Mr Piers Laverty, Mr Les Lawrie, Mr Geoffrey Lehmann, Dr Susan Lever, Mrs Edith McLaughlin, Mr Keith McLaughlin, Mrs Jane McWhirter, Dr Sophie Masson, Mrs Nora Miller, Mr Gino Morelli, Mr John Mulhall, Mr James Murdoch, Mrs Alice Murray, Mrs Alma Murray, Mr Charlie Murray, Ms Christina Murray, Ms Clare Murray, Mr Daniel Murray, Mrs Mavis Murray, Dr Michael Nelson, Ms Penny Nelson, Mr Robin Norling, Mr Mark O'Connor, Mr Greg O'Hara, Ms Maureen O'Hara, Mr John Paul, Ms Gail Pearson, Dr Christopher Pollnitz, Mr Peter Porter, Dr Olaf Reinhardt, Dr Peter Saul, Dr Anurag Sharma (who also kindly sent me a copy of his excellent book on Murray), Ms Karla Sigel, Dr Angela Smith, Ms Ruth Sparrow, Dr Jennifer Strauss, Dr Mohammad Tavallaie, Mr Tom Thompson, Mr John Tranter, Mr Bob Wallace, Professor Chris Wallace-Crabbe, Mr Ken Welton, and Mrs Judith Wright McKinney.

Professor John J. Carmody of the University of New South Wales provided me with information about the likely treatment of Miriam Murray's two ectopic pregnancies.

Associate Professor Bruce Johnson drew on his knowledge of Australian popular culture to give me advice on the music, clothing and mores of Australian students in the early 1960s.

Ms Virginia Fay of the Australia Council kindly supplied me with the *Index of Literature Board Grants* and other publications concerning the Literature Fund's assessments of writers and their projects.

Ms Amanda Marks supplied me with memories, letters, and the photograph of her portrait of Murray, which inspired his poem 'Amanda's Painting'.

Like every researcher, I owe a profound debt to librarians, too often unacknowledged. Mrs Pat Howard of the University of New South Wales Library supplied valuable information on Sydney University life and student mores of the 1950s and 1960s. Dr Marie-Louise Ayres and her highly skilled staff at the Australian Defence Force Academy Library's Special Collection generously spent many days searching for and copying Murray material for me, and followed this up by seeking permissions from recipients of the Murray letters. And the staff of the Manuscripts Room in the Australian National Library, which houses the largest and most important collection of Murray papers, repeatedly put themselves at my disposal, supplying expert advice and patiently feeding me with documents during the weeks I spent in that, my favourite reading-room. Ms Lynne Groves, the Librarian of Taree High School, kindly supplied material from the school archives.

Ms Jan Latham of the University of New South Wales Scientific Illustration Section did sterling work on copying part of Les Murray's photograph collection for me.

Mr Darryl Murray of Tinonee kindly supplied me with the results of his long and painstaking research into the Murray family tree; much about Les Murray's ancestry would have remained obscure to me without his help, and that of Mrs Lily Sambell of Bulby Brush, who supplied much of the information on the Bunyah families.

Mr Gerard Windsor gave me encouragement at a time when I badly needed it, and he also took time from his own writing to read an early draft of this book, suggesting important structural changes, providing many helpful detailed comments and, through his unmatched knowledge of Australian literary history, saving me from several blunders and errors of omission.

I am particularly grateful to the Australian Research Council, which provided me with a generous grant to fund the research for this book: without this vital support, the work would not only have taken much longer, but it is likely it would not have been completed.

Finally, and as always, I return thanks to my own family: to my children Rebecca and Roland, who helped me in my researches to the extent of being grimed from head to foot after an entire day of futile hunting through the half-burned Ellis Collection in the Australian Defence Force Academy Library, and above all to my wife Christine, who took precious time from her own work to read and comment on my typescript, and who kept the home fires burning at a very difficult time in our family life.

To those others who helped me, and whose names I have inadvertently omitted, I offer sincere apologies and thanks.

Peter F. Alexander
UNSW

LES MURRAY'S FAMILY TREE
(direct line in bold)

John Murray IV
m.
Isabella Scott

Children of John Murray IV and Isabella Scott:
- John b. 1824
- **Hugh b. 1826** m. **Margaret Beattie**
- James b. 1827 m. Bridget Ryan
- Agnes b. 1829 m. William Paterson
- Thomas b. 1834 m. Agnes
- William b. ? drowned
- Robert b. 1836 m. Isabella
- George b. 1839 m. Margaret
- Veitch b. 1841 m. Ann
- Walter b. 1843 m. Maria

Children of Hugh and Margaret Beattie:
- Archibald b. 1850 m. Catherine Murray
- Hugh b. 1851 m. Grace Bone
- Alexander (Sandy) b. 1854 m. Isabella Murray
- William b. 1856 m. Fanny Carey
- Isabella b. 1858 m. Robert Andrewes
- James b. 1860 m. (Mina) Wilhelmina Murray
- George b. 1862
- Thomas b. 1865 m. Lavinia Summers
- Robert b. 1867 m. Mary Jane Murray
- **John b. 1848** m. **Isabella Murray**

Children of John and Isabella Murray:
- Margaret m. James Willis
- (Sandy) Alexander Bunyah Allan m. Jane Worth
- **(Allan) John** m. **Emily Payne**
- William m. Sarah Monk
- Bridgid m. John Newell
- (Nellie) Ellen Grace
- Isabella d. infant
- Ada Flora Beatrice m. Robert Paterson
- (Sam) Samuel m. (Allie) Alacque Maurer

Children of (Archie) Archibald:
- Hugh Scott m. Esther Arnold
- (Jim) James m. Jane Monk

Children of (Allan) John and Emily Payne:
- Stanley James b. 1903 m. Fanny (Frances Maude French)
- William b. 1905 d. infant 1907
- (Nettie) Ethel Isabella b. 1907 m. Reg (Wilfred Reginald Murray) Arnall
- **Cecil Allan b. 1909–1992** m. **Miriam Pauline (1915–1951)**
- Myrtle b. 1911 m. Victor Maurer
- (Archie) John Archibald b. 1913 m. Mary Milligan
- Mary Jane b. 1915 d. infant
- (Eric) Leslie Eric b. 1918 m. Edna Tagg
- (Charlie) Selwyn Alexander b. 1922 m. Allice Ferguson
- Ena Agnes b. 1925 m. Cyril Harris

Leslie Allan (1938–) m. **Valerie Morelli (1941–)**

Children of Leslie Allan and Valerie Morelli:
- Christina Miriam (1963–) m. James Gilkerson
- Daniel Allan (1965–) m. Shari Meadows
- Clare Luisa (1974–)
- Alexander Joseph Cecil (1978–)
- Peter Benedict (1982–)

LES MURRAY'S COUNTRY

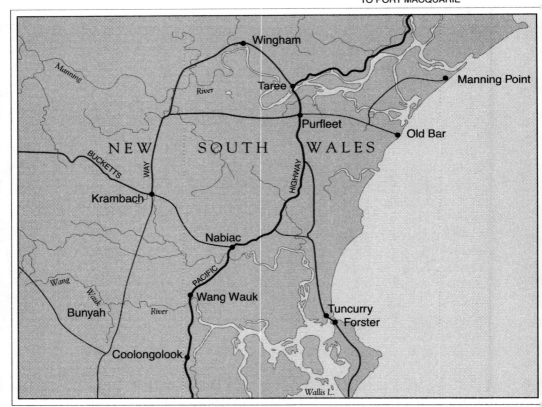

CHAPTER ONE
PRELUDE

~

Do not call it fixity,
Where past and future are gathered.

T. S. ELIOT

At 11.15 on the morning of 18 July 1996 an ambulance drove onto the long bridge over the Manning River outside Taree, and in brilliant winter sunshine sped across it towards Newcastle, the siren wailing briefly as it passed through knots of traffic. The vehicle contained only one patient, a big man with the brassy complexion and sulphurous eyes of someone affected by severe jaundice. The medical records travelling with him named him as a Mr Leslie Allan Murray, and included the results of a CAT scan showing a large liver abscess; the accompanying notes clinically remarked that the patient was a diabetic suffering near-complete renal failure, that there was evidence of gas in the liver abscess, and that septic shock was setting in. Immediate surgery was indicated.

He was in great pain, but sedated into calm. He lay semi-conscious, unable to see the passing forests and the occasional glimpses of scalloped, surf-fringed coast, but knowing exactly where he was because he knew every turn of this road like the inside of his own pocket. The ambulance raced south, over the Manning River, up which his great-great-great-grandmother had sailed in 1851 and beside which the Murrays had prospered and multiplied. Past Purfleet, as on the morning he had come by, aged twelve, behind his mother's hearse, and had seen a then-unknown Aboriginal man, Uncle Eddie Lobban,[1] remove his hat and bow his head in a gesture of mourning never forgotten. Past the turn to Old Bar, where cousin Leila lived with her memories of his childhood; onto the fast multi-lane stretch south to Coolongolook and Buladelah.

This was the length of Pacific Highway that traversed his Country, the stretch, crowded with holiday traffic, that he had fixed in the mind for ever in 'The Buladelah-Taree Holiday Song Cycle':

> It is the season of the Long Narrow City; it has crossed the Myall, it has entered the North Coast,
> that big stunning snake; it is looped through the hills, burning all night there.

> Hitching and flying on the downgrades, processionally balancing on the climbs,
> it echoes in O'Sullivan's Gap, in the tight coats of the flooded-gum trees;
> the tops of palms exclaim at it unmoved, there near Wootton.

Through the edge of the Kiwarrak Forest, over the Bungwahl Creek, down to Nabiac where he had been born fifty-eight years before. The ambulance siren announced his presence now again briefly, and he thought of that birth and how it had killed his mother twelve years later: at least the family had risen far enough for him to have an ambulance now.

South to Wang Wauk where his father had cut timber years before, snigging it out with a bullock-team. Over the Wang Wauk River, which upstream has its humbler beginnings in the creek beside which he had lived all his childhood and youth. It was up that valley, which his family had once owned in its entirety, one of the sacred places of the mind with its forested hills and its winding rock-strewn streams, that there lay the abandoned remains of the tiny house in which he had been brought up, and from which his father had been evicted in such bitterness in the early 1970s. And there, within a kilometre of the ruined foundations of his childhood home, was his beloved Forty Acres, the farm he had planted with fruit trees, the dam he had dappled with lotuses brought from Kakadu, and the little house in which his wife Valerie, packing up at this moment to follow the ambulance, was doing the last-minute checks. As she was about to walk out, her eye fell on the big oil-portrait of him above the sofa, and she burst into tears.

The big man in the ambulance wondered in sedated calm if he would ever traverse these roads again. Through Coolongolook, where he had stood on the banks of the quiet river one evening at the end of 1956, watching the mayflies, and had known that he was going to be a poet. Through the stately forests of O'Sullivan's Gap, where the goannas beg for picnickers' sandwiches; past Wootton and Buladelah, where the still presence of the Myall lakes can be felt, and on south towards the smudge of Newcastle, the steel city, his mother's city, first visited with her at the age of four, all unforgotten:

> John Brown, glowing far and down,
> wartime Newcastle was a brown town,
> handrolled cough and cardigan, rain on paving bricks
> big smoke to a four-year-old from the green sticks.
> Train city, mother's city, coming on dark,
> Japanese shell holes awesome in a park,
> electric light and upstairs, encountered first that day,
> sailors and funny ladies in Jerry's Fish Café.

The pain came in waves which the pethidine allowed him to float over. He had planned to refurbish his parents' graves and had not done it. Now, he thought with drugged satisfaction, his own name could be added to the stone with little extra cost. His one regret was that he had not finished *Fredy Neptune*: now he would die not knowing how it ended.

The ambulance howled its way through early afternoon traffic, and found the John Hunter Hospital forewarned. The big man was wheeled into casualty and checked. The verdict was alarming: 'He's nearly dead'. He was prepared for surgery immediately. Convinced he was dying, he felt neither fear nor regret at the prospect. Wheeled rapidly down wide corridors, he stared unblinking at lights passing rhythmically above him:

> Ribbed glass glare-panels flow
> over you down urgent corridors,
> dismissing midday outside. Slow,
>
> they'd resemble wet spade-widths in a pit;
> you've left grief behind you, for others;
> your funeral: who'll know you'd re-planned it?
>
> God, at the end of prose,
> somehow be our poem—
> when forebrainy consciousness goes[2]

By 4 p.m., within two hours of admission, his chest was being opened, as his wife, struggling towards the hospital through the traffic, was rammed from behind at a traffic light. The last thing he heard, as he sank into drugged darkness, was the surgeon remarking, 'We might lose this one'.

Within hours of his admission the John Hunter Hospital got the first of the hundreds of phonecalls. This harbinger of the storm was from London: 'This is Clive James. How's Les Murray doing?' The writer and broadcaster is a name to conjure with in his native land, and there was a brief fanfare of silence from the woman on the switchboard before urgent internal enquiries began: 'Who is Les Murray?' James was glad to tell her: 'You've got the most important poet in Australia there. I'm sure you'll take good care of him'.[3] And one of his surgeons, Peter Saul, who read and collected Les Murray's volumes, was able to add to this answer: one of the best poets writing in English, his country's foremost literary voice, the unofficial Australian Laureate. Saul could have said, though he did not, that his extraordinary patient was a former farm-boy who could read more than twenty languages, and lift the back of a motorcar by hand: 'This man, who warms cold ground by lying on it, who handparks his car . . .' He did not say that Murray was that rarest of beings, a writer through whom a national consciousness shapes and expresses itself. The receptionist's hesitation is understandable: 'Who is Les Murray?' was not a simple question. To approach an answer to it we have to go back to the beginning.

CHAPTER TWO
THE BEGINNING
1848–1938

In my end is my beginning.

T. S. ELIOT

The story of the Australian Murrays begins on 9 October 1848, when the *Castle Eden*, a sailing vessel of 930 tons, arrived in Sydney, with a load of immigrants from Britain: 14 cabin passengers and 302 government-assisted emigrants, known as 'bounty migrants'. The travellers, crowding the deck for the entry through the narrow gap between the towering sandstone cliffs that guard Sydney's glittering wooded harbour, must have been delighted to arrive: having left Plymouth on 15 June, they had been at sea for nearly four months, with a brief break at the Cape of Good Hope.

Many of the bounty migrants were Scottish. They were paid the equivalent of their fare on arrival in the colony under a scheme introduced in 1835, designed to overcome the shortages of labour in Australia and South Africa. Payment was made after the presentation of testimonials of good character, proof of age from baptismal records, and statements of health and strength: £30 for married men, £15 for unmarried women, £10 for unmarried men, £5 for children.

Among those eager arrivals to the rapidly developing city of Sydney were four brothers and their sister, five of the ten children of John and Isabella Murray of Jedburgh in Scotland. The oldest son, Hugh, arrived with his wife Margaret. The Emigrant Records for the *Castle Eden*, preserved in the New South Wales State Archives, register their arrival:

> Murray, Hugh: Age 22, Shepherd. Native place Jedburgh, Co. Roxburgh, Scotland. Parents—John and Isabella. Mother living at Camptown, Jedburgh, Co. Roxburgh. Church of England. Reads and writes. No relations in Colony. Good bodily health, strength and probable usefulness. No complaints.
>
> Murray, Margaret: Age 22 (his wife). Housemaid. N/P [native place] Co. Roxburgh, Scotland. Parents—Archibald and Margaret Beattie (no address) Presbyterian. Reads and writes. No relations in Colony. Good health. No complaints.[1]

This young and hopeful pair, shepherd and housemaid, stepping down the gangplank into an October spring for the first time, were to become the great-great-grandparents of the poet Les Murray. Hugh Murray's siblings were recorded as James, aged twenty-one, who gave his occupation as gardener, and Agnes, nineteen, William, sixteen, and Thomas, fourteen, all three listed as 'farm servants'.

The Murrays left Scotland as hundreds of thousands of their fellow-countrymen did during the nineteenth century, because of poverty and the great clearances, the process by which millionaire landowners, such as the Earl of Sutherland, forcibly and cruelly evicted the crofters from their ancestral glens, and introduced sheep in their place. Murray (or Moray) is a widespread name, linked with the Firth and the district around Elgin. Les Murray's ancestors had been Lowlanders for generations, established from the seventeenth century in the Border country near Jedburgh, 50 kilometres south of Edinburgh, where for two centuries they made a modest living as tenant farmers.[2] They also made complex intermarriages with the other local families, Veitches, Turnbulls, Scotts, Beatties, Eastons and Rutherfords, and some of these connections were to be continued in Australia.[3]

Every few generations the Murray family line in Jedburgh threw up a brilliant boy who took the first opportunity to leave Scotland and make his way in the world: among those to originate from the tight grouping of Jedburgh Murrays, all related, were General Sir John Irvine Murray, scourge of the rebels during the Indian Mutiny; and an outstanding literary figure, Sir James Augustus Murray, of *Oxford English Dictionary* fame, a fifth cousin, many times removed, of Les Murray. But these glittering connections seem not to have enriched the Jedburgh Murrays, who remained impoverished tenant farmers. 'The finest sight that any Scotsman sees', Samuel Johnson once thundered at the hapless Boswell when he made the mistake of boasting about Scotland's natural beauty, 'is the road that leads him to England', and the jibe was as woundingly true for the little group of Murrays leaving Jedburgh in June 1848 by coach for Plymouth as it had been a hundred years earlier.

Hugh Murray and his siblings were no geniuses, but they were eager to rise out of Scottish poverty. They had been invited to emigrate to New South Wales by Robert Easton, their mother's cousin, who had migrated in 1839 and was working for the Australian Agricultural Company, the largest landowner in New South Wales.[4] Formed in London in 1824, the company was granted a million acres (about 400 000 hectares), part of it stretching along the coast from Port Stephens (230 kilometres north of Sydney) to the Manning River (318 kilometres north of Sydney), and a further part on the other side of the Great Dividing Range, centred on the present city of Tamworth.[5] The company proposed to raise cattle on the coast and sheep inland, and it began importing labour on a large scale to supplement the dwindling supply of convicts; transportation of criminals to New South Wales had officially ended in 1840. Appointed overseer of the company's free men at Gloucester (there was another overseer of convicts), Robert Easton wrote to the Murray boys and persuaded them to come and work under him. They were encouraged by their mother, widowed since 1845 and burdened with ten children, and they seem to have jumped at the chance.[6] The plan was to establish themselves in New South Wales so their mother and the five youngest children could follow.

The *Castle Eden* arrived carrying at least one more passenger than she had sailed with: during the voyage Hugh Murray's wife Margaret had given birth to a son.

> Murray, John: Age 7 weeks. Born on board the 'Castle Eden'. Church of Scotland. Nil reads and writes. No relations in the Colony. Good health.[7]

John, later to become known as 'Bunyah Johnnie', would be Les Murray's great-grandfather. Family tradition held that he had been born in the Bay of Biscay during a terrible storm, but as he was only seven weeks old on arrival in Australia this story was true of his excesses of hospitality and reckless generosity rather than of his birth. It is likely he was born in the Indian Ocean.

Hugh Murray was impoverished, but he had farming experience and he was drivingly ambitious. He and his brothers engaged with the Australian Agricultural Company, and worked for it for three years at Stroud, their sister living there with them. By the time their contracts expired in 1851 they had learned a great deal about farming in Australian conditions, and were ready to strike out on their own. The company was beginning to withdraw from coastal farming to concentrate on its more lucrative sheep-rearing operations inland, and land previously held by it was being offered for lease cheaply to anyone who would take it. The Murray boys, clubbing together, leased land at Kimbriki on the Manning River, about 30 kilometres from its mouth and not far from where the city of Taree would begin to rise in 1854.

In October 1851 they brought out their widowed mother Isabella, still only forty-nine years old. Les Murray's poem 'My Ancestress and the Secret Ballot' would analyse her reasons for coming, and reflect ironically that if the secret ballot, invented in Australia, had spread back to Britain earlier and given the poor some power, she might never have been forced to leave Scotland.[8]

> Put about, wee ship, on your Great Circle course,
> don't carry Bella's Murray daughter and boys
> to the British Crown's stolen Austral land.

> In ten years the Secret Ballot will force
> its way into law in those colonies.
> If the poor can just sit on their non-smoking hand
> till they're old, help will come from Labor policies
>
> and parties, sprung worldwide from that lag idea
> which opens, by evading duellisms of the soul,
> the only non-murderous route to the dole.

With their mother on the bark *Earl Grey* came the five remaining Murray children: John, aged twenty-seven, and Robert, fifteen, both farm labourers, and George, twelve, Veitch, ten, and Walter, eight.[9]

Roads in the interior were still little more than bullock-tracks, and there was fear of Aboriginal or (more likely) bushranger attacks. The Murrays travelled north with their mother in one of the sturdy coastal vessels which would continue to be the main mode of transport until the railways finally replaced them during World War II. The coast along which Isabella Murray and her children sailed in 1851 was and is spectacular. The cliffs and magnificent drowned valleys around Sydney gradually gave way, as they went north, to wooded headlands between which the surf creamed in on long golden beaches. Inland, parallel to the coast, ran the blue barrier of the Dividing Range, heavily forested on its higher slopes, and between it and the coast was a lightly wooded plain which reminded early travellers of English parkland. It was green, fertile and well watered by rivers, some of them wide and deep, which rose in the inland ranges and flowed east to the sea in lazy meanders.

The mouths of these rivers were mostly choked by sandbars, damming up broad coastal lakes where the rivers were too sluggish to force their way through. Where clear estuaries did exist, ports came into being: Newcastle, 180 kilometres north of Sydney on the Hunter River, was developing rapidly by 1848. Another 140 kilometres further north again was the Manning River, its mouth choked by a sandbar which could be crossed only with the most skilful handling by the master of the coaster that would take the travellers upriver to their 'selection', the land they had leased. In later years, Les Murray imagined the coaster arriving at the bar:

> a scraped timber mansion hung in showering
> ropework is crabbing on the tide's flood,
> swarming, sway, and shouting,
> entering the rivermouth over the speedy bar . . .
>
> Seo abhainn mar loch—the polished river is indeed
> like a loch, without flow, clear to the rainforest islands
> and the Highland immigrants on deck, remarking it

keep a hand, or a foot, on their bundles and nail-kegs.
No equipment is replaceable: there's only one of anything,
experience they will hand down.[10]

And having established themselves in this new land, the Murrays prospered. Though they described their new farms as being surrounded by 'primeval forest', the pattern of vegetation they found when they began to settle was largely man-made. Aborigines had settled on the land tens of thousands of years before, and over the course of millennia had altered it radically, by the introduction of the dingo (which had an incalculable effect on the smaller fauna and drove to extinction less efficient predators such as the Tasmanian Devil and Tasmanian Tiger) and, more importantly, by the use of fire.

The custom of burning the land annually, a practical way of clearing land in the wet tropical forests of Australia's northern neighbours, had catastrophic effects in this drier continent. The mighty interior forests were destroyed for ever and the climate altered for the worse by the disappearance of vegetation, so that desertification resulted; on the better-watered coastal fringes, rainforest species retreated to the wettest valleys of the Dividing Range and fire-resistant species such as eucalypts became dominant. Even on the coastal plains, constant use of the fire-stick forced back the forest, burned the humus out of the soils, and produced the open parkland the original white settlers found, and which slowly reforested once the burnings were reduced.[11]

Hugh Murray and his brothers found the Aboriginals no threat, and offered them no violence. Les Murray was to reflect on the original owners of Kimbriki:

Away over past a window is Kimbriki, tribal estate
of one dignified slim old man and the farm of another
my great great grandfather. Both occupied the same land
amicably. Smoke rose beside separate bark roofings.
In the next generation, no tribal heir appeared.
What you presume concerning this will tell you
the trend of your life.[12]

The leased land at Kimbriki was eventually bought by the Murrays (at ten shillings an acre, according to family lore),[13] a homestead was acquired or erected at Mondrook, near Taree, and the family began producing crops on the fertile river-flats, raising cattle in the open forests, and cutting timber for sale to the sawmills.

They also went into business: Hugh Murray opened a general store which supplied settlers in the area on both sides of the Manning, and which prospered. When a post office was established in 1875, Hugh Murray acquired a third source of income by becoming postmaster at a salary of £20 a year.[14] He and his wife built a reputation for generosity and hospitality. And within a few years he had become a considerable landowner, buying land not just at Kimbriki, but also at Bunyah, 30 kilometres to the south, paying thirty shillings an acre, until he owned the entire Bunyah valley to just above Coolongolook,[15] buying blocks and pasturing cattle on the Crown land surrounding them.[16] Hugh owned other land too, at Larry's Flat.[17] The Scottish peasant farmer had come a long way.

In a photograph taken when they were well into middle age, Hugh and Margaret, dressed in their Sunday best, frown fixedly, clearly trying not to blink during the long exposure. Hugh has an irrepressible hillbilly look, which shows itself in his shabby jacket, his straggly unkempt beard and his long hair which, though slicked back for this important event, springs up rebelliously. Margaret, clearly the stronger character, looks a cut above him socially in her black ribbons and her fashionable dress with its cameo at her throat; unlike her husband, she looks straight into the lens, and there is a contained confidence in the gaze of the wide-spaced eyes. They both have the strong, thick-fingered hands of manual workers. A photograph of their homestead at Kimbriki survives too, showing a substantial wooden house and barn, roofed with shingles and linked by a covered way, and in the foreground, standing among chickens and geese, an incongruously large multi-layered columbarium mounted high on posts. All around is open eucalypt forest.[18]

Hugh's brothers married and built similar homes; his sister Agnes married another Scottish migrant, William Paterson, in 1851. With their formidable mother as the head of the family until her death in 1866,[19] the Murrays stayed together and worked together, buying farms within easy reach of each other and developing a powerful regional and clan loyalty that lasted for generations. The red-haired Murray brothers were bristle-bearded, hard-working and hard-swearing, with a strong and apparently inherited tendency to melancholia and whisky.[20]

They not only prospered, they went forth and multiplied exceedingly. Among Isabella's ten children, the first Australian generation, families of ten children remained common. Les Murray's great-great-grandfather Hugh had ten children (nine sons and a daughter, as his mother had done); the poet's great-grandfather, John, in turn produced seven sons and three daughters; the poet's grandfather, John Allan, produced six sons and four daughters. Today (1999) there are well over 2000 direct descendants of Hugh Murray.[21] The descendants of each of his nine siblings are probably as numerous.

Here, I remember all of a hundred years:
Candleflame, still night, frost and cattle bells,

The draywheels' silence final in our ears,
And the first red cattle spreading through the hills

And my great-great-grandfather here with his first sons,
Who would grow old, still speaking with his Scots accent,
Having never seen those highlands that they sang of . . .
A hundred years.[22]

Though Hugh Murray never farmed his land at Bunyah, his eldest son John, immediately after his marriage to his cousin Isabella Murray in 1870, moved there to live and farm. This marriage to a cousin was not unusual for the Murrays: the family links were extraordinarily close, and no fewer than five of Hugh Murray's boys married their first cousins, four of them sisters[23]—not surprising, when a majority of the neighbours for miles were Murrays. This, and the fact that the family was unimaginative in its range of Christian names, so that almost every generation has its John, Isabella, James and Hugh, and sometimes several of them, makes the Murray family tree one of dizzying complexity.[24]

In the wide valley through which runs the stream now known as Bunyah Creek (which after its confluence with the larger Horses Creek becomes the Wang Wauk River), John and his new bride built a house, which they oddly named 'The Parlour'. They were the first white settlers in the area, which its Aboriginal inhabitants, whom the Murrays shouldered aside, had long before named after the wild yams that grew there.[25] Hugh seems to have given John possession of the thousands of acres of hilly country; to distinguish him from the many other Murrays further north, he became universally known as 'Bunyah Johnnie'. Towards the end of the nineteenth century the main track north ran through the settlement of Bulahdelah and over the Manning hill through Bunyah to Krambach, another of the hamlets that dot the valleys, and then on to the Manning. Bunyah Johnnie's house was one of only two on the road, and his generosity to travellers made it a halfway house for those heading to and from the Manning valley: 'So everybody treated it as a kind of way station and would stay there. They never charged them any money for this, they just fed them. Often they had twenty guests'.[26]

But hospitable John Murray and his wife did not long occupy the valley alone. As other potential settlers arrived, John sold land to them at a profit, partly because he needed the money, partly because he owned far too much land to farm himself and wanted to see the area settled. During the terrible drought of the 1880s, he gave material support to the newcomers, helping them to survive. Many of the arrivals were Murrays, either his own siblings or his cousins or nephews. The other pioneering Bunyah families were Patersons, the link through Hugh's sister Agnes holding firm and being reinforced by further intermarriage.[27] Bunyah Johnnie's own ten children were given farms by their father as they reached maturity.

The sixth of these was Les Murray's grandfather, John Allan Murray, always called Allan to distinguish him from his father. And with his generation, a decline in the family's prosperity began to set in. In part this resulted from the steady division of what had once been an ample landholding. The settlement of eastern New South Wales was very swift, and Hugh Murray's opportunity to buy great swathes of countryside at thirty shillings an acre did not recur. Murray family farms diminished rapidly as they were divided between generations of ten children.

Great-grandfather Bunyah Johnnie was perhaps more generous than he could sensibly afford to be, and he was also a less than shrewd businessman. As his grandson Charlie Murray recalled, 'As people came into the valley, he would sell them a piece of land and they would pay it off—there was no time limit set for it—to settle the area. Some paid it, some didn't but that never worried him, although they say the Scots are very canny with money'.[28] Bunyah Johnnie was also, in his cheerful way, a hard drinker and a card-player, and late in life he gambled the family homestead, 'The Parlour', on a game of whist, and lost it to a newly arrived English immigrant named Horace Deer. This was a piece of fecklessness which the family did their best to keep quiet.[29] But his great-grandson would remember:

> My dead relations blur to sepia dust,
> Recede into fable. Great-grandfather John
> Who owned the district, fed it through the drought
> Of the eighties and lost his homestead in a game
> Of whist with an English newchum . . .[30]

Bunyah Johnnie's son, Grandfather John Allan Murray, was a much less attractive figure than his father, with the family faults exaggerated and redeeming features faded. Les Murray was to remember him clearly and without affection:

> I think he was always a bit jealous of his father. He tried to live up to him but didn't have the real generosity to do it, and didn't quite have the resources either. He was a fake-generous host whereas great grandfather had been a genuine generous host. Grandfather was notable for being very generous outside the family and outside the home, but a bit of a tyrant and a pig to people inside the home. One of those. He drank a bottle of spirits a day and occasionally went out and got drunk too. More than occasionally: about

once a month, he and some of his brothers and other old mates would drink for four days and then he'd come back to his regular bottle of schnapps or rum per day.³¹

John Allan had the red-haired, alcoholic pugnacity of his forebears, and a tendency to visit his frequent bellowing rages on his ten children, particularly the two eldest sons, Stanley and the poet's father Cecil. They learned to give him a very wide berth when he was more than usually drunk, but this did not save them from frequent and sometimes vicious beatings, with any implement that came to hand, including the stockwhip, though with its lash doubled back as a concession.³² His wife Emily he never struck: her Irish temper (she had been a Payne) could equal his, and she was the dominant partner in the marriage, taking the big decisions. For all that she cared for him loyally: in the home she waited on him hand and foot, and his son Charlie remembered that on the rare occasions when John Allan went out ploughing, Emily would walk with him behind the oxen, shading him with an umbrella.³³

Alcoholism was to lead to diabetes when he was in his forties: thereafter he never did any physical work, instead taking his sons out of school as soon as each of them reached fourteen, and directing them to work for him. From the age of five they had done 'light' work such as feeding calves and milking for two hours before school. At fourteen Stanley and Cecil, and later Charlie, were put in charge of a trained team of eighteen oxen, and sent into the nearby Wang Wauk forest to cut timber and snig it out, a job requiring strength and great skill. In return they received their pocket money and a vague promise that in due course their father would set them up with a farm of their own. The effect was that they remained completely dependent on him. He continued to order them about at will after they were adults: Cecil would remember being commanded to wait for long hours outside the pub until his father stumbled out, sodden with drink, to be driven home.³⁴ 'Well the sons would get their food and clothes and if they went to a dance or a show they got a bit of money handed to them', John Allan's maid-of-all-work recalled.³⁵ In this way John Allan preserved a tyrannical dominance over his children long after they should have reached independence.

In many ways the Bunyah community was a world unto itself. The valley is still curiously isolated, even though fast driving will bring the traveller into Taree in less than an hour. Before the motorcar became common, after World War II, Bunyah was deeply secluded. The main road north ceased to run through it when the coastal route was put through, and the railway, though hoped for, never came; to this day the only road through the valley, slow and looping as it traverses the curves of the hills, is surfaced with rough gravel, and the few bridges that carry it over the Bunyah Creek are elderly timber structures.

The Bunyah community, cut off, interrelated, and with plenty of space and opportunity to develop eccentricities and peculiarities, took on a character of its own in a short time. Habits such as the male Murrays' regular indulgence in howling, bellowing rages, terrifying their women and children, would have been frowned on and repressed in a town; here they were merely shrugged at and accepted. 'Performing', it was called with mild disapproval. Other more pleasant characteristics of a much older society persisted too: virtually every man (though only the men, curiously) could play a musical instrument, usually the accordion or the violin, and music was a pervasive part of life, as Lily Sambell, one of the Murray girls, remembered: 'You could go into any house and you could have a musical evening. The older people, when they'd come in for their evening meal, they'd pick up their instruments and have a tune before the meal. Uncle Sam used to do that and my father and my brother Jack. Really and truly it was a great atmosphere'.[36]

Many peculiarities of speech developed, or were retained after they had disappeared elsewhere, and there emerged a rich local vocabulary. Much of this related to the few commercial activities of the valley, cattle, timber-getting and the growing of maize. So udders were called 'elders' in the patois of the valley; to poleaxe an animal was to 'peth' it; a cow in calf was 'springing'; to castrate an animal was to 'pick his haggots'; an old cow past milk production was a 'cracker', and a bull castrated after puberty a 'stag'; a tree was a 'stick', its trunk a 'barrel' which could be 'dozy' or have a 'pipe'; unparched maize was 'muttai'; maizemeal porridge was 'pommage'; flowering maize was 'out in tassel' and so on. To confuse someone was to 'minder their brains'; to drive fast was to 'mote'; a ghost was a 'fraid'; a careless and slack person was 'slomicky' ('That old Mother Green is a slomicky, dirty slut I reckon'); an angry man was 'fightable'; 'agen' meant 'by the time that' ('Agen he gets here, I'll have the job done'); 'watertable' was the gutter along the side of a road ('That car nearly run me into the watertable').[37]

These regional words, many of them Scots or northern English in origin, combined with Aboriginal words for plants and animals in the local Kattangal language ('jojo' for a bindii burr, 'carrawak' for currawong), and with peculiarities of grammar and delivery, constituted something close to a Bunyah dialect. They both reflected and reinforced the peculiarity and closeness of the valley community and were part of the birthright of everyone born into it. They also helped to exclude outsiders.

Change was resisted by some of John Allan's generation, who had not much education themselves, and feared that it would lead their children into leaving the valley. Technology was regarded with similar suspicion. John Allan refused to install a telephone for many years, on the grounds that the instrument would attract lightning; when diesel-powered milking machines became available he refused those on similar grounds, grumbling that they 'brought storms'.[38] By that stage in any case his children were doing the milking, so that installing the machines would be of no benefit to himself, and might leave the young people idle. Bunyah had become the home of what was recognisably an Australian peasantry.

Cecil Allan, the poet's father, was born at Bunyah in 1909, the fourth of John Allan's children. According to the family legend, 'His mother did her share of milking fifty cows by hand and then went down and prepared breakfast for the small family she then had, and about half past nine she retired into the bedroom and gave birth to Cecil and didn't get up to make the lunch'.[39] Cecil left school to start his course of serfdom, as unpaid bullock driver and timber cutter, in 1923. Though he was literate, he never finished a book in his life and probably never owned one. 'He started a book called *Robbery Under Arms* once', his son was to recall with affectionate irony.[40] He was shy and timid as a youth, the result of his father's drunken floggings and the cold, experimental beatings inflicted on him by his older brother Stanley.[41] All his life he would have a horror of alcoholism as a result of seeing the effect of drink on his father.

Immensely strong and an untiring worker, he developed a particular love of forestry: he was a great axeman who could chop all day, and had an encyclopaedic knowledge of the trees he cut down. He could tell by tapping a tree that it had a 'pipe', meaning that it was hollow and therefore useless as timber; a glance at the trunk high up would tell him if it was 'dozy' or rotten in places. He could fell a tree so that it dropped just where he wanted it, and took pride in removing it in a way that did not damage other trees: he was a natural conservationist with a deep love of the land. He was the inspiration for one of his son's most effective early poems, 'Noonday Axeman', which Murray would describe as 'tribute to ancestors, attempt to grapple with essential mystery . . . of Australia':[42]

> Between the trees, the tall light reaches me.
> Things are what they are, and that is frightening:
> They require obedience, if they are to be mastered —
> And so many have tried to force their dreams on this planet.

> Things are so wordless. These two opposing scarves
> I have cut in my red-gum squeeze out jewels of sap
> And stare. And soon, with a few more axe-strokes,
> The tree will grow troubled, tremble, shift its crown
>
> And, leaning slowly, gather speed and colossally
> Crash down and lie between the standing trunks.
> And then, I know, of the knowledge that led my forebears
> To drink and black rage and wordlessness, there will be silence.

Cecil took to neither drink nor wordlessness. He gradually became a great teller of tall tales, a skilful dancer, and a self-taught fiddler much in demand at dances in the Bunyah hall. He had great charm and a sly sense of humour. Both then and in later life, he was very popular with women.

In 1937, when he was twenty-eight, still living at home and still completely under his father's heavy thumb, he met a striking-looking 22-year-old nurse from Newcastle, Miriam Arnall, at a Coolongolook tennis match. Her father, Fred Arnall, born in Cornwall into a family of engineers and miners, had become an alum miner at Bulahdelah and later a coal miner in the Hunter Valley; her mother's maiden name was Worth, and the family claimed to be distantly related to the Paris couturiers of that name.[43] George Worth of Coolongolook was nephew to Charles Frederick Worth of Paris.[44] Much less was made of the fact that one of the Worth sisters, Miriam's aunt, had married an Aboriginal.[45] But in later years Les Murray would be more proud of this connection than of the Parisian one.[46]

Miriam Pauline Arnall was the second of seven children, born in Kurri Kurri in the Hunter Valley during World War I, on 23 May 1915. She was highly intelligent and capable, winning many prizes at school in Muswellbrook. Her father died young of miner's phthisis, and the family then moved to Newcastle, enduring great poverty during the Depression. In a period when few women aimed at a career outside the home, Miriam trained as a nurse at the Watt Street Hospital in Newcastle. She had not long qualified when she met Cecil Murray.

There was a family connection between the two young people: Cecil's Uncle Sandy had married a Jane Worth, and Miriam was in Coolongolook to visit her relatives. Nonetheless there was considerable surprise in Bunyah when the meek, put-upon Cecil began showing off this striking young woman, tall and elegant, with her very fair skin, vividly blue eyes and dark hair; she created something of a sensation when he brought her to one of the regular dances in the Bunyah hall.[47] Although there was initial suspicion of her as an outsider ('Our girls not good enough for you, eh Cecil?'), his self-confidence, and his status in the community, rose sharply.

The young couple were married at Merewether in Newcastle on 27 November 1937. The honeymoon was a brief trip by coastal steamer to Sydney and back, and when they returned, they moved into a tiny rundown house, hardly more than a shack, on a 60-hectare (150 acre) section of John Allan's farm, perhaps a kilometre from the main house. This shack, which brother Stanley had previously occupied, John Allan allowed Cecil and his bride to rent for £60 a year—no small sum in 1937, in the depths of the Depression.[48] This rental money he expected Cecil to raise by timber-cutting. As a wedding present, John Allan gave his son the furniture for the house. Dairy herd, farming equipment and everything else needful he would have to find himself: no sense in spoiling the boy.

The Murray wheel had come full circle in just three generations: Cecil had fallen to the level of tenant-at-will, which his ancestor Hugh had left Scotland to escape. It was to a rural shanty that the newly born Leslie Allan Murray would be brought home from the hospital in Nabiac in October 1938. Few poets since Keats can have been raised in humbler surroundings.

CHAPTER THREE
CHILDHOOD
1938–51

It should be noted that children at play are not playing about.

MONTAIGNE

Leslie Allan Murray was born early in the morning on 17 October 1938.[1] The birth, Miriam Murray's first and last, took place in the small and rather primitive Nabiac private hospital, 'Araluen'. Miriam's labour was slow, and another woman, a Mrs Cheers, who suffered from a heart condition,[2] was in the early stages of what was expected to be a difficult labour: as the hospital was too small to attend to both at once, Miriam's 9-pound (4-kilogram) baby[3] was induced. 'Cold steel hurried me from her womb', Les Murray was to write, suggesting a forceps delivery:

> What hour I followed
> the waters into this world
> no one living can now say
> My zodiac got washed away.[4]

And he wondered whether his mother, a city girl and a trained nurse herself, had given permission:

> Sister Arnall, city girl
> with your curt good sense
> were you being the nurse
> when you let them hurry me?
> being responsible
>
> when I was brought on to make way
> for a difficult birth in that cottage hospital
> and the Cheers child stole my birthday?

In fact it is most unlikely that the poet was 'hurried from the womb' by 'cold steel': the standard method of induction was the use of a hooked implement or, more commonly, a finger, to break the membrane and release the amniotic fluid, and birth followed naturally.[5] Murray's was not a caesarean birth, and 'cold steel' would have been involved only if labour had failed to progress, so that a forceps delivery had been required. There is no reason to think it was. A belief in the cold steel and its likely effects on his mother's health, though, would have profound effects on his future.

Cecil, the proud father, missed the event entirely: he had to be home to do the morning milking. Once he had decided on marriage, clearly he could not go on working for his father without wages, and the young couple had determined to build up a herd of dairy cattle, the standard recourse of small farmers in the area. Cecil's father John Allan seems to have been displeased by this show of independence, particularly since it followed an earlier break with his eldest son Stanley, who had left the family farm entirely to strike out on his own. John Allan continued to demand Cecil's help with tree-felling, and the decisive break between them came just a month before the poet's birth.

On 17 September 1938 Cecil had balked at felling a huge tallowwood selected by his father, on the grounds that it was 'dozy'. His father, directing operations as usual from his horse, insisted: 'No, no, he's a sound stick, he wants falling'. And when Cecil defied him, saying the tree was not only dozy, but dangerous, John Allan angrily called in Cecil's favourite brother Archie to do the job.

Archie knew little about bush work: he was a lazy, rather elegant man who loved dancing and who had married just three months before. As he brought the tree down it struck another standing beside it, and there was a menacing sound from above. At Cecil's warning cry, 'Look out!', instead of standing by the stump, the safest place, Archie ran without looking up, and a large section of the treetop snapped off, plunged and hit him squarely on the head, dashing his brains out.[6] His mother Emily, who was credited with the bad gift of second sight, had gone after them that morning to warn her husband that something dreadful was going to happen to Archie, but she failed to find them in the forest.[7] The break between Cecil and his father had been ratified in blood: each blamed the other for this terrible event, and the rift between them would never be healed.

This helps to explain why John Allan charged Cecil and his young wife such a high initial rent for their small farm, why he refused to help them set up their dairy herd, why he was willing to see Cecil struggling, carrying loads on his back for lack of a cart, and why he made no improvements to their house.

The house was the one in which Les Murray came to consciousness, and which he called home until his father was evicted from it more than thirty years later. It was of 'slab construction', meaning that its walls were of thick pit-sawn slabs of wood, often cedar in the early days, set vertically, covered with a roof of shingles, later corrugated iron, and having a floor of stamped earth covered with linoleum or (later) with wooden planks. The shingles leaked, and the slabs of the walls shrank as they aged, leaving cracks that admitted the wind at all seasons in spite of battens nailed over them, and that darkened with blown rain. There exists a photograph of Cecil in the door of this shack, and behind him sunlight streaks through the generous gaps in the walls.

The little house consisted of two main rooms, one of which was used as a living room, the other as the only bedroom, occupied by Cecil and Miriam, and known simply as 'the room'. Les Murray would describe the interior in his poem 'The Lake Surnames'. At one end of the house was an open porch, and to the other end was attached the kitchen, which was a primitive lean-to (a 'skillion' in Bunyah dialect) floored with linoleum. Cooking was at first done in a camp oven, a cast-iron pot suspended over the fire.[8] Later a dilapidated wood-burning stove was installed. In spite of the primitive conditions, Miriam gained a reputation for her cakes and pies.[9] There was of course no refrigeration until ice deliveries began after World War II, and meat was either salted or eaten without delay.[10]

There was no ceiling, so that the fierce sun of the Australian summer beat on the low roof as if on their heads. There was no lining on the walls, no running water, and no electricity: mains power would only reach Bunyah in 1960 and until then lighting was by paraffin lamp. There was glass in only a few of the windows, cardboard in the rest. In winter it was little warmer than living outdoors, and it was greatly inferior to a Scottish crofter's cottage. The toilet was a corrugated iron 'dunny' near the creek bank; when the can was full Cecil would simply tip it into the gully.[11] The basin for washing dishes and faces was a square paraffin tin cut open diagonally, locally known as a Bogan sink; baths were taken on Saturday nights in a tin tub in water heated over the fire. Les Murray, once he passed his babyhood, slept on the western porch: as a concession, at times of blowing rain there was a canvas screen that could be unrolled to shield him, and on fine nights he would watch the stars. This arrangement was locally known as a 'sleepout'. 'We were poor people, hardly had a roof to our mouths', his father would later joke bitterly.[12]

> Childhood sleeps in a verandah room
> in an iron bed close to the wall
> where the winter over the railing
> swelled the blind on its timber boom
>
> and splinters picked lint off warm linen
> and the stars were out over the hill . . . [13]

To begin with, a single child in a country setting, Les Murray was unaware of the depths of their poverty. 'It was the first house I ever saw, I didn't know they came any better. I liked it. But my parents detested that house because to them it was the image of being kept poor, unnecessarily poor, by my grandfather. And by brute circumstance, the droughts.'[14] But as he listened to his parents' increasingly bitter complaints ('Paying £60 a year for this hovel!'), he could hardly fail to share their sense of grievance. In later life, he would convey the sour, gritty essence of poverty with deadly accuracy:

> Lank poverty, dank poverty,
> its pants wear through at fork and knee.
> It warms its hands over burning shames,
> refers to its fate as Them and He
> and delights in things by their hard names:
> rag and toejam, feed and paw—
> don't guts that down, there ain't no more![15]

His parents' 'fate' was clearly personalised: 'Them and He', the class enemy, was not some distant boss, but Cecil's boorish, bullying father. As their dairy herd slowly built up, Cecil and Miriam could have improved the house, but there seemed little point in spending money on what they did not own, and John Allan refused to either give or sell them the farm. They never quite gave up hope that he would relent, but they were wrong.

However, they did not go hungry: they produced much of their own food, for Cecil prided himself on his vegetable garden. Miriam's needle kept them well clothed. There were small luxuries: Cecil, though he drank very little, enjoyed a smoke, and once a week he bet on the horses running at Taree or Randwick, going in to Deer's store at Krambach to place his illegal bets.[16] And gradually, by sheer unrelenting labour, Cecil and Miriam lifted themselves to the point where they could afford to run an old Dodge, all chrome and smoke, a gift from Cecil's mother.[17] This vehicle was the joy of Cecil's life, partly because his mother had given it to him. He recalled only one other gift from her, a watch, which he treasured. He carefully placed it on a log while chopping one day, and it was swallowed by a passing cow.[18]

Financially Cecil and Miriam were always bumping along the bottom. The dairy brought them less than £30 a month during the war, and when things got bad Cecil would get a job working as a road-mender for a while, employment which he regarded as a great humiliation.[19] Seldom did they have more than £200 in the bank, and every so often they slipped into debt; in 1948, for instance, following the bad droughts of the war years, their debt was £298.[20] Drought and shortages of all kinds were to sink deep into their child's consciousness and emerge in one of his brilliant images:

> Pencil-grey and stacked like shillings
> out of a banker's paper roll
>
> stands the tank, roof-water drinker.
> The downpipe stares drought into it.
> Briefly the kitchen tap turns on
> then off. But the tank says Debit, Debit.[21]

Drought was not the only natural menace. Early in 1939, when Les Murray was just four months old, a terrible bushfire swept through the Bunyah valley. Driven by fierce hot westerlies, it flew from the head of the valley to the hamlet of Coolongolook, 10 kilometres away, in half an hour, faster than a horse could gallop, burning all in its path. There was frantic activity as women and children, including Miriam and her baby, were hurried to safety at a swimming hole in the already burnt-out Wang Wauk forest, while Cecil joined the other men and the older boys in fighting the fire. Cecil and Miriam's house caught alight, but with the help of a truckload of men from Krambach, the flames were extinguished.[22] Remarkably, no one was killed, though losses of stock and property were high.[23] Life in the Bunyah valley, with its poor soils and unpredictable climate, was never going to be easy.

For all that the marriage seems to have been a happy one, and Murray's childhood was in many ways idyllic. He grew up in a radiant wooded landscape that would form the background to many of his poems, and abundant though simple food, a good climate, good health and loving parents were advantages he took for granted. He was at first doted on as a single child. For his baptism, in the white-painted Public Hall that since 1926 had formed the centre of Bunyah, and in which the Free Presbyterians met once a month, his mother made a magnificent silken lace christening gown and coat. In 1983 they would be displayed in Sydney as the centrepiece of a National Trust exhibition of dowry items.

> Item 95 Christening Dress & Coat, of the Australian poet Les Murray. Hand-worked silk crepe made by Mrs Miriam Murray (née Arnall) Bunyah, NSW 1938 ... The christening ensemble which she made for her son Leslie Allan, Born 17th October 1938, was used for his christening in the Free Presbyterian Church at Bunyah; kept by her widowed husband for many years after her death, it was passed on to Leslie in time for the baptism of his son Alexander Cecil in 1978.[24]

Cecil and Miriam had considered naming their son Frederick, after one of Miriam's favourite brothers, Fred Arnall. But Cecil also had a distant relative named Fred: this was an unloved and unlovely man, Fred Norrie,[25] who was childless, and who let it be known that he would leave his farm to a child named after him.[26] Cecil, demonstrating the perverse refusal to better himself that he would show several times in life, determined he would not comply, and the child was named Leslie (each of his parents had a brother of that name) and Allan for his grandfather. He would come to dislike Leslie, which he always shortened to Les, would greatly have preferred to be called Fred, and in later life would consider it 'my other name'.[27] He would remember it when he came to write *Fredy Neptune*.

Almost all the scattered inhabitants of Bunyah were members of the Free Church of Scotland, known to its adherents as the 'Wee Free Kirk'.[28] These strictly Calvinist believers stressed the preaching of the Word, disapproved of all instrumental music including the organ ('the deil's kist o' whistles'), allowed the singing of psalms only, and celebrated Communion but once a year. Cecil and Miriam were regular worshippers, Cecil even acting as lay preacher when heavy rains meant a visiting preacher could not get through.[29] And Cecil and 'Mim' were popular members of the congregation, he because he was a hard worker and good company, she because she used her nursing training to provide free medical care to the whole valley.

Her son was to remember her as curt and undemonstrative towards him: 'untactile', he called her after her death.[30] But in the memories of others she was a loving mother: 'Her whole interest was placed around Leslie', one of his cousins, Lily Sambell, would remember.[31] 'She idolised Leslie, of course, he was her only child', Alma Murray would agree, drawing on what she had been told by others.[32] 'A lovely person', another cousin, Leila Griffis, was to call her,[33] and Ellen Harris, a neighbour of the Murrays, echoed the phrase.[34] Women in particular considered her warm and affectionate, competent and generous. She seemed able to do anything, and one of the things she communicated to her son was a firm belief in the equality of the sexes.[35] Though she was refined and town-bred—'aristocratic', an admiring niece called her years later[36]—she took to milking cows, feeding pigs, mucking out and humping milk-pails as readily as to cooking and sewing.

Above all she was public-spirited. Apart from nursing the district, Miriam was remembered more than forty years after her death for the way she organised 'coin evenings' to raise a wedding gift for engaged couples, and for such extraordinary kindnesses as taking on the sole care of the eight-week-old baby of a friend, Mary Rowe, who was having a breakdown: Miriam lived in the Rowes' house and mothered for the baby for weeks until Cecil complained that he and young Les needed her too.[37]

Dairy farming is hard and unremitting labour, and Cecil and Miriam were natural workers. Every morning the thirty or forty cows had to be brought in from their night paddock to the milking shed which, unlike the house, had a concrete floor and running water. There they would be milked, at first by hand, later by diesel-powered machines, a task occupying perhaps two hours, and thereafter sent out to their house paddock. Then Miriam cleaned out the shed while Cecil carried the 8-gallon milk-cans, weighing nearly 40 kilograms each, one by one on his back to the gate to be collected by the milk truck. Each evening the process would be repeated.

During this activity the baby Les would be left on his own, and as soon as he began to crawl he got into trouble. He was intensely active, energetic and daring. One morning he fell off the porch of the house, landing face down on an upturned hoe which came close to severing his nose: he would carry the white scar under his left nostril for the rest of his life.[38] His father belatedly railed in the porch, and thereafter while they were milking his mother would tie him into a high chair with a belt or with one of her stockings.[39] He hated this confinement, and would never forget it.

> Young parents, up at dawn, working. Their first child can't
> be his own babysitter, so as they machine the orphaned milk
> from their cows, he must sit plump on the dairy cement,
> the back of his keyhole pants safetypinned to a stocking
>
> that is tied to a bench leg. He studies a splotch of cream,
> how the bubbles in it, too thick to break, work like
> the coated and lucid gravels in the floor. On which he then dings
> a steel thing, for the tingling in it and his fingers
>
> till it skips beyond his tether. As the milkers front up
> in their heel-less skiddy shoes, he hangs out aslant
> on his static line . . .
>
> Under the bench, crooning this without words to his rag dog,
> he hears a vague trotting outside increase—and the bull
> erupts, aghast, through the doorway, dribbling, clay in his curls,
> a slit orange tongue working in and out under his belly—
>
> and is repulsed, with buckets and screams and a shovel.
> The little boy, swept up in his parents' distress, howls then . . .[40]

In later life he could never bear to wear a seat-belt and would have constant trouble with the traffic police. Barely out of babyhood, he suffered from paroxysms of rage after being confined in this way. Smackings made these worse, and his mother found that sponging him in a tub of water seemed to help; presently he would calm down and then fall dead asleep.[41]

He had the advantages and disadvantages of the only child: focused attention from his parents on the one hand (when they could spare him any at all), isolation on the other. His father's attention was not always welcome: the boy was adventurous, noisy, active, disobedient, and Cecil's upbringing meant that he knew only one method of discipline—beatings. From about the time he turned two, Murray was smacked increasingly severely and often, intensifying to what he called 'frequent harsh floggings for being a bad boy'.[42] His mother would report his misdemeanours to his father when Cecil came in from work, and a beating would follow. In later life he once made a list of the implements he had been whipped with, and could remember twenty-three, ranging from the stockwhip to a razor strop to a milking-machine transmission-belt.[43] A favourite technique was to send the child out to cut a keen and whippy stick to be thrashed with. These beatings would only stop when he became old enough to outrun his father.

His parents had one tall chest of drawers, on the top of which they put the breakable things they wanted to keep out of his hands. Several times they came back from milking to find these precious objects spread out on the floor. Mystified, for he was much too small to have reached them, they kept watch, and found that he had worked out that if he pulled the bottom drawer out all the way, the next a little less far and the third and fourth less again, he could climb the drawers like stairs to reach the top.[44] For this ingenuity he was punished.

Although Bunyah houses are spaced hundreds of metres apart, the neighbours heard these beatings, but without sympathy: 'He got beaten often, but he never got enough', one of them, Ellen Harris (née Hile), would say toughly years later. 'He defied them about everything. He was one of them kinds of kids.'[45] Asked for an example of his misbehaviour, she said that he had torn up his mother's prized flower garden, for no obvious reason. In later years Les Murray himself would come to believe that he was semi-autistic, and therefore very difficult, hyperactive and badly behaved: 'We half-auties have to stimulate ourselves all the time to feel that we're alive'.[46]

He had little to do with other children of his own age, though his relations occupied all the farms around and there were cousins aplenty. Only very rarely was he allowed to visit Aunt Myrtle Maurer, who lived within easy walking distance, and there play with his cousins Leila and Evelyn.[47] He believed that the reason for his lack of contact with other children was his parents' own isolation through what he called 'poverty-shame': a horror of letting others see the details of their threadbare lives. 'I was *never* allowed visits by playmates', he wrote to me years later: 'Home was too demeaning to let the terrible frank eyes of kids see it. But I heard continually of clan and relatives'.[48] As a result he grew up even more of an only child than he might have been if his parents had not suffered this deep shame of poverty.

Even when they were out in Coolongolook or some other nearby village the shame pursued them. Murray would remember seeing a Christmas party at a local shop, and the embarrassment he caused his parents by running to join it:

> I was a toddler, wet-combed
> with my pants buttoned to my shirt
> and there were pink and green lights, pretty
> in the day, a Christmas-tree party
> up the back of the village store.
>
> I ran towards it, but big sad people
> stepped out. They said over me *It's just, like,
> for local kiddies* and *but let him join in*;
> the kiddies looked frightened
> and my parents, caught off guard
>
> one beat behind me, grabbed me up
> in the great shame of our poverty
> that they talked about to upset themselves.
> They were blushing and smiling, cursing me
> in low voices *Little bugger bad boy!*
>
> for thinking happy Christmas undivided . . .[49]

Ellen Hile, a girl nine years older than himself, lived in a house on the hill above the Cecil Murray farm, and often took care of him to give Miriam time for milking. Ellen taught him to walk, and would dress and undress him. 'I was her doll', Murray recalled.[50] She remembered that he learned to speak before he was two, and that he early showed a prodigious memory for nursery rhymes, from 'Baa Baa Black Sheep' to 'Hickory Dickory Dock'. In particular he loved to recite,

> Tiddly-wink the Barber
> Went to shave his father
> Razor slipped
> And cut his lip
> Tiddly-wink the Barber.

'Now I'm Tiddly', he announced to Ellen, and through much of his early childhood the name stuck to him.⁵¹ Identification with literature and through literature had come before he could read.

His hair was red, like that of almost all the Murrays, and his eyes were curiously coloured, one blue, one green, 'like Hereward the Wake', he would joke in later life.⁵² A little after he learned to walk, from about the age of two and a half, he would finish his breakfast in the morning and set off on his own up the hill to the Hiles', where he would have a second breakfast: he seemed always to be hungry, and he would only be thin once, in the year of his marriage. He would then spend most of the day with Ellen, looking at pictures and playing quietly on his own, before toddling back home towards evening.⁵³

But his chief companions were animals. The cows were constant beneficent presences, and they would be invoked many times in his poetry. Many of his most brilliant images were fixed in the mind of childhood, as when a barefoot farm-child on a frosty morning puts his foot under the cow for the delight of 'quick-fade cow-piss slippers'.⁵⁴ He learned that cows, contrary to their stolid reputation, are flighty, nervous creatures, quick to take fright and in need of constant soothing. His parents raised pigs too, to be fed on milk and scraps, and the boy watched them also, with that extraordinary recording vision.⁵⁵ His rag dog was soon replaced by a real one, the family cattle dog named Bluey,⁵⁶ which he loved. There were also several cats, and a large pet goat: a photograph survives of this goat harnessed to a little cart which Cecil must have made, with a chubby small Murray driving it proudly.

He was impatient of all barriers, from the chest of drawers to the seat-belt. Among the places he was forbidden to visit was the Bunyah Creek, for fear that he might drown. The chief barrier between creek and dairy was a railing, low, but too high for a toddler. His Uncle Charlie remembered seeing the small boy calling the dog to stand next to the rail, climbing on its back and onto the fence, perhaps a metre high, then directing the dog to jump over so he could climb down onto it on the other side.⁵⁷ His parents found him down by the stream, watching the bubbles. Another beating followed.

In spite of severe discouragement, gradually he ranged further and further afield, and about the age of four taught himself to swim in that creek.⁵⁸ He avoided the house of his grandfather, 'intemperate, red-faced lunatic' as Murray once called him,⁵⁹ but most of the other wide-scattered houses were friendly, and everyone knew him even if they were not related to him. He slowly developed the habit of long, solitary walks. When his grandmother Emily was dying of cancer in 1941, his mother was asked to nurse her at another Murray farm at Pampoolah⁶⁰ on the lower Manning River. Three-year-old Les had to stay there too, 50 kilometres from Bunyah:

> I got sick of staying there. I thought the place was gloomy and frightening. I'd been very fond of Granny, I thought she was a nice person, but everything had gone gloomy, and I set out one day to walk home. That would have been in 1941. And I was found about eight o'clock that night well along the way. I'd gone about 10 miles tramping along under the moon enjoying myself. I had no fear of the dark.[61]

A little later he saw his first city, when his mother took him to Newcastle to meet her relations. Here he saw many things for the first time, including electric lights, coal, trams, and a double-storeyed house. Years later he would remember:

> Train city, mother's city, coming on dark,
> Japanese shell holes awesome in a park,
> electric light and upstairs, encountered first that day,
> sailors and funny ladies in Jerry's Fish Café.[62]

His mother's family, he noticed, spoke differently. In Bunyah anyone who had died young or unexpectedly was invariably given the title 'poor', as in 'poor Archie', but his maternal grandfather, dead from phthisis, was never called 'poor': it seemed to him a mystery. 'I had three grandparents, while others had four:/where was my mother's father, never called Poor?'[63]

Language increasingly interested him. From about the age of three he pestered his mother about the meaning of words, and he was fascinated for days by a sibilant phrase from the Lord's Prayer, 'trespass against us':[64] he repeated it hypnotically as he toddled about, and years later it would surface in the celebratory poem he called 'The Broad Bean Sermon'. Bunyah folk in general did not care much for book-learning: 'We didn't dwell a lot on readers', one of them, Lily Sambell, remarked dryly in the patois of the valley.[65] The only books in Cecil's house were Miriam's school prizes, but they included a multi-volume encyclopaedia. When Miriam saw that her son was interested, she got him a simple reading book and helped him through it.

About this time he caused amazement in the store at Dyer's Crossing, one of the local hamlets, by reading aloud the names on the biscuit tins.[66] He was barely four when he emerged from under a table at breakfast to ask his visiting Uncle Charlie, 'What's this word?' It was in a then-popular comic strip in the newspaper, 'The Katzenjammer Kids'. Being told the answer, he said, 'Yes, I should have known that', and went back to his reading under the table. Charlie said slowly: 'Do you realise what we've heard?' Cecil said, 'He can't be reading it'. But he was.[67]

Soon he was struggling through his mother's eight-volume *Cassell's Encyclopaedia*, 1923 edition. By the time he went to school at the age of nine, he had memorised much of its text, and presently he read it to pieces. Nearly fifty years later, in June 1994, he was in Yorkshire, being shown round Halifax by a friend, Michael Freeman, when they spotted, in a second-hand bookshop window, a copy of that encyclopaedia, the first Murray had seen since childhood. Murray promptly turned his back on it: 'Check if I'm right. I think I can tell you the abbreviations on the spines of those books. It goes A to Boa, Boa to Con, Coo to Flo, Flo to Isis, Ita to Nav, Nav to Sca, Sca to Zwi, and Index'. 'Perfect', said Freeman, wondering.[68]

Reading the paper whenever he could get a copy made World War II real for the boy. The distant conflict in Europe had initially meant little even to his parents, for Cecil escaped military service because of a crooked leg, broken as a youth and never properly set, and because he was a primary producer and therefore exempt. After the Japanese attacked the US naval base at Pearl Harbor on 7 December 1941, however, even the Murrays in isolated Bunyah sat up and took notice. The Japanese victories of the following months more than fulfilled the fantasies that fear had long prompted in Australia. With the fall of Singapore on 15 February 1942, 15 000 Australians became prisoners of war, and four days later war came home to Australia when Darwin was bombed. Then came a Japanese swing southward, by August threatening Port Moresby, New Guinea. An invasion of Australia seemed imminent.

The government hastily set up a system of aircraft spotters across the country to keep track of aerial movements. Les Murray's Great-Aunt Jane, who suffered from a hormonal imbalance that made her hugely obese, was selected because she was the postmistress and ran the valley's gimcrack telephone exchange from her house: she and Alma would jointly appear as Beryl in *The Boys Who Stole the Funeral*. Aunt Jane was sent a large identification chart of all friendly and enemy aircraft but proved quite unable to tell one from another, and her size made it hard for her to reach a window before the sound of a passing plane faded. She found that young Les was fascinated by the chart, could soon recognise a passing aircraft at a glance, and, as they became more common, could identify them even by the sound of their engines. As soon as one had passed over, Aunt Jane would phone: 'Tiddly, what was that?' Murray was to remark with amusement, 'In a funny way, I actually served in the war'.[69]

The war came to fascinate and obsess him. Some of Cecil's brothers, including Charlie, were in uniform, and the letters they sent back were eagerly shared. The women were engaged in 'knitting for soldiers'. Presently Italian prisoners of war began to appear in the valley, cheerful men who provided welcome unpaid farm labour, made no attempt to escape, and learnt broken English quickly.[70] Les Murray spelled out the war news to himself, and began making elaborate drawings of battles in which Germans and Japanese featured largely. The end of the war, after the atomic bombing of Hiroshima and Nagasaki in August 1945 and before his seventh birthday, made little difference to this activity, which would continue into his twenties. And when he stopped drawing wars, he would write about them well into his maturity, recognising much later, 'I have written about war largely because I am deadly afraid of it'.[71]

Many of the details of the war news he only half understood, and later he would brilliantly recapture his own puzzlement in a poem he called 'The Ballad of the Barbed Wire Ocean':

> No more rice pudding. Pink coupons for Plume. Smokes under the lap for aunts.
> Four running black boots beside a red sun. Flash wireless words like Advarnce.

The reader, in working out that rice could no longer be imported from South-East Asia, that Plume was rationed petrol, that smoking had to be discreet ('under the lap') because cigarettes were supplied only to favourite customers or relations, that the four black boots are the swastika and the sun that of Imperial Japan, finds the culture of World War II as defamiliarised and mysterious as the boy did, spelling out his newspapers with hypnotised fascination under the table.

When the war ended his mother's brother Harry, back from Germany and suffering terribly from war neurosis, occupied a corner of his verandah for a time, smoking 180 cigarettes a day and too vicious and unpredictable to be safely approached. 'That's where I first saw a full blown case of depression', Murray would remark later.[72] But Charlie and other uncles were more forthcoming. The boy loved listening to his uncles telling stories, and naturally imitated their speech. It was not his mother's tongue, but he would come to value it as the language of his birth, and he would make it a poetic tongue, using it in many of his poems, notably *Fredy Neptune*. His ear for dialogue, formed at this time, would be faultless. It was from his uncles too that he first heard poetry other than that of the Bible: 'When they were half drunk they recited Banjo Paterson, and when they were fully drunk they recited Burns'.

But like all children he took the bad with the good: it was at this time that he began swearing like a Digger. 'As a bullocky's child/in a clan of operatic swearers/I first essayed the black poetry'.[73] At four years old he was to be partly cured of this habit by a visiting carpenter:

> My mouth-farting profanities
> horrified Barney McCann,
> the Krambach carpenter staying

> with us to rebuild our bails:
> *Lord, I won't sleep on that verandah*
> *where you sleep! Not tonight.*
> *After what you just said*
> *the old Devil's sure to come for you.*
> *O he's bad, with his claws and tail.*
> My parents smiled uneasily.
>
> Bats flitted, the moon shone in.
> *Will the old Devil get me?*
> I quavered, four years old, through the wall,
> *Will he get me?* The agile long-boned man
> of pure horror, clinging to the outside
> weatherboards like the spur-shouldered
> hoatzin bird in my mother's
> encyclopedia books. *Not if you*
> *knock off swearing. Go to sleep, Leslie.*[74]

The imaginative child was similarly terrified by hellfire sermons in the monthly Free Presbyterian services in Bunyah Hall, and he never forgot one based on 1 Kings 18.44, in which a cloud no bigger than a man's hand would portend the wrath of God on sinners. Knowing himself to be a bad sinner, for why else would his father beat him so, he scanned the sky fearfully for that cloud for many weeks. He read the Bible from cover to cover, and memorised much of it: taking part in a Free Presbyterian quiz on scriptural knowledge, he simply recited. 'I think I'm the only person in the history of that church who ever got a mark of 1200 out of 1200', he would recall with amusement.[75] The superb music of the Authorised Version wove its way deep into his mind: 'The first poetry I *encountered*', he would later call it, with emphasis.[76]

He had plenty of free time, for his education continued to be self-education until he was nine. During 1946 and 1947, starting when he was seven years old, his mother got him lessons from Blackfriars Correspondence school in Chippendale, Sydney, and he loved them: 'That was terrific because you could do a week's work in a day then have the other six days off'.[77] Like all country children he was expected to work on the farm, mainly doing the lighter jobs, feeding the chickens, pigs and poddy calves, or carrying in the wood and the ice. But by comparison with the children he met when he began going to school, he did not consider himself hard pressed. Many of them, he discovered, arrived at school having done two or more hours' heavy work, and faced hours more when they went home again: they would fall asleep with their heads on their desks at the first opportunity.

His first school, at the beginning of 1948 when he was nine years old, was a newly reopened one-teacher affair with fifteen pupils, Bulby Brush Public School, reached by a 6- or 7-kilometre walk through pleasant countryside, usually in company with two of his cousins, Ray Murray and George Maurer; later Lynette Maurer joined them too. Other children rode to school, their horses spending the day grazing in the school paddock.[78] On these walks Murray and his cousins would pick flowers, or fantasise about such things as pirate ships sailing up Bunyah Creek. 'We had a good imaginative life on the way to school.'[79] Or they would catch and kill rabbits, then very common in the valley, 'by closing in on them from three sides, confusing their poor brains'.[80] On occasions they would capture rarer creatures, a sugar glider or a young echidna.[81] On one of these walks Les Murray and George Maurer quarrelled: 'We had a marvellous fight one day, with fence posts, he broke my finger and it's always stayed crooked. There wasn't any malice, it was just animal spirits'.[82]

The young teacher, John Mylan, an enlightened and tolerant man, was not put off by the fact that Murray arrived for his first day's school bearing a long essay on the Vikings, written on butcher's paper. Instead he read it out to the other children. This might have made for a disastrous start to the boy's school career, but, as he would recall, 'they didn't know the fit punishment of nerds and swots, and didn't hold it against me!'[83]

Mylan also seems to have realised that Murray would learn best if left alone, so he was allowed to spend most of his time in the small library in the back room of the school on his own. Though he was now in regular contact with other children for the first time in his life, he continued to be a loner and an autodidact. Mylan, seeing him beginning Douglas Mawson's *Home of the Blizzard*, on the famous explorer's travels in the Antarctic, tried to guide him: 'It's no good to you, Les, that book is too large to take on',[84] but the boy read it from cover to cover. 'Always in the back room, querying those books', was how another of his older cousins, Lily Sambell, remembered him.[85] 'For an only child in the bush, nine is a late age to start socialisation', Murray was to muse in later life, 'or to start acquiring habits of numeracy and externally imposed discipline. I'm still deficient in all those, and look like never acquiring them now'.[86] His account of these deficiencies was accurate, and would remain so.

He spent three years at Bulby Brush, 1948–50, and in 1951, at the age of twelve, began high school. There was then only one high school in the area, at Taree, and to attend it he would have to board with strangers. To avoid this, his parents arranged for him to go to Wyong High instead, for although Wyong was 240 kilometres away, Miriam had a sister there, Aunt Isobel, and he could live with her and her husband Pat Hickling, who ran a poultry farm. The arrangement did not last long.

Aunt Isobel chucked me out after about seven weeks as being uncontrollable. It was really her children who were uncontrollable but they managed to slip the blame onto me. I didn't mind that much, but I quite liked it down there. Dad hadn't wanted to send me away though, he missed me. I suppose Mother did too but she was firm about it because there was no high school within easy reach of us.[87]

He may not have been uncontrollable, but he was certainly difficult, a big, strong twelve year old who was used to being left to himself to do what he pleased, and who had no gift for getting on with strangers. His aunt accused him of teaching her sons to smoke.[88] So back he came, in March 1951, and this time was sent to board in Taree. He had hardly begun to register the fact that Taree High was a quite different proposition from the other schools he had known when there occurred an event, in April 1951, that was to change his life catastrophically. Although he did not know it, his childhood had ended.

CHAPTER FOUR
DEATH OF THE FAMILY
1951–54

My mother died when I was very young.

BLAKE

At the beginning of April 1951 Miriam Murray was thirty-five and apparently in excellent health. She was strong and active enough to go on providing free nursing for everyone in the district, including her diabetic father-in-law Allan, who would ride up every morning demanding 'my needle', meaning his insulin injection, snarl angrily if she had not already sterilised the syringe by boiling it for him, and leave without a word of thanks when he had received it. She continued to do much of the work around the dairy, and to plan eagerly towards her great dreams, another child and a better house.

At the beginning of 1951 one of those dreams appeared about to come true: the ending of the drought years meant that the dairying now produced an income of over £50 a month, and by constant scrimping, by the end of 1950 she and Cecil had saved £620.[1] They now installed diesel-powered milking machines, further increasing output. Allan Murray was still refusing to sell them the farm, but he gave gruff promises that it would be Cecil's when he died: Cecil and his siblings understood this to mean that Allan intended to leave it to Cecil in his will.[2] It was enough encouragement for Cecil and Miriam to order the roofing iron for a new house they planned to erect higher up the slope, and the gleaming corrugated stack sat next to their shabby home like the promise of a better future.

Miriam also continued to hope for another child: it was not by his parents' choice that Les had reached the age of twelve without siblings. At least twice his mother, to her great delight, had fallen pregnant, and the boy, at the age of eight and then again at ten, had been carefully prepared to receive a little brother or sister.[3] Preparation was needed, for he had made it plain that he did not want a sibling: as Miriam told Ellen Harris, he had threatened that if she brought a baby home, he would 'do something to it' or 'throw it off the verandah'[4]—this last presumably linked with memories of his own babyhood fall onto the hoe. Miriam had been worried by his reaction, for he had shown signs of aggression towards other children before, fighting with visiting boys, including his placid cousin Tasman Arnall.[5]

In the event Miriam's worry was misplaced, for she miscarried twice, and was very depressed. These miscarriages may have been caused by the results of an ectopic pregnancy[6] she had suffered when Leslie was five;[7] for this she was rushed to hospital and operated on, spending a week or more in Taree hospital.[8] Her son's recollection was that these repeated disappointments made her colder and more distant towards him: 'She went from being cheerful in my earliest recollections to fairly morose and stern in later ones'.[9]

It may be that concern about her son's reaction made her more willing to have him away from home during another likely pregnancy, and that this was why he was sent first to her sister at Wyong, and then to a boarding house in Taree. At all events, he was away at Taree in April 1951 when his mother began to experience the pain of a second ectopic pregnancy.[10]

In the account he later got from his father, 'She struggled back over from the dairy to the house which is about 120 yards, I suppose, and she was soaking up the blood with sheets. And they were getting red pretty quick apparently, too. She was haemorrhaging like all hell, in other words'.[11] As the bleeding and pain rapidly worsened, her husband telephoned repeatedly for an ambulance to take her to the hospital at Taree. According to Cecil's account, the doctor whose responsibility it was to authorise the dispatch of the ambulance refused to do so. The doctor 'apparently thought the bush folk were using the ambulance as a bit of a taxi service, but the real truth was that he didn't think us important enough to have it', Les Murray would say bitterly.[12]

> I was in the town at school
> the afternoon my mother
> collapsed, and was carried from the dairy.
> The car was out of order.
>
> The ambulance was available
> but it took a doctor's say-so
> to come. This was refused.
> My father pleaded. Was refused.
>
> The local teacher's car was got finally.
> The time all this took didn't pass,
> it spread through sheets, unstoppable.
>
> Thirty-seven miles to town
> and the terrible delay.

> Little blood brother, blood sister,
> I don't blame you.
> How can you blame a baby?
> or the longing for a baby?
>
> Little of that week
> comes back. The vertigo,
> the apparent recovery—
> She will get better now.
> The relapse on the Thursday.[13]

Miriam Murray died in Taree hospital on 19 April 1951,[14] the immediate cause of death being pyelitis,[15] and her son's life was changed for ever. But the circumstances of her death were less clear-cut than Les Murray's rending account suggests, though he would continue to believe the simplified version until he read an early draft of this book when he was sixty years old.

The Bunyah valley was dotted with Murrays, all of them possessing cars at least as good as Cecil's old Dodge; any of them would have come if called. Cecil did not call them. And the doctor, no matter how snobbish or suspicious of 'hillbillies' using the ambulance as a taxi, would have sent it had he been told of Miriam Murray's condition. According to Ellen Harris, herself a trained nurse by this time, the problem was that Cecil refused to tell the doctor what was wrong with his wife, nor would he tell any of his neighbours.

> Cecil wouldn't tell them that she was pregnant, he didn't want any one to know she was pregnant at first. A neighbour [Mavis Murray] came down and she saw—she was a retired nurse see—she could see what was wrong. She immediately rang the doctor and the ambulance because Cecil couldn't get an ambulance to come. He wouldn't tell them that she was pregnant. He wouldn't tell them that she collapsed or that she was haemorrhaging. He could have told them any of those three things and they would have come immediately. He didn't want any one to know she was pregnant because she had lost one before. Mavis came down and she rang the doctor and told him the circumstances and the ambulance and the doctor all came together.[16]

And Mavis Murray, the trained nurse first on the scene, who had quickly realised how ill Miriam was, confirmed that Cecil resisted having Miriam transported by anything but the ambulance:

> See, the ambulance fellows, when he rang them, said to bring her in to town. He wouldn't. Bloody mad, I'd say. He wouldn't. He said they'd have to come out to get her. So they left it and left it and the doctor eventually did send them out to get her. He [Cecil] just wouldn't go in. He had a car and everything.[17]

The questions crowd in. Why did Cecil try to conceal his wife's state from their relatives and other neighbours when he must have realised that she needed immediate help? Miriam, with her training and one ectopic pregnancy already behind her, would certainly have realised this herself. How can one explain Cecil's initial demand that the ambulance come, combined with his refusal to tell the doctor why it was needed? His motives were as mysterious to those on the spot as they remain today.

Perhaps the likeliest explanation lies in the bad blood that had long existed between Cecil and his father. Despite the fact that he was now in his forties, Cecil had remained in humiliating dependency on his father, and bitterly resented it. His marriage to Miriam, the glamorous outsider in self-enclosed Bunyah, was his main claim to respect in his family. So confident and competent in all other areas, Miriam seemed unable to produce a second child. It is not impossible that Cecil, in that family of ten-child families, felt reduced in the eyes of his relatives, particularly his father, because Les remained without siblings. At any rate, it is clear from Ellen Harris's account that Cecil wanted to keep secret from his relatives the fact that his wife was pregnant again, and that he was deeply concerned to hide another miscarriage.

This is likely to be why he would not call on his relations to provide a car to take his wife to hospital when she clearly needed to go. And it also provides an explanation for his bizarre refusal to tell the doctor why the ambulance should be sent. A telephone call from Bunyah had to pass through the local switchboard, which was operated by Les's large Aunt Jane, the postmistress and former plane-spotter: and Aunt Jane, a formidable gossip, listened in to all calls. To tell the doctor, then, was to risk telling all the valley. And, as Les Murray would recall, 'Aunt Jane, Aunt Allie & many of the older women saw all pregnancy as scandalous, a proof that sex had gone on!'[18] Cecil, steeped in Victorian inhibition, had a horror of telling strangers what his son would call 'private stuff'.[19]

This was a crisis, and Cecil was not good in crises. 'In an emergency, he tended to panic', his son was to say.[20] And once the doctor declined to send the ambulance without good reason being given, Cecil displayed all the obstinacy of the poor man who has suffered a lifetime of humiliation, and feels he is being put upon once again. He would have his rights. So Miriam haemorrhaged rapidly for more than three hours,[21] until a single phonecall from Mavis Murray brought doctor and ambulance racing to Bunyah together. The one-way trip in those days took at least an hour.

Though Miriam had lost a great deal of blood, she was operated on in Taree's well-equipped hospital with apparent success. But she seemed to have lost the will to live, in Ellen Harris's view: 'They took her to Taree and well she went through the operation all right but she didn't try to live. You can usually tell if anyone doesn't fight to live because I was a nurse myself. I don't know how long she lived, about a week or so after the operation and then she died'.[22]

Soon after the operation Ellen met Les, white-faced and frightened, at the hospital: 'He said "Is Mummy going to get better?" And I said to him, "Well she can if she keeps fighting," but she wouldn't fight'.[23]

> Everybody in the town
> was asking me about my mother;
> I could only answer childishly
> to them. And to my mother,
>
> and on Friday afternoon
> our family world
> went inside itself forever.[24]

The dying woman was concerned that her husband might take Leslie out of school, as his father had done to him. She made Cecil promise that the boy would be educated, and laid it on him as a sacred charge. 'My mother got me to Sydney University', Les Murray was to say.[25] Her last words, according to Cecil, were 'Whatever will you and Leslie do?'[26]

For a short time the Murray house bustled with black-clad relatives down from the Manning River. Miriam Murray was buried in the Krambach cemetery. As the funeral cortege drove out from Taree, Les Murray saw an old Aboriginal man, 'who stood by the roadside in Purfleet with his hat in his hands and his eyes lowered ... I was twelve then, but that man has stayed with me, from what may well have been the natal day of my vocation as a poet, a good spirit gently restraining me from indulgence in stereotypes and prejudices'.[27] The boy refused to weep at the funeral. 'I wouldn't cry. I stood there cold.'[28] His wound was private, and he would not expose it to the crowd of mourning Murrays. His own relatives, many of them scarcely known, seem to have meant less to him than that respectful stranger in Purfleet. The relatives came, were briefly important with a 'terrible weak authority',[29] and, having done their duty, departed and left him with his father in the empty house.

In later years he chose to forget most of what those first few weeks of his mother's absence were like. But he could not forget the terrible change that came over his father. Cecil, in the agony of his grief, compounded by guilt, went through a collapse that made him quite unable to comfort his son. He wept, terribly and clamorously; he ceased to shave, to wash, to cook; he seemed not to want to live. During the long days he drifted about, gazing vacantly.

His beloved vegetable garden filled with weeds, and cows ate Miriam's flowers. His income from the dairy plummeted.[30] He did not send his son back to school, and the numbed boy did his best to care for his father, behaving as if he were the parent, a responsibility for which he was utterly unprepared:

> For a long time, my father
> himself became a baby
> being perhaps wiser than me,
> less modern, less military;
>
> he was not ashamed of grief,
> of its looking like a birth
> out through the face
>
> bloated, whiskery, bringing no relief.
> It was mainly through fear
> that I was at times his father.
> I have long been sorry.
>
> Caked pans, rancid blankets,
> despair and childish cool
> were our road to Bohemia
> that bitter wartime country.[31]

An earlier poem about this situation, 'The Widower in the Country', well conveys his father's helpless, griefstricken paralysis, and alludes to the pile of roofing iron round which the weeds were now sprouting. Cecil would never use it: it lay there rusting for years, an emblem of his hopes.

> This afternoon, I'll stand out on the hill
> and watch my house away below, and how
> the roof reflects the sun and makes my eyes
> water and close on bright webbed visions smeared
> on the dark of my thoughts to dance and fade away.
> Then the sun will move on, and I will simply watch,
> or work, or sleep. And evening will come on.
>
> Getting near dark, I'll go home, light the lamp
> and eat my corned-beef supper, sitting there
> at the head of the table. Then I'll go to bed.
> Last night I thought I dreamed—but when I woke
> the screaming was only a possum ski-ing down
> the iron roof on little moonlit claws.[32]

His son seemed to get over the shock of his mother's death more easily, but this was illusion. In fact Les was deeply, terribly wounded, and it would be thirty years before he would be able to face her death directly in a poem.[33] It was not just that she had died, though that was bad enough to a boy of twelve who had had her undivided attention all his life. Ellen Harris's remark that Miriam could get better if she wanted to must have struck him to the core. Mummy had not wanted to live; therefore she could not have loved him. He convinced himself, against all the evidence, that she had resented him, had never kissed him: 'I don't remember ever being hugged or touched'.[34] And he thought he knew why: it was because his birth had prevented her from having other children. 'I don't think she liked me all that much because I was an induced birth and after that she always had miscarriages and I think she linked the circumstances of my delivery with her miscarriages. She got a bit dark on me.' And on being asked if his mother had actually told him that her miscarriages were his fault:

> It was sort of half-said in my hearing. I probably blocked it out but not quite quick enough. I think it slipped out in conversation. They [Cecil and Miriam] used to have rows on occasions. It did depress them both that every attempt at a further child ended in a trip to hospital and a big disappointment. They were puritan people anyhow. Sex was never talked about in the hearing of kids. You overheard stuff. It was talked about as an animal function. But it was very much a forbidden matter and dangerous to talk about or get too near. The message that got to me was that it was mortal, it killed you. That sex causes death.[35]

More precisely, he came to believe that he knew who had killed his mother: he had. He was to blame for his mother's dislike of him, and worse still, he had caused her death. His father, in the madness of his grief, screamed at him on at least two occasions that he had killed her, that if he had not been born she would not have died, and the horrified twelve year old had no reason to doubt it.[36]

> From just on puberty, I lived in funeral:
> mother dead of miscarriage, father trying to be dead,
> we'd boil sweat-brown cloth; cows repossessed the garden.
> Lovemaking brought death, was the unuttered principle.[37]

Grief and rage combined with guilt and self-loathing in a terrible neurosis which puberty would presently compound. He escaped from his father as much as he could, spending time at his Uncle Sam Murray's house, playing with his cousin Ray, and he also visited a family at Firefly, the Cornalls.[38] He went on many solitary day-long walks, taking with him a rifle with which he would shoot any wild thing that moved. He was an excellent shot, the result of long practice, and could kill little birds unerringly, no small feat with a rifle, or knock a rabbit sideways on the run.[39] A rabbit not killed outright would have a thin time of it: 'torturing beasts was in part a by-product of the endless war on rabbits', he would write later.[40] In 'The Abomination' he would write of a rabbit dropped into a stump-hole fire, though the animal in the poem is dead. Lighting fires was another sign of the dangerous state into which he was moving.

Cecil had apathetically agreed to have Miriam's mother to live with them and keep house, but Les found the old lady needed more care than she gave, and after a brief time she returned to Newcastle. Hereafter the link with the Arnalls was allowed quietly to wither, as if it had been severed by Miriam's death. Early in 1952, nearly a year after his wife died, Cecil was persuaded to hire a housekeeper, though he could ill afford one. His choice fell on Alma Coleman, a 22-year-old unmarried mother from Markwell, another of the nearby hamlets. Alma moved into the one-bedroom house with her four-year-old daughter Dianne. She would after some years marry one of Les Murray's cousins, John,[41] and she was to prove the first of more than twenty housekeepers over the years, plus another twenty who stayed only one night, as Murray would tell a friend years later.[42] Cecil treated them with scant courtesy, calling each of them in turn 'The Woman'. He would signal rather than speak to them, rattling his cup when he wanted tea, or drawing a circle in the air when he wanted a plate handed to him, a relic of the days when, as a child, he and his siblings had been routinely struck on the head with a strap for speaking at table.[43] Displays of feminine emotion would draw from him a slow shake of the head, followed by, 'She's not strong, the Woman'.[44]

Despite this, Alma was not sorry to get away from home, and thought the way Cecil and his son were living neither primitive nor squalid, for it was very similar to the style in which she had been reared, as one of a family of nine children whose mother had died when Alma was fourteen.[45] She found it natural enough that Cecil used his old Dodge to transport pigs to the saleyards on the seat next to him, that meals were mainly corned beef and fried vegetables, and that clothes were worn until brown and stiff with sweat, and then boiled in a primitive copper outdoors.[46] She found Cecil quiet, undemanding and easy to live with. His son was another matter.

The death of Les's mother, the irrational blame that attached to himself, the collapse of his father, the responsibility of keeping life going: to all these traumas was now added the coming into the house of another woman, in some sense a replacement for his dead mother, and accompanied by a child, like the one she had died from. Alma, tolerant and hard working, took the pressure of responsibility and a lot of the work off him, but his attitude towards her seems to have been equivocal, and to her small daughter Dianne he showed open hostility. Alma thought him strange: 'He was a boy that didn't sort of know how to play with other children because he was an only child'. And she found she could not leave Dianne with him. 'He'd line her up out the front and he'd pelt the tennis ball at her and she'd come in with all these red patches on her and he was using her, I said, like target practice.'[47]

She noticed his treatment of animals too. One day she had just finished the washing, boiling the clothes in the copper in a paddock, when Les appeared with a cat in his arms, and dropped it into the boiling water. The badly scalded animal managed to scramble out and made off in zigzags, screeching. 'Cecil threatened to do it to him.' But the threat did not deter the boy. On another day, she recalled, he fed the kitchen stove with wood until the top glowed red hot, and then dropped the cat (presumably a different cat) on it.[48]

To some extent this was the behaviour of a bored country boy, who had all his life seen animals swiftly and ruthlessly castrated or butchered. The country sport of setting two cattle dogs to pull a cat or rabbit to pieces had not disappeared, and he knew of one case of a country boy chain-sawing a calf in half for the fun of it. In later life he would recall, using the distancing effect of the third person, 'There was a lot of cruelty in those kids. They lived in nature. They saw how casually cruel animals were and they saw how casually cruel people were to the animals. I guess it stirred them and frightened them and they did cruel things out of fear as much as anything. And for power. Usual human mixture of stuff'.[49]

And rough treatment even of other children was not uncommon. Les's cousin Oscar (son of Cecil's coldly sadistic brother Stanley) had crippled another boy, Tommy Hile, by smashing his patella with a mattock, and later had cut off two of the fingers of Tommy's sister Ellen with an axe, and then run away leaving the little girl drawing with her blood on a log, unwilling to go home without her fingers for fear of getting into trouble.[50]

For all that, Les Murray's behaviour was beyond even casual country cruelty, as he came to understand:

> I was a disturbed child. I didn't know then, but looking back on it I was certainly a disturbed child. I was a gentle, good natured, harmless, polite, disturbed child but inside I was a bloody mess. Full of war. Whole days where the mind rotated on nothing but imagery of death, destruction, mayhem and war, savagery. A lot of kids are like that.[51]

He was almost without support and without constraints:

It was a period of a weird mixture of shock and of freedom. It was kind of chaos. In many ways I was Huck Finn for about eight years. I've still got the instincts in me. I've never quite got over the idea of Huck Finn, that one day the bottom will fall out of things and I'll be back sleeping under logs. One day the administrative error of letting me into respectability and comfort will be noticed and cancelled.[52]

Or, as he put it in one of his most powerful poems, 'The Tin Wash Dish':

Shave with toilet soap, run to flesh,
astound the nation, run the army,
still you wait for the day you'll be sent back
where books or toys on the floor are rubbish
and no one's allowed to come and play
because home calls itself a shack
and hot water crinkles in the tin wash dish.

It is a measure of his desperation at this time that he took refuge with some of his father's relations: 'I went over to my Uncle Sam's a lot and he was pretty generous about it. They didn't mind having an extra kid around. They were pretty generous to me. It was to get away from the atmosphere of home a lot, which was Dad just absolutely smashed by grief. He couldn't do much, he'd just burst into tears at any little thing'.[53]

After spending the rest of 1951 in this chaos, he was sent to school again at the beginning of 1952, Nabiac Central School in the village where he had been born. He was placed in the Year 8 class, though he had missed Year 7, the first year of high school.[54] Nabiac Central was small, with only 150 children aged from five to fifteen, almost all of them farm-children like himself, and he (or at least his Bunyah clan) was known to them, for the school was full of Murrays,[55] so that he was accepted without difficulty. But, in an ominous sign, one of them addressed him as 'Nugget': the name was not repeated, but for the first time, he was to remember years later, 'I realised I was fat'.[56]

The headmaster, Mr Greig, a wrinkled dark man 'like an amiable kobold', treated him with compassion, no doubt knowing something about his home life. He got to school in the mornings on the milk truck, having to work for his lift: he was required to alight at each farm gate and heave the waiting 10-gallon (46 litre) milk-cans onto the truck. He would reach school having lifted hundreds of the 50-kilogram cans, in what he would memorably describe as 'the schoolboy's calisthenic, hoisting steel men man-high/till the glancing hold was a magazine of casque armour'.[57]

This constant heavy exercise added muscle to an already large frame: he developed the build of a weight-lifter, and though he did not often show it off, he had extraordinary strength. In his twenties he would when necessary put the nose of his car into a tight parking-spot, get out, lift up the back and move it into place, grinning at the astonishment of his friends and the passers-by.[58] He was a natural heavyweight. This strength, developing in his teens, immunised him from bullying and soon made it impossible for his father to continue to beat him. Instead the neighbours would hear the two of them raging at each other like equals, and on occasions, Ellen Hile asserted, they fought each other with their fists.[59] Murray himself denied this: 'We came close, but I couldn't punch him. Respect. Pity'.[60]

He enjoyed Nabiac Central, continuing there his Bulby Brush routine of isolation and self-directed study. He spent much time by himself in the library, and on days when he did not feel like going to school at all, he would drop off the milk truck before it entered the village, and spend the day reading under the bridge, until it was time to catch the bus that took him home. He read mainly science fiction and war books, he remembered long after.[61] Mr Greig condoned these absences, and in spite of them Murray completed all his tests.[62] He also made sure he was always there on Wednesdays, as that was the day they had educational films: this was the beginning of his lifelong love of films, and he would watch anything on a screen, the flickering seeming to induce a delicious hypnotic state in him.[63]

His intelligence was immediately obvious to the teachers, and his English assignments in particular were the talk of the staffroom. Mr Greig took him for English, and Lionel Gilbert, the biology, art and social science teacher, remembered how the headmaster looked forward to the thirteen-year-old Murray's next essay: 'Doug Greig would say, "One of Les's compositions is here", and we'd go into his office and savour it together. He wrote beautifully, and like an adult: not just the vocabulary, but the ideas too. He expressed himself like an interesting adult'.[64] Murray shone in other subjects too, particularly in Agricultural Biology, where his marks rose into the 90s, a rarity in that school. Lionel Gilbert would remember that he was shy, quiet and attentive, though 'his books were not paragons of neatness'.[65]

The teachers noticed that he was self-contained, a loner, and 'rather sad, to start with'.[66] Characteristically, he would stand solitary by the side of the playground, often in the same spot beside a portable temporary classroom, coolly watching his schoolmates dashing about, and at intervals smiling to himself as if secretly amused. Other children were curious about him, partly because of this aloof air, partly because of his size and height (he stood head and shoulders above the rest of the school), partly because of his huge vocabulary which he liked to display whenever he spoke to them. 'My only social skill in the world was showing off', he would remember.[67] They baited this strange big boy for a little, and he endured it patiently. The youngest pupils, pouring out of the temporary classroom like bees, would buzz him cheekily, and when he pretended to lunge at them, would scream delightedly and run.[68] And he would go back to silence, exile and cunning.

It was at Nabiac that he met a girl he later came to realise had been his first love. She was the adopted daughter of the Greigs, a tall, striking blonde named Marion, with no resemblance to her ostensible parents. Despite this they had raised her to believe that she was their biological daughter, and Mr Greig was very angry when one day a teacher left Marion's record card out on a desk, and the girl learned the truth.[69] The shock was terrible. Though the Greigs were very kind to her, she was tormented by the sense that she did not know who she was, and she grew increasingly depressed; later, as a young student nurse in Sydney, she would kill herself. Something about her miserable sense of alienation made Murray recognise her as a kindred spirit: she was his one female friend throughout his schooldays.

> I met a tall adopted girl some kids thought aloof,
> but she was intelligent. Her poise of white-blonde hair
> proved her no kin to the squat tanned couple who loved her.
> Only now do I realise she was my first love . . .
>
> The slender girl came up on holidays from the city
> to my cousins' farm. She was friendly and sane.
> Whispers giggled round us. A letter was written as from me
> and she was there, in mid-term, instantly.
>
> But I called people 'the humans' not knowing it was rage.
> I learned things sidelong, taking my rifle for walks . . .
>
> Whether other hands reached out to Marion, or didn't,
> at nineteen in her training ward she had a fatal accident
> alone, at night, they said, with a lethal injection
> and was spared from seeing what my school did to the world.[70]

Murray's unfocused rage at what life had done to him concentrated itself on a longing to go into the army: a uniform, a rifle, licence to kill not just animals but 'the humans': that would give him a way of striking back. The militaristic culture of World War II had been reinforced by the Korean War, which began in 1950, and his fascination with things military was stronger than ever.

> I had this idea of going and being an army officer. I could do the short course at Portsea [Officers School] and become a second lieutenant. I don't know why I had that ambition, I wasn't even particularly warlike. I suppose there was a lot of violence in me and boys at that time were war mad, a thing which changed strongly around Vietnam time. But during the fifties boys' culture was deeply military. Because I was a disturbed child I was probably more war-mad than a lot.[71]

It would have been hard to find someone less suited to the military life of discipline, precision and uniformity than this dreamy, vulnerable individualist. But in pursuit of this ambition young Murray, now fifteen years old, dropped out of Nabiac Central School at the end of 1953 after gaining his Intermediate School Certificate in Year 9 of his schooling, intending to wait until he was old enough to enter Portsea Officers School.

Many of the Murray cousins left school after Year 6, never getting to high school even if they wanted to. Cecil's sister Myrtle's four daughters longed to go on but were sent out to work in their early teens, to their lasting resentment, following the pattern set by Cecil and his siblings.[72] Their father did not hold with education. His neighbours by and large agreed: one of them, old John Sambell, growled that 'if you give your children education they get dissatisfied and leave home', and there was much sage nodding of heads.[73] But Cecil, now trying with greater success to put his own life back together, remembered his wife's deathbed commission, and tried to get his son to stay on at school. Or at least, if he was to stay at home, he should help on the farm. But Les, self-willed, angry, confused and too big to beat, would not.

Thus he spent another year, 1954, on his own at the age of fifteen, quarrelling increasingly fiercely with his father, fighting the fires of puberty in his blood, wandering about, on foot or on an old pony,[74] with his rifle. Above all, he read. He would appear at mealtimes, the housekeeper Alma recalled, and as soon as the meal was over, 'he'd go with his book. You wouldn't see him then till next mealtime. He done a lot of reading'.[75] In later years Murray was to come to think that his childhood had been ideal preparation for the course he would follow: 'I was a bit dreamy, solitary and terribly interested in words—a word freak. And that's really enough until adolescence'.[76] He was to consider that his education progressed fastest when it was not interrupted by school. But his father, wishing to fulfil Miriam's dying request, eventually persuaded the boy to agree to two more years of school. In 1955 he would go to Taree High, where he had spent a few weeks before his mother's death. It was an agreement he would bitterly regret.

CHAPTER FIVE
TAREE HIGH
1955–56

There is no end to the violations committed by children on children, quietly talking alone.

ELIZABETH BOWEN

Les Murray was sixteen years old when he came to Taree High School for the second time, at the beginning of 1955. His previous stay, ended by the death of his mother, had lasted just a few weeks four years earlier. After his 'Huckleberry' years of running wild, interrupted by stints at small friendly bush schools, where everyone knew him, Taree[1] was something very different. Though the town had fewer than 10 000 inhabitants, that made it a city in Murray's eyes, and this would be his first extended experience of one, though he had visited Newcastle twice, and had often been into Taree with his father to shop.

There was no school bus to Taree, and his father was too busy to take him. Cecil had by this time given up his dairy herd and gone back to his bachelor occupations of timber-getting and bullock-driving; his work for the Masonite company meant that he sometimes camped out in an old tram-car in the bush during the week, cutting timber in distant forests on the lower Myall River.[2] It was agreed that Les Murray would have to board in Taree during the week, going home only at weekends. At first he had a shared room in the house of a Mrs Gibbs, next door to the Peter's Creamery. Most of his fellow boarders were young and boisterous workers in the creamery. Mrs Gibbs, eighty years old but very much in control, made no attempt to stop them when one night, soon after his arrival, they laid hands on young Murray and inducted him into their society by forcibly holding the scared youth down, removing his trousers and coating his genitals with boot-polish, amid howls of laughter: 'greasing his bearings', they called it.[3] He bore this ritual humiliation stoically: 'It does you no harm, I suppose'. This was the society he lived in outside school hours.

Yet in some ways it was better than living at home. For one thing, he had access to the Peter's Creamery showers: he could shower all day if he pleased, and for the first time since the death of his mother, he was really clean. The shower on the farm had consisted of a zinc bucket with holes, mounted on a beam in the dairy, and the pleasure lasted no more than a minute: the endless Creamery showers were a luxury he never tired of. The other advantage of boarding house life was that he got away from his father, and by now he was finding even weekends back in Bunyah a trial: 'Going home to Dad was a mixed blessing. He did his best, he was just wrecked'.[4]

But it was during the day that he had real need of stoicism. Taree High was a much larger school than any he had experienced: in 1955 it had nearly 800 pupils, and many of them were well known to each other because they lived in town. In addition they had already been through three years of high school together. Murray, as a newly arrived country boy in class 4A, was an outsider on two counts.

He was not just new, he was odd: he had no social graces except trying to impress by showing off his vocabulary and his huge general knowledge: this worked on the teachers, but irritated the students. 'I didn't have any idea at the time that it was a dreadfully dangerous thing to do because it can get you regarded as a nerd, a swot and all sorts of dangerous pond life.'[5] He had a slight speech impediment which made him pause before getting certain words out, as if he were fighting down a stammer: he would keep this for life. He was shy, quiet, immature and puppyishly anxious to be liked, particularly by the girls. To make matters worse, he was visibly a country boy and poor: there was about him an indefinable sense that he was uncomfortable wearing shoes, and his shirt would not stay in his trousers.[6] The absence of running water in his home could be deduced, for though his body was clean, thanks to Peter's Creamery, his clothes were grubby and smelled.[7] He suffered from bad acne, which he picked at constantly.[8]

And he was very big. He had by now reached his full height of just under 6 feet (180 cm) and he had his father's broad shoulders and barrel chest. His weight was already 15 stone, or more than 95 kilograms, though he was not particularly corpulent, most of that weight being bone and muscle.[9] In school photographs he is taller and broader than the masters. He would have been a very useful member of the rugby XV, but he had no interest in sport of any kind and did not know enough to hide his disdain for it.[10] He was a natural victim.

The pupils in his year, about fifty of them divided into two classes, turned on this new, strange boy, and he was mercilessly baited. He accepted this patiently, as he had at Nabiac Central, expecting that they would grow tired of it. But whereas at Nabiac he had been part of a large clan of Murrays who would stand up for him if things got too bad, and the baiters had been part of his world of the rural poor, for whom there might be consequences from Murray neighbours if they went too far, here he was defenceless and undefended.

It was the girls who particularly fixed on him. Other boys at the school believed it was because the girls thought they should be best in subjects such as English, History and Art, and Murray quickly showed that he could easily outdo them.[11] Murray himself believed that they were in some sense revenging themselves for slights at the hands of other boys:

> Something or other was working in them. I suspect that it was by no means entirely their own fault. They had probably had a bugger of a time from other boys and here was one that was such a droob, such a helpless weirdo, that they could get their own back on the male race . . . They were probably having a hell of a time with their own identity and their own fears because in that merciless world of teenage girls, nobody's ever pretty enough and nobody's ever got few enough pimples and nobody's ever got the right clothes. It's merciless, merciless. You need a valve, something to take it out on.[12]

Murray was the ideal victim because it was easy to raise a laugh against him, and because when persecuted he retreated into a dumb, miserable silence. 'If goaded he would just sit and withdraw into himself, you know what I mean?' recalled one of the girls who tormented him most pitilessly.[13] She also noticed, and misunderstood, his hunger for and fear of sex, recalling forty years later, 'He seemed particularly to dislike girls. He would say "Stupid women" and had no time for you. I got the impression he couldn't stand women. To tell you the truth I was very surprised when I heard he'd married'.[14] Naturally his fellow-pupils, though they knew he had lost his mother, had no conception of the terror that warred constantly with his longing for a girlfriend. Murray himself was only half aware of it:

> Oh I probably sent out signals that said No touchy, keep away, frightened of you! this kind of thing. I particularly copped persecution at the hands of about ten of the girls in that class. They were worse than anyone. The boys used to get bored with persecuting me sometimes but this particular bunch of girls found it an insatiable delight. The rest of them kept their distance as they always do. They don't take part in the bullying but they don't give you any sympathy or comfort at all. They are afraid of getting any on them, persecution of themselves.[15]

The method his fellow-pupils fixed on was relentless mockery of Murray's size. 'The way that they got me was to say that I was fat. I wasn't particularly, at the time, but that was their way of dealing with me.'[16] He was addressed by a plethora of fat-names: 'Tubby', 'Nugget', 'Fatso' and worse, in a varied but unrelenting campaign that gradually broke down his already tottering self-esteem.

Murray did not imagine this treatment. One of his fellow-pupils, Robin Norling, recalled, 'There's no doubt that his view the girls were getting at him is right. The trouble was that he wanted to be liked by them, and showed it; and his social strategies were sadly lacking. He tried to show off to them intellectually, and didn't succeed'.[17] The boys joined in half-heartedly, making fun of him by clumsy practical jokes such as loading his schoolbag with bricks and waiting to see him lift it, a jape that backfired when he swept it up effortlessly; they also treated him with contempt, sniggering at everything he said, with sidewise glances for approval from the girls. 'The kind of cruel things you do', one of them would remark, 'to the lowest order of kid in a school'.[18]

Some schoolboy wit among them named him 'Bottlebum', and many called him nothing else for two years. He learned to regard as a friend any boy who derided him only in public, to protect himself, and was sensible in private.[19] There were three or four of these, including Ralph Suters and Bob Wallace. Wallace often invited Murray round to his home, and in later years was amazed to hear that he had not liked the school.[20] The only one who never taunted him, and addressed him as 'Les' even in public, Colin McCabe, he gratefully regarded as his best friend, and never forgot him.

But it was the girls, whose company he longed for and feared, who refined the mockery. It was one of them who seems to have originated the name many of the girls used for him, 'Bottom'. With its combination of crude reference to his size, Shakespearian echo[21] and a suggestion of his place in this society, it was an inspired piece of cruelty. Had it been used once or twice it might soon have been forgotten: but it was used consistently for the two years he was at Taree High, and it would make a return, with terrible results for Murray, more than thirty years later. And Bottom the sexual fool was how these girls loved to see Murray.

> I would have treated them with my usual mixture of shyness, bluster and fear. That gets you nowhere, that gets you taken after. I used to have strings of sixteen-year-old girls hanging after me screaming with laughter and provoking me into making more of a fool of myself. And coming on to me, making various motions towards being my girlfriend in order to dismiss any such idea and howl some fresh ridicule. I'd make some evasive reply to escape, and that would cause more merriment. It was hell, it was proper functioning hell.[22]

The death of his mother had already fixed in him a terror of sex: this persecution, taking the form of constant sexual attraction and rejection, turned the knife in the green wound, and went on doing so for two years. Reasoning it through in maturity, he would come to think he was the victim of 'a kind of attempted psychic castration of people who are out of fashion in some way', at the hands of his schoolmates. 'Species always breed back towards the middle, towards the average. And they will do their best to prevent breeding on the part of the non-average.'[23] It is this reflection that underpins one of his most misunderstood poems, 'Rock Music':

> Sex is a Nazi. The students all knew
> this at your school. To it, everyone's subhuman
> for parts of their lives. Some are all their lives.
> You'll be one of those if these things worry you.
>
> The beautiful Nazis, why are they so cruel?
> Why, to castrate the aberrant, the original, the wounded
> who might change our species and make obsolete
> the true race. Which is those who never leave school . . .
>
> It's the Calvin SS: you are what you've got
> and you'll wrinkle and fawn and work after you're shot
> though tears pour in secret from the hot indoor clouds.

These years of quiet cruelty, helplessly endured, were to prove one of the vital formative experiences of his life. It was as crucial as that other terrible psychic wound, with which it was linked, the death of his mother. At Taree High, he would come to see, he was the victim of an organised, powerful majority, a mob with leaders who set the fashion and who had decreed his torture and exile. And there was no appeal against his sentence. 'Nothing a mob does is funny', he would say in *Fredy Neptune*, his most detailed study of this phenomenon.[24]

Those who tried to break ranks and show him human warmth at Taree High were pulled into line:

> For example, the only girl in the school who ever initiated a conversation with me was a cousin called Elizabeth King. The day after this friendly yarn, though, I saw her in the playground being earnestly Spoken To by other girls, all casting glances in my direction—and these were the last looks she ever did cast in my direction. She had seemingly got her peer-group orders, and I ceased to exist. And she wasn't even in my accursed year, but several years lower.[25]

He was made to drink deep of the bitter waters: he would never forget, and in his poetry he would make that terrible time live again for ever:

> Those years trapped in a middling cream town
> where full-grown children hold clear views
> and can tell from his neck he's really barefoot
> though each day he endures shoes,

> he's what their parents escaped, the legend
> of dogchained babies on Starve Gut Creek;
> be friends with him and you will never
> be shaved or uplifted, cool or chic.
>
> He blusters shyly—poverty can't afford instincts.
> Nothing protects him, and no one.
> He must be suppressed, for modernity,
> for youth, for speed, for sexual fun.[26]

In his later writing he would recognise the universality of his situation at Taree High: every society has its victims, every society its torturers. He would always be on the side of the outcast: the poor, the powerless, the odd, the unemployed, the unfashionable. For the victimisers, the enforcers of fashion, he would find many names: 'the humans', he had called them as an angry child, later 'the snobs', 'the mob', 'the Nazis', 'the police'. In a sense he would never get over this experience: 'Merely crossing a schoolyard, even today', he would write in 1983, 'can fill me with muscle-tightening horror'.[27] It was Taree High that turned him decisively against enforced conformity, intellectual gangs, particularly literary and academic ones, and the mob-persecution of any individual, even those he disagreed with, often women: Lindy Chamberlain, Helen Demidenko, Pauline Hanson.

The sexual pressure on him was increased by his home life. After some months boarding with Mrs Gibbs, he moved to another boarding house nearer the school, run by a Mrs Cox. Here he shared a room with a signal worker on the railways, whom Mrs Cox would annoy by calling him 'our male telephonist'. This man was very successful with women, though in Murray's view 'you wouldn't have noticed him in a crowded place'.

> I think he was just enthusiastic. He must have been persuasive. He'd come off shift at midnight, and he'd quite often bring home a girl from one of the trains that passed through in those dark cold hours of the night. He'd put them back on the next train in the morning. His passion was fornication, he used to bring girls home and have his way with them in the room that we shared. I had to stay asleep. My orders were to stay asleep. So I heard a certain amount of human urgency.[28]

These experiences Murray made the mistake of relating to some of his schoolmates, who hated the tone with which he tried to keep control of his urgent desires. 'They wanted to be romantic about all that stuff. But when it was talked about at all by me, it was talked about in the coolest most scientific way, as if done by ants on Mars.'[29]

Some of the teachers could see what was happening, and pitied him. 'Why didn't one of them say so?' Murray would ask bitterly years later. 'It would have been like a glass of water in Hell.'[30] But they felt unable to intervene. All of them, of course, heard his nicknames.[31] As his art teacher, James Murdoch, remarked, 'I knew Les came from the country, and that he was very isolated. I remember him because he was different from the others, and he wasn't happy at school. Not interested in sports. He was teased and set apart: Bottlebum, the other boys called him, I remember. But I found him very well behaved, and very respectful in class'.[32] The English master, Keith McLaughlin, recalled, 'He was gauche and clumsy: pupils and staff both felt he was out of things socially. Also he was very big, and very clever'.[33]

Les Lawrie, the physical education teacher, treated him with kindness and excused him from the weekly exercises. This was half compassion, half self-interest on Lawrie's part: it was a requirement of his job to 'pat' or steady the pupils as they came over the vaulting box, and the year before he had badly hurt an arm in catching a boy named John Hartcher, who weighed 13 stone (82 kilograms). Murray was 6 inches taller than Hartcher and broader by a good deal, so that Lawrie regarded him with trepidation: 'Les was hard to forget, I can tell you. He's big now: well he wasn't much smaller then. And the sight of him coming over a vaulting box at you, out of control, he was usually out of control, and you've got to pat him—I tell you it was a formidable sight'.[34]

Murray avoided all physical activity other than the cadets, which he loved, and which provided cause for further scorn. Cadets had ceased to be obligatory for all boys in the year he arrived at Taree High. Most boys gratefully ceased to attend, but Murray was so keen that he wore his cadet uniform whenever possible. He was rapidly promoted to be sergeant, and wore the stripes with pride, though the cadet master thought him too sloppy to be a soldier.[35] He was however the star of Taree High's five-man Rifle Team, posing proudly with them in a photograph in *The Torch*, the school magazine.[36]

His military interest grew steadily during this time of misery at Taree: the unrelenting victimisation produced a smoldering, impotent resentment that made him long to be part of some powerful group and in a position to strike back at his tormentors: 'Imagine the teeth-clenched eerie delight of fellows pouring bombs out on Germany, the number of schoolyards they were killing'.[37] He was later to realise that at this time he was going down a path that could have led to terrible things:

> Slim revenge of sorority. He must shoot birds,
> discard the love myth and search for clues.

> But for the blood-starred barefoot spoor
> he found, this one might have made dark news.[38]

He seems only once to have turned on his tormentors by bloodying the nose of the next boy to call him Bottlebum, which he could easily do, for he was stronger than any two of them. He flattened his opponent, a boy named Worth, without difficulty. But fighting back, he found, merely drew more attention to him: he was accused of bullying ('Pick on someone your own size!') and he could not fight the girls.[39] He confined his red-eyed hatreds to killing small creatures on the farm.

He lived an internal life in self-defence, a life of which his teachers and fellow-pupils knew nothing, building up a private mythology to give himself strength. One of the stories that consoled him was that of Samson, who had always been his favourite character in the Bible. 'He had a bugger of a time but he brought the whole world down on their heads.'[40] Murray loved films, and saw as many as he could. One of these in particular provided him with a parallel to his own situation, and he saw it until he knew the dialogue by heart from beginning to end. It was *From Here to Eternity*, the Fred Zinnemann love-and-war hit of 1953,[41] set in Hawaii in the build-up to the attack on Pearl Harbor. Murray identified strongly with Private Prewett, the powerful boxer played by Montgomery Clift, who refuses to fight again because he once killed an opponent, and who is persecuted relentlessly by his corrupt company commander. His only friend, played by Frank Sinatra, is killed for trying to defend him. Prewett breaks and deserts just before the Japanese attack. *From Here to Eternity* explored Zinnemann's recurrent theme of the crisis of moral courage, requiring an individual to face his conscience and choose between maintaining his personal integrity or conforming to external demands. This was a lesson Les Murray was already drawing from life.

> I loved that movie, I really did. I suppose subconsciously it reflected a lot of things that were happening to me. There was this persecuted absolutely lone fellow, who had one friend, played in the film by Sinatra, who was killed in a fight. I suppose it was that and other military fantasies that got me through Taree High School.[42]

The other great attraction of the film, though Murray did not mention it in later years, was the sultry love scene, particularly daring for its time, in which Burt Lancaster and Deborah Kerr embrace on the beach as the surf rolls over them.

In his art class Murray expressed pain, anger and grief continually in his drawings: those around him noticed but did not understand what they were seeing. One of his fellow-pupils, Robin Norling, who later became an important artist, recalled that 'At a time when the rest of the class had moved on to madly sophisticated abstract art, he was still drawing his one subject, which was soldiers, tanks, war machinery, generals. He was crazy about war. Like a kid'.[43] The art teacher, James Murdoch, found that whatever subject he asked the students to paint, from a bowl of flowers to a landscape, Murray 'would manage to introduce some Nazis, German soldiers in their German helmets. Bullets going everywhere, battle scenes. I would ask him what was the relationship of what he'd painted to what I'd set, and he always had a good explanation'.[44]

Murray was good at explanations that covered up the gaps in his work. According to Les Lawrie, 'He had a reputation as a bull artist, with his exam papers. The economics teacher [Bill Allen] said Les Murray wrote a pretty good romance when he didn't know what to put in his economics exam'.[45] On the other hand he had extraordinary knowledge of most unexpected areas. In one of the first art classes, James Murdoch told the group that they would be studying pre-Columbian art. Could any of them name one pre-Columbian civilisation? The rest of the class was utterly stumped, but Murray's hand went up: 'Ah, sir, do you mean the Aztecs, the Maya, Zapotec, Totonac, and Teotihuacán civilisations, the Toltecs . . .' He knew them all, Murdoch would recall years later.[46] Who could fail to detest such a classmate?

And in English and History he was the outstanding pupil of his year. The English teachers, Keith and Edith McLaughlin, were particularly impressed by him from the start. 'He was interesting to teach, more than most pupils, because he was genuinely interested in words. He owned a dictionary, a *Concise Oxford* I think, and he looked words up and remembered them, and used them, very unusual words sometimes. He used words like an adult. I enjoyed teaching him.'[47]

Murray's vocabulary impressed his fellow-pupils too. Each year the school magazine, *The Torch*, carried a class report on the senior pupils. The report for class 4A in 1955 devotes a doggerel couplet to each pupil, including 'Les at English is a whiz/Is a dictionary in that head of his?'[48] By the next year there had been little change, the report for class 5A noting, 'Les could well make his home in a dictionary'.[49] Perhaps for his own amusement, he would sometimes misuse the polysyllabic words he threw at his schoolmates. Robin Norling was to say, 'I remember him threatening to "transubstantiate someone through a wall". Not that he was violent, this was just bluff and horseplay'.[50]

Murray played up to this image of himself as a 'brain' and a 'whizz with words'. It was a big improvement on himself as sexual clown. His fellows knew that at what they all called 'playtime' he took himself off to the library to read his way through the school *Encyclopaedia Britannica*. 'Kids would say to him,

"Where are you up to now?" ' Norling remarked later, adding, 'He set out to be preposterous. He could talk about anything. I would say he had a very lonely life'.[51] Other pupils were less sympathetic: 'He chose not to socialise, and then blamed others for isolating him', one of them said coldly years later.[52]

Nor did Murray hesitate to argue with the teachers if he thought they were wrong about some fact or opinion. It was not just that he read the encyclopaedia: he appeared to remember everything he read. His memory was already as retentive as a mantrap. Bob Wallace was impressed:

> He had a huge brain for history and had all these quotes up his sleeve: in Modern History he would virtually take over the class. Same in English. We admired his talent. When he spoke out he knew what he was talking about. He argued with teachers, and wasn't often proved wrong. He had a few battles that way with the McLaughlins, but they liked him though they were a bit wary of him.[53]

Particularly bright pupils could take certain subjects, including English, at Honours level, which meant sitting a separate examination at the end of the School Leaving Certificate year. The McLaughlins encouraged Murray to do English Honours, and tutored him with pleasure. It was with them that he first began reading poetry in a concentrated way, focusing particularly on Gerard Manly Hopkins and T. S. Eliot, who were set for study,[54] but also ranging much more widely than he was required to do. In a single weekend on the farm he read the whole of Milton's poetic output, particularly relishing *Samson Agonistes*, and it never struck him that this was an unusual way for a schoolboy to spend his free days.[55]

Eliot was the first Modernist writer he encountered, and the American poet's pervasive melancholy struck a painful chord with him: in later years he would come to hate Modernism as a manifestation of cultural depression. 'Modernism's not modern: its true name's Despair/I wear it as fat. And it gnawed off my hair', he would write.[56] He also disliked what he saw as Eliot's 'desertion of egalitarian America for snobbish English high culture'.[57] It would be many years before he could visit Eliot's memorial stone in Westminster Abbey and half-make his peace. 'I said to him as he was lying there horizontal and I was standing up vertical, I said "You were a damn good poet but I still wouldn't want to meet you".'[58]

Despite the fact that he had already begun to live poetry, when Edith McLaughlin asked for a contribution for the school magazine at the end of 1955 and again in 1956, he provided not poems but short stories. In 1955 he published a lightly humorous, autobiographical piece about school cadets in which a particularly sloppy cadet is punished by 'Sergeant Thompson, a precocious young pimple-faced lad'.[59] This sketch, though confidently written, is notable chiefly for being his first publication of any kind.

By the following year, 1956, however, he was able to turn out a Faustian yarn entitled 'Mr Cuthbert and the Devil',[60] a polished piece of work for a seventeen year old, concise, well-expressed and with a neat plot twist. Lucius J. deVere Cuthbert (the name speaks volumes about this country boy's ideas of the big world) is engagingly pleased at having raised the devil: 'A smile of faint surprise suffused his pale, sharp features'. And Satan is sketched with quick, sure detail: 'He took an expensive-looking cigar from the air, [and] lit it with a clawed fingertip'. Satan agrees to provide Cuthbert with great wealth and not even claim his soul in return, on one condition: that none of the wealth be put to religious use during the first year. Cuthbert agrees joyfully, realising only when it is too late that if any of the money he spends is then used by another person for any religious purpose, his soul is forfeit.

Murray continued to put most of his effort into work not set by the school. He noticed some German texts in Keith McLaughlin's office and asked about them. Taree High taught both French and Latin, but at Nabiac there had been no possibility of doing so and it was now too late for Murray to pick up those subjects. He envied the pupils who were taking them. One of his clear memories of his mother was of her telling him, then aged four or five, while they sat out in the moonlit garden, that English was not the only language, and that there was another language called French of which she knew a little.[61] As Keith McLaughlin realised,

> I think he felt inferior to students who were doing languages. I'd done German at university, and had some German texts, primers on learning German and so on. One day he asked me if he could borrow one, and gradually he borrowed most of them and used them. I think he just wanted to have another language. The school didn't teach German, but he was interested in it himself.[62]

Murray discovered that he had a natural aptitude for languages, in which his astoundingly tenacious memory played a large part, and his German developed rapidly. Murray's paternal grandmother had had a German cousin named Johann von Holstein.[63] In addition there were German families in the Bunyah valley, and the Murrays had intermarried with some of them, such as the Maurers,[64] so that he felt he had a German link. This was the first of the languages he learned consciously; in the years that followed he would come to read a score of them with ease.

His schoolwork he continued to take lightly, doing it rapidly and tending to put in just enough effort to get by. On English he spent more time, one day remarking to the physical education master Les Lawrie, who lived near his boarding house and occasionally gave him lifts home after school, that he was not enjoying reading Shakespeare. 'There are Australian poets too, you know', said Lawrie, mentioning Henry Lawson, Judith Wright, Kenneth Slessor and others.[65] This was a revelation to Murray, who came the next day to take up Lawrie's invitation to borrow and read a volume of Lawson's verse. 'But he wasn't very impressed by him', Lawrie recalled.[66] All the same, as Murray gratefully recorded in an article he wrote for the school magazine in 1988, Lawrie had alerted him to the existence of Australian poets, 'whose ranks I would soon attempt to join'.[67] He got hold of an anthology, *The Boomerang Book of Australian Verse*, and there encountered for the first time the work of Douglas Stewart, being greatly impressed by Stewart's poems about Aboriginal rock-art.[68] 'When I was shown . . . poetry written in my own country about things I knew or was interested in, the magic happened', he would tell other schoolchildren years later.[69]

His father, worried by what young Les was to do in life, drove in to Taree to consult Keith McLaughlin, who was also the Guidance Counsellor. 'The father was a good solid bloke, a timber-cutter: busy cutting poles in 1956. A solid ordinary chap. He told me Les's mother had died when he was young, and the father had raised him alone.'[70] McLaughlin advised Cecil to send his son to the University of Sydney if he could get in.

Les Murray did the Leaving Certificate at the end of 1956. The possible marks for each subject were Honours (in English and Mathematics), A (meaning a first-class pass), B (second-class pass) or Fail. The English Honours examination was held on a Monday morning, and to the McLaughlins' deep disappointment Murray missed it, having failed to get back in time after his weekend in Bunyah.[71] He had simply mistaken the time.[72] Because the examination could not be taken again, he had to sit the ordinary examination in the afternoon. As a result he got only an A, rather than the hoped-for Honours in English. He scored As also in Economics and Art, and Bs in his remaining subjects, Modern History (another disappointment), Biology and Geography. He was quite happy with this outcome, as it assured him of a Commonwealth Scholarship to study at Sydney University.

He left Taree High School without regrets at the end of 1956: those red-brick buildings would always remind him of suffering. It would be twenty years before he returned, having been invited back in 1977 to talk to the pupils about poetry. After giving his talk he walked meditatively around the school with Edith McLaughlin. As they were parting Murray quietly delivered a matter-of-fact summary, without self-pity: 'I had one of the hardest times of my life here'.[73]

Back in Bunyah, on the hot afternoon of Christmas Day 1956, after the miserable midday corned-beef dinner with his father, he wrote his first poems, ten of them, in a single burst. They were short, all about machinery and the effects of light on oil or steel, heavily influenced by Hopkins's images, 'like shining from shook foil'.[74] One of these ten first poems in particular stayed in Murray's mind, a poem in which he tried to describe the light on the railway lines at Gloucester Station. It was a poem of covert farewell, for Gloucester was the station from which he would leave for Sydney University. Though he would later say they were 'terrible', at the time he read his poems with pride: 'I can do this', he thought with excitement.

Some days before he had taken his old pony, Creamy, and gone on one of his day-long rambles from Bunyah, thinking about what he was going to do with his life. By late afternoon he was in an old timber-mill he sometimes visited, on the riverbank at Coolongolook, nearly 10 kilometres from home. Dow's mill, now long gone, was already falling into ruin, weeds growing through the floor, the remaining machinery rusting quietly, the big circular blades on the walls dimming.

> Down a road padlocked now
> steel discs and weeds sprawled
> in a room whose rusty hair
> was iron cornrows, and its brow
>
> a naily timber lintel
> under which I'd gaze across
> the river at Midge Island
> as the tide turned on its pintle . . .[75]

The place seemed a symbol of the decay of his father's timber-getting lifestyle. He determined he would turn his back on that, and he would never be a dairy farmer either. As he would put it in a verse-letter to the poet Dennis Haskell, 'At eighteen, I made a great vow/I would never milk another bloody cow'.[76] He stood a long time watching the mayflies circling over the still water, thinking about his future, and with a sense of inevitability he realised that he was going to be a poet.[77] A few years later he would put some of the excitement of this discovery into a fine poem, 'Spring Hail', in which a boy realises that he owns Pegasus:

> It was time, as never again it was time
> to pull the bridle up, so the racketing hooves
> fell silent as we ascended from the hill

above the farms, far up to where the hail
formed and hung weightless in the upper air,
charting the birdless winds with silver roads
for us to follow and be utterly gone.

This is for spring and hail, that you may remember
a boy and a pony long ago who could fly.[78]

CHAPTER SIX
SYDNEY UNIVERSITY
1957–58

*Out of the Fifties, a time of picking your nose
while standing at attention in civilian clothes
we travelled luxury class in our drift to the city
not having a war, we went to university.*

LES MURRAY[1]

Murray arrived in Sydney early in March 1957, accompanied by his father: he was overwhelmed by the size of the city, which he had previously visited only twice and that briefly.[2] The first visit had been with his mother, and afterwards he could recall only that they had seen a Dutch submarine near Luna Park, and had taken a ferry ride; the second time, when he was seventeen, he was brought by his father, whom he exhausted in a search for the Museum of Applied Arts and Sciences in Ultimo.[3]

Now his father found lodgings for him in Allawah, in the south of Sydney, with a family named Campbell. His Commonwealth Scholarship paid him £7 a week, enough to cover his university fees and his board and lodging. 'In Sydney at that time it would pay your board at a boarding house or a private family and leave you maybe a little bit over for coffee and books. It was fairly well calculated for the late fifties', Murray would recall.[4] He found the city exciting but intensely alien, and in later weeks would hang around Central Station for the pleasure of hearing trains announced as leaving for Gloucester or Taree, and for the sight of country folk arriving, with their homely clothes and familiar speech, even as he knew instinctively that his own values were being challenged and might be transformed:

> I haunted Central Station in my turn
> to hear names, or a suitcase called a port
>
> this even as I was learning to judge landscape
> not for food, but blasphemously, as landscape . . .

The next day, when the university term began, he arrived at Sydney University by train to register as a Bachelor of Arts student, wearing his only suit and accompanied by his father, who struck up an enthusiastic acquaintance with a pretty female student and afterwards often asked about her.[5] The university, founded in 1852, is Australia's oldest; in 1957 it had just over 10 000 students and was expanding rapidly, with new buildings springing up to house the growing student body. The campus is magnificently sited, its eminence giving it sweeping views over the city centre, and its main buildings, nineteenth-century Tudor-Perpendicular-Gothic sandstone structures, gave an illusion of great age, deeply attractive in a young country. Old buildings and young people: it was an ideal combination for which nothing in Murray's country upbringing had prepared him, and he was delighted by oriel windows and gargoyles, carillons, hammer-beams and stained glass.

His age-cohort included a particularly talented group of people whom their country would presently hear of: Clive James, Germaine Greer, Robert Hughes, Bruce Beresford, Bob Ellis, Mary Gaudron, Michael Kirby, John Bell, Richard Wherrett, Geoffrey Lehmann, Richard Butler, Mungo MacCallum, Richard Walsh, Colin Mackerras and Laurie Oakes, together with others who would never become well known, but whom Murray would respect and learn from.

After his experiences at Taree High, he expected to have to endure mockery at Sydney University, and was delighted when there was none. Quite the contrary: universities at their rare best feed and encourage the unusual, and Murray's one social skill, intellectual display, here gained him rapid respect. In any case Orientation Week, with which the academic year began, was a kind of wild bazaar of stalls featuring the various university clubs competing for student interest with any stunt they could dream up. Exotic dress and eccentric behaviour were everywhere on display.[6] Murray immediately realised he must shed his suit.

On his third day, wandering slightly dazed around the campus alone, his father having returned to Bunyah, Murray made a lifelong friend when he struck up a conversation with another new student named Walter Davis.[7] Davis, the son of a welder from western Sydney, was as nervous as Murray about starting university. He had been educated in a Catholic school and was very timid about this, his first step into a non-Catholic world.[8]

Suspicion and even hostility between Catholics and Protestants, largely an Irish import, was widespread in Australian cities until the 1950s, when job advertisements still commonly specified 'No Catholics need apply'. Davis, as much as Murray, expected attack. After they had introduced themselves and spoken briefly about their backgrounds, the subject of religious denominations came up. 'I'm Catholic', said Davis nervously. 'It doesn't make a difference to you, does it?' In Bunyah, despite the preponderance of Free Presbyterians, there had been little sectarianism. Murray's paternal grandmother had been born a Catholic and several of his cousins were Catholics,[9] but though Murray had heard his parents remark on the difference between them and their neighbours, he had been uninterested.[10] So the idea that anyone could fear admitting to being Catholic was slightly startling to him. His antennae, finely tuned to persecution after his victimisation at Taree High, drew him to Davis, and as a result he began to take an interest in Catholicism.

Through Davis he quickly made contact with the Newman Society, the main Catholic social group on the campus, attending their meetings regularly and at mealtimes sitting at the Newman Society table in Manning House (the women's club, much frequented by men) or the University Union. Religious groups played major social roles among the students of the time, as they had since the university was founded in 1852. In addition to the large and very active Newman Society, there was a passionately engaged Anglican Evangelical Society, reflective of Low Church dominance in Sydney's Anglican diocese, and a much more liberal pan-Protestant grouping, the Students Christian Movement. One of the most dramatic changes that would sweep the university in the next decade would be the marginalising of these religious groups, but at this stage they were a powerful force in student life. A straw in the wind was the Libertarian Society, a small band of atheists, freethinkers and proto-hippies. Their time would come. Though he began with the Newman Society, Murray was soon making friends in each of these groups and moving easily between them.

Among the friends he made in the Newman Society were Greg O'Hara, Tony Coady, Jeremy Nelson, Mick Byrne and Elisabeth Knowler, the girl whom Walter Davis was to marry. Davis persuaded Murray to attend one of the weekend camps the Newman Society organised, and he had long conversations with the Newman Society chaplain, Roger Pryke.[11] He gradually built up a large circle of Catholic friends at the university. One of them was Mike Molloy, who would become one of the best cinematographers Australia has produced.[12]

Murray also made many non-Catholic friends, including Peter Wagner, who would teach Murray about Judaism, and whose friendship Murray would never cease to value.[13] Wagner, whose mother was seriously ill, was something of a solitary, locally famous for having failed Philosophy 1 five times.[14] According to a fellow-student, Clive Kessler, Murray seemed drawn to Jews who were marginalised in the Sydney University Jewish community (itself marginalised), including Wagner, Kessler's sister Naomi and Vernon Kronenberg.[15] Naomi Kessler felt in Murray a strong sense of shared exclusion, as she recalled:

> I was painfully shy but tried to hide it and I was overwhelmed by my total incapacity to operate in the world of the successful, WASPish, well kempt private-school-educated students on the one hand and the members of the Libertarian society on the other who, now with hindsight but not then, appear as a bunch of self-indulgent, pretentious poseurs ... Les was always for me a sort of male counterpoint to my own dreaded Angst as an outsider. How much easier it might have been if I could have spoken to him of that outsider status—but my sense of my own social incompetence forbade it.[16]

Murray would come to see Jews, like Aboriginals, as often disregarded bearers of essential values, and in *Fredy Neptune* he would link them in the person of the mysterious guardian and guide, the Jewish-Aboriginal Sam Mundine.

Students still lived in a world that had been formed by World War II and only slightly modified by the Korean conflict, though it was about to undergo a revolution fed on sharp changes now being imported, mostly from America, into popular culture in Australia. Rock music had arrived only in 1955, when Bill Haley and the Comets had blasted it in a film called *The Blackboard Jungle*.[17] A cloud small as a man's hand had appeared. Beginning with Presley's first international hit, 'Heartbreak Hotel', in 1956, imitation Elvises sprouted across Australia. In 1958 ABC TV, which had begun broadcasting two years before, would begin carrying 'Bandstand' and in 1959 'Six O'Clock Rock', programs that for most Australian adults were the first encounters with the rock scene.[18] But in 1957 little of this registered on campuses: student values remained relatively conservative, and unquestioned except by a tiny minority. As a group, Australian students had yet to be radicalised or politicised by the Vietnam War. Their music was not yet rock, but jazz and folk. Murray, largely tone-deaf, generally avoided music altogether.[19]

Male students wore their hair college-boy short, aesthete-long, or in a Roman cut, and they dressed smartly, many even wearing ties. Women students wore tight sweaters and tartan skirts, or baggy jerseys and tight pants or pedal-pushers, or (though decreasingly) twin-sets and pearls; the heavy eye makeup, beehive hairstyles and pale lipstick of the early 1960s had yet to appear. They treated each other, generally, with decorum: sexual intercourse, as Larkin famously remarked, would not begin until 1963. Murray began discovering a whole new world:

> We learned to drink wine, to watch Swedish movies, and pass
> as members, or members-in-law, of the middle class
> but not in those first days when, stodge-fed, repressed,
> curfewed and resented, we were the landladies' harvest.[20]

In the first week Murray saw a poster advertising a 'Writers, Artists and Composers Group', heard an announcement about it in an English lecture, and attended its first meeting. Not many people did, and they included no composers. The only painter was an ex-Riverview student, Robert Hughes, blond and suave in a bow-tie,[21] who did not return for a second meeting.[22] The organiser was a bright slim boy two years younger than Murray, Geoffrey Lehmann. Lehmann announced that he wrote poetry, and asked if anyone else did. He later recalled: 'There was this rather moon-faced boy, a couple of years older than me, from the country, at the back of this group of about fifteen people. That was Les. He indicated he wrote poetry. We arranged that we'd both bring our poetry to the university one day that week, and later that week we met with a girl called Libby Sweet'.[23]

The three of them retired to one of the university's sports ovals, sat down under some trees behind the Physics building, and there read verse to each other through the hot afternoon. Libby Sweet,[24] whom Murray thought well described by her surname, was too shy to read her work ('Oh no, no, they're just little things, little things');[25] in any case it had early become clear to her that her role in this group was that of audience.[26] Lehmann and Murray, emboldened by her admiring presence, declaimed to each other. Lehmann, years later, would remember Murray's shy delivery, his face decorated with three or four scabs as if he had scratched mosquito bites, and the vividness of his imagery:

> I think there was a poem on this occasion, called 'The Refugees', and the last line, 'Flowing, their faces pinched and white/Like peristalsis through the dirty gut of night', which was pretty good for a bloke about seventeen, very impressive. And I thought this bloke looks a bit unprepossessing, but this is a terrific poem. And there was another about an afternoon thunderstorm, about 'a thunder-wardrobe in the sky', an image of a wardrobe banging. I thought this fellow has something. I told him that. I don't think he'd shown his poetry to anyone at that stage. I said 'These are pretty terrific poems'.[27]

Lehmann, though he came from a working-class background, had won a scholarship to an expensive Anglican school, Shore. There he had distinguished himself in a range of activities, had begun writing poetry at fourteen, and had gained entry to Sydney University at the age of fifteen, though he had elected to wait until he was sixteen. He was confident, intense and self-absorbed, and he had read more modern poetry than Murray, so that he set about energetically editing and improving Murray's poems.[28] Murray accepted his advice meekly and gratefully, and he glowed at Lehmann's praise: 'Geoff was one of the first people to think that my poems had some promise'.[29]

Lehmann's praise had to be paid for though, for when he did not like a poem he would say so, emphatically. His dark, cold face would glow with triumph when he was about to annihilate one of Murray's efforts.[30] After more than a year, when they knew each other better, Murray admitted to Lehmann that he had come to dread showing him his poems because in so many cases Lehmann would toss them back with the terse comment, 'Bullshit, Murray!'[31] At meals he would join Murray at the Newman Society table in the Manning: some distance away they would see the smart set at a table with Clive James, Robert Hughes and Germaine Greer.

Sweet was to remark of Hughes, who would in time become one of the English-speaking world's most influential art critics, 'He was somehow more important than the rest of us'.[32] Slim and elegant, he was given to such outré items of dress as black roll-neck sweaters or pink bow-ties.[33] Clive James was at this time much less impressive in spite of being very good looking:[34] he struck other students, unable to see the pain he was covering up, as loud-mouthed, arrogant and in danger of becoming an alcoholic.[35] Greer, who had arrived from Melbourne in the summer of 1959 in pursuit of a member of the Libertarian Society, Roelof Smilde,[36] and who took to the society and its raunchier outgrowth, the Sydney Push, like a duck to water, attracted attention by her ineluctable intellectual conversation, and by her appearance in the student review at the end of the year as a tube of striped toothpaste.[37] Murray would always feel excluded by groups like that at Greer's table.

In that first week of his first term Murray had introduced himself to Clive James under an arch near the old Fisher Library steps. James had earlier noticed his striking figure at Redfern Station, looking, as he later put it, 'as if Sidney Greenstreet had been given the role of Ginger Meggs'.[38] James was already working on his deadpan witty growl, in an early version of which he delivered a brief, amusing monologue on the origins of medieval drama, flourishing his ever-present cigarette for emphasis, his long hair flopping over his face. But Murray was not to be browbeaten. 'The origins of drama in the West', he told James firmly, 'lie in this': and he began to chant a medieval Mystery play, in Latin. James listened nonplussed.

Then the two of them spoke of Allied and Japanese military aircraft, 'the Brewster Buffalo and the F4U Corsair, the lumbering Mavis flying-boat and the wonderful Ryan-inspired Mitsubishi Zero-Sen fighter the Imperial Army and Navy stayed content with for too long'.[39] Murray knew them all from his wartime plane-spotting service, when he had scanned the skies for Aunt Jane; Clive James, he came to believe, was obsessed by military aircraft because his father, being flown back to Australia in an American plane after long imprisonment, torture and starvation by the Japanese during the war, had died when the aircraft crashed. Murray recognised someone almost as wounded as he was himself. 'He used to talk a lot about military aircraft in the Pacific War', Murray said, adding compassionately, 'It was fairly obvious it was because he was looking for the plane that would bring his father back'.[40] James would movingly use as the epigraph for his *Unreliable Memoirs* Andromache's speech to the dead Hector: 'Our child is still but a little fellow, child of ill-fated parents, you and me. How can he grow up to manhood?'[41]

But it was from Lehmann that Murray learned most. He admired Lehmann's urbane, learned poems, and liked evoking his high, hysterical laugh: the two of them became close friends. At first he was abashed by Lehmann's private-school education ('I have what Aborigines call Big Shame, I shrink from better-dressed people', he would say),[42] but when he met Lehmann's father Leo, a broad-shouldered, rough-handed workman who for thirty years had operated a Sydney ferry from Lavender Bay and who was much like Cecil Murray, he felt more confident. Lehmann's small, shabby home, surrounded by driftwood and assorted plumbing collected by Leo, had the same strengthening effect.[43]

Lehmann was reading Arts/Law, and in later life he would go on to become not just a distinguished poet, but the author of a standard reference work on Australian tax law. At this time, though, his chief interest was literature, and he and Murray soon began hanging round the editorial office of *honi soit*, the university's weekly paper since 1929, and those of *Hermes*, the annual Undergraduate Association journal, and *Arna*, the annual Arts faculty magazine, and contributing poems to these publications.

Murray continued his self-education at Sydney University. Although he registered to read English 1, Preliminary German and Psychology 1, he soon ceased to attend lectures and buried himself in the stacks of the old Fisher Library, a fine sandstone Gothic building completed in 1909 and now known as the MacLaurin Hall.

> We were reading Fisher Library, addressing gargoyles on the stair,
> drafting self after self on Spir-O-Bind notepaper . . .

Here he would be encountered in the reading room, poring over a Sanskrit dictionary or a Finnish grammar, and emerging to tell wondering and amused groups over coffee in the Manning of his latest discoveries.[44]

> The reading-room beams supported heraldry
> and a roof like a steep tent.
> Mine was a plan-free mass querying
> Of condensed humans off the shelves,
> all numbered, the tribal, the elderly.[45]

Plan-free his reading might be, but it was not disorderly, nor was he just playing with languages: his Spanish rapidly became good enough for him to produce several excellent translations of Lorca's poems.[46] In later years these included 'Canción del Jinete', which he thought 'beautiful beyond words', and in reply to which he wrote 'Civil War Incident'.[47] He produced translations of Italian poetry too, including Ungaretti's 'Un' intera nottata'.[48] His other great interest remained films, and he became a devotee of the university film society, and a regular patron of Sydney's many cinemas, building up an encyclopaedic knowledge of movies.

Neither of these activities was calculated to get him through his examinations. 'Because my study habits at Sydney University consisted of reading every book in sight and yarning and seeing the movies and not doing any study I went crash on my face at the end of the year in the exams.'[49] He failed both English 1 and Psychology 1, and scraped a bare pass in Preliminary German,[50] though one of his German lecturers in later years, Michael Nelson, would describe him as a brilliant student of the language.[51]

Failure at this time was common: 55 per cent of first-year English students failed in 1955 and 1956, and overall, 30 per cent of first-years in Arts failed during the late 1950s.[52] Murray was in any case faintly contemptuous of the English course, which included no Australian writers: 'a major in English made one a minor Englishman', he would say wittily later.[53] All the same, his results were a shock to him, and a very unpleasant surprise to his father. The immediate effect was that his Commonwealth Scholarship was withdrawn, and he would now have to find the funding for further study himself.[54]

He retired bruised and rueful to Bunyah at the end of the year, and there followed a period of fierce quarrels with his father, who told him he was good for nothing. There were particularly angry scenes when Murray refused to help with any of the heavy work around the farm, digging postholes, grubbing out stumps and the like. 'That's the way you earn your living, it's not mine', he would tell his father, but this was a difficult line of argument to sustain at a time when he needed his father to pay for his next year of study. All the same Cecil, driven by his wife's dying wish, agreed to give him £5 a week.

This was no small matter to Cecil Murray: his total income during 1958 would prove to be only £670, and the lost Commonwealth Scholarship had been worth more than half that. By the end of 1958 Cecil, though he did all he could to raise his income, including acting as rural mailman and doing deliveries of meat and groceries from the store at Krambach in his old stationwagon,[55] would have just £80 and ten shillings in his account with the English, Scottish & Australian Bank.[56]

Over the next few years some of Murray's new friends would visit Bunyah: Lehmann and Greg O'Hara came together, Lehmann thinking the farm and its valley magnificent, and O'Hara being astonished at its primitiveness. Virtually nothing had changed since Miriam died, Cecil refusing to move on. The symbolic roofing iron still lay rusting beside the old shack;[57] dust sifted through the cracks between the wall-slabs. The impression was one of great squalor, as O'Hara remembered:

> Because of having no refrigeration other than the bush meat safe, Cecil and Les lived mainly on tinned food. When they had emptied the contents into their saucepan, they simply threw the tins out the door. Over the years, the house had become surrounded by hundreds of rusty tins and numerous bottles, so Les and I were never short of targets when we'd shoot off a few rounds from his .22 rifle.
>
> The toilet was a typical bush dunny, away from the house and near the top of the creek bank. When the can was full, Cecil would simply tip it over the bank.
>
> Lighting in the house was by kerosene lamp. Cecil would not stay up late as reading was difficult. His only diversion was to listen to his battery-powered radio for a bit before going to bed. This was one of the pre-war console models, powered by a car battery which would go flat and reception would depend on his being diligent enough to keep it charged.[58]

One day Cecil discovered a red-bellied black snake living in that radio, kept pleasantly warm by the valves.[59]

All of Murray's friends were impressed by his father, a square man who seemed composed entirely of muscle and bone. Cecil Murray struck O'Hara as earthy, coarse, solid, admirable, and immensely strong. According to Bob Ellis, Cecil looked as if he had been carved out of a solid block of wood, and he could lift the back of a car with one hand.[60] Lehmann remarked that he could have been parachuted into eleventh-century peasant life without a moment's friction.[61] His snoring at night was elemental, all-embracing, deafening, and tactfully he would stay awake until his visitors had gone to sleep.[62] He had a fine stock of bush stories, mostly true, on which his son would draw for years, and a puckish sense of humour. He asked O'Hara to help him by pulling his finger, and when the mystified visitor did so, Cecil emitted a reverberant fart, the purpose of this exercise being to embarrass the shy youth: he succeeded entirely.[63]

But Cecil was also capable of better jokes, as when he accused a later visitor, John Mulhall, of shooting one of his cows: Mulhall had been out shooting all afternoon, had returned to Sydney on the late train, and in the evening the cow failed to appear. The others defended Mulhall loyally, while Cecil grew more enraged at the loss he had suffered; and he was letting loose a torrent of abuse when the cow walked into the milking shed, in perfect health. Cecil was silenced, but only for an instant. Then with one of his sly grins, 'Mulhall always was a bloody bad shot', he said.[64]

Murray, by contrast, remained an excellent shot: he carried his rifle everywhere, shocking Lehmann by firing at hawks overhead and at crimson rosellas rocketing through the trees—he was capable of bringing down the rosellas[65]— or of setting a playing-card in the top of a post ten metres away, edge on, and splitting it in half.[66] One vivid unpublished poem, written by 1961, he entitled 'The Eagle Shooter':

> It was a day as cold as crystal
> And I rode out on the rust-red mare
> There was a wind in the nervous bluegums
> But I could only watch him winding
> A deadly thread in the perfect sky
>
> He pivoted and hung, and hunted
> Till I shot him with my dark
> Rifle from where I sat my saddle:
> I see him yet, a wrecked thing drifting
> Down the ringing air, and I
>
> Full of deepest heart's own winter
> Ride to pick my eagle up . . .[67]

On another occasion he killed, with a rifle, 'twenty-three assorted thrushes, tits, wagtails and wrens'.[68] The rosellas at least were not wasted: Cecil Murray liked eating them, and one of his son's unpublished jottings would include a little quatrain:

> There was a man of olden time
> Who loved to dine off parrots
> En casserôle or baked with thyme
> Or boiled and served with carrots.[69]

Cecil was troubled by his son's apparent indolence. At the end of one of these visits, Cecil put him and his friends back on the train to Sydney. As it began to move out of Gloucester Station, he called out to Murray, 'Well, are you going to get a job?' 'Yes, OK, I'm going to get a job', replied Murray, who had been nagged by Cecil all weekend. 'What are you going to do?' Cecil cried enthusiastically, trotting to keep up with the train. 'I'll apprentice myself to a fornicator', shouted Murray, and his friends saw Cecil stop, put both hands into what remained of his hair, and try to raise himself off the platform by it.[70]

CHAPTER SEVEN
TRYING AGAIN
1958–60

~

Few have been taught to any purpose who have not been their own teachers.

JOSHUA REYNOLDS

Somewhat chastened, Murray returned to Sydney University at the beginning of 1958 to try to recover his position, registering again for English 1 and Psychology 1 and this time adding Elementary Chinese. The Campbells, with whom he had lived in Allawah during 1957, were not keen to have him back, and he found alternative lodgings with a family in Croydon Park. They soon asked him to leave, and he moved on to a house in Burwood, owned by a widow named Mrs Wythes, of whom in later years he would recall little other than that she had a very pretty daughter, Margaret, with only one arm. Margaret had once been the target of a bag-snatcher, who had collapsed in shock when Margaret's artificial arm came off in his grasp, an anecdote that Murray enjoyed and would use in *Fredy Neptune*.

Murray's landladies needed great tolerance, for he was extraordinarily untidy, personally grubby (the glory days of Peter's Creamery showers far behind him), and kept most irregular hours. To make matters worse he often did not pay his rent. Greg O'Hara, who got to know Murray in 1958 through Walter Davis, recalled, 'What little money he got, Les would shamelessly waste on things like cigars, American cigarettes and general good living for a couple of days. Often, he wouldn't leave enough to pay his rent or even for something decent to eat'.[1] He was constantly hungry as a result, and took to hanging around the Union unashamedly cadging food off other people's plates, and appropriating anything anyone left, saying off-handedly, 'Waste not, want not'.[2] His friends would usually buy him a meal, and those who did not know him well he repaid by his constant flow of tall bush stories, heard from his father, and treasures from his astoundingly wide reading. 'Nobody used to mind too much', O'Hara remembered, 'because Les was always such good company to have at table'.[3] He was content to sing for his supper: 'You can buy Murray with a meat-pie', Lehmann would remember him saying cheerfully.[4]

He gradually reverted to the habits of his Huckleberry years. As his appearance and behaviour grew more eccentric, he became one of the characters of the university, pointed out with pride to freshers, particularly as his reputation as a poet grew. A quatrain he coined casually at this time flew from mouth to mouth:

> I shot an arrow in the air,
> It fell to earth in Taylor Square
> Transfixing, to my vast delight
> A policeman and a sodomite.[5]

In later years he would be embarrassed by this squib, and would do his best to disown it.[6]

At a time when students dressed much more formally than they do towards the end of the millennium, he wore army surplus clothing, including a motley collection of camouflage shirts, webbing belts, berets and desert boots of a type known as 'brothel creepers'; presently, to increase his income, he would join the Naval Reserve, and go about dressed as a sailor in navy blue jerseys and sailor's caps. His teeth had never had the attention of a dentist, and they were green, crowded and carious.[7] He had a curious way, when talking about something that really interested him, of smiling a beatific, childlike smile, raising his eyes to the ceiling and keeping them there: and as he spoke the middle fingers of both his hands, on the table in front of him, would extend and then describe small circles in the air in unison while he unreeled his brilliant monologue. He was very amusing, and easily amused: his laugh, which sounded frequently, was a witches' cackle, falsetto, maniacal, infectious. He loved an audience, and collected one effortlessly.

Some of his habits took getting used to. Geoffrey Lehmann was to recall trying to persuade him to wash more frequently:

> We went one day to see two not good German films, at the old Lyric Theatre in George Street. I was sitting next to Les. And there was just this terrible stench [loud laugh], and when you're sitting through two terrible movies in German, and this dreadful effluvium rising around you—I gave him a talk about wearing underpants, and washing them.[8]

Murray was not in the least put out to have Lehmann's advice: on the contrary, he was enlightened, and grateful. At Bunyah, where the Murrays' only water-supply had been a small rainwater tank, washing was a luxury chiefly reserved for cows' teats, and he had no idea that underclothes existed. In later years he would say that he had discovered them, with such items as saucers, toilet paper and handkerchiefs, when he first met the middle class at Sydney University. But he was glad to learn. From now on, when he stole socks from Woolworth's as he had been in the habit of doing since Taree High,[9] he added underpants to his haul.

His height and heavyweight build, the country background of which he spoke often, his uncut and thinning hair, his odd, unembarrassed habits such as picking up a plate and licking it thoroughly at the end of a meal, or going barefoot—then absolutely not done—or rolling his own cigarettes and teaching deeply impressed middle-class students how to do so,[10] all these combined incongruously with his nimble and muscular intelligence, his sparkling conversation and his apparent knowledge of everything under the sun. His speech, similarly, combined broad Bunyah dialect with learned allusions and quotations in half a dozen languages including Chinese and Dutch.

Many of his free and easy habits of dress and behaviour would become commonplace on campuses within a decade or two: though neither he nor his fellow-students knew it, he was the future. To his contemporaries he was a fascinating conundrum who could be neither snubbed nor defeated in argument; he was impossible to characterise and impossible to ignore. He was of course aware of this, and played it up. 'It's my mission to irritate the hell out of the eloquent who would oppress my people', he was to say years later, 'by being a paradox that their categories can't assimilate: the Subhuman Redneck who writes poems'.[11]

He succeeded in both delighting and irritating many. 'Loathsome Les', one of the German lecturers, Michael Nelson, called him.[12] Some of the smarter students affected to think him a buffoon or gaby, and avoided him. Geoffrey Lehmann was to recall with deep regret an occasion when he was walking down Broadway with Colin Mackerras (one of five notable brothers[13] and later to be a professor of Chinese) and another student named John Sheldon.[14] Mackerras looked back to see Murray a block or two behind them, hurrying to catch up. 'Oh look, there's that awful Les Murray person', he said, 'Let's *run*!' The three of them took to their heels, and with Murray waving and calling out to them, jumped on a bus and disappeared. Lehmann came to rue this as a shameful act of treachery towards his friend: 'I thought whatever he does to me in the future I can't ever complain, it was a terrible thing to do'.[15] Murray however took no umbrage: compared to his experiences at Taree High, this was as nothing.

It was Lehmann and another student poet, Brian Jenkins, who in 1958 took Murray to Repins, a popular coffee shop in King Street, to meet Lex Banning. Banning suffered from cerebral palsy and his body never ceased its slow involuntary writhing, while to speak he had to suck in a throatful of air with an audible 'whoop' before each sentence; but the charm of his conversation was such that after a few minutes in his presence his athetosis became irrelevant.[16] He was a poet whom Murray greatly admired. The younger man shyly showed Banning his poems, and was grateful for his criticism: 'He was one of the early witnesses of my efforts to write poetry, the first real, practising, downtown poet to see and comment on my prentice work. He gave me the encouragement I needed, and to a degree the model I needed, to gather up my courage and choose the course my life has taken'.[17] Murray saw Banning as part of a tradition of Australian writing in which Murray himself would presently find a central place. To him, Banning occupied a position 'midway between the older Sydney tradition, derived in part from Norman Lindsay and the earlier Slessor, of highly literary tropes and the use of figures and dramatic cruxes from European high art . . . and a later forties and fifties tradition of the Well-Made Poem, usually having contemporary imagery and centred in current reality'.[18]

Banning was profoundly convinced of the pre-eminence of poetry as a literary form. On one occasion he had interrupted a lecture being given by another poet, John Thompson, who had jokingly defined poetry as the wine of literature. 'No, John', cried Banning from the back of the hall, 'No. The cognac!'[19] For Murray, who was still writing short stories and flirting with other forms of prose, Banning's teaching would prove decisive. 'I don't believe myself prose is better than poetry for anything, except possibly for running a government administration', he would say in later years, only half jokingly.[20]

Murray would treasure the memory of this meeting, referring to it when he paid tribute to Banning after his death,[21] and he may have had it in mind when he made reference to Repin's and Lorenzini's, a wine bar in Elizabeth Street and another of Banning's favourite watering holes, in an important early poem, 'An Absolutely Ordinary Rainbow'.[22] Murray was to come to dislike it, as Yeats disliked 'The Lake Isle of Innisfree', because ignorant readers sometimes spoke as if he had written nothing else,[23] but he was proud of having written it. It had begun as a poem about the coffee shops in which so much of Sydney's literary life went on,[24] and gradually focused on the operation of the dreaming or poetic mind, which in his view operates below the level of the conscious, and above the level of the body, which Murray regards as a powerful part of the intelligence, with subconscious thought processes of its own. 'That weeping man just stood up in my mind, and demanded to be written.' The pentagram, he was to say, was the 'key image, but only an image'.[25]

Although he was concentrating more on poetry, he managed to pass his three subjects at the end of 1958, and to his and his father's relief, his scholarship was restored to him for 1959. On the strength of this success he returned to Bunyah triumphant at the end of 1958, and one catches a glimpse of him there in what is apparently the first of his letters to survive, dated 12 December 1958, to Greg O'Hara:

Dear Gregory,

God save the Queen—and seeing this letter has got off to such a personal and intimate start, how are you?

... I am sitting in an enormous Edwardian chair, leather bottomed and magisterial, and the pressure lamp is chortling away in front of me. To stimulate the flow of eloquence, I have just brewed coffee, and will beg indulgence to stop here and drink off the first cup.

Delightful, but a little weak. I have therefore added a quick jerk of Bushell's Essence of Coffee and Chicory, which brings the mix up to ambrosial standard. Now to proceed.

He then discusses at length a dirty-joke-telling contest he had engaged in, unfortunately without recounting any of the jokes, before continuing:

Comedy of this type—the *satirical* type—is perhaps the best weapon the culture has to enforce its ways, combining ritual, humour and vicarious relief. For instance, when I tell the one about the old and the young rooster, I am at once (a) exorcising, by simple word magic, perversion, male sexual jealousy and youthful pride (b) extolling the wisdom of age on an allegorical level—use of animals voicing human problems, and so on, in the manner of the very widespread habit of oral storytellers and (c) perhaps ritually exorcising larvated homosexuality in myself, as well as having a titillating little experience of social defiance. Such jokes, like just about all humour, are the very acme of conformity, in fact. Revolt is a rather solemn matter. Tragedy is more in its line. No one was ever martyred with flames of laughter, but it is a much more hideous and permanent way of mortifying heretics. Unfortunately, but quite naturally, devoted and fanatical bodies never have it—the Church could have rid itself of Luther, for example, by spreading funny stories about him, his build, his habits, and so on, but, out of considerations of charity and truth, it chose argument, with what results you see about you. Still, Communists don't laugh either—I sometimes think the hardest thing in the world to do is to laugh and still believe . . .[26]

This letter well illustrates his conversations at the time, with their mixture of earthy humour, curious learning, hard experience (his remarks about society martyring a heretic in flames of laughter have Taree High just under their surface), and something approaching wisdom, unexpected in a country youth who had just turned twenty. He signed himself, to the Catholic O'Hara, as 'Your Canting Calvinist Comrade Leslie A. Murray ("A" standing, of course, for "Adamantine-and-brass-bossed-shield-of-the-true-Faith")'.

Back in Sydney for the academic year 1959, he registered for English 2, German 1 and Chinese 1, and changed lodgings again, starting the year with a German family in Five Dock. Here he spoke German at breakfast, and continued his rapid progress in the language: in later years native speakers such as his student friend Olaf Reinhardt considered his German impeccable.[27] He loved studying Chinese, and in later years would regret not having got further with it. 'Chinese is lovely. I like characters.'[28] He did very little in English: Mick Byrne would remember Murray scribbling a 2500-word English essay while carrying on a conversation at a table in the Union, and at the end fabricating a reading-list, of which he told Byrne proudly that the first item was a real book, though he had invented all the others. When they next met he complained bitterly to Byrne, who was immensely amused, that he had been given only a Beta plus for this essay, and railed at the lecturer who marked it as 'a hired mediocrity'.[29]

In spite of his intentions of working steadily, the manifold delights of university life were engaging more of his attention.

> In that supermarket of styles, with many a setback
> we tried everything on, from Law School Augustan to rat pack
> and though in Chinese my progress was smooth up to K'ung
> and in German I mastered the words that follow Achtung
> in my slow-cycling mind an eloquence not yet articulate
> was trying to say Youth. This. I will take it straight.[30]

He paid little attention to politics, though he did oppose the cession, under American pressure, of Dutch New Guinea to Indonesia.[31] He also acted in a revue skit that attacked French policy towards Algeria, where a savage war was moving towards the crisis of the early 1960s. In the skit, a group of French aesthetes captured an Algerian Arab, tied him to a chair, inserted *plastique* explosive in his mouth, all the time talking over him in the jaded pretentious jargon of Existentialism, and blew his head off.[32]

It was early in 1959, on Shakespeare's birthday, that he published his first poem, in the university weekly *honi soit*. Clive James, its literary editor at the time, was so pleased with the poem, 'Property', that both he and Geoffrey Lehmann memorised it:[33] James could still quote it verbatim when interviewed a quarter of a century later.[34]

> In my secret garden
> I kept three starlings,
> In my secret locket,
> Three copper farthings.

> One zinc-grey evening
> The birds escaped me,
> And a crippled man stole
> My shining money.
>
> The starlings wandered
> Till three hawks took them
> And now my agents
> Have caught the cripple.[35]

The echoes of Auden in that suggest the direction his reading was now taking: Auden, with his military metaphors and love of nursery rhymes, as well as his long, flexible, colloquial lines, was to be an influence for some years. Another early presence was Yeats, the Yeats of *The Rose* or *The Wind Among the Reeds*. His voice is audible in the very title of another Murray poem of this period, 'Love after loneliness':

> Plucking the petals of a song,
> Tossing them to float and fall
> A girl went wandering along
> At evening by the city wall:
>
> And I stood far off in dismay
> Lost in the ebbing of the day.

It was Lehmann who suggested he try different material. Lehmann had at school read Virgil, had fallen in love with the Georgic on apiary, and nursed the ambition to write poetry about farming, about which he knew nothing. As a result he was fascinated by Murray's endless stories about country life, replete with little details such as how his father Cecil had used a tree-stump as a seat until it had been polished by use to a mirror-like finish. 'Les, you're terrifically lucky', he told Murray, 'you've got all this material ready to your hand'.[36] Lehmann would years later get access to country material through the stories of his first father-in-law, Ross McInerney, and put it to use in *Ross' Poems*.[37]

Country themes first made their appearance in print, however, in the short stories Murray continued to turn out. In July 1959 he and Lehmann produced a publication they called *Kam*, which ran for only one issue, and which (as well as Lehmann's contributions and those of a few of their friends) contained an early, lifeless Murray poem, 'The Englishman', and a short story, '1943', in which a sympathetic but uncomprehending farm-boy meets a neurotic old soldier who has killed too much and is going off his head.

The annual undergraduate magazine *Hermes* in 1959 contained a better Murray story, 'Red Cedar', which dramatised his father Cecil's cruel treatment at the hand of Murray's grandfather. In 'Red Cedar', set in the context of Cecil's world of bullock-driving and timber-getting, a grizzled old man horrifies a child by telling him how he was deliberately crippled by the boy's wicked grandfather.[38] Both '1943' and 'Red Cedar' depict a child's discovery of the cruelty of the adult world, a discovery that had come too early to Murray.

His country experience began to appear in his poetry only a little later, first in a fragment entitled 'Evening at Home', which he published in *honi soit* in October,[39] and more successfully in a brilliant little character sketch he called 'The Trainee, 1914':

> Ah, I was as soiled as money, old as rag,
> I was building a humpy beside a gully of woes,
> Till the bump of your drum, the fit of your turned-up hat
> Drew me to eat your stew, salute your flag.
>
> And carry your rifle far away to your wars:
> Is war very big? As big as New South Wales?

Those final naive questions, with their darting insight into the mind of the speaker, were a sign of things to come. In Clive James's opinion, Murray's recognition of the importance of the Australian landscape was an imaginative leap of the utmost importance both to him and to Australian literature; it was a large part of the secret of Murray's penetration of what was vital to Australian culture, helping to make him what James called 'a ground-level satellite'.[40] James, himself monolingual at this time, was immensely impressed by Murray's grasp of languages. 'His mind is naturally cosmopolitan', he would say, 'yet he remained focused on his own country—an act of real imagination, comparable to Larkin's focus on his own surroundings and circumstances'.[41]

It was in 1959 that Murray made one of the lasting friendships of his student days. At the end of the university's first term (of three) his German landlord got tired of his mess and asked him to leave. He chanced upon an advertisement on the Union noticeboard: a student named Robert Ellis was looking for a room-mate. Murray went along to meet him. Ellis considered himself to have second sight, and he had foreseen his next room-mate: 'I knew that the next person I lived with would be like, I thought, Jimmy Porter out of *Look Back in Anger*. I knew he would be a wild bohemian, angry and mad. And Murray turned up, and he was a bit bigger than I expected, but he was otherwise just right'.[42] Ellis tended to think of himself as an Angry Young Man: *Look Back in Anger*, John Osborne's hit of 1956, had a strong appeal for him.[43]

Murray and Ellis turned out to have a lot in common: Ellis was from northern New South Wales,[44] had endured a strict religious upbringing in a small-town setting, and was busy trying to remake himself at Sydney University. He was in slow revolt against his Seventh-day Adventist beliefs, as one of the witty epigrams he produced at this period suggests:

> Keeping on the straight and narrow
> But for this would pall:
> He whose eye is on the sparrow
> Also lets it fall.[45]

Ellis would go on to become a successful playwright and scriptwriter, film-maker and political spin-doctor. He was intelligent and eager to experience life, and the scorn he would learn by working for the then Australian Broadcasting Commission had not yet affected his manner. His lank hair tumbled over his face and his words tumbled over each other in his enthusiasm to get them out in his gravelly voice. He slouched about in a crimplene suit in which he sometimes showered before standing out on the roof to dry.[46]

At this time he was living in the Raffles Hotel in North Bondi, then owned by one Abe Saffron, who would presently become well known to the police. Ellis was four years younger than Murray, but they got on well from the first, and Murray and he shared room 10 in the Raffles Hotel for the next year. They liked young Saffron too, usually breakfasting with him before they left for the university, and he left for Kings Cross, where he was sinking to the top of Sydney's crime world.

Before he met Murray, Ellis had been a conventional small-town boy. He soon ceased to be so, as he recalled:

> Les didn't seem much different then than he is now. He wasn't quite as bald. He certainly was more like 15 stone than 22 stone, but he was big and he had many of the distinguishing characteristics like the green teeth, witch's giggle, the filthiness, the complete disorder of clothing. I was quite tidy and tended to wash clothes before I met him, but I picked up many of his bohemian tendencies out of sheer force of charismatic example, I guess. Les was charismatic.[47]

The two of them had soon created unparalleled squalor in room 10. 'Clothes were essentially a form of mulch that had fallen on the floor', Murray would recall, 'a mulch of writing paper, ink, clothes, wet towels. Ellis went in heavily for the wet towels. He was never willing to pick up a wet towel. They got trodden in a bit'.[48]

Ellis greatly admired Murray, envied his writing and strove in vain to equal it.[49] Under Murray's influence he began drinking first coffee, which he had never tasted, and then alcohol. 'I remember your dread of the Wrath on first tasting coffee', Murray would write with amusement in one of a fine 'spiral of sonnets' he dedicated to Ellis years later.[50] Ellis shared Murray's passion for films, and the two of them spent much of their time in cinemas together. And Ellis presently discovered sex and dedicated himself to fornication, thereby leaving Murray behind.

Ellis did his best to encourage his friend to lose his virginity, but failed. Murray was only slowly conquering his horror of sex to the extent of talking freely to the women who often clustered to listen to him when he held forth in the Manning, but the idea of inviting one of them out was still a terror to him. 'I liked women, and enjoyed their company, but any movement towards the erotic filled me with desperate misgivings, and I would bolt', he wrote later.[51] When left alone with a woman he would freeze and begin a desperate deflection tactic, talking rapidly, indistinctly and compulsively, 'motor-mouthing' as he called it, until she left him in bewilderment or boredom.[52] 'I was, and remain, quite incapable of interpreting female signals', he was to say, 'or distinguishing between flirting and what primatologists unpleasantly term presenting. I never dared assume a sexual invitation could be real, if directed at me'.[53] But his evasions were getting harder to sustain. The infected sexual wound, caused by the circumstances of his mother's death and exacerbated by the girls of Taree High, was gradually gathering to a head.

At the end of 1959 Murray failed Chinese because he had absented himself from the examination, but scraped passes in English and German. This was not good enough for the Commonwealth Scholarship board, and he now irretrievably lost his scholarship.[54] His long-suffering father reluctantly agreed to pick up the bills once more. When Murray returned to Raffles Hotel in February 1960, after the summer holidays, he found that he and Ellis had been thrown out for untidiness, the manageress, Mrs Ross, having been itching to get rid of them.

Ellis had not yet returned to Sydney, and Murray took himself off to another hotel to wait for him, reading D. H. Lawrence novels because his English lecturers had passed on F. R. Leavis's recommendation of them. Years later he recalled that *The Plumed Serpent* had been the final straw: 'I regarded Lawrence with great suspicion at all times but that one convinced me that he was not my cup of tea. I chucked the book at the wall and said I will read no more of this idiot'.[55] It was the beginning of his conscious reaction against Modernism.

He and Ellis took a room in Strathfield, and it was while he was living here, in Lent term 1960, that Murray made three new friends on campus, outside the old Union building: a zany half-Jewish Catholic fresher named Peter Barden and two of Barden's former schoolmates from Waverley College, Ken Welton and John Mulhall. Barden thought Murray one of the most interesting people he had ever met:

> He looked like a page out of a crumpled R. M. Williams catalogue. He was wearing moleskin trousers and a blue cotton shirt with button-down pockets which had in those days the inevitable packet of Lucky Strikes in them. We were talking for some obscure reason about Alfred North Whitehead. Les made some terrible adolescent pun involving blackheads and whiteheads which I have forgotten. Somehow Ernest Hemingway came up. Les said 'Hemingway taught me everything I know about modern poetry'.[56]

Having thus engaged Barden's curiosity, Murray proceeded to impress him with his friendliness, his learning, his jokes and his unconventionality. Barden's own Monty Pythonish sense of humour helped to keep Murray's depression at bay, and he soon became a regular member of Murray's circle. They discovered that one of Barden's cousins was Cecil Murray's bookie in Krambach.[57] Barden did not much understand or like Murray's poetry, and told him so: this honesty did not sour their friendship.[58] As Ellis recalled,

> There was much coffee drinking and a fair bit of flagon wine, much pool playing, incredible conversation. Barden, who was somewhere between a diseased polecat and a great Bunyanite writer-preacher, was a ferocious personality the like of which I haven't seen outside Ireland. He was very Irish, not in his accent, but in his attitude, a great romantic and a man who would happily have fought duels of honour. Murray adored him.[59]

Barden shared Murray's interest in things military, and he, Murray, Welton, Mulhall and Bruce Muddle, a trainee clerk in the court system, formed what they called The Army of the Four Colonels. The fact that there were five of them was part of the cuckoo logic of the name. Murray, now twenty-one, tended to dominate this group; the others constituted what a female friend of Murray's, Penny McNicoll, called 'the Merry Men to Les's Friar Tuck'.[60] They were four years younger than him, and with their teenage antics they became the circle of schoolmates he had longed for but had never had at Taree High.

They organised marathon pub-crawls, though Murray, with his inherited horror of alcoholism, was never a big drinker; they read poetry to each other on the Manly ferry and on trains; they ostentatiously refused to stand for the national anthem in cinemas, Murray talking seditiously and loudly in Gaelic through the music, and the others gamely making similar noises.[61] With Barden, Murray went on a walk down the coast from Bondi through the Waverley cemetery and on to Coogee and beyond: his poem 'A Walk with O'Connor', written in 1967, would commemorate this hike.

The Four Colonels also engaged in several long bushwalks together, taking the train out to the Holdsworthy army reserve on the Woronora River. On one of these walks, in March 1961, the others bet Murray, who had turned up at the station barefoot, that he could not walk all weekend without shoes. By way of accepting the bet, for £5, a very large sum to him, he dropped his cigarette, covered it with the ball of his big bare foot and very deliberately ground it out. The others might as well have handed over the money at once.

Once they reached the reserve he stripped and plunged into the river, and proceeded to impress his friends by swimming fast enough down one long stretch to keep pace with them as they walked. He emerged to offer them another bet: for another £5 he would do without trousers all weekend. Once they had accepted, he fabricated, out of his belt and Barden's scarf, a loincloth which he wore for the next two days. A photograph survives of the weekend, with Murray, pale and hirsute, posturing in this primitive attire like a stone-age savage armed.[62]

One of the waterholes along the river was particularly dark and grim looking, and Barden said it was inhabited by a bunyip. Murray, who had an encyclopaedic knowledge of the medals and awards of nations ranging from Japan to the Soviet Union, and who was fond of inventing honours for the Army of the Four Colonels, offered to invest anyone brave enough to swim in it with 'the Order of Grendel's Mother'. No one took him up.[63]

John Mulhall had brought along a *Teach Yourself Norwegian*, which he had been working on assiduously in the hope of impressing the others. He did not succeed, for he found that Murray knew much more Norwegian than he did, and in fact could speak the language with fair fluency; Murray also had more than a smattering of Danish. With relish Murray quoted George Borrow, the legendary linguist and traveller, triumphantly chanting as he tramped along the banks of the Woronora in his loincloth, 'The man who twenty tongues could talk/And twenty miles a day could walk'.[64]

It was on one of these walks that Murray spent his only night in jail. Barden, walking ahead, suddenly shouted, shocked, that he had found a corpse. Forty years later Murray had forgotten no detail: 'A fellow lying all desiccated and very dead wearing a brown windcheater and what had been a white shirt, stained. A pair of brown trousers and rubber sandals. And lying face down. One of his arms had been lying in the water and the yabbies had eaten the flesh off it'.⁶⁵ The corpse's ankles were tied, his clothes had been weighted with large stones, and it was clear he had been murdered. Rattled by the discovery, the group walked to Woronora Dam and telephoned the police. It was by now growing dark, and as Murray could give the constabulary no address (he was between landladies) he was locked in a cell for the night, along with Barden, who thereafter happily boasted that he had once been Murray's cellmate.⁶⁶ The next morning they led the police to their grisly find: the corpse was never identified.

On their return from this walk, Welton, who had lived in Alice Springs where his father practised medicine, was being keenly questioned by Murray on the hunting techniques of Aborigines of the centre. Suddenly Welton dropped to his knees, peering at the railway platform, to the puzzlement of the crowds in Wynyard Station. 'We catch 'im here, boss', he cried excitedly, and Murray and Barden instantly fell in with the game, the three of them gabbling fake-Aboriginal to each other as they loped along following the invisible spoor.⁶⁷

> I would remember routines we had invented
> For putting spine into shapeless days: the time
> We passed at a crouching trot down Wynyard Concourse
> Tell each other in loud mock-Arunta and gestures
> What game we were tracking down what haunted gorge . . .
> Frivolous games
> But they sustained me like water.⁶⁸

Murray needed the sustenance of such frivolities, for though his new friends were hardly aware of it, his life was now very slowly spiralling down into chaos. His increasingly manic cheerfulness was an attempt to hide from himself the fact that a crash was not far away. 'I was going off my head. It was very slow and it was very gentle. It was what they call a slow breakdown. You don't know you're having it.'⁶⁹ Nor could he know that the crisis would come through sex: no hunting games would save this Actaeon.

CHAPTER EIGHT
IN THE PIT
1960–62

~

Things fall apart; the Centre cannot hold;
Mere anarchy is loosed upon the world.

W. B. YEATS

Murray and Ellis found their Strathfield landlady, Mrs Boucher, a woman of paralysing meanness. The breakfast she supplied consisted of half an inch of porridge in the bottom of a plate, and eventually her two lodgers, after enduring this for six months in 1960, 'went down the drainpipe', as Murray put it, to avoid paying her the last fortnight's rent: 'She hadn't deserved it'.[1] She was probably glad to see them go: although Murray was not, as Peter Barden observed, 'overly fond of abluting',[2] on one occasion Mrs Boucher had come home unexpectedly to find him standing unclothed in her bathroom, using her toothbrush.[3] Given the state of his teeth, she had reason to be peeved.

She also objected to the girls he began bringing home in emulation of Ellis, who never seemed to have difficulty in persuading women to share his bed although his thin neck and long nose at this time gave him a marked resemblance to an emu.[4] One of Ellis's trophies, which he kept proudly taped to the wall, was a ten-shilling note one woman had given him, and he was vexed when Murray purloined it for food. On one occasion, finding that Murray had returned to their room with Mike Molloy and two sisters, Ellis nobly gave Molloy his own bed: 'I remember there was a night when he and Molloy had two sisters, whose name escapes me, in two single beds and I was lying furious and erect on the floor trying to contain my curiosity. They were certainly very heavily petting though no penetration took place'.[5] Murray perhaps found Ellis's curiosity about his relations with women unnerving.

In 1960 Murray met a big-eyed, vivacious girl named Penny McNicoll, who was working in the offices of *honi soit*, and he was attracted to her. For her part, she had read some of his poetry and thought of him as a celebrity:

> One day in the winter of 1960 a rather burly character in a navy top and a navy beret came into the office and just sat down as if he had all the time in the world. It was the most interesting thing that happened in our week. So we all

sat around and chatted. He put some things in the chief editor's in-tray [Richard Walsh, whom Murray would in future years encounter as the head of the publishing house Angus & Robertson]. Anyway it was Les, and he and I went and had coffee and had a long talk that afternoon. I had never met anybody like him. He was hugely clever, and witty and very engaging in all sorts of weird, whimsical, irritating ways. His sense of humour was wonderful and wild and his courtly imagination was intermittently irritating and appealing . . . I've always been absolutely switched on by the sheer brilliance and gift and generosity of the man.[6]

He told her he came from Bunyah, and when she doubted that such a place existed, he told her it was between Forster and Gloucester; when she lightly quoted 'Dr Foster went to Gloucester', he interrupted to tell her the religious and political significance of that and several other nursery rhymes; he seemed to know everything. She was tremendously impressed. She told him about numerology, and how her days were dominated by the totals of her bus tickets. He received this information gravely, and confided in return that he was deeply attracted to the idea of becoming a Catholic.[7] He was increasingly feeling about Catholicism, 'I belong to that'.[8]

McNicoll, who would later become well known as the novelist Penny Nelson,[9] became a lifelong friend of Murray, and they saw each other constantly after he became literary editor of *honi soit* for two terms during 1960.[10] She found his poetry very beautiful, and was haunted, for reasons of her own, by 'Dolores',[11] which ends:

> But sweet Dolores had to choose
> Old Belial or Honest John;
> She went to hell in snakeskin shoes
> Unloved by either one.

She liked the courtliness with which Murray treated her and other women, the way, for instance, that he would join the tips of his spread fingers on meeting a woman, and bow from the waist.[12] Above all, she loved the way he made her laugh. But she was worried by his reaction when she kissed him: 'It was as though he'd not been kissed. He was an innocent, an absolute innocent. I felt terribly guilty after that, I thought Oh shit! This is too serious, this is deep stuff to him'.[13] It was, though she did not know how deep. But it was with Ellis, whom she met subsequently, that she began a passionate affair, and one that he would commemorate in his film *The Nostradamus Kid*.[14]

Ellis in fact formed the habit of pursuing Murray's female friends. He slept with another girl attracted to Murray, Ros Bateman, who some years later became mentally unstable and committed suicide. 'There may have been some reason why I pursued and tupped Les's girlfriends', Ellis was to say coolly, without relating this observation to his jealousy of Murray's writing. Only gradually would Ellis come to recognise that he envied Murray's abilities: 'Resentment of Les's fame', he would remark, 'is quite easy to have'.[15]

He thought it deeply unfair that Murray did no work for examinations and still got through English 3 and Indonesian & Malayan at the end of 1960,[16] while Ellis could slave and fail.[17] One area in which Ellis easily outclassed his friend was in the collection of women: sleeping with Murray's women friends when Murray would not do so himself was an affirmation of this. Murray himself believed that Ellis, having been an unwanted child, 'has a fierce need to test love by betraying all who love him'.[18] At one stage Ellis confessed to Murray that he suffered from an inferiority complex. 'Nonsense, Robert', Murray said briskly, 'There's nothing complex about your inferiority'.[19]

Flirting, whether under Ellis's influence or not, proved dangerous for Murray: he was playing with fire. 'I feared they [girlfriends] would die, by my fault; when abortion came in, I feared to cause one, but above all I feared the awful ridicule which would certainly greet any approach on my part . . . The prime site of my illness, then, was sexual. Common enough'.[20] He was indeed ill, though his friends were slow to realise it. Under constant sexual pressure, his personal life gradually drifted into disorder.

In the middle of 1960 he ceased to share rooms with Ellis, and went through a rapid succession of landladies. Some he fled to avoid paying the rent, but most initiated his moves, often after just a week or two. Among his papers in the National Library is an unpublished sketch, 'Notes from the House of Mrs Harvey':

> Excuse me, dear.
> Yes, Mrs Harvey, I—
> You're not a tidy boy.
> No, Mrs Harvey . . .
> Books piled on the floor
> But, Mrs Harvey—
> The other boys are good.
> (Oh, Mrs Harvey!)
> It's not like in my day . . .
> No, Mrs Harvey.
> Murders and all.
> Yes, Mrs Harvey, they—
> And then there is your rent.

Yes, Mrs Harvey, I—
You have till Tuesday, then.
Yes, Mrs Harvey.[21]

One of these landladies, a Mrs Moxham, he drove to a nervous breakdown in just a fortnight;[22] another pretended to have a heart attack to get rid of him. A landlord asked him to leave because he thought Murray was homosexual.[23] Yet another threw him out for eating his pudding before his main course.[24] 'There was something about me which gave them the grues or the horrors and they'd find an excuse to get rid of me', he would recall later.[25] This experience of giving people 'the horrors' he would later transfer to his hero Fredy Boettcher.

He thought of himself as 'going feral', as he would put it later;[26] in fact, he was gradually spiralling into nervous breakdown. He wrote to Lehmann in August 1960, 'I'm in the dark night of the soul just now—self-doubt, self-criticism, feelings of impotence and decay and Christ knows what are at me like rats at a wheat bag. Without exaggeration, I'd be glad of affection from a dog at the moment'.[27] His study of psychology in 1957 and 1958 enabled him to put a name to the condition he suffered from, though doing so did not cheer him up: 'It's no fun, being manic-depressive. The label doesn't help at all'.[28]

Having lost Penny McNicoll and Ros Bateman to Ellis, he loved from afar a girl named Ann Radford who failed to notice him,[29] was flirted with by another, whom he managed to 'talk out of my life',[30] before he took up with another of *honi soit*'s staff, Jackie Campbell. She was not conventionally pretty, she habitually wore her fair hair in a bun, she was shy to the point of silence and Ellis would ungallantly describe her as 'breastless',[31] but she was highly intelligent and sympathetic, and men were attracted to her. Her father, like Clive James's, had died in the crash of an American plane while being repatriated after years as a Japanese prisoner of war.[32] In the pages of *honi soit* she was described as 'one of the most hardworking members of staff besides holding the Lady Joyful prize for cuddlesomeness. Unfortunately, none of us have had much opportunity to try out Jackie's worth in this direction'.[33]

After the *honi soit* dinner at the end of 1960, Murray, Barden and a friend named Harry Newton, all happily inebriated, went off to Murray's favourite coffee-house in Kings Cross, the Jedda, and Jackie Campbell went too. Murray's spirits were not depressed by the fact that he had failed German 2, a German lecturer, Michael Nelson, saying to him with mixed admiration and sarcasm, 'Even if you're a poet, you should attend lectures',[34] as Olaf Reinhardt remembered. Afterwards Murray saw Campbell home from the Jedda, and at the door kissed her goodnight, probably the first girl he had kissed rather than been kissed by. 'See? I *must* have been mellow, eh?' he wrote to a friend, Mick Byrne.[35]

The friendship blossomed at a film group conference they both attended at Newport, a northern suburb, and afterwards, as Murray told Byrne, 'on North Sydney station, en route to Roseville, where Jackie lives in a Legacy hostel in term-time, we became engaged. Hooked I am, and never a man lost his freedom with more alacrity or less regret'.[36] In fact he had engaged himself rather casually, and as the relationship progressed he came to rue it. Jackie Campbell, very happy, took him to meet her family in Bathurst, and as the whole thing became more real to Murray, he began to panic. Himself as lover, married man, father: the thought could not be borne.

He did not have the courage to tell Jackie Campbell, and in fact wrote for her the charming poem he would publish under the title 'Love After Loneliness',[37] but under the pressure of his relationship with her, his slide into mental instability became rapid. Years later he would recognise, 'I was going that way already, but the crisis came when I attempted to form an engagement with Jackie Campbell. The engagement, the stress it caused, sent me loopy. I got madder as things got more serious'.[38] His behaviour, bohemian and irregular before, now became completely erratic. 'I reeled away into sleeping rough: I suffered total lack of energy, a state of bonelessness, painful, jagged mental confusion.'[39] He drank a good deal, and he took to the copious use of amphetamines, then freely available: they gave him the illusion of having his energy back. Campbell, deeply hurt, put up with this for a while and then sharply broke her engagement with him. 'She got sick of my behaviour and dismissed me from the Presence,' Murray would say simply.[40]

He had by now passed eight of the required nine units and seemed within easy reach of taking his degree, but he could not summon the energy to do so. He did not register at Sydney University during 1961, partly because of his mental state, partly because his father was now unable or unwilling to support him further;[41] instead he drifted about on the fringes of student life, spending much of his day in the *honi soit* office, which was then in a cottage near the Union building, and sometimes sleeping there as well, or on his friends' floors.

In spite of his small income from the Naval Reserve, in which he had served since 1960, he was now desperately short of money; he piled up small debts, pawned his watch and his typewriter to his father's intense annoyance, and ceased to look for lodgings. He gradually drifted into sleeping in parks or buildings sites, like Samuel Johnson in his early years in London. Often he would spend the night in one of the new buildings rising on the campus. He slept on a plastic sheet and a blanket, emerging in the morning to slap the cement dust off himself as the builders arrived.

The Carslaw building was one I slept in a lot. All you needed was shelter and concealment. As long as you got up before the workers got there you were okay and you could go and wash the cement dust off you in the showers. There were plenty of good showers around the place. I might have been hungry. It was good for my figure and I was very clean.[42]

He was not always successful in getting rid of the cement: 'Les's grey period', his friend Mick Byrne would laughingly call this.[43] In warmer and dryer weather he would sleep on Bondi golf-course, or in a cave at Diamond Bay, or in a disused army base at Dover Heights, or under a rock overhang near the Bondi sewer outfall: Ellis spent one night there with him and was terrified on waking to find that he was only inches from rolling off the cliff-edge.[44]

Murray began taking any odd job he could find, and he found many. Fredy Boettcher's life of rapid scene-shifts was his at this time. He became, in his own words, 'a well-read scholarly derelict'.[45] During these two years he worked for some months in the post office stores, doing very little until someone noticed and sacked him.[46] He spent some months at the Public Service Commission, but turned up so seldom that he embarrassed Greg O'Hara who had recommended him for the job.[47] He considered that working at anything other than his poetry was a complete waste of his time: 'Who wanted a bloody job? I hated the idea of jobs. I was terrified of them. I mean, what good had work ever done my father? He never had a job in his life that he wanted to do'.[48]

He worked in the electrical branch of the State Railways, resigned, and took up again a year later, this time in the catering branch. Just before leaving at the end of this second stint he and a rat-faced[49] co-worker, also about to be sacked, surreptitiously ate a turkey prepared for the New South Wales Railways Commissioner, picking the flesh away from the inside so that later when an attempt was made to carve it, the shell collapsed with a sigh.[50] The Commissioner must have become wary of employing university students, for Ellis, who worked for the railways a little later, when sent to swab out a toilet, carelessly used a bucket of creosote and tarred the room. 'The Commissioner came in and could barely find his way out!' Murray recalled with one of his characteristic cackles of laughter.[51]

There was not much to laugh about in these derelict years. When things grew desperate he would go 'into exile', as he termed it,[52] to Bunyah, where his father was tolerant of him once he saw how ill he was. His psychological distress showed itself in physical ailments, including mysterious muscular pain, and bleeding and suppurating gums. He mooned about the farm and tried to continue to work, giving friends like Greg O'Hara long accounts of his research into Danish philology. But his letters, the handwriting of which bespeaks distress at this time, have a manic touch.

> My regards to all. Tell 'em I'm studying to be a warlock, and welcome donations of hair, skin, toenails, blood, St John's wort, mandragora, poxpus, bluestone, gall—tell 'em anything!' [May 1961]
>
> Me, I'm alive, which is enough. I've got a mouthful of suppurating china-ware [and] the beginnings of a cold ... Dotty? Yes—congratulations. [Greg O'Hara had written that he sounded 'dotty'.] You'd be about the latest to join the 'Certify Murray' Association (Inc. in Bunyah, representatives in Hell and Sydney, capital, Murray's debts.)
>
> No job. Movement is pain, save that of the jawbone and pen-hand ...[53]
> [June 1961]

Though he had little understanding of what was wrong with him, he did his best to nurse himself, writing to Penny McNicoll:

> What I really do here in this arcadian Bunyah (oh, it exists! you bet your Colonial life it does!) is cut down bushes, rest, write letters, rest, eat sparingly, rest, write verse, rest, look after the farm, rest—Tennessee Williams'd love this farm, I assure you, save for the fact that the only erotic activity that occurs here is confined to the cattle and the vegetable marrows. Lewd fruit, those cucurbits![54]

These last remarks were deceptive: in fact his misery was increased at this time by the fact that his father had acquired a mistress, Mrs Smart, and moved her into the Bunyah house.[55] Murray liked to believe that his father remained constant to the memory of his dead mother, and he was not gracious to 'Frau Smart', as he called her. Cecil would never go to bed with her while his son was in the house, and he made no move to marry her. 'The old man is dreadfully slow', the puzzled woman once complained to Murray, who gave her no sympathy.[56] He bitterly resented both her and her son, a sailor on leave from HMAS *Leeuwin*, who walked about the farm killing creatures with a hunting rifle.[57] In the tiny one-bedroom shack the three of them drove each other to distraction, while Cecil tried to keep the peace. Murray did his best to make the interlopers feel unwelcome, and suffered himself. 'Me, I go to bed whenever possible', he wrote to Greg O'Hara, 'or creep around with my nerves hanging out, smoking and picking rows. Oh, for a calf to whip!!'[58]

The poetry he wrote in this blackening period, much of it remaining unpublished, included translations from Lorca, poems in response to him,[59] and fine descriptions of Bunyah and the ghosts of his lost past:

> Beyond the windows, heaving trees
> Fill their darkness with white rain,

> What the wind-ghost with his breath
> Mourns and breaks begins my death
> I cannot build the past again.⁶⁰

In his depression, he tried to lift himself above these circumstances, telling McNicoll that he was doing his best to keep writing.

> The things I write about are mainly religious or metaphysical—I'm concerned with relations between human time and eternity at the odd points where they meet and illuminate each other, eg. where matter becomes immortal, or spirit enters time 'for a season'. (It happens.) This heirophanic [hierophantic] thinking works both ways of course: calling on men to witness the world of spirit and, almost, calling on that world to witness us. Like Octavio Paz said in a poem I once translated: the Mass is 'an incarnate pause between this and timeless time'. Joints and junctions like that, arising in the oddest places, are my meat, not, I'm ashamed to admit, people.⁶¹

As an analysis of one of his main themes, this was deeply perceptive: he would illuminate the intersection between the physical and spiritual worlds in poems from 'The Burning Truck' (which he had had the idea for in 1960, when 'this truck came up in my mind, and I just followed it to see what would happen')⁶² and 'An Absolutely Ordinary Rainbow', through to *Fredy Neptune* and beyond.

And this intersection and struggle were being played out in his own life: 'You accuse me of believing in God. I do, but the misery is, I don't *serve* Him. I serve my silly vanity most of the time'.⁶³ All the same, he believed, 'We're all so close to eternity (my name for where I think God lives) that we stumble over the doorstep quite often, no matter who or what we are'.⁶⁴ And by illustration he quoted a poem he had recently written:

> Cliffs think eternity
> Is stone
> Sheep fear, resignedly
> It's bone.
>
> Blood knows eternity
> Is perfect, red
> Lions bear it to the kill
> Within their tread
>
> The snake knows it is coiled
> Because he knows—

> I am less wise than he
> I just suppose
>
> Saints take eternity
> For guide,
> And earth approaches it
> As bride.[65]

His concerns, in the depths of his depression, were profoundly spiritual, as they would continue to be for the rest of his life. It was about this time that he read Rudolf Otto's *The Idea of the Holy*:[66] more than thirty years later he could call it 'the most influential book of theology I ever read'.[67] And in spite of the stresses on him, he was continuing to produce poetry, and to publish it. One of the poems he wrote at this time, 'City of Tigers', though never published, was a vivid evocation of the terrors that haunted him:

> Down the scoured limestone stairs
> The tigers tread on pads of quiet.
> Who goes, who goes this night of dreams
> This windless night of lantern moon? . . .
>
> Secretly they fan and hunt
> These tigers—who can tell their course?
> Who cries, who runs, this drumming night
> Who is broken? Bleeds the moon?
>
> Along the high streets, tigers go —
> Jesus save me from the sight.
> Who goes, who goes, this night of blood
> This ancient night of lantern moon?

'I can't explain it at all', he told Geoffrey Lehmann, 'it just popped out on the paper, and I don't know much about it, save that I'm scared it may be a true verdict'.[68]

Honi soit continued to carry regular contributions from him, and towards the end of 1961 he returned to Sydney to help Lehmann edit the Arts Faculty journal *Arna*. It contained two poems by Murray, in one of which his characteristic voice emerges clearly for the first time: this was 'The Japanese Barge':

> . . . A Barge
> Arrived one night on the beach,
> Lugged in on the night-tide, queer
> Foreign and Japanese.

> It wallowed,
> The rudder-post frozen with coral
> Up the bay and grounded, reaming
> Water, bow dug in sand. Phantom
> Soldiers disembarked and scattered.
>
> We found some buttons and a tin
> Of mud-fused cigarettes; no more . . .
>
> That night
> The tide withdrew it, whispering
> Out of the shallows. None saw it go
> Out to the deep night, drowning
> Into the dark of mind and ocean.
>
> The samurai did not come back at dawn
> And we forgot to talk of battles.[69]

This strange, dreamlike vision, conveyed using a technique that would be paralleled in 'The Burning Truck', was sparked off by nothing more obviously significant than a tin of Japanese cigarettes Ken Welton had shown him.[70] Some of his best poems were to come direct and unannounced from the dreaming mind, and 'The Japanese Barge' was an astonishing poem for a Bunyah youth of twenty-two.

It was during this terrible period of depression, in 1961, that his work began to appear in commercial journals for the first time. Early that year the Sydney journal *Southerly* carried two poems by him, 'Veterans'[71] and 'The Englishman'.[72] He was delighted, partly because *Southerly*'s editor was Kenneth Slessor,[73] whose own fine poetry Murray greatly admired, partly because his first attempt to make his mark on a reading public outside the university had suffered a setback when the poet Douglas Stewart,[74] long-serving editor of the Red Page of the *Bulletin*, famous for its publication of new Australian writing, responded to his earliest poems with a terse note: 'You have obviously put more thought into the covering letter than into any of the poems'.[75] Murray, at first downcast, had learnt from this rebuff: 'He was right!' he would remark.[76] Hereafter he submitted a steady stream of highly polished poems to *Southerly* and the *Bulletin*, and continued to publish short stories, one of which was accepted by ABC Radio in 1962.[77]

But by the middle of 1961 he was desperate, seriously concerned that he was on the edge of insanity. His sleep was interrupted by terrible nightmares. He suffered constant hunger and began losing weight, and his begging for food in the Union had begun to take the form of imitating a dog, sitting up with cocked paws, whining dolefully and snapping at scraps thrown to him: few of his friends thought this funny.[78] He borrowed money and did not return it, until one day an exasperated creditor, Ian Boden, by way of replying to another appeal for cash, while Lehmann and others looked on, ceremoniously burnt a five pound note in front of Murray's starting eyes.[79]

He was by now working at Central Station doing accounts, a task for which he was singularly ill-fitted, as he was, and would remain, formally innumerate, though very quick to do rough mental calculations, visualising figures in terms of their proportions to each other. Instinctively he felt he must get away from Sydney, from his friends and the university; at the same time he shrank from Bunyah and Frau Smart. He rang his father's brother, Charlie Murray, to say he needed to get completely away. As Charlie recalled:

> Then one day I got a phone call from him and he said he was going walkabout around Australia. And he said 'I'm having trouble', he said, 'I go to sleep at night, I have nightmares and all I see is these figures. I think I'm going mad', he said, 'so I'm going to go walkabout. I didn't tell Dad because he'd stop me from going, so I don't want you to let him know until I'm well on the way'. I said 'OK'. He said 'I think I need it bad'. I said 'OK, I understand'.[80]

Setting off with £18 in his pocket, Murray hitch-hiked to Melbourne in July 1961, to stay for a while with Tony Coady, one of his Sydney University friends, who had rooms in Carlton. He ended up spending three months with Coady, who found him a fascinating companion. 'How is it you know so many languages?' Coady asked once. 'After the first seven it just comes naturally', said Murray with panache.[81]

He tried to earn a living in Melbourne by selling, door to door, filters designed to be fitted to the screens of black-and-white television sets, thereby supposedly converting their pictures into colour; these filters he had to buy from the manufacturers and sell on at a profit. He sold only one—not surprisingly, as the filters did not work. The money he got from this one success he at once spent on a dinner for Coady and his wife. He had no money to pay Coady rent, and instead offered him batches of poems, which Coady carefully preserved.[82]

In letters he wrote to Penny McNicoll one catches a glimpse of him and Mick Molloy, another university friend now living in Melbourne, drinking beer, listening to Mahalia Jackson records, cursing Melbourne and trying to throw a table knife into the back of an elderly chair until the landlord came up to ask them to pipe down.[83] Coady introduced him to Vincent Buckley, who offered to publish a few of Murray's poems. Murray gratefully accepted, telling Lehmann, 'He doesn't like me much, but he will talk to me'.[84] Buckley also promised Murray a couple of his own poems for publication in *Hermes*, the annual Undergraduate Association journal of Sydney University, for which Murray was still acting as co-editor.

But Murray was right to think Buckley did not like him: after he had left Melbourne he heard from Coady that Buckley had remarked to academic and literary friends, 'Very promising poet, young Murray, but a terrible Nazi you know'. He was hurt by this calumny, but presently came to think it a compliment 'that this established poet should feel so threatened by a total unknown that he would try to blight my reputation in the bud like that'.[85] All the same Murray would never forget Buckley's malice, and in later years would say sharp things about the older man.

On his trip down to Melbourne, in a truckies' cafe at Tarcutta near Gundagai,[86] Murray had rewritten and condensed 'The Burning Truck', and he now summarised it for McNicoll and quoted its ending:

> Over the tramlines, past the church, on past
> You and me, and thence out of the world
> With its disciples.

adding, 'which makes you reread the whole thing, (I hope). Like the idea?'[87] When Lehmann read this version he criticised the dullness of 'you and me', suggesting instead 'past/The last lighted window', an improvement Murray at once adopted.[88]

And it was with the revised version that he achieved his ambition of getting poems published in the *Bulletin*, the most famous and important Australian literary journal, while he was in Melbourne late in 1961, and just after the death of the famous Red Page, the major literary section that had been started by A. G. Stephens in 1896. Douglas Stewart, the editor, was delighted with 'The Burning Truck' and with another poem reflecting Murray's military interest, 'Deck Chair Story'. 'The Burning Truck', in particular, made it clear to Stewart that a major new poetic voice was speaking.

Younger readers took note too: the poet Chris Wallace-Crabbe,[89] whom Murray met in Melbourne at this time,[90] was to remember being astounded by 'The Burning Truck': 'How on earth a young poet could come up with a self-sustaining image like that I scarcely know, and it immediately established him in my mind as a poet of great gifts'.[91] He would grow more certain of Murray's importance as he saw more of his work: towards the end of the century he would say unhesitatingly, 'He's a terrific genius'.[92] The novelist Christopher Koch, then primarily a poet, wrote to Stewart from Italy asking who was the old Digger who wrote 'Deck Chair Story'.[93] This enquiry was to initiate a long and close friendship between Koch and Murray. Even from the depths Murray was making his voice heard.

But he could not rest anywhere at this time, and he had not come away to reproduce in Melbourne the situation he had fled from in Sydney: after three months he was on the move again, to Adelaide. Looking back he would recall this trip:

> Today, a sequence from that equivocal season
> Danced in my memory:
> I saw myself away in South Australia,
> Still a novice, but learning,
> Having already felt frost through my blanket,
> Learned how to dig a hip-hole, to sleep quickly,
> How to camp in good cover, especially in cities . . .
>
> All that day, I had traversed the German country
> —Vast fields of September, distant adobe houses
> Hungry, such was my mood, for the exotic,
> I'd listened for German in casual talk overheard
> In winecellar towns at peace with their horizons.

His terrors and inadequacies haunted him:

> I walked on and on
> Upbraiding myself with melancholy pleasure
> For past insufficiencies, future humiliations:
> 'You are always at fault. Nor will this ever change,'
> Saith the inner Voice,
> Wise alien liar.[94]

From Adelaide he hitched into Central Australia, heading for Alice Springs, 'Out of the fenced and fertile South-east districts/And, just on sundown, entered the waterless kingdom'. He had a dangerous lift to Alice Springs, with two gun-crazy Melburnians who shot at all the wildlife they saw from the car, and who discussed coolly how easy it would be to shoot Murray and bury him beside the road. Their passenger, who could shoot better than either of them, kept smiling and hoped this talk would remain nothing more than that.

Through Alice Springs, like a man pursued, he continued to Darwin with an equally dangerous insurance inspector, who was constantly drunk and who kept Murray drunk too, and from Darwin he pressed on into the back-blocks of western Queensland: 'I covered all states except Western Australia and Tassie.

I enjoyed it too. I just drifted along. I had this talent for sleeping rough so it didn't cost me much'.[95]

He certainly tried everything by way of saving money on hotels. Once in Queensland he asked a Presbyterian minister for a bed for the night, and might have got it had he not slid into a theological dispute with the man: when Murray grew angry he was sent on his way into the dark. Then or on another occasion he shared the sleeping-place of a large but timorous watchdog in a backyard shed.[96] 'He stayed and kept me warm', Murray recalled about the animal: 'He wanted to come with me the next day, but dogs hitch poorly'.[97] He often had nothing to eat, and flesh fell away from him so that he was soon thin, and his massive structure of bone was very evident.

Sometime in November 1961 he was in the Northern Territory, riding in a cattle-truck between Tennant Creek and Carnooweal, and in the night he felt the illness 'blow off me'.[98] He believed himself to be cured, and returned, gaunt but calm, to Sydney and to his greatly relieved father. But the release was an illusion, and in Sydney the depression settled on him once more. In his despair he took off for Melbourne a second time, but travelling no longer seemed to help and he returned gloomily to Sydney. Like Stephen Dedalus in *Ulysses*, he was homeless everywhere.

He now fell back on the Sydney Push for support and comfort. The Push (the term meant a gang of larrikins) had originally formed around the Libertarian Society, whose guru was John Anderson, Professor of Philosophy at Sydney University. More of an activist than a scholar, Anderson was a gaunt Scot who dismissed religion, patriotism, romanticism and morality. The university senate thought him shocking and censured him; a State MP called him 'a curse upon this country'; delighted students flocked to him.[99] The Libertarian Society was based on his ideas, but its adherents intended to put them into practice in their social, sexual and political lives, something Anderson himself resiled from as he aged. 'Endorsing Pareto's analysis of sexual guilt as a repressive social mechanism', Clive James was to write, 'the Libertarians freely helped themselves to each other's girlfriends'.[100]

But the Push combined town with gown. To the Libertarians were added assorted Sydney intellectuals (including Murray's early master, Lex Banning) and a sub-rout of traditional jazz fans, sailors and small-time gamblers and crooks. 'The world of crime started just where the Push finished', Clive James would remember, 'and often the edges overlapped'.[101] The favourite meeting place of this disparate group was the Royal George Hotel in Sussex Street, filled with smoke, beer, loud talk and indifferent jazz, but there were also various 'Push houses' round Sydney. One of these, at 2 Glen Street, Milson's Point, almost under the Harbour Bridge, was leased by Brian Jenkins, the student poet who earlier had introduced Murray to Lex Banning. Jenkins compassionately invited Murray to move into the Glen Street house, even though Murray was penniless and could not contribute to the rent.

Here he was allowed to doss down on the overcoat of a Canadian denizen, and after some weeks graduated to a bed. The Glen Street house was run like what would later be known as a commune; as Murray put it, 'We pioneered that stuff before all the blue-prints came from America'.[102] Perhaps a dozen people occupied the house, drifting in and out of relationships with one another, in rebellion against conventions of all kinds and thereby reproducing conventional morality inverted. It was an effortfully immoral lifestyle, with a great deal of heavy-duty love-making and drinking. Betrayal was done all the time, and they told each other, in vain, that jealousy was passé.

It was clear what the men got out of this arrangement, for there was a steady supply of new wide-eyed young women eager for thrills: 'The women came and went, but the men went on forever', one of them remarked.[103] While the women lasted, the historian Anne Coombs noted, 'who they had sex with would determine their status in the group'.[104] When they fell pregnant, the hat would be passed round to pay for an abortion; such donations were the closest anyone came to responsibility.

The Push hated euphemism, as Murray noticed:

> Everything had to be called by its hardest possible name in the Push. So girls interested in lots of sexual activity were called the Cunt Push. Judy McGuinness[105] used to pick up the phone and say 'Milson's Point Home for Fallen Ladies'. Often on the other end it would be her poor mother. They played hell with the social mores of parents and folk of that sort. That was a lot of the point. It wasn't so much who you were having sex with, it was who you were having sex against.[106]

Murray was not having sex for or against anyone, and was rather resented for it. He noted clinically the men who were there only for the easy women; he noted with pity such figures as the girl who slept under the stairs, and who would be woken by men wanting sex: whimpering and cursing, she would always submit.[107] Not surprisingly, the Push would die of feminism.

'Aloof in a Push squat, I thought I was moral, or dead', Murray would write.[108] He took great quantities of methedrine, and in spite of it was overcome with torpor. Flaccid with depression and accidie, he simply slept all day, and sat round and talked desultorily at night, listening for hours to the hypnotic sitar ragas of Ravi Shankar.[109]

The Glen Street house had a magnificent view down the harbour, and immediately outside the windows swooped the roller coaster of Luna Park:

> Where I lived once, a roller coaster's range
> of timber hills peaked just by our backyard cliff
> and cars undulated scream-driven round its seismograph
> and climbed up to us with an indrawn gasp of girls.[110]

A good deal of the fun indoors seemed to him just as mechanical and unspontaneous. He was anaesthetised by his childhood and youth, describing himself to Lehmann as 'Me! Whom the Lord decreed celibate, and Satan made potent, or vice versa'.[111]

Occasionally he would voice his despair to the other inmates of the house: 'When I was living with the Push in Milson's Point, I came out one morning, looked morosely around the assembled scrags and said: "Well, I've had my weekly wet dream. Now I've got nothing to look forward to"'.[112] And there was a response: one of the Push girls, Carol, came and slipped into his bed in her underclothes. In vain. He froze, the memory of Taree High still fresh on him, and simply talked at her until she gave up and staggered away dazed with words.

> Once Carol from upstairs came to me in bra and kindness
> and the spider secreted by girls' derision-rites to spare
> women from me had to numb me to a crazed politeness.
> Squeals rode the edge of the thrill building.[113]

Fredy Boettcher would suffer that same numbness, but in his case made physical. All the same, though Murray did not realise it, sexual acceptance of the sort Carol offered him was gradually salving his wound. And it was in Sydney, in 1962, that his life quite suddenly turned around. Depression lifted without warning, in the inexplicable way that the disease has, and he met Valerie Morelli.

CHAPTER NINE
HALT AND TURN
1962

~

She shall do him good and not evil all the days of her life.

PROVERBS

Valeria Gina Maria Morelli, always known as Valerie in Australia, was born in Budapest on 1 August 1941.[1] Her father, Gino Morelli, born in 1913, was a Hungarian of Swiss descent, his father József being a prosperous lawyer whose large household was complete with maids, a chauffeur and governesses to teach little Gino six languages. At the age of twenty-four, Gino met Valerie's mother, Berta Linder, a strikingly attractive blonde Swiss, while he was working for a Hungarian bank in Zurich, and they married in August 1939: war broke out in September. Gino, called up by the Hungarian air force, took his new wife to Hungary, a satellite of Germany during the war. He served with the Hungarian forces, working first as a translator (those six languages serving him well) and then, when the Hungarians invaded Russia in support of the Germans in 1941, as a sound recording engineer for the Hungarian propaganda department, recording interviews with Hungarian soldiers on the Russian front. He was engaged in this work when Valerie, his first child, was born: he got compassionate leave to return for the event, and again after his son Stephen was born in April 1943.[2]

In March 1944 the Nazis, suspicious that Hungary was trying to detach itself from what was by now clearly the losing side, seized control of the country, and conditions deteriorated sharply. Early in December 1944, as the Wehrmacht fell back on Budapest and advancing Russian forces pressed forward into Hungary, three-year-old Valerie and the baby Stephen were dispatched with the last Red Cross train to safety in Switzerland, on the strength of their mother's nationality. That same day, 6 December, Gino and Berta were arrested by the Hungarian Nazis on suspicion of having helped Jews: the bank for which Gino had worked in Switzerland was Jewish-owned, and Gino's stepmother was Jewish. Gino eventually bought their release with a hidden store of gold coins, but his brother-in-law in Switzerland, into whose care the children were delivered, was told by the Red Cross that Gino and

Berta had been taken by the Nazis and were probably dead by now. 'Till this point we've had three children', the brother-in-law told his wife stoutly, 'Now we have five'.³

In a series of hair's-breadth escapes, first from Hungarian Nazis, then from Russian troops bent on rape and rapine, Gino and Berta fled Hungary for Romania, having to move east because the routes west were closed by the beginnings of the Iron Curtain. For a time Gino made a dangerous living in the Bucharest black market, one of his business associates being Peter Abeles, who would eventually become an Australian tycoon.⁴ By the end of 1945 Berta was able to rejoin their children in Switzerland, and Gino followed some months later. The family lived in Switzerland until 1950, Gino supporting his family first by working as a book-keeper, later by selling encyclopaedias door to door on a bicycle. In 1950 they emigrated to Australia, arriving in Sydney on the *Goya* in November.⁵ Valerie, whose home language had changed from Hungarian to Swiss-German, was nine on her arrival in Australia. In later years Murray would evoke this time in 'Immigrant Voyage', working from his wife's vivid memories:

> Pattern-bombed out of babyhood,
> Hungarians-become-Swiss,
> the children heard their parents:
> Argentina? Or Australia?
> Less politics, in Australia . . .
>
> Dark Germany, iron frost
> and the waiting many weeks
> then a small converted warship
> under the moon, turning south.
>
> Way beyond the first star
> and beyond Cap Finisterre
> the fishes and the birds
> did eat of their heave-offerings.
>
> The Goya was a barracks:
> mess-queue, spotlights, tower,
> crossing the Middle Sea.
>
> In the haunted blue light
> that burned nightlong in the sleeping-decks
> the tiered bunks were restless
> with coughing, demons, territory.

After a period in migrant camps at Bonegilla on the Murray River and in Nelson Bay ('the dry-land barbed wire ships/from which some would never land'),[6] they stayed with friends in Sydney, then rented a house in Cronulla in Sydney's south, where Gino took any job he could find: as a storeman for Taubman's Paints, as a cosmetics salesman, as the book-keeper for a frozen fish company. Their story could have been that of any of the millions of European migrants who were flowing into Australia in these postwar years.

Gino was a particularly good salesman, and he eventually moved into real estate: for twenty years he part-owned an estate agency, Burgis & Morelli, in the Sydney suburb of Beverly Hills.[7] Gino's father József, ruined by the war, joined them in Sydney in 1955, just before the Hungarian uprising, and would live with them for the rest of his long life.[8] Gino built a house in Loftus, and Valerie attended a convent school in Sutherland, for though Berta was a Zwinglian Protestant by upbringing, under Gino's influence Valerie and Stephen were raised as Catholics, and in later life the faith of both would be unwavering.

In 1956 the Morellis moved to Chatswood, and here Valerie finished her high school education at another convent school, Monte Sant' Angelo, before going to Sydney University in 1959 to read languages. Her aim was to become a teacher. Her already wide knowledge of European languages, combined with keen intelligence and self-discipline, meant that her work was as focused as Murray's was erratic, and she made steady progress through her degree. She was calm, good-humoured, and possessed of quite uncommon common sense. She was also beautiful, having the looks of her paternal grandmother, Cornelia: at this time she wore her dark brown hair shoulder length, framing her round face; through her swept-up spectacles her blue eyes were shrewd and sympathetic. 'Friendly, open, natural', her fellow-student Olaf Reinhardt was to call her, adding that she seemed not to care about the fashions that so obsessed other women students at the time.[9]

She first met Murray before he met her. In 1960 they were both in German 2, and at the end of the year the students were summoned, in alphabetical order, for oral tests which involved each in reciting a poem, sight-reading a prose passage, and then engaging in German conversation with the examiner. Miss Morelli, at the end of this minor ordeal, was asked to send up Mr Murray. On a bench outside the German department she found a figure in a blue naval jersey, with a sailor's little white pork-pie hat perched on the back of his head; his hair was cow-licked, Baby Hughie-style, across his forehead. He was studying his German text intently, probably because he had not troubled to look at it before. 'Excuse me, you're Mr Murray?' asked Valerie: 'They're expecting you upstairs'. Murray gave her a startled, unseeing glance, leapt to his feet without a word and went in.[10] Afterwards he would have no memory of this encounter with her.

In 1961 Valerie did German 3; Murray had dropped out. It was not until the end of 1961 that she saw him again, after his walkabout, and was struck by how thin and gaunt he had become: his ribs stood out sharply. At Easter 1962, the adventurous German department decided to put on a medieval Passion play, in late medieval rhyming German. It was to be produced by one of the lecturers, Len McGlashan, who had discovered the manuscript in Innsbruck, and directed by Oliver Fialla. All rehearsals, and the final performances, were in the Great Hall, and McGlashan enthusiastically recruited anyone who could speak a word of German into the very large cast. Valerie agreed to be wardrobe mistress, designing and running up costumes at a moment's notice and playing non-speaking parts in the crowd scenes. Murray, who had registered again in 1962 to read German 2 and Indonesian & Malayan 2, played Satan, wearing a red suit of crushed velvet sewn by Valerie, and a pig-mask through the eye-slits of which he could see virtually nothing. This was a serious handicap, for at the end of one scene he was required to leap off the stage, and on the opening night he sprang blindly into the front row, and landed on the Governor of New South Wales.[11]

He did, however, now see Valerie for the first time: as she tried his costume on him for size, she noticed that he gave her a great sidelong look. 'He actually made me take a bit of eye contact. We didn't do very much of that because he was terribly shy.'[12] As he did with women, he spoke to her very fast, in a clipped monotone through immobile lips, like an unpractised ventriloquist: she thought of it as 'Aussie malespeak'. 'And it was all very intelligent and lots of tangential thinking and unusual vocabulary and in the end I became embarrassed about saying I beg your pardon, I beg your pardon. It was going past me much too fast and he wouldn't even look at me, speaking out of the corner of his mouth.'[13] This terrified fending-off, his usual reaction to women, gradually subsided. Valerie's central-European background meant that she spoke German as well as he did, and could match his displays of knowledge about Danish or Spanish with her native Hungarian, or Italian or French. And while he was a poet, she had a lovely singing voice, some of Murray's friends considering that she could have had a career as a great singer.[14]

Bob Ellis would remark that Valerie was 'like an identikit drawing of the perfect woman for Les. They come out of the same cookie cutter. Her European extraction didn't hurt either. He was always fascinated with things German, Hungarian, Swiss, and she was the perfect roll-your-own European woman for him'.[15] Valerie's natural friendliness and openness gradually calmed

Murray's fears and he found himself deeply attracted to her, though in one of their earliest conversations he had told her he intended to become a Trappist monk.[16]

She began noticing that they kept meeting, as if by chance, and then one day saw that he had spotted her from across the busy Parramatta Road, and that he dodged through six lanes of traffic so as to walk past her and greet her with pleased surprise, not even stopping to talk. 'There was no strong attraction for me to begin with', Valerie would recall. 'I used to be comfortable in his company and I was curious.'[17] Presently he summoned the courage to invite her to a film, and then another. One day they arranged to take a train together to the Blue Mountains for a walk. The night before the walk he was flattened with influenza, and in his Push squat no one woke him until hours after they were to have met at Central Station: he rushed there, sneezing with chagrin, and found Valerie still waiting for him four hours after the agreed time. Even though Murray firmly believed himself to be repulsive to women, this sign of her steadfastness must have given him a clear signal, and after this the progress of their relationship was rapid.

She took him home to meet her parents and her spry grandfather József, and he helped her father Gino paint the kitchen of their Chatswood house. The initial meeting was not a success, and not just because Murray was no painter: Gino, with all the energy of the immigrant determined to make good, rapidly sized Murray up and decided that the potential of this aspiring poet to keep his only daughter in luxury was nugatory.[18] In this judgement he was absolutely right. On the other hand he admired Murray's linguistic skills: Gino essayed a few of his six languages on this strange new friend his daughter had brought home, and was astounded at the response: years later he would say flatly, 'Les is a language genius'.[19]

As it turned out, the young people took matters out of the hands of Gino and Berta. About a month after the play and shortly before Valerie's graduation, on 25 April 1962, Anzac Day, they went together to Lane Cove park. As they wandered around the rifle range there, Murray said to Valerie without ceremony or preparation, 'You're the girl for me. I want to marry you. What do you think?' 'OK', she replied simply.[20] Her parents were far from enthusiastic, but they would soon be persuaded by events.

One morning early in August 1962, after a night in which Murray and Ellis had broken into the staff club at Sydney University and gorged on cheese, stale biscuits and wine, they emerged blinking into the sun in the great Quad, and Ellis announced to Murray that he was forswearing fornication. In celebration of this solemn moment he and Murray inflated Ellis's remaining condoms and allowed a stiff breeze to swirl these grotesque balloons satisfyingly around the old buildings:

> The day you gave up fornication
> we took your WetChex and, by insufflation,
> made fat balloons of them, to glisten aloft in the sun
> above the Quad, the Great Hall, the Carillon—
> and that was Day One in the decade of chickens-come-home
> that day kids began smoking the armpit hairs of wisdom.[21]

Although the poem does not say so, it was Day One because as Ellis (very briefly) renounced sex, Murray at last took it up. And it was soon after this that Murray's and Valerie's chickens came home. The ribald Ellis was to opine that Murray and Valerie had lost their virginity together and conceived their first child on the same night, in the back of her father's Holden.[22] It was in fact a Ford Falcon, and it was still in the garage, for Murray had not yet learned to drive.[23] He was soon, joyfully and without embarrassment, telling his friends:

> Valerie and I are getting married in the church of Our Lady of Dolours at Chatswood on Sat. 29th Sept, that is to say this very month. Wally Davis will be best man, Maureen Dalton [Valerie's best friend] will be bridesmaid. Why are we getting married so precipitately and at such an untoward time, you ask? My boy, we have to. You'd be surprised how few regrets I have at the moment, all the same . . . Ah, lad, I feel so good this spring, you wouldn't *believe*—I could spit clear to Turkey, I could catch geese on the wing, I could—but enough, enough.[24]

Gino and Berta were shocked and troubled, but they accepted the *fait accompli*. Cecil Murray, neither shocked nor worried though his son had nothing whatever to marry on, calmly said 'Ah well, you made your bed, now lie on it'.[25]

Murray's university friends were more taken aback: Peter Barden's reaction was to seize his father's whisky bottle, blaspheme, and drink a great stoup: later he recovered enough to take Murray out to a celebratory lunch.[26] Ellis's reaction was more complicated: 'I guess I was injured', he would say slowly, years later.[27] He had come to depend on Murray more than he realised. Within a short time he would be showing signs of instability, and the Cuban Missile Crisis at the end of the year would send him fleeing hysterically into the Blue Mountains with Penny McNicoll and another friend, Ian Masters, to avoid the Wrath to Come.[28] On realising the next morning that Sydney had not been reduced to radioactive rubble, Ellis ran from the car and (according to Masters' account) was found weepingly haranguing a petrol bowser.[29]

McNicoll, undiplomatically invited by Murray to meet 'the best of women', was later to give a faintly acerbic description of Valerie as 'a wary, smiling, pleasantly spoken brown-haired student who wore glasses, and whose long fingernails were painted with frosted apricot nail polish'.[30] But, she added with reluctant admiration, 'this was the woman who'd dared give Les some advice about clean clothes and personal hygiene'.[31]

Lehmann, an outspoken atheist, was interested to know how Murray was going to cope with marriage to a Catholic. Murray tailored his reply to his friend's expectations:

> Les said 'I'm going to be getting married to Valerie, and I really do want to become a Catholic. There's only two problems. Number one I just don't believe in God. And number two, I'm emotionally incapable of praying!' [laughter] Anyway he was obviously able to overcome the problems.
>
> So I said to Les, 'Look man, it's all right to become a Catholic, nothing wrong with that. But when you do, don't write bloody poems about God. You don't want to become like Francis Thompson and write that kind of rubbish.' I was alarmed at the thought of bardic religious poetry coming over him, which it never has, actually. His religion is very discreet in his poetry.[32]

In fact Murray, who had never abandoned the Christianity of his upbringing and had clung to it most passionately in the depths of his depression, was now well along the road to changing his denominational loyalty. Catholicism had a profound attraction for him, and it came partly through his contact with Catholic friends like Walter Davis and his wife Elisabeth:

> I liked the way that they could be religious and yet laugh. I'd never struck that before. They could laugh at the most sacred things and not dismiss them. They could be loyal while laughing. This struck me as a wonderful liberation. And I was fascinated by the idea of the Eucharist. It absolutely wowed me. Anybody who's interested in imagery has to be interested in that type of fusion, metaphor taken all the way to identity.[33]

From the start he associated religion and poetry: to him, religion was a long and perfect poem, the fullest possible expression of a vital aspect of existence. He found the Roman Catholic insistence on transubstantiation and such dogmas as the Assumption of the Virgin Mary particularly attractive, partly because he associated them with resistance to the Enlightenment, and the enforced orthodoxies of intellectual and political life:

> I like those things because they are damned good elaborations of the Poem, but [also because] they are such an offence to the gentiles. I love those parts of the Church, the harder it gets to believe the happier I am with it. The sense that at least somewhere there are propositions at utter variance with the dogmas of secular French-Revolution Modernism is wonderful. A counter-balance to

what I find a terribly oppressive, arrogant, narrow, bullying kind of atmosphere. Most of the things that have been said about Catholicism in the past really apply to the modern Inquisition. The Inquisition is not the Catholic one but the Modernist one.[34]

Catholicism reached below logic, below sense, in a way that delighted him; it overlapped poetry in this, as (for him) Protestantism did not. As he would put it in a short poem, 'Distinguo',

> Prose is Protestant-agnostic,
> story, explanation, significance,
> but poetry is Catholic:
> poetry is presence.[35]

Language was another factor drawing him to the Church: he loved the music of the Bible, and of the Mass. But deeper than all rational influences, he would say in later years, was 'a matter of my darkly realising I *belonged* there—call that a call, maybe. I do, among some hearers'.[36]

Though he would not be baptised into the Roman Catholic Church until 1964,[37] he would live as a faithful, practising Catholic from this time on, attending Mass at least once a week. Religious belief, he asserted, was the one barrier to the blackness in the heart of man. 'The only agency I see which may help humans, all of them, endure and delight in peace is God's grace. Any blockage of that in their lives, and they are open to blood sacrifice, of themselves and others'.[38] His, however, would never be Valerie's serene certitude of belief: he wrestled continually with his faith and would be constantly rethinking it. In his poetry he would consider it vital not simply to restate the foundations of his faith, but to 'make it new'. And he would come to feel that some of his most intractable antagonists in this process were Catholics.[39] All the same, from this time forth his Christianity was newly alive, a philosophy and belief system that gave structure and meaning to every aspect of his being, the base of all his ideological positions, the still centre around which his world turned. 'Catholicism's a complete way of life', he would say with conviction decades later.[40]

The mixed-marriage ceremony, starting at 4 p.m. on 29 September 1962 in the church of Our Lady of Dolours, Chatswood, was conducted by Monsignor Harrington. Murray, slim and handsome in a hired grey suit, was calm up to the moment Valerie in her white wedding dress joined him in the aisle. He then began to sweat, as he put it, 'like an Arabian marathon runner performing in a coon-skin coat',[41] but Valerie steadied him and got him through it, as she would get him through everything to come. The congregation was composed of his university friends (including Ellis, Lehmann, Molloy, Peter Wagner, Penny McNicoll, Barry Oakley, Barden, Welton and Mulhall), and of polyglot Morelli friends in profusion: as Murray recalled, 'People with names like Nagy and Hunyor, Moszny[42] and Pilat shook my damp hand, wishing me well in many kinds of English and German'.[43]

A much reduced party then went on to a small reception at a place called the Windsor Gardens; Cecil, who had been subdued and ill at ease during the wedding, all his Free Presbyterian instincts recoiling from the Catholic setting, gradually cheered up as people noticed and were pleasant to him and to Mrs Smart.[44] There were decorous, heavily accented speeches. The Army of the Four Colonels then elaborately presented Murray with a Japanese officer's sword by way of farewelling him from their ranks, their Monty Pythonish mumbo-jumbo watched in polite bewilderment by the European section.

Afterwards the reduced army went sorrowing away to a much more lively party in Paddington. They all imbibed strong waters, and early in the morning John Mulhall said to Barden, 'Welton just came in through the window'. 'So what?' said Barden woozily. 'The window was closed', said Mulhall. Ken Welton, badly cut, was found lying in a small pool of blood. In the course of the confusion attendant on patching him up, one of their friends, Mike Limerick, arrived with the news that the state government, in one of its periodic fits of morality, was ordering the shutting of all brothels. 'Can't you just see the headlines?' crowed Mulhall: 'LES MURRAY WEDS: BROTHELS CLOSE'.[45]

The honeymoon consisted of a weekend spent in a borrowed flat overlooking Mona Vale beach, and it was only here that the eternal aspect of what they had done came home to Murray. For him and Valerie, marriage was permanent. 'The next thing we do as final as that will be to die', he told O'Hara soberly. 'It gives you powerfully to think: I'm still realising it. I think Valli is farther along the road to comprehension that I am.'[46] In fact, Valerie was ahead of him at this time on many roads, psychological, social and spiritual: he had missed out on great swathes of life. He would slowly grow to understand that she was the best thing that would ever happen to him, though at this time he naturally chiefly appreciated her physical beauty and warmth: 'Isn't she lovely, though? Her beauty fascinates me afresh every day'.[47] His friends concurred that she was much too good for him. More surprisingly, all his friends liked her very much, and he lost none of them.

Slowly, painfully, Valerie would undo what he believed the girls of Taree High had done to him; she offered him unconditional unwavering love, a home, solace for his lost mother, and a way back to mental health, though his recovery would be far from instantaneous. 'When young lips have drunk deep of the bitter waters of Hate, Suspicion, and Despair', Kipling once wrote, 'all the Love in the world will not wholly take away that knowledge'.⁴⁸ Murray's Black Sheep years were over, but Valerie would have to continue to tolerate their effects for decades to come.

He and Lehmann edited the Undergraduate Association's annual *Hermes* at the end of the year. It contained a poem Murray entitled 'Halt and Turn', dedicated 'for V'—'in gratitude for loving me in spite of my being a sleazy bum', as he told Lehmann.⁴⁹ The poem recognises what she had done for him in giving him a refuge from the storm of life, and apologises for what she would continue to have to do:

> Descending into the level country
> I saw, as far as the wind could blow
> The naked trees were leaning away
> From the blind gift of the snow . . .
>
> Weary's the way beyond the weariness
> That brings me home to your hearth
> Forgive me if my shoeprints leave
> Some dead snow on your path.⁵⁰

CHAPTER TEN
THYRSIS AND CORYDON
1962-65

~

*Together both, ere the high Lawns appear'd
Under the opening eyelids of the morn,
We drove a-field.*

MILTON

The newlyweds took a tiny flat at 5 Mansfield Road, Glebe, enjoyed, as Murray told Greg O'Hara, 'showers à deux, cabbage-salad suppers taken in bed, learning to keep house',[1] and tried to finish their studies at Sydney University at the end of 1962, without much success. Valerie, ill with recurrent bouts of flu, pregnant, and shaken by the change from the comfortable routine of living with her parents and spending all her Education Department grant on herself, failed her Education Diploma examination, but was allowed to begin teaching at Kogarah without it, on the strength of her bachelor's degree.[2] Her pregnancy would soon make it impossible for her to continue. Murray, who had done no work all year, failed both German 2 and Indonesian & Malayan 2. With that, he abandoned his attempts to finish his degree: he would not try again until 1969.

Reluctantly, he took a temporary job at the University of New South Wales library,[3] the first element of what would prove to be a long association with Sydney's second-oldest university.[4] He followed this with a temporary clerkship in the Commonwealth Office of Education in Miller Street, North Sydney.[5] He and Valerie were poorly off, for though they had married on her Education Department grant, the promise of support from Cecil (his £5 a week continuing to arrive faithfully) and help from Valerie's parents, the grant was about to end, and both Cecil and the Morellis were now experiencing crises.

The Morellis had been disturbed by Valerie's marriage, and their son Stephen, who had a very strong religious vocation, now announced that he was joining the Order of Christian Brothers.[6] Stephen would be a teacher in the Order for many years, and would then live among the Gumbaynggirr people near Kempsey, recording and preserving their language and culture and becoming their foremost scholarly exponent.[7] His parents found the loss of both their children in quick succession very hard to take, though they adjusted to it in time.[8]

Cecil's crisis was much worse, and it had been signalled by a single, isolated sentence in one of Murray's letters to Greg O'Hara, on 20 October 1962: 'Dad has lost the farm'. In July 1962 Cecil's terrible old father John Allan had died, in his eighties, nursed on his deathbed by Cecil, the only one of his children willing to care for him at the end.[9] All his life he had promised that Cecil would inherit the portion of the farm he and Miriam had lived on, and John Allan had told all his other children that the land was Cecil's. But when the will was read, it specified merely that all the land John Allan had owned, including the 150 acres Cecil had worked since 1938, was to be sold to whichever of his sons wanted to buy it, and the proceeds divided equally between his children. This will was an old one, made soon after Cecil's birth, and though it was believed a later will had been drawn, the office of the solicitor who acted for John Allan had suffered a fire, and any later will had been lost.[10]

Cecil was bitterly hurt and angry. The cost of buying the land he lived on and loved was approximately £1200,[11] and his share of the inheritance would have been very close to that sum;[12] if there had been a shortfall he could perhaps have raised it as a loan, though in July 1962 his bank balance stood at just £36, 5 shillings and a penny.[13] But he refused to buy what he and all his siblings knew to be his: the injustice was intolerable to him. Not for the first time, his obstinacy would cost him dear: this time he lost not his wife, but the land that was his heart's blood.

His brother Eric, in the last years of John Allan's life, had persuaded the confused old man to sell him a large part of the family farm for £1200, and had cadged large sums of money from him, for towards the end John Allan would sign and hand over blank cheques even to a drinking-acquaintance in a bar.[14] Eric also owned two other farms. He now bought Cecil's land, and at first gave his brother permission to go on living in the shack as long as he pleased. Cecil had passed from dependence on his father to dependence on his brother, a bitter blow even though he got on well with Eric.[15] His younger brother Charlie considered that Cecil had been treated utterly unjustly, but could do nothing about it.[16] 'Grandfather, who hated Dad, left the place to *all* his children, to be sold and the profits divided, and, well, Dad didn't have enough money to buy it from his loving brothers and sisters', Murray wrote savagely to Penny McNicoll.[17]

But worse was to come. In the early 1970s Eric would deed the land to his son Leith, and Leith told Cecil he needed the timber from the shack to make farm gates. Cecil resisted impotently for a while, and then despondently left his home of forty years, moving some miles down the valley to an equally small house on a hill owned by a neighbour, Leo Hile. Cecil occupied this house in return for keeping an eye on Hile's cattle.[18] The act of charity on Hile's part showed up Cecil's siblings' lack of love very sharply.

This quiet but cruel series of events produced a bitter resentment in Cecil, and cold anger in his son. 'Those are the facts', he wrote after describing the whole miserable business to Penny McNicoll: 'Don't think I could bear to comment on them'.[19] For Les Murray, as for his father, the Bunyah valley was a sacred place, the Country they belonged to. 'I think that landscape means something', he had written soberly to Greg O'Hara: 'Every rock up there is, and this is no joke, a friend of mine. Obstinately, it remains Home'.[20] He would come to feel its loss intensely. It was as much a part of him as his ancestry was. When he was offered, and accepted, an honorary doctorate of letters from the University of New South Wales in 1998, he would muse, 'The only title I've ever valued was "Cecil's boy from Bunyah"'.[21]

It was now quite clear that he should not continue to depend on his father for income. But to be independent Les Murray would need a permanent paid position of his own. While he looked for it, he took another of his temporary jobs, this time as a labourer with the Stores department of the State Railways, where his phenomenal physical strength stood him in good stead.[22]

He began scanning the papers for any position that looked likely to suit his talents, and in that period of full employment, soon found an advertisement in the *Sydney Morning Herald* for one that should have suited him perfectly: translator at the Australian National University. Strongly supported by letters from Len McGlashan of the Sydney University German Department[23] and from Penny McNicoll's father David, publisher of Consolidated Press,[24] he was flown down to Canberra to be interviewed and thoroughly tested on his knowledge of languages. He was promptly appointed to the position of translator at the Institute of Advanced Studies, part of the Australian National University,[25] at a salary of just under £20 a week.[26] It was a tremendous tribute to his abilities, for this twenty-four year old with no degree was able to satisfy the university authorities, including J. J. Graneek, the University Librarian,[27] and Constantine Kiriloff, the head of the Translations Unit, that he could translate any of the languages of western Europe. Years later Kiriloff would attest to Murray's 'excellent knowledge of Germanic and Romance languages'.[28]

Relieved and delighted, Murray felt himself to be capable of great things: after a nostalgic Easter 1963 at Bunyah, and just before moving down to Canberra, in a single sitting, he wrote 'Spring Hail', the poem that evokes his youthful decision to devote himself to poetry. He knew that it was one of his best poems so far, and he thought it 'a gift'.[29] He hitched down from Sydney to the national capital a week before Valerie, in April 1963, and began settling into the government house they were given at 77 Burn Street, Downer, a rawly new suburb which was then the northern edge of Canberra. His friends thought this a startling transformation: the catatonic down-and-out of just a few months before was now a suburbanite home-owner with a sought-after academic position. 'So long as [Valerie's] with me, and so long as I can still write, I don't care if I go respectable, radical, rechabite or renaissance', he joked.[30]

The house, for which the university-subsidised rent was only £3 and 15 shillings a week,[31] had four bedrooms, and it was empty of everything except built-in wardrobes and a solid-fuel heater, which they soon found they needed, for Canberra can be bitterly cold. 'The size of the place scares me!' Murray told his friends.[32] It is not in fact a large house, but he was comparing it with the shack in which he had been brought up. Valerie's parents helped them furnish the rooms, and her mother sewed curtains for the large picture windows, but they had no phone, no fridge, no washing machine.[33] Houses on the other side of the road were still being built, for Canberra was rapidly growing: Murray, with his gift for snapping up unconsidered trifles, found the many building-sites fine sources of firewood for the solid-fuel heater.[34] Years later, he would come to recognise that his post at the ANU, and this house, his and Valerie's first, had been part of his salvation. Bob Ellis would remark to him in 1998, 'This is the house that saved your life, Les. You were sliding into shapeless bohemianism, and you could have been lost'. Murray agreed.[35]

He took up his new position with the Institute of Advanced Studies on 16 April 1963,[36] and found the job in many ways ideal for him. The Australian National University, with the accent on 'National', was at this time optimistically regarded as the Australian answer to MIT. Brilliant young scholars were recruited from around the world and given tenured Chairs on large salaries; a significant number of them settled in with happy sighs and did no further stroke of work. The university was magnificently funded and equipped, and (according to Murray's student friend Olaf Reinhardt,[37] who made the move to Canberra four years after the Murrays did) its library collection made that of Sydney University look chaotic and inadequate.[38]

One of the university library's many resources was the Translation Unit. This now consisted of Murray and his supervisor but legal equal, Constantine Kiriloff; they were nominally under the direction of Jack Graneek the University Librarian, but were practically autonomous. Graneek became a good friend of Murray's; he had been trained in Hull, under Philip Larkin, and often talked to Murray about him.[39]

Kiriloff and Murray kept academic hours, meaning that Murray would turn up for work at about ten in the morning and leave when the work was done. He acquired an enormous bicycle, on which he would ride into one of the concrete-lined storm-water drains that run through Canberra: he referred to this as 'the Mussolini Canal', and along its mostly dry bed he would cycle all the way from his house into the ANU campus, his head visible sliding rapidly along just above ground level, a tuft of hair blowing off the top so that it looked, as Geoff Lehmann remarked, like 'a balding innocent onion'.[40]

The university library office he shared with Kiriloff was spacious, light, and lined with dictionaries and grammars; they had a generous grant to buy any more they needed. Constantine Kiriloff, who would later become Professor of Chinese at the University of Canberra and work himself to death, was at this time a portly, strong-featured, dark-haired man who favoured herringbone tweed and narrow ties; he spoke English as if he had learned it from books, as indeed he had.

Born in Siberia, he was a childless, driven scholar who had lived in China, working for the French police in Shanghai and as Liaison Officer with the American Red Cross in Hangkow and Peking; he had also worked for the Kuomintang government as a translator, and among other curious tasks, had translated Mme Sun Yat-sen's speeches to the Central Committee into Chinese for her, as she was fluent only in English.[41] At the ANU he translated all the Slavonic languages, including Old Church Slavonic, as well as Chinese and Japanese. Murray greatly admired his ability: 'Kiriloff was a wonderful being. What he knew he knew'.[42]

> My Chekhovian colleague who worked as if under surveillance
> would tell me tales of real life in Peking and Shanghai
> and swear at the genders subsumed in an equation.[43]

Kiriloff's stories would stand Murray in good stead when he came to write the final book of *Fredy Neptune*—Kiriloff appears there as Ilya Chaikin.

For his part, Murray translated at sight German, Swiss-German, Dutch, Danish, Swedish, Norwegian, French, Italian, Spanish and Portuguese,[44] though this did not mean he could speak all these languages with fluency. In addition he was at this time capable of translations from Malay, Scots Gaelic, Afrikaans, New Guinea Pidgin (which he had learned in order to help Greg O'Hara, who now worked in Papua New Guinea), and he had what he modestly termed 'a smattering' of Hungarian.[45] Over time he would add several more languages, including Latin and a good deal of Kattangal, the language of the Aboriginal people around Bunyah. Among the languages he could read with effort, but did not master, were Greek and Armenian: Murray in later years doubted that he had ever studied Armenian,[46] but his notes in that language are among his papers in the National Library.[47]

He would also correct the English of his academic clients, who occasionally thought this impertinent and argued with him, in vain. One of them tried to prove his point by appealing to the *Oxford English Dictionary*, but Murray disputed the dictionary definition too. Kiriloff, astounded, asked how he dared do such a thing: 'We Murrays own the bloody language', Murray replied cheerfully: 'My cousin [Sir James Murray] wrote the dictionary'.[48]

Academics would drop into the Translation Unit with books, articles or objects inscribed with text in any language known to man, demanding translations, and Murray and Kiriloff obliged. There was a waiting list of six months for typed versions of translations, but the Translations Unit would supply instant verbal translation. Murray's first job, bizarrely, was an Italian article on nodular cutaneous diseases of Po Valley hares,[49] and this proved a fair indication of his future tasks, which ranged from legal articles in Danish to entire novels in Portuguese. Ignorance of the subject, however, proved no obstacle to his providing instantaneous translation:

> Sometimes you wouldn't know what you were reading off. One fellow brought in an article illustrated with beautiful pictures that looked like lamps and lanterns, street lights and treasure chests, and I said 'What are these little things I'm reading about anyway?' He looked at me with big eyes: 'How the hell can you be translating this stuff without knowing what it is?' He said 'They're foraminifera' [marine protozoans]. I had no idea.[50]

Murray and Kiriloff took pride in only being defeated once, by a mysterious coin whose three-word inscription, in what Kiriloff thought was a central Asian script, they could not decipher.[51] Nothing else floored them, though a Finnish book on myxomatosis came close: combining their skills, and with the aid of Finnish grammars and dictionaries, they translated it triumphantly.[52]

Murray enjoyed the work, and particularly enjoyed being able to question all the experts in various fields who were constantly knocking on his door: here was a treasure-house of all the latest facts, better than reading the *Encyclopaedia Britannica* at Taree High:

> I was a translator at the Institute:
> fair pay, clean work, and a bowerbird's delight
> of theory and fact to keep the forebrain supple.
>
> I was Western Europe. *Beiträge, reviste,
> dissertaties, rapports* turned English under my
> one-fingered touch. Teacup-and-Remington days.
>
> It was a job like Australia: peace and cover,
> a recourse for exiles, poets, decent spies,
> for plotters who meant to rise from the dead with their circle.[53]

The pay was adequate, and the Murrays' home life blissfully happy: their first child, Christina Miriam, was born on 7 May 1963, 'weighing about 7 pounds net. and of a mauve colour', as Murray told Greg O'Hara.[54] Peter Barden came down from Alice Springs to be her godfather, and stayed for weeks.[55] She gave Murray a shock, for she had the beautiful face of his mother, after whom she had been named, and as she grew would come to look more and more hauntingly like the dead woman. Given Murray's tormented feelings about his mother, this produced in him a very complex response towards the baby. To begin with, however, he delighted in her beauty and in every aspect of her development.[56] 'Isn't it a horrible pity we can't remember what was happening in our brains in those first weeks and months?' he asked Lehmann. 'Say, when we began to distinguish Me from Other and Other-like-Me from Tall Shape—but you can't even talk about it, can you?'[57]

Valerie proved herself a chef and baker of Miriam's calibre, and Murray was soon writing, after a christening for the first child of one of his university friends, Brian Jardine, 'Val had prepared an enormous spread of savouries, cream puffs, fudge, cake, coffee . . . suffice it to say I almost ate myself sick'.[58] He began putting on flesh rapidly, his mass soon rising to 100 kilograms:[59] it would go higher,[60] though his immense strength always enabled him to carry his weight gracefully. Valerie, when taxed by one of his friends with being too good a cook, replied dryly, 'All Leslie needed was access to a full fridge'.[61] Larkin wrote a poem about getting up at night to use the toilet; Murray would write one about rising to visit the fridge.[62] And it was not so much that he ate a lot, as that he loved rich food. In particular, his dairy-farm upbringing meant that he had a passion for cream and butterfat: as Valerie put it, 'Les likes butter with his butter'.[63] Like Samuel Johnson, he would never forget his times of near-starvation and begging for scraps, and he ate as if preparing for their return. The habits of poverty would never leave him: 'Starvation is never more than three days away', he would remark.[64]

Valerie went back to teaching at the end of 1963, getting a post at Dickson High School, only a few hundred metres from 77 Burn Street, so that their income was now a comfortable one. But she had not been there long before she found herself pregnant again: the Murrays' second child, Daniel Allan, was born on 30 January 1965, and rapidly came to have his sister's good looks. Murray, with the bad example of his father and grandfather before him, was an overly strict parent: he began smacking Christina with a rolled-up newspaper when she was just fifteen months old, and both children learned to fear him.[65] Olaf Reinhardt, who was now living near them in Canberra, recalled meeting the Murrays coming back from church one Sunday. Murray told him with grim relish that little Christina, no more than four years old, had talked during prayers, and was going to get a belting when they got home. In later years she had forgotten the beating (according to Valerie, it never eventuated),[66] but Christina vividly remembered having to wait for it.[67]

Canberra, a custom-built capital that was still only a sketch of the splendour to come, struck Murray as artificial and soulless. There was little to do: 'The entertainment situation's poor, but then so's the transport after dark, and it adds up to this: there's nowhere to go at night, and if there were, there'd be no way of getting there'.[68] By day, on the other hand, there was much to see—if they only had a car:

> The War Memorial, Mt Stromlo [observatory], Cotter Dam, Duntroon (it's an open [military] camp), Mt Ainslie, Black Mountain, Red Hill lookout, where you can go at night and sit in a circular coffee shop on the spine of the hill and see all Canberra spread below you, enticing as the lights of Babylon, and on the other side of the ridge, mysterious dark lands full of dim mountains and mist.[69]

Babylon it was not. The city was chockful of the middle class he found so alien: 'Dull streets of decorous homes in which uniform people, or so it seems, live according to some extension of the Public Service Act, with rules for dress, for untidiness at weekends, for duty, for spontaneity and for, God knows, maybe even copulation'.[70] Middle-class rules were imposed on the Murrays too: the city Council began to write to him demanding he mow his lawn and tend his garden, which he allowed to grow wild. He resisted until the letters began to threaten eviction, and then he went out, hired a back-hoe, and (to Peter Barden's huge amusement) ploughed the entire garden under, a process he would repeat once or twice a year henceforth.[71]

These and similar demands increased his irritation, and when it deepened into his usual depression he would burst into a tirade like those favoured by his Murray ancestors:

> I've had a bad attack of the old taedium vitae lately. Can't say why, but then one never can. It'll pass. I need a tonic. Like escape from Canberra, which would, without the least fragment of a doubt, be the deadest, dullest, most worthless, ephemeral, baseless, pretentious, pathetic, artificial, over-planned shithouse of a town I've ever laid eyes on. I'd set it alight, some days, but I'm sure they'd merely put the fire out with dull, unimaginative efficiency and go on as before. Sod the place![72]

But Canberra and his translation job were, as Murray had said, only 'cover' for his real work. 'There's no such thing as a job that will give you enough time to write', he would remark,[73] but the translation post came close. After a pause of some months following the move, he was beginning to gestate again. He gave Greg O'Hara one of his rare descriptions of the poetic process:

> I wouldn't be surprised if the themes start shifting away from the 'bush' to the city, and the imagery too, but we'll see. I've got that tickling feeling in my cerebrum which usually makes itself felt just before a poem arrives, and the familiar feeling that accompanies a constellation of half-images slowly gathering into groups—but we're not allowed to say too much about that, or Herself gets angry with us, and won't give us poems.[74]

Just before moving to Canberra, he had sold 'Spring Hail' to an American journal, the *Literary Review*, telling Greg O'Hara joyfully, 'I sold a poem the other day to an American outfit, and will be receiving a tenner [£10] later this year when they publish it. A tenner! That's three times as much as I ever got for a poem before', adding modestly, 'Of course, it was a superlative poem'.[75] He was also being noticed in the newspapers, delightedly telling O'Hara, 'Do you know what? A critic said the other day I'm the biggest thing in Aust. poetry since Judith Wright. It's nice to know someone other than V. and I think so. I'm the biggest thing in *anyone's* poetry since Yeats, *I* say'.[76] By September 1963 he was complaining about Canberra winters, and in parentheses mentions that he is writing poetry again:

> All nights in Canberra are chilly and miserable, of course, but this is a windy, rain-ridden one, and to step much beyond the door means certain drowning in the thick, glabrous clayey mud. I'm sitting in front of the fire in a chair Val's parents gave us when they got their new lounge suite, glass of muscat at my elbow, little daughter Christina sucking a pensive thumb in her pram—she gets bored if she has to spend all her free time in the nursery, which is at the other end of the house—unfinished poem on the floor to work at when I've finished writing to you, Valerie puttering around in the kitchen, singing and running taps, and the rain outside gusting and spinning and hooting along with the wind.[77]

And his poem very well conveyed the atmosphere of Canberra, where the new Lake Burley Griffin had begun to fill under the downpour:

> Eavesdropping rain
> A quiet car
> A sense of mountains
> In the air,

Dark houses sleeping
Beneath the freez-
ing drip of Europ-
ean trees,

Lost paddock and stone
Under the lake . . .[78]

But there was a still more exciting event on the horizon: his first book. Since late in 1962 he, Geoffrey Lehmann and Brian Jenkins, his Push squat host, had been planning to publish a joint volume. As he told Greg O'Hara on New Year's Eve 1962: 'Of the book: it's been arranged (by Lehmann with Wentworth Press) that Jenkins, Lehmann and I issue a joint volume next— ah, *this* year, so long as the Commonwealth Literary Fund's willing to support us . . .'[79]

In the event, the Literary Fund disappointed them, but Murray offered the book instead to ANU Press, part of whose brief was to publish the work of members of the university. He was now making many literary contacts, the steady appearance of his brilliant early lyrics in the pages of the *Bulletin*, *Southerly* and *Woroni*[80] giving him a rapidly growing reputation. But it was not enough to write magnificently: to ensure his first book's success, he needed to be part of the small circle that influences how writing is received. This circle he and Lehmann began to cultivate.

The Murrays already knew A. D. Hope, who occupied the Chair of English at the ANU, and who was probably the most internationally recognised of Australia's poets.[81] Meeting Hope through his translation work, Murray had invited him and his wife to dinner that night at Burn Street. He knew that smoked salmon was considered a chic thing to serve, and in his lunch hour he had gone out excitedly and bought an entire smoked salmon for £5, then a considerable sum. He sent it home triumphantly in a taxi, phoned Valerie and told her to bake it. 'I don't think you bake smoked salmon', Valerie protested, but Murray insisted. 'Like everybody else in Australia at the time, I was learning the habits of the next class up', he would grin years later. 'We were all getting promoted on class.'[82] So the Hopes dined with the young Murrays on baked smoked salmon, perhaps the rarest dish ever served by one Australian poet to another.[83]

Alec Hope, slim, dapper, impish and a great ladies' man, was in many ways quite unlike Murray, but they got on very well. Hope liked Murray's poetry, and over the years would be a great help to the younger man, writing him letters of reference, introducing him to people who could advise and help him, and generally keeping a fatherly eye on him. Murray felt that Hope's poetry made the error of believing that the eighteenth century was the way to the future, but he enjoyed Hope's company, was always grateful for the support Hope gave him, and sympathised profoundly with him during the long years of dementia that would close Hope's life.[84] 'Wise, humane and friendly' were the adjectives he used to characterise Hope at this time.[85]

The Canberra poet David Campbell had in 1964 become Poetry Editor of the *Australian*, and that same year Murray began sending him a stream of his recent poems, 'The Away-Bound Train', 'Widower in the Country'[86] and 'Beside the Highway', as well as slightly earlier ones such as 'Spring Hail' and 'Noonday Axeman'. Campbell could not fail to be impressed by the power of this new voice, and Murray then sent him the entire manuscript of the new joint volume: in December 1964 Campbell strongly recommended that ANU Press publish it.[87] The Press, advised by A. D. Hope, agreed.

By now Brian Jenkins had withdrawn from the venture, stung by the sharpness of Lehmann's criticism of his work.[88] Murray took advantage of the extra space to include another newly written poem, one of his best of this period, 'Driving Through Sawmill Towns'.[89] His contributions as they were finally printed included many poems with echoes of other poets, as one might expect from a young man's first work: Yeats could be heard in 'Property', 'Love after Loneliness', and 'Tableau in January'; Slessor in 'Privacy'; Eliot (despite Murray's detestation of him) in 'Agitation', 'A New England Farm, August 1914' and 'The Winter Rising'. But the best of Murray's poems, including 'The Japanese Barge', 'The Burning Truck', 'The Widower in the Country' and 'Noonday Axeman', were clearly his own: already, one aspect of his mature, characteristic voice had arrived.

He and Lehmann discussed many possible titles, until Murray, as he told David Campbell,

> had a brainwave, and looked up my battered old copy of Virgil's Eclogues and found a quote which fitted the bill perfectly: one about two young Arcadian singers who meet by chance under a whispering ilex tree and decide to have a contest.[90] We're not competing, Geoff and I (he'd beat me hollow) but the idea of two poets practising their art together under a tree gives the book a certain unity, I think, besides appealing to us in a general sort of way'.[91]

The Eclogues had personal resonance for Murray, who had been introduced to Virgil by Brian Jenkins:

> I used to read whole slabs of the Latin just to get it inside my head and get a strong feeling of it. His [Virgil's] is very difficult Latin of course, but I learned the way you could closely pack and articulate a stiff, difficult language. They're an interesting set of poems about people very like my own. They're about small

country people gradually losing their hold on the land and being pushed out by other interests. That made me sit up and take note.[92]

The Ilex Tree was published by ANU Press late in 1965,[93] and its proud authors were delighted with the printing, though Murray hated 'the ridiculous lime green cover with a kind of an abstract slug on it'.[94] Murray's contributions were only a small selection of the hundreds of poems he had written by this time, many of which survive unpublished. Given that it was a first book by two young poets (Murray was twenty-six and Lehmann twenty-four) it drew a surprising amount of critical attention.

First off the mark was Ronald McCuaig, in the *Canberra Times*, announcing that Murray was 'a visionary poet at his best', and confessing he was tempted to compare the volume with the *Lyrical Ballads* of Coleridge and Wordsworth; Murray was, he added, a more dynamic Traherne. He drew particular attention to 'The Burning Truck', 'which astonishes me as much today as it did when I first saw it in the *Bulletin*'.[95] This poem also struck the anonymous reviewer in *Current Affairs Bulletin*, who called it 'one of the most remarkable and memorable short poems of the decade'.[96]

The poet Vivian Smith, in the *Bulletin*, called *The Ilex Tree* 'the best first book of poems by really young writers to have appeared in Australia for a considerable time'. He considered 'Noonday Axeman' and 'The Away-Bound Train', now among Murray's most anthologised poems, to be 'marred by imprecisions of language and portentous Eliotic statements', but he recognised Murray as 'a poet of exciting possibilities'.[97] S. E. Lee, in *Southerly*, picked out the strangely haunting quality of Murray's war poems, particularly 'A New England Farm, 1914', and 'Manoeuvres', and found 'Noonday Axeman' the most ambitious of his poems dealing with everyday experience.[98] Ronald Dunlop, in *Poetry Australia*, perceptively remarked that the focal point of most Murray poems is landscape, real or imagined, and that his concern with the past implies concern for the future, instancing particularly the magnificent elegiac close of 'Driving Through Sawmill Towns'.[99] Felicity Haynes in *Westerly* commended Murray's 'economy and smooth polish'.[100]

There were no entirely negative reviews, though the *Age* thought both Murray and Lehmann had produced a number of uncertain poems,[101] and W. Hart-Smith, in a long and sharp article in *Poetry Magazine*, produced a classic back-handed compliment when he said 'nearly every one of Murray's poems is worth working on'.[102] Several critics commented that Murray's work was 'too restrained'. One of these was the anonymous critic of the *Times Literary Supplement*,[103] and another was Roy Fuller, in the *London Magazine*, for *The Ilex Tree* was also noticed in Britain:

Both [Murray and Lehmann] are accomplished technicians, surprisingly mature and unstraining writers, and by frequently assuming personae other than their young selves avoid first-book dangers of monotony and excessive introspection. Mr Murray's usual objective correlatives are Australian landscapes and townscapes, but he is always conscious of history, ancestors, character. Though really he leans on no other poet, there is a measured Frostian tone about this work—indeed, one sometimes feels that his restraint is too severe, that he could inject more sensational interest (and with advantage) if he cared to do so. He describes women in small towns 'in calendared kitchens', and a possum 'ski-ing down/The iron roof on little moonlit claws', but such touches of brilliance are comparatively rare.[104]

Most critics resisted the temptation to compare Murray and Lehmann, but those who did, Felicity Haynes in *Westerly* and the anonymous *Times Literary Supplement* reviewer, judged Lehmann the 'stronger, more confident poet'.[105] Murray, used to deferring to Lehmann, probably agreed. *The Ilex Tree* was an undoubted success, and at the end of 1965 it won the Grace Leven Prize of £100 for the best volume of poetry published in Australia that year, thereby ensuring Murray and Lehmann even more public attention.[106] They were launched.

Their rising reputations evoked increasingly pressing invitations to take part in poetry readings and conferences, in Sydney and further afield: in 1967 he and Lehmann travelled to Armidale, at the invitation of an academic named Derek Whitelock, to attend a 'Writing School' at the University of New England, the first of many such gatherings Murray would take part in.[107] In Armidale Murray stayed at Robb College, and met Kenneth Slessor and Judith Wright, with both of whom he struck up friendships. He loved Wright's early sensuous and unexpected imagery, and had the tact not to tell her he thought her later work increasingly wooden and programmatic, the result (Murray believed) of her husband Jack McKinney's abstract and intellectual influence on her.[108]

For her part Wright, who disliked conformity, seems to have been taken by his casualness, his tattered shorts, and his habit of grinding out his cigarette-butts with a bare foot.[109] Seeing him do this for the first time, she said to him approvingly, 'You'll do'.[110] He was clearly a real non-conformist in a world of pretenders. Wright came from a distinguished and wealthy squatter background, an inheritance she was trying to live down, and when she spoke to Murray of their link with the land, had virtually no comprehension of his terribly deprived background.[111] Murray was polite, rather as D. H. Lawrence was when Edith Sitwell complained to him about the miseries of her millionaire childhood.

He was particularly pleased to meet Kenneth Slessor in Armidale: Slessor's was the name that came first to Murray's mind when he listed Australian poets, and this was not just because Slessor, as editor of *Southerly* in 1961, had published the first Murray poems to appear outside university journals. Although Slessor had fallen silent since publishing *One Hundred Poems* in 1944, Murray considered his *Five Bells* the greatest poetry to come out of Australia, and he often named Slessor as his model and master.[112] Other Australian writers concurred: the novelist Christopher Koch would write to Murray in 1977, 'You descend in a perfect line from Ken: themes of Australia and themes of Europe co-existing in your work, double-faced, contradictory, and yet in harmony, because the mix is in perfect harmony with our history, with what we *are*'.[113]

Slessor invited Murray to visit him in Sydney, and Murray did, becoming a good friend of the older man, as did Lehmann. Occasionally they would dine together at Lehmann's house or at Slessor's. Slessor was a generous host, serving excellent food with fine wines, the fare always spiced with good conversation. He went out of his way to help many young poets as he helped Murray and Lehmann. With his pink scrubbed skin, immaculate bow-tie and Cheshire cat smile,[114] Slessor was a *bon vivant* of great charm, and his presidency of the Sydney Journalists' Club gave him considerable literary influence long after the Muse had quietly ceased to visit him.

Murray himself was rapidly gaining literary influence, and others were soon seeking his help and advice. In June 1965, even before *The Ilex Tree*'s publication, he was contacted by the editor of the journal *Poetry Australia*, Grace Perry, and asked to put together a special edition of her magazine dedicated to the work of poets of Canberra and the Monaro.[115] In agreeing,[116] he inadvertently took sides in the civil war that was now breaking out in Australian poetry.

Perry was a wealthy medical doctor whose avocation was poetry, and she had for years edited the Poetry Society's journal *Poetry Magazine*.[117] Murray had met her while giving some readings with Geoffrey Lehmann and Keith Smith at the Ensemble Theatre in North Sydney.[118] She was a woman of immense charm, energy and good humour, and Murray found her enthusiasms very hard to resist.[119] In 1964 she had lost a power struggle with a group of writers who succeeded in stacking a meeting of the Poetry Society and ousting Perry as editor. She, in dudgeon, took the address list of *Poetry Magazine* and founded a rival publication of her own, *Poetry Australia*, which tried to highlight the best writing being produced in Australia in order to foster a national poetry with the confidence to be itself.

The victorious group who had ousted her continued to run *Poetry Magazine* until 1970, turning it into the flagship of what was portentously called 'New Australian Poetry', much of which in fact took its inspiration from the United

States. Around these two rival publications, with their rival views of the direction in which Australian poetry should be moving, passionate groups formed, each thinking itself the wave of the future. This split, in Murray's view, was the nub of the war which would energise Australian poetic circles in the 1970s, and in which he would play a major and fertile role.[120]

Murray would always feel himself to be an outsider, but he now had the friendship of some of the most influential figures in Australian writing, and was rapidly becoming a name himself. Already by the end of 1965, however, he was looking for more worlds to conquer. And to find them, he came to feel he would have to live for an extended period outside Australia. 'Not live in exile, at least not in extenso, but I did want the big finishing school of travel', he was to say.[121] He began casting his eyes abroad.

CHAPTER ELEVEN
THE ANTIPODES
1965–68

∼

To arrive in a distant city,
Walk up streets
Full of strange prices, languages, traffic, faces . . .
To search for yourself awhile, then, with a gesture,
Step across your heart
And set off inland . . .

LES MURRAY, 'ANOTHER CONTINENT'

Murray was particularly pleased with The Ilex Tree's British reviews, for this was still the period when an Australian artist felt he had to gain recognition in Britain to be secure of acceptance at home. He knew he was not fated to live and die a translator at the ANU. Even before the book's publication, from 16 September to 2 October 1965, he had made his first trip out of Australia, to Britain, as one of two Australian delegates to the British Commonwealth Arts Festival Poetry Conference in Cardiff: Murray had been nominated by the ANU, and his fellow delegate was the poet James McAuley. The Arts Festival Poetry Conference, an official attempt to strengthen literary ties within the former Empire, opened with great fanfare by Prince Philip, was not a success. It had been chosen as the site of an assault by a group of British performance poets, and writers primarily interested in words on the page were driven to the peripheries.

Murray noticed the first signs of what was to come when he took the train to Wales, having flown in to Heathrow. Sharing his carriage was a loud couple, whom he presently discovered to be the British 'jazz poet' Michael Horovitz and his wife Frances. Horovitz wrote and delivered poems in an aggressive grungy style that consciously echoed that of the American Beat Generation, and that would gain in passion as the Ban the Bomb movement shaded into increasing resistance to the Vietnam war: he liked to think of himself as the centre of a British Beat group he would call The Children of Albion.[1] As the name implies, he claimed the tradition of Blake, but was much closer to that of the Sitwells, whom Leavis described as belonging to the history of advertising rather than that of literature. Now Horovitz attracted Murray's attention by proclaiming to his fellow travellers, 'My best poems are written in semen on my wife's belly'. Frances, a better poet than her husband, smiled a little tightly.[2] Horovitz was rehearsing: he would use the same line during the conference, and his wife, in the audience in a loose hippie frock apparently made of cheesecloth, would smile the same smile. 'Whatever the semen poems were like', Murray would remark dryly, 'I reckoned they'd have to be better than what he was reciting on stage'.[3]

Horovitz and other performance poets, including Jeff Nuttall and the Scot Alexander Trocchi, who was one of the chief organisers of the conference, drank quantities of whisky, poured foul-mouthed scorn on what they considered 'conventional' poetry, and organised 'happenings' involving such tactics as leading a pig onto the stage[4] or demanding that the gathering produce a poem in celebration of their fellow poet Mao Tse-tung.[5] They succeeded in taking over the conference with what Murray would call 'drugged Californication'.[6] The Nigerian playwright Wole Soyinka, Murray, McAuley and others like them quietly withdrew to the pubs and clubs of Tiger Bay.

This was Murray's first experience in life, rather than writing, of the spirit he would later recognise back in Australia, and which he would, rather loosely, come to call Modernism.[7] He would come to see it as the continuation and fruit of the Enlightenment, which in his view had been a disastrous overemphasis of human intellect, and a turning away from the spiritual. He thought of its Cardiff manifestations as 'the Bomb Culture',[8] and in his view poetic values would see off this loud intrusion:

> Three a.m., Tiger Bay. In the only
> club still open, the Sheik's Tent,
> James McAuley and two Welsh students
> are discussing enjambment.
>
> Uptown, the Bomb Culture's just opened
> its European run,
> discounting many things on its counter:
> calm tradition is one;
>
> here, though, cheesecloth, fuzzed menace and Sin
> are all mortified to death
> to find themselves kindly dismissed
> for talk of Wordsworth . . .[9]

Murray went off with some Cardiff friends he had made, including the poet Vernon Watkins, who had been a friend of Dylan Thomas, William Plomer,

Roy Campbell and many others. Murray also saw a lot of Watkins's friend Henry Treece, a self-proclaimed 'anti-cerebral' poet, who offered the young Australian advice on writing, to which he listened carefully.[10] Murray read them some of his latest work, including a new poem that he carried in his hip pocket, 'Evening Alone at Bunyah', the first piece in which he had touched on his Gaelic background.

> This country is my mind. I lift my face
> and count my hills, and linger over one:
> Deer's, steep, bare-topped, where eagles nest below
> the summit in scrub oaks, and where I take
> my city friends to tempt them with my past.
>
> Across the creek and the paddocks of the moon
> four perfect firs stand dark beside a field
> lost long ago, which holds a map of rooms.
> This was the plot from which we transplants sprang.
> The trees grew straight. We burgeoned and spread far.
> I think of doors and rooms beneath the ground,
> deep rabbit rooms, thin candlelight of days . . .
> and, turning quickly, walk back through the house.

Murray later recalled with pleasure that the poem made him many Welsh friends.[11] Among these were some young and enthusiastic drinkers, the research student Gareth Griffiths, Peter Bement, who would later become an Anglican priest, and an eccentric painter and playwright, Alan Osborne.[12] Griffiths (who would in time emigrate to Australia, partly because of Murray's influence)[13] and Bement became his lifelong friends.

When the conference sputtered to its rancorous close, with Horovitz and his friends triumphant among the ruins, Murray went up to Scotland to visit his cousin Ray Murray, with whom Murray had often visited as a child, and who was now studying to become a minister in the Free Presbyterian Church. Les Murray then flew to Denmark and hitched from there into Germany and down the Rhine to Switzerland, polishing his languages as he went. He found the skills he had acquired in Central Australia served him well in Europe too. 'I was good as a tramp and lived on virtually nothing', he would recall.[14] He headed for Zurich, having promised Valerie to look up her relatives there, and was made welcome by them. At the insistence of one of Valerie's uncles he drank his only glass of absinthe, and by the time he flew from Zurich to Sydney he had less than five Swiss francs left, so that Valerie's cousin had to pay his airport tax.[15]

Back in Canberra, he found he could not get Europe out of his mind. The translation position was comfortable and permanent, and the university offered to sell him the Burn Street house for £5500.[16] It would have been an excellent investment and Valerie was keen to have it, but Murray was resolute: they were going to leave Canberra for Europe, and would need all their resources for the trip. 'My advice was always Les's hindsight', Valerie would recall ruefully. 'I would say "We've got to do it" and much later he would say "Oh, we should have done it".'[17]

He was increasingly irritated by Canberra's bureaucracy: among other things, it kept an eye on the health of ANU employees, and it insisted that Murray see a dentist (something of which he had a horror) and lose weight in accordance with a scale called 'the height to weight ratio'. The Morellis' Sydney dentist, a polyglot Ukrainian named Bermann, reeled back when Murray opened his mouth—his long dentist-phobia was all too evident in the black craters—and decreed that seven ruined teeth would have to come out.[18] This Murray endured, talking to Bermann in many languages through a mouth full of ironmongery.

> From five to nine, in warm Lane Cove,
> and five to nine again at night,
> an irascible Carpatho-Ruthenian strove
> with ethnic teeth . . .
>
> . . . Pausing to blow
> out cigarette smoke, he'd bite his only
> accent-free mother tongue and return below
>
> to raise my black fleet of sugar-barques
> so anchored that they gave him tennis elbow.
> Seven teeth I gave that our babies might eat
> when students were chanting Make Love! Hey Ho!

But weight loss was a different matter, and though he struggled valiantly with diets for a while, they seemed to make no difference. The height to weight ratio, which called for him to shed 12 of his 100 kilograms, came to symbolise for him all the pettinesses of officialdom, and it was oddly linked in his mind with another kind of enforced conforming zeal, the self-righteous intolerance that increasingly characterised the anti-Vietnam war protests that now rocked the ANU campus.

Murray opposed the war, but the arrogance and veiled menace of the demands that he sign petitions and join protests put his back up. He was outraged to hear that students who did not oppose the war were being failed by a radical tutor. This was a phenomenon he recognised: the student-police of Taree High come again. For his part, he refused ever to be part of a gang, as he would make plain in 'Demo' and in a poem he called 'Memories of the Height-to-Weight Ratio':

> But there was a line called Height-to-Weight
> and a parallel line on Vietnam. When a tutor
> in politics failed all who crossed that, and wasn't
> dismissed, scholarship was back to holy writ.[19]

Murray was increasingly itching to get away. In the middle of 1966, sliding into depression again, he felt he must go walkabout as he had in 1961, and he hitch-hiked alone across the Nullarbor plain to Western Australia, leaving Valerie and the children in Canberra. Peter Barden, who had himself gone through a miserable wandering period, was now working as an engineer for a huge iron-ore mine, Mount Goldsworthy Iron Ore Development, east of Port Hedland, and Murray called on him. He found he could not stay even a day unless he became an employee of the mine, and Barden got him a temporary job as a cook, helping to prepare 417 meals three times a day.[20] They saw a little of the dramatically stark countryside on Barden's 50cc Honda motor-cycle, though at the risk of their lives, for with Murray on the back, Barden found it fiendishly hard to keep the front wheel on the road.[21] Murray was soon sacked for laziness, the head cook telling him scornfully, 'You wouldn't work in an iron lung, mate'. 'You don't have to work in an iron lung', Murray retorted: 'It's the ideal billet'.[22]

The ANU and Jack Graneek had been very patient with him because of his excellence as a translator, but this long disappearance raised eyebrows, and a worried Valerie had been hard-pressed for explanations. Murray now found that the Institute of Advanced Studies was, as he put it, starting to 'circle my job'.[23] He began to gather what money he could lay hands on. In 1966 Douglas Stewart, impressed by *The Ilex Tree*, had written asking him to allow Angus & Robertson to see his next manuscript:

> I was going overseas on my Grand Tour early the next year, and so I went down to Lower George Street, to that tall warren above Robinsons' map shop, the old building in The Rocks whose ancient steel-cage lift used to creak upwards at the speed of sap rising in a tree, and made the acquaintance of Douglas; the resulting friendship lasted till I had the sad job of reading some of his superb poems at his funeral . . . Brash as ever—at least it's understood as brashness when you are still young—I asked Douglas for an advance on my next book of verse, to which he agreed with a gentle smile, adding that he wasn't sure any

poet since Henry Lawson had got one. They hadn't dared to ask. The £200 Douglas advanced me on the firm's behalf at that time helped me greatly on my trip abroad.[24]

With the £200, Stewart gave Murray a piece of advice: 'Maintain a reasonable liaison with rhyme'.[25] Murray would.

Early in 1967 he resigned his position at the ANU, secured letters of reference from Con Kiriloff,[26] A. D. Hope, Derek Whitelock and others, and flew to Britain again at the end of April 1967, leaving Valerie and the children to follow him once he had found somewhere for them all to live. His only British friends were in Cardiff, and he returned there, looking up Gareth Griffiths and Peter Bement as soon as he arrived. They were on their way out to a stag party for a friend of theirs named Davis, and they urged Murray to go to bed after his long flight. He refused, and to their admiration spent the night of 2 May 1967[27] drinking and roistering with them and Davis in Merthyr Tydfil, as he would remember in poetry rich with the influence of Dylan Thomas:

> The first night of my second voyage to Wales,
> Tired as a rag from ascending the left cheek of Earth
> I nevertheless went to Merthyr in good company
> And warm in neckclothing and speech in the Butcher's Arms
> Till Time struck us pintless . . .

He then made the mistake of chasing a great deal more beer than he was used to with a very hot curry:

> Fair play, it was frightful. I spooned the chicken of Hell
> In a sauce of rich yellow brimstone. The valley boys with me
> Tasting it, croaked to white Jesus. And only pride drove me,
> Forkful by forkful, observed by hot mangosteen eyes,
> By all the carnivorous castes and gurus from Pant
> My brilliant tears washing the unbelief of the Welsh.[28]

In the back of Griffith's little Hillman Minx on the way back to Cardiff, with Peter Bement driving because he was the least drunk, the combination of exhaustion and alcohol suddenly overcame Murray and he passed out, his heavyweight wrestler's form slumping onto Griffiths and pinning him into a corner of the car. The others had the utmost difficulty in dragging him up to bed when they arrived.[29] 'In those days I thought I was made of inexhaustible matter', Murray would remark, 'and it was one of the first times I found I wasn't'.[30]

In the days that followed his friends helped him find a small flat, at 7 Herbert Terrace in Penarth, a pleasant stone terrace house since converted into a trendy office. They also advised him on the purchase of a secondhand car, a green 1963 model Ford Cortina, the first car he ever owned.[31] He had first driven only after meeting Valerie, when her father Gino rashly allowed him the use of his Ford; he rapidly became a skilful but impetuous driver, who accumulated speeding fines.

After he had been in Wales for two months, Valerie and the two children joined him in June 1967. They soon found that they were going through their savings much faster than they had expected, and that finding and keeping a job was going to be difficult: the unemployment rate in Cardiff was 15 per cent. Murray got a job as a janitor for BBC Wales, sweeping floors, but soon got the sack. With some difficulty he found another job with the Dock Labour Board, but was dismissed again as soon as they found that he could not count.[32]

The Murrays lived on their dwindling savings for the rest of the year, seeing Wales in the Cortina and falling in love with it. 'They say that your first foreign country's the one you're always drawn back to', Murray would remark. 'It's true. Mine was Wales.'[33] He loved the green and beautiful countryside, with slate-grey villages huddling under menacing hills, and he liked the Welsh. Gareth Griffiths' father told him of the dodges by which people in the valleys got through the Depression, of how in Pant, for instance, they stole electricity through illegal connections to the power-lines, and how as the village policeman Prosser patrolled up the hill, preceded by warning calls from local children, wires were removed as he climbed, and the lights went out 'like the Titanic sinking'.[34] Murray loved this image and would use it in 'Three Tries at Englynion':

> Instructive to watch a whole mountain
> Town grow progressively dark
> Like a great ship sinking at night
> As the police walk upward.

They went further afield, driving up to Scotland in August for the wedding of his cousin Ray to Roberta McPherson. The poet, Valerie and their children also travelled to Devon and Cornwall in September.[35] As the autumn advanced they drove about blackberrying, which gave Murray a pleasing but illusory sense of connection with the land: 'The best blackberries in Britain grow between Cardiff and Barry Dock'.[36]

He continued to write, producing during these months in Wales a series of poems touching on aspects of the Eucharist in everyday life, including those astonishingly powerful poems 'The Abomination' and 'Blood'.[37] In Herbert

Terrace too he wrote that fine villanelle, 'The Commercial Hotel', about an Australian town such as Mungindi or Mullumbimby, and 'Prosper the Commonwealth', about the Gloucester (NSW) cattle-sales, as he told Lehmann.[38] And he tried to make a living by his verse. He wrote off to any academic contact he had, offering readings of his work, and gave a few, to an Adult College at Grantley Hall near Ripon, and to another college at the end of August.[39] But these engagements paid very little: in Ripon, for two talks he received only ten guineas and his board.[40]

As winter came on the Murrays found themselves in a corner, their savings all but gone and no work to be had. Late in October, they found themselves running short of money even for food. To accompany their remaining two pounds of dried peas, Valerie had to decide between buying some Hungarian bacon or half a pig's head for sixpence: she plumped for the pig's head, and they baked it.[41] Even Murray's sunny Micawberism had its limits. In desperation, he decided to leave his family in Wales and go to London on his own in the hope of finding work. In his absence, Valerie did something they had not previously contemplated: she applied for the dole, going along to the Social Security office in Cardiff, where she was interviewed with a child on each knee. When the kind interviewing officer asked her when she had last seen her husband, she, to her own mild surprise, burst into tears. 'It worked beautifully', she remembered later.[42]

Meanwhile Murray had had an equally unexpected piece of luck of his own. On his arrival in London on 28 October, he called at Australia House to see if there was any mail for him (Australians in Britain then routinely used the High Commission as a post office), and found a telegram from the Secretary of the Commonwealth Literary Fund in Canberra, advising him that the Fund had awarded him a Fellowship for 1968, worth $3000.[43] He was surprised and delighted, for though he had applied for the Fellowship before leaving Australia, he had had no expectation of success. Buoyed by this news, he returned at once to Wales to rejoice with Valerie, and the two of them impulsively decided to move to Scotland, which Murray thought of as the home of his ancestors.[44]

In August they had visited Inverness and had loved it; now, in early November 1967, they drove there in the Cortina and rented a seventeenth-century cottage, a small place with half-thatched, half-slate roof and thick white-washed walls, at Westhill on Culloden Moor, to the east of Inverness. In Herdsmuir Cottage, not far from the site of the bloody eighteenth-century battle of Culloden,[45] they spent the winter of 1967–68, being adopted by a local cat which Murray named Douglas because it was black, and which was able to get into the cottage no matter how carefully they locked it out.[46] At the start of the new year, Murray began to keep a scrappy traveller's diary, with only the briefest of notes to record the days:

January 1: Foyers waterfall [a local beauty spot]. Weather wet & cold, hillside slippery.

January 2: Inverness—everything closed! Worked on poem [probably 'A Walk with O'Connor'].

January 3: Big snow at last! Pines bedecked, flakes size of florins.

January 4: Ardclach bell tower & Aulsie Bridge—saw 40 grouse and 7 pheasants.

January 5: Car broke down. New battery transplanted. More snow.

January 6: Up Sutherland coast to Caithness. Wick, thence night at St Clair Hotel, Thurso.

January 7: Thurso to John o' Groats, views of Stroma Is. & Orkneys agleam with snow. Bitter cold on Dunnet Hd.

January 8: Shopped, slept and typed poems. Heard of inclusion in Borestone Mountain anthol. Deo Gratias. [Borestone Mountain was an American poetry award, the winning poems being published in an anthology.]

January 9: To Fort William, visited W. Highlands Museum. Lots of Jacobite relics incl. Secret Painting.

January 10: Shopped, slept, scribbled, finished 'If a Pebble Fall'. [This cerebral poem was published in *Southerly* the following year.][47]

January 11: Shopping spree, finished 'A Walk with O'Connor', wrote letters, comp[osed] quatrain on Art.

As the entries suggest, he was greatly enjoying seeing Scotland, and he loved the first northern winter he had experienced as much as his children did: Christina's earliest memories would include making a snowman on Culloden moor.[48] She and Daniel were beautiful children, Christina blonde and her brother dark: a visiting friend of Murray's described them as 'stunning'.[49] Murray travelled a good deal with his family, rejoicing in the possession of a car, visiting Skye, and making many day trips to such places as Cawdor, the Great Glen, and Gordonstoun, a tourist with plenty of time.[50] On these trips, and while at home in the cottage, he polished his Gaelic (a language he had studied intensively while still in Australia), being particularly interested in the Skye variant of the language.[51]

In addition, and apparently combining the activities seamlessly, he constantly thought about and wrote poetry. He was immensely productive. Neither hasting nor resting, he moved in steady progression from the completion of one poem to the gestation of the next. His diary records the process by which he would spend some days simply thinking about the next poem, then its beginnings, development and completion in a little over a week. The entries from 21–28 January 1968 are typical:

Sunday January 21:	Suffered from cold. Wrote letters, went to Mass, moaned.
Monday January 22:	Prepared Gaelic, sniffled, thought.
Tuesday January 23:	Shopped, borrowed Aust. books from Library—'research' (sic).
Wednesday January 24:	Stayed at home, began Krambach poem after seeing 'Blowup' [a film]—no causal connection!
Thursday January 25:	Lived quietly, continued Krambach poem.
Friday January 26:	Shopped, continued Krambach poem.
Saturday January 27:	Don Kirby [a Sydney friend] rang, may visit next week. Finished Krambach poem—or a mutation of it.
Sunday January 28:	Went to Burghead, saw catacomb-like Roman well. Thence Mass and polishing of poem. Venison for dinner.

'The Krambach poem' cannot be identified with certainty; it may have been 'Windy Hill', published in *The Weatherboard Cathedral*. Two days later, on 30 January 1968, he records the beginning of the next poem: 'Scribbled without result', and the next day, 'Wrote to some effect perhaps—remains to be seen'. His energy and application were prodigious.

And he was constantly experimenting with poetic forms, turning out sonnets, ballads, englynions, senryu, tanka, rondels, triolets, sestinas, villanelles, loving technical challenges and seeking them out for the sheer joy of overcoming difficulty. This fertile restlessness, like his insatiable lust for new languages, was part of that love affair with words which would continue all his life.

He wrote compulsively, partly because writing gave him a pleasure nothing else could equal. Years later he would tell a BBC interviewer:

> It's wonderful, there's nothing else like it, you write in a trance. And the trance is completely addictive, you love it, you want more of it. Once you've written the poem and had the trance, polished it and so on, you can go back to the poem and have a trace of that trance, have the shadow of it, but you can't have it fully again. It seemed to be a knack I discovered as I went along. It's an integration of the body-mind and the dreaming-mind and the daylight-conscious-mind. All three are firing at once, they're all in concert. You can be sitting there but inwardly dancing, and the breath and the weight and everything else are involved, you're fully alive. It takes a while to get into it. You have to have some key, like say a phrase or a few phrases or a subject matter or maybe even a tune to get you started going towards it, and it starts to accumulate. Sometimes it starts without your knowing that you're getting there, and it builds in your mind like a pressure. I once described it as being like a painless headache, and you know there's a poem in there, but you have to wait until the words form.[52]

He also clearly thought of composition as a spiritual process rather than primarily an intellectual one. Years later he would write to a friend, 'I've always, as you know and as I managed to capture in the poem "Satis Passio", dimly pursued the idea of successful art as a *presence* rather than any sort of construct of ideas. The "real presence" of art—the provenance of that notion will be obvious! I think it is an invoked spirit, and the technique's the invocation'.[53] And to him, poetry involved the rational mind, the dreaming mind and the body, three elements acting in concert to produce utterance as full as human beings are capable of:

> You've got to be able to dream at the same time as you think to write poetry . . . You think with a double mind. It's like thinking with both sides of your brain at once. And if you can't do that, you can't write poetry. You can write expository prose, but poetry is as much dreamed as it is thought and it's as much danced in the body as it is written. It's done in your lungs. It's done in every part of your muscles—you can feel it in your muscles.[54]

Perhaps paradoxically, absence from Australia focused his mind sharply on home. In Herdsmuir Cottage or in hotels while travelling, he wrote poems about Bunyah, Krambach and Sydney, just as Joyce, in Trieste and Zurich, wrote fixedly of Dublin. There was some intersection between his surroundings and his subject matter, as when in 'A Walk with O'Connor' (a poem he would describe as 'a dialogue about the life of action')[55] he recalled his 1961 hike down the Sydney coastline with Peter O'Connor Barden, when the two of them tried in vain to translate the Gaelic on a monument to Irish republicanism in Waverley cemetery.

> At Waverley, where the gravestones stop at the brink,
> Murmuring words, to the rebel's tomb we went,
> An exile's barrow of Erin-go-bragh and pride
> In grey-green cement:
> We examined the harps, the hounds, the lists of the brave
> And, reading the Gaelic, constrained and shamefaced, we tried
> To guess what it meant . . .

He perhaps reflected with pleasure that now he could have translated it fluently. His present voluntary exile in Scotland made his Celtic heritage peculiarly alive to him, just as his Catholicism was given spice by the proximity of Culloden, that site of a catastrophic setback for Catholicism in Britain.

But much of the time in his imagination he lived in Australia, thinking about it constantly, and borrowing Australian books along with Gaelic texts from the Inverness library. It was in Herdsmuir Cottage that he first read Thomas Kenneally, and here too that he spent a week reminiscing about Sydney University with a visiting friend from those days, Don Kirby.[56] Kirby wrote to Lehmann, 'It is hard to describe the joy of finding this magnificent Celt in such a setting',[57] but in truth Murray knew himself to be a displaced Australian rather than a Celt come home. A constant stream of letters passed between him and his father.[58] On a trip to Glenfinnan, Ballachulish and Oban he recorded in his diary for 14 February 1968, 'Intimations of violin poem', intimations that rapidly yielded 'Ill Music', a fine poem about one of his Bunyah cousins and his particular form of the Murrays' inherited black depressions.[59] It was in Scotland too that he made his first attempt to convey the rhythm and feeling of Aboriginal poetry, in 'The Rock Shelters, Botany Bay'.[60] Kirby wrote to Lehmann, 'Les has written volumes of extremely good poetry which I have been reading over the last few days', adding, 'Still occasionally it is impolite to listen to Les; always it is absolutely necessary to read him'.[61]

On 18 February 1968 the Murrays left Herdsmuir Cottage, discovering as they went that the cat's name really was Douglas,[62] returned to Wales, helped Gareth Griffiths move to his new post at the University of East Anglia,[63] did some sightseeing in Cambridge and London, and then took their Cortina on a ferry from Harwich to the Hoek of Holland, planning to spend several months touring the Continent.

Murray was terrified by the Dutch traffic, not surprisingly, as he repeatedly forgot that he should be driving on the right.[64] His spoken Dutch rapidly became fluent with use, and he found the people friendly, the big skies over the flat landscape evocative, and the art and architecture fascinating. In his little diary he recorded in detail the way features of the houses changed as they journeyed; in the Rijksmuseum in Amsterdam he noted, 'Decided for Vermeer & Cuyp against Rembrandt'.[65] Into Belgium they went, finding it 'Catholic but dull' (though Murray loved the Waterloo battlefield centre), staying in youth hostels or cheap hotels; and on into France, where Murray looked for and found his Celtic traditions: 'Brittany unmistakably part of Celtdom. Square granite houses, themes of death and pain. Trees pruned into cripple shapes. Ancient stone crosses, *calvaires* tremendous—also saw piled human bones in ossuaries . . . Impressed by emph[asis] on pain of thieves in *calvaires*'.[66]

In Paris, where Murray loved the Eiffel Tower on sight, he and Valerie had arranged to meet and travel with Bob Ellis, who unexpectedly turned up with what Murray resignedly called 'his current bedmate—latter foisted on us for the trip'.[67] Together they all visited museums, churches and galleries without number; they spent two days in the Louvre, Murray surprised at not being disappointed by the *Mona Lisa*.[68] In the crowded car the party of six then set off southwards to Sens on 25 March 1968, calling at too many magnificent chateaux, irritated by spats between Ellis and his girlfriend, by fleas in the cheap hotels and by gastric flu which felled them one by one, starting with Ellis.[69] At Brive, on the way to Lascaux, there was what Murray termed 'a fairly painless rupture', and Ellis and his friend returned to Paris.

The Murrays continued, fasting and making frequent stops, to Biarritz, where they were impressed by the buildings but sneered at the beach. They then drove by way of Roncevalles into Spain, where at Zaragoza Murray 'kissed relic of BVM de Pilar',[70] talked to peasants in Burgos, changing languages with his usual ease, saw snow in the Cathedral square in Avila, hated the traffic in Madrid, and dodged the Prado, 'thoroughly sick of museums', though knowing he would regret doing so.[71] They fled Madrid's crowds for Toledo, where they were deeply impressed by the bullet holes still visible in the walls of buildings near the rebuilt Alcázar, symbol of Catholic resistance during the Civil War.

But it was futile to try to avoid crowds, for this was Holy Week, in which every major Spanish city is packed with penitents being watched by tourists. The Murrays tried with increasing difficulty to see Toledo, Cadiz and Gibraltar, where Murray noticed a donkey with an enormous erection pointing it at Africa.[72] They were in Granada on Easter Sunday 1968, hearing Mass in the cathedral amid vast throngs and wishing the other tourists elsewhere.

Murray recorded wittily in his diary: 'Petulance: he came into the world and found it occupied'.[73]

The sights of Europe now flashed before their increasingly jaded eyes: Alicante, Barcelona, Ripoll, through Andorra (where Murray bought a flick-knife and tried snails for the first time)[74] and over the Pas de la Case in deep snow into France, seeing castellated Carcassonne (which could not fail to impress them), Nîmes, Avignon (where they battled more crowds to see the 'Papal' palace), and on up the Rhône valley to Valence and Switzerland, which they reached with relief on 21 April 1968. This was for Valerie the kind of ancestral place Scotland was for Murray, and she slipped into Swiss-German with a sense of home-coming. 'Lunched in German near Murten', Murray recorded contentedly.[75]

They were received with what Murray called 'dour affection' by Valerie's relatives in Zurich. They spent the next week relaxing after their travels, though for Murray this meant having the time to type out copies of his latest poems to send to editors, as he did whenever he had a batch ready. Among the mail waiting for him in Switzerland had been acceptances from *Meanjin* and the *Sydney Morning Herald*.[76] And he continued to write, producing a poem called 'Seven Cities' on 2 May.[77] On 28 April 1968 they had a wonderful time when they visited St Gallen, where Murray registered and absorbed the baroque magnificence of the monastery library. The poem that resulted later, 'Three Interiors', is a superb example of his ability to create art that does not so much convey experience as produce it:

> The softly vaulted ceiling of St Gallen's monastic library
> is beautifully iced in Rococo butter cream with scrolled pipework
> surf-dense around islands holding russet-clad, vaguely heavenly
> personages who've swum up from the serried volumes below.
> The books themselves, that vertical live leather brickwork,
> in the violin-curved, gleaming bays, have all turned their backs
> on the casual tourist and, clasped in meditation, they pray
> in coined Greek, canonical Latin, pointed Hebrew.
> It is an utterly quiet pre-industrial machine room
> on a submarine to Heaven, and the deck, the famous floor
> over which you pad in blanket slippers, has flowed in
> honey-lucent around the footings, settled suavely level and hardened:
> only the winding darker woods and underwater star-points
> of the parquetry belie that impression. What is below
> resembles what's above, but just enough, as cloud-shadow,
> runways and old lake shores half noticed in mellow wheat land.

Who, faced with a choice between reading that and seeing the room itself, would not choose the poem?

But as usual he was as much concerned with Australia as with Europe: the news from Sydney was of terrible bushfires sweeping the east coast, and it combined in his mind with an increasing homesickness for what he called 'unconquered things', issuing in another fine poem of this period, 'The Fire Autumn', in which he evokes the forests of his childhood with brilliant clarity.[78]

> We have been to see autumn in Europe. It is beautiful but
> Humanized to despair in those poor remnant woods,
> With tourist paths leading to every bit of Waldeinsamkeit . . .
>
> At this stage of the lasting Culloden, watching
> Such galaxies shine through the redcoats and wear them to tin,
> Like a distant coast beyond shimmer, too still for cloud,
> The trees of my forests and breakaway mountains are feathering
> With gold of emergence, with claret, cerise, liquid green,
> Faint blues fat with powder, new leaves clustered thick down the length
> Of charcoal-stiff bark. Brush water is licking stones clean.[79]

The poem gave him, he was to say with careful irony, 'a start towards a vision of the metropolitan world as a means of driving us into transcendence, which I see as its best discernible function'.[80]

After a week they were rather reluctantly packing again, this time for Italy: 'V. tired of trip', Murray recorded wearily. 'All keen to go home'.[81] They left on 2 May 1968, but they did not get far. Forty kilometres outside Zurich, in Siebenen, another car struck theirs lightly and Murray drove straight over a low brick wall. No one was hurt, but the Cortina was destroyed. Fortunately they had insured it. They were obliged to settle into the Gasthof Kreuz in Siebenen and wait for their insurance cheque to arrive:[82] it took only a week but it seemed to them a year, during which Murray ate hugely out of sheer frustration.[83] Valerie's parents were dumb-struck when they heard about the accident: Berta's mother had been killed in Siebenen in a car-crash in 1939.[84]

When the insurance cheque arrived the Murrays hired an Opel Kadett and continued their journey, through the St Bernard tunnel to Lugano, beautiful among its hazy, Chinese mountains, and on through Como, Milan and the Appenines to Pisa: 'Climbed leaning tower, naturally'.[85] Baby Daniel had a tantrum high on one of its polished, railless levels, terrifying his father.[86] And so through Florence to Rome, where they lived outside the city at a hotel on Lago di Bolsena, driving the 60 kilometres to see St Peter's and the Vatican.

Murray found he was more interested in Etruscan remains outside the city than Roman ones in it.[87]

By now both they and their finances were exhausted, and at the end of May they drove rapidly north, avoiding Paris because of the 1968 riots which had now broken out in the city. As radicals from all over Europe converged gleefully to join the fun, Murray and his small family carefully skirted the city, crossed Belgium and took the ferry to Britain. Within a week Murray had put Valerie and the children on board one of the last liners regularly plying the Australia run, the P&O *Fairstar*: they sailed on 6 June 1968 on the long voyage home via Trinidad, Curaçao and Panama.[88] Having seen them on board, Murray went ahead of them by air, intending to find a job and somewhere for them to live. He assumed, with his usual sunny optimism, that this would not be difficult.

Murray was to deny that they had gone to Britain with the thought of settling there permanently, as so many Australian artists from Peter Porter to Clive James still did. 'My "reply" to the expat. generations was to succeed *from home*', he would write.[89] The stay had reinforced in him the knowledge that he was, finally, Australian. He drew his strength, Anteus-like, from the soil of his own continent: henceforth he and his family would live there, come what might. The European interlude was over.

CHAPTER TWELVE
THE VERNACULAR REPUBLIC
1968–71

To forge in the smithy of my soul the uncreated conscience of my race.

JAMES JOYCE

Murray went back to Canberra on his return to Australia, and stayed for a fortnight with Walter and Elisabeth Davis while trying to find his feet again. He had no money and nowhere to live, and he was glad when, shortly before Valerie and the children arrived by sea, Geoffrey Lehmann offered him the loan of a house in Lavender Bay. In 1942, during the scare caused by the shelling of harbourside suburbs by Japanese submarines, Lehmann's father Leo had noticed that prices for waterfront property had collapsed overnight. Moving fast, he bought, for £300, a large Lavender Bay property on which stood three houses: a magnificent double-storey house with iron-lace verandahs, a fine sandstone terrace, and a smaller terrace in an advanced state of disrepair: it was this third house the Murrays now gratefully occupied. And here Valerie and the children rejoined him after their five-week voyage. Leo's purchase would find a place in *Fredy Neptune*:

> Newcastle had been shelled from a sub, and Sydney raided.
> A man with a German name had snapped up a mansion and two houses
> right on Sydney Harbour for three hundred pound the morning after
> when half the toffs were doing a bolt.[1]

The house had beautiful views, and the Murrays would wake to see, between their toes, the sun rising over the Harbour Bridge and the site where the new Opera House would stand.[2] But it was empty of even the most basic amenities (they had to buy a tiny stove to cook on) and the upstairs floorboards were so rotten that only strategically placed sheets of corrugated iron saved them from crashing through to the equally decayed floor below. Lehmann, when appealed to, let them move into the second, stone terrace house, which was crammed with Leo Lehmann's possessions: a bower-bird, he had filled the place with tools, bottles of watch-cogs, spools of thread, old china, chests of buttons and (bizarrely) a drawer of water-pistols.[3]

Valerie begged the Department of Education for a job, and was given one at North Sydney Boys High School. On the strength of this income they found a small ground-floor flat at 1/10 Commodore Street, Waverton.[4] Valerie walked to work, depositing Christina (now aged six) in the North Sydney Demonstration School, while Daniel (now four) was in a kindergarten across the road. Murray stayed at home and wrote. From now on, and for many years, it would be Valerie's income that they depended on as their primary source of support. Murray felt what he called 'an outdated but incorrigible shame'[5] at being supported by her, and his repeated failures to find a bearable job, month after humiliating month, gradually brought him to the point of desperation. He found the inability to support his family a profound challenge to his masculinity: in later years he would attempt, in poems like *The Boys Who Stole the Funeral* and *Fredy Neptune*, to move towards a new definition of what it means to be a man in the late twentieth century and beyond.

When by the end of 1968 he had still found nothing despite Australia's prosperity and full employment, he determined to go back to Sydney University and finish his degree in the hope that the testamur would open doors for him. In 1969, therefore, he registered for German 2 and Linguistics 1, did the minimum amount of work required, and got a bare pass in both, thus completing his bachelor's degree,[6] 'the most mediocre degree Sydney University ever awarded', he would joke later.[7] Within a year, his own poetry would be studied at universities.[8] Even before he graduated,[9] he was being invited to speak about his work on campus, giving a talk on 'The Language of Poetry' to Sydney University's English department on 20 October 1969. The talks he had given in Britain proved to be the first of many such talks he would give on campuses around the world.[10]

The degree, however, did him no tangible good at all and his demoralising misemployment continued. Valerie endured, rather than enjoyed, her teaching, and though her parents were tactful, they seem to have felt that their doubts about her marriage had been justified. This was a time of great and growing pressure for Murray. A. D. Hope, on being applied to for another letter of reference, asked rather plaintively why Murray did not last in any of the jobs Hope helped get him. 'Well I try, Alec', Murray told him earnestly, 'but sooner or later, along comes some bastard who thinks he can give orders to a Murray!'[11]

He did not, however, sit and mope. He wrote poetry steadily, and, more surprisingly, he took to political agitation of a literary type. His time abroad had made him focus very closely on what it meant to be Australian, and he was increasingly an active nationalist and republican. This was the development of a position he had held for many years. He was to say that he had become a republican while still at school, when his father tried, and embarrassingly failed, to take him to Newcastle to see the Queen, on a tour of Australia early in 1954: the old Dodge died in the attempt and they never got there.[12] The fifteen-year-old Murray found himself reflecting on how odd it was that they were trying so hard to see a woman to whom they meant nothing whatever. He became convinced, he was to say, of 'the sheer unbridgeability of archaic rank'.[13]

By 1963, before he first went overseas, his ideas had developed to the point where he could, half-jokingly, set out his 'master-plan for Australia' in a letter to Greg O'Hara, going into great detail. The first point of his plan involved the declaration of an Australian republic. Others included the flooding of the centre of the continent, the breaking up of the states into dozens of smaller units of local government (he provided a map), the abolition of 90 per cent of prisons since he regarded imprisonment as barbarous and ineffective, a ban on American records and trashy magazines to foster Australian cultural values, and the institution of Swiss-style universal part-time military training. Important points in his republican program included:

5   Financial aid to artists and to such things as the book trade, Aust. Orchestras etc . . .
7   Isolationist foreign policy, or rather one of dignified relations with other states, fidelity to treaty obligations, but *no* kow-towing, especially cultural.
8   Freedom of speech—you've got to give 'em *some* sort of safety valve.
9   Abolition of tax on persons living in areas in need of development, plus land grants, high wages etc.
10 Deportation of superfluous labour to the above for limited periods and given the above conditions.
11 Transfer of Nat[ional] capital to Alice Springs.
12 Erasure of Canberra . . .
13 Immediate citizenship for all Aborigines, severe punishments for discrimination against them.
14 Stiff taxes on luxury goods . . .
19 Free, unbiased (except against bourgeois dullness & hypocrisy) education . . . Bourgeois slant to be got rid of, even if it means getting rid of half the teachers.[14]

Though some of this was light-hearted, he was deadly serious about the need for Australia to shake off the political shackles that bound it to Britain, and the cultural ones that tied it to the United States. Three elements stand out in his program. He wanted an Australia that stood on its own feet politically, neither stooping nor strutting; he wanted his country to take pride in an indigenous culture; third, he wanted an Australia that cared for all its people, including Aborigines and those, such as his own people, who lived poverty-stricken in isolated or undeveloped areas. His economics were dirigiste and socialist. Thirty years later, he would maintain much the same stance.

The notion of an Australian republic was radical indeed in 1963; thirty years later it would still be only a dream, and though some of his other dreams would come to pass (universal citizenship for Aborigines would follow a referendum in 1967, and serious government support for the arts would come not long after), others, such as cultural independence for Australia, would remain to be worked for as hard as ever.

Murray was not content to merely wish: velleity was not one of his weaknesses. He set about moving energetically towards his vision for his country, and soon after his return from Britain he was writing to the Prime Minister, John Gorton, urging on him the adoption of a new Australian flag:

> What I would like to see promoted in this country is the continued growth of a warm, unstrident, confident and pretty nearly unconscious Australian patriotism, a natural thing which would make it quite simply absurd to regard us as some sort of superior colonials, however warmly we might still adhere to the British Commonwealth or any other such notion. For a nation of this sort, I do not think even our present rather handsome modification of the British Blue Ensign would be appropriate.[15]

And he included a design of his own, featuring two boomerang shapes and four seven-pointed stars, green on gold. He would never abandon his campaign for a new flag. Over the years to come he would press many different designs of his own on political heavyweights like Jim Cairns, or the Governor-General Sir Paul Hasluck,[16] and be fobbed off with courteously evasive replies.[17]

He even announced the founding of a new 'Australian Commonwealth Party', which put forward (chiefly in letters written to the papers by himself) some of the ideas he had first advanced to Greg O'Hara in 1963, including regional development, education reform, the need for cultural independence, and a passionate rejection of what he called 'Australia's present mercantile-opportunist economy'. The party's membership consisted chiefly of himself and Max Fabre, a psychologically fragile fellow-student from Sydney University, and Murray would later say it was designed partly to lend Fabre support and give him an interest.[18] Fabre had a strong physical resemblance to Rasputin, and when he was in a particularly fragile state would let his fingernails grow very long, and refer to himself as 'One'. He would later move to New Zealand, and from there write Murray a letter that began, triumphantly, 'I have found a wife. She is not my wife'.[19]

But though the Australian Commonwealth Party was not to be taken entirely seriously, Murray's letters to the newspapers were intended to both amuse and challenge. 'Australia will be a great nation, and a power for good in the world', he declared in one letter to the *Bulletin* in 1972, 'when her head of state is a part-Aboriginal and her prime minister a poor man. Or vice versa'.[20] The 1972 elections put an end to the party's always-transparent pretentions to electoral support.

But in another area, Murray's political energies achieved real success. He brought to the attention of those in positions of power his 1963 proposal that governments should directly support artists. By 1969 one of his Sydney University friends, Dick Hall, was private secretary to Gough Whitlam, the leader of the Federal Labor Party in opposition. Murray was a strong Labor supporter at this time, though as a student he had regarded socialism as a spent force, writing 'Requiem for a Revolutionary Army' in valediction of it.[21] Hearing Murray's ideas on funding for the arts, Hall suggested that he should put them into the form of a policy paper for the Labor Party: Murray did, in 1969, and he subsequently published a revised version of it in *Australian Quarterly*.[22] He accompanied it with letters to such Labor figures as Barry Jones[23] and Doug McLennan,[24] urging his ideas on them and the party. He also prodded journalist friends into writing on the same subject.[25] In sum, he worked up a skilful and effective lobbying campaign that developed great momentum and would make itself felt for years.

His original paper was a deeply felt protest that artists should live in poverty while those who studied their work could earn comfortable salaries, and a proposal that artists who had achieved distinction should be given a state salary of $5000 a year for five years. Over the years he would return to this theme many times, changing and elaborating his proposals.[26] But even this, his first contribution, would have a major effect on ALP policy on the arts, for though the details of his paper were not followed, its major thrust, 'that artists of real merit or substantial promise be seen as having a *right* to a decent income',[27] would influence the Whitlam government when it set in place the Australia Council after its election in 1972. When Murray argued for income-spreading for artists, to reduce their tax-burden in good years, Whitlam adopted a modified version of his scheme.[28] And although Murray never felt content with the results of his efforts, he would be mildly gratified, years later, to come across his phrasing in Australia Council literature.[29]

His greatest contribution to Australian independence, however, would be his help in giving Australians a culture to take pride in, and in that sense his poetry is his most important republican statement, together with his many critical celebrations of Australian art, primarily literary. Now he gathered the poems he had written since *The Ilex Tree* and prepared them for publication by what he regarded as his country's chief publisher, Angus & Robertson, who had given him the £200 advance when he left for Europe. *The Weatherboard Cathedral*, as he entitled his second volume, would appear at the end of 1969.

It was the first volume of which he was sole author, and it contained some of his most characteristic poems to date, including 'An Absolutely Ordinary Rainbow' and 'A Walk with O'Connor'. It also revealed his satiric gift, in poems like 'Senryu', which one critic would call 'a mind-teaser that increases in importance the more I think about it':[30]

> Just two hours after
> Eternal Life pills came out
> Someone took thirty.

The Weatherboard Cathedral was confident, daring, experimental, and powerfully Australian: its title announced Murray's intention of pressing the claims of his father's weatherboard shack as the repository of spiritual values as important to Australia as those of any cathedral.

The volume drew even more enthusiastic reviews than *The Ilex Tree* had done. Kenneth Slessor, in the *Daily Telegraph*, called *The Weatherboard Cathedral* 'a new and vital impulse at a time when poetry in general is faltering between the outworn attitudes of the past and a sterile and graceless modernity', remarked that it was 'full of magnificent poetry', and continued, 'Murray's Australianism is overwhelming but never ostentatious. He says all that Lawson and Paterson tried to say but with infinitely more passion and subtlety'. Slessor particularly admired 'Evening Alone at Bunyah', Murray's first tribute to his home valley and to his father.[31]

Other reviewers were equally complimentary. Alan Riddell, in the *Sydney Morning Herald*, called Murray 'one of the most gifted poets now writing in Australia';[32] his fellow poet R. A. Simpson called *The Weatherboard Cathedral* 'an assured book that ranges widely'.[33] Jim Tulip remarked that there might not be a 'weatherboard cathedral' in Australia, but that there was a maker of one was beyond doubt: 'He nails his big lines and straightforward rhythms to the page with the same "dour shirtsleeve joy" as his ancestors took in making their homes in the lonely New South Wales countryside'.[34] Geoffrey Lehmann called him 'one of the strongest poets to emerge from this country in recent years', compared him to James Dickey, and described his strengths as 'absolute rightness of image, the ability to produce the unusual but accurate sensory phrase, wit and depth both present at once'.[35] Keith Harrison compared him to Frost in his sense of place.[36]

But other critics, perhaps feeling that the praise heaped on him for *The Ilex Tree* now needed redress, complained that *The Weatherboard Cathedral* was

The Murray family, gathered at Bunyah in November 1926 for the silver wedding anniversary of the poet's paternal grandparents, Allan and Emily Murray: among the assorted great-uncles and great-aunts, the poet's father Cecil is in the top row, third from the right; his sadistic older brother Stanley is next to the right, wearing the bow-tie. In the middle row, fifth from the left, with her hair slicked over her forehead, is Aunt Myrtle, who was so terribly burned as a child. To the right from Myrtle along the middle row are, in order, the poet's Aunt Nettie, who during his childhood lived just across the creek from his parents' shack, then his paternal grandparents, Emily and John Allan, with Aunt Ena on John's knee. In the bottom row, Uncle Charlie is the small boy fourth from the left, with Uncle Eric next on the right.

The poet's grandparents, Emily and John Allan Murray, photographed about 1940.

The first known photograph of Les Murray. He is seated among his mother's fowls, at the age of one year in 1939. The effects of the terrible bushfire which swept through Bunyah some months before are observable in the dead trees behind.

Les Murray at Bunyah, aged two, being propelled in a home-made pram by his mother Miriam, about 1940.

Les Murray driving his pet goat at Bunyah, c. 1943.

Taree High: the cadet sergeant, 1956.

'distinctly inferior to his early volume',[37] or said that Murray now seemed 'at a loss to know what to sing'.[38] Rodney Hall regretted 'the smoko manner in poetry'.[39] And the reviewer in Meanjin paid him an ironic compliment akin to the one that had greeted The Ilex Tree: 'Les A. Murray is a rural wanderer, writing in the manner of The Prelude, relaxed, but confident that the poet himself, his environment, and his impressions are the substance of poetry'.[40]

On the whole, though, Murray had reason to feel pleased with the reception of The Weatherboard Cathedral, and he earned some money from it— in contrast to The Ilex Tree, the contract for which had awarded him and Lehmann nothing at all. The publicity brought him notice from one of his former schoolmates at Taree High: Robin Norling wrote to him, with clumsy jocularity, 'I'm afraid I always thought you a little mad—finding you've become a poet reinforces my opinion of you'.[41]

It seemed to Murray that an important, and neglected, aspect of Australian culture lay in the large body of Aboriginal oral poetry that had been collected by researchers, but of which too little had been published. In July 1969 he proposed to Angus & Robertson that he should edit a volume of Aboriginal verse in translation, and the publisher was receptive to the idea.[42] Murray needed an income to live on while he did the work, however, and he now approached the Minister in charge of Aboriginal Affairs, Mr Wentworth, for support; Wentworth referred him to Dr H. C. Coombs, then Chairman of the Council for Aboriginal Affairs. Coombs gave Murray a most enthusiastic reception, and promised him that money would be found: he was also Chairman of the Australia Council for the Arts, and he told Murray that a fellowship would be arranged, with attachment to the Institute of Aboriginal Studies at the Australian National University.[43] Coombs, who had gradually drawn into his own hands a range of positions of power in Aboriginal affairs, was also the head of the Institute, and Chancellor of the ANU.

On the strength of this verbal promise, Murray naively and joyfully moved himself and his family to Canberra at the beginning of February 1970,[44] Valerie having dutifully resigned her teaching job. They rented a house at 7 Giles Street, Kingston, in Canberra, at $28 a week. The rent was more than they could afford, but they expected that once Murray's fellowship came through they would benefit from the ANU's housing subsidy as before. But week followed week, and there was no word from Dr Coombs. Murray continued optimistic: 'Dr Coombs, the Chairman of the Council for Aboriginal Affairs, is currently writing letters to himself as Chairman of the Aust. Council for the Arts, recommending that I be given a grant from there, pleading that I'm a good fellow, a deserving case, proponent of a worthy project etc. I hope fervently that he agrees with himself', he told his friend Mick Byrne.[45]

But there was only silence. Murray's increasingly puzzled letters to Coombs drew non-committal responses, and when he asked directly, 'When is the money going to start?' Coombs's office responded that they knew nothing of any money. Murray was now seriously alarmed. All his attempts to see Coombs were frustrated, and after months of being fobbed off by Coombs's understudies, including Jean Battersby and Charles Perkins,[46] he received a letter informing him that the Council for the Arts had decided not to fund his anthology.[47] He was hard hit. The Arts Council 'had turned my project, which would have produced a valuable and unprecedented publication, into a nightmare of humiliation for me', he would write to a later Australian Prime Minister, William McMahon, 'and I could no longer bear to think about it'.[48]

The move to Canberra had disrupted the Murrays' lives and left them thousands of dollars out of pocket. Shocked and disillusioned, Murray reached the bitter conclusion that he had been insufficiently radical for Coombs, who had quietly dropped him and the Aboriginal poetry project. Enraged by what he saw as Coombs's treachery and by what he called 'this cynical torment at the hands of a bureaucratic machine',[49] he decided that Coombs wanted a revolution and had realised that Murray's volume would not help the cause: 'The idea was to be as socially divisive as possible and bring on the revolution. And one of the things that they were trying to do at the time was to get the Aborigines to hate the white people . . . I wasn't going to be divisive enough. I would have produced a peaceful reconciling book but he wanted division. He wanted hatred'.[50] Coombs was one of the most distinguished Australians of the postwar era, and most historians would regard the notion that he 'wanted hatred' as absurd. But Murray also came to think that there were other dangerous men in high places: it was at this time, in May 1970, that he saw the historian Manning Clark, at a private party in David Campbell's house, wearing what Murray believed to be the Order of Lenin.[51]

It is possible that Murray had misunderstood Coombs, more probable that Coombs had made a rash and optimistic promise to Murray and subsequently changed his mind, or realised he could not deliver what he had pledged. 'And Les was easy to ignore—he wasn't going to make a big fuss', Valerie remarked without bitterness.[52] At all events, the fellowship on which Murray had depended proved a mirage, and he and his family were now stranded. They sank rapidly into debt.

As so often, Valerie proved their saviour, getting a teaching post in Canberra at Telopea Park High School where she had taught before they left for England,[53] 'liking it without great enthusiasm, if you follow me', as Murray told Mick Byrne.[54] In fact, as Murray admitted, 'the poor girl is pretty depressed, mainly about the future . . . She loathes her birthdays, and the sense of time passing'.⁵⁵ He mentioned to Lehmann his own 'repeated bouts of sadness'.⁵⁶

Murray desperately appealed to Canberra friends in the Public Service, did some rabbiting on David Campbell's farm for pocket-money, and collected letters of recommendation from contacts like A. D. Hope: presently, to his great relief, he was offered a temporary clerkship in the Prime Minister's Office,⁵⁷ which he called 'Gorton's Garden of Toadies'.⁵⁸ Here he helped to answer the Prime Minister's mail, writing 'careful noncommittal letters, designed to reveal nothing, help noone [sic] and give nothing away',⁵⁹ talked to his co-workers, and read books with his feet up on the desk. He also used the Prime Minister's stationery to write to friends like Mick Byrne. 'Another letter from Les', Byrne's wife would say on the arrival of an important-looking envelope marked 'Prime Minister, Canberra'.⁶⁰

Murray liked the work, and got on well with his superiors, though he subverted the office by asking his colleagues why they were wasting their lives like this. 'If you had your choice, what would you really like to go off and do?' Years later he met his former boss, Jack Reedy, who told him, 'I lasted about two years after you were in that job, you got to me, you got to the whole branch.' Reedy had resigned from the Prime Minister's Department and founded a business selling musical instruments, as he had always wanted to do.⁶¹

Murray liked Canberra only a little more than before, though he was good-humoured in verse, where he poked wry fun at the already confusing system of circles on which Canberra's roads are designed. With money borrowed from his father, he had bought a little Mazda 1200 in mid-1970,⁶² a car light enough for him to hand-park with ease, and he expressed sympathy with interstate motorists who got lost regularly in the capital's labyrinth:

> The interstate driver soon discerns
> That twelve identical statues of Burns
> Are unlikely even in this braw town
> And that there are Circles, interwound
> To test, by his cunning and his mettle,
> Whether he shall go home, or settle.⁶³

He drove like Jehu, collecting many traffic fines over the years, and when reproved by friends, remarking complacently and irrelevantly that he had been born on the same day as Evel Knievel, the American stuntman. Since Knievel had broken many of his bones more than once, this was no comfort to Murray's nervous passengers.

The Murrays resumed their Canberra social life, seeing the Davises, the Hopes and the Reinhardts, all of whom had helped Murray when he was down.

He even began offering help to others, such as the nationally renowned commentator who sought Murray's advice on winning a bride, thereby proving that he had little judgement in his choice of guide. Valerie however was able to right the balance. The commentator wanted detailed guidance on whether he should invite the girl to a picnic (too informal?) or a restaurant (too formal?), could he pay her as many as three compliments or was that too many for one day, and would it be forward to notice her lovely pale stockings? He was so nervous that he drank immoderate amounts of the Murrays' cheap red wine, and irritated Valerie by spewing it all over the hall carpet. Murray was amused by such manifestations of the physical, perhaps because he did not have to clean them up:

> I remember the day that Messer Calvo
> having eaten a whole roast fowl at luncheon
> with lettuce, onions, borage, honey, apples
> and drunk two flagons of my good Médoc
> rose suddenly from his place with strangling mien
> and at a staggering run, beset with arches
> all down the halls,
>   invented the festoon.[64]

Murray called the commentator 'mad as a meat-axe',[65] but also described him with affection as

> a dear, graceless, clumsy, straight-up-and-down bachelor friend of ours, a political wizard, who's in love and wants to show us his lady. We'd laughed ourselves into knots the previous night when he came to ask our advice on romantic matters, and noted down all we told him under headings; it was like a strategic plan laid out by a cuckoo general. We hope the wench is *very* kind and understanding.[66]

She was.

The Murrays even had relatives in Canberra by this time, for one of Valerie's aunts now lived there with her son, a 115-kilogram weight-lifter and shot-putter named Béla Magassy. Béla had helped Murray move in when they arrived, 'and—Zowie!—the furniture just floated into the house', Murray reported.[67] When they were subsequently invited to the Magassys for dinner they found Béla out, and his mother noticed that he had left a bar loaded with his heaviest weights in the living room where he had been puffing and grunting earlier in the day. 'Oh, now we'll be tripping over them all evening', she said in dismay. Murray lifted the bar in one hand, like a suitcase: 'Where will I put them?' he asked, as Béla's mother literally gaped.[68]

Murray resumed his poetry readings, earning $20 on 16 August 1970 for a reading for the Arts Council of the Australian Capital Territory.[69] At Thomas Kenneally's invitation he attended a Global Village Conference at the University of New England, where he met Bruce Dawe.[70] The two men liked each other on sight, admired each other's writing, and would correspond irregularly from then on. They had a great deal in common; among other things, they were both from poor country backgrounds, from which each derived a strong sympathy for the underdog and a deep suspicion of privilege, and they were both Catholic converts from Presbyterianism, though they never spoke of religion.[71] Their poems had similar colloquial edge, and sometimes similar subject-matter.[72]

Dawe later remembered Murray's technique at this conference, when he had been irritated by a condescending speaker, of asking the man an apparently guileless question, and when he got a dismissive answer, asking a more sophisticated question and another, until the speaker was in over his head, floundering haplessly.[73] Dawe, who with his laconic delivery and craggy country-boy persona was as easy as Murray to underestimate, got a deal of quiet enjoyment out of this demonstration of the bullfighter's art.

As usual Murray found that a job kept him from his work, and he applied for a Commonwealth Literary Fund Fellowship, 'as a ratline by which I may escape the ship of State'.[74] And towards the end of the year, his luck began to turn: on 26 October 1970 it was announced that he had won the Open section of the poetry competition set up to commemorate the bicentenary of Captain Cook's exploration of the east coast. Murray had submitted a poem-sequence, 'Seven Points for an Imperilled Star', a series of seven poems that together summed up his feelings towards his country. They included a long and important poem, 'Toward the Imminent Days', which he had written in honour of Lehmann's marriage to Sally McInerney in July 1969, 'The Ballad of Jimmy Governor', a finely compressed ballad about an Aboriginal outlaw that he had worked on during March 1970,[75] and 'The Conquest', which, like 'The Ballad of Jimmy Governor', considered relations between whites and Aboriginals.

> Philip was a kindly, rational man:
> Friendship and trust will win the natives, Sir.
> Such was the deck the Governor walked upon.
>
> One deck below, lieutenants hawked and spat.
> One level lower, and dank nightmares grew.
> Small floating Englands where our world began.

The Captain Cook Bicentenary Celebrations prize-money, $2500, was enough to allow the Murrays to clear their debts to Cecil Murray and other friends: they paid with relief.[76] To put the sum in context, the average male income in Australia for 1970 was $3848, and Australian writers quoted in *Australian Author* that year had gross earnings of well under $2500.[77] Murray's Cook Prize, then, which gained him great publicity, was at least equivalent to the average annual income of Australian writers at this time.[78] To add to his pleasure, he was awarded a six-month Commonwealth Literary Fund Fellowship for 1971.

On the strength of these two triumphs, he and Valerie decided to move back to Sydney. She had been unsettled by their continual shifting, by Murray's succession of unsatisfactory jobs, and by the deep depressions that continued to affect him. In the grip of these he would give terrifying displays of temper, particularly intimidating Christina and little Daniel: in later years Valerie would remember screaming at him to pull himself together.[79] At the end of 1970 she left Murray in Canberra, and moved to Sydney with the children to live with her parents in Chatswood while she searched for a house: she had deeply regretted not buying the Burn Street house, and was determined not to make that mistake again. Murray could not face the unspoken reproaches of his parents-in-law, with whom he was in any case never comfortable for more than very brief visits: even when he left Canberra he chose to live on his own for a period, in a dank sandstone house in Wollombi. He also went to Adelaide for a time, visiting a cousin, Judy Murphy, and her husband Tony Gibb. Here he also met once more his university friend Ros Bateman, who made it clear that her affection for him was not yet dead, though he treated her with great propriety.[80] 'It was a difficult time', Valerie would say later, with understatement, though she added, 'Our marriage was never really on the brink'.[81]

Early in 1971 she found a small house, at 27 Edgar Street, Chatswood, not far from her parents' home in Sydney's north. It was a modest red-brick-and-tile cottage on a steep hill, and its back garden would soon be overlooked by the first of the glittering multifaceted glass towers of Chatswood's shopping centre, which Murray would capture in 'Mirror-glass Skyscrapers': but at $22 750 she thought they could afford it. The Murrays took a loan of $14 000 from a building society, and Valerie signed the purchase papers on 11 March 1971.[82] She began teaching at Turramurra High School at the same time.[83] She thought of the house as a way of ensuring that they would not keep moving: 'That gave us a fair bit of stability for a good long while because we were paying it off'.[84] Murray rejoined her soon after: they held a big housewarming for friends ranging from Ken Slessor to Geoff Lehmann, and they would happily occupy the little house on Edgar Street for fourteen years, until the end of 1985. These would be years of trial, consolidation, and growing success.

CHAPTER THIRTEEN
THE TEST OF FAITH
1971–74

And when Peter was come down out of the ship, he walked on the water.

MATTHEW

For the next six months of 1971, as they got used to life in Chatswood, Valerie taught and Murray wrote: by September he had virtually completed his next book of verse, which he planned to call 'The Work Against Mortality'.[1] In the event it would appear in mid-1972 as *Poems Against Economics*, a title that among other resonances would contain a protest against the way economists like Dr Coombs could control an artist. Murray tried in vain to persuade the publisher to print one of his designs for a new Australian flag on the cover.[2] He did not abandon this idea, and thanks to his characteristic persistence, his next volume would carry the design.[3]

Once the six-month fellowship expired, though, at the end of July 1971, all the old pressures reasserted themselves. He tried once again to secure a clerkship with the Commonwealth Public Service, was offered one with the Department of Labour and National Service, but refused to have anything to do with sending National Servicemen to Vietnam, a war he by now strongly opposed. He appealed to Prime Minister McMahon 'for a measure of understanding and, perhaps, mercy', styling himself 'clerk class 1',[4] and received one of the suavely non-committal replies he had himself become expert at writing for the Prime Minister.

In deep gloom he took a dead-end clerkship with the Commonwealth Education Department (which his friend Christopher Koch called 'the Writer's Iron Lung'),[5] the second time Murray had had one there, and appealed to his university contacts for something better. In July 1971 he secured an interview with Leonie Kramer, Professor of English at Sydney University, and begged her for a university job: 'Not an exalted academic post, of course: research assistant, translator, even trolley-pusher in Fisher Library would do'.[6] Kramer, an extremely tough woman who sent many beggars away empty, flatly refused to help him, and he, hurt and angry, responded by writing to her as soon as he got back home, demanding that she remove all his work from the Australian literature courses of the university. Kramer consulted the university's lawyers, learned that he had no legal right to make such a demand, and sent a memo to members of her department ordering that study of his work should continue.[7] Murray bore her no lasting ill-will, and in later years they would be allies in Australia's battle of the books. But the incident reinforced the deep ambiguity of his attitude to universities and academics: though he could run intellectual rings round most academics without getting out of his chair, and though in years to come he would graciously accept various honours from universities, in his depressed moods he thought of universities as centres of privilege from which he and 'his people' were excluded, and by which they were mocked and derided.

His continuing failure to find tolerable employment brought him to a momentous decision late in 1971. Bored to stupefaction by his clerkship with the Education Department, he cleared his desk one day and told his superior 'I'm going home'. His boss was sympathetic: 'Are you sick?' 'No', said Murray, 'There's nothing to do. I'm going home for ever'.[8] And he did. He had decided that, come what might, he would never take another of the despised 'jobs': he would live by his real work. His boss subsequently rang several times asking if he would like to change his mind,[9] but Murray had enough courage, faith in his gift, and luck in his wife, to be able to stand firm as a freelance poet for the rest of his life. Twenty years later he would tell a friend, 'I've never regretted my leap out of cover employment, & I know I'd never have written as well if I had not leapt'.[10]

For all that, it was not easy. He thought of himself as living like a farmer, patching a living out of bits and pieces of poetry, lecturing, editing and reading. A better analogy is perhaps that of an Aboriginal or Bushman hunter-gatherer group: there would be feast-times when Murray speared a rare prize or fellowship, but in between they depended on Valerie's unspectacular but steady gathering at Turramurra High.

He came to think of his poetry as his religious vocation, the Trappist life he had been considering when he met Valerie, silent communion with a sheet of paper in his cell. As he would put it a decade later to a friend, the Welsh poet John Barnie:

> I really have to go on finding grace enough to trust in Divine Providence, which has so far never let us down. I have to go on having the grace not to sacrifice myself, in this case to some wage-earning job, if I could get one with my record and at my age. While ever I go on doing this work, we will be provided for, barely but sufficiently. I think I'm really in one of the darker sayings of Jesus, the sort that make me ultimately cleave to him above any other contender: I'm in the one which promises a person damnation if they put wife

or child or father or mother before Christ.[11] This quasi-priestly work of poetry is Christ, for me; it's His life as I can live it by my efforts—or to put it another way, it is my Christ-nature made real and effective in the world. If I go back to one of the conventional (and in most people perfectly laudable) sacrifices, that of keeping my family, I will be lost. Difficult religion, this one.[12]

He now focused all his efforts on his poetry, and he worked tremendously hard. From 1971 his occasional appearances at poetry readings became a steady stream of engagements for readings, tours and conferences: a poetry reading in Broome in July 1972, a Waratah Festival organised by Father Edmund Campion for St Mary's Cathedral in October 1972, a lecture to the Teachers' College in Wollongong the same month. He threw himself into such talks and readings, even though he was so nervous of public speaking that he scarcely dared make eye-contact with his audience, gazing instead at a corner of the ceiling as he half-read, half-recited. Despite being an ordeal, such occasions were not only useful publicity, the oxygen on which a writer depends, they were vital sources of income now that he was a free-lance poet.

His readings were highly effective, for unlike many poets he could, at his best, voice his own poems to perfection, and would rehearse a new poem carefully until he had got its delivery to his satisfaction. And in the social chatter that surrounded such events he shone too. The critic Carol Treloar would recall the effect of his Johnsonian conversation, wide-ranging, original and authoritative, on a buzz of bored writers and their fans:

> I remember innumerable poetry readings and one or two lunch (or counter lunch?) parties in Sydney where Les, leather cap on balding head, would genially and unassumingly begin to yarn. And quickly the noisy impassioned convolutions of debate would disentangle themselves, the beer cans and mugs of rough claret would waver and hang in awkward midair suspension, the glazed eyes of introversion would resurface and home towards him, and sundry desperado litterati and comrades would listen . . . It is the art of story-telling and rich sense of the past (however legendary) that comes on so strong in Les Murray the man. And in Les Murray the poet.[13]

In March 1972, as part of a Commonwealth Literary Fund tour of South Australia, he attended Writers' Week at the Adelaide Festival for the first time, enjoying himself, meeting many of his fellow-writers, including the visiting luminaries Allen Ginsberg,[14] Lawrence Ferlinghetti[15] and Andrey Voznesensky.[16] Murray admired the ageing Beats no more than he did the apparatchik, and when he noticed that they were treated with much more respect than the Australian artists, all his Bunyah hackles rose: 'There was some sour comfort', he snorted, 'in the fact that the visiting poets . . . were felt to be the sort of people more appropriately treated as stars than as genuine, first-rate writers'.[17] Humble subservience to foreign writers was a form of colonial cringe he hated to see. All the same, he was comfortably lodged in a university residence, and evenings in the seventh-floor bar of the Australia Hotel, where he was able to renew literary friendships, exchange gossip and enjoy conversation, went far to make up for inequalities of hospitality.

He was in Western Australia (where he wrote 'Cycling in the Lake Country')[18] on a tour funded by the Commonwealth Literary Fund, then on its last legs, when *Poems Against Economics* appeared in June 1972.[19] The volume got mixed reviews. By now, with two volumes already behind him, he had been typecast, both by his supporters and by critics: he was the poet of the countryside in subject matter, and a conservative in style, straightforward and accessible. *Poems Against Economics* unsettled both those views, and the critics showed their bewilderment.

The volume consisted of three sections: the Cook Prize-winning 'Seven Points for an Imperilled Star', which subtly raised a range of questions as to what kind of country Australia was, and where it should be going; 'Juggernaut's Little Scrapbook', which pressed sharp spurs of satire into the national hide; and 'Walking to the Cattle-Place', a complex and learned series of meditations on the significance of the cow-culture in which Murray had been raised, and which drew on his curious and varied knowledge about other cattle-cultures, ranging from Celt to Sanskrit to Zulu. He was putting forward alternative values to those of the bureaucratic bean-counters, and doing so with serious intent, and the volume had a complex thematic unity, the individual poems of his previous volumes giving way to a *livre composé*.

'There have been no great technical innovations at any stage of his career', Bob Adamson's journal *New Poetry* grumbled, 'and at times Murray's poems have tended to ramble'.[20] From *New Poetry*, which regarded technical innovation as equivalent to poetic excellence, this was a severe condemnation. In fact, in the new volume Murray was experimenting with a new form of long, meditative poem, one that moves repeatedly from startling observation to new understanding in a series of ascending pulses, slow to make its point but richly repaying openness and thought on the part of the reader. It was a form he was to make his own, though *New Poetry* did not notice. This was the first shot across his bows from the group of poets that had formed around one of Murray's poetic rivals, John Tranter, and for which *New Poetry* was a mouthpiece; it would not be the last.

More sympathetic readers, who had liked Murray's earlier work and expected to find more of the same, found themselves struggling with the intellectually demanding poems of the 'Walking to the Cattle-Place' sequence: the poet and critic Geoff Page confessed, 'The basic problem with such breadth of reference is reader ignorance'.[21] In fact, much of the sequence makes an immediate impact, deriving its power from Murray's vivid observation and his intuitive sympathy with animals:

> A sherry-eyed Jersey looks at me. Fragments of thoughts
> That will not ripple together worry her head
>
> It is sophistication trying to happen . . .[22]

In the volume as a whole Murray was advancing an alternative view of what Australia had been and could still be, a place of values deeply rooted in the land and capable of being developed into a distinctively Australian, and distinctively spiritual, culture. His critics were not yet ready for his vision.

Still other readers, hoping for poetry of harmless escapism, were taken aback by a poet who applied himself to political commentary about 1970s Australia with a savage polemical edge. He had already sharply identified and tagged the book-keeper spirit that reduces all of life and culture to what can be bought and sold, the stultifying power that in the 1990s would come to be called 'economic rationalism':[23]

> All night I talked to the treetops
> I told them Make very small leaves
> For the ringbarking spirit has come
> And has stolen our country . . .
>
> My arm a lever already,
> In the planner's aurora, I smoke,
> Thinking ahead, perhaps far
> To a savage Nuremberg on economics.[24]

And he took his stand, in a brilliant little satiric quatrain he called 'Incorrigible Grace', on a quite different set of values:

> Saint Vincent de Paul, old friend,
> My sometime tailor,
> I daresay by now you are feeding
> The rich in Heaven.

He also now began to make highly effective use of the Aboriginal poetry he had been prevented from publishing, using its strange rhythms and flavours in 'Stockman Songs':

> Going to Rubuntja, the cattle-train. Banging two trailers . . .
>
> My wife's uncle Blue-tongue, grass seed man. He tastes of spinifex.
>
> The clumsy bull has written a cheque on the cow's flank.
> In the dust of her flank, in the fur, a long water cheque . . .
>
> The iron gnamma-hole tja:, a hot white flowering tja:na:
> A finch lives under the drinking trough. His dance country.

This was an elaboration of the way he had used Aboriginal words in 'The Ballad of Jimmy Governor', terms such as 'white lady' (methylated spirits and powdered milk) and 'jimbera' (a man of mixed race). But it was not just Aboriginal vocabulary and speech patterns he was voicing in his work: increasingly he set about giving poetic utterance to ordinary Australians of every kind, the architects and builders of the weatherboard cathedral, using for them the Bunyah dialect of his childhood and youth.

> My country is Kiltartan Cross
> My countrymen, Kiltartan's poor

said Yeats's Irish Airman: Murray speaks with the same pride of Bunyah. He uses a vocabulary his father would have found natural, and which imparts a strong sense of place to his poetry:

> The ticks on her elder are such
> Muscatels of good blood.
>
> If I envy her one thing
> It is her ease with this epoch.
> A wagtail switching left-right, left-right on her rump.[25]

It is not just the use of the Bunyah word 'elder' for 'udder'; the wagtail switching left-right produces a little shock of displacement for the European reader who knows that a northern wagtail bobs up-down and never sits on cattle, and who registers the newness of the Australian bird with a vivid pleasure.

The same pleasure in renewing vision is produced more generally by Murray's pervasive vernacular: ring-barkers, yellow-box logs, possums, utes, iron roofs, sheep that prop, lakes that die of thirst—a whole range of references that Australian readers accept unthinkingly as their birthright reveal Murray's work as the poetry of a confident but unassertive nationalism. The mere opening of a poem such as 'SMLE' brings a northern hemisphere reader up with a start: 'January, heat'. The same is true of both title and opening lines of 'Cycling in the Lake Country', which entices the reader into thoughts of Wordsworth, and then dispels those thoughts by placing us among Western Australia's desert salt-lakes: 'Dried phlegm of lakes/that die of thirst'. There is a puckish humour at work in this cultural wrench, but also deadly serious intent. Murray was engaged in a vital enterprise that would occupy him for much of his career: the production of a beautiful, flexible, Australian poetic language, an enterprise akin to what Eliot in 'Little Gidding' called 'the purification of the dialect of the tribe'.

Poems Against Economics in fact was full of experiments, of new beginnings, and Murray would develop many of them in his future work. Yet for all its innovation, which was recognised by critics like Jim Tulip,[26] Roger McDonald[27] and Tom Shapcott,[28] his remained a voice that was unmistakably Australian and his own. As the critic in the *Sydney Morning Herald* put it: 'It has always been a mark of greatness that an artist's work should be immediately recognisable, bearing the unmistakable hallmark of its creator. In this sense, Murray's art is as individual as that of G. M. Hopkins. It is also uncompromising in its demands'.[29] And as before, his work was noticed outside Australia, Peter Porter writing of him in the *Observer*, 'His poetry is dense, referential and exuberant: I could not imagine it being written in Britain or America'.[30]

Murray's was no longer a new voice in Australian poetry: by 1973, at the age of thirty-four, he had become a new voice in world poetry, and an established figure in his own country. His rapidly growing literary prominence, combined with his intellectual and political leadership on the issue of funding for the arts, meant that he was a natural and popular recipient of government funding even before the 1972 election victory of Gough Whitlam, many of whose ideas on state patronage and cultural independence he had anticipated and articulated with such effect. In fact, late in 1971 Murray was awarded a six-month grant of $4000 for the first half of 1972, and the dingo was driven from his door for a little longer.

Murray's was a republic of the mind, particularly of the imagination: he believed that if Australians could take imaginative possession of their country, the republic would have arrived. When the Whitlam government, which he strongly supported during its short, frenetic period in office, was dismissed by Sir John Kerr on 11 November 1975, Murray would be enraged, but within a few months he would also be able to see hope in what had happened:

> In at least two very different ways, the republic is already here. It can be argued that we have been a republic of sorts since November 11 last year [he wrote in 1976]. Anyone who believed that the Crown might still act as some sort of

ultimate talisman of political decency was undeceived that day ... The other republic, the one we have to discern, is inherent in our vernacular tradition, which is to say in that 'folk' Australia, part imaginary and part historical, which is the real matrix of any distinctiveness we possess as a nation, and which stands over against all of our establishments and colonial elites. This is the Australia of our deepest common values and identifications, the place of our quiddities and priorities and family jokes.[31]

He wrote with increasing confidence as a spokeman for the country he was helping to bring into being. But it would not come about without resistance and struggle, a struggle as much literary as political. He now embarked on a new aspect of his career. He was about to take a leading part in Australia's long literary war.

CHAPTER FOURTEEN
THE BATTLE OF THE BOOKS
1974-76

For savagery, dishonesty, bullying, ill-will and poorly disguised jealousy, I have never seen a piece of academic criticism quite equal that regularly practised by authors on each other. Literature just seems to be informed by this greater joie de vivre.

LES MURRAY[1]

One way of viewing the movement of art history is to see it as a series of pendulum swings, one generation moving forward by reacting against the art of their immediate predecessors, and in their turn suffering rejection by the following generation. By 1974 many poets of Murray's generation were energetically elbowing aside the group who had dominated Australian poetry for the previous quarter-century, A. D. Hope, R. D. FitzGerald, Judith Wright and James McAuley. But though united in rejection, they could find little agreement on the way forward, and increasingly they turned on each other. More generous arts funding in the 1970s intensified these battles, which now became a struggle for real resources: Murray's successful lobbying for funds had unintentionally added explosive fuel to the flames. Funding success was partly a matter of peer review, and an enhanced reputation and well-placed allies could make the difference between getting a large grant or struggling with a succession of dead-end jobs as Murray had struggled for years.

The energy released by this fierce competition was immensely enriching, and it promoted the emergence in Australia of a number of poets, the best of whom were the equal of any in the English-speaking world at the time. Among them were Murray, Bruce Dawe, John Tranter, Bruce Beaver, Thomas Shapcott, Rodney Hall, Robert Adamson, Michael Dransfield and Vicki Viidikas, but many other names could be added. Cliques constantly formed, fell apart with bitter recrimination, and reformed with variations. There was an upsurge of new, mostly short-lived little magazines, often mimeographed, with such titles as *Our Glass*, *Mok*, *Crosscurrents* and *The Great Auk*; there were poetry readings at Monash University and La Mama in Carlton, Melbourne, the Harold Park Hotel in Sydney, and at Friendly Street in Adelaide; there were contests such as the annual Balmain poetry and prose competition, and the emergence of new publishing houses such as Grace Perry's South Head Press (founded to insulate her from any more takeover attempts) and Michael Wilding and Pat Woolley's Wild & Woolley, as well as the introduction of Queensland University Press's important Paperback Poets series. Murray's steady activity was part of a rich ferment of Australian poetry.

By the early 1970s the intensifying literary tension between rival groups of writers had produced clear battle lines, forming up behind (or within) the two national poetry magazines, *Poetry Australia* and *New Poetry*. As Murray saw it, the struggle was between that loose and shifting group of poets who became known as 'the Generation of '68' (named and headed by John Tranter, but including Robert Adamson, Martin Johnston, Michael Dransfield, Ken Bolton, John A. Scott and, later, John Forbes, John Jenkins and Gig Ryan, and whose flagship was the journal *New Poetry*) on one hand, and those who opposed them on the other.

New Poetry was the successor to *Poetry Magazine*: having ousted Grace Perry as editor in a branch-stacking coup in 1964 (the quarrel coming about because she had wished to publish foreign poetry in translation),[2] the victorious group itself split in 1970, when some of its members became uneasy about the amount of space being given over to American and British poets. The result was the appearance, in February 1971, of *New Poetry*, edited initially by Adamson and Carl Harrison-Ford, later by Adamson alone.

New Poetry spoke for the Generation of '68 (whose name was intended to evoke the passions of that year, compounded of anti-Vietnam demonstrations in the English-speaking world and student revolt on the streets of Paris) in being angrily anti-establishment, radical, revolutionary and iconoclastic: its spirit was shaped by rock music, drugs, Vietnam protests, and a belief in poetry as a weapon.[3] The Generation of '68 explicitly set themselves against 'ethics, morality, religion and mythology'.[4] Adamson, a wild young man who had discovered poetry in prison when he first heard the lyrics of Bob Dylan, was a natural voice for the group, bringing to their pronouncements an underworld edge which gave his allies an agreeable frisson. The Generation of '68 expressed a strong antagonism to 'traditional' Australian poetry. In place of this tradition they elevated the writing of the American Beats and their British disciples, and (in time) newer American poets such as John Ashbery.

Equally determined to encourage movement in Australian poetry, but much less impressed by American or British models, Grace Perry's magazine *Poetry Australia* provided an alternative, and more eclectic, prescription for change. Its ultimate model was Harriet Monroe's *Poetry* magazine, and its dual aim was fostering Australian verse by encouraging beginners to develop their gifts, and publishing the best work available from Australia and the world.[5] It carried no editorial comment, it used the best printers and paper though Perry's finances were always stretched, and it tried to present the very best poetry to be found in English and any other language. Partly because the *New Poetry* group had thrust her from the Poetry Society editorship, there was bad blood from the start between *Poetry Australia* and *New Poetry*.

Murray had already associated himself with Perry in editing the Canberra Poets issue of her magazine in February 1966, and the grudging review of *Poems Against Economics* by *New Poetry* had been enough to remind him of it. He had in any case a low opinion of Adamson's poetry,[6] an opinion that extended itself to Adamson's journal. He found almost incomprehensible the admiration of the Generation of '68 for the kind of writing that had wrecked the Commonwealth Poetry Conference in 1965.

By 1973 Grace Perry, for all her energy and overwhelming presence, was tired and ill with a potassium deficiency disease which robbed her of vitality, so that increasingly she was obliged to retreat to her country home in Berrima. She approached Murray, and asked him if he would edit her journal in a caretaker capacity until she recovered. He readily agreed to become what he called 'her locum tenens' (Perry still worked as a medical doctor), for he had long dreamed of having control of a literary magazine. 'I've always wanted a magazine of my own', he would muse in 1997, 'but I'll never get one because it would take a lot of money and I haven't got a backer'.[7] This was his chance. Both he and Perry initially thought of this as a short-term arrangement, but Murray was to remain acting editor of *Poetry Australia* for seven years, until 1980.

This position, and his growing literary prominence, gradually made him a natural centre for opposition to the Generation of '68. Writing in 1982, Tom Shapcott would remark of Tranter and Murray:

> They have been seen—they have set themselves up—as opposition leaders: each has consciously cultivated their separate 'school'. Tranter's recent anthology *The New Australian Poetry* claims the desirable new grouping, with Tranter firmly mid-centre. Murray for some years now has sent followers out to corner the Commentary Market, and the poems of his acolytes Kevin Hart, Alan Gould, Geoff Page, Robert Gray and Roger McDonald appear in very central places indeed.[8]

Murray would deny that he aspired to lead anything like a formal group, but his emphatic rejection of the Tranterites and the derivative form of Modernism they advocated caused him to be widely perceived as heading the resistance to them. His work on *Poetry Australia* provided him with a major weapon in this resistance.

Perry paid him nothing ('I'm in this game for my health', he would joke wryly),[9] and worked side by side with him as far as her energy would allow. Every few weeks Murray would go to her surgery in Lyons Road, Five Dock, and 'read the drawer':

> This meant sifting through the one or two deep filing cabinet drawers which filled up with contributions seemingly within hours... I would reduce a pile of work eighteen inches or two feet thick to a loosely stacked half-inch or so of work good enough to publish unaltered, plus perhaps a like amount of work showing enough gleams of quality to warrant my scribbling editorial suggestions all over the manuscripts and entering into negotiations with the authors. And then there would be all the verse submitted by people wanting evaluations, advice and the like. This was a firm part of the magazine's effort, and all seekers of evaluation and advice got it, often at length. A very few resented the hard things I sometimes had to tell them, and even without that the strain of bringing the bad news to people about the worth of their cherished effusions never grew less.[10]

He very much enjoyed the work, finding it challenging but not so time-consuming as to keep him from his own work. He rapidly showed himself to be an outstanding editor, and in fact had already had a good deal of practice. His fellow editors on *honi soit*, back in 1960, had written of him, 'Wields a blue pencil with cruel accuracy',[11] and he seemed to have an editorial eye that led him to pounce unerringly on the weak line, the tired word, the clumsy punctuation: he did not hesitate to point them out and suggest improvements.

Poets he thought promising would get their work back fringed with dozens of suggested corrections and improvements in Murray's beautiful, always legible hand. With close friends like Penny McNicoll, who had become Penny Nelson in 1964,[12] he could be joky but sharp: 'You are *forbidden* to have "etched on my wall" as the last line of the poem, *etched* is a worn-out word—scarcely any bite left in it—and the line is, agonizingly, a syllable short. "Ye've played a bum note there, Sean!" (P. Sellers, 1958)'.[13] He would question individual words and suggest alternatives, he did not scruple to move a comma, and occasionally he would suggest radical surgery. Rejecting two poems by Duncan Miller, he wrote of a third, 'This is the one! How about condensing the other two into a preface to this, say 6–8 lines and using the Fiddens Wharf title for the resulting single poem? If you do this, please send us the result—and more of your other poems too. Avoid prosiness, though. Good luck. Les Murray ed. Poetry Aust'.[14]

Some young writers were hurt by his firmness ('"Why do you write so badly" I think is the way you put it, Ho Ho Ho', Gary Catalano wrote to him),[15] and there is no doubt that he made enemies. But others came to realise how helpful his sharp comments were compared to the polite, brief rejections of lazier editors. 'I found your harsh criticism stimulating', Barry O'Donoghue wrote bravely, 'Not out of any personal pleasure at being attacked, but because it provided me with impetus and a foundation on which to re-structure and re-create my poetry'.[16]

Nor did established writers escape his advice: 'If you can't say anything, then don't', he wrote in the margin of a Dennis Haskell poem, adding 'Syntax? Condense. Perhaps delete. I'd use a stanza break here', and so on all down the margin,[17] to Haskell's slightly tense gratitude.[18] 'If all editors took so much trouble, we'd all be happier', Hal Colebatch told him,[19] and others echoed the praise.[20]

A. D. Hope envied Murray's poise and certainty as an editor, saying with relish, 'Les of course solves the problem that we all have as an editor, he just puts on the mantle of a highland chieftain imperiously, and says Yea or Nay'.[21] Rosemary Dobson was very hurt to have a poem she had sent him returned with the comment, 'Sorry Rosemary, I can't publish your poem, it's too long and prolix—Les'. She took it to Alec Hope and appealed, 'It's not, is it?' The tactful Hope looked through it and told her it was not: 'But it was, you know', he confessed to Mark O'Connor.[22] To O'Connor himself Murray once wrote, 'Congratulations, this time you have put the dull bit at the end where I have chopped it. I'll publish your poem. Les'.[23] O'Connor was to tell him, 'You're the only editor I've ever had. The others were merely selectors'.[24]

Murray was particularly frustrated by the writers who only just fell short of the required standard, but never seemed able to rise despite all his efforts and advice: 'I think I grieved for every single case of just too little talent, every case where the number of silk hairs on the sow's ear just could not be made to increase despite all rubbing with editorial unction'.[25] Again and again he had to give the same advice: 'Cultivate concision, try to be more vivid, learn about imagery, remember poetry is an art not a confessional, cultivate precision, avoid waffle, don't rely on vague generalisations, let us see and feel with you, avoid ancient poeticism, and most commonly of all, please read some poetry and try to get an idea what it actually is'.[26]

He was soon carrying on an enormous correspondence, all his side of it handwritten, as contributions poured in on him from aspiring or established poets. He soon developed the habit of replying on postcards, a custom he would retain for the rest of his life. Even Valerie got them, though in writing to her Murray would drop into German for particularly personal matters. His script, rounded, fluid and sensuous, remained legible no matter how small he wrote, and he seemed to get as much onto these cards as anyone else could into a letter. He was always on the lookout for unusual cards, and bought them wherever he went: he had William Plomer's genius for finding them.

Poetry Australia specialised in occasional issues devoted to introducing Australian readers to poetry they might not otherwise encounter: during Murray's tenure (and he oversaw issues 49 to 72) there was a Dutch-Flemish issue, a Scottish and Irish Gaelic issue, and issues on Francis Webb and American poetry. Murray's linguistic skills and his foreign contacts stood the journal in good stead; he was able to correct the many errors of the Dutch translator, and it was Murray who both initiated the Gaelic issue and found the right person to edit it, the poet and scholar Ruaraidh MacThómais.[27]

These special issues were often very good business: the Dutch and Belgian governments took 8000 copies of the Dutch-Flemish issue, and the print-run on it was 10 000, 'large for a specialist literary magazine anywhere', as Murray said proudly.[28] Proofing, laying out and cutting up the journal was a huge task, 'the equivalent of bringing out a paperback book—a slim volume of verse—every three months', Murray would say. 'It was good fun.'[29]

In spite of the journal's title, he declined to think of Australia as his sole province, and he published poetry from Canada, South Africa, the United States, New Zealand and Papua New Guinea; there were also Russian, Portuguese and German poems in translation, while after his visit to the Struga poetry festival in 1974, much Balkan material began to appear in his pages, along with Austrian poetry sent to him by the poet Herbert Kuhner whom he had befriended in Struga. Something of Murray's own cosmopolitanism and urbanity came through in *Poetry Australia*'s pages. Through his widening contacts he secured contributions from such luminaries as Ted Hughes, Seamus Heaney, Richard Murphy and Margaret Atwood.

He was also constantly on the lookout for new Australian talent, and among those who first published with *Poetry Australia* during his time as editor were Robert Gray, Peter Goldsworthy, Andrew Lansdown, Jennifer Rankin, Geoffrey Lehmann, Peter Porter, Kevin Hart, Peter Redgrove, Alan Gould, Gary Frances, Jennifer Hampton, William Burns, Paul Lake, John Foulcher, Jamie Grant, and Dennis O'Driscoll.[30]

He particularly welcomed submissions from writers on the other side of the Poetry Society split. A number, including the greatly gifted John Tranter,[31] whose early work had in fact been published by Perry and who resented what he regarded as Murray's takeover of *Poetry Australia*,[32] approached him in toe-dipping letters, asking whether they would be considered. 'I was amused at the self-protective tactics of this', Murray wrote, 'and always wrote back telling them not to be mad, that they'd be welcome to submit their material, but making no false promises as to its acceptance'.[33] He was determined to make the quality of submissions the test of whether they went in, no matter who they were from: as he told the expatriate poet Craig Powell, 'I'd print Beelzebub's eldest bastard if his poem was good enough'.[34]

For all Murray's good intentions, the split was not healed by his signals across the gulf, and as his reputation grew, he came to be seen as more of a threat by those who disliked his opinions. And those opinions were being widely disseminated. In addition to his work for *Poetry Australia*, which increasingly reflected his own wide tastes, he was of necessity earning other income by literary reviewing, at first for the *Sydney Morning Herald*, beginning in June 1973,[35] and gradually, as the acuity of his judgement and the extraordinary range of his reading drew attention, for many other publications as well. He was a rare combination, in a reviewer, of immense breadth of reference, generosity and extreme sharpness, and his opinions came to carry considerable weight; he was lionised at gatherings such as the Orange Festival of the Arts in 1973, and on reading tours such as to Tasmania in October the same year, for he now wore three hats, those of poet, editor and critic, and was carefully listened to. He was aware of this, and like T. S. Eliot, he consciously avoided commenting in print on contemporary poets whose work he did not admire, fearing to be thought jealous or malicious.

The Generation of '68 did not always feel the same compunction. When Murray's next volume, *Lunch & Counter Lunch*, appeared in October 1974, John Tranter in a review began by remarking, as if suppressing a yawn, that the volume was 'much what one would expect', slyly congratulated Murray on having become 'less jingoistic and more thoughtful', and remarked on his having produced 'a rather too clever sequence of sonnets about the poet's days at Sydney University' and 'a witty and extended exercise on the theme of broadbeans' (smack! though in retrospect it is Tranter who receives it, for 'The Broad Bean Sermon' would be one of the most widely admired and anthologised of Murray's poems). And Tranter then zeroed in on his main complaint, which was that Murray declined to dance to an American tune:

> It is worth noting, though, that there has been a growing interest in current overseas experiment among many of the younger local writers and readers of poetry, and it is difficult to fit Murray anywhere into this picture, so localised are many of his concerns.
>
> The avant-garde internationalist may find the scent of gum leaves a little overpowering in this book, and the author's insistence on a carefully articulated 'plain speech' a definite limitation to areas of experiment and possible discovery.[36]

And he concluded, with the satisfaction of the man finishing off a good job, 'In all, *Lunch & Counter Lunch* offers a varied, well-balanced and nourishing diet of home-grown poems'. Martin Johnston began his review on almost exactly the same note as Tranter: 'Les Murray's new book of poems, with its be-all and end-all title, is very much what one would have expected'.[37]

Apart from the Generation of '68, *Lunch & Counter Lunch* was welcomed by enthusiastic critics. David Malouf described the new volume as 'of astonishing dexterity and scope', and added boldly: 'There is no doubt about Murray's stature. He is a powerful poet, with all the gifts, one might want to assert, of a potentially great one. This new book reveals him at a point of crisis. Whichever way he now turns, it will be the key work of his career'.[38] Malouf also remarked on Murray's courage in raising ideas and issues so unfashionable in the Australia of the 1970s. His analysis was both sympathetic and extremely acute:

> The book is meant to make us uncomfortable. It is the work of an intelligent man who distrusts our modern intelligence and whose preferred faculties, one guesses, would be intuition, psychic vision, but also the countryman's plain commonsense and even plainer sense of decency. What I meant is that if what we have here is a conservative mind it is a very critical, complex and flexible one—and given the current climate, to be a conservative as Murray is might be the most way-out form of radicalism. There is in these poems a feeling of going hard against the tide. It is what gives them their strong sense of energy, but also, I think, a rather edgy, aggressive, defensive tone.[39]

Not everyone agreed with Malouf about the aggression. 'Murray's has become a very individual voice', Katharine England wrote, 'distinctively but not aggressively Australian, urbane, tolerant, detached but not unconcerned'.[40] Kevin Hart challenged head-on Tranter's notion that Murray was predictable, remarking, 'the area in which Murray is working—the purification of the Australian vernacular into a poetic language—is, I think, the most interesting and rewarding area of experimentation at the moment'.[41]

From the Australian expatriate Peter Porter, in a private letter, came praise that Murray particularly valued: 'I want you to know how much I admire the poems in "Lunch and Counter Lunch". With this book you become the best poet writing in Australia, and one of the best anywhere in the English-speaking world'.[42] Murray had met Porter through Geoffrey Lehmann in 1973 and had liked him at once in spite of finding him somewhat intimidating: he greatly respected Porter's opinion.

And Murray must have felt a particular satisfaction when Robert Gray, who seemed to be a recruit to the Generation of '68 but who would elude all categorisation and much else besides, managed to praise him in the pages of the enemy's journal, *New Poetry*:

> I don't know that many people have realized that in Les Murray we have one of the major Australian poets.
>
> I'm aware he writes a lot that detracts from such a stature—the 'yarning' poems, the heavy whimsicality and humorousness, the usually grating small poems—but at 38 he does have already a body of work one can speak of, I believe, alongside that of Slessor, Hope, Wright and Webb ... Les Murray is not just technically skilful, he is a masterly technician.

In contrast to Tranter, Gray picked out 'The Broad Bean Sermon' for particular praise: 'I must write about "The Broad Bean Sermon" in a separate paragraph—this is surely a classic; this most beautiful poem, about fecundity, tolerance, diversity, presented with so much sensuous detail, which reminds one of the great things of which Les Murray is capable'. And Gray, going on to compare Murray's recent work with that of the later Auden, remarked, 'the concentration and precision of his language has never been greater than here. He is someone of the highest craftsmanship and intelligence'.[43] Murray had carried off these plaudits under the guns of the enemy.

Only years later, and after repeated slights from the Generation of '68, would Murray reply, and then straightforwardly, in a review of a set of recordings of Australian poets reading their own work, in 1976. To Bob Adamson he was kindly and generous, but clear-sighted:

> A man with a slender but fitfully genuine gift, he has to work rather desperately to sustain an overblown legend he once whomped up for himself out of hysteria and bullying and gang warfare in a time and milieu which was receptive to such strategies ... It is the spirit behind all the promotions and posturings and literary triple-takes, behind the polemics and the interminable rather pathetic public displays of complex naughtiness and 'erudition', behind the dashes to Canberra and elsewhere to fight off the challenge of younger bucks. It seems least active, least devouring, when he returns to his spirit-country up there on the Hawkesbury estuary, that intricate country of mudflats and mangroves and fishermen. There, he can be simple, and approach a personal centre from which he may yet do good, even very good work. When changing fashion strips the legend away, I think the Hawkesbury will save him.[44]

John Tranter was neither thug nor fraud, and Murray liked him personally and greatly admired his gifts, so that there is in his remarks on Tranter's work a genuine regret for opportunities lost:

If most of Adamson's work at this stage can be classed as poetry for people who don't know what poetry is, that of John Tranter must be called poetry for people who don't *like* poetry ... With Tranter's work, mannered, controlled, discussing feeling rather than evoking it and disciplined out of any simplicity or largesse, we reach an era of wholly conscious art, an era in which poets must try to convince intellectuals that poetry really is a high-order, non-trivial, productive thing, worthy of serious regard. We thus get a poetry which approaches the condition of say, calculus, and foregoes all human identification. It becomes intensely respectable, but with an imposed and rather despairing respectability. Poetry has frequently been a courtier art, but no despot of the past ever made us perform contortions half as severe as those demanded by the kings of our new academic cities-of-refuge.[45]

And with that Murray passed on. Most of the time he was too busy with his increasingly demanding writing to spend much time troubling himself about others. In any case, as Valerie noticed, he had an extraordinary capacity for dealing with an issue, giving it his complete concentration, and then putting it behind him and moving on. Posterity would judge between him and the Generation of '68, whose already dated name would soon fall out of use. After some years members of the group would seek to deny the links between them: Tranter, asked about his alliance with Adamson, would reply that it no longer existed.[46]

But while the alliance lasted its members exerted great influence in Australia's small literary world, and in the case of some of them, enmity to Murray was the effect of visceral dislike of his opinions, compounded with envy of his gifts.[47] 'I know he's wrong—*but you've got to hand it to him*', as Ken Bolton would summarise and exemplify this attitude.[48]

The publication in 1976 of the selection Murray called *The Vernacular Republic* gave many critics reason for a reassessment of Murray's by now very substantial poetic achievement. 'In the whole of Australian poetry only Slessor and Wright have a more satisfying achievement', wrote Robert Gray, adding, 'And Murray is a young poet yet, only 38'.[49] Peter Porter went further: 'I would rather read Murray's poetry than that of any but a handful of writers working in English today'.[50] Several critics saw his title as an accurate pointer to his national importance: 'He is like a modern equivalent of the Gaelic bards who recorded, exhorted, celebrated and made beautiful the life of the tribe around them', wrote Roger McDonald.[51] And Carol Treloar remarked, 'The poems work collectively towards an unwritten cultural statement about the present and ideal quality of Australian life ... Murray seems to have a kind of cultural mission comparable in intent to Yeats', adding that Murray showed more compassion than the Irish poet to those with whom he does not identify.[52] His poetic reputation continued to grow, though he had some regrets about publishing a selection: 'When you sign up for a Selected Poems', he told Craig Powell, 'it's hard to believe yourself any longer in the first flush of poetic youth'.[53]

Meanwhile he had added another arrow to his quiver. His reviews imperceptibly shaded into yet another form of writing, the essay. Increasingly, reviews such as that just quoted, in which he discussed recordings of Tranter, Adamson and others, wittily titled 'More Wow Than Flutter', were long enough to constitute an essay length, carefully argued survey of contemporary Australian poetry, and he was as active in producing them as he was fertile of poetry. In addition, from the early 1970s he began turning out a stream of highly polished, powerfully argued essays on the theoretical underpinnings of his own work, and on the definition of Australian culture and its place in the world.

He conducted, for instance, a brilliant, mutually respectful debate with Peter Porter on the Boeotian and Athenian influences that feed into Australian poetry.[54] Boeotia, north-west of urban-minded, slave-holding Athens, was scorned by Athenians as rude, boorish and stupid, its arts condemned as old-fashioned and tedious. Murray, who had first felt the sting of exactly this scorn at Taree High, pointed out that Hesiod and Pindar were Boeotians, and that the only great Athenian poets were dramatists. 'Boeotia, in her perennial incarnations, replaces theatre with dance or pageant—or sport; philosophy she subordinates to religion and precept, and in politics, she habitually prefers daimon to demos . . . she clings to older ideas of the importance of family and the display of individual human quality under stress'.[55]

He took his stand firmly on the Boeotian side of the argument and reinterpreted such literary forefathers as Slessor as Boeotians too, arguing that 'in any sense broad enough to admit the great majority of Australians, our culture is still in its Boeotian phase and any distinctiveness we possess is still firmly anchored in the bush'.[56] He rejected the false contrast between metropolitan and provincial (he did not have to say that his own poetry refuted it) but he also firmly placed the Generation of '68 (whom he tactfully did not name) as Athenians, living in a world of fashion, coterie-art and the pursuit of artistic innovation as an *effect*: their modernist rituals 'could be seen as repetitive, cyclic and derivative, and the practitioners, with one or two exceptions, lacked the necessary talent or even intelligence'.[57]

He produced essays extrapolating from his personal concerns, such as the problems of reading and teaching his poetry, and other essays on nationally important topics, central to his thought, such as the definition of an Australian republic, the need for state funding for the arts, the troubled relationship between poets and the academic world, the ramifications of the race debate in Australia, and the urgent need to nurture an Australian spiritual sense. These essays were widely read when they first appeared, in journals such as *Quadrant*, and they attained permanent life when he reprinted them in the volumes of prose he published irregularly from the late 1970s—*The Peasant Mandarin: Prose Pieces* (1978), *Persistence In Folly: Selected Prose Writings* (1984), *Blocks and Tackles* (1990), *The Paperbark Tree* (1992), and *A Working Forest* (1997).

Murray rapidly emerged as an important poet-essayist, in the tradition of Eliot. His prose style, lucid, erudite, logical and urbane, was almost as flexible and sensitive as his poetry, and he helped to stimulate, guide and feed debate on issues that were to be central to Australian national life. 'One of Australia's natural and assured essayists', the critic and author Brian Matthews would call him.[58] His influence was felt and acknowledged by politicians such as Kim Beazley,[59] scholars such as Bernard Smith[60] and Rhys Jones,[61] and writers and thinkers such as Donald Horne.[62] Often he was seen to be well ahead of the debate, as on republicanism and arts funding, and his views were commonly unfashionable: neither criticism troubled him. By the 1980s he had become an important and widely acknowledged voice in the public debates shaping Australian cultural life.

He continued to collect distinctions and honours. On 5 January 1974 he got the good news that the Literature Board was giving him another grant for the next year; on 3 May he heard that the Boarstone Poetry Award was including 'The Flying Mural', one of the poems from *Lunch & Counter Lunch*, in their volume *Best Poems of 1973*. In June 1974 he won the National Book Council Award of $1000 for *Lunch & Counter Lunch*, and was invited to attend the Struga Poetry Festival in Yugoslavia at the end of September, all expenses paid. He took the opportunity afforded by the trip to give readings in both Britain (where he stayed with Peter Porter in London, the two becoming close friends)[63] and Denmark, where Aarhus had become a centre for the study of Australian literature. This was the first such foreign reading tour he had attempted. It was enough of a success financially for him to plan more, as his reputation in Europe grew: the *Times Literary Supplement* became a regular outlet for his latest poems from the mid-1970s.

But even as he travelled and chatted in a multitude of tongues to the poets who gathered at Struga, on beautiful Lake Ohrid ('like a successful, populated Lake George')[64] and read aloud to great crowds from a bridge over the town's river, the event being televised nationally, he was itching to write poetry. On the cardboard back of one of his writing-pads, among the addresses of poets he was meeting, he was jotting down images as they occurred:

> Freedom is the angel of imprisonment
> The temporary angel of entrammelment
>
> Innocent as a spoon
>
> Belly dancers—like boughs in a current, rhythmically shaking their leaves
>
> Limbs of the harbour put out yachts
>
> Ships of all flags on the spring tide
> Steel walls chained and wrinkling ride
>
> Boy with a jackplane/making moustaches of wood

'I'm spoiling to write some poems', he told Valerie, 'probably a run of short lyrics, giving the long meditative mode a rest for a while'.[65] The poems of his next volume were already on the way: several of the images he jotted down at Struga would find their place in 'Impulse Resisted on the Manly Ferry', a poem of sexual temptation and self-restraint that makes punning use of the name of the Sydney suburb.

His bold experiment in going free-lance seemed to have succeeded: he was not sinking but standing, and even striding. His combined income from grants, publication, editing and reviewing, together with Valerie's steady labour as a teacher, meant that by the end of 1974 Murray was able to realise a long-held dream: he bought part of the farm from which his father had been evicted. On 5 November 1974 he paid $8456 for a section of the farm known to the Murrays as 'the forty acres',[66] and within weeks began the erection of a tiny prefabricated weatherboard house there, not much larger than a suburban two-car garage and costing just $12 000.[67] His intention was to move his father back onto the land that in Murray's view had always been his. He made the mistake of agreeing to have ceilings only eight feet (244 cm) high to save money, with the result that the little house, no bigger than Cecil's original shack, proved exhaustingly hot in summer: but in 1975, when his father finally moved in, Murray felt he had a toehold in his ancestral country, his spirit place, again. More than that, he felt he had gone some way towards righting the terrible wrong visited on his father.

In the triumphant poem he wrote about the purchase, 'Laconics: The Forty Acres', taking its form from an Irish Gaelic original,[68] he names its previous owners, his Great-Uncle Jim, his Grandfather Allan, his Uncle Reg who bought it when his father could not, and his cousin Leith who evicted his father. He allows Leith (whom he would later get along with well enough when the two became neighbours)[69] a shred of anonymity by calling him 'Brett':

We have bought the Forty Acres,
prime brush land.

If Bunyah is a fillet
this paddock is the eye.

The creek half-moons it,
log-deep, or parting rocks.

The corn-ground by now
has had forty years' grassed spell.

Up in the swamp
are paperbarks, coin-sized frogs—

The Forty, at last,
our beautiful deep land

it was Jim's, it was Allan's,
it was Reg's, it is Dad's—

Brett wanted it next
but he'd evicted Dad

for bitter porridge
many cold returns.

And the poem ends with a beautifully restrained paean of praise for his Homeland, a busy planning of pleasure, a joyful acknowledgment of possession:

And the orchard will go there
and we'll re-roof the bare pole barn.

Our croft, our Downs,
our sober, shining land.

The friends who knew how much this purchase meant to him wrote to congratulate him: 'I read somewhere a poem of yours from which I learnt that you had become a propertied member of the landed gentry', joked Con Kiriloff. 'I remember well how nostalgia crept into your voice whenever you mentioned Bunyah.'[70] From this point on Murray planned to move back to Bunyah himself as soon as he was earning enough from his writing to be able to do so, though he was aware of the dangers isolation would present: 'The point of writing in the city is, of course, not libraries but *friends*',[71] he told Penny Nelson.

From now on he spent his holidays back in Bunyah: the little hot house on the forty acres became to him all that Thoor Ballylee was to Yeats, but with the difference that Murray had been born and brought up at Bunyah, and belonged to it finally. His children came to love Bunyah too: Cecil indulged them completely and let them smoke, ride horses, swim in the creek and generally run wild on the property, much as Murray had done in his Huckleberry years. The contrast with their father's strict discipline made them look forward to every holiday: it was a family joke that Christina would arrive at Bunyah laughing and leave crying. She particularly loved her grandfather's vivid stories of his childhood and youth, and the endless tales he could spin about a wonderful imaginary underground world.[72] These tales had first been told to Les Murray, in his childhood.[73]

Murray now resumed his Sydney University habit of inviting his friends down to Bunyah, and proudly showing them around. They noticed that Murray did no work whatever on the farm. One afternoon he took a new friend, the writer Jamie Grant, to see his father digging a hole for a fence-post. When they reached the spot where Cecil was labouring in the heat, Murray sat himself comfortably on the post to enjoy the spectacle. 'I dug a hole once', he remarked to Grant. His father straightened up, crimson and streaming sweat: 'Not on my bloody farm you didn't', he growled.[74]

Much of Murray's poetry now focused itself with renewed sharpness on his home valley, and the contrasting values of bush and city: he believed that the rural values and decencies from which he drew his own strength were central to Australian culture. It was in 1976 that he wrote one of his best-known poems on the subject, 'Sydney and the Bush', which would appear in his next volume:

> When Sydney and the Bush meet now
> there is antipathy

and fashionable suburbs float
at night, far out to sea.

When Sydney rules without the Bush
she is a warder's shop
with heavy dancing overhead,
the music will not stop

and when the drummers want a laugh
Australians are sent up.
When Sydney and the Bush meet now
there is no common ground.

It was early in 1976 too that he wrote an extraordinary cycle of poems, 'The Buladelah-Taree Holiday Song Cycle', in which he drew on the oldest manifestations of Australian rural culture, Aboriginal oral poetry. During his planning of the ill-fated volume of Aboriginal poetry, he had read and greatly admired Ronald M. Berndt's translations of the Wonguri-Mandjikai Moon-Bone Cycle of poems from Arnhem Land.[75] Around Christmas 1975, on a trip to Bunyah, he conceived of writing a cycle of poems in the style and metre of Berndt's translation.

> As I thought about it, I realised it would be necessary to incorporate in it elements from all three main Australian cultures, Aboriginal, rural and urban. But I would arrange them in their order of distinctiveness, with the senior culture setting the tone and controlling the movement of the poem. What I was after was an enactment of a longed-for fusion of all three cultures ... The poem would necessarily celebrate my own spirit country.[76]

Murray focused it on the annual holiday migration of families to the bush or the sea, 'going back to their ancestral places in a kind of unacknowledged spiritual walkabout', as he put it, 'looking for their country in order to draw sustenance from it. Or newcomers looking for the real Australia'.[77] He wrote the poem in thirteen sections, as in the Moon-Bone Cycle, producing it in two bursts about a month apart, the hiatus coming between sections six and seven.

The Jindyworobak poets of the 1940s had been mocked for the thinness of their understanding of Aboriginal culture, and Murray was taking a great risk with this daringly experimental poem: sharp knives were waiting to accuse him of cultural arrogance, or ignorance, or daring to speak for Aboriginal people. That he brought it off triumphantly is a tribute not just to his powers as a poet, but to his deep knowledge of Aboriginal culture and to his refusal to admit the inevitability of cultural apartheid in Australia. 'It's a reconciling poem', he told the scholar Laurie Hergenhan.[78]

David Malouf, lecturing on Caliban's naming-magic, would remark on 'the extraordinary way our own Aborigines have possessed the land in their minds, through folkstories, taboos, song cycles, and made it part of the very fabric of their living as we never can'.[79] Murray, always opposed to the division of Australians, always on the lookout for convergence, riposted crisply, 'We can, and some of us do, possess the land imaginatively in very much the Aboriginal way',[80] and his poem richly demonstrated what he meant.

> It is good to come out after driving and walk on bare grass;
> walking out, looking all around, relearning that country.
> Looking out for snakes, and looking out for rabbits as well;
> going into the shade of myrtles to try their cupped climate, swinging by one
>   hand around them,
> in that country of the Holiday . . .
> stepping behind trees to the dam, as if you had a gun,
> to that place of the Wood Duck,
> to that place of the Wood Duck's Nest,
> proving you can still do it; looking at the duck who hasn't seen you,
> the mother duck who'd run Catch Me (broken wing) I'm Fatter (broken wing),
>   having hissed to her children.

Like all of Murray's work, the poem cycle is a magical naming and evocation which gives everyone who reads it the sense of possession, of being possessed by this land, which he rejoiced in. The cycle concludes with a subtle evocation of Australian spirituality, the word 'holiday' reverting to its original meaning, in poetry so simple that the reader cannot see how it is done, but so effective as to suspend the breath:

> People go outside and look at the stars, and at the melon-rind moon,
> the Scorpion going down into the mountains, over there towards Waukivory,
>   sinking into the tree-line,
> in the time of the Rockmelons, and of the Holiday . . .
> the Cross is rising on his elbow, above the glow of the horizon;
> carrying a small star in his pocket, he reclines there brilliantly,
> above the Alum Mountain, and the lakes threaded on the Myall River, and
>   above the Holiday.

Little that has been written in the twentieth century can match the power of this. The sequence was at once recognised as the achievement it is, and it won the C. J. Dennis Prize of $1000, news Murray received with pleasure in Brisbane, where he was travelling with his son Daniel and Jamie Grant, in September 1976; that same month Murray heard from the Director of the Australia Council that he had been awarded a Senior Literature Board Fellowship of $10 000 a year for three years.[81] The battle of the books would continue for decades, but Murray was not allowing it to paralyse him.

March 1961: On a hike down the Woronora River, Murray bet that he could spend the weekend without shoes or trousers—and won. *(Photograph: John Mulhall)*

Les Murray in the doorway of a shed on his father's farm, Bunyah, c.1962.
(*Photograph: John Mulhall*)

Woronora River, 1962: Peter Barden standing by to repel pirates. (*Photograph: John Mulhall*)

At Bunyah, 1962: Les Murray conducting a slave auction over Peter Barden.
(Photograph: John Mulhall)

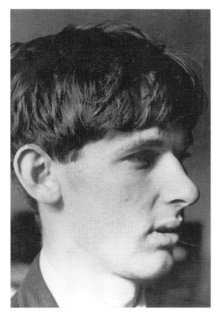

Bob Ellis at Sydney University in 1962, photographed by Peter Barden, who added a caption: 'Well actually the emus were all on my mother's side!'

Les Murray clowning at Bunyah: the farmer warning intruders off his land.
(Photograph: John Mulhall)

Valerie Morelli, photographed by her father Gino about the time Murray met her.

CHAPTER FIFTEEN
PUBLIC AND PRIVATE
1977–81

~

It is more shameful to doubt one's friends than to be duped by them.

DE LA ROCHEFOUCAULD

Murray's family continued to grow. He and Valerie had had a third child, Clare Louisa, on 16 May 1974, and another, Alexander Joseph Cecil, in May 1978. The little house on Edgar Street began to seem too small, and another room would be added in 1983, so that Daniel would have a bedroom of his own. Murray continued to work tremendously hard at his desk through these years, but according to his daughter Christina, he simply declined to do anything that looked like housework.[1] She was eleven when Clare was born, but regularly had to change the baby's nappy for him, and she also had to come home from school almost every day at lunchtime to feed Clare.[2] In 1975 Valerie went back to teaching, at Crows Nest Boys High, where she would be the English as a Second Language teacher for the next decade, with time out on maternity leave.[3]

Murray remained a strict, even severe, parent, particularly when in the grip of the bouts of terrible depression that continued to affect him, and Daniel and Christina continued to fear his entirely unpredictable rages. Christina was still occasionally beaten with a belt until she reached puberty, and she was grateful to sit out of his reach at family meals.[4] Valerie did her best to restrain her husband, but her success was limited. 'Les maintains staunchly that he may lose his temper, but then the episode is finished', her diary recorded: 'I know on the other hand that we live in a lightning-strike zone and it will strike again and again'.[5]

But Murray began to mellow and relax with the arrival of Clare in 1974. From the time she first smiled, at six weeks, she could charm him, and as she grew Christina and Daniel noticed enviously that she seemed able to get away with anything. Even Clare was smacked, once, at the age of three,[6] but soon after Alexander's birth Murray stopped the beatings: 'Suddenly it all dropped off me. I thought no, you don't do that'.[7] There would continue to be random slaps directed mostly against Daniel: Murray's upbringing, good and ill, could not simply be discarded at will. But the cold premeditated hidings, always rare, were at an end. Valerie he never struck, and in their occasional verbal quarrels his children noticed that she gave as good as she got in vocabulary and volume.[8]

He was often away from home, visiting a rapidly lengthening list of campuses as a writer in residence: at the University of New England in May 1978, in Edinburgh and Stirling from February to May 1981, at Newcastle University in 1982, at the University of New South Wales from April to May 1983, Sydney University in 1984 and again in 1985, at La Trobe University in 1988 and so on. He made a great impression on campuses, for though he never ceased to regard public intellectuals as 'journalists, parasites and social climbers, the enemies of my blood',[9] he remained one of the most agile, energetic, wide-ranging and sure-footed of intellectuals himself. 'I have a lot of time for scholars', he would write, 'as distinct from the criminal social dynamic enshrined in universities'.[10]

He also travelled constantly to give readings, in Tasmania in October 1981, in India in 1987, Tasmania again in January 1988, Britain in May 1988, Armidale in July 1988, and shorter visits without number to read to schools, for he was inexhaustibly generous to students of his work. He was a striking figure at poetic gatherings, and almost everyone seems to have found him instantly likeable, as the poet Alan Gould would remember:

> I had to go down to a Poetry 1975 Festival that was being organised by Grace Perry at Macquarie University. I went down in the capacity of being the editor of a magazine called *Canberra Poetry*—it was for the region—and I was accompanied by Mark O'Connor and Kevin Hart.
>
> We were all in rooms at Dunmore Lang College. The first time we went down to dinner there was an enormous fellow in a vermilion shirt—I say vermilion forcibly, because it was very bright—and the trousers of a double-breasted suit—he put the jacket on later in the evening, I think. We just stood in the queue behind him, exchanging the kind of pleasantries one does; and then later in the evening, he read a poem about brush turkeys. The three of us from Canberra voted the line 'Turkey work, turkey work' as the best line of the week; and from then on we had easy bantering-type sessions.[11]

Gould's reaction to Murray was typical of his impact at these gatherings. He attracted attention by his size and his dress: he often wore a baseball cap to cover his large balding head, and a vast jumper, knitted for him by Valerie, which appeared to have been designed to use the last of two dozen batches of different wools, and whose dazzling multi-coloured stripes ran to the horizon. In later years he wore other brilliantly striped sweaters knitted for him by the poet Jennifer Compton, and to which she gave names: 'The Gorgeous Hydrangea', 'The Vasty Fields of France'.[12]

He was hard to miss at first sight, but it was once he began to read that he really drew attention. Not all his readings were successful, but when he overcame his nervousness and found the venue to his taste, his performance could be very striking. Eyes turned up as if in a trance, he recited rather than read his wonderful poems, the hushed room seeming to light up with flashes of beauty and emotion, inexhaustibly renewed. The contrast between his massive physical presence and this verbal nimbleness, all swerve, slash and pirouette, was astonishing, and he knew it. Years later he would describe his reading in 'Performance', written after seeing a firework display at Krambach:[13]

> I starred last night, I shone:
> I was footwork and firework in one,
>
> a rocket that wriggled up and shot
> darkness with a parasol of brilliants
> and a peewee descant on a flung bit;
> I was busters of glitter-bombs expanding
> to mantle and aurora from a crown,
> I was fouettés, falls of blazing paint,
> para-flares spot-welding cloudy heaven,
> loose gold off fierce toeholds of white,
> a finale red-tongued as a haka leap:
> that too was a butt of all right!
>
> As usual after any triumph, I was
> of course inconsolable.

Such successes left him depressed and with the feeling that he did not deserve the praise, he would explain years later: 'Acclaim, applause, recognition used to leave me feeling absolutely wrecked. You knew you'd have to pay for it'.[14] Or, as he put it to Geoff Page, 'The receipt of affection from hundreds of people can throw me into a despond for days!'[15]

The longest of his absences from home at this time was the stay he made at Edinburgh and Stirling, from February to May 1981. His appointment at Stirling was the result of an earlier meeting with an academic from there, Angela Smith, who had encountered Murray at a conference in Fiji in January 1980. She was impressed by his poetry, by his prodigious memory, and by his love for Scotland: 'On a conference trip I found myself beside him on a boat to a small island. I was amazed, as we chatted, at his knowledge of Scotland—he had total recall of all the landscape, features of places we talked about, where roads bent to avoid lochs and so on'.[16] For his part, he thought Angela Smith 'a deeply sensible scholar and the kindest of people'.[17] Smith, who taught Commonwealth Literature in Stirling, arranged the residence in 1981 for Murray, and his arrival for the start of it was propitiously marked by the appearance, in the *Times Literary Supplement*, of one of his most cerebral poems, 'Bent Water in the Tasmanian Highlands'.[18]

For all the interest he had in his Gaelic background, he did not feel at home in Scotland, and he was increasingly struck by the colonialism of the country, which he feared was well on the way to becoming 'Scotlandshire'. After having trouble with immigration at Heathrow on 14 February, he noted in the pocket diary he kept during the visit: 'Country which invited me did not control its own immigration matters'.[19]

His Edinburgh flat, to his gloom, had a bath and no shower: Murray's weight was now approaching 130 kilograms, and a bath was of little use to him. 'And, dryland point, I always felt nervous about wasting water in a bath!' he would say years later.[20] Between 27 and 30 March he wrote a longing poem about showers, telling his diary, 'Finished shower poem, slowly and savouringly—only 46 days now till I get one!'[21] Not surprisingly, 'Shower' is a cascading, luxurious, tropical affair:

> From the metal poppy
> this good blast of trance
> arriving as shock, private cloudburst blazing down,
> worst in a boarding-house greased tub, or a barrack with competitions,
> best in a stall, this enveloping passion of Australians:
> tropics that sweat for you, torrent that braces with its heat,
> inflames you with its chill, action, sauna, inverse bidet,
> sleek vertical coruscating ghost of your inner river . . .

Part of the time he had to cook for himself, a problem he solved 'by buying tins of rice-cream and pouring them down my throat without plates because it saved on washing-up'.[22] In Edinburgh he met Peter Porter, with whom he had stayed on a previous visit to London: on this occasion the two renewed their friendship, though Murray found Porter somewhat intimidating: 'as usual felt put in shade by PP's fluent conversation, which makes me tonguetied'.[23] In a poem he would write for Porter's seventieth birthday in 1999, Murray would show his gratitude to Porter:

> Thank you for much hospitality.
> A pillar of good talk all night
> you were, and of company by day.[24]

Once he moved on to Stirling he met again the Canadian poet and critic Dennis Lee,[25] first encountered in Fiji and whose work he liked. He also saw a great deal of Angela Smith and her hospitable husband Grahame. For their sake he liked Stirling University, and when its funding was savagely cut the next year he wrote a powerful letter to Britain's Prime Minister Margaret Thatcher, on 9 October 1981, begging her to reconsider. He begged in vain, though Stirling would survive and, in 1992, give Murray an honorary Doctorate of Letters.[26]

The best result of his time in Scotland, however, was that the distance from home somehow gave him the objectivity and courage he needed to broach in poetry the terrible subject of his mother's death and all it had meant to him. His diary records his struggle to write 'The Steel' and the other poems of the deeply moving series for his mother:

Wed 1 April: Meant to work on difficult poem abt. Mum's death but dodged that by writing letters.

Thur 2 April: Troglodytic day, happily spent writing a card to the Morellis, then a poem about the spiritual quality I call sprawl; typed poem ['The Quality of Sprawl'] in evening and sent to Alan Gould . . . Feel I've entered a rising wave as reg[ards] Poems—but will it survive interruption of C'hagen trip? [He was to go on to read in Denmark after finishing his Scottish stay.]

Sat 4 April: Did repairs to essay on interest ['First Essay on Interest', a poem].[27]

Mon 13 April: Clerical celibacy (& lay continence) are not only valuable as witness, but ways of dying for others.

Wed 15 April: Began writing the dangerous, unavoidable poem on Mum's death (30 years ago this Sunday)—will have to show it to Dad if it works, and respect his wishes. Horrible prospect of his grief & anger. Got some distance with poem, retreated to bed and insomnia.

The poem about his mother was 'dangerous' because of his awareness of the causes of his own mental instability: he was risking a breakdown in facing his ghosts. But he gritted his teeth and pressed forward:

Thur 16 April: Went on with poem, stirring deep feelings & buried stuff . . . (Night) Rough draft of poem finished now. Will let it sit for a while.

Good Friday 17 April: Failed to dispel melancholy.

Holy Saturday 18 April: . . . Then read Gunn's The Silver Darlings & let the poem percolate.

Easter Sunday 19 April: Worked on poem, with misgivings.

20 April: Worked on poem in forenoon . . .

22 April: Worked on Mum's poem in ev[enin]g.

23 April: Poem three-quarters done, but seems to have stuck. Sat over it for hours, then went out to do business.

25 April: Snow gone by yesterday afternoon leaving pleasant memory of heavenly meringue! Worked on poem, endured frustration & some breakthrus. Bed early.

Sunday 26 April: Stir crazy in arvo: went to see Lees, but found DL [Dennis Lee] busy on vital typing. Another seven days completed, and so's the poem, at least in preliminary form. Will type up tomorrow and let sit again, for maturing.

Mon 27 April: Wrote letters in forenoon . . . typed up First poem for my Mother and Midsummer Ice sep[arate]. from main sequence.

29 April: Bought presents for home, wrote letters, thought of additions to Steel (Mum's poem).

Sat 2 May: Worked on Mum's poem, refining & polishing, getting points clear.

And on the point of finishing this, one of his most searching and powerful poems, written with tears as he told a friend years later,[28] he doubted the worth of his work and feared the exposure he brought on himself and his family:

> Sun 3 May: Finished fair copy (hand) of poem, began typing it up. Feel cold and depressed. How much of my work really travels, or would travel if allowed? The poem as typed is *true*—and delivers me & my family into the hands of the snobs. But so what?
>
> Mon 4 May: Finished typing Steel this morning.[29]

He also realised how much he had forgotten his mother:

> The death of our very closest seems to set off a mechanism of forgetting in us, and when Mum died I was silly enough to stay stunned for too long, and thereby lose much that I should have held onto. Which meant that I, of all people, piled more death on top of her temporal death, and failed in my duty of memory.[30]

The sequence so drained him that after it he wrote nothing for three months.[31] But in due time, having opened this vein, he would structure the whole of his next volume, *The People's Otherworld*, around his mother, 'the urban and semi-urban world of mining and engineering, the world of the Arnalls, my mother's people'.³²

He spent a brief stint in Denmark, doing readings arranged by two new friends, with both of whom he stayed. They were the Welsh poet John Barnie, who would help him to get a selection of his work published in Denmark in the form of a chapbook he called *Equanimities*,³³ and the Australian expatriate Bruce Clunies Ross, whom he had met in Aarhus in 1978 and again in Augsburg in 1979, where Clunies Ross was delighted by his courage in criticising Patrick White at a conference largely devoted to the novelist.³⁴

Murray, who had met White on several occasions and thought him a curmudgeon, said briskly of his writing, 'He has a tin ear and is intellectually thin',³⁵ an opinion that an assembly of very serious German White-worshippers in Augsburg thought blasphemy. It was exacerbated when Murray added defiantly, 'And he can't write!' Clunies Ross, a man of great erudition and cultural depth, was to recall with amusement, 'So when he walked out of the session, everyone just stood as far away as possible'. He added, 'I think Les is the complete antithesis of White and I really like that'.³⁶

He would become a good friend, whom Murray looked up whenever he revisited Denmark (where Clunies Ross was struck by the fluency of Murray's Danish),³⁷ and he would prove one of the most penetrating and appreciative critics of Murray's work. Towards the end of the century he was to say that Murray, in the way of great poets, had 'changed the whole tradition of Australian poetry', adding,

> His ability to write that highly polyphonic poetry which is operating at so many levels all the time consistently, no one else [in Australia] can do that. There is no other modern poet who can do it either. I often think that Les is almost like a metaphysical poet transposed into the modern world. Les has fulfilled that idea of the major poet who reorders the whole tradition, because we all look at the past in Australian poetry differently now that Les has arrived, and one of the differences is that he's actually raised it up. I mean, for instance, we think more of [Charles] Harpur now that Les has arrived. He's made us go back to Harpur and see things in Harpur that perhaps we didn't see before . . . Before Les we had two traditions running side by side: the ballad or vernacular tradition, and as it were the high tradition—even in Judith Wright—but he combines them brilliantly in all those great serious poems with titles like 'The Dream of Wearing Shorts Forever' which is a serious poem, but a very funny one as well.³⁸

Although Murray had enjoyed himself in Europe, he was glad to board the Qantas flight for Australia:

Tues 12 May: On to QF002 for home! . . . Slept as much as poss—easy on 5/6 empty aircraft. Retained sleeping-seats next to me in face of Indonesian soccer team, Singapore to Sydney. Different if they'd been League players.

Thursday 14 May: Home at last! Praise God, all well. Bunyah tomorrow.[39]

In spite of his dislike of being away from home, he found time to attend a bewildering whirl of writers' festivals, as his international reputation grew: in Struga in 1974, Rotterdam in 1977, 1979, 1989, and 1998, Venice in 1979, Aarhus in 1978, and Adelaide in 1972, where he again met Wole Soyinka the Nigerian playwright, this time liking him less than he had in Wales in 1965. He also met Ted Hughes, for whom he would write 'Anthropomorphics' and who would influence him by reaction. Murray liked Hughes, enjoyed his animal poems, and would strive to avoid imitating them when he wrote *Translations from the Natural World*. But he was deeply suspicious of Hughes's reworking of biblical material. 'Don't go to him for your religious instruction', he would advise John Barnie in later years: 'He's a sensationalist and a witch'.[40]

Murray returned to the Adelaide Festival in 1976 and 1988, and attended writers' gatherings in Fiji in 1980 and Melbourne in September 1988, made a wide-ranging Literature Board-funded tour of the United States and Canada in 1980 with David Malouf and Vincent Buckley, and so on as long as his energy lasted. He kept up this travelling even after he became a diabetic, financial need driving him to use his energy to the limit.

The trip with Malouf and Buckley, Murray's first visit to North America, had its ticklish side according to the account Murray subsequently gave Mark O'Connor. Two rooms had been booked at most stops for the three poets, so that two of them had to share. Murray, though he thought Buckley 'a failed poet and a toad',[41] and would have much preferred a room to himself, had to share with him repeatedly. He continued to smart from his belief that Buckley had told friends in Melbourne, in 1961, that Murray was a Nazi ('It's still believed by some'),[42] and he retaliated by calling Buckley 'Vin Blank', or later, 'Vin Ordinaire'.[43] In later years he recalled with relish the American critic Stanley Kunitz asking him during this tour, 'This old Professor Burkley—who saddled you with him?'[44]

On this trip, at a lunch in the flat of the Canadian-born poet Mark Strand in Greenwich Village, Murray met Joseph Brodsky, who greatly admired Murray's poetry: in a review Brodsky had remarked, 'it would be as myopic to regard Mr Murray as an Australian poet as to call Yeats an Irishman. He is, quite simply, the one by whom the language lives'. He now strongly advised Murray to change his American publisher Persea, whose distribution was poor: on his advice Murray switched to Farrar Straus & Giroux, who would handle his American publications from then on. Murray was grateful to Brodsky, and liked him in spite of his long, obscene stories about Tsarist guards officers: 'He comes from St Petersburg after all. I get along with Russians and he of all Russians I get along with best. That's one fellow I wouldn't mind spending a week with at all'.[45]

The West Indian poet Derek Walcott was invited to the lunch too, and knocked for a long time downstairs without being heard. When he was eventually admitted Murray asked him why he had not simply climbed the fire escape. 'You're thinking this fucking black man is going to climb up a fire escape?' said Walcott, who believed that to do so would invite being shot as a burglar. 'Oh, that's right, you're black, yeah', said Murray. 'I forgot.'[46] Murray would continue to meet Walcott at various international poetry gatherings: in 1989, he recalled, Walcott and he were drinking in a big square in Rotterdam, talking about their humble origins: 'Walcott slouched back in profound self-satisfaction and general benevolence and he said, "Les, when you was a young man masturbatin' on your farm, did you ever think that one day you would be sitting here in Europe hobnobbing with Susan Fucking Sontag?"'[47]

Murray hated being without his family on these journeys, and rejoiced in the few on which Valerie could accompany him: after the Rotterdam Festival in 1977, for instance, which Murray attended with Kevin Hart, Alan Gould and Tom Shapcott, he and Valerie travelled together through Ireland, the UK, Austria and central Europe, Murray being much impressed by Budapest, 'one of the most splendid cities I've ever seen'. More than that, it was Valerie's birthplace:

> It was moving to stay in the house Valerie was born in . . . and to meet the uncle who carried her through the street fighting in 1944 to catch the last Red Cross train to Switzerland. A fine bloke. The family was fabulously hospitable, and very moved to have V. back among them however briefly. In Dublin we stayed with Seamus Heaney, a fine man from the North, and fed our souls on ancient treasures.[48]

He enjoyed being the guest of Heaney and his wife Marie, though he thought the Irish poet the most guarded of human beings, who followed to the letter his mother's injunction, 'Whatever you say, say nothing'.[49] But he also thought Heaney 'a most generous spirit'.[50]

Steadily growing recognition of Murray's powers brought an increasing stream of prizes: the Grace Leven Prize, which he had first won for *The Ilex Tree*, he received again for *The Boys Who Stole The Funeral* in 1980; he also won the Australian Literature Society Gold Medal for *The People's Otherworld*, as well as the New South Wales Premier's Prize for Poetry, the

Canadian-Australian Literary Award, the Christopher Brennan Award and the National Book Council Banjo Award, all in 1984; the Christopher Brennan Award, the Fellowship of Australian Writers poetry prize and the Canada-Australia Literary Prize, all in 1985; the Bicentennial Prize, the Paul Harris Award from Rotary International and the South Australian Premier's Prize, all in 1988, and so on steadily, culminating in the big international awards he began to collect in the 1980s, the Petrarch Prize in 1995, the T. S. Eliot Prize in 1997, the Queen's Gold Medal for Poetry in 1999. In 1998 he and Derek Walcott would be named as potential Poets Laureate in succession to Ted Hughes, who died in October that year,[51] an honour from which Murray at once publicly excused himself on the grounds that 'it would be wrong for me to serve the head of a foreign power'.

From sales of his books, fees for readings, prize-money and grants, he made a precarious and undependable living. For all his optimism and his literary success, his would remain a very thin and uncertain income, only once in his life rising to $40 000 a year, during 1992–96, when he had a four-year Keating Fellowship. He accepted relative poverty as the price of his vocation. His children had to endure the sneers of friends who noticed that their father was always at home: 'Doesn't your Dad work?' Christina was asked scornfully.[52] But in fact he worked without ceasing, constantly thinking, writing (always longhand, with a black Pentel pen, erasing by covering the offending word with an impenetrable block of black ink), then typing the result on his manual typewriter, pecking it out with the crooked middle finger of his right hand, which his cousin George Maurer had broken years before on the way to school. He was aware that his writing brought his children mockery, and he was sensitive about how he wrote of them: 'Few poems I've made mention our children/That I write at all got you dork names/More might have brought worse', he would write in a poem for his eldest daughter.[53]

When he was in the throes of composition he did not welcome intrusions. On one occasion two smartly dressed, crew-cut young Americans knocked at 27 Edgar Street: Murray ambled barefoot down the passage and filled his front door. The young men explained that they were calling from the Church of the Latter-Day Saints, with a special offer for him: they would leave with him a free copy of the *Book of Mormon* if he would agree to read it and discuss it with them when they returned next week. Murray smiled the smile of the village idiot, with which he had entrapped many a superior speaker at conferences: 'Ah, nah', he said slowly. 'Save your time and your money. I've already read it'. 'And what did you think of it, sir?' asked the young men eagerly. A long pause from Murray, and then, benignly, 'I thought it was rubbish'.

The young men fell back, conferred with quick glances, regrouped: 'This is an important matter, sir. You should take it to the Lord in prayer'. 'I have', said Murray. The young men, even if they could see the trap, could not avoid it: 'And, sir?' 'He thinks it's rubbish too', said Murray. With a delighted eldritch cackle he told Mark O'Connor, 'They went away with little broken words'.[54]

While unwanted visitors got brushed off inventively, he and Valerie continued to lead very active social lives, and the range of friends they entertained at small dinners or large parties in the little house on Edgar Street was strikingly wide: postmen found themselves rubbing shoulders with poets, academics with tree-surgeons. Murray made friends easily, and was profoundly loyal to them, to the extent of injuring his own interests in supporting theirs, as he did in joining Mark O'Connor's campaign against the Literature Board. And he joined O'Connor in spite of recognising very clearly that the younger poet was not without his faults. In 1983 Murray told John Barnie that O'Connor's most recent poetry was, as he put it,

> okay, but not really good: there's more intellect, and intellectual determination, in it than poetry, I fear. He is a fiercely ambitious man with areas of obsession in him ... he hates and scorns many of my known opinions and attitudes, notably Catholicism, which is a major obsession ...` there's quite a lot of hostility mingled with his feelings of gratitude and prudent alliance.[55]

In spite of this clear-sightedness, Murray was prepared to help O'Connor in a fight he thought just, even though he himself paid a high price for the alliance.

He tended to laugh a little at O'Connor's obsessions, though, and wrote a witty poem commenting on one of them, O'Connor's desire to reform English spelling. This was 'The Cwdeitar' ('The coup d'etat') which expresses Murray's view that phonetic spelling begs the question of whose pronunciation and current spelling are to be privileged, and suggests both authoritarianism and parochialism:

> Let the enemy's culture rot in the *fycan* libraries!
> People transliterating *oevasiez* books would be *delt widh*.
> Political opponents were given outback farms
> and criminals exiled. I remember well
> the silence of a planeload of white sex offenders
> going to be parachuted into Ethiopia
> and the jokes of the women loading them aboard;
> I remember bishops dancing on Rainbow Snake Day

and the General driving his enormous armoured
Holden Lyrebird, SR-1, to the races
in his moleskin uniform, under banners reading
ENNI PIEPL WYRTH A CRYMPAT HAEZ A NEITIV LAENGWIX.

On the other hand Murray had a lot of sympathy for O'Connor's interest in environmentalism, considering as he did that a good farmer was of necessity a good environmentalist. The two of them made several trips together to acquaint themselves with bits of Australia they did not know. In 1980 Murray, with O'Connor, Alan Gould and a young friend, Piers Laverty, made a lengthy trip to the far west of New South Wales, to see that parched and beautiful area, travelling in Murray's battered Toyota HiAce van, which from time to time broke down, to Murray's embarrassment.[56] Murray nosed around every tiny settlement they passed through, particularly seeking out regional museums and ambling round them, alive with curiosity about some new aspect of his country.

And in 1981, when O'Connor was Writer in Residence at James Cook University, engaged in writing his fine poems of the Barrier Reef,[57] Murray, Gould and the anthologist John Leonard drove up to Townsville to meet him, coming across Peter Barden on the way, in Mackay. Barden, who had temporarily returned to Australia from the United States to work on the Burdekin project, struck Gould as 'exactly the kind of pal you'd expect Murray to have from university days. He was also unkillable—very lean and full of rascality'. Murray might not have been lean, but he was as 'unkillable' as Barden. The two of them sat up yarning and drinking beer all night, while Gould dozed, and at dawn they tried in vain to persuade him to join them in climbing a local eminence to see the sun rise. Murray then drove all day to Townsville on no sleep: Gould was immensely impressed. 'He was in his forties then, so there was some considerable physical resilience', he would say with admiration.[58]

Gould, Leonard and Murray went camping on Dunk Island, an expedition organised by O'Connor, who took them to the Coral Cave. The sea was unusually rough, and Murray did not enjoy the water taxi ride out to the island. 'It's wonderful Mac, isn't it?' said Gould, who called everyone 'Mac'. 'I can manage', said Murray tautly, 'if I just concentrate on the horizon'.[59]

He and the others erected their primitive tent, a canvas sheet slung over a rope tied between trees, facing the sea, to get the benefit of the sea breezes. O'Connor knew better, placing his parallel to the beach. In the night a heavy tropical storm came up, blew straight through Murray's shelter, and soaked him and Gould to the skin. As soon as morning came Murray bundled all his possessions into a large dripping swag tied at the top, dumped it on the wharf, and sat beside it smoking cigars until the water taxi that had brought them arrived at one in the afternoon. He intended to take no further part in camping.[60]

He kept up his friendships with men and women he had met at Sydney University, from the Four Colonels (Peter Barden, who had by now emigrated to the United States where Murray would see him whenever he visited that country, John Mulhall, an advertising executive in Sydney, and Ken Welton who had moved to Queensland) through Bob Ellis (by now an editor and film-maker), Penny Nelson (a novelist), Mick Byrne (working for the post office, as he would do all his life),[61] Greg O'Hara (working among Aborigines in Tennant Creek), Dick Hall (who having been personal private secretary to Gough Whitlam was now a senior journalist), the academic Olaf Reinhardt and his wife, Libby Jones and her academic husband Alec, and Walter and Elisabeth Davis, living in Canberra. Writers ranging from Kenneth Slessor, Douglas Stewart and Geoff Lehmann to Christopher Koch, Mark O'Connor, Peter Porter, Peter Goldsworthy, Chris Wallace-Crabbe, Alan Gould, Robert Gray and Jamie Grant and his wife Margaret Connolly met and remet at the Murrays'.

Murray had met Robert Gray and Jamie Grant at a seminar for *Poetry Australia* at Macquarie University in 1975, and had become friendly with both of them, liking them as personalities and poets. After this meeting he would pay unexpected visits to Grant, sometimes startling Grant's friends and relatives with what they thought odd behaviour. On one occasion, while Murray was helping Grant to move house, Grant's slim sister-in-law walked into the still unfurnished living room and found Murray lying sprawled, mountainous on the bare floor. 'What are you doing, Les?' she asked in concern. Without moving or taking his eyes off the ceiling, Murray rumbled, 'Gravity, my dear, has more effect on me than it does on you'.[62] It was through Grant that Murray met his literary agent Margaret Connolly, who would act for Murray from 1989. She married Grant in September 1990.

Robert Gray's lapidary poems Murray greatly admired, but he found Gray the most elusive of men. 'Bob Gray seems to have gone into smoke, as he frequently does', Murray would write to friends like the Canberra poet Geoff Page: 'I'll grab him when he de-volatilises'.[63] Gray repeatedly accepted the Murrays' invitations to dinner, and then would phone to cancel at the last minute. By way of reciprocating, he would invite the Murrays to a meal, and then be out when his guests arrived.[64] 'Robert Gray—if that's who he really is', Murray would say, chuckling.[65]

And there were friends who fitted into no category other than that they and Murray liked and respected each other. One such was Piers Laverty, whose distinguished ancestry included both Mackerrasses and Nathans;[66] his father, Peter Laverty, was Director of the New South Wales Art Gallery, and one of his uncles was Murray's university friend Dick Hall.[67] Laverty and Murray met at Hall's beach-house at Eira Beach in the National Park south of Sydney in 1970, when Murray was thirty-one. Laverty, then fifteen years old, was a confused and rebellious teenager with no idea of what to do with his life. Murray, perhaps seeing something of his own difficult youth in Laverty, invited him to meals, relished his company, guided his reading, and gave him quiet advice without seeming to do so. 'I looked upon Les as being my university', Laverty would say later.[68] More than that, Murray acted as an older brother to Laverty at a time when the latter was distant from his own family.

When Laverty trained as a potter Murray took a close interest in his progress,[69] and in 1985, when Laverty smashed his pelvis in a bad motor-accident, Murray visited him nearly every day during the eleven weeks he spent in hospital, and with his father Cecil spent most of Christmas day with him there, smuggling in a bottle of whisky to cheer him up. Laverty would go on to make a living as a tree-surgeon, and his bluff defensiveness, rough beard and powerful build made many obtusely underestimate him, as they underestimated Murray. To see Laverty in the context of his beautiful house, stuffed with books and objets d'art, or his sumptuous workshed, built with the air and care of a cathedral, or to hear him talk about literature, in which his knowledge was wide and his taste excellent, could be a revelation. 'Piers will tell you he's a tree-lopper', Murray once warned me half-jokingly, 'and if you believe him you'll be severely punished'. Laverty was a partial model for Forbutt in *The Boys Who Stole The Funeral*.[70]

Murray showed his capacity for friendship, and his generosity towards those who could never repay him, most clearly in his handling of the many students of his work who wrote to him from all over the world. He corresponded tirelessly with them, just as he was tireless in helping Australian students, whom he would agree to meet and tutor for hours on end. Every famous author is pestered by unwanted correspondence: Murray seemed absolutely to welcome it, and he went to astonishing lengths to help students. On two separate occasions he invited my own students to spend days as his guest so that he could answer their hundreds of questions, gracefully dealing with intrusions and gaucheries. An earnest Iranian, Mohammad Tavallaie, sent him pages of babu questions such as, 'Why, how and when did God create the world?'[71]

Murray did his manful best with them. 'I know I got the *When* right', he told me with a cackle: 'It was in the Beginning'. One of these students, Karla Sigel, a highly intelligent American, he later took the trouble to visit in Kentucky in 1991, out of concern for her problems and interest in her progress.[72]

Among the many overseas admirers he wrote to repeatedly was Anurag Sharma, a young Indian student from Jaipur, to whom Murray wrote many times, beginning in May 1990. Discovering the difficulties Sharma had in obtaining his work, Murray generously sent him copies of many books, poems and articles. He read with interest Sharma's responses to his writing and commented on them, so that the two developed a dialogue that gives a fascinating glimpse of two highly intelligent men, from quite different cultures, engaging one another in a discussion that was fruitful to both although they never met in the flesh. Sharma, in 1997, published in India a study of Murray's writing, *A Dimension of the Angel*, for which Murray supplied a brief introduction and which he had tried hard to get published in Australia.[73] Sharma praised Murray's use of Indian influences in his 'Walking to the Cattleplace' sequence, and Murray was heartened: 'Your thesis justifies my temerity, all those years ago, in borrowing magpie-fashion some fragments of ancient Indian wisdom about Mother Cow and related matters'.[74]

But their correspondence was not confined to literature: Murray rejoiced with Sharma on the birth of his daughter ('My blessings on the little girl herself; may she have a long and auspicious life'),[75] the completion of his thesis and his first academic job, and told Sharma of his struggles with depression, his travels and his children. The letters that passed between them rapidly developed a genuine human warmth, a tribute to the talent of each for friendship across the barriers of space, age and culture.

Some of Murray's closest friendships were pen-friendships. Among the most striking of these is that with John Barnie. Though Murray and Barnie met whenever Murray returned to Wales, it was chiefly as a correspondent that each confided in the other. Murray's long and deeply personal letters to Barnie were given added warmth by Barnie's depression, poverty and personal problems: Murray could throw off his intense shyness and reserve when faced with someone who shared his own difficulties, and Barnie's physical remoteness made him a safe repository of very frank judgements on subjects ranging from theology to the state of Australian letters. Murray's letters to him, all of which Barnie preserved, constitute one of the clearest and most detailed records of the poet's personal and intellectual life.

In spite of Murray's proclaimed dislike of academics ('Intellectual here means one who processes foreign thought for Australian use, and then enforces it', he grumbled to Philip Hodgins),[76] he had many academic friends, ranging from Sharma to Kevin Hart, and from Angela Smith to Olaf Reinhardt. Soon after I met him at a reading I had organised on the campus of the University of New South Wales in September 1982, he invited me to dinner, a particular act of kindness to a very junior academic.

Only recently arrived in Australia, my wife and I were slightly awed at the prospect of dining with this famous man, and afraid that all his talk might be of Australian literary figures whom we did not know. But he and Valerie expertly put us at ease, talking about everything from the pernicious influence of British publishers on the Australian market to the history of his mother's family (he had invited his cousin Tasman Arnall, also an academic at the University of New South Wales, to meet us), while Valerie served her delicious food and Murray packed it away effortlessly, thickly slathering everything on his plate with butter and swallowing it without checking his conversation for a moment. Between courses he proudly took us out into the moonlit garden to admire his crop of broad beans, luxuriant despite the heavy clay soil.

His mind was richly stocked: he seemed interested in everything I had to tell him, and he could add to it and return it to me enhanced by some new setting. His general knowledge was astonishingly varied and detailed. Somehow during the evening the subject of alum came up, and no one was sure what it was, or what it was used for. No one except Murray: 'A styptic in medicine; also kitty litter! A mordant in dyes, too'. He loved to talk, and he loved to listen. His genius for friendship with a wide range of people was one of the many ways in which he transcended boundaries and rejected conventions, an aspect of his complex personality of a piece with the baseball cap he occasionally wore to black-tie gatherings.

But he could lose friends too. In October 1978 he began to feel that Grace Perry was cooling towards him at *Poetry Australia*, and he reluctantly considered resigning.[77] In the event things were smoothed over for another year. But late in 1979 Perry eased him out of his 'locum' and replaced him with her lawyer, John Millett, who had been Managing Editor. The arrangement between Murray and Perry had always been unwritten and undefined, so that he only discovered she had resumed control when poems he had accepted were rejected by her, to the bewilderment of poets all over the country. 'That cost me a deal of face, but I've since grown it back, and hold no grudges', Murray wrote stoically. At the time, though, he was both hurt and puzzled, for he had very much liked Grace Perry and thought she liked him:

> The peculiarity of Grace was that she had two voices. She had a kind of outgoing extrovert charm and good humour and bounding energy that was

expressed in one voice, and occasionally, mostly at poetry readings, when she read her poetry, there was a strange, lost-little-girl voice that she used to read in. I thought, 'That's weird. It sounds like another personality'. That was the personality that wrote her poems. And when I suddenly got terminated in 1980 from the magazine, I had to puzzle over why, and I thought in the end, it was the little girl voice that sacked me.

It was the cheerful, outgoing friend of mine called Grace Perry who hired me, and with whom I got along, and it was that other personality that sacked me because that was the kind of jealous, clenched inner being that Grace's poetry represented.

And it was threatened by the fact that the magazine was getting beyond Grace's grip and beyond her control, and more importantly, beyond her talent. People were publishing in it who were beyond anything Grace could reach, and somehow the unstated final limit on the magazine was that it wasn't allowed to outgrow its founder. She allowed it to outgrow its founder to a good degree. It floated high but eventually it had to be reeled in.[78]

Murray had enjoyed working for *Poetry Australia*, not least because it kept him intimately in touch with the latest poetry being produced, and put him in a position to help the talented young writers he discovered, tutored and published. Many of these had become personal friends: it was during his time at *Poetry Australia* that he grew close to such writers as Mark O'Connor (whose long sequence 'I-land' he had been delighted to publish, but whose driving ambition made Murray wary), Robert Gray (whom Murray thought the best imagist poet in Australia), Peter Goldsworthy (a doctor whom Murray half-jokingly called Australia's Chekhov, and whose understanding wife Helen he was able to talk to about his blackest periods),[79] Jennifer Rankin, Peter Porter, Kevin Hart, Alan Gould, the Austrian poet Herbert Kuhner and Jamie Grant. Hart and Gould had attacked the Generation of '68 in a long poem in heroic couplets, 'The Harrowing of Balmain', of which Murray was the hero.[80]

He valued and maintained his friendship with each of them, and would be deeply hurt when he came to believe that Hart, a talented poet ('one of our supreme poetic craftsmen', Murray called him)[81] and whose conversion to Catholicism Murray had celebrated in a poem of pain and rejoicing entitled 'The New Moreton Bay', had turned against him in future years. The falling-out was in fact occasioned by little more than warnings from a mutual acquaintance that 'Kevin's not your friend, you know'[82] (warnings which Hart much later denied had any substance), followed by a review Hart wrote for the Melbourne *Sunday Age*,[83] and of which he sent Murray a preview copy. It contained (amid many compliments) criticism of some of Murray's weaker poems.

Murray's depression had weakened his sense of proportion in such matters and he was profoundly wounded.[84] But the loss of Hart's friendship, which Murray continued to regret, was exceptional: Murray's friends were in general deeply supportive of him. And in the early 1990s he had need of them, for he was about to enter the valley of the shadow. This would be the period of his most painful literary and political struggles.

CHAPTER SIXTEEN
ANGUISH & ROBBERY
1978-92

~

Force, and fraud, are in war the two cardinal virtues.

HOBBES

Having lost the job he loved at *Poetry Australia*, Murray fell back on another outside post he had taken on in 1978, acting as one of the two poetry readers for Angus & Robertson, Australia's premier publisher and the firm that had published his own books since *The Weatherboard Cathedral* in 1969. The firm had been taken over in the 1970s (the first of a number of takeovers that would presently see the firm fall into Rupert Murdoch's hands and become a tributary of Harper Collins) and for a while under its new management seemed in danger of disappearing, but the energetic intervention of Richard Walsh, whom Murray had known as a student editor of *honi soit*,[1] saved it. 'Richard Walsh was ready to keep it alive, and I got the job of being its "poetry poison taster" as they called it', Murray recalled.[2]

In fact he offered himself for the job: he considered that Rodney Hall, who was advising Walsh at the time and whom Murray disliked, was killing the Angus & Robertson poetry list.[3] Murray approached Walsh: 'Get rid of Rodney and I'll get you back what Angus & Robertson's always had, which was the best poetry list in Australia'.[4] Walsh agreed, paying Murray $1000 a year: 'He's absolutely famous for utter meanness', Murray would remember wryly. After a decade's inflation this payment would rise to a still-risible $2000,[5] and Murray was so lacking in business acumen that when Margaret Connolly, one of Australia's best literary agents, began acting for him in 1989, she found that he was omitting to collect even this paltry sum.[6]

Connolly, who would continue to act for Murray for many years to come, found him an endearing client:

> I like doing things with Les. He's very entertaining to work with, and he's also someone you're very fond of. You always get the business right or you don't have the friendship, but he's more someone you're friendly with. And he's

entertaining because he gets into lots of straits and then comes and confesses to me what he's done. And I have to help him out. Les thinks he doesn't want to bother you about something or that he's going to waste a lot of your time, but it's often something on which five minutes in the beginning would save five hours in the end.[7]

But though he sometimes muddled business arrangements, he was an utterly professional writer and editor. It was his task, at first shared with the poet Vivian Smith, to read the poetry manuscripts that poured in to Angus & Robertson, mostly unsolicited, and to make a recommendation on them. He would come in to the Angus & Robertson offices in Ryde once a week to scan new arrivals quickly, making an almost instinctive judgement, rejecting most at once, and writing brief and incisive reports on the few that caught his eye. Tom Thompson, who worked with Murray at Angus & Robertson in later years and who would clash with him repeatedly, recalled: 'He was a tremendous reader, because he could give you a report or write you a one page blurb which was totally imbued with a phenomenal knowledge, and genuine generosity, there was just no doubt about that. I couldn't fault him as a reader. That's what you wanted from him. You wanted someone who lived poetry'.[8]

Murray did live poetry, and his many surviving reader's reports are models of their kind. He could be ruthlessly brief in rejecting an author he thought unworthy of the Angus & Robertson list:

> A vast unselective collection of the verse of a minor poet whose slight talent faded a long time back. As a Selected or Collected, this'd have no commercial prospects, as X[9] rightly has no substantial reputation. A plodder, alas, made worse by American models he took up in Canada. Weaknesses: Lack of poetry, mostly.[10]

Of another poet who submitted a volume entitled 'The Alchemist':

> He's now clearly played out his tiny vein of ore—and is in fact an *anti*-alchemist in that he can change fool's gold into even more worthless indeterminate rubbish.[11]

And of a third:

> This poor, laborious, rather dim performance poet survives by parrotting the sensibility of the 70s in chopped prose to the converted & the immature. The results on paper are inexpressibly bad & embarrassing. *Not* A&R standard.[12]

And another:

Prosy, relying on readers' complicity rather than on poetic effect, of which there's none.[13]

Nor was he a great respecter of established reputations. Of a much-puffed 'ethnic' poet, whom the multi-cultural wave had carried beyond her depth, he wrote:

> I've never been impressed with [the poet]'s work, at all; it all sounds to me like Literature, in the bad sense, smooth, soulful, empty, respectable, no life in it anywhere, except in the quietly dogged determination to be seen as a sensitive artist. I wouldn't entertain it.[14]

But where he liked the poetry, particularly if he thought it had something new and unpopular to say, he was powerful in its support. Of the work of Peter Kocan, Australia's only would-be political assassin (he was restricted to a mental hospital for trying to kill Labor Party leader Arthur Calwell in 1966), he wrote:

> Splendid verse of searing effect, directed like a laser at the squalid bullying dishonest era we live in. This book is so good, so honest and so brave it should be published immediately, out of sequence. It will draw the flak of tyrants, which can be turned to its commercial advantage, but mostly it will do honour to the house that publishes it.[15]

Of poems by Harry Cummins, he commented:

> This book *is* a goer. A highly intelligent, fiercely independent-minded poet, saying often forbidden things in accents based in part on D H Lawrence & Anglo-Saxon alliterative models, he deserves to be published—and he'll need the large-format size of book because of his long lines! So many *utter* surprises in his imagery: I'm delighted. (eg, N. Qld mtns the colour of baked trout! Perfect.)[16]

Murray had a powerful grasp of the structure of a proposed book, and he could home in on the author's main themes like a missile. Of a manuscript by Alan Gould he wrote:

> Taken as a whole ms., I think this is the richest, freest, most musical ms. of poetry Alan's yet done. The various and Monaro poems at the beginning have a crispness & physicality that delight me, as much as the sheer intellectuality & wise surprise I always get from Alan, and the internal contrasts in those are well set off by the comic end-piece on that unutterable (but actual!) Queanbeyan wine. The choral symphony part of the book of course returns to, but I think

also culminates, Alan's older grand themes of the ocean and planetary life: I think it's masterly, in its detail and its enormous architecture.

As he did in Gould's case, he sometimes offered entirely practical advice on the timing of the books he recommended:

To bring this ms. out as a book wd. entail queue-jumping, which might be justified in view of the large sales the musical performance next Nov. would generate [Gould had written the libretto for a Bicentennial Choral Symphony], but I leave that to you.[17]

And he was, as Thompson had said, generous, willing to let poems change his mind, even if he did not click into their groove at once: 'Yes, I'd publish this. I don't resonate with every word in it, but too much of it is too good for me to ignore'.[18]

His judgements were confident, and he stood by them with great determination. If Walsh chose not to publish a poet Murray had recommended, he accepted that as a commercial decision, and of the business side of publishing he had only the foggiest conception.[19] But he would fiercely contest the issue if Walsh tried to publish a writer Murray thought not worthy of the Angus & Robertson imprint. Early on they clashed, and Murray threatened to leave:

They learned quickly that if they didn't take my advice big trouble would ensue. I would resign. Richard Walsh once tried to impose [a poetaster] on me and I said 'No. [He] is not good enough for the A&R list.[20] You're not associating my name with rubbish like that', so it was dropped instantly. He behaved himself after that, he left it to me. So I got him the best list and this went on through the rest of the 1970s and through the 1980s.[21]

His threat won the day, for it was recognised that if he went, much of Angus & Robertson's stable of poets would go with him. He took control of the poetry list, and it came to bear his stamp very clearly for twelve years, from 1978 to 1990, to the frustration and anger of poets like Adamson and Tranter, who felt themselves to be shut out by him. They were only half-right: Murray was to say he would have published Tranter and Forbes, and others, if they had submitted their work.[22]

Many of the writers Murray had published in *Poetry Australia* now found favour at Angus & Robertson, as well as others he discovered during his time at the publisher: Geoff Lehmann, Robert Gray, Peter Goldsworthy, Alan Gould, Jamie Grant, Geoff Page, John Foulcher, Julian Croft, Philip Hodgins, Andrew Lansdown[23] and others appeared on the A&R list during his tenure. The Generation of '68 over-simply came to think of many of these as Murray supporters. It would be more accurate to say that Murray supported them, and he did so because he thought them fine poets.

He also brought in, or cemented in place, a broad spectrum of poets no one could have accused of being his acolytes, ranging from the performance poet Billy Marshall Stoneking (whose volume *Singing the Snake* Murray strongly recommended) to Gwen Harwood. During the twelve years he spent with Angus & Robertson, working closely with the editor, Sue Phillips, who greatly admired Murray and who was married to Richard Walsh, he delivered what he had promised, the best Australian poetry list of any publisher.

But this was not enough to save him during the upheavals that followed Rupert Murdoch's decision to merge his seven publishing companies in Australia, in 1989. The staff of a much bigger Murdoch company, Collins, were brought in over the heads of the Angus & Robertson management, as Murray recalled:

> There came the day when the staff at Angus & Robertson's were sacked more or less en masse and were replaced by frightened operatives from Harper Collins—the new breed of publishers who know that their job probably will last for six months and they'll have their throat cut and they eat each other in the meantime. It's a rotten game. Young university women with frightened faces who are trying to be more politically correct than each other to survive a bit longer than the others.[24]

Even before this period he had found the business world's ruthlessness in the handling of staff breathtaking, sending to his friend Chris Wallace-Crabbe a card with a wry little limerick, the first he had written:

> Said the magician 'Could I have afforded
> to resign on the spot when you ordered
> me to saw the Fat Lady
> in half before payday,
> I would have. I find wage cuts sordid.'[25]

In the changeover Tom Thompson, a Collins employee, became publisher of Literature at Angus & Robertson. Murray scented danger at once: Thompson, dark and raffish, was a poet associated with the Tranter–Adamson group. More than that, Murray had twice strongly advised Angus & Robertson against publishing Thompson, and Thompson knew it,[26] for Walsh had the bad habit of communicating to rejected authors Murray's crisp reports on them, though Murray remonstrated crossly with him about this.[27]

Trouble soon came, beginning with Thompson asking Murray to cut back on his recommendations, of which Thompson thought there were too many: he particularly wanted to reject Lansdown and Gould. Murray won on both (the Gould volume subsequently won an award), but he agreed to several of Thompson's alternative suggestions, including the publishing of a Tranter ally, John Forbes, whose work he respected, to Tom Thompson's secret surprise.[28]

But this was just the opening skirmish, and the struggle soon intensified. When Thompson said he wished to publish the work of Ken Bolton, whose verse Murray thought without merit, Murray dug in his heels. 'It's not poetry', he said flatly, and when Thompson persisted, Murray produced what he optimistically considered his trump card: a newly drawn contract with Angus & Robertson, secured for him by Margaret Connolly. It was from this point that she became his agent. The contract specified that no poetry manuscripts were to be accepted without Murray's prior consent and that he was to be sole poetry reader.[29]

Thompson had written quietly to Bolton, 'I don't want to antagonise Les Murray till January, so you won't get a firm offer in a letter with the early 1991 date of publication till mid January ... Would $1000 be alright as an advance?'[30] He thus showed that he intended to challenge Murray's previously undisputed control of the poetry list. Bolton later said he had refused the advance. Thompson also passed Murray's dismissive comments about Bolton's verse on to Bolton, via a mutual friend, and somewhere along the line malicious additions were made, to the effect that Murray considered Bolton's work 'unChristian':[31] Murray, on learning of this years later, would deny having used the term, adding 'it's not relevant', and pointing out that he had strongly supported the work of non-believers like Alan Gould.[32] But Bolton, deeply hurt, penned an angry letter of protest to Angus & Robertson.[33] Bolton would nurse his grievance for years, and then strike back at Murray with a poem and reviews intended to annoy.[34] He failed in this desire, however, for Murray did not read them.[35] He continued to resist publication of Bolton's work by Angus & Robertson and succeeded in blocking it.

Battle was now joined, but it was a battle in which Murray, despite the formalisation of his contract, was outmatched from the start. Thompson was an extremely shrewd user of organizational structures ('You go about publishing for empowerment', he would say),[36] and he rapidly out-manoeuvred Murray, who cared more about poetry than about power. Thompson pirouetted round him ('I am skipping about as if I had jazz ballet shoes', he told Bolton gaily)[37] by commissioning Bob Adamson to edit a volume of Christopher Brennan's work for the Imprint Lives series, over which Murray had no control. 'I did it deliberately because Adamson has consistently been probably the

Valerie Morelli's graduation from Sydney University, May 1962, just days after Les Murray had proposed to her.

Les Murray in the *honi soit* office, Sydney University, September 1962, the month of his marriage to Valerie Morelli.

Les Murray and Valerie Morelli on their wedding day, 29 September 1962.

The marriage party at Our Lady of Dolours, Chatswood, 29 September 1962: left to right, Cecil Murray, the groomsman Walter Davis, the bridesmaid Maureen Dalton, Les Murray, Valerie Murray, Valerie's parents Berta and Gino Morelli, her brother Stephen Morelli, and her paternal grandfather Jószef Morelli.

The married man: Les Murray in December 1962.

'Teacup and Remington days': the Translation Unit, Australian National University, Les Murray and Con Kiriloff in their office, 1963.

A family party at the Morellis, early 1963: from left, Valerie's brother Stephen, Les Murray, Valerie (with Christina becoming evident), and her parents Berta and Gino Morelli.

only poet who has worked out of Brennan's Balmain', Thompson would say.³⁸ He subsequently published a volume of Adamson's own work on the grounds that it was autobiographical, not poetic.

And there would be more. Murray might be sole poetry reader, but Angus & Robertson in 1990 hired a reader for the publisher's Classics series: this was an active and intelligent woman, Drusilla Modjeska, an Australian of English descent who had acquired her Polish name through a brief marriage. Although Modjeska was not hired to read poetry manuscripts, Thompson felt aided by her, for (according to him) she questioned some of Murray's rejections of poets, to Murray's steadily increasing distress. He was now deep in depression and quite unable to cope with any pressure. His chief remaining ally in the firm, Sue Phillips, left in June 1990, declaring herself unable to work with Thompson.³⁹ Hereafter Murray was exposed and alone. Friends like Jamie Grant could see what was happening, but were powerless to intervene.⁴⁰ Thompson wrote to Bolton: 'The Murray thing brews on, and is perpetually dangerous and long-standing ... Of course as far as he is concerned the issue is over now, but new ones loom large (who will I reject next for instance) ... I think this month is very hot emotionally, to those who are large among us'.⁴¹

Thompson also adopted the simple stratagem of not acting on Murray's recommendations. As Murray recalled later,

> What they did was reject everything that I recommended to them, make sure that nobody who was associated with me got published. It took a while for the penny to drop, but John Tranter was clearly privy to the operation because he described it in an article in *The Union Recorder* in Sydney University. He said it must be very frustrating to get none of your recommendations accepted.⁴²

In fact Tranter's piece was an interview in *Hermes*, which appeared after Murray's resignation had become common knowledge. Tranter did indeed have sources of information inside Angus & Robertson.⁴³ Thompson certainly kept some of Murray's enemies informed, telling Bolton in August 1990 that he expected a reaction from Murray, 'as I have just finally rejected Peter Kocan for the third time'.⁴⁴

By March 1991 the editor Nikki Christer had come to agree with Tom Thompson that 'it's time for Les to move on'; she proposed Tranter as his replacement.⁴⁵ On 10 June 1991 Murray, by this time profoundly depressed, accepted defeat and resigned from Angus & Robertson sick at heart: he had taken to calling the firm 'Anguish & Robbery'.⁴⁶ At the end of his final Reader's Report, he wrote,

> I have a clear perception, which I can no longer hide from myself, that your other advisor or advisors on poetry are determined to eliminate from the list all poets not strictly obedient to a 1970s leftist ideology ... So be it. I am frankly tired of justifying my sole criterion of literary, as distinct from ideological, quality. If it is the intention of the firm to shift to ideologically based, affirmative-action publishing, I can only signal my inability to lend my name to any list that may result. Accordingly, I resign, with effect from the date of your reading this, from my post as your poetry reader.[47]

Tom Thompson was quoted in the press release to the effect that 'we accepted his resignation reluctantly'.[48] For a brief time he acted as reader himself, and then called on Adamson for advice. The Generation of '68 had taken the citadel, just as at this time they were, in Murray's opinion, attaining a dominant influence in the Literature Board's awarding of grants. 'I hope you're not too depressed, or endangered', Murray wrote to Philip Hodgins, 'by the Great Massacre of real writers the Lit. Board allowed itself this year?'[49]

Nobody at Murdoch's new giant publishing house seemed to care much about the price Angus & Robertson now paid: Murray, along with some of Australia's best writers, including Robert Gray, Jan Owen, Peter Goldsworthy, Peter Kocan, Hal Colebatch, Jamie Grant, Geoff Page, Alan Gould and Andrew Lansdown, left the firm[50] and several of them took their next books to Heinemann, where Jamie Grant's brother Sandy was Managing Director.

During his side-show years at Angus & Robertson Murray had continued his real work, and his landmark volumes continued to appear, slowly but regularly: *Ethnic Radio* in 1977, *The Boys Who Stole The Funeral* in 1980, a revised and enlarged edition of his selected poems, *The Vernacular Republic: Poems 1961–1981* in 1982, *The People's Otherworld* in 1983, and *The Daylight Moon* in 1987. Angus & Robertson had lost the services of a man who was by now widely recognized as one of the major poets in English. 'It is just imaginable that there are still one or two readers left in Australia', Martin Duwell wrote of *The People's Otherworld*, 'who haven't yet realised that we have in our midst a poet of extraordinary accomplishment and strength'.[51] And with his going came a sharp change at Angus & Robertson: on Adamson's advice, in 1991 the firm published Tranter's *The Floor of Heaven* and Adamson's *Wards of the State*. With Murray out, the Angus & Robertson poetry list became more varied, but it also became, as the poet and literary historian Dennis Haskell would tactfully put it, 'more mixed in quality'.[52]

Murray now experimented with publishing his work himself, in partnership with Margaret Connolly and her husband Jamie Grant. They called their venture Isabella Press, Murray at last finding a chance to bestow his ancestress's name on one of his offspring. But Grant and Connolly discovered that he had no grasp of the business of publishing. He had only the vaguest ideas about a publisher's costs and overheads, and seemed to imagine that if the author got 10 per cent of the retail price of a book, the publisher must be pocketing the remaining 90 per cent.[53] He also alarmed Grant by offering to publish the works of other writers: 'He kept on turning up at our doorstep with all these maniacs who had written books and he then became very bitter towards us for being reluctant to publish them. Only temporarily, you know. As soon as we said "Well, we're not going to have this publishing company any more, it's closed down", he calmed down'.[54] Isabella Press published only one book, Murray's *Translations from the Natural World* in 1992, the distribution being handled by Heinemann; it then folded, and Murray published his next book, *Collected Poems*, in 1994, with Heinemann.

Tom Thompson himself lasted only two years longer than Murray, resigning on 7 May 1993.[55] And by 1993 the once dominant force in Australian poetry was thinking of withdrawing from poetry publishing altogether: 'Adamson, Tranter et al may have conquered a city on the point of slipping beneath the waves', Murray told Philip Hodgins.[56]

But the waves were rising on other shores too: Heinemann itself presently went out of poetry publishing, so that Murray published only one volume with them. He then migrated again, to the innovative Sydney publisher Duffy & Snellgrove, the cautious Michael Duffy having become a good friend while he was editor of the *Independent Monthly*, for which Murray wrote from 1993 on.[57] After 1995 Michael Duffy would be his publisher. But the ending of the conflict at Angus & Robertson changed little as far as the larger struggle in Australian literature was concerned: it was just one campaign in an ongoing war. Murray would remain a stormy petrel, as the reaction to that extraordinary volume *The Boys Who Stole The Funeral* amply illustrates.

CHAPTER SEVENTEEN
STEALING THE FUNERAL
1979–81

You call me misbeliever, cut-throat dog,
And spit upon my Jewish gabardine,
And all for use of that which is mine own.

SHAKESPEARE

Of the volumes Murray published in the 1980s *The Boys Who Stole The Funeral* was the most striking departure for him, as in it he explored a new form, the verse-novel, trying, as he said, 'to reclaim ground for poetry which the novel, the film, etc. have filched from us over the past couple of centuries'.[1] His reclamation of lengthy narrative for Australian poetry would have repercussions in the work of poets as diverse as Alan Wearne, John A. Scott and Dorothy Porter, and the ripples would spread to the United States.[2]

In 140 sonnets, formal or irregular, Murray told the story of two city boys, Kevin Forbutt and Cameron Reeby, who steal the body of Forbutt's great-uncle from a funeral parlour and take it to the country in fulfilment of the uncle's wish to be buried in his home town, an echo of the importance many Aboriginal people attach to returning the remains of a dead person to his or her spirit country. The poem continues Murray's examination of the Boeotian-Athenian divide, but it also examines such issues as the impact of feminism and the need to rethink masculinity, as well as the role of Aboriginal culture in defining what is Australian.

Murray considered that the traditional idea of the masculine had reached a crisis-point: as he would tell Angela Smith, *The Boys Who Stole The Funeral* is structured by the view that

> men have collapsed, are baffled, not knowing, after the collapse of the military idea-and-culture, what to do next; I don't know whether this collapse of the traditionally masculine is a cause or a symptom of the queer stoppage I feel in our world down beneath all the furious playing of variations on things long known . . . the ageing trendies furiously defending the year 1968 and the mandarinate of mere style it seemed to promise . . .[3]

And of this crisis, feminism was a corollary. Murray looked at feminism chiefly through the figure of Noeline Kampff, a two-dimensional caricature of the feminists he met, mainly on university campuses, in the late 1970s. This was a period when certain campus feminists felt the need to out-macho men, and the results were designedly not pretty. Noeline Kampff speaks entirely in clichés and curses, expresses confused hatred and despair, and pours a bucket of blood over Reeby in a symbolic abortion or human-sacrifice scene: by creating her, Murray offered himself as a target for feminists on the lookout for one, and the offer was accepted gleefully. 'My God, how they'll hate you when they read it', Chris Koch warned him: 'Sharpen your dirk, you'll need it!'[4]

Koch was right. For years Murray would be lacerated on campuses by demonstrators who disrupted his talks with angry speeches masquerading as questions, and who on at least one campus, that of the University of New South Wales in 1983, displayed posters attacking him, wrote obscene comments in lipstick in the male staff toilet he used, and sent him anonymous envelopes of excrement.[5] He had had similar though less extreme experiences at Newcastle University the year before.[6] In this way those who vilified him demonstrated both the truth of Murray's caricature, and their lack of understanding of it.

By contrast, the reviews he got were mostly respectful, but in Australia there were few thorough-going encomiums compared with his previous books,[7] and there was a groundswell of negative comment, from critics ranging from John Forbes[8] to John Douglas Pringle.[9] This was in strong contrast to the very enthusiastic overseas reception of the volume when it was published in Britain and America.[10] There was also what Murray termed 'a strong whispering campaign' against the *Boys*. 'It was blocked from getting several major prizes', he told a friend.

And having begun, the campaign against him did not let up for many years. His literary opponents in the Battle of the Books regarded *The Boys Who Stole The Funeral* as a godsend, for it allowed them to say openly what they had muttered behind their hands for years. 'Conservative' became the code-word routinely used for him, meaning, as Murray put it to John Barnie, 'Enemy, Fascist, Shoot-on-sight'. And this was exaggeration born of fact: many of his opponents, and some of his friends, among them Bob Ellis[11] and Gareth Griffiths,[12] casually referred to him as a fascist. In a few years he would be writing to Penny Nelson, 'I barely go out of the house now, for fear of radical attack and of the disgust that overtakes me when forced to watch trendy identification-rituals. Fifteen years of being called Murray the Fascist have rather exhausted me, I fear'.[13]

Murray should have been able to take pride in the achievement of *The Boys Who Stole The Funeral*. His infectious pleasure in language is evident everywhere in this volume. Samuel Johnson remarked disapprovingly of Shakespeare that he could not resist a pun; the same is true of Murray, who plays with words as a dolphin does with water. He also spins surprising and inevitable images endlessly, apparently effortlessly; by this stage in his career he was in complete control of his art, using rhyme and conventional stanzaic forms as easily as free verse. The freshness of his observation and his ability to convey images vivid as flames is evident everywhere: from the description of a jet fighter that 'floats up the valley/with a sound like a long plunger rising/in a sonorous tube, and slams over' (poem 104), to a compelling evocation of the obscene challenge posed by a bikie gang, urban violence personified, or the description of someone sinking into sleep and being jolted half-awake by 'that abyssal start/sheer drop, that is said to come/from the heart shifting speeds'—an experience that, although it is universal, had not been described before.

Yet the reception of *The Boys Who Stole The Funeral* was not welcoming. Even some of Murray's friends, too scrupulous of language and morals to call him names, were uneasy about the volume: among these was Geoff Lehmann, who for weeks kept a copy he had borrowed from Murray, unable to return it for fear of having to say what he thought of it.[14] A chill had already set in between them, exacerbated by factors including Lehmann's painful divorce following a crisis when his wife Sally left him for Peter Porter in 1977.[15] 'I was punished for seeing him [Lehmann] in his awful humiliation', Murray would come to believe,[16] a view Lehmann dismissed.[17]

There were other factors in the cooling-off, including that Lehmann had dissuaded Murray from visiting a mutual friend, Steve Wilson, when Wilson was dying of malignant melanoma in 1979. Murray subsequently came to believe this was because Wilson was considering converting to Catholicism and Lehmann, an atheist, did not wish Murray to influence him.[18] In this Murray was mistaken; Lehmann had had a falling out with Wilson and was unenthusiastic about Murray's visiting him, but had no thought of keeping the dying man out of the arms of the Church. In fact Wilson, among whose close friends was a Catholic nun, became a Catholic convert a fortnight before his death.[19] For his part Lehmann believed it was his inability to praise *The Boys Who Stole The Funeral* that gradually led to a permanent break in a friendship which had lasted nearly a quarter of a century, and which each had valued.

There were others who had mixed feelings about the volume too, including Murray's friend Peter Goldsworthy, to whom Murray wrote,

> I'm delighted that *The Boys* pleased you, but I can't quite agree that I've been unsympathetic to Noeline Kampff. The point with her—perhaps I didn't make it clear enough—is that she's *trapped*. 'When you can't get a mask off it makes

you murderous.' She's as trapped in her anger and the received clichés she has allowed to feed it as poor Reeby is in his habit of spasmodic violence under pressure. Neither of them can live without external supports—Reeby seems for a moment to be pulling free of his regret for his lost career in science, but NK's whole homage is to her 'platoon', the Movement; the blood she tips over Reeby is her oblation (one of many? or her desperate substitute for the abortion expected of her? the point's left deliberately ambiguous) to her peer group ... I *did* try to vary her, make her more rounded, but I was almost violently repulsed: she *had* to be like that. Characters do have their own logic, and once they come alive they pursue it; I found that out in writing *The Boys* ... you'll have 'got' the ghastly appropriateness of Jennie Dunn's retribution carried out on a now-silenced NK's face/mask. [Dunn scalds Kampff's face with boiling water.]

I may surprise you, though by telling you there's almost nobody in the novel I have more sympathy for than for NK. Her nearest parallel in my past work is the Weeping Man in the poem An Absolutely Ordinary Rainbow. He is a human absolute, and she has tried to be one; her cliché is the hideous music of that attempt.[20]

Feminist anger and retribution he would have to endure, misplaced though they were, but there was another attack he had not so clearly anticipated, from those who thought he had no right to 'appropriate' Aboriginal names, rites and customs. He had risked their wrath in having Kevin Forbutt undergo an initiation rite at the hands of two mysterious characters, the Birrugan and the Njimbin, the spelling of whose names changes constantly (Birroogun, Berrigan, Nimbin) to make it plain that they have reference well beyond any single racial group.

Murray came across 'Birrugan' in the scholarly work by Professor J. S. Ryan of the University of New England, author of *The Land of Ulitarra*;[21] only after writing his poem would Murray find the same name in a work on the Gumbaynggirr people produced by Valerie's brother Stephen, where the name is translated as 'Jesus'.[22] Both Birrugan and Njimbin were chosen precisely because they allowed cultural references that included, but went well beyond, the Aboriginal. In particular, Murray surrounded the Birrugan and Njimbin with Christian imagery, focusing on the 'Common Dish' from which Kevin eats, and which is Grail, chalice, camp-meal, and the sum of common human experience and human suffering. As always, he was interested in finding points of commonality, rather than division, between Australians.

This did not save him from a sharp letter from Judith Wright, who had spent years fighting for Aboriginal causes, was in 1980 incensed by Premier Charles Court's actions in Western Australia in allowing mineral exploration near sacred Aboriginal land at Noonkanbah, and now thought that she saw a similar enemy in Murray. She wrote, on 16 June 1980, telling Murray that she had read *The Boys Who Stole The Funeral* 'as always with great appreciation of your powers'. But she then accused Murray of inflicting the rite of subincision on Forbutt, pointing out that this terrible ritual never spread to the east coast, and accusing Murray of having 'illegitimately transplanted over many hundreds of miles a rite the pair would never have recognized while tribal structure survived and initiations were carried out'. Wright added pointedly, 'Poetic licence within our own culture is one thing, but beyond it is another'.[23]

And she went on to tell Murray that she was organising a display of manuscripts by Australian authors, in support of the notion of an Aboriginal Treaty: 'Any chance of your responding with a manuscript from the book—even if you still don't believe in any agreement with the Aborigines over an equally illegitimate invasion?'[24]

Murray liked Wright, and in 1973 had proposed to the Whitlam government that she be made Governor-General, a proposal Whitlam apparently seriously considered.[25] But Murray recognised at once the real menace of her letter to him. For all its bantering tone, this double accusation of having both misrepresented and 'illegitimately invaded' Aboriginal culture had the potential to be a lethal thrust of the type that had destroyed the reputation of the Jindyworobaks, and Murray could not ignore it. If Wright could press her accusation home, she would do him immense and lasting harm. He had no reason to doubt that she would; her rejection of her own squatter background made her unsympathetic to Murray's pleading for his rural people and their values.

His response, given the menace he faced, was admirably sure-footed and elegant. He began by giving Wright a lesson in Aboriginal culture by way of gently asserting which of them most needed it:

> You seem, on a first reading of my verse novel, to have interpreted the visionary initiation sequence as being based on the Northern and Central Australian rite of subincision, and you rightly point out that this never came anywhere near the east coast. Now, while it's true that the novel adverts to subincision once or twice early on, Kevin Forbutt's experience at the hands of the Birroogun and the Njimbin has nothing to do with that rite; it's based on Eastern Australian 'clever-feller' or witch-doctor initiations as described by Elkin in *Aboriginal Men of High Degree*, plus some material, including the variable-variant names of the Birrugan and the Nimbin, taken from Professor Ryan's *The Land of Ulitarra* . . . You may have noticed the prominence given to crystals in my cheerful but fundamentally respectful *fantaisie* on the Aboriginal rite; that's

characteristically Eastern Australian. The wise men magically remove the 'ordinary' inner organs of the initiand and replace them with special, powerful ones. Because I was working along a fine line between Aboriginal and Western metaphors about crystal, purity, etc., I deliberately kept it ambiguous whether Kevin was getting a 'new' soul or having his existing one polished and clarified. I can't find anything in the relevant part of *The Boys* to suggest that subincision is going on there, and geographical misplacement of a ritual is not the sort of mistake I'd make. Besides, while my rite has a strong Aboriginal flavour and contains Aboriginal elements, e.g. the crystals, the flying into the sky with the aid of magical cords etc., it also contains many Western and Christian themes, and its real centre is the Common Dish, the democratic grail of common experience and common suffering which I put strongly over against the older European aristocratic grail of spiritual privilege attained only by an elite. Me versus Patrick White there, I guess!

He then strongly defended his right to draw on Aboriginal culture:

I haven't quoted anything verbatim from any existing or past Aboriginal rite, but have created what in music would be called a fantasia or set of variations involving some Aboriginal themes and elements. And surely one must be free to do this sort of thing. If all Aboriginal culture is to be locked up in sacred secrecy, how can it contribute its richness and flavour to the conversation of mankind? How can it assist the claim of the Aborigines to respect and consideration? It is one of the strongest arguments they have got, in a hard world.

And Murray subtly accused Wright, and the many white intellectuals who took her line,[26] of a cultural authoritarianism that was abhorrent to him, and harmful to Aboriginal and wider Australian culture:

Being Australian, I'd face creative death if I were to be confined scrupulously within a permitted 'European' or 'Western' range of culture, just as I think an Aboriginal artist would if he were segregated within a rigid tribal tradition in which he was prohibited from taking any account of the post-Conquest realities of his world. As soon as you even *meet* another culture, your own becomes inadequate and in that measure decadent—and that's a fact which excites me, because it's liberating, full of possibilities unknown within the strict fences of cultural Apartheid.

For all his goodwill towards her, he flatly refused to join Wright's Treaty campaign, which he saw as essentially and dangerously divisive:

> I couldn't bring myself to underwrite anything that looked like a proposal to divide the Australian people. And to keep them divided. Your passion may be Justice, or perhaps Restitution; mine is Reconciliation. Both are probably unattainable, in anything approaching a final degree, but mine inclines me to a position closer to the Jindyworobaks and Xavier Herbert, a Creole notion which, if all facts of parentage and kinship were truly admitted on both sides, has a good deal of present reality as well as future attractiveness.[27]

Wright was clearly rattled by Murray's overwhelming response: she had gone after what she thought was an easy target, and now found herself on the back foot instead. Nor did she defend herself against his charge that she was working to divide Australia both culturally and racially, except to point out to him that some Aboriginals had asked for a Treaty. For the rest, 'I make no comment on your other statements except to say that Aborigines, for the most part, now hate us so intensely and have so deep a contempt for our way of life that the last things most of them want are to be part of it . . .'[28] And with what Murray saw as veiled menace, she asked if she could display Murray's letter in her Treaty exhibition.

Murray was polite enough not to question her right to speak for Aboriginals in this way, but he did point out what he had hinted before, that the notion of a clear racial divide between 'Aborigines' and 'whites' was a construct, not least because of the high proportion of people of mixed blood in the Aboriginal communities:

> If, as you say, the Aborigines now thoroughly hate us and despise our way of life, then many if not most of them must be hating a part of themselves. And I can't wholly credit the motivations or respect the demands of folk who are denying part of their own background, who can't come to any reconciliation with a side of their ancestry. Intermixing is a fact, and it is dishonest to deny it.

As so often with Murray, a subtle subtext is also present here: Wright's bitter statements on behalf of Aboriginals, he was delicately hinting, expressed a dangerous inner division. He wholeheartedly endorsed her view of the need to recognise Aboriginal links with the land, but argued for its widening:

> I am horrified by Charlie Court's wholly self-assertive and vicious actions over the Noonkanbah thing, but what could you say to a white farmer up in my country who saw his land resumed and wrecked without any hope of appeal to liberal opinion or the United Nations? I've seen this done; it happens wholesale, for example, with dam-building projects. And you can't tell me that their land isn't heart's blood, as you put it, to many white country people. As Bunyah

is to me. My point here is that *all* of us, especially all of the poor, are under the same threat as the Noonkanbah people, and your Treaty threatens to set one section of the poor against another section . . .

Instead he presciently suggested an alternative course, though the *Wik* debate and the discussions that would follow it were still decades in the future: 'My instinct now is that what we need is not a treaty . . . but something much harder: a fundamental reexamination of land tenure over the whole continent, so as to arrive at something *everyone* can agree upon'.[29] And with that, he agreed that she might display his letter as she had asked: 'Use it with my blessings, so long as you use this one along with it. If I'm to be your Aunt Sally—and better me, perhaps, than a less experienced one—then I want you to display *all* of my case.[30]

But Wright was now in full retreat, though she could not bring herself to admit that Murray might have a spiritual link with his land akin to the Noonkanbah people's with theirs, and she argued that white farmers had done great damage to Australia. Murray, who did not idealise his people, agreed, arguing only that 'the Aborigines are willy-nilly in the same boat as us', and repeating that 'the thing requires repairs and maintenance to the whole boat, not just to certain cabins, however deserving, however justifiably resentful'.[31]

Wright told him that she had decided against displaying the letters, and rejected the charge that she was using him as an Aunt Sally. Murray apologised: 'I guess it's just that, coming from where I do, I sometimes feel a little embattled in the fairly conformist liberal atmosphere of Australian literary and intellectual circles. My caste is one which yours excludes, by and large, from its liberalism'.[32]

The final moves of this fascinating contest came when he proposed that the two of them publish their letters to each other, as what would obviously be an important contribution to an ongoing national debate. Wright countered after many months of silence by suggesting instead, in 1983, that both sides of the correspondence be quietly lodged in the National Library. Murray had moved on by this time, and agreed. For him the debate had never been one of political point-scoring, and he had no wish to hurt her. And it is characteristic of him that at no stage in this debate did he mention to her that he had Aboriginal cousins, for his grandmother Emily Worth had a sister who had married an Aboriginal: he kept in close contact with some of these Aboriginal cousins, including Vicki Grieves, who in the future would run the Aboriginal medical service in Taree.[33]

But the central themes of *The Boys Who Stole The Funeral*, and the debate with Wright, underscored for him a decision he had been moving towards for years: he was determined to move back to his home valley, in part to affirm in his own life the values he had asserted for so long in his poetry.

> I'd like to go home and live amongst my people as a way of saying to them that they don't have to feel relegated or wholly defensive. In this country, the bush has tended, certainly all of this century, to be a place where city money buys out the real farmer and the descendant of the early settler, and uses the land as a tax shelter and a bauble of privilege. But you'll have to read all about this in (or between the lines of) the Boys. After that, if I don't go home soon, my country readers will start to grow cynical about me. I half-deliberately painted myself into that corner . . . When we get up there, I'll be able to scrap all that Sydney-or-the-Bush stuff and get on with my bigger and always-underlying theme, which is holiness.[34]

He believed he was on the point of going home, and he half-knew that he was going to have to face all the Bunyah demons of his childhood again.

CHAPTER EIGHTEEN
AUTISM AND ISOLATION
1981–87

~

*. . . live like some green laurel
Rooted in one dear perpetual place*

W. B. YEATS

By 1981 the Murrays' fourth child, Alexander, was three years old, a beautiful child whom Murray found it a joy to be with. But he was causing increasing anxiety. After seeming to develop naturally for nearly two years, he suddenly appeared to fall back: speech which had begun to develop fell away into silence, he could not be toilet-trained, he was obsessive, showed no ability to play imaginative childhood games, showed little reaction to his parents and no fear of danger, and would consume nothing but milkshakes, nuts and honey.[1] He required constant vigilance, for he would run away from home given the least opportunity, and he responded to any raised voice of rebuke by terrified screaming, or by running through the house crashing through doors. The Murrays fought back coldly frightening intimations that the boy might be mentally handicapped.

In September 1981, unable to bear the uncertainty any longer, they took him to a local Child Assessment Centre and had him tested. The results came through on their wedding anniversary, 29 September 1981: Alexander was autistic. Murray was to say that this news was one of the hardest things he had to bear in his life: he struggled to accept it, finding Valerie, as often before, 'way out ahead of me, to come to terms with this development'.[2] Years later he would recall that on hearing the news, 'I did a thing I now know was very Aboriginal: I fell back on country for solace, picturing to myself every cutting & bend on the road from home [Bunyah] to Gloucester. When I'd done that, I'd recovered my inner balance'.[3]

But full acceptance did not come easily. For years Murray would listen eagerly to stories of supposed autists who suddenly began to talk in full sentences, and would continue to hope that Alexander would 'come right, or at least, like his father, right enough to "pass" in the world'.[4] There would be no sudden miracles for Alexander, in spite of his parents' prayers, but in time, with devoted unceasing care and many years of expert teaching, he would begin to make eye contact, to speak, and to interact with those around him. He would be one of the chief sorrows and blessings of his parents' lives.

Murray began to learn all he could about autism, a neurobiological disorder that affects physical, social, and language skills. The term was first used by the psychiatrist Leo Kanner in the 1940s to describe children who appeared to be excessively withdrawn and self-preoccupied. The syndrome usually appears before three years of age, as it had in Alexander, though the earliest signs are quite subtle. Autistic infants appear indifferent or averse to affection and physical contact, though attachment to parents or certain adults often develops later: Murray was to come to believe that he himself had been partly autistic in rejecting affection from his parents. Speech develops slowly and abnormally (it is often atonal and arhythmic) or not at all. It may be characterised by meaningless, noncontextual echolalia (constant repetition of what is said by others) or by strange mechanical sounds. Inappropriate attachment to objects may occur: in Alexander's case, these ranged from palm-trees to pineapples, and in general he seemed to worship fruit while refusing to eat any. There may be muted reaction to sound, no reaction to pain, or no recognition of genuine danger, yet autistic children are extremely sensitive. Usually the syndrome is accompanied by an obsessive desire to prevent environmental change, and frequently, rhythmic body movements such as rocking or hand-clapping.

Certain kinds of autists, once called idiot savants, now known as Aspergers, show astonishing visual or numerical skills, doing calculations instantly, or knowing all there is to know about narrow fields: in Alexander's case, this would be soil types, and in his teens he could draw elaborate soil-maps of areas as diverse as Bunyah or the American prairies. Again, Murray saw parallels with himself, speculating that his verbal precocity and polymathic knowledge were linked with the condition. And as autism isolates its sufferers and numbs them to pain, Murray's hero and alter-ego Fredy Boettcher would be afflicted by hyper-anaesthesia, or complete loss of feeling. Aided by the splinter of ice that Graham Greene said lurks in the heart of every artist, Murray would gradually turn the tragedy of Alexander's condition to poetic use.[5]

Almost at once after the shock of this diagnosis in September 1981 there was another, as Murray told John Barnie:

> Our other big news is, we suspect, consequent upon the first: we seem to have got pregnant again, one more time than we ever meant to. Valerie is apprehensive, because of the statistics on the birth of defective children to ageing mothers . . . but the odds are heavily our way, and I'm hoping that the fine old family name of Isabella will now get the run I thought it had missed out on.[6]

But his foremothers (having had the short-lived Isabella Press) would miss further memorialisation: Peter Benedict was born in a breech delivery on 25 May 1982, the Murrays' fifth and last child. A Literature Board grant for 1982 and a Writer in Residenceship at Newcastle University gave them a breathing space and allowed Valerie to take fifteen months off teaching, relief she sorely needed to cope with these burdens. 'She badly needs a rest, after a straight decade of teaching and raising the family', Murray wrote, though he added that this 'rest' merely meant reducing her jobs by one.[7]

Valerie's diary, begun in 1982 to keep track of Alexander's development, records her endless, patient struggles to toilet-train him, the constant alarms when he disappeared as he did several times a week in spite of barbed wire and locks ('Alex runs away over back fence—a man runs him down in James St and takes him to police station'),[8] his irritating obsession with scattering small objects like buttons, macaroni or spots of ice-cream on the floor, her delight when he began to say his first distorted words, and her exhaustion at coping with the housework and with the new baby Peter during all this. No one, reading these uncomplaining diaries, could fail to admire her strength and courage, or wonder how much Murray could have written without her.

Alexander's need for the special autistic school at Forestville, and Peter's arrival, meant that the Murrays' well-developed plans to move to Bunyah were put on hold for several more years, and it would not be until 1985 that they were able to transfer themselves. By then Alexander had advanced to the point where he could cope with a school in Taree, and Murray erected on his Forty Acres a second, slightly larger house than the one in which Cecil lived, separated from it but standing so close together that they constitute one dwelling, linked by a small conservatory.

The momentous move from Chatswood to Bunyah was made on the last day of 1985, Murray having persuaded Valerie to try country life for one year. They did not sell their Chatswood house, so that if Bunyah proved intolerable to Valerie they would be able to move back. Meanwhile Christina and Daniel, she a 22-year-old tutor in Animal Husbandry at Sydney University, he a 19-year-old student half-way through a degree in Metallurgy at the University of New South Wales, shared the house until they had a falling out and Daniel had to leave. The Murrays would not sell 27 Edgar Street until 1998.

Murray need not have worried about his family's reaction to the move. Valerie could cope with almost anything, and she and the three younger children, Clare, then eleven, Alexander, seven, and Peter, two, all loved Bunyah. The utter peace, the restrained magnificence of the valley with its high wooded hills and rolling farmland, the fact that country living proved cheaper than staying in the city so that Valerie was presently able to give up teaching altogether (after a year as a helper to a handicapped girl at Taree High) and devote herself to her family, all these things persuaded them that the move had been the right one. Above all was the relief of finding that Alexander fitted into his new school without problems and in fact seemed to improve rapidly at Bunyah. He adopted Murray's own childhood practice of going for immensely long walks through the friendly countryside, and his parents could follow his progress through phonecalls from farmers many kilometres away: 'Your boy's just gone by here'.

If Valerie had had doubts about living with her father-in-law, they gradually dissipated. Cecil, like his son, had to be urged to wash more frequently, and would always irritate Valerie by what Murray called 'furtive uncivilisation and self-neglect',[9] but he was good-humoured, generous, kind to the children and constantly amusing. His eyesight was deteriorating and he would undergo a cataract operation in April 1986, but his spirit was dauntless: he continued to enjoy dancing and music, and would celebrate his eightieth birthday, in February 1989, with a large party which ended with him and his brother Eric serenading the departing guests with fiddle and accordion out on the road at 2.30 in the morning.[10]

He continued to enjoy unsettling city visitors by playing the country bumpkin, displaying rough country manners with a sly sideways glance to catch their reaction, or casually saying things to shock. Peter Barden's wife Ann, on a visit to Bunyah, was among those tested in this way. Knowing that she had a particular love of dogs, Cecil announced that his dog was sick: 'I'd better get the vet kit, I s'pose'. Ann was all interest: 'What sort of vet kit do you have?' Wordlessly, Cecil went to a cupboard and got out two rifles.[11] Such jokes had a neat pincer-effect on the victim: to show shock was to be laughed at, to conceal it suggested you expected country folk to behave like this. It was a form of rural one-upmanship very hard to counter, as Cecil knew, and he enjoyed himself quietly.

Oddly enough, it was Murray who found Cecil difficult: 'Dad and I are stuck, to a large extent, in the relations of 1951–7, my adolescence, when he was wrecked by depression & grief and I was orphaned by that & Mum's death', he told a friend.[12] In addition, though the Murrays from now on worshipped faithfully each week in St Bernadette's, the handsome red-brick church in Krambach, to the end of his life Cecil pointedly ignored his son's Catholicism and would never accompany them.

For all that, Murray had longed to make the move for many years, and was delighted to be settled on home soil. He wrote to John Barnie, who had recently moved back from Denmark to his native Wales,

> I've done a Barnie, as you see, and gone home! It's all working more smoothly than it seemed it might, given a last-minute hitch over Alex's schooling, but now he goes 40 miles a day by bus . . . The lotus I brought back from the Nthn Territory in 1984 are rioting in the house dam, and I go in danger of becoming a lotus-eater. Rare trips to Sydney are irksome now—I really had had a bellyful of that life.[13]

'I think I'll become a venerable dead author, benign and remote', he added in another letter.[14] To me he explained later:

> In a way, I came home in order to annul any dimension of social rise in my life, to strip away any appearance of 'having tickets on' myself. Locals who knew me as a boy accept me in this spirit, I think—and I suspect many of our arriviste literati take it, rightly, as an affront. As MacDiarmid wrote of the Socialist MacSpaunday group:
> > 'unlike those yellow twicers
> > I am *of*, not *for*, the working classes'.[15]

Being Home at last was a constant, quiet joy to him, and very productive of poetry, as he contentedly told an academic friend, Christine Alexander.[16] His Sabine farm would be immortalised in poems about its dams covered in beautiful magenta lotuses, the birds that dashed themselves against the house windows until Murray pasted up cut-out cardboard hawk shapes to warn them off, the sixty-year-old china pear trees that had survived the destruction of an earlier house, and near which he planted an accompaniment of fruit saplings. As he put it invitingly in a verse letter to the West Australian poet Dennis Haskell,

> I think you'd like it here, in our glade
> of fruit saplings that now nearly manage shade
> and soft grass, beside the lotus dam
> and our other trees. Some year you must see them.
> Trees, space, waterbirds—things of that ilk,
> plus people of my own kind, are the milk
> and honey I came home for. Not dairying,
> that drudgery, poor, imprisoning, unvarying.[17]

Apart from his fruit trees, Cecil's vegetable garden and a few chickens, Murray used the land rather as indigenous Australians might have done from the dawn of Bunyah's history: he lived on it, hunted over it (though now only very occasionally, with Cecil's old shot-gun, of which only one barrel functioned), delighted in its beauty, and burned it annually. Cecil, in the years when he had been without a farm of his own, had most missed being able to burn his own grass. This ritual burning at the end of winter, Murray then insisted, was beneficial—a view he would later change in light of the evidence that the practice, persisted in over thousands of years, had deforested and desertified the continent, exhausted its soils and dried its climate, sharply reducing the range of Australian flora and fauna unable to survive drought and fire, a horrifying impoverishment.[18] He gardened a little, but inexpertly: Valerie interrupted one phone conversation with me to call urgently through the door, 'Leslie! Don't pull that out, it's a rose'. In summer he enjoyed roaring back and forth on a large ride-on mower (once inadvertently rolling it into the dam),[19] and he was a dab hand with a chainsaw.

Mostly he wisely stuck to his last, like the master-craftsman he had become. Once settled in on the Forty Acres, he began to produce a fine set of poems following the cycle of his first year back at 'my dear Bunyah', as he called it to Angela Smith;[20] it would be published as *The Idyll Wheel* in 1989. 'What I yearn for is what I've got in large measure: a warm cocoon to spin silk in as our winter comes on. I'm spinning some good silk, too, I think . . .'[21]

This 'good silk' began to appear in his next volume of poetry, *The Daylight Moon*, published by Angus & Robertson in 1987, and bearing on its cover a photograph of the little shack in which Murray had been brought up, symbol for him of all the happiness and misery of Bunyah, symbol also of his physical return to his roots. Murray tended to print his poems in the order in which they had come to him: in this case the point at which he moved to Bunyah is clear, for the volume, from page 39 on, was full of his childhood memories transmuted into vivid poetry: he was working on 'Roman Cage Cups' when he made the move. The later poems of the volume crystallise experiences ranging from his work on the milk truck as a muscular schoolboy, to the stories he had heard from his father and uncles, and memories of himself as an infant among cattle. He was returning in imagination to his hard time, the time between his mother's death and his arrival at Sydney University. It was dangerous territory.

The volume was very well received, both in Australia and in Britain, for he had now, after two futile attempts,[22] succeeded in being published in the United Kingdom, having been taken up by Michael Schmidt's excellent Carcanet Press.[23] British and American press reaction was warmly welcoming. 'If he is anything', Derek Walcott wrote of him in the *New Republic*, 'he is Roman in the way that Ben Jonson was Roman, firm-based and pillared with scholarship, way above the tiny hawkers below in the market'.[24] Peter Scupham, in *Poetry Review*, called him 'Australia's unofficial laureate',[25] the first time the phrase was used of him. Karl Stead, in the *London Review of Books*, remarked on his 'wonderful gift of phrase', and commented, 'More than any other poetry I can think of, except perhaps the early work of Judith Wright, his has caught the distinctive feel of the Australian experience'.[26] The Poetry Society in Britain made *The Daylight Moon* its Commonwealth Spring Choice in 1987, to Murray's pleasure: 'but in a way I'm sad at how resented that'll be back home here, & how I'll be sniped at by some Austrns. for the crime of "making it abroad"!'[27]

He was publishing hard at this time, for just before the move to Bunyah he had also found time to produce three books which together reflected his constant thinking about what it means to be Australian. *The Australian Year*, ostensibly a coffee-table book about the Australian seasons, is in fact crammed with Murray's passionate love and curious knowledge of the Australian landscape, its flora and fauna and its ways. It is full of such felicities as his description of an attacking magpie's 'silent, arrowy flight', 'white-painted bee-boxes forming Hopi pueblos', and 'white bloodwood trees dripping their crimson kino stickily down their trunks till the ground around is brittle with rusty glaze'. In prose, as in poetry, he handed Australians their country seen for the first time in brilliant images.

His second book at this time was his *New Oxford Book of Australian Verse*, a survey of Australian poetry in which he allowed each poet no more than three poems, in an effort to avoid seeming partisan in his choice. This was in contrast to *The New Australian Poetry*, edited by John Tranter in 1979 as a vehicle for the Generation of '68, and *The Younger Australian Poets*, edited by Robert Gray and Geoffrey Lehmann in 1983 to represent those whom Tranter had downplayed. The resulting selection is in part a reflection of Murray's view that 'ours isn't a towering Alpine tradition, as you know, but a low, rolling poetic landscape of many little hills and secret waterholes'.[28] In part, the volume was a revolutionary statement about Australian national traditions. As usual he was looking for what brings Australians together, nationally and culturally:

> It'll be the first Aust. anthology to make a firm point of mixing pukka and popular poetic traditions together, and will illustrate, at many points, the ways in which they flowed together and fused. That's really the nub of it, I think: fusion, abolishing or at least rearranging the class-categories of 'high' and 'low' inherited from the aristocratic European past. Both traditions need each other . . .
>
> Between these two poles there's a poetry of, I guess, national self-acceptance, which takes Australia unselfconsciously as the centre of things because that's where we live. Geoff Page, Alan Gould, Roger McDonald (tho' he seems to have given up poetry now), Rhyll McMaster, Geoff Lehmann, Bob

Gray (though he's a bit Acmeist),[29] me—lots of us work in this mode. Bruce Dawe was into it early . . .[30]

He lamented the fact that intransigence over money on the part of the scholar Ted Strehlow's widow forced the removal of six pages of marvellous Aranda and Loritja poetry,[31] but in spite of this the anthology, which was the first to include Frank the Poet McNamara as well as Barry Humphries and 'The Bastard from the Bush', gave him immense pleasure: 'It has lots of sprawl, no little irreverence, and will catch hell when it comes out', he wrote gleefully to Angela Smith.[32]

In this he was mistaken, for even in Australia the volume was on the whole well received. Though the critics thought it 'eccentric', there was a consensus that, as Chris Wallace-Crabbe put it, it was 'a rattling good book for dipping in and getting the flavours'.[33] Vivian Smith particularly approved the choice of young poets, the ballad and folk material, and the range of Aboriginal verse presented.[34] 'The most readable anthology of Australian verse I have ever encountered', said Peter Porter.[35] One of the few negative voices was that of Vincent Buckley: 'Murray has muffed it'.[36] The Tranterites largely ignored the volume, but other reviewers made a point of saying that Murray had showed them up: David Rowbotham, in the *Courier-Mail*, remarked, 'What Les A. Murray has done to (and for) Australian poetry in probably its darkest hour, its invasion by bogus practitioners producing the unreadable, makes this book a source of amazement. The *New Oxford Book of Australian Verse* represents a rescue operation, and presents new vision'.[37]

Murray's other compilation, also made during his months of reading for the Oxford book, was an *Anthology of Australian Religious Poetry*. In this, as in his Oxford anthology, he pointedly eschewed all annotation, glossing, biography or commentary, as a protest against the way literary critics, in his view, 'summarize and interpret and manage literary texts, so that most students think that the text is just a sort of primitive, unreal thing from which the real stuff of interpretation arises'.[38] He used the broadest definition of 'religious', trying to include all religious traditions in Australia, including that of reaction against religion, but he held to the criterion that to be included the verses had to be poetry: 'Books of poetry which actually give primacy to the poetry in them are quite rare in our age'.[39] He wrote to the poet Philip Salom,

> I guess I'm prepared for some flak over the relig. anthology. It'll confuse them, mind, since it's all religions, not just Christianity. It's a survey of how the religious impulse has found poetic embodiment in Australia. Interesting—did I tell you this—by far the largest amounts of Christian poetry and of poetry in general which one could properly see as religious have been written since World War II. No decline visible—in fact the very opposite of one.[40]

The volume drew little flak, and was in fact warmly received. Chris Wallace-Crabbe was to describe it as 'fascinating and substantial: whatever its lacunae, it alters our whole understanding of Australian poetry'.[41]

Wallace-Crabbe's reference to 'lacunae' was something of a private joke. On the publication of the first edition of Murray's volume Vincent Buckley had phoned Wallace-Crabbe to ask how many poems he had in Murray's anthology. 'Four or five', said Wallace-Crabbe: 'How about you?' 'Only two', said Buckley sourly, 'but the cunt is always trying to do me down. And guess how many of his own poems he's put in?' Wallace-Crabbe guessed 'Eight'. 'More', said Buckley. 'Twelve, eighteen?' guessed Wallace-Crabbe. 'Twenty-four!' said Buckley, with the air of man who has proved the evil of the enemy beyond doubt. The anecdote well illustrates the Sydney–Melbourne divide.[42] When Murray brought out a second edition of the volume, in 1991, he reduced his own contributions to eighteen, but he also removed both of Buckley's poems.

The volume was more than just another anthology to him. In Murray's view, poetry and religion were intimately connected, in that poetry was the fullest possible expression of some aspect of life, while religion was the deepest expression of the whole of life itself. In his terms, then, religions were the greatest of poems.[43] Like all poems in his view, religions involve the three vital elements of the conscious mind, the dreaming mind and the body. As he put it in one of his most profound poems, 'Poetry and Religion':

> Religions are poems. They concert
> our daylight and dreaming mind, our
> emotions, instinct, breath and native gesture
>
> into the only whole thinking: poetry.
> Nothing's said till it's dreamed out in words
> and nothing's true that figures in words only.
>
> A poem, compared with an arrayed religion,
> may be like a soldier's one short marriage night
> to die and live by. But that is a small religion . . .
>
> There'll always be religion around while there is poetry
>
> or a lack of it. Both are given, and intermittent,
> as the action of those birds—crested pigeon, rosella parrot—
> who fly with wings shut, then beating, and again shut.

In the course of his reading for these two anthologies, in January 1986, he discovered the work of Philip Hodgins, a young Melbourne poet who was slowly dying of leukaemia, and whom Murray considered a real find. 'His poems are graced with an immense calm', Murray would write, and he particularly admired the way Hodgins 'combines a minute recollection of farming life on the riverine plains of northern Victoria with a true understanding of country people and the vast embodiment the hard bare slog of their lives slowly confers on them'.[44] In the years remaining to Hodgins Murray would befriend him, successfully recommend the publication of his work by Angus & Robertson, and rejoice in each year and each poem Hodgins managed to snatch from death. Hodgins (with Murray, Robert Gray, Paul Kane and the chef Stefano di Pieri) played a major part in founding the Mildura Literary Festival, which Murray tried to attend every March, believing it much the best literary festival in Australia; after Hodgins's long-foreseen death in August 1995 he liked to think of it as the Philip Hodgins Literary Festival, though it was never formally named that.[45]

But Murray himself was now suffering the first of a series of physical ailments, outriders of a much more serious psychological storm which had been building up in him since his writing of 'The Steel', the poem in which he faced his mother's death. In 1987 he turned forty-nine, and was beginning to show his age. He was still strong enough to astound friends like Robert Gray by lifting the back of the Toyota HiAce van he drove ('It's only a tin box', he told Gray, grinning),[46] but he was now almost completely bald and what little hair he had was greying fast. About this time he was diagnosed as a diabetic, as his father and grandfather had been before him, though the disease was at first controlled with tablets alone. As it worsened insulin injections would become necessary: he took these easily, and on occasions he would casually inject himself in the thigh through his trouser-leg while talking animatedly, thereby deeply impressing my children.

By the end of the 1980s his weight was peaking at a formidable 160 kilograms, and although his strength allowed him to carry it, he avoided exercise if he could. Gray, on a visit to the Chatswood house shortly before the Murrays left it for Bunyah, recalled Valerie telling Murray to walk Gray to the station: 'You need the exercise, Leslie'. Murray and Gray walked perhaps a hundred metres up the road before Murray, puffing, sat on a wall telling Gray 'Let's stop for a yarn'. After fifteen minutes' chat he looked at his watch: 'Valerie'll be expecting me back about now. You can find the station on your own, can't you, Bob?' And he trundled back home.[47]

Still, he retained his immense strength. When Bob Ellis moved into his house in Palm Beach, in 1976, Murray helped him with his furniture, a task that proved difficult because the truck could not be brought right up to the house, and everything had to be carried across a hundred metres of rough ground. Towards the end of this task, when Ellis and his other helpers were exhausted, Murray went back to the truck and found that one of the heaviest items had been forgotten, a large refrigerator. Murray bent his knees, hugged the fridge, straightened up with it, and carried it on his own across the broken ground, laughing at his friends' awed offers to help him, finally lowering it delicately into position in the kitchen.[48]

But he showed increasing signs of wear as the 1980s passed and his fiftieth birthday approached. For years he had been conscious that his hearing was very gradually failing, writing a sadly funny poem about it, in which he indulged to the full his Shakespearian love of puns:

> Hearing loss? Yes, loss is what we hear
> who are starting to go deaf. Loss
> trails a lot of weird puns in its wake, viz.
> Dad's a real prism of the Left—
> you'd like me to repeat that?
> THE SAD SURREALISM OF THE DEAF.
>
> It's mind over mutter at work
> guessing half what the munglers are saying
> and society's worse. Punchlines elude to you
> as Henry Lawson and other touchy drinkers
> have claimed. Asides, too, go pasture.
> It's particularly nasty with a wether.
>
> First you crane at people, face them
> while you can still face them. But grudgually
> you give up dinnier parties; you begin
> to think about Beethoven; you Hanover
> next visit here on silly Narda Fearing—I SAY
> YOU CAN HAVE AN EXQUISITE EAR
> AND STILL BE HARD OF HEARING.[49]

'I found the deafness that I slid into infinitely slowly from, I'd say, my teens onward, to be very seductive, as well as an increasing nuisance', he told Peter Goldsworthy, adding, 'it was the invitation to Autic Island, the World of One'.[50] He tended to dominate conversations so that he knew what was being said, irritating some of his friends: 'How do you know you're going deaf, Les?', asked Jamie Grant satirically.[51] Murray eventually submitted to an operation, telling Geoff Page jocularly, 'Drs Black & Decker are going to ream my inner ear out'.[52] The skilful doctor's name was actually Tjiong, and Murray's hearing was saved by the insertion of an artificial stirrup bone in his left ear in an operation in Taree on 10 February 1987. He was astonished by the improvement:

'When Dr Tjiong finally pulled the dressing out every truck in Taree ran over my ear because I hadn't heard them for years'.[53]

But trouble of a more serious kind, not to be cleared by an operation, was gradually growing in him. The return to Bunyah, he would come to believe, would have to be paid for. 'If home conceals Old Bad Stuff you had not mastered the first time around, going back there, perhaps especially as you approach your fifties, is an invitation to crisis.'[54] His complex childhood wounds were being reopened by his return to Bunyah and his now-constant examination of the past in his poetry. And as at Taree High, where injuries had been rubbed freshly raw by the jibes of his schoolmates, he now grew increasingly sensitive to what he considered constant attacks on him by journalists or jealous minor poets exercising the cruel Australian privilege of poppy-lopping. And it was at this point that his torments at Taree High, decades before, reached out to touch him again.

CHAPTER NINETEEN
THE POWER OF THE DOG
1987–89

*O the mind, mind has mountains; cliffs of fall
Frightful, sheer, no-man-fathomed. Hold them cheap
May who ne'er hung there.*

HOPKINS

At the end of 1987 the constant sniping Murray had endured for years reached a climax over his publication, in the *London Review of Books*,[1] of a poem about venereal disease, 'Aphrodite Street':

> So it's back to window shopping
> on Aphrodite Street
> for the apples are stacked and juicy
> but some are death to eat.
>
> For just one generation
> the plateglass turned to air—
> when you look for that generation
> half of it isn't there.

Murray was talking about the generation who had come to sexual maturity after the introduction of the Pill, and he was using AIDS as a way of commenting on the demeaning sexual ethos he had first encountered at Taree High, Aphrodite posing as the source and central criterion of all human value, being endlessly pressed upon the young through peer influence, television programs and magazines in which to be young, self-focused, sensuous and beautiful was put forward as the ideal, to the terrible cost of those who could not conform:

> Age, spirit, kindness, all were taunts;
> grace was enslaved to meat.
> You never were mugged till you were mugged
> on Aphrodite Street.

> God help the millions that street killed
> and those it sickened too,
> when it was built past every house
> and often bulldozed through.
>
> Apples still swell, but more and more
> are literal death to eat
> and it's back to window shopping
> on Aphrodite Street.

His poem went completely over the head of some of his readers. He was immediately attacked, with extraordinary venom, by those who seemed to believe that AIDS was solely a disease of homosexuals, and who misinterpreted his poem as an attack on that group. The Australian poet Alan Wearne, writing to the *London Review of Books*, raged:

> I know a number of homosexuals who have the Aids antibodies. I certainly have a bisexual friend with the disease. Obviously Les A. Murray knows no one in these categories, for behind all the attempt at artifice (an attempt which I find collapses into doggerel) simply lies the stark vision of what we Australians term 'poofter-bashing'. Faith, hope and love matter little with this man, it seems: for by 'Aphrodite Street's' standards there's nothing like kicking a person, group, race or nation when they're down; or worse still, a poet attempting to play God, cheering on the kickers.

Wearne also attacked the paper for publishing Murray's poem, concluding, with all the vitriol he was imputing to Murray, 'Many an obese glutton has died of a cardiac arrest, or related heart disease. Perhaps I should write a poem on this topic. Would you publish it?'[2]

Murray replied good-humouredly, patiently pointing out that AIDS 'threatens us all', and explaining that in any case it was merely the peg on which he had hung his poem: 'I was memorialising a certain demeaning sexual ethos which has been dominant in Western society for a generation, one which tends to destroy faith, hope and love, and families, and the lives of children. It is a sort of idolatry'.[3] To his friends he remarked tolerantly that he could sympathise with Wearne, who had spent ten years 'writing an unreadable verse novel I may have described to too many people as a "sexual Hansard".'[4] But neither reason nor good humour could save him from another surge of attacking letters from British gay activists accusing him of being 'hate-filled' and 'homophobic', and his increasingly pained responses merely gave them more publicity for their cause.[5] His opponents were not interested in understanding him or his poem.

Wearne's cruel sneer about him as an 'obese glutton', echoed by the reference of another *London Review of Books* correspondent, John Fletcher, to his 'anatomy',[6] could not have failed to remind him of the years of fat-names he had endured at Taree High, and in this sensitised state he probably made a mistake when he accepted an invitation to read his work to the Taree Rotary Club. The event, in March 1988, was very well attended, several former Taree High teachers and pupils being present in the crowd of 150, and the reading was a great success. While he was still wrapped in the glow of the congratulations that followed, he was approached by a former school fellow, who had been one of his most relentless and subtle pursuers thirty years before. She talked to him for a little, and then, to remind him of those days, dropped into the conversation the name she had used on him so often: 'Bottom'. Murray was stabbed to the heart: though he concealed the fact and continued the conversation, he got away from her as quickly as he could and went home wounded to Bunyah.

The next day, as he was out driving, he began to weep, not understanding why, and having begun, he could not stop. 'What the hell is this?' he asked himself fearfully.[7] He suffered painful tingling in his fingers. Back home, he lay on the sofa curled up like a caterpillar to which a cigarette has been applied, tears oozing from shut eyes. He had had many episodes of black depression before, and it was a long time before Valerie realised that this was something different and more serious. 'Another testy evening from Les—cyclonic depression', her diary would record stoically.[8] He suffered from indigestion, something he had never experienced before; his always-crowded mind now became congested, crammed with ideas he could not formulate clearly or nimbly enough, so that they tumbled over each other and made him incoherent.

The helpless weeping would sometimes go on for days; at other times it would last a few hours, and then he would be up and at the table, writing a poem. 'Poetry's the only kind of thinking, or action, that my disease hasn't touched', he told John Barnie.[9] His powers of recovery were astounding, for when he was in the depths of depression he endured misery beyond description. Years later, asked if he believed in Hell, he would reply soberly, 'I've been there. I've had depression. There is nothing worse. You know, when your brain boils in your head. Misery beyond all bloody description. It's fearsome and you don't deserve any of it'.[10] Hardest of all was the knowledge, as the depression lifted, that it would return before long. As he told Bob Ellis, 'Having a depressive attack is like the first scene from *Macbeth*. You chase the witches away and get their cauldron. Then you cut your head off and put it in and boil it for four or five hours and you take it out, put it back on your shoulders, and say "I'm going to do this again tomorrow"'.[11] This miserable state he would endure for eight years.

His body chemistry altered, and he found he could no longer endure to smoke, a habit he had always enjoyed. He could not go near Taree High. And from being a daredevil driver, he now became oddly nervous, and cliff roads or high bridges reduced him to whimpering terror. Peter Barden, now living in San Francisco with his wife Ann, would remember how Murray, on the cliff road to a local beauty spot, Muir Woods, suddenly began to shake and put his hands over his eyes and say 'Oh Jesus! Oh Christ! Oh Jesus!', alarming them both terribly.[12] His poem 'Corniche', written in November 1992,[13] would describe the condition vividly:

> The first time, I'd been coming apart all year,
> weeping, incoherent; cigars had given me up;
> any fall off a steep road and I'd whimper past in low gear
> then: mortal horror. Masking my pulse's calm lub-dup.
>
> It was the victim-sickness. Adrenalin howling in my head,
> the black dog was my brain. Coming to drown me in my breath
> was energy's black hole, depression, compere of the predawn show
> when, returned from a pee, you stew and welter in your death.

He became increasingly sensitive to negative criticism, and naturally believed he encountered it everywhere, in spite of repeated evidence of his success and acclaim. On 2 March 1988 he was awarded the South Australian Premier's Prize for poetry ($12 500), and the Bicentennial Prize of $5000; buoyed by these successes, he travelled down with Valerie and Alexander to receive them. But the ceremony itself was a shambles, with the Premier remarking in his speech that many people had advised him against giving Murray the award, and this grudgingly given honour saddened Murray, spoiling the whole occasion for him.[14]

Although he continued to receive invitations to readings and conferences, he accepted fewer of them, and with greater difficulty. He had always hated going away without Valerie and his children; now, in his miserably vulnerable state, it took all his courage to do so, and he only kept it up because these trips constituted a major part of his income. He became increasingly convinced that a majority of his fellow Australian writers despised and hated him, that the honours he received in Australia were hypocritically offered, and that cliques of his enemies were constantly plotting to do him harm by shutting him out of anthologies, prizes or awards, or by boycotting the writing of those associated with him.

Murray did have literary enemies, some of whom did what they could to hurt him, in part because he dominated the Australian literary scene like a mastodon among gazelles, in part because they feared he was out to hurt them. 'I have this queer, queasy feeling that I've finally been Declared Black', he wrote to Philip Hodgins in complaining about the strange paucity of reviews of *The Daylight Moon*.[15] This was largely imagination on his part: the volume was well reviewed, and it won the National Poetry Award in 1988, while 'The Tin Wash Dish', a poem he had finished too late for inclusion in the volume, won the ABC Bicentennial Prize for the best short poem. He continued to pile up public successes, while irrationally believing himself to be shunned and loathed.

In August 1988 Murray accepted the invitation to be keynote speaker at a conference on 'Writers and Academics', which Christine Alexander, the writer Gerard Windsor and I organised at the University of New South Wales. Other participants included Donald Horne, Brian Matthews and Harry Heseltine, whom Murray considered friends, and Frank Moorhouse, Fay Zwicky and John Tranter, whom he did not. On the eve of the conference I got a brief letter from him: 'Dear Peter, No creaky excuses: I'm simply not prepared to have social contact of any sort with a couple of the people you've invited to speak at the conference, so I'm not coming. It's no use: public ... conflict, however gladiatorially exciting, is just not for me. It's inefficient, and robs me of concentration'.[16] He enclosed his paper, 'The Lecture Halls of the Fisher King', to be read on his behalf at the conference. I put this to the gathered delegates, and was surprised at the fierceness of the rejection that followed: 'If Les hasn't the grace to turn up', growled one red-faced speaker, 'we don't want to hear him'. And the majority voted against having the paper read. This was a heavy loss to the conference, for 'The Lecture Halls of the Fisher King' is one of his most brilliant pieces, written in sixty short numbered paragraphs, any three of which would have provided more food for thought than some of the papers that were read.

1. The first 140 years in the development of Australian literature in English, from Barron Field's 'Kangaroo' to the early Sixties of this century, proceeded without significant academic involvement or help.

2. The establishment of other lines of patronage before the universities took up Australian literature in any large or convinced way may yet save our literature from a wholesale repudiation of the 'common' reader.

3. An academic-led literature is a gentrified suburb, but the unconstrained reader is the objective correlative.

5. The spirit of the age, as sedulously cultivated in universities and among their graduates, makes it curiously hard to admit or assume that Australian literary studies can be undertaken out of love . . .

10. The little magazine as we have known it is a relic of the era of literary modernism and now artificially prolongs that era.

11. Universities, like any patron, can determine the subject matter, the attitudes and the tone of all but the strongest and most individual writing— and thus to study any but the strongest and most independent of current writing is merely to admire oneself in the mirror.

13. Literary studies are vital in establishing and maintaining accurate texts. Authorial intention has been shown as a fallacy in criticism, but not as yet in the textual editorial sphere. Where discoverable, it should be respected, except where it is wrong.

14. It is the special glory of academics not to set or follow fashion, but to counteract it on behalf of texts which it injures or obscures. They exist to keep the unread read, and to defend its real qualities. For a literary academic to treat any author as bygone is a betrayal of trust.

18. Inexplicable literary hatreds arise more often from the prick of an editorial pencil than from that of a critical pen.

19. Academics and authors despise each other most when each has it in mind to exploit the other. When this impulse is dormant, each merely considers the other his dependant, if not his natural servant.

20. Publishers, in turn, despise both academics and authors because they depend on both but effortlessly exploit both.

21. Publishers can exploit academics and writers alike because the former have an assured income and the latter do not.

23. For savagery, dishonesty, bullying, ill-will and poorly disguised jealousy, I have never seen a piece of academic criticism quite equal that regularly practised by authors on each other. Literature just seems to be informed by this greater joie de vivre.

50. Those who say the author is dead usually have it in mind to rifle his wardrobe.

57. The Enlightenment will crumble and disappear because its disappearance can be imagined. To imagine poetry disappearing, however, is paradoxical.

60. Sixty observations on any subject whatever should suffice.[17]

Despite his continued public good humour and stout common sense, he was sinking further into depression, as his inability to face the conference showed. There was a more dramatic form of this fear a little later in the year, when he was due to fly to America for a reading in New York: he went down to Sydney on his own to catch the plane, and at the last minute was unable to do so, phoning Valerie in deep distress from the airport to announce that he was returning home.

On 28 October 1988, just after his fiftieth birthday, his depression had deepened to the point that he had his first big panic attack: he experienced a sharp, continued, vice-like pain across his chest, and was convinced he was having a heart attack. Valerie rushed him in to the Taree Hospital for monitoring. After a frightening overnight stay in the cardiac ward, and extreme unction from the Catholic chaplain, a battery of tests revealed no physical problem, and he was put on medication. As he told John Barnie:

> My disease is an all too common & quite chemically-based one: clinical depression. The treatment's no longer the subliterary Freudian couch, which rarely works, if ever it does: to my relief, I'm on medication instead, & am promised full recovery by Christmas or before, tho' I have to go on with the tablets for 6 mths or so to prevent a relapse. It seems I'd gone acute, & the phantom heart attack was an unconscious scream for help. And help came, thank God.[18]

But the hope that he would recover 'by Christmas' was much too sanguine. Having fallen into the jaws of what he, following Winston Churchill, called 'the Black Dog', he stayed there year after year. Medication succeeded medication: Tofranil, Valium, Lithium, Prozac, none produced a lasting effect, though Murray rather enjoyed taking them. Xanax proved best for him, though the relief it gave was slight.[19] As he told me in 1994:

> So I suppose for the next six years I was mad as a loon in many ways. But I was able to go on working in between attacks. It does take away your energy. It means I've been less productive than I could have been. In the old days I could write both poetry and prose. I can't write prose much any more, because I just haven't got the energy. It goes down a black hole.[20]

He often woke in deep misery in the early hours of the morning, 'your troubles and terrors ripping into you with a gusto allowed them by fatigue and the disappearance of proportion',[21] the experience Larkin describes in 'Aubade'. He also continued to have the phantom heart attacks at intervals, and though his conscious mind knew he was not dying, his reaction was always one of ungovernable terror and frantic demands to be rushed to hospital. The death of his mother lay deep beneath this black misery; several of the panic attacks were triggered by merely looking at his daughter Christina, whose resemblance to her dead grandmother was now eerie to him. As Christina, who had never been told of the resemblance, recalled her puzzlement:

> I actually triggered panic attacks and I could see it was me doing it and I couldn't figure out why. I could see him looking at me strangely . . . apparently I was triggering them by my appearance. He would look at me like it wasn't me. It was odd. It didn't occur to me at the time—I didn't know why he was doing it—but he would just look at me like he was looking through me and then go quiet.[22]

The next minute he would be begging her to get her stethoscope and listen to his heart, and though his pulse was slow and regular, nothing would settle him but a trip to a hospital.

These crisis-points were dramatic punctuations, but the continuing text of his depression was made up of the hours he spent each day weeping on the sofa, waiting for the cloud to lift so that he could work again—until the next time. He became at such times, as he put it himself, 'a great baby utterly dependent on his wife'.[23] He could wear only stretch-knit clothes and draw-string pants. His bouts of anger became harder to control. Valerie tried to restrain his aggression in his many contacts with traffic policemen, who repeatedly stopped him for driving without a seat-belt, or for speeding: in December 1989, for instance, driving back across the continent from Perth, 'I low-flew home at speeds of 160–180 km. in honour of my imminent licence disqualification for speeding', as he told Philip Hodgins with maniacal glee. 'At those speeds, speed is a visible thing, glassy and streamy, a sort of eerie crystal grown on high concentration, hard to keep in focus but narcotic when you do'.[24]

Policemen were sometimes intimidated by his sheer size and the sense of unhinged aggression he projected in his contacts with them: he had always regarded the police as symbols of the many ways in which the privileged maintained their dominance over the poor. Jamie Grant recalled being driven by him when a motorcycle policeman stopped them for overtaking a line of law-abiding motorists at speed while not wearing a seat-belt. Murray claimed his speedometer was broken, adding, 'And as for the seat-belt, there's this letter'.

The Murrays' Canberra home, 77 Burn Street: Bob Ellis and Les Murray revisiting it in April 1998 during the making of Ellis's film about Murray, *Bastards from the Bush*.

The Scottish sojourn: Les Murray, Christina and Daniel on Culloden Moor, February 1968, while they lived in Herdsmuir Cottage. *(Photograph: Don Kirby)*

Les Murray and Valerie at the wedding of Geoffrey Lehmann to Sally McInerney, July 1969.

Kenneth Slessor and Les Murray at the housewarming party, 27 Edgar Street, Chatswood, April 1971.

Les Murray with Anne and Bob Ellis on their wedding day, 17 December 1977, Mona Vale Anglican Church, Pittwater Road, Sydney.

He handed the policeman a letter from a psychiatrist, Dr Michael Richardson of Taree, to the effect that 'if constrained by a seat-belt, Mr Murray has a tendency to become severely distressed'. Murray was in fact not constantly under Dr Richardson's care, but drew on him, usually by telephone, for information about the chemical causes of depression. The policeman took in the letter, Murray's great size, and the strange look in his eyes: he returned the letter very slowly, said 'Drive carefully, sir', and left the scene.[25]

On another occasion, on the Pacific Highway near Taree, Murray invited a young policeman, who was remonstrating with him for not wearing his seat belt, to 'Just shoot me'. 'I beg your pardon, sir?' said the policeman, startled. 'Shoot me', said Murray: 'My offence is clearly unpardonable, and I'm sick of my life. Blow me away with that cannon of yours!' Valerie said in an urgent whisper, 'My husband is very ill'. The young man leapt onto his motorbike and roared away without another word.[26]

During these years of misery Murray alienated many people, including some who knew him well, by his apparent moroseness, the occasional savage comments that escaped him in letters or on cards, and the way he broke appointments of long standing. This was the period, for instance, when he held up Angus & Robertson's publication of Geoffrey Lehmann's volume of Australian parodies, *The Flight of the Emu*, to Lehmann's irritation, simply because it contained a mild parody on Murray's work by Laurie Duggan.[27] Those who were angered by such lapses had no idea that they were dealing with a man standing in a flame, constantly gripping himself to avoid screaming, able to function at all only by the exercise of immense, unremitting will.

It was in this state that he had to face the climax of his struggles at Angus & Robertson. Such tensions exacerbated his condition, as he recognised. 'My sanity is returning', he wrote hopefully to me at the end of 1989, 'tho' I'll probably always have to steer clear of Aust. literary/intellectual circles'.[28] But his eventual release, still years away, would come neither through isolation nor aid of psychiatrists, but through the action of a minute life-form swarming in his intestine: Escherichia coli.

CHAPTER TWENTY
FIGHTING THE BLACK DOG
1989–92

*I am but mad north-north-west; when the wind is southerly,
I know a hawk from a handsaw.*

SHAKESPEARE

Murray started 1989 with a bang. In the New Year's Honours list he was made an Officer of the Order of Australia, one of only two literary figures to receive the honour that year,[1] and henceforth could subscribe himself AO, though he seems never to have done so. He was in some doubt as to whether to accept the honour, and it was some time before he decided that he could. His depression had made him gloomy about the direction the country was taking, he had disliked the Bicentenary celebrations of 1988 ('the Bison Tannery', he dismissively called them), and he suspected that the idea of honours based on the British system was another form of colonial cringe. 'I still don't quite know how to respond to the idea of getting the medal', he told Penny Nelson.[2] After deliberation he accepted gracefully.

Another honour, a few months later, was more easily adjusted to. In May 1989 the federal Treasurer, Paul Keating, announced a generous Creative Fellowships scheme, under which particularly talented artists would receive an income of $40 000 for each of four years: Murray was selected as one of the inaugural Fellows.[3] It was a recognition both of his poetry and of the role he had played in arguing for a guaranteed minimum income for artists, and he accepted it rejoicingly, though a reading tour in Tasmania, to which he was already committed, meant that he could not attend the announcement ceremony itself, Valerie accepting the fellowship in his place: for the organisers she proved a face-saving addition to the all-male lineup.

Murray continued to talk optimistically, fearfully, obsessively, about his depression, filling page after page of letters to his friends with descriptions of how much better he was. More realistically, he would sometimes scribble briefly, 'I'm a bit less mad, I think. Or a bit less the wrong sort of mad'.[4] At home, Valerie had much to endure, as her Journal records:

> Another unreasonable explosion . . . They seem to be a daily event lately—a desperate need for a surge of adrenalin. Wonder how much more I can take.

The slightest excuse is enough for a tantrum;—there's no disciplining the children except *sotto voce* in case it's taken as a convenient springboard for another scene, when Les is on a downer. Symptoms: inattentive if not completely deaf, deliberately mishearing or misinterpreting a situation, mean taunts—he's especially malicious towards his father, not that there's no provocation there![5]

Murray struggled with great courage to overcome this 'madness', or at least to continue to function as an artist when all he felt able to do was lie and weep, or eat. Compulsive nervous eating was one long-term symptom of his disease, as his corpulence showed, and during the misery of the late 1980s his weight rose to an extraordinary 160 kilograms.[6] He continued to travel whenever he could during this eight-year black period from 1988 to 1996, though he continued to think of each of these trips as 'a crowded loneliness'.[7] In retrospect it is astonishing how much energy he managed to draw on in spite of dragging the Black Dog everywhere he went.

It would be tedious to detail his journeys, but in these years they included conferences or readings at the Rotterdam Poetry Festival in June 1989, to Tasmania and Western Australia the same year, rapid flights to Japan, Israel, the United Kingdom and the United States in 1990, a trip round the Kimberleys in August 1990 with the artist Michael Leunig, a long trip through the United States and Canada in 1991, a visit to Britain and Denmark in 1992, Britain and France in March 1993, two trips to Europe in 1994, two more in 1995, and so on without respite. In addition he made the three- or four-hour drive to Sydney many times each year to visit schools or give readings at one of Sydney's universities.

His friends worried about this: 'Someone of his weight and age ought not to have to travel constantly to make a living', Mark O'Connor would say.[8] Murray's size made flying claustrophobic and uncomfortable for him, particularly since he could never afford anything but economy class. But travel was vital to his income, and many aspects of travel he thoroughly enjoyed, particularly the reception he got from foreign audiences. A few of his poems, like 'The International Terminal', recorded this facet of his life with his usual vividness, reaching takeoff in its final lines: '—and airborne, with a bang, this five-hundred-seat/theatre folds up its ponderous feet'.

He thoroughly enjoyed his trip to the Jerusalem Poetry Festival in February 1990, finding Israel a nation 'powerfully charged, full of resonances'. As he told Philip Hodgins:

> I had lunch in Gehenna on Sat., looking up at Mt Zion above me. Gehenna is the ravine next to this very comfy artists' colony [Mishkenot Sha'ananim,

meaning 'The Restful Abodes'] in which we're being spoiled rotten. All built of a peachy beige limestone full of quartz, Jerusalem has a towering presence without skyscrapers, like a transmuted Edinburgh(!) & the Mayor at our reception on Sun. referred to David the Psalmist as our earliest local colleague . . . Today, my skin's still a-tingle with the mineral salts of the Dead Sea, tho' I did shower. Judea down there, & up here too, reminds me of the Flinders Ranges, & I notice the many gum trees here are S[outh] A[ustralian] species.[9]

He visited the Church of the Holy Sepulchre, and hated it, finding it full of big votive lamps and dark-faced icons;[10] in time to come, *Fredy Neptune*'s hero, visiting it during World War I, would have the same reaction:

> I drifted down stone streets like gorges, down alleys of stepped floor
> to where I hadn't known I was going: the Holy Sepulchre,
> huge awful cave church with cliffs inside, and caverns
> and soldier tourists, and glass lamps in front of deathly pictures:
> I heard a trooper growl *Easy seen why Christ didn't stop here!*
> Black clergy all over, with their hands out.
>
> . . . and when I stumbled up, out, they were calling the noon prayer
> from all the minars. It was muttering and chanting, that whole city,
> it was swarming to God, from one end to the other,
> men in fur hats nodding, as they read books to a wall,
> women in red wigs, nuns and Muslim nun-wives,
> friars and liars and some soldiers not swearing at all.[11]

Murray's fascination for languages extended easily to Hebrew, and he had long conversations with Hebrew scholars in which he pursued a theory that God was working through evolution, that, in some sense, evolution was God:

> I asked learned Jews about the name the 'something even stranger' on its one visit to Earth as it were unmediated, not via the voice or the flesh of a man, had meant by telling Moses that its name *eyeh asher eyeh*, literally 2 future tenses of the defective verb 'to be' joined by 'who'—'I will be who I will be' *or* 'I will be (the one) who will be'. Did this support the idea of a living end & culmination of evolution, who by *becoming* eternal would always have existed? Yes, there was an ancient Rabbinical paradox to that effect. And cd it, did it, also signify 'I am the one who *really* exists'? Yes, idiomatically that's closer to it.[12]

He considered biblical scholarship itself to be a type and pattern of evolution, in the way it constantly tested, shifted, challenged the text it addressed, while leaving that text finally unaltered but perhaps better understood. As he would put it in a poem written in October 1994:

Mother and type of evolution,
the New Testament of the scholars
may be likened to a library catalogue
of the old type, a card index console
of wooden drawers, each a verse.
And you never know which ones are out,
stacked up, spilt, or currently back
in, with some words deleted
then restored. And it never ends.

The title he would choose for this poem showed what he thought scholarship ultimately achieved with the sacred text it worked on: 'Each Morning Once More Seamless'. He enjoyed his conversation with the Hebrew scholars.

He had a less pleasant interchange on leaving Israel: at the airport Shin Bet, the Israeli internal security service, took him into a small room, searched him, and questioned him with great thoroughness about his political views. 'I'll never know what drew their attention to me, but it was detailed'. When asked, Murray told them that he was sure they and the Arabs would settle their differences in the long run, and that he did not have a solution to offer. The Shin Bet men feigned incredulity: 'You're a poet and you haven't got an opinion?' 'I'm not that kind of stereotype poet', Murray replied. Privately, at the time, he was of the view that 'the Arabs will recover none of Palestine',[13] though by 1998 he would have changed this opinion.[14]

The Japanese trip was equally brief, in August 1990, but he had the pleasure of taking Valerie with him, for the Japanese paid all costs and treated the Murrays with great generosity. They flew via Guam, and Murray found Japan 'a rich & crowded adventure, full of impressions; it was even fascinating to be effectively illiterate again'.[15] He shared a Japanese-style room with Valerie, sleeping on tatami mats and kneeling at the low table; they travelled widely, being shepherded everywhere by their hosts, visiting temples without number, enjoying Japanese food and even playing pachinko, the pinball game that besots millions of Japanese workers.[16] Murray's size drew admiring attention everywhere, and he constantly heard the word 'Sumo'.[17]

One result of this sustained peripateticism was that both on paper and in the flesh he became an established presence on the poetic landscape of Europe, the only Australian poet of his generation to achieve this distinction. Once Carcanet in Britain began publishing his work in 1986 his power became increasingly widely recognised there, and translations of his work into German, Italian, Dutch, Swedish and Norwegian followed in the next decade. His astonishing abilities as a linguist helped here: not only could he communicate easily when he travelled and read on the European continent, but he was capable of correcting his translators, and did so. Contrary to the popular view, he believed that almost all poetry could be translated successfully, and he had the knack of choosing outstanding translators: Margitt Lehbert for German, Marie-Christine Hubert for Italian, the scholar Martin Leer for Danish and Maarten Elzinga for Dutch.

He also declined to be defeated or confined by the war at Angus & Robertson, then still in progress. In January 1990 he accepted the job of Literary Editor of *Quadrant*, a journal of which *Encounter* was the British equivalent, and which like it had been founded with CIA funds as a way of countering Soviet cultural influence in the West. *Quadrant*'s new young editor, Robert Manne, was moving the magazine 'out of its Cold War depressions into a sprightlier phase', as Murray told Peter Goldsworthy,[18] but Murray knew that the coded expletive 'conservative' would now be attached to him even more firmly. He refused to be cowed: 'I am now the Literary Editor of *Quadrant*, a bit on the Ben Hall basis that the secret police of our culture will hang me anyway, so I'll earn it', he told Philip Hodgins defiantly.[19] He had in fact had a long association with *Quadrant*: many of his most important long articles, including those on the need for an Australian republic, had been first published there during the 1970s. The new task took only a few hours each week, and as usual he found the work of editing thoroughly enjoyable.

A large part of this job was the commissioning, not of poems, but of reviews of the dozens of books that flooded in each month. It is characteristic of Murray's thoroughness as an editor that he skimmed these, chose the best for review, and then read each one before he sent it out to a reviewer. And it is characteristic of his fairness that he refused to tell his reviewers what he thought of the volumes they received, until after they had sent in their reviews, which he published whether he agreed with them or not.

He was right about the obloquy that would attach to him for taking on this job. 'I have always felt the publishing of literature in *Quadrant* had other purposes than the disinterested support of writing', John Tranter wrote to him, in refusing his friendly invitation to contribute a poem or two. And Tranter added, 'my own honest belief is that the poetry has always been seen by that organisation [*Quadrant*] as at the best window-dressing, and at the worst a way of making the magazine's other purposes look as though they had the implicit support of its best literary contributors'.[20] There was to be no peace between Murray and the Generation of '68, for all his continued amiable signals.

Murray was angry at the suffering Philip Hodgins and others endured as a result of Tranter's 'takeover' of the Literature Board. There is no evidence to support Murray's view that the Tranterites had 'taken over' the Literature Board: even had they succeeded in doing so, the regular turnover of Literature Board advisers made it impossible for any clique, no matter how well-placed, to keep control of it for long. But Murray suffered severely from the belief that he was fighting a losing battle against powerful and triumphant enemies. To John Barnie he remarked, in 1992: '"Peer" review has been a vicious failure here, & subsidy has flooded us with Politically Correct rubbish'.[22]

His poetry naturally reflected the terrible mental strain of these years: '2 or 3 "bad" days a week I'm down to', he told Penny Nelson hopefully.[23] This was the period when he was writing the poems that would appear in the second half of *Dog Fox Field* in 1990, a volume that would focus on his son Alexander, for Murray's own mental stress had drawn him closer to his autistic child.

Since the little chapbook *Equanimities* (1982), Murray had dedicated each of his volumes not to any individual but 'To the Glory of God', thereby stressing his central theme: he had adapted the Jesuit motto *Ad Majorem Dei Gloriam*, reasoning that God's glory could not be increased. But in addition many of his volumes had a private dedicatee: his Bunyah heritage in *The Weatherboard Cathedral*, Valerie's immigrant background in *Ethnic Radio*, his parents jointly in *The Daylight Moon*, his mother's family in *The People's Otherworld*, and now Alexander in *Dog Fox Field*. By way of hinting at this dedication, Murray used for the cover a photograph of a superb portrait doll of Alexander, made by Valerie, among whose many understated artistic gifts was the modelling, painting and firing of chinaware dolls, which she would then dress in finely stitched handmade clothing. The Alexander doll has a haunting quality, what Murray called 'the innocent unearthliness of autism'.[24]

A few of the poems focused on Alexander himself, among them 'Like the Joy at His First Lie':

> Today, at eleven and a half,
> he made his first purchase:
> forty cents, for two biscuits, no change
> but a giant step into mankind.

But the best of the poems in *Dog Fox Field* more generally explore the possibilities of the non-rational mind. The title poem, powerfully moving, examines a theme Murray would pick up again in *Fredy Neptune*: the Nazis' mistreatment of the feeble-minded, selected because they were unable to construct a simple sentence using the words 'dog', 'fox' and 'field'. Their fate was at first castration, and later extermination in specially designed vans:

> These were no leaders, but they were first
> into the dark on Dog Fox Field:
>
> Anna who rocked her head, and Paul
> who grew big and yet giggled small,
>
> Irma who looked Chinese, and Hans
> who knew his world as a fox knows a field.
>
> Hunted with needles, exposed, unfed,
> this time in their thousands they bore sad cuts
>
> for having gazed, and shuffled, and failed
> to field the lore of prey and hound
>
> they then had to thump and cry in the vans
> that ran while stopped in Dog Fox Field.

And this cruelty he compared, as often before, to his own treatment at Taree High and since: the children the Nazis killed were disposed of not because they were feeble-minded, but because they, like the victims of the communists, were identifiably different, like Jews, Romanies, homosexuals or kulaks. And the fashion-police were still active:

> Our sentries, whose holocaust does not end,
> they show us when we cross into Dog Fox Field.

It was now that he began to produce the poems that analysed what had happened to him at Taree High, among them 'A Torturer's Apprenticeship' and 'The Past Ever Present'.

But there was in this volume an occasional harshness and anger that made some of the later poems seem strained and opaque in a way not explained by experimentation: Murray might imagine that his illness was not affecting his ability to write poetry, but the pressures under which he was living showed. Though, like each of his books, it contained poems of the highest intensity—'Tin Wash Dish', 'The Ballad of the Barbed Wire Ocean', the title poem and 'The Emerald Dove' were among the best things he had written, and his renewed use of rhyme in this volume is often highly effective—*Dog Fox Field* would not be remembered as his best volume. It won the Grace Leven Prize for 1990, but some critics glowered: Kevin Hart commented that 'at their worst these poems are merely boos or hurrahs',[25] while Noel Rowe grumbled that a number of the poems 'are little more than rhythmical commentary'.[26] Christopher Pollnitz found in the volume 'a long drought . . .

only relieved by poems of anger and psychological distress'.[27] 'For *Dog Fox* I had two good notices in Oz & the rest stinkers', Murray told Penny Nelson stoically.[28]

Even as he came under increased pressure in Australia, however, his reputation continued to grow in Britain, where readers were delightedly discovering a backlog of his poems, and where his asperities were mitigated by distance. 'I sell better in the UK than at home now', he told Penny Nelson, '& get far better reviews'. He had just returned from a triumphal tour of Britain, in April 1991: 'hectic but productive', he told Nelson, 'good, big audiences, masses of sales, lots of radio'.[29] It was true that the difference between Australian and overseas reviews of his work was striking: British literary journals were heralding *Dog Fox Field* with headlines like 'One of the few poets there are who remind you how few poets there are',[30] while in the United States the *New Yorker* termed him 'by far the best Australian poet since A. D. Hope, and one of the most accomplished poets now writing anywhere in English'.[31]

Dog Fox Field was made the Poetry Society's 1991 Spring Choice in the United Kingdom, perhaps because emerging in it were other quite different poems, explorative of non-rationality, of a type he would fruitfully follow up for his next volume. These were poems in which he investigated the minds of animals, poems such as 'Masculeene, Cried the Bulls' and 'The Cows on Killing Day', in which he gets into the minds of the creatures he knew so well, producing an alienation effect more successful than any but the very best 'Martian' poem:

All me are standing on feed. The sky is shining.

All me have just been milked. Teats all tingling still
from that dry toothless sucking by the chilly mouths
that gasp loudly in in in, and never breathe out.

All me standing on feed, move the feed inside me.
One me smells of needing the bull, that heavy urgent me,
the back-climber, who leaves me humped, straining, but light
and peaceful again, with crystalline moving inside me.

It was appropriate that these animal poems should strike a strong chord in Britain, for the first one written had had a British source. Entitled 'Bat's Ultrasound', it had been touched off as early as 1985 by Murray's coming across two curious Welsh englynion consisting entirely of vowels, with the exception of one consonant, 'r':

Oer yw'r Eira ar Eryri,—o'ryw
Ar awyr i rewi;
Oer yw'r ia riw 'r ri,
A'r Eira oer yw 'Ryri.[32]

The lines mean 'Cold is the snow on Snowdon's brow/It makes the air so chill/For cold, I vow, there is no snow/Like that of Snowdon's hill'. This literary curiosity inspired the astonishing technical tour de force in which Murray represents the ultrasound of the bat in words that appear nonsensical, but are not:

ah, eyrie-ire; aero hour, ey?
O'er our ur-area (our era aye
ere your raw row) we air our array,
err, yaw, row wry—aura our orrery,
our eerie ü our ray, our arrow.

A rare ear, our aery Yahweh.

Murray, writing to the Welshman John Barnie, called 'Bat's Ultrasound' an 'English-language cynghanedd'. It is almost delirious word-play combined with sheer technical innovation of a power none of his 'experimental' contemporaries could equal, and in the poems of *Translations From the Natural World* he gave it free rein. He thought of it, and 'The Cows on Killing Day', as having stood up in his dreaming mind and demanded to be written,[33] as the Weeping Man in 'An Absolutely Ordinary Rainbow' had stood up so many years before.

He found it hugely liberating to get away from his usual concerns for a while, as he told Angela Smith: 'It's a rest from the human, and from making myself ill by worrying about social-cultural stuff that's probably ephemeral anyway'. And he added:

Since finishing Dog Fox, I've . . . moved into a big long project I've deliberately kept vague and instinctive, finding my way rather than planning. It's tentatively titled Presence, with the subtitle Translations from the Natural World. It successively touches the lives of many animals, birds, even plants and insects and fish, sometimes giving a sense of their life from the outside, more often by pretending to translate their 'speech'—living things do all talk, I say, but they don't talk human language, or always speak with their mouth. I'm trying to be neither Walt Disney nor Ted Hughes, and enjoying the constraints: no hands, no colour vision if they're mammals . . . not much metaphor or sense of time, no consequences, no mercy, but no vindictiveness either etc. Equally good fun are the new senses and powers, such as flight, the ability to see thermals in air, to hear and talk in infrasound (the elephants do this), to see heat when I'm a snake, to detect scents beyond the human range, to live forever until you die.[34]

Translations From the Natural World, published by his and Jamie Grant's short-lived Isabella Press in 1992, was a great critical success, restoring the faith of readers who had disliked the tense and irritable later poems of *Dog Fox Field* and who knew nothing of the suffering Murray was undergoing.

Murray had had a deep understanding of and sympathy with animals since the days when, as a lonely farm-boy making his own amusements, he had regarded animals like his goat, the dog and the cows as his companions. Now back on the farm, living with his father again less than a kilometre from the ruins of his childhood home, he took pleasure in the company of his dog Doug and his cat Fauna McDonald, and two literary cockerels, Patrick (who was white) and Manoly (who was not). In Murray's view, Doug believed he could talk; certainly when spoken to the sagacious animal produced in response a throaty gargle which sounded peculiarly like garbled speech: 'The civil white-pawed dog who'd strain/to make speech-like sounds to his humans'.[35] Murray's 'Two Dogs', however, talk in smells, in a work of passionate empathy:

> Enchantment creek underbank pollen, are the stiff scents he makes,
> hot grass rolling and rabbit-dig but only saliva chickweed.
> Road pizza clay bird, hers answer him, rot-spiced good. Blady grass, she adds,
>   ant log in hot sunshine. Snake two sunups back. Orifice?
> Orifice, he wriggles.

Keats had remarked that he pecked about the gravel with small birds; Murray showed the same negative capability with showers of fire-tail finches in 'MeMeMe':

> Present and still present don't yet add up to time,
> but oscillate at dew-flash speed, at distance speed. Me me me
> a shower of firetail (me me) finches into seed grass
> flickers feeding (me) in drabs and red pinches of rhyme.
> All present is perfect . . .

He showed astonishing technical control over his lines, writing 'MeMeMe' in the quick, high monosyllables of the finch, entangling 'Strangler Fig' in complex syntax intertwined, voicing 'Insect Mating Flight' in the high thin whine of insect wings. And as if trying to find his limits, like Hughes's Wodwo, he made poetic excursions beneath the skins of creatures as diverse as echidna, elephant (whose infrasound voices rumble 'Dawn and sundown we honour you, Jehovah Brahm/who allow us to intone our ground bass in towering calm')[36] and even snail, for which he adopts the pulsing, ceaseless, slow measure of Christopher Smart:

> By its nobship sailing upside down,
> by its inner sexes, by the crystalline
> pimpling of its skirts, by the sucked-on
> lifelong kiss of its toppling motion . . .[37]

And he could sum up a whole animal world of incomprehension and tragedy in four lines, as in 'Goose to Donkey':

> My big friend, I bow help;
> I bow Get-up, big friend:
> let me land-swim again beside your clicky feet,
> don't sleep flat with dried wet in your holes.

He was clearly a poet at the height of his powers, moulding language creatively to his will, able to say anything he chose in the way he chose, combining a huge range of sympathetic experience with the muscular ripple of original thought.

The critics took a little while to adjust to this change in his direction. 'Murray is attempting to change perspective, to "talk for the animals", as it were', John Foulcher remarked, adding:

> Consequently, his structural focus has a disarming unfamiliarity; this poetry has far more in common with Hopkins than with that other literary zoo-keeper, Ted Hughes, and seems to rival the fashionable 'language poets' in its technical dexterity. Murray's work differs from this latter group, though, because he actually has something to say.[38]

Foulcher also spotted the fact that, as he put it, '*Translations From the Natural World* is a profoundly spiritual book'.[39] In general the critics were impressed by this new evidence of his expanding range. 'Murray is a poet who contains multitudes', the critic Dennis Haskell would remark,[40] and nowhere is this clearer than in the cascading variety of these subtle, robust spiritual rejoicings, for all that animal poems are just one aspect of his multitudinous output.

The people of his valley interested him just as much. More than thirty years before, he had told Greg O'Hara that every rock of his country was a friend of his.[41] Every house, every bridge, every turn of the road was too: each had its story, and it was a profound experience to go for a drive with him and hear them, as I did on two occasions. He could read every detail of the landscape like the pages of a loved book. Up there on the hill was the little house in which his father had lived after being evicted; that big ridge was named for the English new chum to whom his great-grandfather had lost his house in a game of cards; this bridge was named for Aunt Lavinia, who had dominated the local council; that was the steep incline on which his father's steering had failed, twice; below that crest the wedgetail eagles nested; this was the turn on which Murray had accidentally killed a kangaroo with a joey in her pouch, an event he profoundly regretted. Bunyah was heart's blood to him, as he had told Judith Wright, and as he spoke a listener seemed to feel its pulse. He reproduced the experience of these drives in two poems, 'Aspects of Language and War on the Gloucester Road', and 'Crankshaft', named for the shape of the poem on the page, as the speaker gestures to left and right, but a title also containing a pun that becomes clear in the final stanza.

He had always considered that his title, to the Bunyah valley in general and the Forty Acres in particular, was based on his links with and love of the area. Partly as a result, he was unperturbed by the *Mabo* decision of the High Court in July 1992, which recognised that native title had not been extinguished across all of Australia, and which opened up a spate of land claims by Aboriginal groups. He wrote to John Barnie:

> Three tribes have already put in a claim for the Kimberleys, in West Aust. I don't know whether you noticed, but I discreetly gave Aust. back to the Aboriginals in my film [*The Daylight Moon*, made by Don Featherstone in 1990], justifying my ownership of our place & my rights to & in that whole 'country' exclusively in Aboriginal Law terms. Which they admit. I suspect we'll end up, away on ahead, with a mixed system based on Aboriginal tenure and customary use.[42]

He identified increasingly closely with his Aboriginal cousins during these years, often seeing them socially. With his usual speed he also began studying vocabulary lists of the local language, Kattangal, of which there was only one remaining fluent native speaker, Ella Simon; when she died, Murray became one of the most knowledgeable of Kattangal students, though he would have denied any such claim. Henceforth he would make fruitful use of local legends in his poetry, including the mysterious poem he entitled 'One Kneeling, One Looking Down'.[43]

He liked to imagine that the anticipated new code of legal possession, when it arrived, would give more security to the rural poor, of whatever race, than they had under a system that allowed indebted farmers to be evicted from their land by bankers and lawyers. In one of his most successful satirical poems,

'The Rollover', written in July 1992, he joyfully and wittily imagined the tables turned:

> Some of us primary producers, us farmers and authors
> are going round to watch them evict a banker.
> It'll be sad. I hate it when the toddlers and wives
> are out beside the ute, crying, and the big kids
> wear that thousand-yard stare common in all refugees.
> Seeing home desecrated as you lose it can do that to you.
>
> There's the ute piled high with clothes and old debentures.
> There's the faithful VDU, shot dead, still on its lead.
> This fellow's dad and granddad were bankers before him, they sweated
> through the old hard inspections, had years of brimming foreclosure,
> but here it all ends. He'd lent three quarters and only
> asked for a short extension. Six months. You have to
>
> line the drawer somewhere. You have to be kind to be cruel.
> It's Sydney or the cash, these times. No one buys the Legend of the Bank
> any more. The laconic teller, the salt-of-the-earth branch accountant:
> it's all an Owned Boys story. Now they reckon he's grabbed a gun
> and an old coin sieve and holed up in the vault, screaming
> about his years of work, his identity. Queer talk from a bank-johnny!
>
> We're catching flak, too, from a small mob of his mates,
> inbred under-manager types, here to back him up. Troublemakers,
> land-despoiling white trash. It'll do them no good. Their turn
> is coming. They'll be rationalised themselves, made adapt
> to a multi-national society. There's no room in that for privileged
> traditional ways of life. No land rights for bankers.[44]

For all its wit, and I have heard Murray's reading of the poem to a large city audience rapturously received, the satire has an undertone of bitterness: the vision would remain just that, small farmers like his own people would go on being evicted in just the way he describes, and the economic rationalists, he feared, would retain the whip hand. But he would go on fighting them. Auden's cynical line, 'Poetry makes nothing happen', was not one he subscribed to.

CHAPTER TWENTY-ONE
BECOMING A NAME
1992–94

~

I cannot rest from travel: I will drink
Life to the lees: all times I have enjoy'd
Greatly, have suffer'd greatly, both with those
That loved me, and alone; on shore, and when
Thro' scudding drifts the rainy Hyades
Vext the dim sea: I am become a name.

TENNYSON

By the early 1990s Murray's Country was well on the way to becoming a place of literary pilgrimage, and not just to the streams of school and university students who sought him out. Established scholars also were paying tribute. The first major academic book on him appeared in 1992, Laurence Bourke's *A Vivid Steady State*,[1] but several others, long planned, came to nothing, and Murray, paranoia still stalking him, became convinced that widespread dislike of him was behind the sequence of disappointments.

A book of essays on his work, prepared by Bruce Clunies Ross, was abandoned after long delays which Murray was convinced had been designed to kill the project. Then an American friend, the writer Paul Kane, with whom Murray had several times stayed outside New York, was in the mid-1990s planning a critical monograph on Murray to appear in Oxford University Press's Australian Writers series, but did not complete his task. Murray, disappointed, thought Kane 'adept at keeping his head down. And so responsive to Aust. literary values'.[2]

A different fate befell a detailed study of Murray's work by the Newcastle academic Christopher Pollnitz: this was stopped by Murray himself in 1990, when he saw a draft, on the grounds that Pollnitz thought him a misogynist.[3] Murray quickly regretted what he had done: as he told John Foulcher, 'Stopping this book did Chris' career all sorts of no-good and he was *wroth*. I got a bad conscience about it all when L. Bourke's book came out, because Bourke had the wit not to show me his ms. before he published it, as Pollnitz had done . . . I felt bad indeed, punishing Pollnitz for dealing openly with me!'[4] For though on second thoughts, when his depression lifted a little, he had changed his mind and given his permission, the volume never appeared, as by October 1990 the publisher, Oxford University Press, had decided to terminate the contract.[5]

These events fed Murray's sense of being the target and victim of a conspiracy. 'The Left, or rather those who learned in the 60s to use Left jargon for their own career ends, set upon me first, not I upon them', he wrote to Wallace-Crabbe:

> This was just after your & Vin's attempt to capture Oz poetry failed in the early 60s & the Hall-Shapcott one took off with anti-Viet. powering it & the Tranters et al leaping aboard. Me-mories. As to the mad theorists, I don't mind them. They've freed us from the academy. If the Author's dead, then twice dead are parasite critics on vast professorial salaries.[6]

Wallace-Crabbe was a professor of English at the University of Melbourne.

Despite the frustration of these false starts, they constituted clear evidence that academic and popular interest in his work continued to grow. There were other little signs of his eminence. In June 1992 Bob Ellis's thirteen-year-old daughter told Murray he was 'in the new Macquarie Dictionary'. 'Oh yes, what do I mean?' Murray joked, but he was pleased at the reference in the volume.[7] 'And you died in 1976', the girl added: she had misunderstood the reference to the appearance in that year of his first *Selected Poems*. 'Ah, Jen', said Murray, delighted, 'when you've got that behind you, you're invincible!'[8]

He was appearing on film as well as on paper. The film-maker Don Featherstone had in 1990 made *The Daylight Moon*, a film about Murray and his work he enjoyed taking part in. It fed his lifelong love of films, which as early as 1985 had led him to act a horse-doper and car-thief in the film *I Own the Racecourse*.[9] *The Daylight Moon* was screened in Australia in 1991 and in Britain, on ITV, in 1992: 'as a result my anonymity over there is *blown*', he told Penny Nelson with feigned regret after a March 1992 tour there during which crowds of hundreds were drawn to his readings, and he seemed to be recognised everywhere.[10] There would be other films, among them one by Bob Ellis, *The Nostradamus Kid*, for which Murray served as part of the inspiration for the character of McAlister.[11] Murray even wrote a film script himself, in 1992, for a super-Imax movie about Antarctica, made by John and Susanna Weilley of Heliograph Films, which showed around the world.[12] In later years the ABC would screen documentaries about him made by itself and by Ellis. His interest in filmic techniques, and his belief that they could be adapted to poetry, would show itself clearly in *Fredy Neptune*.

Murray was in any case an instantly recognisable figure by the early 1990s, made even more so by the poem 'Self-Portrait from a Photograph' which he wrote and published in March 1992. It had been sparked off by a photograph of himself taken by his father-in-law, Gino Morelli:

> A high hill of photographed sun-shadow
> coming up from reverie, the big head
> has its eyes on a mid-line, the mouth
> slightly open, to breathe or interrupt.
>
> The face's gentle skew to the left
> is abetted, or caused, beneath the nose
> by a Heidelberg scar, got in an accident.
> The hair no longer meets across the head
>
> and the back and sides are clipped ancestrally
> Puritan-short. The chins are firm and deep
> respectively. In point of freckling
> the bare and shaven skin is just over
>
> halfway between childhood ginger
> and the nutmeg and plastic death-mottle
> of great age. The large ears suggest more
> of the soul than the other features:
>
> dull to speech, alert to language,
> tuned to background rustle, easily agonised,
> all too fond of monotony, they help
> keep the eyes, at their sharpest, remote,
>
> half-turned to another world
> that is poorer than this one, but contains it . . .

The sharp awareness of ageing that he showed in that poem was growing on him. The operation he had undergone on his left ear in 1987 had been a complete success, but his other ear was now almost entirely deaf and early in 1992 he underwent an operation on that also. This time there was an unexpected price: pinching of the facial nerve, caused by an oedema that developed after the operation, produced Bell's palsy.[13] The facial muscles on the right side were badly affected, and for months afterwards he looked as if he had had a severe stroke, one side of his face fallen and his speech badly slurred. His right eye was also inactivated, as a result of which he had a fall during a trip to Queensland at Easter 1992, and broke his right wrist, so that he could neither write nor drive. He was depressed by this, by the palsy, and by people who told him he was improving when he knew he was not. Only when Alexander said he was getting better, nearly a year later, did he believe it.[14]

Valerie had health problems at this time, too. In July 1992 she broke her foot badly in a fall in the garden, tearing ligaments: Murray trundled her indoors in a wheelbarrow and called a doctor. The foot took nearly a year to heal completely, though she was up on crutches doing housework within three weeks. During the short period while she was virtually immobilised Murray and Clare had to take her place, mothering Cecil and the younger children while Valerie directed from a chair. Clare, aged eighteen in 1992, was under stress herself, fleeing her Taree school at this time because of bullying, a pattern her father recognised with depressing clarity: he wrote for her the angry and sympathetic poem 'Where Humans Can't Leave and Mustn't Complain'.

His two older children, who had not lived with their parents since the move to Bunyah, both married at this time. Christina, now twenty-nine, married a fellow veterinarian, James Gilkerson, on 8 February 1992, at Berrico: the guests had to fight their way there through a tremendous rainstorm that flooded all the creeks. Christina, still occasionally annoyed at her father for his severity towards her as a child, and for what she saw as his domineering style of argument in her adulthood, declined to be given away: 'I am not property'. In the beautiful epithalamium he gave her for a wedding gift, with the wish 'may you/always have each other, and want to', he affirmed this as his own belief:

> I am awed at you, though, today,
> silk restraining your briskness and gumption,
> my mother's face still hauntingly in yours
>
> and this increase, this vulnerable beauty.
> James is worthy of his welcome to our family.
> Never would I do, or he ask
> me to do what no parental memories
> could either: I won't give you away.
>
> But now you join hands, exchanging
> the vows that cost joyfully dear.
> They move you to the centre of life
> and us gently to the rear.[15]

Christina was moved to tears when Murray read this beautiful affirmation of parental love during the ceremony.[16]

Daniel, aged twenty-eight, married Shari Meadows on 10 October 1993, and would add a law qualification to his metallurgy degree the next year. Shari was Jewish, and her family resisted the union, a reaction with which Murray sympathised: 'We met them on Sun. this week, & they're nice. Not the gorgons they tried hard to appear in order to repel Daniel. Aus. Jewry is very proud of its record low marrying out rate, only 9 per cent. We never resented their efforts: it is after all the stated law of their people. I hope only that the marriage is good'.[17]

At the civil wedding Daniel crushed underfoot a glass wrapped in a beautiful old shawl, and his parents and the other guests danced a shuffling hora. 'Great amity and warmth prevailed', Murray reported.[18] But Daniel, who had long been alienated from both his parents, was angered when his father made a clumsy speech, not having realised in advance that he would be called on for one.[19] The rift with his eldest son, of which this was just the latest manifestation, was a matter of abiding grief to Murray, who did all he could to heal it, including going into debt to help buy Daniel and Shari their first house. But his efforts at reconciliation were without lasting effect: he came to believe that Daniel had inherited what he thought of as the Murray depression. He and Christina, however, were able to draw together again after years of coldness. His three younger children seem always to have regarded him and their mother with untroubled love.[20]

Alexander turned fifteen in 1993, a great source of joy and pain to his parents. He had improved to the point where he could conduct a brief but genuine conversation, making eye-contact and varying the intonation of his voice. But even his improvement brought grief, as Murray told John Barnie: 'Our Alec is ashamed he's not in real secondary school, just in the Support Unit class. Bitter, to be just bright enough to sense your deep relegation, eh?' Just as bitter to be the parents. Murray had refrained from writing about Alexander directly, but in 1993 he produced one of his most powerful poems, 'It Allows a Portrait in Line-Scan at Fifteen':

> He retains a slight 'Martian' accent, from the years of single phrases.
> He no longer hugs to disarm. It is gradually allowing him affection.
> It does not allow proportion. Distress is absolute, shrieking, and runs him at
>   frantic speed through crashing doors.
> He likes cyborgs. Their taciturn power, with his intonation.
> It still runs him around the house, alone in the dark, cooing and laughing.

> He can read about soils, populations and New Zealand. On neutral topics he's
> illiterate.
> *Arnie Schwarzenegger is an actor. He isn't a cyborg really, is he, Dad?*
> He lives on forty acres, with animals and trees, and used to draw it continually.
> He knows the map of Earth's fertile soils, and can draw it freehand.
> He can only lie in a panicked shout *SorrySorryIdidn'tdoit!* warding off conflict
> with others and himself.
> When he ran away constantly it was to the greengrocers to worship stacked
> fruit.
> His favourite country was the Ukraine: it is nearly all deep fertile soil.
> Giggling, he climbed all over the dim Freudian psychiatrist who told us how
> autism resulted from 'refrigerator' parents . . .
> He is equitable and kind, and only ever a little jealous. It was a relief when that
> little arrived.
> He surfs, bowls, walks for miles. For many years he hasn't trailed his left arm
> while running.
> *I gotta get smart!* looking terrified into the years. *I gotta get smart!*

No one has written with greater sensitivity, or more movingly, about the joy and pain of autism.

The growth of his children to adulthood, Christina's and Daniel's weddings, and the accompanying sense that he was being moved 'gently to the rear' increased Murray's consciousness of the passage of time. He complained about loss of memory, telling Penny Nelson that the Black Dog chewed it up,[21] and he did show very occasional lapses, such as when he and Wallace-Crabbe were doing a reading together at Berwick near Melbourne, and in the middle of the audience questions that followed, Murray unexpectedly turned to Wallace-Crabbe: 'Chris, could I print "The Crims"?' This was a fine ballad of Wallace-Crabbe's. 'I'm afraid it's already been used, Les.' Murray looked perplexed: 'Who published it?' 'You did, in *Quadrant*', said Wallace-Crabbe.[22]

But the truth is that Murray's memory was still much more tenacious than that of anyone else he knew. He never took notes, his astonishingly wide reading being stored in his head; even though he lived a very busy life, making appointments for readings, tours, broadcasts and book launches many months in advance, he kept no appointment diary, believing that writing things down was an admission of failure. Nor would he carry a camera when he travelled, for the same reason: his ability to remember just where a road in Scotland curved round a loch, which had astonished Angela Smith in Fiji, meant that he could replay his travels at will on his inward eye. On one of his visits to Peter Barden, whom he continued to call on whenever he visited North

America, Barden took him back to Muir Woods outside San Francisco. 'Bring your camera', Barden advised. 'I don't have a camera, mate', Murray scoffed, 'I've got a memory!'[23]

He retained his youthful good humour and disdain of formality, and was very good company. As a guest of others, or in formal settings, he behaved with propriety, but there was often to be seen a satirical glint in his eye, as if he considered this middle-class role-playing more than slightly artificial: there was about him something of the attitude his teachers had observed in the solitary boy at Nabiac school, standing by the side of the playground observing his fellows and smiling quietly to himself.

To be his guest at Bunyah was to see a different side of him, unbuttoned, relaxed, sometimes scatologically witty, sprawling, endearingly casual. He cared little about conventional table manners, for instance, and after one meal (he had had two large helpings of pork and roast vegetables) I observed him raise his plate to his lips, tip it up and drink the gravy. He contemplated the plate for a moment with a pleased expression, then raised it again and licked it very carefully from end to end, with great relish. To all appearances it needed no washing after that. After another such meal, when we had eaten perhaps half of a very large leg of mutton, he stood at the sink watching Valerie wash the dishes while I dried up, and while he talked to us he abstractedly picked up the roast by the protruding bone and picked it clean, as one might eat a toffee-apple.

A fortunate visitor to Bunyah might also be shown a symbol of his vastly eclectic interests, in the shape of what Murray called 'The Great Book'. This was a large, hard-covered ledger-book, which Murray had adapted as a commonplace book or scrapbook. Into this he copied any poem that particularly caught his fancy, including rare fragments such as the poem by Penny Nelson's uncle, Adam McCay, which began, 'The loveliest whore in Darlinghurst was in the family way'. This started on so high a note, Murray added with a cackle of laughter, that McCay was never able to go on with it: Murray himself had added a second line, 'In spite of her diamond pessaries and jewelled whirling spray'. Into the Great Book went postcards, newsclippings, cartoons, like the one 'of a great sink in which there were today's dishes, yesterday's dishes, dishes from the nineteen-thirties, nineteenth century dishes, pre-Reformation dishes, Classical dishes, dishes from the Ice Age. [loud laugh] They got thinner as you went down, there were fewer of them, but away down deep in that water they were there!'[24] His children loved the Great Book, and Clare begged for and secured a promise that it would be left to her.

The official recognition of his work, which had come in the form of the Order of Australia in 1989, was reinforced in 1992 when the federal Justice Minister, Senator Michael Tate, flew to Taree with his advisers to consult Murray on the wording of a new oath of allegiance, to be taken by immigrants becoming naturalised Australians. Minister and poet met in a Taree wedding reception centre, and Murray began by telling Tate that Australia should not have an oath, but a pledge.[25] Tate agreed. Murray, who thought the existing pledge (with its demand for loyalty to the Queen) 'hopelessly grovelling', then proposed his alternative, which he considered adult by contrast:

> Under God, from this time forward
> I am part of the Australian people.
> I share their democracy and their freedom
> I obey their laws
> And I expect Australia to be loyal to me.

Senator Tate was bemused by the last line: he asked Murray what reward he wanted for his work, and Murray asked to be present when the pledge was first used.[26] In the event his wording was adopted with modifications:

> From this time forward (under God)
> I pledge my loyalty to Australia and its people
> Whose democratic beliefs I share
> Whose rights and liberties I respect
> And whose laws I will uphold and obey.

Murray's reciprocal last line was dropped, to his disappointment: but the visit showed the honour in which he was held by those in power. For some time he had been Australia's pre-eminent poetic voice abroad; increasingly he was being treated as the national poet inside the country too.

This impression would be greatly reinforced when, in 1999, Prime Minister John Howard called on him to help draft a new Preamble to the Constitution, to be put to the population in a referendum on whether Australia should become a republic. 'I've called on Australia's best writer to help me draft the Preamble', Howard told journalists. And on being asked who he was referring to, he responded, 'Les, of course'.[27] There was no need for him to mention Murray's surname. As the unofficial laureate, Murray had a national voice, and he was prepared to use it.

By 1993 Murray was convinced that what he saw as the Tranter–Adamson group's takeover of the Literature Board could not be reversed, and, egged on by Mark O'Connor, he began a concerted attack on it in the newspapers. 'Time's up for Literature Board', cried the headline of one of the earliest of his articles,[28] in which he argued that the board should now be dissolved, and replaced with 'a couple of clerks and a computer' administering a scheme for supplementing the royalties of artists: 'Under this, the Government would simply give every author the difference between the royalty paid them by their publisher and the list price of all books of theirs sold during that year. This payment would be reducible on a sliding scale that would reflect the author's income from extra-literary sources'.[29] He proposed to eliminate the Literature Board's subsidies to publishers: books that needed subsidy, he suggested, did not deserve publication, and Literature Board funding was merely giving non-books a non-run before they were pulped. He calculated that his scheme, apolitical, unselective and making readers the judges of which writers should be rewarded, would cost no more than the existing arrangement.

The Australia Council's Chairman, Rodney Hall, a former Chairman, Michael Costigan, and others, including Tom Thompson and Marion Halligan, fought back.[30] The level of the replies Murray received was not always high: Thompson contemptuously advised Murray to 'stick to counting cows'.[31] Peter Craven, in the *Times Literary Supplement* (for the debate spread to British publications), made a point of remarking on Murray's corpulence.[32] Murray replied with restraint, 'whatever the causes of my corpulence, I do find it a useful test of intelligence and character in others', a point perhaps too subtle for Craven.[33] Rodney Hall, early in 1993, argued that Murray's own generous funding from the Literature Board had deprived others,[34] a point Murray characterised as the 'cruel and humiliating divisiveness which his own system of patronage fosters'.[35] Hall did not mention that he had himself received 'about $500,000' in Literature Board grants.[36]

For all that his barb went home as it had been intended to, and it was reinforced by Murray's hearing from Mark O'Connor that board members regarded grants to Murray ('our token fascist')[37] as justification for not funding his friends. Murray agonised long over this, and then decided that he would never again accept a grant from the body on which he had depended for so long, and whose funding he had put to such good use. Others of his friends took the same difficult decision, including Jamie Grant, Hal Colebatch and Peter Kocan.[38]

This was a particularly courageous and self-sacrificing move for Murray to have made, and it was tested when, some months after he had opened his campaign against the Literature Board, he was assured privately that a second multi-year Keating Fellowship was his for the asking: 'Of course you can have another Keating, Les'.[39] He had in fact already unsuccessfully applied for one, and he regarded this offer as 'a bribe meant to discredit and silence me':[40] he determined not to take it up. Valerie regarded his renunciation of Literature Board funding with alarm: 'It's all very well to make a point, but what are we going to live on?'[41] And Mark O'Connor, who did not follow Murray in this step, blamed himself for having provoked Murray to it.[42]

The public debate would continue for years, with increasing bitterness.[43] Mark O'Connor, a particular sufferer from Literature Board neglect, founded ACRA News, a publication devoted to exposing the iniquities of the Literature Board grants, and in doing so hardened the resistance of some of the board members to his applications.[44] Women writers associated with Murray continued to apply with success: the poet Jemal Sharah, who was Murray's goddaughter, told him, 'I'm a woman and I'm ethnic. They can't lay a glove on me'.[45] Women, in Murray's view, could 'use the Literature Board's categories against them, but blokes can't do anything. Blokes are helpless, and that's the way it is'.[46]

Murray believed he paid a price for his attacks on the Literature Board, in that the newspapers were sending him to Coventry. The publication in 1992 of *Translations from the Natural World* had been triumphant, winning both the New South Wales and Victorian Premiers' Prizes for 1993 and the National Book Council Banjo Award, worth $7500. 'I've swept the pool of major prizes here with *Translations*', he told John Barnie, 'and the papers hate me so much, still, for attacking the sacred Aust. Council that no word of my feat has appeared anywhere'.[47] This belief was largely the result of his ongoing depression: in fact he was seldom out of the spotlight for long, and the Australia Council debate assured him of frequent and often positive publicity. Australians love hating their government and bureaucracy, and Murray's reputation as the people's poet was cemented by this controversy.

Partly in the hope of defeating those he feared were trying to silence him, late in 1993 he revived plans to start a magazine of his own, to be called The Cream: 'the idea's to entertain, & to feed the long-starved aesthetic senses without the depressive accompaniments of dissention & anger'.[48] He recruited Jamie Grant to the idea, and planned also to invite the help of Louise Adler, the playwright Alex Buzo, John Clarke, Margaret Connolly, Robert Gray, Clive James, the poet Kate Jennings, Christopher Koch, Robert Manne, Denis O'Driscoll and Brian Turner, a little check-list of those he respected and felt able to call upon, though not all of them were his personal friends. He even produced a publishing proposal, giving the rules of the journal:

> Writing, in any form, of the highest possible standard only . . .
> No politics without spin
> No critical jargon
> No reviews
> No academic 'publish or perish'.[49]

Alas, he might have added 'No money', and the idea came to nothing. In 1998 Mark O'Connor would try to interest him in launching another publication, this time using the Internet: Murray demurred, not wanting to learn a new technology.[50]

Since his fall into deep depression in 1988 he had cut back sharply on his output of prose: now, under the dual need to replace the lost Literature Board funding and keep himself in the public eye, he began publishing a regular column in the *Independent Monthly*, beginning in October 1993.[51] Under the joky by-line 'Our Man in Bunyah', he aired many of his unpopular and radical opinions, which even at their quirkiest made compelling reading. In 'Assault with a Deadly Metaphor', in October 1993, he brought a poet's insights into language to bear on the need for a new Australian political vocabulary of equality to replace the dead imported vocabulary of class and of 'left' and 'right', 'centre and margin'. The latter metaphor he subjected to particularly sharp scrutiny:

> This is the old Inner Circle game, Where The Action Is, the picture of reality by which most lives are secretly shamed and relegated, and it is probably as old as the first chieftain's court. In Western civilisation, Athens and Rome boosted it mightily, and every tinpot kingdom and empire and literary circle has reinforced its tyranny . . . There are many kinds of marginality, from the sexually crippled to the rural poor, but common features can be discerned. All of the deeply marginal know the same rules, by rote: that the fundamental attitude of the human world is predatory contempt. That the idea of 'rights' is laughable. That politeness is merely delayed refusal. That achievement is murder. That attainments differ in value depending on the attainers . . . And that to attempt rescue from marginality while leaving one's fellows there is to be accursed. Even if the rescue is in terms one's fellows in relegation could not share. This is the sort of inner damage one old cultural metaphor can do. Like class, to which it is intimately related, it is a form of assault.[52]

A sonorous buzz is audible in his bonnet, but the voice is also unmistakably that of a man who has been deeply and continuously hurt by what he is describing, and who keenly desires to save others from the same hurt.

In others of these *Independent Monthly* pieces he came up with apparently outrageous suggestions that turn out to have a real Swiftian edge to them, as when in 'A Modest Proposal' he suggested the emptying of Australia's prisons by means of a wholly new kind of amnesty: every time a police constable was convicted of wrongdoing, one prisoner should be freed; every time a police officer was imprisoned, three prisoners should be released; for a magistrate, twenty or thirty; for a police minister, a quarter of the prison population. In extreme cases, such as when a chief magistrate and a prisons minister were in jail simultaneously, it might be necessary to buy in prisoners from other states to have enough to release. Since Murray was writing at a time when both the chief magistrate and the minister for corrective services of New South Wales had not long before been in prison simultaneously, this was very sharp satire indeed.[53]

In another of these articles he gave vent to some of the brilliant aphorisms into each of which he could pack enough thought to fill an article:

> Republics are for those who dream of rising socially; monarchies are for the self-relegated.
> The kangaroo has never heard of Australia.
> Class is triage.
> In practice, equality is shapely, youthful, neatly dressed people before they open their mouths.[54]

Murray could not be ignored, and in fact was gaining increasing recognition in Australia and abroad. In March 1994 he was nominated as Professor of Poetry at Oxford. He was amused, and honoured: 'I won't get it, not this time: James Fenton will. But the mere notion bespeaks great kindness on the part of its proponents, toward one who really couldn't profess a liking for roast potatoes!'[55] He was clear-sighted: as he had predicted, James Fenton was elected, though the British journal the *Economist* condemned Fenton as a 'Pommy bastard' for the 'ruthless tactics' he had used to ensure his victory. 'Mr Murray is a better poet', it added flatly, describing him for its non-literary readers as 'a sheep-farmer from New South Wales who resembles Humpty Dumpty and writes marvellous poetry'.[56] Murray did not share the *Economist*'s indignation, or that of letter-writers to *The Times*.[57] 'It would have been a terrible commute for me', he joked.[58]

But the nomination showed the growth of his reputation in Europe, bolstered at this time by the translation of his best poems into German: 'At present,' he told Peter Barden, 'we have the rare social distinction of a live-in translator, Mrs Margitt Lehbert from Berlin'. Lehbert spent weeks at Bunyah while she and Murray polished the poems Hanser Verlag would publish in the selection entitled *Ein ganz gewöhnlicher Regenbogen* ('An Absolutely Ordinary Rainbow') in 1996. Lehbert did a beautiful job, though in spite of Murray's help her knowledge of Australia was inferior to her knowledge of English, and she translated 'Diggers' as 'miners', a blunder Murray blamed himself for having missed.

His editing of *Fivefathers*, a selection for British and European readers of the poetry of five male Australian poets (Kenneth Slessor, Roland Robinson,

David Campbell, James McAuley and Francis Webb) of the generation before his own, what Murray significantly called 'the Pre-Academic Era',[59] also drew attention outside Australia, immediately becoming a Poetry Book Society recommendation in Britain.[60] Murray regarded this as 'evidence that new polycentric ideas are replacing an older imperial snobbery which was really a disguised form of English national protectionism in the arts'.[61]

And he continued to travel very often to the northern hemisphere: in 1994, for instance, he did a reading tour of Italy, Germany and Britain in May and June, and in October and November returned for another tour of Britain, Ireland and Germany. He was concerned to raise the profile in Europe, not just of his own writing, but of Australian culture generally. Behind his standard others would advance. That standard was about to ride higher, for his poetic output was rising to a peak. And the key event in shaping his next two volumes would prove to be the death of his father.

CHAPTER TWENTY-TWO
KILLING THE BLACK DOG
1994–96

Human life begins on the far side of despair.

JEAN-PAUL SARTRE

In 1994 Cecil Murray was eighty-five years old, and his magnificent constitution was beginning to break down. Like his father before him, he had been a diabetic for the last twenty years of his life;[1] his son, a few years before, had developed the same condition.[2] Just before Christmas 1993 Cecil had a severe hypoglycaemic attack, and Murray feared he was dying; though he made a recovery, routine X-rays revealed he had a lung cancer, probably the result of smoking hand-rolled cigarettes since 1919. 'You've got the butt you can't put out', his son commiserated with him.[3] 'Seems the cancer isn't progressing fast, at all, but it's there, and not to be removed at his age of 85', Murray wrote to Angela Smith: 'A sleeping tiger in the cage of his ribs'.[4] Cecil came back home to Bunyah, but he was more subdued after this, and presently began showing signs of loss of memory and confusion.

His father's decline focused Les Murray's mind on the bush values of self-sufficiency and decency that Cecil represented to him, and family stories formed a central theme of the poems he was writing. Often these were counterpoised deliberately against the materialism, fashion pressures and coterie values he saw in much critical writing in Australia. In 1993 the academic Jennifer Strauss edited *The Oxford Book of Australian Love Poems*, which Murray, whose work was not included in it, disdainfully characterised as containing not love-poems but sex-poems: 'poems of sexual display and advertising', he called them.[5] By way of a delicate corrective, in May 1994 he wrote and dedicated to Strauss 'Australian Love Poem', a queer and moving account of a school-teacher, never quite sacked for paedophilia but moved from school to school, who for many years had lived with Murray's Aunt Nettie, just across Bunyah creek from the Murray home. The teacher, young enough to be Nettie's son, had given her solace in a loveless and childless marriage, and had nursed her devotedly in her dotage. In the years when Christina had spent childhood holidays at Bunyah this man had occasionally made suggestive comments to her when she visited her great-aunt, until one day, when he attempted to fondle her, Christina struck him and would not go back.⁶ Murray liked him and Nettie's husband Reg tolerated him, but on the day Nettie was taken to a nursing home he left the farm and was never seen again.

> As she got lost in the years
> where she would wander,
> her boy would hold her in bed
> and wash sheets to spread under.
>
> And when her relations carried her,
> murmuring, out to their van,
> he fled that day, as one with no rights,
> as an unthanked old man.

Murray was fascinated by the complexities of this relationship, the contemned and outcast figure finding refuge on the farm, giving his aunt love in return for shelter, nursing her devotedly as she turned into the little girl he had always wanted, and then disappearing 'as one with no rights'. It was love of a richness, strangeness and complexity beyond the scope of Strauss's volume, and she rightly saw his dedication of the poem to her as a reproach.⁷

He finished it just too late for inclusion in his *Collected Poems*, which Heinemann brought out in 1994. Murray chose for its cover a Brueghel painting, *The Strife of Lent with Shrove-Tide*, depicting an exceedingly well-fleshed man, with an uncanny resemblance to Murray, stoically offering his cheek to two scrawny and malevolent figures, one of whom is taking a large bite out of it. Murray told Philip Hodgins it was a 'pic. of me & Fay [Zwicky] & Sr Veronica [Brady]'.⁸ Even his most embittered opponents recognised the wit and courage of this cover: 'It's a masterfully wicked joke, and you have to applaud it', Ken Bolton conceded, in an otherwise unbalanced and angry article designed to annoy Murray,⁹ and having the sneering Taree High-style title 'Requiem for a Heavyweight'.¹⁰ In the article Bolton mocked Murray's accounts of his torments at Taree High with the words 'Ah, poor baby!', not realising how vividly he was illustrating the persistence of the bullying spirit Murray had identified there.¹¹ But Bolton's frustrated rage was a perverse compliment: the publication of the *Collected Poems* meant that no one could now ignore the astonishing range and power of Murray's achievement.

The reviewers recognised the weight of the volume, their comments often going well beyond its impact as literature. 'Murray's poetry is central to an ambitious cultural project', wrote Philip Mead: 'This project takes the form of a long and complex quarrel with the post-modern world and, more positively, expresses itself as a massive renovation of humanism'.[12] Alan Gould considered that readers would return to the volume 'for the illumination his work casts on the character of Australian civilisation and the nature of existence itself'.[13]

Overseas critics were no less enthusiastic about this new revelation of his stature, which in the United States was entitled *The Rabbiter's Bounty*.[14] The *Georgia Review* termed him 'one of the most important writers in English today'.[15] *Poetry* (Chicago) said he was 'the most arresting and angular poet to come out of Australia since Judith Wright and A. D. Hope'.[16] British journals echoed the sentiment, *Poetry Wales* calling him 'without doubt, the major poet to have emerged from Australia so far'.[17] The *Spectator* said he wrote 'like one of Botticelli's angels'.[18] And the *Times Literary Supplement*, linking him with Heaney, Walcott and Brodsky in what it called 'an internationally recognised pantheon of poets', commented: 'Murray does not just extend the teleology of his own family into that of Australia but into that of the world as a whole. Few poets can manage such a weighty transition so smoothly, and that Murray is able to do this is the true mark of his stature'.[19]

The 'teleology of his own family' was much on his mind in this period. By the time he left for his second reading tour of 1994, on 3 October, Cecil was rapidly deteriorating. Murray, 'running on approval and adrenaline',[20] gave twenty readings in thirty days, and even found time to write a poem in Derry, amid dawning hope of a peace settlement:

> Almost surprised to have been
> delivered to the same house
> as I went to sleep in, I unglue
> my mouth, and flap back the bedclothes.
>
> Brickwork is dawning, and pooled streets
> which are floors of that red sea.
> Time enough, for descending stair-depths
> on a smile, dispelling hosts' privacy.
>
> The salmon were scabbard and blade
> in the shops of Ireland;
> mist formed like manna on dusk fields.
> Glassed prison cells jutted single there
>
> like nuclei filled with police
> inside membrane-cubes of mesh . . .
>
> But the dream-tunnel I travelled in
> to here was individual and is gone

forever, into all I'll bring soon,
afresh, to that old collective, language.²¹

All through his trip, though, he worried about his father, and wrote repeatedly about him to his friends. 'He's incoherent sometimes, & prone to wander off', Murray told Peter Barden from Scotland. 'This has only set in this year, and I really hope it won't be prolonged'.²² A CAT scan at the end of October 1994 revealed that Cecil had a duck-egg sized and inoperable brain tumour. 'Dad's resigned to dying & keen to be gone, & I have to find the resources to deal with the farewells & the care, so long as we can give it at home. No more hectoring him out of depression & urging him along, as I've been doing, really, ever since Mum died. That's over'.²³ Murray's own depression seemed to be relaxing its grip: 'I have a curious feeling Dad may take it with him, when he goes, though I don't at all blame him for it'.²⁴

He also felt that his father's approaching death was at last freeing him from juvenility, for in his father's mind Murray had never progressed beyond the age of fifteen: 'So: adulthood is finally rushing upon me', he told Peter Goldsworthy.²⁵ Cecil still had flashes of his old style: 'I'll be all right when I stop dying', he said cheerfully to his sister on the phone at the beginning of December.²⁶ He refused at first, out of modesty, to let Murray or Valerie wash or shave him, but they were anxious to spare him from hospital which he hated.

Cecil's brother Eric, with whom he had built up a warm friendship in their last years, died on 23 December 1994, but Cecil himself hung on, Valerie nursing him heroically as he lost the use of his right side. Murray was convinced that his father did not want to spoil Christmas for the family by dying before it: 'Dad quietly made a supreme effort & had this one final Christmas with us, at his old place at table', he wrote to me.²⁷

He was concerned about his father's spiritual preparedness for death, and screwed up his courage to ask Cecil if he had forgiven his father and brothers.

Sorry Dad, but like
have you forgiven your enemies?
Your father and all them?
All his lifetime of hurt.

I must have, (grin). I don't
*think about that now.*²⁸

This almost unconscious letting go of resentment seemed to Murray to be true forgiveness, a process of which the act of conscious forgiving was only the start: this was an insight that would inform the final stanzas of *Fredy Neptune*.

By 3 January 1995 Cecil was no longer able to walk, and reluctantly they took him in to Taree hospital, where Murray visited him. He gripped the steel bed-frame with still-powerful hands. 'Yes, you're busting to talk', he told his son, 'but I can't talk any more, I'm too busy dying'.[29] He died at 5 a.m. on 6 January 1995, the feast of the Epiphany as Murray noted,[30] and was buried beside Miriam in Krambach cemetery on 10 January. Half-way through the eulogy in the Bunyah church, with Bob Ellis and Piers Laverty among the large congregation, Murray realised, 'I was managing very good aplomb because I hadn't started grieving but rather had largely finished grieving: I'd been helping Dad with his 43-year mourning for Mum all that time and really mourning him as well. And now I could lay the burden down . . . Queer to be an adult, too'.[31]

He disposed of his father's few possessions thoughtfully, clothes to the St Vincent de Paul Society, rare items such as ancient cricket boots to the State Museum, which displayed them prominently. The elegy he wrote for his father in April, 'The Last Hellos', has this same mixture of grief and relieved acceptance, implicit in the sob of the opening line, and the quiet submission in the second:

Don't die, Dad—
but they die.

This last year he was wandery:
took off a new chainsaw blade
and cobbled a spare from bits.
Perhaps if I lay down
my head'll come better again.
His left shoulder kept rising
higher in his cardigan.

He could see death in a face.
Family used to call him in
to look at sick ones and say.
At his own time, he was told.

The knob found in his head
was duck-egg size. Never hurt.
Two to six months, Cecil.

I'll be right, he boomed
to his poor sister on the phone
I'll do that when I finish dyin.

Don't die, Cecil.
But they do . . .

> Your grave's got littler
> somehow, in the three months.
> More pointy as the clay's shrivelled,
> like a stuck zip in a coat.
>
> Your cricket boots are in
> the State museum! Odd letters
> still come. Two more's died since you:
> Annie, and Stewart. Old Stewart.
>
> On your day there was a good crowd,
> family, and people from away.
> But of course a lot had gone
> to their own funerals first.
>
> Snobs mind us off religion
> nowadays, if they can.
> Fuck thém. I wish you God.

The colloquial rightness of the stress on 'thém' robs Murray's calm dismissal of the anti-religious of sting, and in the last sentence he and his father are united in belief and practice as they had never been in life. Poems like this, and the great sequence on his mother, made it clear that in the poetry of human grief he had no modern peer.

The sense of renewal and healing he felt after the death of his father showed in his acceptance, in March 1995, of an invitation from New College, an Anglican college of the University of New South Wales, to give a lecture in a series organised by Christine Alexander: Murray proposed to talk about his depression, something he could not have faced before the death of his father. 'I was, and to a happily lesser extent still am, in the process of getting over a serious depressive breakdown, and wasn't at all sure I would have the energy for the writing of lectures, on top of my grimly maintained persistence in writing poems', he told Bishop John Reid. 'I wasn't sure the disease had left enough grace or hope in me to share with people—I've had to use cerebration instead, plus simple surrender, to get along. And, like more folk than will admit it, I wasn't sure I was good enough to present myself as a very public, high profile Christian. But—I'm prepared to give it a go, in the older Aust. way!'[32] The moving and quietly triumphant lecture, delivered to a packed audience at New College on 11 November 1996, and the publication that resulted, *Killing the Black Dog*, would be his frankest and most courageous approach yet to the sources and symptoms of his disease.

In March 1995 he wrote one of his most powerful poems to date, 'Burning Want', in which he revisited all his painful memories of his deprived childhood, his mother's death, his father's grief, his own miserable years at Taree High. This was the poem, he would later say, that 'initiated his recovery from depression'.[33] It would be truer to say that the death of his father initiated the process, of which the poem was just one sign. 'It's a bit unforgiving', he wrote to me about 'Burning Want', 'but I've tried & can't *do* forgiveness, on this material. Not till it's fully *out*, stated & cured. If ever it is cured, as distinct from obliterated. We can hope'.[34]

There is a new jauntiness about other poems written at this time, including the witty syncopated piece 'Tympan Alley', which pays homage to Valerie's singing. Her coloratura renditions of the songs of the 1920s and 1930s, often in harmony with Clare's soaring soprano, were a frequent feature of the little Bunyah house:

Adult songs in English,
avoiding schmaltz,
pre-twang:
the last songs adults sang.

When roles and manners wore
their cuffs as shot as Or-
tega y Gasset's,
soloists sang

as if a jeweller raised
pinches of facets
for hearts as yet unfazed
by fatty assets.

Adult songs with English;
the brilliantine long-play
records of the day
sing of the singlish,

the arch from wry to rue,
of marques and just one Engel,
blue, that Dietrich played;
euphemism's last parade

with rhymes still on our side
unwilling to divide
the men from the poise,
of lackadays and lakatois—

and always you,
cool independent You,
unsnowable, au fait,
when Us were hotly two,

not lost in They.[35]

The pied butcherbirds, magnificent singers, listened with heads cocked to Valerie's music, and whole groups of them in the Bunyah valley could flute 'Wild again, beguiled again', though no matter how rapt their attention, they never learned the next line. Murray would capture this scene in 'Singing to the Butcherbird', written at the University of New South Wales during a Writer in Residenceship in the second half of 1997.

Wild again, beguiled again
the black & white butcherbird sings
in the top of a sunny pine;
most of his kin sing similar:
it's the local butcherbird tune.

Though they listen fascinated
they can never learn the next bars:
a simpering, whimpering child again
Not much simper in a bird;
they enter the world in their coffin.

He needed to get away from Bunyah after his father's death, which had left both him and Valerie exhausted. The chance was provided by a big German literary award, the Petrarca Preis: DM40 000, computing equipment (of which he made no use) and an all-expenses paid trip to Avignon to receive the award.[36] It was the most prestigious European award he had yet received, and it lifted his spirits: he was the first non-European winner in the twenty-year history of the prize. With the aid of a small legacy from his father, he was able to take with him Valerie, Alexander, eighteen, and Peter, thirteen, and he combined the time on the Continent with a brief residence at Trinity College Oxford and a week in a cottage in Hay-on-Wye, for the festival. He was a great collector of odd names, and in Hay was delighted to spot a kite shop called 'Way on High'. On this trip too he made a visit to his Stirling friends Angela and Grahame Smith, who had visited Bunyah in 1984 and 1993, and would return in 1998.

He collected the prize at Avignon on 17 June 1994, and the Murrays were all accommodated in a hotel of such luxury that they had never experienced anything like it. They hoped hard that they would not have to pay for any part of their stay.[37] Murray bought a beret in the hope of looking like a local, and he and Valerie chatted in French and German until the muscles of their faces ached from the unaccustomed exercise. There were daily organised trips into the smiling countryside, the only one of which Murray did not enjoy was a drive up Mont Ventoux, which Petrarch, inventor of tourism, was reputedly the first man to climb for aesthetic reasons: all Murray's horror of mountain roads returned, and he held his beret before his eyes while Valerie urged him to think of Holland, 'luxe, calme et volupté'. It worked.[38] For the rest, it was '3 days of picnics with damask & silver, Chateauneuf du Pape & a counter tenor, and dinners where the waiters whipped silver domes off our plates in unison at the nod of their chief, and the food was paradisal in every course'.[39]

He followed this up with more readings in Barcelona, where the Murrays were 'knocked sideways', as Murray put it, by Gaudi's Sagrada Familia cathedral,[40] some lazy days in a borrowed house near Llança near the French border, a brief stop in Paris for Valerie to admire the fine portrait head of Murray that a Canadian sculptor, Jonathan Hirschfeld, had made in May 1993, and a happy visit to Bruce Clunies Ross and his pretty wife Anna Maria in Denmark: Clunies Ross had laid in the bottle of Glen Murray whisky he always got for the poet's reappearance.[41] This European tour was by far their most expensive holiday ever, and by the end of it Cecil's legacy and much of the prize money had been exhausted. Murray thought it worth every penny: 'I'm specially glad it was such a success in Valerie's eyes. She'd deserved and needed it for so long'.[42]

The Hirschfeld portrait head, which has never been cast or exhibited, was a portent: Murray had now achieved such national prominence that a queue of portraitists began to form, eager to paint him. Among them were the New Zealander Rose McKinley, Helen Potter, Margaret Ackland and Lee Zaunders, whose large painting of Murray, which he and Valerie thought particularly successful, would hang above the Murrays' sofa for years. Other portraits of the poet would appear in the annual Archibald portrait competition in Sydney year after year, as different artists struggled to convey his likeness. Many of them failed, the massive physical presence masking for them the agile delicate strengths of the mind: the only artist who could catch that was Murray himself, and it was a portrait of internalities scattered across many poems. Even he, when he painted a self-portrait of what could be seen, tended to produce a caricature, as in 'Levities of the Short Giant':

> Afternoon, and the Short Giant takes his siesta
> on a threadbare ruby sofa which, being shorter than he,
> curves him into the half moon or slice-of-pawpaw position,
> hull down, like a deep-timbered merchantman, with both hands on deck,

his stubbled head for poop and lantern, and at the bow
twin figureheads: bare feet with soles the earthen green
of seed potatoes, rimmed with old paintings' craquelure.
Massive mosquito-scabbed legs slope down into dungaree;
asleep in his own arms, he makes odd espresso noises.

One of the artists who painted him was an elegant ex-Zimbabwean, Amanda Marks; her portrait of Murray, seen from behind seated in a little boat, pleased him immensely while she was working on it, and he wrote a poem about it, 'Amanda's Painting', before her changes produced a painting he liked less well.

> In the painting, I'm seated in a shield,
> coming home in it up a shadowy river.
> It is a small metal boat lined in eggshell
> and my hands grip the gunwale rims. I'm
> a composite bow, tensioning the whole boat,
> steering it with my gaze. No oars, no engine,
> no sail. I'm propelling the little craft with speech.
> My shirt is apple-red, soaking in a salt birth-sheen
> more liquid than the river, my cap is a teal mask
> pushed back so far that I can pretend it's headgear.
> In the middle of the river are cobweb cassowary trees
> of the South Pacific, and on the far shore rise
> dark hills of the temperate zone. To these, at this
> moment in the painting's growth, my course is slant
> but my eye is on them . . .

Marks's account of the rich animal life in Zimbabwe fascinated him, and during another trip to Europe, in September 1995, he produced a brilliant covert miniature self-portrait, 'Dreambabwe':

> Streaming, a hippo surfaces
> like the head of someone
> lifting, with still-entranced eyes,
> from a lake of stanzas.

This had all the wit and courage of his *Collected Poems*' Brueghel cover, and caught with preternatural exactness the half-dazed ecstasy occasionally visible even at his poetry readings, a penumbra of the state in which he composed. He was facing down his demons with increasing panache, and believed he had the Black Dog by the throat. Its death, however, came at a high cost, and one that he had not at all anticipated.

In mid-afternoon on 12 July 1996 he was pottering around the garden at Bunyah when he stopped, gripped himself, and leaned against the water-tank, white and sweating. 'I'm in terrible pain', he told Valerie: 'I can't understand it, you're going to have to take me to out-patients'. 'It's just indigestion', she reassured him cynically, suspecting that he was having another of his panic attacks. But when the cramping, upper-abdominal pain was worse after some hours, she drove him in to the Manning Base Hospital in Taree. A resident physician conducted an electrocardiogram, which was normal, and ruled out a heart attack, and he was sent home again with some antacid tablets, after three hours in casualty.[43]

He was back again four days later, on 16 July, with a letter from his GP, Dr Gosling, stating that Murray had a suspected case of cholangitis (inflammation of the gall bladder) as well as a temperature and abdominal tenderness. For three days he had been increasingly jaundiced and suffering severe abdominal pain. An ultrasound check of the gall-bladder was ordered, together with a battery of other tests. The ultrasound showed that there was 'fat or a mass' on the liver, and a CAT scan was ordered for the next day; it revealed an abscess on the liver. By 17 July 1996 his condition was worsening: he grew short of breath so that oxygen had to be administered, and tests showed that the sugar levels in his urine were steadily rising. He was, in Valerie's words, 'bright brass yellow and his eyes the colour of corn-fed egg-yolks'.[44] By the morning of 18 July his doctors were growing uneasy: their patient was showing signs of kidney failure and septic shock, and it was decided to send him to a tertiary hospital with specialised liver surgeons. By 11.15 a.m. he was in the ambulance on his way to the John Hunter Hospital in Newcastle. Sedated and calm, he remembered his mother's death, decided that his own name could easily be added to the stone on his parents' graves, reflected that his family had risen in the world if they could now travel by ambulance, and wondered serenely if he would ever drive these familiar roads again.[45]

Valerie, clearing up at home to follow him to Newcastle, took a last look at the Lee Zaunders portrait of him above the sofa and broke down.[46] She controlled herself until the point where, five minutes from the John Hunter Hospital, she stopped at a red traffic light, and after she had been stationary for a minute or so another driver slammed into the back of her car. It was the last straw. 'I threw a proper Mediterranean seven', she would say later:[47] she screamed, tore her hair, wept with her face on the bonnet. By the time she reached the hospital Murray was being operated on.

'It is fair to say that when he arrived he was nearly dead', Dr Jon Gani of the John Hunter Hospital would say later. Murray had severe septic shock and a large abscess under the left side of his liver. The operation on 18 July was to drain the abscess. The last thing he heard, as the anaesthetic took effect, was the voice of his surgeon: 'We could lose this one'.[48] The pathology report from the operation revealed the infection was caused by escherichia-coli, a bacterium usually found only in the intestinal tract: it seemed likely that a fish-bone or chicken-bone had perforated either his stomach or intestine, releasing the bacteria. At first the operation seemed to have been successful, though Murray was kept under continual sedation in the Intensive Care Unit. His problems included complete kidney failure and severe septic shock: 'This is as bad as it gets', one of his specialists remarked.[49] Continual renal replacement therapy, mechanical ventilation (his lungs were badly congested) and repeated blood transfusions kept him alive.[50] He received extreme unction from both the Anglican and Catholic chaplains.[51]

Piers Laverty, who well remembered Murray's care for him after he smashed his pelvis in 1985, made the four-hour return trip from Sydney two or three times each week to be with Valerie in this time of fear, taking her out for lunch and telling her comforting stories when it seemed that Murray's life hung by a hair: '"Les told me that he had a dream and he met Death and Death said it didn't want him for a long time". And that seemed to cheer her up. I never told her that I made it up'.[52]

For some days Murray seemed to be improving, and then his condition deteriorated again, so that he had to have further surgery on 28 July. Surgeons now found that the abscess had failed to drain: worse, the tissue surrounding the liver was necrotic. 'We decided to remove the section of liver affected by the abscess', Dr Gani was to say. 'This amounted to between 10 and 12 per cent of the organ—about the size of a standard margarine container.'[53] Murray returned to the Intensive Care ward with larger drains, was given more blood transfusions, and was kept sedated and ventilated. Valerie sat by his unconscious form all day and every day, watching the vineyard of tubes that linked him to life, listening for the theme from the first movement of Beethoven's fifth symphony (V for Victory as she thought of it hopefully) from a machine that warned of dropping blood-sugar levels, reluctantly leaving at night, exhausted, to sleep in Clare's student room in Newcastle.

Within two days Murray began passing urine, and it was clear the second operation had been more successful than the first. He was no longer sedated with drugs, though his coma persisted. He began to stir on 30 July 1996 and deliriously tried to pull out his tubes; on 1 August he opened his eyes; on 4 August he said his first word since arriving in hospital: a nurse asked him if he knew who he was, and he replied 'Yeah'.

The hospital knew too: within twelve hours of this unconscious large patient's admission, the staff had been startled by the phone-call from Clive

James in London.[54] Soon the switchboard was dealing with dozens of enquiries a day, most of which it referred to Murray's agent, Margaret Connolly. She, to stave off the avalanche, put out regular press statements on Murray's condition, which the newspapers printed, so that the whole country, and Murray's friends abroad, followed his progress with anxiety. Phonecalls, telegrams, letters and bouquets poured in. When he was pronounced out of danger there were relieved newspaper articles: 'Poet Cheats Death'.[55]

Murray, who was for a long time unable to take in the fact that he had been unconscious for twenty days (it had felt like half an hour to him), said later that he had 'awakened to find my State funeral in full swing ... the biggest demonstration of public love and concern that will ever come my way, I'm sure, and only the Generation of '68 stayed aloof from it'.[56] He surfaced with a craving for Chinese soup, which Valerie brought in for him, and with a weak giggling enjoyment of a joke about President Paul Kruger of the Transvaal in 1895 opening a new synagogue in Johannesburg with the sincere prayer, 'I open this synagogue in the name of our Lord Jesus Christ amen'. 'Perhaps things are as reconciled and sensible as that where I'd nearly gone', he told Angela Smith.[57]

His hand was unable to write, but he composed in his head a poem, 'Bottles in the Bombed City', for his British publisher Michael Schmidt, whose Carcanet Press offices had been destroyed by a big IRA bomb that wrecked the Corn Exchange in Manchester. 'I didn't know I liked Manchester till they blew my publisher there to smithereens!' he told Geoff Page.[58] The medical imagery flowed naturally from his own situation: 'They gave the city a stroke. Its memories/are cordoned off. They could collapse on you'. The John Hunter Hospital put out a statement that he had improved to the point where he was 'conscious and verbal', a phrase he loved and would use as the title for a future book of poems.

He tottered out of the hospital at last on 16 August 1996, his weight down to just over 100 kilograms (he had lost 30 kilograms, most of it wasted muscle),[59] and was very glad to get home to Bunyah again. But still more pleasing was a psychological change, which he had become aware of even before he was conscious of the public affirmation: the Black Dog had left him.

> I no longer come down with bouts of weeping or reasonless exhaustion. And I no longer seek rejection in a belief that only bitterly conceded praise is reliable. I'd always seen women in the unwounded parts of my mind as simply fellow humans: now I may be able to see them that way altogether. If I have a regret, in the sudden youth and health of my mind in its fifty-eighth year, it is that I've got well so late in my life, as in a poem I started writing for my wife Valerie before the Big Sick and finished after it:[60]

After a silver summer
of downpours, cement-powder autumn
set in its bag. Lawns turned crunchy
but the time tap kept dribbling away.

The paddocks were void as that evening
in early childhood when the sun
was rising in the west,
round and brimming as the factory furnace door,

as I woke up after sickness.
Then it was explained to me
that I'd slept through from morning
and I sobbed because I'd missed that day,

my entire lovely day.
Without you, it might have been a prophecy.[61]

CHAPTER TWENTY-THREE
FORGIVING THE VICTIM
1996–98

~

And I took all the blame out of all sense and reason,
Until I cried and trembled and rocked to and fro,
Riddled with light.

W. B. YEATS

Murray badly needed to believe that he had shaken off the Black Dog, and the last thing he wanted was a passionate public controversy of the sort that in the past had so often deepened his depression. Yet that was what he got, soon after leaving hospital. The focus was Australia's most controversial historian, Manning Clark, whom Murray had known slightly while they both lived in Canberra, and whom he had run into subsequently when they both visited the Hermannsberg Mission in Central Australia in 1987.[1]

In May 1970 Murray had met Clark at the Canberra home of a mutual friend, the poet David Campbell: at the time Murray, unemployed, was doing some rabbiting on Campbell's farm for pocket-money. Clark was wearing a striking medal, which Murray, who had had a fascination for military and other decorations since childhood, recognised as the Order of Lenin, a Soviet decoration distributed copiously inside Russia,[2] but awarded to very few foreigners. Seeing Murray's stare, Clark tapped the impressive medal proudly, saying 'It's real, you know, not the stuff students wear. It's a real gong'.[3] Through Murray's mind darted the thought, 'Doesn't he know how much blood is on it?'[4]

He later looked up the medal in the Australian National University library, and satisfied himself that Clark had indeed been wearing the Order of Lenin. Though he thought this as shameful as wearing a Nazi decoration, he did not want to expose Clark, and it was only eight years later he chanced to mention it to an academic friend, the political scientist John Paul: 'What would you think of a senior Australian historian who wore the Order of Lenin at a private dinner-party?'[5] Paul was incredulous, and asked Murray to describe what he had seen. 'Lenin's head in relief in silver [it was actually platinum], edged with ears of grain in gold, and red enamel above', said Murray. Paul later mentioned Murray's story to a journalist friend, Peter Kelly.[6]

On 24 August 1996, while Murray was recovering from his operation, the Brisbane *Courier-Mail* ran a story by Kelly suggesting that Clark, who had died in 1991, had been a Soviet agent of influence who helped to select Australian diplomats; the newspaper used as evidence Murray's sighting of his Order of Lenin. It also quoted an academic, Geoffrey Fairbairn, who in 1970 had seen the same medal worn by Clark at drinks at the Soviet Embassy, where Clark's wife taught English to the staff, and where Clark himself tutored the Ambassador.[7] Fairbairn had been deeply distressed to see the historian wearing the Soviet decoration, which he identified with certainty as the Order of Lenin.

Members of the Clark family angrily denied that Clark had ever been awarded the Order of Lenin, arguing that it must have been a lesser Soviet award, resembling a large coin, which Clark had received from the Russian Communists in 1970: unfortunately this could not now be found. For weeks a passionate controversy swirled through Australian and British papers.[8] It was given a partisan edge by the fact that Clark had been closely associated with the Australian Labor Party. Labor politicians entered the fray in his defence.[9]

Murray was the only living witness, Fairbairn having died in 1980, and he was badgered for interviews until he was exhausted.[10] He came under tremendous pressure to deny that he had seen Clark wearing the Order of Lenin, but refused to do so, though he hated being the centre of the controversy.[11] The medal he had seen and described to John Paul could not be mistaken for any other Soviet decoration, certainly not for something resembling a simple coin. Nor was it credible that Clark had merely bought or borrowed it (though Murray tactfully did not point this out), for Fairbairn had seen him wearing it at the Soviet Embassy, the one place Clark would not have dared wear it had he not had a right to.

Given Clark's frequently affirmed Leninist sympathies, it is not clear that any Soviet medal could do his reputation much further harm: he twice accepted invitations to tour the Soviet Union—in 1958 after the suppression of the Hungarian uprising and again in 1970 after the Czech uprising was crushed—while in his shameful book *Meeting Soviet Man*, published in 1960, he had several times compared Lenin to Christ.[12] For a time after his first visit to the USSR he had clipped his beard so as to give himself a striking resemblance to Lenin.[13] At the very least, as a letter to the *Economist* put it, 'the fact that the privately humane Clark proudly wore an ersatz Lenin medal on many occasions shows, for a supposedly great historian, a remarkable lack of knowledge or care about the career of one of the 20th century's monsters'.[14] Clark had in word and deed openly supported a system soaked with the blood of

100 million victims, and Murray had no wish to point the moral. He refused to comment further on the matter.

Publicity much more pleasant to him came with the publication, a month after he left hospital, of his latest volume of verse, defiantly entitled *Subhuman Redneck Poems*. The cover illustration was a photograph by Graham McCarter of Cecil Murray in the overgrown garden of the Bunyah house, wearing his bush-hat and holding his violin and bow, the very image of a rugged redneck musician. Many of the poems spoke for Cecil and for Murray's people, the rural poor, against those who would patronise and suppress them: perhaps 10 per cent of the volume's poems, as a result, were passionately indignant. The critic Don Anderson, whose judgement Murray respected, picked out this group of poems for condemnation and listed them by name, calling them 'vile'.[15] Murray felt they had hit the target: 'He named all the right ones', he remarked with a grin.[16]

Anderson was right to remark on the unevenness of the volume—all Murray's volumes are uneven, though as Bruce Clunies Ross would remark, 'There's "less good" and "good", but it's very hard to find really inferior Murray'.[17] But perhaps Anderson had failed to see that Murray's *saeva indignatio* in defence of the 'redneck', the poor, the common man, was as vital and energising to him as Yeats's use of the occult was to the Irish poet. And other critics recognised that, as Elizabeth Lowry put it, 'Murray's poetry, grounded as it is in the assertion of the private claims of the individual against public pressures, might just conceivably be liberal in the original sense of the word'.[18]

Anderson's criticisms, though, did not extend to the bulk of the book, which was made up of poems as strong as any Murray had written: he was clearly a poet at the height of his powers, as Anderson affirmed:

> He is a great poet of grief—here for his father, as he was for his mother in *The People's Otherworld*. He is one of Australia's premier poets of the natural world . . . His gift for similes that leap off the page like brush-fires is everywhere on display: 'You slept like a salt tongue, in gauze'; 'childhoods among bed-ticking midnights/blue as impetigo mixture' (and note the rich double-entendre in 'bed-ticking'); a woman's hair is 'like teak oiled soft to fracture and sway'. He is a master of economy.[19]

Other critics saw these strengths too. The poet Sophie Masson, responding to Anderson's negative comments about the angry poems in the volume, wrote: 'There are surely so many other things in the collection—beauty and tenderness, great pain and loss, and an unerring eye for the numinous word and the almost unbearable, yet exquisite, image—and the taking of enormous risks, both personally and artistically'.[20] It was perhaps above all the sense of suffering endured, accepted and overcome that gave the volume much of its power. And as Anderson recognised, Murray remained what he had been from the start of his career, one of the best nature-poets in the language, as in 'Dead Trees in the Dam':

> Odd mornings, it's been all bloodflag
> and rifle green: a stopped-motion shrapnel
> of kingparrots. Smithereens when they freaked.
>
> Rarely, it's wed ducks, whose children
> will float among the pillars. In daytime
> magpies sidestep up wood to jag pinnacles
>
> and the big blow-in cuckoo crying
> Alarm, Alarm on the wing is not let light.
> This hours after dynastic charts of high
>
> profile ibis have rowed away to beat
> the paddocks. Which, however green, are
> always watercolour, and on brown paper.

His description of two deaf women signing to one another, too, has a magical rightness to it, particularly in the brilliant imagist connection with Chinese calligraphy:

> Two women were characters, continually
> rewriting themselves, in turn, with their hands
> mostly, but with face and torso too
> and very fast, fluttering like the gestures
> above a busy street in Shanghai.[21]

He could produce repeatedly the same deadly accurate bounce and stab, transfixing images like a bird, unerringly, as in 'Comete' with its description of a woman's long hair:

> Uphill in Melbourne on a beautiful day
> a woman was walking ahead of her hair.
> Like teak oiled soft to fracture and sway
> It hung to her heels and seconded her
> As a pencilled retinue, an unscrolling title
> To ploughland, edged with ripe rows of dress,
> a sheathed wing that couldn't fly her at all,
> only itself, loosely, and her spirits.
>   A largesse

of life and self, brushed all calm and out,
its abstracted attempts on her mouth weren't seen,
nor its showering, its tenting. Just the detail
that swam in its flow-lines, glossing about—
as she paced on, comet-like, face to the sun.

Subhuman Redneck Poems was a great critical success. It won Murray the premier British poetry award, the T. S. Eliot Prize, worth £5000, and television news helicopters thwacked the skies above the Forty Acres and floated down into the paddocks around the little weatherboard house as journalists competed for interviews. Murray's neighbours, to whom helicopters usually meant a medical emergency or police aerial-spotting for marijuana, were tremendously impressed.

Those Australian critics who had been peddling the view that his poetry had gone off badly since the 1970s gradually fell silent, though with apparent reluctance: 'For this he gets the T. S. Eliot Prize', lamented Ken Bolton in a review of *Subhuman Redneck Poems*.[22] By contrast *Time* magazine devoted a full-page encomium to his work, calling him 'a national conscience-pricker', and quoting one of the T. S. Eliot Prize judges, the poet Ruth Padel, as saying, 'He is a good example of a poet who becomes universal by being very particular'.[23] And, what pleased Murray even more, the volume was a great popular success, selling more than 10 000 copies in Australia, an astonishing figure for a book of poetry in a country of only 18 million people.[24] Australians had proved again that they were willing to identify with his sometimes lonely struggle against literary and political fashion.

But that energising and stressful conflict never came to an end in spite of his occasional victories, and it was important to him that it should not. By February 1997 he was engaged in another ideological struggle, this time with Robert Manne, editor of *Quadrant*, for which Murray had acted as Literary Editor since 1989. Manne had from the start of his tenure sought to reposition *Quadrant* politically, and Murray, who at first had supported the move, gradually came to oppose it on the grounds that Manne was going too far. Murray thought *Quadrant* almost the last publication standing out against the left-wing fashions he deplored, and he did not want to see it abandon that position. The crisis came when he clashed with Manne over the Helen Demidenko affair.

In 1994 Demidenko had published an acclaimed first book, *The Hand That Signed the Paper*, a novel focusing on killings in the Ukraine by communists before and by Nazis during World War II. Before its publication, on 22 September 1993, it won the Australian/Vogel Literary award. In June

1995 Demidenko also won Australia's premier literary prize, the Miles Franklin Award, a range of critics and commentators lauding her and her work.

But with that the tide turned. Beginning on 9 June 1995, criticism of the novel began to appear, centring on allegations that the book was anti-Semitic.[25] There was no agreement on this, and on 3 July 1995 the novel won another prize, the Association for the Study of Australian Literature's Gold Medal. Then came a dramatic development. On 19 August 1995 it was revealed that Demidenko was not the daughter of a Ukrainian immigrant, as she had claimed, but the offspring of two English migrants: her real name was Helen Darville. There followed a storm of controversy, some of the critics who had previously praised her work now joining the many others who turned on her, attacking her as a fraud, a plagiarist and an anti-Semite.[26] Her book was hastily dropped from the 1995 shortlist of the Victorian Premier's Literary Awards.[27]

Murray, who had not thought much of *The Hand That Signed the Paper*, felt intense sympathy with Demidenko/Darville once she came under a storm of often vicious personal abuse. 'She was a young girl, and her book mightn't have been the best in the world, but it was pretty damn good for a girl of her age [twenty when she wrote it]. And her marketing strategy of pretending to be a Ukrainian might have been unwise, but it sure did expose the pretensions of the multicultural industry', he would remark.[28] The ferocious, massed attack on her was a phenomenon he recognised from Taree High, and he would do his best to stand against it wherever it found a victim. He considered that Darville's crime lay in showing up proponents of multiculturalism, and in 'talking about dangerous material, the Holocaust and, more dangerous still, the immense slaughter, the killing fields, of the Communists—you're just not allowed to mention that stuff. The Communists have an enormous interest in suppressing all that history'.[29] The claim that her novel was anti-Semitic he thought unsustainable, a view shared by level-headed Jewish and gentile commentators such as Andrew Riemer, Peter Singer, Thomas Kenneally and Leonie Kramer.[30]

The first of Murray's responses was a poem, 'For Helen Darville', which he published in *Subhuman Redneck Poems*, in which he draws attention, as Darville had, to the fact that the victims of communism vastly outnumber those of Nazism and deserve equal pity:

> The Six Million are worth full grief:
> it isn't enough to be stunned—
> but showing up your elders' multiculture
> so easily is what got you shunned,

> that, and pity for the greater working class
> which their dream made work in the ground,
> eighty million in a darkening red flag
> outspread under ice, under grass.

Subsequently, in 'A Deployment of Fashion', he would link the attack on Darville with the wider phenomenon of attacks on those judged outcasts (from Lindy Chamberlain to Pauline Hanson) by society's fashion police, the journalists, academics and others who form opinion:

> In Australia, a lone woman
> is being crucified by the Press
> at any given moment.
>
> With no unedited right
> of reply, she is cast out
> into Aboriginal space.
>
> It's always for a defect in weeping:
> she hasn't wept on cue
> or she won't weep correctly.
>
> There's a moment when the sharks are
> still butting her, testing her protection,
> when the Labor Party, or influence,
>
> can still save her. Not the Church,
> not other parties. Even at that stage
> few men can rescue her.
>
> Then she goes down, overwhelmed
> in the feasting grins of pressmen,
> and Press women who've moved
>
> from being owned by men
> to being owned by fashion,
> these are more deeply merciless.
>
> She is rogue property,
> she must be taught her weeping.
> It is done for the millions.
>
> Sometimes the millions join in
> with jokes: how to get a baby
> in the Northern Territory? Just stick

> your finger down a dingo's throat.
> Most times, though, the millions
> stay money, and the jokes
>
> are snobbish media jokes:
> Chemidenko. The Oxleymoron.
> Spittle, like the flies on Black Mary.
>
> After the feeding frenzy
> sometimes a ruefully balanced last lick
> precedes the next selection.

In later years he would advocate 'a law or UN Convention outlawing the use of concerted opinion as a weapon of social control—ie the deployment of fashion against any individual or group'.[31]

Robert Manne, by contrast, joined in the attack on Darville, in a long article in *Quadrant* in August 1995, republished in the *Sydney Morning Herald*. Murray, writing to disagree with him, accused him of having been 'duchessed by the Left' who were out to silence *Quadrant* and steal it. He told Manne he was disgusted by anyone who joined a gang to pick on an individual, and for good measure added that he was aware that Manne was trying to have him removed from *Quadrant's* editorial board.[32]

There were disputes also between Murray and Manne on such issues as the printing of an article by Hal Colebatch claiming that Manning Clark had been anti-Semitic: Manne, who did not agree, rejected the piece, against Murray's advice. Murray, like Manne, thought Colebatch mistaken, but felt he deserved a hearing. Colebatch subsequently got his opinion into *Quadrant* as a letter, which Manne countered editorially.[33] The issue was important as a symptom of the struggle now in progress. On 21 July 1997 Manne wrote to the Committee of Management of the magazine asking for support in sacking Murray.[34]

'I'm fighting for my survival as Lit. Ed. of Qdt.', Murray told Christine Alexander in February 1997: 'Rob Manne's out to dump me as he shifts politically. We'll know soon who is to go'.[35] In the event, it was Manne who went, Murray having the support of Committee of Management members such as Leonie Kramer for his view that under Manne's direction *Quadrant* was in danger of losing its independent voice in Australian journalism. In addition to the Demidenko affair, committee members seem to have felt that *Quadrant* was failing to take an independent line on the issues of racial politics that were now convulsing Australian public life.

Murray himself rather agreed with Manne's line on racial issues, telling Geoff Page, 'On Wik [the High Court ruling that Aboriginals could lay claim, on grounds of traditional ownership, to land on the Australian mainland], I'm comfortable with it, and probably closer to the Dodsons [Mick Dodson and his brother Pat were both prominent Aboriginal spokesmen] than to the Howards [Prime Minister John Howard]'.[36] But committee members considered, as Manne reported to the press, that Manne had changed *Quadrant* to the point where the journal 'is indistinguishable from any other magazine of opinion, that it has lost its anti-leftist bite, and that only one line has been run on Mabo and Wik and the stolen children'.[37] Finding the board unwilling to remove Murray, and in fact keen to back him, Manne resigned.

Murray, telephoned by a journalist and asked to comment on events, replied that he valued *Quadrant* as a voice that added variety to editorial expression in Australia, that he had nothing against Robert Manne, and hoped that the Left, which had tried to seize control of *Quadrant*, would now treat Manne well in spite of the fact that he had failed to deliver the magazine to them.[38]

In many of his dealings with the newspapers, which he had tended to regard as weapons of war, he was now more relaxed. In 1997 the *Sydney Morning Herald* was still taking what Murray called 'the Aust. Council's line against me',[39] alleging that he had had huge amounts of Literature Board support and deserved no more.[40] In March 1997 the newspaper unwittingly printed in its letters column a spoof response, written by Murray's friend Piers Laverty: 'As a taxpayer who has no truck with poets or people of that ilk, I was horrified by the picture . . . of Big Les lollygagging about the Bunyah Health Farm, stuffing himself with larks' tongues and the like . . . all paid for by the taxpayers'.[41] Pleased with this, one weekend Murray amused himself by copying his dead father's crabbed, turn-of-the-century handwriting, and produced in it a letter which he dispatched to the *Sydney Morning Herald*, supporting Laverty's line, sourly disapproving of Murray's 'grant-bludging', but revealing that 'Les's big government handout' was the mainstay of the local economy of the Bunyah valley: 'I know some butchers might have to go out of business if they didn't supply Murray's weekend whoopee parties with lawyers and pen-pushers at his estate as he has the hide to call it'. The letter was signed 'Cecil Murray'. Again the newspaper fell for the hoax,[42] only two days later grumbling gamely that 'someone has been having a lend of the *Herald*'.[43] Murray had reached the point where playfulness was replacing anger.

He was winning other, more personal battles too. With his new-found confidence in facing his past, he made his peace with some fellow pupils from Taree High. It was at this time that he began exchanging Christmas cards with a few of them, such as Ralph Suters and Robin Norling. He was even drawn to Barbara O'Neill, who as Barbara Montgomery had been one of the girls who had tormented him most actively. Some years before she had approached Murray and invited him to a Taree High School class reunion: in refusing it, he had reminded her of his treatment at her hands and those of her friends. He needed to put the matter behind him. O'Neill pleaded defensively, 'We were only sixteen'. 'I was only sixteen', Murray replied evenly. Later he would remark, 'We said a lot in that one exchange'.[44] Victim and victimiser each had something to forgive, a profound and original insight that would inform the ending of *Fredy Neptune*.

Now he heard that O'Neill was dying of stomach cancer. Murray screwed up his courage and visited her in Taree's Manning Base Hospital several times, to her surprise and pleasure. As O'Neill neared her end Murray visited her for the last time, and as he left, gave her a big kiss of forgiveness on the cheek, to which she responded with warmth. 'We both understood what we were saying', Murray would recall later.[45] The torments of Taree High were behind him at last.

His long process of reviewing and accepting his life was given added energy during these years by the process of self-examination that collaborating with a biographer entailed. From the end of 1994 onwards he submitted to long interviews which involved an often painful reliving of his past and the raking up of many old embers. I warned him that I might discover and reveal uncomfortable things about his background: 'Anything you can find, you can use', he repeated confidently. These lengthy interviews intensified during the second half of 1997, when he was Literary Fellow at the School of English, University of New South Wales; with his earlier harried visit in mind he had feared being 'pelted by the feminists' there, but the angry wave had passed its peak. Instead he found the university a pleasant change from Bunyah life, a change he registered in 'Prime Numbers':[46]

> Normally I live in the country,
> work, garden, parry thrusts from the *Herald*,
> but two days a week I fly in
> to a cubicle in the Stacked City,
> an every-coloured brick university
> that is built on top of itself
> like a brain's lobes and evolutionary layers
> on the last rock before Botany Bay.
>
> The inner streets of this oppidum
> are paved with grey carpet, and inmates
> lie on them for cool negotiations
> or to write in big pads. Footsteps with vocal

> animate the stairs and little squares;
> odd walls not yet built over
> catch sun and frecklings of leaves;
> a coffee shop may form round a stairwell . . .
>
> Back above the racehorse-named streets
> in Overlap City, I'm really a specimen,
> a mountain to geographers . . .

But even as he submitted to exploration, mapping, classification, he was inspecting, analysing, writing himself, putting the final touches to the volume he would call 'my secret autobiography':[47] *Fredy Neptune*.

CHAPTER TWENTY-FOUR
FREDY MURRAY
1993–

O body swayed to music, O brightening glance
How can we know the dancer from the dance?

W. B. YEATS

Since finishing *The Boys Who Stole The Funeral* in 1979, Murray had been thinking of writing another long narrative poem, partly because he had found the earlier poem so enjoyable to write and wished to renew the experience, partly because he had things to say that only a long poem could accommodate. *The Boys Who Stole The Funeral* had been an affirmation of the values he admired in the Australian context. In 1992 he proposed a more ambitious project, for which the whole world would be the backdrop: *Fredy Neptune*.

The book began, he was to say, just as *The Boys Who Stole The Funeral* did, when the figure of the hero stood up in his mind and demanded attention: 'I'll never know where he came from, he just stood up in the poem. Fredy's poem. He wanted to be told. Forbutt did the same, he stood up and said there was a man who needed burying'.[1] Murray had great faith in the importance of the few poems that came to him in this dreamily compulsive way: the first of them had been the weeping man in Martin Place, in 'An Absolutely Ordinary Rainbow', and among their number he counted the animal poems of *Translations from the Natural World*.[2] German-Australian Fredy Boettcher stood up in his mind and said 'Write me'. And Murray did, to find out what happened: 'I write basically to discover it'.[3]

Fredy Boettcher, he was to say, was much like himself. 'Fred' was the name Murray wished he had been given. Indeed, during his periods of depression, Valerie responded to his sudden mood changes by calling him 'Les' when he was cheerful, and 'Fred' when the Black Dog had him: 'Les is at least two people', she would remark.[4] Like Murray, Fredy Boettcher is a farm-boy from the mid-north coast of New South Wales, and there are many parallels between creator and creation, ranging from the fact that Fredy's father is the victim of persecution by his neighbours, as Cecil Murray had been wronged by his family, to the fact that Fredy, like Murray, is alienated from his mother.

Above all, Fredy is imprisoned in a body without feeling, so that he is cut off from the world, a state that Murray felt he himself suffered, psychologically if not physically. As early as 1961 he had written to Geoffrey Lehmann,

> Heard from a friend of mine the other day that you assert that I regard people as 'unreal ideas' or some such. You're pretty near the mark, too, and it worries me. I even wrote a poem about it. [He then quotes a juvenile, obscure poem, 'Session in Camera', a Yeatsian colloquy between Soul and Body, and comments on it.] You see? It's my old theme of lack of communication once more.[5]

Fredy Boettcher's condition, which Murray identified as macular anaesthesia, is not dissimilar to one symptom of severely autistic children, who show little response to pain, and who, to break through the anaesthetic barrier, beat their heads. Some can be comforted by the sensation of gentle squeezing.[6] Alexander's condition lies somewhere in the background of Murray's description of Fredy Boettcher's, and the portrait of the German boy Hans, whom Fredy saves from the gas chambers, owes much to Alexander. Fredy's condition, then, can be seen as a physical parallel to the autist's inner anaesthesia.

In Fredy Boettcher's case, anaesthesia is brought on by the horror of seeing a group of Armenian women being burned by Turks during the Armenian genocide of 1915, and being powerless to intervene or save them. Murray drew for this scene on a terrible poem by the Armenian Atom Yarjanian,[7] who himself died in the genocide:

> The twenty sank exhausted to the ground.
> 'Get up!' The naked swords flickered like snakes.
> Then someone fetched a pitcher of kerosene.
> Human justice, I spit in your face.
> Without delay the twenty were anointed.
> 'Dance!' roared the mob: 'This is sweeter than the perfumes of Arabia!'
> They touched the naked women with a torch.
> And there was dancing. The charred bodies rolled.
>
> In shock I slammed my shutters like a storm,
> Turned to the one gone, asked: 'These eyes of mine—
> How shall I dig them out, how shall I, how?'[8]

This image of burning paralleled one Murray had already explored in poetry: one of his aunts, Myrtle, had been terribly burned in a childhood accident, and when small he had often wondered over the webbing of scar that covered her to the end of her life. He had conveyed something of her agony in 'Cotton Flannellette':

Lids frogged shut, O *please shake the bed*,
her contour whorls and braille tattoos
from where, in her nightdress, she flared
out of hearth-drowse to a marrow shriek
pedalling full tilt firesleeves in mid air,
    are grainier with repair
than when the doctor, crying *Dear God, woman!*
No one can save that child. Let her go!
spared her the treatments of the day.

Now the burning women of Yarjanian's poem came to serve as a symbol of the mob persecution which Murray termed 'the police', and which for him summed up much that was worst about human nature in the twentieth century. The Armenian genocide, he believed, had inspired Hitler,[9] who several times referred to it in his table talk.[10] Murray's passionate opposition to the creeping nihilism of his time, his steady affirmation that life itself is sacred, would be the dominant theme of the poem, as it had been of his entire output to this point. It was what he called 'the central statement of the book'. 'In this century well over a hundred million people have been murdered by police ... Another hundred million have died in uniform in wars, but the ones that I particularly have been haunted by, all my life, ever since I learned of it, are these unarmed victims of ideologies, tribalisms, that sort of thing.'[11]

This spirit of mob persecution represented all he was determined to go on identifying and fighting, whether it showed itself in playgrounds, literary coteries, political witch-hunts or in the gulags of totalitarianism: he would stand with the persecuted, the marginalised, the poor, the isolated and the oppressed wherever he recognised them. He identified with them instinctively. As he wrote to his friends Walter and Elisabeth Davis:

> In my mind I always cast myself in the loner-outcast role. You know how we each have a poem in us, and 'cast' ourselves and others in its narrative? One is reality, two or three is company, many more than that's a lynch mob, is how my poem goes. There! Now the answer's down to its essence for you. I do tend to be more trustful of very big groupings, eg the biggest church, nations etc.—people rather than their state-apparatus I mean—because the quotient of intimacy there is low as compared with what's likely in a smallish mob.[12]

Fredy Boettcher is isolated not only by his loss of feeling and the immense somatic strength he shares with his creator, but by his simplicity, his lack of education, his being a foreigner wherever he goes, and the fact that he feels compelled to hide what has happened to him. Murray chose to make him

German partly because of his own fluency in that language, partly because Germans were persecuted in Australia during World War I, when the story starts, but partly because he considered that the history of the Germans was central to the twentieth century, and he wanted to compress it all into the poem:

> It is the story of the Twentieth Century, it is *the* big story, the fate of the Germans and the fate they then visited on others. I'm telling it from way out on the periphery. A man who was in the German orbit but was well out towards the edge and was occasionally spun in towards the centre a bit and spun off again and had this intricate destiny of his own.[13]

It was important to him that *Fredy Neptune* not be an intellectual or forebrain poem: Fredy's life was to be primarily involved with feeling, or its lack, rather than ratiocination. His was to be principally the thought of the body and of the dreaming mind. Accordingly Murray sought and found non-literary styles and models for the work. The poem is written almost entirely in the dialect of the Bunyah valley, the speech he had learned from his father and uncles, though he infused it with transliterated German idioms to convey the subtle mental flavour of a narrator who thinks in two languages. Even the spelling of 'Fredy' in the German manner is part of this bilingual flavouring. To manage this blending convincingly even in a brief poem would have been a feat; to sustain it for 10 000 lines is astonishing.

And since the hero is an uneducated man, Murray was determined to convey him in appropriate terms: the techniques of the poem are determinedly non-literary in their inspiration. Murray drew them from his father's stories, from comic-strips such as *Superman*,[14] which, he liked to recall, had first appeared in the year in which he was born,[15] and above all from the films he had loved since childhood, and of which he had an encyclopaedic knowledge.

> I learned from movies how to frame sequences, how to move quickly, how to keep the thing in focus and yet moving. People are used to going at great speed in movies, they're used to literature taking a lot more time. I noticed some of my critics have been saying the book moves very quick, I suppose partly because there's a lot in it. I thought yeah well where I got that from is two things. One is that Fredy's looking back into the past, and when you're reminiscing you call up a lot of stuff fairly close together. The other thing is how to frame it, and I got that mostly from films.[16]

The rapid cuts, the scene-shifts and the depiction through action are filmic techniques which give the poem some of its bounding energy, and its driving speed. In 1993, about the time he began writing the immense poem, he had told Philip Hodgins: 'How you do directions, if you really want to know, is you cover 'em over with vivacity, & you show the directed action as already starting—not "he walked across the yard & got into the ute" but show him doing sthg. or seeing sthg. as he crosses the yard, then show him *in* the ute. Movie technique, all of it'.[17] And the dreamlike unreality of a damaged character who drifts half-conscious through life, yet because of unusual physical powers finds himself involved in many of the central events of his time, is also perhaps borrowed from a particular film, *Forrest Gump*, though Murray was to say he had not seen it until December 1998, having 'stayed away from it deliberately'.[18]

Given *Fredy Neptune*'s immense length, and the complexity of its blank-verse *ottava rima* stanzas, Murray's progress on the verse novel, as he called it before its publication, was very rapid. He began it early in 1993, and finished it on 28 June 1997, publishing it book by book, as he completed each one, in the *Adelaide Review* and in *PN Review*.[19] His progress can be traced through his correspondence. In July 1993 he was telling Penny Nelson:

> I'm writing a vast verse-novel at the moment, abt. a German-Australian sailor named Fred Boettcher, and for some events in Palestine & nearby in 1917–18 I've relied v. much on a long-forgotten book by a Capt Sutherland who served, with Hudson Fysh, Ross & Keith Smith & half the other famous Aust aerial pioneers, in No. 1 squadron AFC [Australian Flying Corps]. The other day I happened for the first time in decades to drop in to the War Memorial in Hyde Park [central Sydney], & there was a portrait of that same man, who hadn't provided one in his book. It reminded me irresistably of the Canadian actor Donald Sutherland—same long head & face, to a T, except translated into dark and saturnine colouring. A family face, very clearly.[20]

And in a postcard to her, just a month later, he was adding: 'Book 1 of my long verse novel appeared in the Adelaide Review this month, and I'm abt. 3/4 of the way through Book 2, & wishing I cd get some books on circus strong-men acts & the like. For Bk 3 I'm also reading Mein Kampf. Now there's a Boys' Own story!'[21]

By May 1994 he was writing to Walter and Elisabeth Davis about mass killings, like the Holocaust,

> that the world keeps rather determinedly quiet about eg 7 million Ukrainians, perhaps 10 million Russian small farmers, millions of Chinese under Japan and Mao. And perhaps 4–5 million Indians at Partition, and the Armenians, and the native Formosans etc etc. We may need a term besides genocide, for Very

Big Slaughters that aren't primarily racial. A larger term that includes genocide. Myriocide? Democide?[22]

Book 2, 'Barking at the Thunder', was published in 1994, while he was writing Book 4. By 4 August that year he was telling Peter Goldsworthy, who had written to him about the hardships of the blind whose sight is partly restored, 'If you think the sight-restored get it hard, wait till you read what Fred cops in Book 4! At the moment he's in Kentucky trying to kidnap the chief madman from a private & very shonky sanatorium'.[23]

On 19 December 1994 he told me he was running into occasional problems, and being slowed by them: 'When you hit a difficult patch, the poem will stop you, actually. When you get puzzled you can't write any further. You have to stop and think that one through. Then you are allowed to write that, and you can go on. Sometimes you can run along for a while, then you'll hit another snag. A snag is telling you to think deeply'.[24]

He wrote the poem in the way someone from an oral culture might tell a story—the way his semi-literate father had told stories—working from a loose frame of ideas and improvising as he went. In his head was a basic plan that he noted on the cardboard backs of writing-pads, and he shuffled these to find an appropriate order for the events as the story unfolded.[25] 'I'm working from the pattern I learnt from my father, I think, which is start a story and it runs along. It's a well-known oral literary tactic. Chinese professional storytellers used it'.[26] Book 3, 'The Somatic Nobility' (later renamed 'Prop Sabres'), was published in 1996, with Book 4, 'The Police Revolution', following later the same year. The finished volume, published by Duffy & Snellgrove, was launched in Sydney on 19 July 1998.

Fredy's story covers the period of the great twentieth century German drama, from before World War I to the aftermath of World War II, and it ends with Fredy Boettcher's response to Hiroshima. The burning of women anaesthetised him; the realisation that this new and terrible burning was for everyone sets him on the road to recovery. One of the themes of the poem is the reflection that World War II had produced an equality of suffering, women as well as men, soldiers at the front and civilians in the rear. Fredy Boettcher's condition, a horror of injustice, begins to break down with his realisation of the universality of suffering. The poem ends with an extraordinary realisation that he must forgive the innocent, forgive those whose suffering he had on his conscience.

The revelation comes in a fumbling conversation with what Murray called 'his inner man, his deeper self, who's been running the whole thing all the time', while the retarded boy Hans plays with a tennis ball, the mindless random pulses punctuating Fredy's advances in awareness:[27]

> You have to pray with a whole heart, says my inner man to me,
> and you haven't got one. *Can I get one?*
> Forgive the Aborigines. *What have I got to forgive?*
> *They never hurt me!* For being on our conscience.
> I shook my head, and did. Forgiving feels like starting to.
> That I spose I feel uneasy round you, I thought to them, shook my head
> and started understanding. Hans served, and the ball came bounding back
> like a happy pup. Forgive the Jews, my self said.
>
> That one felt miles steep, stone-blocked and black as iron.
> *That's really not mine, the Hitler madness*—No it's not, said my self.
> It isn't on your head. But it's in your languages.
> So I started that forgiveness, wincing, asking it as I gave it.
> When I stopped asking it, cities stopped burning in my mind.
> My efforts faded and went inwards.[28]

Having forgiven Aborigines, Jews and women, Fredy is told to forgive God:

> I shuddered at that one. Judging Him and sensing life eternal,
> said my self, are different hearts. You want a single heart, to pray.
> Choose one and drop one. I looked inside them both
> and only one of them allowed prayer, so I chose it,
> and my prayer was prayed and sent, already as I chose it.

And with that his sense of feeling returns to him, with pain and joy.

Fredy's strange growth towards feeling, which is a growth towards moral maturity, parallels Murray's own in life and art. He remarked of the angry poems of *Subhuman Redneck Poems*:

> I'm not interested in all that stuff now. I wrote it out of my system. Two ways: I wrote that out directly in *Redneck*, but over a much longer period, five years, I wrote it in *Fredy Neptune*. Fred is the turning of it right up to the level of poetry. A lot of the *Redneck* poems in fact are fairly gentle and sweet. There's only a few of them that are angry. Fred is the whole rage and horror turned into art. Really I think my depression as much as anything was about horror, about the unbearable, so I think—There's a lot of me in Fredy.[29]

He would also remark to me, when asked about his religious beliefs:

> My contribution to religious thought has been that God has to share in our disaster and to be punished for what had been done. To take on our nature including the dreadful things we do to each other ... If a great deal of pain is involved—the pain of the innocent—then He who provided the opportunity for it to happen has some responsibility for it as well.[30]

He admitted that this erosion of God's righteousness was close to heresy ('It skates along the edge'), but he defended it.[31] 'God has to be punished by humans not least because He alone can bear the punishment.'[32]

And with the completion of *Fredy Neptune*, Murray felt that he had reached a new acceptance of the darkness that had begun to fall on his life with the death of his mother, and a forgiveness of the God who had allowed it. It was a turning away from the old, for him, a putting on of the new. The ending of *Fredy Neptune* brought new problems of its own: 'Lately I had a period when I thought I wasn't writing very well. I think it was because I'd finished *Fredy* and I was trying to rediscover myself as the non-depressive me', he would say.[33] But they were problems he found liberating, and he felt the volume decisively marked the end of his former life. *Fredy Neptune*'s publication was greeted with the award to Murray of the Queen's Gold Medal for Poetry,[34] and he was gratified, for into that book he had distilled the essence of what life had taught him. It marked a closure, in his mind, more profound that anything except death. When I jokingly told him that since he had not yet died I could not end this book, he responded without hesitation: 'End with *Fredy Neptune*. And let your last sentence read, "And then Murray turned, and disappeared into his fiction"'. And with that, Murray turned and disappeared into his fiction.

EPILOGUE

As the end of the millennium approached, Murray and Valerie lived where they hoped to die, in his ancestral valley. They continued to occupy the modest little Hardiplank house that nestles out of sight of the road, at the end of the rough drive that begins between the Habsburg-yellow gateposts, bumps over steel cattle-grids, winds past the lotus-dam with its dead trees, and terminates with a welcome from the poet, issuing rumpled, barefoot and affable from his study, glasses pushed up onto the dome of his bald head, and from his wife, calm and hospitable no matter how unexpected the visit.

Their two youngest children lived with them. Peter was studying information technology and was devoted to oblique, unexpected speech, fast driving, solitude, and computer games. Alexander was about to start working in a local nursery, where his love of fertile soils and natural growth would find full expression. Clare was a talented post-graduate student at the University of New South Wales's College of Fine Arts.

Christina and her husband James, both veterinarians, lived in Sydney: their daughter Grace Eleanor Murray Gilkerson was born on 28 December 1997. Daniel was a lawyer working in industrial relations, and he and his wife Shari lived in Sydney with their daughter Hannah Rose Murray, born on 7 December 1998.

NOTES

Abbreviations

ADFA	Manuscripts Collection, Australian Defence Force Academy, Canberra.
AS	In the possession of Angela Smith, Stirling, Scotland.
ASh	In the possession of Anurag Sharma, Jaipur, India.
CA	In the possession of Christine Alexander, Sydney.
CP	In the possession of Christopher Pollnitz, Newcastle.
CW-C	In the possession of Chris Wallace-Crabbe, Melbourne.
GL	In the possession of Geoffrey Lehmann, Sydney.
GO'H	In the possession of Gregory O'Hara, Tennant Creek, Northern Territory.
JB	In the possession of John Barnie, Wales, UK.
JG	In the possession of Judith Green, Sydney.
JT	In the possession of John Tranter, Sydney.
KB	In the possession of Ken Bolton, Adelaide.
LM	In the possession of Les Murray, Bunyah.
MT	In the possession of Mohammad Tavallaie, Teheran, Iran.
NLA	Manuscripts Collection, National Library of Australia, Canberra.
PA	In the possession of Peter Alexander, Sydney.
PB	In the possession of Peter Barden, San Francisco.
PG	In the possession of Peter Goldsworthy, Melbourne.
PN	In the possession of Penny Nelson, Sydney.
RS	In the possession of Ruth Sparrow, Redwood Park, South Australia.
TT	In the possession of Tom Thompson, Sydney.
VM	In the possession of Valerie Murray, Bunyah.
WD	In the possession of Walter and Elisabeth Davis, Canberra.

All interviews were conducted by Peter Alexander unless otherwise indicated.
All poems not otherwise attributed are by Les Murray.

1 Prelude

1   Les Murray later learned his name: Eddie Lobban was well known to the Purfleet community. Murray's addition to the typescript of an early draft of this book: PA.
2   'You Find You Can Leave It All'.
3   Interview with Clive James, Cambridge, 3 January 1999.

2 The Beginning, 1848–1938

1   New South Wales State Archives Office, reel 56 4/4904, Main Migrant Lists, *Castle Eden*: arrived 9 October 1848.
2   Joan Murray, *The History of the Australian Murrays from Roxburghshire, Scotland*, pp. 7–10.

3   Les Murray, 'The Bonnie Disproportion', in *The Paperbark Tree*, p. 112.
4   A. K. Frost, *Paterson Easton Family History*, pp. 11–12.
5   A. K. Frost, *Paterson Easton Family History*, p. 16.
6   Les Murray, 'The Bonnie Disproportion', in *The Paperbark Tree*, p. 112.
7   New South Wales State Archives Office, reel 56 4/4904, Main Migrant Lists, *Castle Eden*: arrived 9 October 1848.
8   Victoria and South Australia were the first states to introduce secrecy of the ballot (1856), and for that reason the secret ballot is referred to as the Australian ballot. In Great Britain the secret ballot was finally introduced for all parliamentary and municipal elections by the Ballot Act of 1872. In the USA, the Australian ballot system was extensively adopted after the presidential election of 1884.
9   New South Wales State Archives Office, reel 59 4/4920, Main Emigrant Lists, *Earl Grey*: arrived 15 October 1851.
10 'Physiognomy on the Savage Manning River', first collected in *The Daylight Moon*.
11 Les Murray gives a finely detailed account of this process in 'Eric Rolls and the Golden Disobedience', published in *Quadrant*, December 1982, and republished in *A Working Forest*, pp. 148–66.
12 'Earth Tremor at Night', first collected in *Subhuman Redneck Poems*.
13 Interview with Charlie Murray, Newcastle, NSW, 2 April 1997.
14 Joan Murray, *The History of the Australian Murrays from Roxburghshire, Scotland*, p. 24.
15 Interview with Charlie Murray, Newcastle, NSW, 2 April 1997.
16 Les Murray's annotations (December 1998) to an earlier draft of this book: PA.
17 A. K. Frost, *Paterson Easton Family History*, p. 20. Larry's Flat is now known as Krambach.
18 The photographs are reproduced in Joan Murray, *The History of the Australian Murrays from Roxburghshire, Scotland*, pp. 28–9.
19 According to her death certificate, she died of Icterus Arcites (jaundice).
20 Interview with Les Murray, Sydney, 19 December 1994: 'The Murrays are depressives from back and back and back'.
21 Joan Murray, *The History of the Australian Murrays from Roxburghshire, Scotland*, p. 24. In addition I am particularly indebted to Mr Darryl Murray of Tinonee, who supplied me with detailed and painstakingly gathered information on the Murray family in Australia.
22 Les Murray, 'Noonday Axeman', first published in *The Ilex Tree*.
23 John, Archibald, James and Robert married respectively Isabella, Catherine, Wilhelmina and Mary Jane, all daughters of their Uncle James; their brother Alexander married Isabella, daughter of their Uncle Robert. In the previous generation two of their father Hugh's brothers, Thomas and Robert, had married sisters.
24 Hugh's children's generation is particularly confusing. Five of the boys married their cousins, two of whom were named Isabella, and the boys' sister was also Isabella.
25 Kattang, the local Aboriginal language, also has a very similar word, *ba:nja*, meaning 'candlebark' or kindling. Les Murray thinks this the more likely derivation: Les Murray's annotations (December 1998) to an earlier draft of this book: PA.
26 Interview with Les Murray, Bunyah, 19 December 1994.
27 Yet another family, the Hookes, owned land at Bunyah, but never settled there themselves: Les Murray's annotations (December 1998) to an earlier draft of this book: PA.
28 Interview with Charlie Murray, Newcastle, NSW, 2 April 1997.
29 Interview with Les Murray, Bunyah, 19 December 1994.
30 'Evening Alone at Bunyah', first published in *The Weatherboard Cathedral*.

31 Interview with Les Murray, Bunyah, 19 December 1994.
32 Interview with Les Murray, Bunyah, 19 December 1994.
33 Interview with Charlie Murray, Newcastle, NSW, 2 April 1997.
34 This is the account Cecil gave his daughter-in-law: interview with Valerie Murray, Bunyah, 17 December 1996.
35 Interview with Mavis Murray, Taree, 6 April 1997.
36 Interview with Lily Sambell, Bunyah, 17 December 1996.
37 These examples were all listed by Les Murray, perhaps for an article he did not complete, in 1967: Murray Collection, MS5332, Box 1, Folder 2: NLA.
38 Interview with Charlie Murray, Newcastle, NSW, 2 April 1997.
39 Interview with Les Murray, Bunyah, 19 December 1994.
40 Interview with Les Murray, Bunyah, 11 August 1997.
41 Les Murray, *Killing the Black Dog*, p. 16.
42 Murray's 'Comments on Poems', sent to Lehmann in preparation for readings Lehmann organised at the Ensemble Theatre in Sydney during 1964: GL. The version of the poem quoted is from *The Ilex Tree*: Murray made changes for subsequent publication.
43 Interview with Les Murray, Bunyah, 19 December 1994.
44 Les Murray's annotations (December 1998) to an earlier draft of this book: PA. Les Murray also claimed that through his relationship with Vicki Grieves he was distantly a Dumas.
45 Interview with Les Murray, Bunyah, 28 August 1996.
46 He heard from one of his Aboriginal cousins, Vicki Grieves, that their common ancestors the Worths may have been Jewish; pleased with this suggestion, he tried to substantiate it but could not. Letter, Les Murray to Angela Smith, 7 March 1998: AS.
47 Interview with Lily Sambell, Bunyah, 17 December 1996.
48 Though he never altered the £60 p.a. rent, and inflation after 1950 rapidly reduced the sting of it.

3 Childhood, 1938–51

1 Birth certificate: LM.
2 Interview with Les Murray, Bunyah, 19 December 1994.
3 Interview with Valerie Murray, Bunyah, 17 December 1996; she was told the details of Les Murray's birth by his father Cecil.
4 'The Steel', first collected in *The People's Otherworld*.
5 I am indebted to Prof. John J. Carmody of the University of New South Wales for this information.
6 Interviews with Les Murray, Sydney, 18 November 1997, and with Charlie Murray, Newcastle, NSW, 2 April 1997.
7 Interview with Les Murray, Sydney, 18 November 1997, and 'In a Working Forest', in *The Paperbark Tree*, p. 383.
8 Interview with Charlie Murray, Newcastle, NSW, 2 April 1997.
9 Interview with Lily Sambell, Bunyah, 17 December 1996.
10 'I still wince a bit at corned beef': Les Murray's annotations (December 1998) to an earlier draft of this book: PA.

The Green Man: Les Murray photographed by Valerie, 1980.

Murray's collection of massively striped sweaters gradually became a trademark: Les Murray, photographed in 1982. (*Photograph: Newcastle Herald*)

Les Murray with historian Manning Clark at Hermannsburg Mission near Alice Springs, April 1987. Murray regarded Clark as a dangerous man, but it is Clark's face that is filled with suspicion here.

In 1988 Clive James did a series of TV interviews with famous Australians: here he sits between painter Lloyd Rees and Les Murray.

25 December 1989: one of the annual Christmas photographs of the Murrays and friends assembled in the garden of Valerie's parents' house in Chatswood. From left to right, standing: Valerie, son Alexander, Les Murray, daughter Christina, Murray's friend and agent Margaret Connolly, Piers Laverty, Jamie Grant, son Daniel, Anthony Lawrence, Daniel's wife Shari, Valerie's brother Stephen, her mother Berta, daughter Clare, Les's father Cecil, Valerie's father Gino Morelli. Sitting, next to the 'civil white-pawed dog' Doug, is son Peter.

Cecil Murray in the garden at Bunyah, April 1993, less than two years before his death. (*Photograph: Graeme McCarter*)

Les Murray, January 1980, 'Self-portrait from a Photograph'. *(Photograph: Gino Morelli)*

Les Murray, a lover of any aspect of film, enjoying himself acting in a Queensland Health Department TV advertisement, November 1993.

Les Murray reading at the National Gallery, Canberra, in 1993. The recital with eyes upturned, trance-like, was characteristic of these performances.

11 Greg O'Hara's 'Reminiscences of Les Murray' [1995]: PA.
12 Les Murray, 'The Human Hair Thread', in *Persistence in Folly*, p. 7.
13 'The Sleepout', first collected in *The Daylight Moon*.
14 Interview with Les Murray, Bunyah, 19 December 1994.
15 'The Tin Wash Dish', first published in *Dog Fox Field*.
16 Interview with Ellen Harris, Bunyah, 9 October 1996.
17 Interview with Les Murray, Sydney, 18 August 1997.
18 Interview with Les Murray, Sydney, 16 December 1998.
19 Interview with Les Murray, Bunyah, 19 December 1994.
20 The statements of Cecil's account with the English, Scottish & Australian Bank have been preserved from 1945 on: PA.
21 'Rainwater Tank', first published in *Ethnic Radio*.
22 Interview with Ellen Harris (née Hile), Bunyah, 9 October 1996.
23 Interview with Ellen Harris (née Hile), Bunyah, 9 October 1996, and Les Murray, 'In a Working Forest', in *The Paperbark Tree*, p. 377.
24 Quoted in Penny Nelson, 'The Dowry', in S. Falkiner (ed.), *Room to Move*, Sydney: Allen & Unwin, 1985, p. 68.
25 Norrie had married Cecil's Aunt Annie.
26 Interview with Les Murray, Sydney, 4 August 1997.
27 Interview with Les Murray, Sydney, 4 August 1997.
28 The Free Church of Scotland was formed as the result of a breakaway from the Church of Scotland in 1843; in 1900 the Free Church united with the United Presbyterians to form the United Free Church.
29 Interview with Shirley Lantry, Maitland, 27 August 1996.
30 Unpublished letter, Les Murray to the author, 18 August 1998: PA.
31 Interview with Lily Sambell, Bunyah, 17 December 1996.
32 Interview with Alma Murray, Taree, 17 December 1996.
33 Interview with Leila Griffis (née Maurer), Old Bar, 27 August 1996.
34 Interview with Ellen Harris (née Hile), Bunyah, 9 October 1996.
35 Les Murray's annotations (December 1998) to an earlier draft of this book: PA.
36 Interview with Shirley Lantry, Maitland, 27 August 1996.
37 Interview with Lily Sambell, Bunyah, 17 December 1996.
38 Interview with Les Murray, Bunyah, 28 August 1996.
39 Interview with Ellen Harris (née Hile), Bunyah, 9 October 1996.
40 'Infant Among Cattle', first published in *The Daylight Moon*.
41 Interview with Les Murray, Sydney, 18 November 1997. The sponging treatment was described to Valerie Murray by Cecil Murray: interview with Valerie Murray, Bunyah, 16 December 1996.
42 *Killing the Black Dog*, p. 16.
43 Interview with Les Murray, Bunyah, 8 October 1996
44 Interview with Charlie Murray, Newcastle, 2 April 1997.
45 Interview with Ellen Harris (née Hile), Bunyah, 9 October 1996.
46 Telephone interview with Les Murray, Bunyah, 17 August 1998.
47 Les Murray's annotations (December 1998) to an earlier draft of this book: PA.
48 Unpublished letter, Les Murray to the author, undated [6 October 1998]: PA.
49 'The Holy Show', to be published in *Conscious and Verbal*.

300   NOTES (CHAPTER 3)

50   Interview with Les Murray, Bunyah, 28 August 1996.
51   Interview with Ellen Harris (née Hile), Bunyah, 9 October 1996.
52   Interview with Les Murray, Bunyah, 4 September 1998.
53   Interview with Ellen Harris (née Hile), Bunyah, 9 October 1996.
54   'Birds in Their Title Work Freeholds of Straw', first published in *Poems Against Economics*.
55   For instance, 'Blood', first published in *The Weatherboard Cathedral*.
56   This almost legendary animal was 'remembered' by Les Murray's daughter Christina, who had been born long after Bluey's death (interview with Christina Murray, 11 July 1997), and it would appear in Les Murray's magnificent elegy for his father, 'The Last Hellos', first collected in *Subhuman Redneck Poems*.
57   Interview with Charlie Murray, Newcastle, NSW, 2 April 1997.
58   Telephone interview with Les Murray, Bunyah, 3 February 1999.
59   Interview with Les Murray, Sydney, 18 November 1997.
60   This was a farm bought in 1880 by George Murray: Joan Murray, *The History of the Australian Murrays from Roxburghshire, Scotland*, p. 49.
61   Interview with Les Murray, Bunyah, 19 December 1994.
62   'The Smell of Coal Smoke', first published in *The People's Otherworld*.
63   'The Smell of Coal Smoke'.
64   He mentioned this phrase and his fascination for it in a reading at Sydney Grammar School, 15 October 1998. I am grateful to Mrs Libby Jones for this information.
65   Interview with Lily Sambell, Bunyah, 17 December 1996.
66   Interview with Alma Murray, Bunyah, 17 December 1996.
67   Interview with Charlie Murray, Newcastle, NSW, 2 April 1997.
68   Interview with Les Murray, Sydney, 11 August 1997.
69   Les Murray, 'My Country Childhood', in *Australian Country Style*, June–July 1991, p. 18.
70   Interview with Ellen Harris (née Hile), Bunyah, 9 October 1996.
71   'Les A. Murray', in *Australian Literary Studies*, Vol. 12 (2), October 1985, p. 268.
72   Interview with Les Murray, Bunyah, 9 October 1996.
73   'The Devil', first collected in *Subhuman Redneck Poems*.
74   'The Devil'.
75   Quoted in M. Daniel, 'Poetry is Presence: An Interview with Les Murray', *Commonweal*, vol. 119, 22 May 1992, pp. 11–12.
76   Unpublished letter, Les Murray to Mohammad Tavallaie, 9 September 1993: MT.
77   Les Murray, 'My Country Childhood', in *Australian Country Style*, June–July 1991, p. 18.
78   Interview with Lily Sambell, Bunyah, 17 December 1996.
79   Interview with Les Murray, Sydney, 19 December 1994.
80   Les Murray, 'From Bulby Brush to Figure City', in *The Paperbark Tree*, p. 339.
81   Interview with Les Murray, Sydney, 18 November 1997.
82   Interview with Les Murray, Sydney, 18 November 1997. It was the middle finger of his right hand.
83   Interview with Les Murray, Sydney, 18 November 1997.
84   Interview with Lily Sambell, Bunyah, 17 December 1996.
85   Interview with Lily Sambell, Bunyah, 17 December 1996.
86   'From Bulby Brush to Figure City', in *The Paperbark Tree*, p. 337.
87   Interview with Les Murray, Sydney, 18 November 1997.
88   Interview with Les Murray, Bunyah, 8 October 1996.

4 Death of the Family, 1951–54

1. Cecil Murray's bank statements of account with the English, Scottish & Australian Bank: PA.
2. Interview with Charlie Murray, Newcastle, NSW, 2 April 1997.
3. Interview with Les Murray, Sydney, 10 November 1996.
4. Interview with Ellen Harris (née Hile), Bunyah, 9 October 1996.
5. Interview with Alma Murray, 17 December 1996, and letter from Tasman Arnall, Les Murray's cousin, to Christopher Pollnitz, 15 May 1989: CP.
6. An ectopic pregnancy is one in which the conceptus (the products of conception—that is, the placenta, the membranes, and the embryo) implants or attaches itself in a place other than the normal location in the lining of the upper uterine cavity. The site of implantation may be either at an abnormal location within the uterus itself or in an area outside the uterus. Ectopic pregnancies outside the uterine cavity occur about once in every 300 pregnancies, and are one of the major causes of maternal deaths. I am grateful to Prof. John Carmody of the University of New South Wales for this information.
7. Interview with Alice Murray, wife of Cecil's brother Charlie, Newcastle, NSW, 2 April 1997.
8. Interview with Ellen Harris (née Hile), Bunyah, 9 October 1996.
9. Interview with Les Murray, Bunyah, 19 December 1994.
10. Two ectopic pregnancies are a relatively rare coincidence and one that suggests Miriam Murray had suffered a pelvic infection at some stage. It is possible that her son's view that she had sustained permanent hurt at his birth had foundation, but more likely that the first ectopic pregnancy had resulted in infection. I am grateful to Prof. John Carmody of the University of New South Wales for this information.
11. Interview with Les Murray, Sydney, 18 August 1997.
12. Les Murray, *Killing the Black Dog*, p. 14.
13. 'The Steel', first collected in *The People's Otherworld*.
14. Extract, Death Certificate, Miriam Murray, D1856: LM
15. Inflammation of the mucous membrane of the pelvis of the kidney.
16. Interview with Ellen Harris (née Hile), Bunyah, 9 October 1996.
17. Interview with Mavis Murray, Taree, 6 April 1997.
18. Les Murray's annotations (December 1998) to an earlier draft of this book: PA.
19. Telephone interview with Les Murray, Bunyah, 3 February 1999.
20. Interview with Les Murray, Sydney, 18 August 1997.
21. Interview with Les Murray, Sydney, 18 August 1997.
22. Interview with Ellen Harris (née Hile), Bunyah, 9 October 1996.
23. Interview with Ellen Harris (née Hile), Bunyah, 9 October 1996.
24. 'The Steel', first collected in *The People's Otherworld*.
25. Interview with Les Murray, Sydney, 19 December 1994.
26. Les Murray's annotations (December 1998) to an earlier draft of this book: PA.
27. Les Murray, 'The Human Hair Thread', in *Persistence in Folly*, p. 7.
28. Conversation, Les Murray with Bob Ellis in the Seedwillow Production film *The Bastards from the Bush*, screened on ABC television, 1 September 1998.
29. 'The Steel', first collected in *The People's Otherworld*.
30. Statements of account, Cecil Murray with Scottish, English & Australian Bank: PA.
31. 'The Steel', first collected in *The People's Otherworld*.
32. 'The Widower in the Country', first published in *The Ilex Tree*.

33 Not until 1981 would he be able to begin the sequence on her, in writing 'The Steel', while in Stirling, Scotland.
34 Interview with Les Murray, Sydney, 10 November 1996.
35 Interview with Les Murray, Sydney, 10 November 1996.
36 Interview with Les Murray, Sydney, 10 November 1996.
37 'Burning Want', first collected in *Subhuman Redneck Poems*.
38 Les Murray's annotations (December 1998) to an earlier draft of this book: PA.
39 His university friends testified to his accuracy: Greg O'Hara's, 'Reminiscences of Les Murray' [1995]: PA, and interview with John Mulhall, Chatswood, Sydney, 16 July, 1997.
40 Les Murray, *Killing the Black Dog*, p. 17.
41 John was the son of Les Murray's Great-Uncle Sam.
42 Unpublished letter, Les Murray to Geoffrey Lehmann, undated [end 1958]: GL. Some of those who wished to leave after one night Cecil managed to persuade to stay on, and at least one subsequently became a good friend, returning to Bunyah several times. This was the adventurous Englishwoman Nora Miller: letter from her to the author, 29 June 1997: PA.
43 Les Murray's annotations (December 1998) to an earlier draft of this book.
44 Unrecorded conversation with Les Murray, Sydney, 16 December 1998.
45 Interview with Alma Murray (née Coleman), Bunyah, 17 December 1996.
46 Interview with Alma Murray (née Coleman), Bunyah, 17 December 1996.
47 Interview with Alma Murray (née Coleman), Bunyah, 17 December 1996.
48 Interview with Alma Murray (née Coleman), Bunyah, 17 December 1996. Years later Les Murray would comment with good humour, 'I was always kind to spiders. And my cruelty to other creatures is now so transmuted into compunction that I recently found myself herding an eel back up a gully into the dam it had washed out of. How many of us eel-shepherds are there?' Les Murray's annotations (December 1998) to an earlier draft of this book: PA.
49 Interview with Les Murray, Sydney, 18 November 1997.
50 Interviews with Ellen Harris (née Hile), Bunyah, 9 October 1996, and with Les Murray, Sydney, 18 November 1997.
51 Interview with Les Murray, Sydney, 19 December 1994.
52 Interview with Les Murray, Sydney, 19 December 1994.
53 Interview with Les Murray, Sydney, 19 December 1994.
54 Interview with Lionel and Margaret Gilbert, Armidale, 3 September 1998.
55 Interview with Lionel and Margaret Gilbert, Armidale, 3 September 1998.
56 Conversation, Les Murray with Bob Ellis in the Seedwillow Production film *The Bastards from the Bush*, screened on ABC television, 1 September 1998.
57 'The Milk Lorry', first collected in *The Daylight Moon*. The smaller, lighter cans referred to earlier were those for cream.
58 Interviews with Robert Gray, Sydney, 11 August 1997, and with Valerie Murray, Bunyah, 9 October 1998.
59 Interview with Ellen Harris (née Hile), Bunyah, 9 October 1996. Her house was on the hill above the Murrays', and she remembered them as fighting 'a lot'.
60 Les Murray's annotations (December 1998) to an earlier draft of this book: PA.
61 Unpublished postcard to Peter Goldsworthy, 15 May 1991: PG.
62 Interview with with Les Murray, Bunyah, 28 August 1996.
63 Interview with Les Murray, Sydney, 19 December 1994.
64 Interview with Lionel and Margaret Gilbert, Armidale, 3 September 1998.

65 Interview with Lionel and Margaret Gilbert, Armidale, 3 September 1998.
66 Interview with Lionel and Margaret Gilbert, Armidale, 3 September 1998.
67 Interview with Les Murray, Sydney, 19 December 1994.
68 Interview with Margaret Gilbert, Armidale, 3 September 1998.
69 Interview with Lionel and Margaret Gilbert, Armidale, 3 September 1998.
70 'Burning Want', first collected in *Subhuman Redneck Poems*.
71 Interview with Les Murray, Sydney, 19 December 1994.
72 Interview with Leila Griffis (née Maurer), Old Bar, 27 August 1996.
73 Interview with Les Murray, Bunyah, 28 August 1996.
74 Sindbad, soon to be replaced by Creamy. Interview with Les Murray and Valerie Murray, Bunyah, 8 October 1996.
75 Interview with Alma Murray, Bunyah, 17 December 1996.
76 Les Murray in *Writers in Action: the Writer's Choice Evenings* (ed. Gerry Turcotte), p. 87.

5 Taree High, 1955–56

1 Taree lies 16 kilometres above the mouth of the Manning River. Established in 1854 as a private town, it was proclaimed a municipality in 1885 and a city in 1981; its name derives from the Aboriginal tareebin, or tarrebit, referring to a local wild fig, the 'sandpaper fig'. Situated on the Sydney–Brisbane rail line and the Pacific Highway, 130 kilometres northeast of Newcastle, Taree is the principal city of the Manning River district. Its population in 1955 was under 10 000; in 1998 it was about 17 000.
2 Interview with Alma Murray, Bunyah, 17 December 1996.
3 Interview with Les Murray, Bunyah, 28 August 1996.
4 Interview with Les Murray, Sydney, 19 December 1994.
5 Interview with Les Murray, Sydney, 19 December 1994.
6 Interview with William Burrell, Les Murray's cadet instructor, Taree, 27 August 1998.
7 Interview with Keith McLaughlin, Taree, 28 July 1998: 'I think being a farm-boy, he didn't wash very often'. Also interview with Jane McWhirter (née Liddell), Forster, 3 August 1998: 'He smelled'.
8 Interview with Jane McWhirter (née Liddell), Forster, 3 August 1998.
9 Interview with Les Lawrie, Les Murray's physical education teacher: also letter to the writer from Les Lawrie, 31 July 1998: PA.
10 Les Murray, 'From Bulby Brush to Figure City', in *The Paperbark Tree*, p. 339.
11 Interview with Bob Wallace, Taree, 3 August 1998. Wallace was one of Murray's classmates.
12 Interview with Les Murray, Sydney, 19 December 1994.
13 Interviewed in Forster, 3 August 1998. The interviewee asked that quotations not be attributed to her by name.
14 Interviewed in Forster, 3 August 1998. She asked that quotations not be attributed to her by name.
15 Interview with Les Murray, Sydney, 10 November 1996.
16 Interview with Les Murray, Sydney, 19 December 1994.
17 Interview with Robin Norling, Sydney, 3 August 1998.
18 Interview with Robin Norling, Sydney, 3 August 1998.

19 Les Murray, 'From Bulby Brush to Figure City', in *The Paperbark Tree*, p. 339.
20 Interview with Bob Wallace, Taree, 3 August 1998.
21 The class was studying Shakespeare in English: interview with Keith and Edith McLaughlin, Taree, 28 July 1998.
22 Interview with Les Murray, Sydney, 19 December 1994.
23 Interview with Les Murray, Sydney 19 December 1994.
24 *Fredy Neptune*, 'Barking at the Thunder', p. 88. In conversation with Bob Ellis he remarked 'Nothing a mob does is clean'. In the Seedwillow Production film *The Bastards from the Bush*, screened on ABC television, 1 September 1998.
25 Les Murray, *Killing the Black Dog*, pp. 18–19.
26 'A Torturer's Apprenticeship', first collected in *Dog Fox Field*.
27 Les Murray, 'On Being Subject Matter', in *The Paperbark Tree*, p. 189.
28 Interview with Les Murray, Bunyah, 6 August 1998.
29 Interview with Les Murray, Bunyah, 20 March 1995.
30 Interview with Les Murray, Bunyah, 6 August 1998.
31 Interviews with William Burrell, Taree, 27 August 1998, with James Murdoch, Woodburn, 3 Aug 1998, and with Keith and Edith McLaughlin, Taree, 28 July 1998.
32 Interview with James Murdoch, Woodburn, 3 August 1998.
33 Interview with Keith and Edith McLaughlin, Taree, 28 July 1998.
34 Interview with Les Lawrie, Taree, 27 July 1998.
35 Interview with William Burrell, Taree, 27 August 1998.
36 *The Torch*, 1955.
37 Interview with Les Murray, Sydney, 7 October 1997.
38 'A Torturer's Apprenticeship', first collected in *Dog Fox Field*.
39 Unrecorded telephone conversation with Les Murray, Bunyah, 26 November 1998.
40 Interview with Les Murray, Sydney, 19 December 1994.
41 It won eight Oscars, including for Best Director. I am indebted to Assoc. Prof. Bruce Johnson of the University of New South Wales for information about the film.
42 Interview with Les Murray, Sydney, 19 December 1994.
43 Interview with Robin Norling, Sydney, 3 August 1998.
44 Interview with James Murdoch, Woodburn, 3 August 1998.
45 Interview with Les Lawrie, Taree, 27 July 1998.
46 Interview with James Murdoch, Woodburn, 3 August 1998.
47 Interview with Keith McLaughlin, Taree, 28 July 1998.
48 *The Torch*, 1955, p. 60.
49 *The Torch*, 1956, p. 39.
50 Interview with Robin Norling, Sydney, 3 August 1998.
51 Interview with Robin Norling, Sydney, 3 August 1998.
52 Interview with fellow-pupil who requested anonymity, Newcastle, 3 August 1998.
53 Interview with Bob Wallace, Taree, 3 August 1998.
54 Interview with Keith and Edith McLaughlin, Taree, 28 July 1998.
55 Interview with Les Murray, Sydney, 19 December 1994.
56 Unpublished postcard, Les Murray to John Barnie, 7 November 1993: JB.
57 Les Murray's annotations (December 1998) to an earlier draft of this book: PA.
58 Interview with Les Murray, Sydney, 20 December 1994.

59 Les Murray, 'Cadet Entwhistle and the Sergeant', *The Torch*, 1955, p. 29.
60 *The Torch*, 1956, p. 24.
61 Interview with Les Murray, 19 December 1994.
62 Interview with Keith McLaughlin, Taree, 28 July 1998.
63 Interview with Les Murray, Sydney, 20 March 1995. His von Holstein ancestor would appear in *Fredy Neptune* as 'the man in the second book, "Barking at the Thunder" who married the servant girl back in Germany and had a good marriage out of it and whose letter back to the family was refused'.
64 Les Murray's paternal Aunt Myrtle had married Victor Maurer.
65 Les Murray's annotations (December 1998) to an earlier draft of this book: PA.
66 Interview with Les Lawrie, Taree, 27 July 1998.
67 'Flumine Pereant Illae', in *The Torch*, Bicentennial edition, 1988, pp. 10–11.
68 Interview with Les Murray, Sydney, 25 August 1997.
69 Les Murray's 'Preface' to John Palmer (ed.), *Poems for Senior Students*.
70 Interview with Keith McLaughlin, Taree, 28 July 1998.
71 Interview with Keith and Edith McLaughlin, Taree, 28 July 1998.
72 Interview with Les Murray, Sydney, 19 December 1994.
73 Interview with Edith McLaughlin, Taree, 28 July 1998.
74 'God's Grandeur': Hopkins's opening line, 'The world is charged with the grandeur of God', is a fair summary of one of Murray's most enduring themes.
75 'Coolongolook Timber Mill': on 23 November 1998 Les Murray sent me the unpublished typescript, with a note: 'This describes the evening in early December 1956 in Dow's old timber mill at Coolongolook when I decided poetry wd. be my life's venture'. PA. The poem will be published in *Conscious and Verbal* in 1999.
76 'Extract from a Verse Letter to Dennis Haskell', first published in *The Daylight Moon*.
77 Les Murray in conversation with Bob Ellis in the Seedwillow Production film *The Bastards from the Bush*, screened on ABC television 1 September 1998. In 1998 he told a BBC interviewer, on 'Desert Island Discs', that this decision had come to him on 6 December 1956.
78 The poem would be written in April 1963: Les Murray's 'Afterword' in Alexander Craig (ed.), *Twelve Poets 1950–1970*, p. 219.

6 Sydney University, 1957–58

1 'Exile Prolonged by Real Reasons', first published in *The People's Otherworld*.
2 Interview with Les Murray, Bunyah, 21 September 1998.
3 He alludes to this trip in 'Big Shame', written in 1998 and to be published in *Conscious and Verbal*.
4 Interview with Les Murray, Sydney, 19 December 1994.
5 Interview with Les Murray, Bunyah, 21 September 1998.
6 Clive James gives a vivid description of Orientation Week in chapter 13 of his *Unreliable Memoirs*.
7 Interview with Walter Davis, Canberra, 23 November 1996. Walter Francis Davis was born in 1940 and brought up in Western Sydney. After leaving Sydney University and marrying

8 Interview with Walter Davis, Canberra, 23 November 1996.
9 Including the four children of his father's sister Myrtle.
10 Les Murray's annotations (December 1998) to an earlier draft of this book: PA.
11 Interview with Mick Byrne, Sydney, 15 July 1997.
12 Films to his credit include *2001* and *Mad Dog Morgan*.
13 Peter Wagner became Librarian to the NSW Police Force. In 1995 Les Murray would dedicate to him a poem, 'For Sydney Jewish Museum', first collected in *Subhuman Redneck Poems*. 'Awful poem, too', he would grimace later: 'I'll write him a good one some day'. Les Murray's annotations (December 1998) to an earlier draft of this book: PA.
14 Unrecorded conversation with Prof. Clive Kessler, Sydney, 9 December 1998.
15 Unrecorded conversation with Prof. Clive Kessler, Sydney, 9 December 1998.
16 Email, Naomi Kronenberg (née Kessler) to the author, 13 December 1998: PA.
17 Bob Rogers with Denis O'Brien, *Rock 'n' Roll Australia*, p. 3. I am grateful to Assoc. Prof. Bruce Johnson of the University of New South Wales for drawing my attention to this text.
18 Bob Rogers with Denis O'Brien, *Rock 'n' Roll Australia*, p. 49.
19 This at any rate was his own assessment of his musical ability. Valerie Murray was to contest the point: 'Les can carry a tune, and has quite a wide taste in music'. Les Murray added, 'I'd never play anything I couldn't win . . .' Valerie Murray's and Les Murray's annotations (December 1998) to an earlier draft of this book: PA.
20 'Sidere Mens Eadem Mutato', first published in *Lunch & Counter Lunch*.
21 The description is from Penny Nelson's memoir, *Penny Dreadful*, p. 150.
22 Interview with Libby Jones (née Sweet), Sydney, 12 September 1998.
23 Interview with Geoffrey Lehmann, Sydney, 5 September 1998.
24 In 1970, after an earlier marriage, she was to marry Alex Jones, who had been at Shore with Lehmann, and who became a Senior Lecturer in English at Sydney University.
25 Quoted in an interview with Geoffrey Lehmann, Sydney, 5 September 1998.
26 Interview with Libby Jones (née Sweet), Sydney, 12 September 1998.
27 Interview with Geoffrey Lehmann, Sydney, 5 September 1998.
28 Interview with Geoffrey Lehmann, Sydney, 5 September 1998.
29 Interview with Les Murray, Sydney, 19 August 1997.
30 Interview with Les Murray, Sydney, 19 August 1997.
31 Interview with Geoffrey Lehmann, Sydney, 5 September 1998.
32 Interview with Libby Jones (née Sweet), Sydney, 12 September 1998.
33 Interview with Pat Howard, Sydney, 29 September 1998.
34 Interview with Pat Howard, Sydney, 29 September 1998.
35 Interview with Mick Byrne, Sydney, 15 July 1997.
36 Anne Coombs, *Sex and Anarchy: The Life and Death of the Sydney Push*, p. 113.
37 Interview with Mick Byrne, Sydney, 15 July 1997.
38 Interview with Clive James, Cambridge, 3 January 1999. Sidney Greenstreet was the amply fleshed film-star, perhaps best remembered now for a role in *Casablanca*; Ginger Meggs is a long-time Australian cartoon character, a rumpled red-haired boy perpetually wearing horizontally striped jumpers.
39 Les Murray, 'Corsair Over the Rift Valley', in *Blocks and Tackles*, p. 209.
40 Interview with Les Murray, Sydney, 4 August 1997.
41 Clive James, *Unreliable Memoirs*: the quotation is from the Iliad, XXIV.

(Note: item starting "Elisabeth Knowler he became a civil servant in Canberra, continuing to live there after his retirement." precedes item 8.)

42 Conversation with Bob Ellis, in the Seedwillow Production film *The Bastards from the Bush*, screened on ABC television, 1 September 1998.
43 Interview with Geoffrey Lehmann, Sydney, 5 September 1998.
44 Interview with Penny Nelson, Sydney, 3 April 1995.
45 'Incunabular', a poem he wrote in 1998 at the University of New South Wales and would publish in *Conscious and Verbal*.
46 Unpublished letter, Les Murray to Geoffrey Lehmann, undated [end 1958]: GL.
47 Unpublished letter, Les Murray to Geoffrey Lehmann, 28 August 1960: GL.
48 Unpublished letter, Les Murray to Geoffrey Lehmann, 28 August 1960: GL.
49 Interview with Les Murray, 19 December 1994.
50 Les Murray's transcript of academic record, University of Sydney.
51 Recorded telephone message, Michael Nelson to PA, Sydney, 24 September 1998.
52 W. F. Connell et al., *Australia's First*, p. 73.
53 'Sidere Mens Eadem Mutato', first published in *Lunch & Counter Lunch*.
54 Les Murray's speech at the launch of *Subhuman Redneck Poems*, Leslie McKay's Bookshop, Double Bay, Sydney, 27 September 1996.
55 Greg O'Hara's 'Reminiscences of Les Murray' [1995]: PA.
56 The statements of Cecil Murray's account with the English, Scottish & Australian Bank for 1958: PA.
57 Interview with Walter Davis, Canberra, 23 November 1996.
58 Greg O'Hara's 'Reminiscences of Les Murray' [1995]: PA.
59 Interview with Geoffrey Lehmann, Sydney, 5 September 1998.
60 Interview with Bob Ellis, Sydney, 13 July 1997.
61 Interview with Geoffrey Lehmann, Sydney, 5 September 1998.
62 Interview with Geoffrey Lehmann, Sydney, 5 September 1998.
63 Greg O'Hara's 'Reminiscences of Les Murray' [1995]: PA.
64 Peter Barden's taped 'Reminiscences of Les Murray', recorded at Pasadena, California, 20 April 1995: PA.
65 Interview with Geoffrey Lehmann, Sydney, 5 September 1998.
66 Interview with John Mulhall, Sydney, 16 July 1997.
67 Unpublished letter, Les Murray to Geoffrey Lehmann, 17 June 1961: GL.
68 Unpublished letter, Les Murray to Greg O'Hara, 5 May 1963: GO'H.
69 Unpublished poem, Murray Collection, MS5332, Box 3, Folder 20: NLA. Cecil's parrot-eating is also mentioned in Les Murray's poem 'Aspects of Language and War on the Gloucester Road', first published in *The Daylight Moon*.
70 Interview with John Mulhall, Sydney, 16 July 1997.

7 Trying Again, 1958–60

1 Greg O'Hara's 'Reminiscences of Les Murray' [1995]: PA.
2 Greg O'Hara's 'Reminiscences of Les Murray' [1995]: PA.
3 Greg O'Hara's 'Reminiscences of Les Murray' [1995]: PA.
4 Interview with Geoffrey Lehmann, Sydney, 5 September 1998.
5 Published as 'East Sydney' in *The Weatherboard Cathedral*, p. 23.
6 For instance, at the launch of *Fredy Neptune* in Sydney, 19 July 1998.
7 Interview with Bob Ellis, Sydney, 13 July 1997.

8   Interview with Geoffrey Lehmann, Sydney, 5 September 1998.
9   Les Murray, 'Flumine Pereant Illae', in *The Torch*, Bicentennial edition, 1988, p. 10.
10 Interview with Dr Olaf Reinhardt, Sydney, 16 September 1997.
11 Conversation with Bob Ellis, in the Seedwillow Production film *The Bastards from the Bush*, screened on ABC television, 1 September 1998.
12 Interview with Penny Nelson, Sydney, 3 April 1995.
13 His brothers were (Sir) Charles the conductor, Malcolm the political commentator, Alistair, onetime headmaster of Sydney Grammar School, and Neil.
14 In 1998 Sheldon was teaching at Sydney Grammar School.
15 Interview with Geoffrey Lehmann, Sydney, 5 September 1998.
16 Interview with Les Murray, 19 August 1997.
17 Les Murray, 'My Earliest Master', in *Blocks and Tackles*, p. 75.
18 Les Murray, 'The Wine and the Cognac', in *Blocks and Tackles*, pp. 79–80.
19 Les Murray, 'The Wine and the Cognac', in *Blocks and Tackles*, p. 79.
20 Les Murray at the launch of *Fredy Neptune* in Sydney, 19 July 1998.
21 Les Murray, 'My Earliest Master', in *Blocks and Tackles*, pp. 74ff.
22 'An Absolutely Ordinary Rainbow', first published in *The Weatherboard Cathedral*, was written while the Murrays were living in Britain, late in 1967: unpublished letter, Les Murray to Geoffrey Lehmann, 14 January 1968: GL.
23 Interview with Les Murray, Sydney, 2 September 1997.
24 Lecture by Les Murray to a class on 'After Modernism', University of New South Wales, September 1998.
25 Les Murray's 'Afterword' in Alexander Craig (ed.), *Twelve Poets 1950–1970*, p. 219.
26 Unpublished autograph letter, Les Murray to Greg O'Hara, 12 December 1958: GO'H.
27 Interview with Dr Olaf Reinhardt, Sydney, 16 September 1997.
28 Interview with Les Murray, Sydney, 19 December 1994.
29 Interview with Mick Byrne, Sydney, 15 July 1997.
30 'Sidere Mens Eadem Mutato', first collected in *Lunch & Counter Lunch*.
31 Unpublished letter, Les Murray to the author, 20 December 1998: PA. The transfer of the western half of New Guinea to Indonesia did not happen until 1962, but it was clearly on the cards by 1960.
32 Unpublished letter, Les Murray to the author, 20 December 1998: PA.
33 Interview with Geoffrey Lehmann, Sydney, 5 September 1998.
34 I interviewed him in the UK, 3 January 1999. James also quoted the poem in 'His Brilliant Career', *New York Review of Books*, vol. 30, 14 April 1983, pp. 31–2.
35 *honi soit*, Thursday, 23 April 1959, p. 6.
36 Interview with Geoffrey Lehmann, Sydney, 5 September 1998.
37 Published in 1978.
38 'Red Cedar', *Hermes*, 1959, pp. 48–9.
39 *honi soit/Tharunka* 1 October 1959, p. 8.
40 Interview with Clive James, Cambridge, 3 January 1999.
41 Interview with Clive James, Cambridge, 3 January 1999.
42 Interview with Bob Ellis, Sydney, 13 July 1997.
43 John Osborne's play was his first hit: its exhilarating outbursts of rage against contemporary society helped define the group who called themselves 'The Angry Young Men' (including Osborne, John Amis and Alan Sillitoe) and whose radical and anarchic views appealed to Ellis.

44 Robert James Keith Ellis was born on 10 May 1942 in Murwillumbah, northern New South Wales, and had a strict Seventh-day Adventist upbringing.
45 Unpublished letter, Ellis to Greg O'Hara, 3 October 1962: GO'H.
46 Interview with Les Murray, Bunyah, 21 September 1998.
47 Interview with Bob Ellis, Sydney, 13 July 1997.
48 Interview with Les Murray, Sydney, 10 November 1996.
49 Interview with Bob Ellis, Sydney, 13 July 1997.
50 'Sidere Mens Eadem Mutato', first published in *Lunch & Counter Lunch*.
51 Les Murray, *Killing the Black Dog*, p. 19.
52 Interview with Valerie Murray, Bunyah, 8 October 1996.
53 Les Murray, *Killing the Black Dog*, p. 20.
54 Interview with Les Murray, Sydney, 19 December 1994.
55 Interview with Les Murray, Sydney, 19 December 1994.
56 Peter Barden's taped 'Reminiscences of Les Murray', recorded at Pasadena, California, 20 April 1995: PA.
57 Peter Barden's taped 'Reminiscences of Les Murray', recorded at Pasadena, California, 20 April 1995: PA.
58 Peter Barden's taped 'Reminiscences of Les Murray', recorded at Pasadena, California, 20 April 1995: PA.
59 Interview with Bob Ellis, Sydney, 13 July 1997.
60 Interview with Penny Nelson (née McNicoll), Sydney, 3 April 1995.
61 Interview with Penny Nelson (née McNicoll), Sydney, 3 April 1995.
62 Photograph in the possession of John Mulhall.
63 Interview with Ken Welton, Gympie, 16 August 1998.
64 Interview with Ken Welton, Gympie, 16 August 1998. The quotation is from *Lavengro*.
65 Interview with Les Murray, Sydney, 10 November 1996.
66 Peter Barden's taped 'Reminiscences of Les Murray', recorded at Pasadena, California, 20 April 1995: PA, and interview with Ken Welton, Gympie, 16 August 1998.
67 Peter Barden's taped 'Reminiscences of Les Murray', recorded at Pasadena, California, 20 April 1995: PA.
68 'The Wilderness', first collected in *The Weatherboard Cathedral*.
69 Interview with Les Murray, Sydney, 19 December 1994.

8 In the Pit, 1960–62

1 Interview with Les Murray, Sydney, 19 December 1994.
2 Peter Barden's taped 'Reminiscences of Les Murray', recorded at Pasadena, California, 20 April 1995: PA.
3 Greg O'Hara's 'Reminiscences of Les Murray' [1995]: PA.
4 As John Mulhall noted on the verso of a photograph of Ellis that he took at this time, and now in the possession of Les Murray.
5 Interview with Bob Ellis, Sydney, 13 July 1997.
6 Interview with Penny Nelson (née McNicoll), Sydney, 3 April 1995.
7 Penny Nelson's memoir *Penny Dreadful*, pp. 151–3.
8 Les Murray, BBC interview, 'Desert Island Discs', 1998.

310 NOTES (CHAPTER 8)

9 Her father was (and is) a distinguished newspaperman and sometime poet, David McNicoll, who became the Publisher of Australian Consolidated Press. She married Michael Nelson in August 1964 and divorced him, after two children, in 1978. In 1981 she married Albert Gillezeau, whom she left in 1987 for Michael Kesteven. Her first novel, *Medium Flyers* (1990) was well received, and she followed it with *Prophesying Backwards* (1991), *Beyond Berlin* (1993) and with a volume of memoirs, *Penny Dreadful* (1995). In 1998 she lived in Sydney.
10 *honi soit*, 29 September 1960, p. 8, lists the paper's staff under the heading 'They Went That Way, Officer'.
11 Published in *The Ilex Tree*, p. 16.
12 Penny Nelson's memoir *Penny Dreadful*, p. 153.
13 Interview with Penny Nelson (née McNicoll), Sydney, 3 April 1995.
14 Made in 1994: Ellis is thinly disguised as Kenneth Elkin, and McNicoll as Jenny O'Brien.
15 Interview with Bob Ellis, Sydney, 13 July 1997.
16 Transcript of Les Murray's Academic Record, University of Sydney.
17 Interview with Bob Ellis, Sydney, 13 July 1997.
18 Unpublished letter, Les Murray to Penny Nelson (née McNicoll), 24 March 1992: PN.
19 Interview with Bob Ellis, Sydney, 13 July 1997.
20 Les Murray, *Killing the Black Dog*, p. 20.
21 Unpublished poem, Murray Collection, MS5332, Box 3, Folder 20, NLA.
22 Greg O'Hara's 'Reminiscences of Les Murray' [1995]: PA.
23 Interview with Les Murray, Sydney 20 March 1995. He flatly denied being homosexual.
24 Interview with Valerie Murray, Bunyah, 8 October 1996.
25 Interview with Les Murray, Sydney, 20 March 1995.
26 Interview with Les Murray, Sydney, 19 December 1994.
27 Unpublished letter, Les Murray to Geoffrey Lehmann, 17 August 1960: GL.
28 Unpublished letter, Les Murray to Geoffrey Lehmann, 17 August 1960: GL.
29 Unpublished letter, Les Murray to Geoffrey Lehmann, 28 December 1960: GL.
30 Unpublished letter, Les Murray to Mick Byrne, 26 December 1960: PA.
31 Interview with Bob Ellis, Sydney, 13 July 1997.
32 Interview with Les Murray, Sydney, 4 August 1997.
33 *honi soit*, 29 September 1960, p. 8, 'They Went That Way, Officer'.
34 Interview with Dr Olaf Reinhardt, Sydney, 16 September 1997. Reinhardt also remembered that in the final German examination, Murray had answered only the first set of questions, worth 22 per cent, and passed over the questions worth 78 per cent. Told about this afterwards, he said mildly, 'Oh God. Oh well, I suppose I should read the instructions'.
35 Unpublished letter, Les Murray to Mick Byrne, 26 December 1960: PA.
36 Unpublished letter, Les Murray to Mick Byrne, 26 December 1960: PA.
37 Originally called 'Chant du Chevalier': unpublished letter, Les Murray to Geoffrey Lehmann, 28 December 1960: GL. It would be published in *The Ilex Tree*.
38 Interview with Les Murray, Sydney, 4 August 1997.
39 Interview with Les Murray, 4 September 1998.
40 Interview with Les Murray, 4 September 1998.
41 Interview with Les Murray, Sydney, 20 March 1995: 'I had no money and Dad had no more'.
42 Interview with Les Murray, Sydney, 10 November 1996.
43 Interview with Michael Byrne, Sydney, 15 July 1997. Byrne was born in Bankstown in 1938, the son of a bus-driver. He did not complete his degree, and worked for the postal service for thirty-five years. Les Murray regarded him as one of his close friends.

44 Interview with Bob Ellis, Sydney, 13 July 1997.
45 Interview with Les Murray, Sydney, 18 November 1997.
46 Interview with Michael Byrne, Sydney, 15 July 1997.
47 Greg O'Hara's 'Reminiscences of Les Murray' [1995]: PA.
48 Interview with Les Murray, Bunyah, 19 August 1997.
49 The description is Les Murray's: interview with him, Sydney, 20 March 1995.
50 Interview with Les Murray, Sydney, 20 March 1995.
51 Interview with Les Murray, Bunyah, 18 August 1997.
52 Unpublished letter, Les Murray to Geoffrey Lehmann, 29 July 1961: GL.
53 Unpublished letters, Les Murray to Greg O'Hara, 11 May 1961 and 23 June 1961: GO'H.
54 Unpublished letter, Les Murray to Penny Nelson (née McNicoll), 13 July 1961: PN.
55 Unpublished letter, Les Murray to Greg O'Hara, 23 June 1961: GO'H.
56 Telephone interview with Les Murray, Bunyah, 3 February 1999.
57 Unpublished letter, Les Murray to Greg O'Hara, 23 June 1961: GO'H.
58 Unpublished letter, Les Murray to Greg O'Hara, 23 June 1961: GO'H.
59 Notably 'The Scream', quoted in an unpublished letter, Les Murray to Geoffrey Lehmann, 29 July 1961: GL.
60 'Assault of the Elements: quoted in unpublished letter, Les Murray to Geoffrey Lehmann, 29 July 1961: GL.
61 Unpublished letter, Les Murray to Penny Nelson (née McNicoll), 20 July 1961: PN.
62 Interview with Les Murray, 2 September 1997.
63 Unpublished letter, Les Murray to Penny Nelson (née McNicoll), 20 July 1961: PN.
64 Unpublished letter, Les Murray to Penny Nelson (née McNicoll), 20 July 1961: PN.
65 This is the version he published in *Arna*, 1962, p. 65. In his unpublished letter to Penny Nelson (née McNicoll), 20 July 1961, the last stanza ran: 'Saints find eternity/A guide/And oceans know it is/Most wide.': PN.
66 Rudolf Otto's *The Idea of the Holy: An Inquiry Into the Non-Rational Factor in the Idea of the Divine and its Relation to the Rational*.
67 Unpublished letter, Les Murray to Mohammad Tavallaie, 9 September 1993: MT.
68 Unpublished letter, Les Murray to Geoffrey Lehmann, 17 June 1961: GL.
69 *Arna*, 1961, p. 30.
70 Interview with Les Murray, 19 December 1994.
71 *Southerly*, no. 1, 1961, p. 42.
72 *Southerly*, no. 3, 1961, p. 39.
73 Kenneth Slessor (1901–1971) became a journalist, while also writing poetry now considered among the best produced in Australia. He lived mostly in Sydney, often within view of the harbour, which features strongly in his verse. His *Five Bells* (1939) is commonly regarded as the best volume of Australian poetry to appear before Les Murray's own work. Though Slessor wrote virtually no original poetry after 1944, he continued to be a major literary figure, through his editing of the anthology *Australian Poetry* (1945) and *The Penguin Book of Australian Verse* (1958). He also wielded great influence, in the period when Les Murray was coming to prominence, through his work on the Sydney *Sun* (1945–57), *Daily Telegraph* (from 1957), and *Southerly* (1956–61) and through his voice on the Commonwealth Literary Fund Advisory Board, and the National Literature Board of Review.
74 Douglas Stewart (1913–1985), New Zealand-born poet and editor, edited the Red Page of the *Bulletin* from 1940–61; in 1961 he became poetry editor at Angus & Robertson until 1971, but continued an active literary career as writer and critic thereafter. *The Fire on the Snow*, a verse-drama for radio, was his greatest literary success, but he wrote many other

plays, as well as much poetry, short stories, edited volumes of verse, and copious criticism. He was a great and generous encourager of younger poets from Judith Wright to David Campbell and Rosemary Dobson.
75 Interview with Les Murray, Sydney, 25 August 1997.
76 Les Murray's annotations (December 1998) to an earlier draft of this book: PA.
77 Unpublished letter, Les Murray to Greg O'Hara, 20 October 1962: GO'H.
78 Interviews with Bob Ellis, 13 July 1997, and with Mick Byrne, 15 July 1997.
79 Interview with Geoffrey Lehmann, Sydney, 5 September 1998.
80 Interview with Charlie Murray, Newcastle, 2 April 1997.
81 This is the account Coady gave Chris Wallace-Crabbe: Interview with Wallace-Crabbe, Sydney, 8 September 1995.
82 Interview with Tony Coady, Sydney, 13 November 1998.
83 Unpublished letter, Les Murray to Penny Nelson (née McNicoll), no date (first page missing): PN.
84 Unpublished letter, Les Murray to Geoffrey Lehmann, undated [1961]: GL.
85 Telephone interview with Les Murray in Bunyah, 3 February 1999.
86 Les Murray's 'Afterword' in Alexander Craig (ed.), *Twelve Poets 1950–1970*, p. 218.
87 Unpublished letter, Les Murray to Penny Nelson (née McNicoll), no date (first page missing): PN.
88 Interview with Geoffrey Lehmann, Sydney, 5 September 1998.
89 Chris Wallace-Crabbe (1934–), poet, editor and academic, has published nine volumes of verse, and edited three major anthologies. Since 1968 he has taught English at the University of Melbourne. At the time he and Murray first met he had published only his first volume, *The Music of Division* (1959), but was already building a major poetic reputation.
90 Murray mentions him in an unpublished letter to Geoffrey Lehmann, 29 July 1961: GL.
91 Interview with Wallace-Crabbe, Sydney, 8 September 1995.
92 Interview with Wallace-Crabbe, Sydney, 8 September 1995.
93 Telephone interview with Christopher Koch, Tasmania, 9 April 1995. C. J. Koch (1932–), poet and novelist, is best known for his novel *The Year of Living Dangerously* (1978), but has also written others, *The Boys in the Island* (1958), *Across the Sea Wall* (1965), *The Doubleman* (1985) and *Highway to a War* (1995). *Across the Sea Wall* was savagely reviewed, perhaps in reaction to the praise lavished on *The Boys in the Island*, and the great success of *The Year of Living Dangerously* restored his reputation.
94 'Recourse to the Wilderness', first collected in *The Weatherboard Cathedral*.
95 Interview with Les Murray, 19 December 1994.
96 Greg O'Hara's 'Reminiscences of Les Murray' [1995]: PA.
97 Les Murray's annotations (December 1998) to an earlier draft of this book: PA.
98 Interview with Les Murray, Sydney, 18 November 1997.
99 Anne Coombs, *Sex and Anarchy*, p. 7.
100 Clive James, *Unreliable Memoirs*, p. 137.
101 Clive James, *Unreliable Memoirs*, p. 139.
102 Interview with Les Murray, 19 December 1994.
103 Quoted in Anne Coombs, *Sex and Anarchy*, p. 212. Coombs's book is the most complete history of the Push.
104 Anne Coombs, *Sex and Anarchy*, p. 213.
105 She was the sister of Paddy McGuinness.
106 Interview with Les Murray, 19 August 1997.

107 Interview with Bob Ellis, Sydney, 13 July 1997.
108 'The Head-Spider', first collected in *Subhuman Redneck Poems*.
109 Les Murray in BBC interview, 'Desert Island Discs', 1998.
110 'The Head-Spider'.
111 Unpublished letter, Les Murray to Geoffrey Lehmann, 29 July 1961: GL.
112 Unpublished letter, Les Murray to Greg O'Hara, 7 February 1963: GO'H.
113 'The Head-Spider'.

9 Halt and Turn, 1962

1 Valerie Murray's birth certificate, Murray Collection, MS5332, Box 1, Folder 2: NLA.
2 Interview with Gino Morelli, Sydney, 21 July 1998.
3 Interview with Gino Morelli, Sydney, 21 July 1998.
4 Les Murray's annotation (December 1998) to an early draft of this book: PA.
5 Interview with Gino Morelli, Sydney, 21 July 1998.
6 'Immigrant Voyage', first collected in *Ethnic Radio*.
7 Interview with Gino Morelli, Sydney, 21 July 1998.
8 Interview with Gino Morelli, Sydney, 21 July 1998.
9 Interview with Olaf Reinhardt, Sydney, 16 September 1997.
10 Interview with Valerie Murray, Bunyah, 8 October 1996.
11 Les Murray, talk to the Library Society of the University of New South Wales, 25 August 1997.
12 Interview with Valerie Murray, Bunyah, 8 October 1996.
13 Interview with Valerie Murray, Bunyah, 8 October 1996.
14 Interview with Bob Ellis, Sydney, 13 July 1997.
15 Interview with Bob Ellis, Sydney, 13 July 1997.
16 Interview with Valerie Murray, Bunyah, 9 October 1998.
17 Interview with Valerie Murray, Bunyah, 8 October 1996.
18 Interview with Valerie Murray, Bunyah, 8 October 1996.
19 Interview with Gino Morelli, Sydney, 21 July 1998.
20 Interview with Valerie Murray, Bunyah, 8 October 1996.
21 'Sidere Mens Eadem Mutato', first collected in *Lunch & Counter Lunch*.
22 Interview with Bob Ellis, Sydney, 13 July 1997.
23 Les Murray's annotation (December 1998) to an early draft of this book: PA.
24 Unpublished letter, Les Murray to Greg O'Hara (then living in New Guinea), 12 September 1962: GO'H.
25 Quoted in unpublished letter, Les Murray to Greg O'Hara (then living in New Guinea), 12 September 1962: GO'H.
26 Unpublished letter, Les Murray to Greg O'Hara (then living in New Guinea), 12 September 1962: GO'H.
27 Interview with Bob Ellis, Sydney, 13 July 1997.
28 The incident is hilariously described in an unpublished letter, Les Murray to Greg O'Hara, 4 November 1962: GO'H, and in Penny Nelson's *Penny Dreadful*, pp. 191ff. In a subsequent letter Les Murray opined, 'I don't agree that his running away during the scare was prudent—I call it at best neurotic, at worst cowardly. And most funny, too . . .' Unpublished letter, Les

Murray to Greg O'Hara, 28 November 1962: GO'H. The farce would be reflected in Ellis's film *The Nostradamus Kid*.
29 Unpublished letter, Les Murray to Greg O'Hara, 4 November 1962: GO'H.
30 Valerie Murray denied wearing such nail polish.
31 Penny Nelson, *Penny Dreadful*, p. 169.
32 Interview with Geoffrey Lehmann, Sydney, 5 September 1998. Francis Thompson (1859–1907) is best known for 'The Hound of Heaven', describing the poet's flight from God, the pursuit, and the overtaking.
33 Interview with Les Murray, Sydney, 20 December 1994.
34 Interview with Les Murray, Sydney, 20 December 1994.
35 Murray wrote 'Distinguo' in September 1989: unpublished letter, Les Murray to Judith Green, 13 September 1989: JG. The poem was first collected in *Dog Fox Field*.
36 Unpublished letter, Les Murray to Judith Green, 13 September 1989: JG.
37 Les Murray's 'Chronology', supplied to the author: PA.
38 'Les A. Murray', in *Australian Literary Studies*, vol. 12 (2), October 1985, p. 268.
39 Notably Sister Veronica Brady, who Murray came to believe 'hates the ground I walk on'. He believed this was partly because she idolised Vincent Buckley, whom Les Murray thought 'a failed poet and a toad'. Interview with Les Murray, Sydney, 20 December 1994. Brady attacked Les Murray on theological and personal grounds in such articles as 'What Will Suffice', *Helix*, nos 21–2, 1985, pp. 112–20.
40 Unpublished letter, Les Murray to Judith Green, 13 September 1989: JG.
41 Unpublished letter, Les Murray to Greg O'Hara, 20 October 1962: GO'H.
42 At the time he spelled it Moriszegy in the letter to O'Hara, but the name was actually Mozsny: Les Murray's MS annotation to the TS of an early draft of this book, December 1998: PA.
43 Unpublished letter, Les Murray to Greg O'Hara, 20 October 1962: GO'H.
44 Unpublished letter, Les Murray to Greg O'Hara, 20 October 1962: GO'H.
45 Peter Barden's taped 'Reminiscences of Les Murray', recorded at Pasadena, California, 20 April 1995: PA.
46 Unpublished letter, Les Murray to Greg O'Hara, 20 October 1962: GO'H.
47 Unpublished letter, Les Murray to Greg O'Hara, 5 October 1962: GO'H.
48 'Baa, Baa, Black Sheep'.
49 Murray's 'Comments on Poems', sent to Lehmann in preparation for readings Lehmann organised at the Ensemble Theatre in Sydney during 1964: GL.
50 *Hermes*, 1962, p. 70.

10 Thyrsis and Corydon, 1962–65

1 Unpublished letter, Les Murray to Greg O'Hara, 20 October 1962: GO'H.
2 Unpublished letter, Les Murray to Greg O'Hara, 4 November 1962: GO'H.
3 Unpublished letter, Les Murray to Greg O'Hara, undated [5? October 1962]: GO'H.
4 He would have two periods as writer in residence (1983 and 1997), would deliver many readings and lectures over the years, would be appointed to the University of New South Wales Council, and in 1998 would receive an Honorary D. Litt.
5 Interview with Les Murray and Valerie Murray, Bunyah, 28 August 1996.
6 Interview with Gino Morelli, Sydney, 21 July 1998.

7 Among his publications is *Gumbaynggirr Dreaming, vol. 1, Stories of Uncle Harry Buchanan*, translated by the Gumbaynggirr Language and Culture Group. Interview with Gino Morelli, Sydney, 21 July 1998. Les Murray would draw on Stephen Morelli for much Aboriginal lore, and refers to him respectfully as 'my poison-brother fellow' in the poem 'Big Shame': relatives to be avoided under Aboriginal kinship rules often carry the 'poison' prefix in English.
8 Unpublished letter, Les Murray to Greg O'Hara, 31 December 1962: GO'H.
9 Interview with Charlie and Alice Murray, Newcastle, NSW, 2 April 1997.
10 Interview with Charlie Murray, Newcastle, NSW, 2 April 1997.
11 In an interview, Sydney, 10 November 1996, Les Murray said the land would have cost £5000; but, according to Charlie Murray, the government valuation at the time was £8 an acre, or £1200 for the 150 acres Cecil worked.
12 Interview with Charlie Murray, Newcastle, NSW, 2 April 1997.
13 Statement of Cecil Murray's bank account with the English, Scottish & Australian Bank: PA.
14 Interview with Charlie Murray, Newcastle, NSW, 2 April 1997.
15 'Dad and Eric had driven bullocks together, & Eric always sought Dad's advice & was dependent on him. Some of their kindness after Mum's death (she'd disliked them) came under Edna's influence, I'm sure. She was my favourite aunt & their house is described in "Towards the Imminent Days" parts 4 & 5' first collected in *Poems Against Economics*: Les Murray's annotation (December 1998) to an earlier draft of this book: PA.
16 Interview with Charlie Murray, Newcastle, NSW, 2 April 1997.
17 Unpublished letter, Les Murray to Penny Nelson (née McNicoll), 19 June 1964: PN.
18 Interview with Les Murray, Sydney, 10 November 1996.
19 Unpublished letter, Les Murray to Penny Nelson (née McNicoll), 19 June 1964: PN.
20 Unpublished letter, Les Murray to Greg O'Hara, 28 November 1962: GO'H.
21 Telephone conversation with the author, 21 September 1998.
22 Unpublished letter, Les Murray to Greg O'Hara, 4 November 1962: GO'H.
23 Unpublished letter, Les Murray to Greg O'Hara, 4 November 1962: GO'H.
24 Unpublished letter, Les Murray to Greg O'Hara, 7 February 1963: GO'H.
25 Founded in 1946, the ANU was originally confined to graduate study. In 1960, when Canberra University College (founded in 1929) became part of the university, undergraduates were admitted for the first time. Affiliated with the university are the Institute of Advanced Studies, the unit responsible for doctoral degrees, and research schools of medicine, physical and biological sciences, social sciences, and Pacific studies.
26 Telephone interview with Les Murray, Bunyah, 1 October 1998.
27 Jack Graneek had come to the ANU from Northern Ireland: he was a scholar of the Classics and Hebrew. His wife Myra, ten years his senior, taught in the German department.
28 Letter of reference for Les Murray, 26 April 1967: Murray Collection, MS5332, Box 1, File 2: NLA.
29 Les Murray's 'Afterword' in Alexander Craig (ed.), *Twelve Poets 1950–1970*, p. 219.
30 Unpublished letter, Les Murray to Greg O'Hara, 31 December 1962: GO'H.
31 Unpublished letter, Les Murray to Greg O'Hara, 5 May 1963: GO'H.
32 Unpublished letter, Les Murray to Greg O'Hara, 5 May 1963: GO'H.
33 Interview with Valerie Murray, Bunyah, 8 October 1996.
34 Unpublished letter, Les Murray to Greg O'Hara, 5 May 1963: GO'H.
35 Telephone conversation, Les Murray with the author, 4 September 1998.
36 Unpublished letter, Les Murray to Greg O'Hara, undated [?March/April 1963]: GO'H.

37 Interview with Olaf Reinhardt, Sydney, 16 September 1997.
38 Interview with Olaf Reinhardt, Sydney, 16 September 1997.
39 Les Murray's annotations (December 1998) to an earlier draft of this book: PA.
40 Interview with Valerie Murray, Bunyah, 8 October 1996.
41 Unpublished letter, Les Murray to Greg O'Hara, 23 September 1963: GO'H.
42 Interview with Les Murray, Bunyah, 8 October 1996.
43 'Employment for the Castes in Abeyance', first collected in *Ethnic Radio*. 'Kiriloff used to curse about it too because in Russian there are three genders and six cases and if a paragraph consists of many lines of mathematics and three or four lines of language you don't know what the case, number and gender of all those things are in the mathematics.' Interview with Les Murray, Bunyah, 8 October 1996.
44 Interview with Les Murray, Bunyah, 8 October 1996.
45 Les Murray's annotations (December 1998) to an earlier draft of this book: PA.
46 Les Murray's annotations (December 1998) draft of this book: PA.
47 His notes on both Greek and Armenian (and in their scripts) are among his papers in the Murray Collection, MS5332, Box 2, Folder 15: NLA.
48 Interview with Les Murray, Bunyah, 28 August 1996.
49 Unpublished letter, Les Murray to Greg O'Hara, 5 May 1963: GO'H.
50 Interview with Les Murray, Bunyah, 8 October 1996.
51 Interview with Les Murray, Bunyah, 28 August 1996.
52 Interview with Gino Morelli, Sydney, 21 July 1998.
53 'Employment for the Castes in Abeyance', first collected in *Ethnic Radio*.
54 Unpublished letter, 7 May 1963, Les Murray to Greg O'Hara: 'At four o'clock this afternoon my good wife was delivered of a daughter, weighing about 7 pounds net. and of a mauve colour': GO'H.
55 Unpublished letter, Les Murray to Geoffrey Lehmann, undated [1963]: GL.
56 'Christina has six teeth, can *nearly* walk (given a bit more daring, she *could*, the little wretch!), calls everyone Daddy and is really beautiful now.' Unpublished letter, Les Murray to Penny Nelson (née McNicoll), 19 June 1964: PN.
57 Unpublished letter, Les Murray to Geoffrey Lehmann, 29 July 1961: GL.
58 Unpublished letter, Les Murray to Greg O'Hara, 23 September 1963: GO'H.
59 Interview with Les Murray and Valerie Murray, Bunyah, 28 August 1996. Valerie: 'You [Les Murray] were fifteen and a half stone then [in 1964]'.
60 It peaked at just under 160 kg in the late 1980s: interview with Valerie Murray, Bunyah, 9 October 1998.
61 Interview with Jamie Grant, Sydney, 18 April 1995.
62 'Three Interiors', first collected in *The People's Otherworld*.
63 Interview with Valerie Murray, Bunyah, 9 October 1998.
64 Les Murray's annotations (December 1998) to an earlier draft of this book: PA.
65 Interviews with Valerie Murray, Bunyah, 8 October 1996, with Christina Murray, Sydney, 11 July 1997, and with Daniel Murray, Sydney, 9 August 1997.
66 Les Murray's annotations (December 1998) to an earlier draft of this book: PA.
67 Interview with Christina Murray, Sydney, 11 July 1997.
68 Unpublished letter, Les Murray to Greg O'Hara, 5 May 1963: GO'H.
69 Unpublished letter, Les Murray to Greg O'Hara, 5 May 1963: GO'H.
70 Unpublished letter, Les Murray to Greg O'Hara, 5 May 1963: GO'H.

71 Peter Barden's taped 'Reminiscences of Les Murray', recorded at Pasadena, California, 20 April 1995: PA.
72 Unpublished letter, Les Murray to Greg O'Hara, 7 August 1963: GO'H.
73 Interview with Les Murray, Bunyah, 28 August 1996.
74 Unpublished letter, Les Murray to Greg O'Hara, 5 May 1963: GO'H.
75 Unpublished letter, Les Murray to Greg O'Hara, undated [?March/April 1963]: GO'H.
76 Unpublished letter, Les Murray to Greg O'Hara, 31 December 1962: GO'H.
77 Unpublished letter, Les Murray to Greg O'Hara, 23 September 1963: GO'H.
78 'The Canberra Remnant', first collected in *The Weatherboard Cathedral*.
79 Unpublished letter, Les Murray to Greg O'Hara, 31 December 1962: GO'H.
80 The *Bulletin* published 'The Burning Truck' and 'Deckchair Story' in 1961. *Southerly* published 'Manoeuvres' in no. 1, 1964, p. 41. It had previously published other poems of his, in no. 1, 1961, p. 42, and no. 3, 1961, p. 39. *Woroni* would publish 'Driving Through Sawmill Towns' in 1964.
81 When I decided to emigrate to Australia in the 1970s, I enquired among literary academics of my acquaintance at Cambridge. Those who were not Australian specialists knew of only two living Australian writers, White and Hope.
82 Interview with Les Murray and Valerie Murray, Bunyah, 28 August 1996.
83 Interview with Les Murray and Valerie Murray, Bunyah, 28 August 1996.
84 Interview with Les Murray, Bunyah, 23 September 1997.
85 Murray's 'Notes', as guest editor, *Poetry Australia*, no. 8, February 1966, p. 4.
86 Completed late in September 1964: unpublished letter, Les Murray to David Campbell, 23 Sept 1964: Murray Collection, MS5332: NLA.
87 Unpublished letter, Les Murray to David Campbell, 16 December 1964: Murray Collection, MS5332: NLA.
88 Interview with Geoffrey Lehmann, Sydney, 5 September 1996.
89 Interview with Les Murray, Sydney, 19 August 1997.
90 Les Murray is referring to the opening lines of Virgil's seventh Eclogue.
91 Les Murray to David Campbell, 8 February [1965], Murray Collection, MS5332: NLA.
92 Interview with Les Murray, Sydney, 19 August 1997.
93 It was not published until after Les Murray's return from Europe in mid-October 1965.
94 Interview with Les Murray, Sydney, 19 August 1997.
95 *Canberra Times*, 11 December 1965, p. 11.
96 *Current Affairs Bulletin*, vol. 39 (3), 26 December 1966, pp. 44–5.
97 *Bulletin*, 12 February 1966, p. 48.
98 *Southerly*, vol. 26 (2), 1966, pp. 126–32.
99 *Poetry Australia*, vol. 2 (10), June 1966, pp. 31–4.
100 *Westerly*, no. 3, December 1966, pp. 90–4.
101 *Age*, 10 September 1966, p. 23.
102 *Poetry Magazine*, no. 1, 1966 pp. 28–30.
103 *Times Literary Supplement*, 15 December 1966, p. 1172.
104 *London Magazine*, January 1967, pp. 86–7.
105 Felicity Haynes in *Westerly*, no. 3, December 1966, pp. 90–4; anonymous, in *Times Literary Supplement*, 15 December 1966, p. 1172.
106 The Grace Leven Prize, awarded by the Perpetual Trustee Company, is still awarded annually: Les Murray had won it three times by 1998.

107 Interview with Geoffrey Lehmann, Sydney, 5 September 1996.
108 Interview with Les Murray, 23 September 1997.
109 Interview with Les Murray, 23 September 1997.
110 Telephone interview with Les Murray, Bunyah, 1 October 1998.
111 Telephone interview with Les Murray, Bunyah, 1 October 1998.
112 For instance, in an interview he gave Graham Croker for *Uniken*, University of New South Wales, 5 August 1997.
113 Unpublished letter, Chris Koch to Les Murray, 18 August 1977: Murray Collection, MS5332, Box 10, File 69: NLA.
114 The description is that of Vivien Smith, in a fine poem entitled 'Twenty Years of Sydney'.
115 Les Murray refers to this commission in an unpublished letter to David Campbell, 27 June 1965: Murray Collection, MS5332, Box 10, Folder 69: NLA.
116 It would appear in February 1966: *Poetry Australia*, no. 8. Les Murray included Mackenzie Munro, David Campbell, A. D. Hope, J. R. Rowland and himself, with 'Evening Alone at Bunyah' and 'The Insolent Familiar'.
117 The Poetry Society, founded in Sydney in 1954 to encourage the study of poetry, had from 1954 published a journal, *Prism*. This was superseded in 1961 by *Poetry Magazine*, a bi-monthly edited by Perry until 1964, when Adamson and his group ousted her in a branch-stacking coup.
118 Les Murray, 'Inside Poetry Australia', *Quadrant*, April 1983, pp. 16–24.
119 'He refers to her as 'having beaten down my resistance with a drumfire of words': unpublished letter to David Campbell, 27 June 1965: Murray Collection, MS5332: NLA.
120 Telephone interview with Les Murray, Bunyah, 1 October 1998.
121 Les Murray's annotations (December 1998) to an earlier draft of this book: PA.

11 The Antipodes, 1965–68

1 The name was taken from the title of a Horovitz anthology, *Children of Albion*, 1969. Other members of the loose Jazz Poetry group were Christopher Logue, Roy Fisher, Pete Brown, and Spike Hawkins.
2 Telephone interview with Les Murray, Bunyah, 1 October 1998.
3 Telephone interview with Les Murray, Bunyah, 1 October 1998.
4 Telephone interview with Les Murray, Bunyah, 1 October 1998.
5 Telephone interview with Gareth Griffiths, Perth, 2 October 1998.
6 Unpublished letter, Les Murray to John Barnie, 13 April 1983: JB.
7 It was in fact only a fringe element of Modernism, a term usually used so broadly that it would certainly encompass Murray's own writing.
8 *Bomb Culture* was the title of a work by Jeff Nuttall.
9 'The Cardiff Commonwealth Arts Festival Poetry Conference 1965, Recalled'. The poem was first collected in *Ethnic Radio*.
10 Email from Gareth Griffiths to the author, 2 October 1998.
11 Murray's 'Afterword' in Alexander Craig (ed.), *Twelve Poets 1950–1970*, p. 219.
12 Telephone interview with Les Murray, Bunyah, 1 October 1998.

13 Telephone interview with Gareth Griffiths, Perth, 2 October 1998. Griffiths would become Professor of English at the University of Western Australia.
14 Telephone interview with Les Murray, Bunyah, 1 October 1998.
15 Telephone interview with Les Murray, Bunyah, 1 October 1998.
16 Interview with Valerie Murray, Bunyah, 9 October 1998.
17 Interview with Les Murray and Valerie Murray, Bunyah, 28 August 1996.
18 Unpublished letter, Les Murray to Penny Nelson (née McNicoll), 19 June 1964: PN.
19 'Memories of the Height-to-Weight Ratio', first collected in *Subhuman Redneck Poems*.
20 Interview with Les Murray, Sydney, 18 August 1997.
21 Peter Barden's, taped 'Reminiscences of Les Murray', recorded at Pasadena, California, 20 April 1995: PA.
22 Peter Barden's, taped 'Reminiscences of Les Murray', recorded at Pasadena, California, 20 April 1995: PA.
23 'Memories of the Height-to-Weight Ratio', first collected in *Subhuman Redneck Poems*.
24 Les Murray, 'A House that is a Home', in *Blocks and Tackles*, pp. 48–9.
25 Les Murray, 'Eulogy for Douglas Stewart', *Southerly*, vol. 45 (2), June 1985, p. 127.
26 A copy of this exists in the National Library, dated 26 April 1967: Murray Collection, MS5332, Box 1, File 2: NLA.
27 Murray gives the date in a letter to Geoffrey Lehmann, 20 June 1970: GL.
28 'Vindaloo in Merthyr Tidfyl', first collected in *Poems Against Economics*. Pant, a village near Merthyr, was the home of Gareth Griffiths.
29 Telephone interview with Gareth Griffiths, Perth, 2 October 1998.
30 Telephone interview with Les Murray, Bunyah, 1 October 1998.
31 Interview with Les Murray and Valerie Murray, Bunyah, 28 August 1996.
32 Interview with Les Murray and Valerie Murray, Bunyah, 28 August 1996.
33 Interview with Les Murray and Valerie Murray, Bunyah, 28 August 1996.
34 Telephone interview with Gareth Griffiths, Perth, 2 October 1998.
35 Unpublished letter, Les Murray to Geoffrey Lehmann, 17 September 1967: GL.
36 Interview with Les Murray and Valerie Murray, Bunyah, 28 August 1996.
37 Murray's 'Afterword' in Alexander Craig (ed.), *Twelve Poets 1950–1970*, p. 219.
38 Unpublished letter, Les Murray to Geoffrey Lehmann, 17 September 1967: GL
39 Unpublished letter, Valerie Murray to her mother, 29 August 1967: Murray Collection, MS5332, Box 1, File 1: NLA.
40 Unpublished letter, Derek Gains, Deputy Warden, Grantley Hall, to Les Murray, 19 June 1967: Murray Collection, MS5332, Box 1, File 1: NLA.
41 Interview with Les Murray and Valerie Murray, Bunyah, 28 August 1996.
42 Interview with Valerie Murray, Bunyah, 28 August 1996.
43 Telegram to Les Murray, 27 October 1967: Murray Collection, MS5332, Box 1, File 1: NLA.
44 Interview with Les Murray and Valerie Murray, Bunyah, 28 August 1996.
45 The battle of Culloden (16 April 1746) was the last battle of the 'Forty-five Rebellion,' when the Jacobites, under Charles Edward, the Young Pretender (Bonnie Prince Charlie), were defeated by British forces under William Augustus, Duke of Cumberland.
46 Interview with Les Murray and Valerie Murray, Bunyah, 28 August 1996.
47 *Southerly*, vol. 28, 1968, p. 273.
48 Interview with Christina Murray, Sydney, 11 July 1997.
49 Unpublished letter, Donald Kirby to Geoffrey Lehmann, 12 February 1968: GL.

50 Les Murray's pocket diary for 1967–68, Murray Collection, MS5332, Box 5, File 34: NLA.
51 Entry for 15 January 1968: Les Murray's pocket diary for 1967–68, Murray Collection, MS5332, Box 5, File 34: NLA.
52 Les Murray in BBC interview, 'Desert Island Discs', 1998.
53 Unpublished letter, Les Murray to John Barnie, 13 January 1984: JB.
54 Les Murray in Gerry Turcotte (ed.), *Writers in Action*, p. 87.
55 Murray's 'Afterword' in Alexander Craig (ed.), *Twelve Poets 1950–1970*, p. 219.
56 Brother of the distinguished jurist Justice Michael Kirby. Don Kirby stayed with the Murrays in Inverness from 10 to 16 February 1968.
57 Unpublished letter, Donald Kirby to Geoffrey Lehmann, 12 February 1968: GL.
58 They have all been lost, but Les Murray refers to his rejoicing in getting mail, and his worries when there is a mail-strike in Sydney, in his pocket diary for 1967–68: Murray Collection, MS5332, Box 5, File 34: NLA.
59 Published in *The Weatherboard Cathedral*.
60 'The Human Hair-Thread', in *Persistence in Folly*, p. 11.
61 Unpublished letter, Donald Kirby to Geoffrey Lehmann, 12 February 1968: GL.
62 Interview with Les Murray and Valerie Murray, Bunyah, 28 August 1996.
63 Telephone interview with Gareth Griffiths, Perth, 2 October 1998.
64 For instance, 2 March 1968, Les Murray's pocket diary for 1967–68, Murray Collection, MS5332, Box 5, File 34: NLA.
65 8 March 1968: Les Murray's pocket diary for 1967–68, Murray Collection, MS5332, Box 5, File 34: NLA.
66 15 March 1968: Les Murray's pocket diary for 1967–68, Murray Collection, MS5332, Box 5, File 34: NLA. A *calvaire* is a roadside shrine, usually a carved wooden representation of Calvary.
67 20 March 1968: Les Murray's pocket diary for 1967–68, Murray Collection, MS5332, Box 5, File 34: NLA.
68 21 March 1968: Les Murray's pocket diary for 1967–68, Murray Collection, MS5332, Box 5, File 34: NLA.
69 28 March 1968: Les Murray's pocket diary for 1967–68, Murray Collection, MS5332, Box 5, File 34: NLA.
70 3 April 1968: Les Murray's pocket diary for 1967–68, Murray Collection, MS5332, Box 5, File 34: NLA. 'BVM' means Blessed Virgin Mary.
71 8 April 1968: Les Murray's pocket diary for 1967–68, Murray Collection, MS5332, Box 5, File 34: NLA.
72 Interview with Les Murray and Valerie Murray, Bunyah, 28 August 1996.
73 14 April 1968: Les Murray's pocket diary for 1967–68, Murray Collection, MS5332, Box 5, File 34: NLA.
74 18 April 1968: Les Murray's pocket diary for 1967–68, Murray Collection, MS5332, Box 5, File 34: NLA.
75 21 April 1968: Les Murray's pocket diary for 1967–68, Murray Collection, MS5332, Box 5, File 34: NLA.
76 21 April 1968: Les Murray's pocket diary for 1967–68, Murray Collection, MS5332, Box 5, File 34: NLA.
77 It does not appear to have pleased him, for it was not published.
78 Murray's 'Afterword' in Alexander Craig (ed.), *Twelve Poets 1950–1970*, p. 219.
79 Published in *The Weatherboard Cathedral*.

80 Murray's 'Afterword' in Alexander Craig (ed.), *Twelve Poets 1950–1970*, p. 219.
81 27 April 1968: Les Murray's pocket diary for 1967–68, Murray Collection, MS5332, Box 5, File 34: NLA.
82 They received 2280 Swiss francs for the Cortina. Les Murray's pocket diary for 1967–68, 10 May 1968, Murray Collection, MS5332, Box 5, File 34: NLA.
83 5 May 1968: Les Murray's pocket diary for 1967–68, Murray Collection, MS5332, Box 5, File 34: NLA.
84 Les Murray's annotations (December 1998) to an earlier draft of this book: PA.
85 12 May 1968: Les Murray's pocket diary for 1967–68, Murray Collection, MS5332, Box 5, File 34: NLA.
86 Les Murray's annotations (December 1998) to an earlier draft of this book: PA.
87 Interview with Les Murray and Valerie Murray, Bunyah, 28 August 1996.
88 Interview with Les Murray and Valerie Murray, Bunyah, 28 August 1996.
89 Les Murray's annotations (December 1998) to an earlier draft of this book: PA.

12 The Vernacular Republic, 1968–71

1 *Fredy Neptune*, 'Lazarus Unstuck'.
2 Interview with Les Murray and Valerie Murray, Bunyah, 28 August 1996.
3 Interview with Les Murray and Valerie Murray, Bunyah, 28 August 1996, and with Geoffrey Lehmann, Sydney, 5 September 1998. According to Lehmann, his father used the water-pistols on troublesome dogs.
4 Interview with Les Murray and Valerie Murray, Bunyah, 28 August 1996.
5 'Patronage Revisited', in *The Peasant Mandarin*, p. 23.
6 Transcript of Academic Record for Les Murray, University of Sydney: PA.
7 Interview with Les Murray and Valerie Murray, Bunyah, 28 August 1996.
8 The first Honours thesis on his poetry was written by Dianne Ailwood in 1970, and published in *Southerly*, vol. 31(3), 1971, pp. 188–201.
9 He graduated in absentia on 30 May 1970: unpublished letter, 17 April 1970, H. McCredie (Registrar, University of Sydney) to Les Murray, Murray Collection, MS5332, Box 1, File 5: NLA.
10 Unpublished letter, Les Murray to Phil Roberts, lecturer in English, University of Sydney, 20 October 1969, Murray Collection, MS5332, Box 1, File 1: NLA.
11 This is the account Hope gave Mark O'Connor: interview with O'Connor, Canberra, 3 July 1997.
12 Les Murray's annotations (December 1998) to an earlier draft of this book: PA.
13 Les Murray, 'Sidelined by the Elite Republican Guard', *Independent Monthly*, November 1995, p. 65.
14 Unpublished letter, Les Murray to Greg O'Hara, 23 September 1963: GO'H.
15 Unpublished letter, Les Murray to the Rt Hon. John Gray Gorton, 26 January 1969, Murray Collection, MS5332, Box 1, File 1: NLA.
16 Unpublished letter, Les Murray to Governor-General, November 1972, Murray Collection, MS5332, Box 1, File 2: NLA.
17 Unpublished letter, Jim Cairns, MHR for Lalor, to Les Murray, 12 October 1972, Murray Collection, MS5332, Box 1, File 1: NLA.

322   NOTES (CHAPTER 12)

18   Les Murray's annotations (December 1998) to an earlier draft of this book: PA.
19   Unpublished letter, Les Murray to the author, 20 December 1998: PA.
20   *Bulletin*, 2 December 1972, p. 5.
21   Quoted in unpublished letter, Les Murray to Geoffrey Lehmann, 29 July 1961: GL.
22   'Patronage in Australia: A Critique and Two Proposals', *Australian Quarterly*, vol. 44(3), September 1972, pp. 67–80.
23   Unpublished letter, Barry Jones to Les Murray, 16 November 1972, Murray Collection, MS5332, Box 1, File 2: NLA.
24   Unpublished letter, Sen. Doug McLennan to Les Murray, 30 October 1972, Murray Collection, MS5332, Box 1, File 2: NLA.
25   Stuart Sayers, Literary Editor of the *Age*, wrote to him on 20 November 1969 (Murray Collection, MS5332, Box 1, File 1: NLA) promising an article on the subject of literary patronage, in response to a letter from Les Murray, now lost.
26   For instance, in articles he entitled 'Patronage Revisited', reprinted in *Peasant Mandarin* pp. 1 and 22, and originally published in 1972 and 1977. See also 'The Noblesse Trap: the Ills and Possibilities of Arts Patronage' in P. Coleman (ed.), *Double Take*, Melbourne: Mandarin, 1996, pp. 63–99.
27   Les Murray, 'Patronage in Australia', *The Peasant Mandarin*, p. 16.
28   Unpublished letter, September 1972, Sen. Doug McLennan to Les Murray (Murray Collection, MS5332, Box 1, File 2: NLA), in response to Les Murray's sending him an advance copy of his article on this subject, 'Patronage in Australia: A Critique and Two Proposals', subsequently published in *Australian Quarterly*, vol. 44(3), September 1972, pp. 67–80.
29   Les Murray, 'Patronage Revisited', *The Peasant Mandarin*, pp. 22–3.
30   Graham Rowlands, *Makar*, vol. 5 (4), December 1969, pp. 32–4.
31   *Daily Telegraph*, 18 October 1969, p. 17.
32   *Sydney Morning Herald*, 22 November 1969, p. 16.
33   *Age*, 6 December 1969, p. 17.
34   Jim Tulip, *Southerly*, no. 2, 1970, pp. 148–151.
35   *Bulletin*, 7 February 1970, p. 43.
36   *WLWE Newsletter*, no. 18, November 1970, pp. 45–6.
37   Evan Jones, *Nation*, 13 December 1969, pp. 22–3.
38   Peter Ward, *Australian Book Review*, December 1969/January 1970, pp. 60–1.
39   Rodney Hall, *Australian*, 24 January 1970, p. 19.
40   K. L. Goodwin, *Meanjin*, vol. 30(3), September 1971, p. 373.
41   Norling to Les Murray, 16 November 1969, Murray Collection, MS5332, Box 1, File 1: NLA.
42   Unpublished letter, Les Murray to Angus & Robertson, 24 July 1969, Murray Collection, MS5332, Box 1, File 1: NLA.
43   Interview with Les Murray and Valerie Murray, Bunyah, 28 August 1996; also unpublished letter, Les Murray to Mick Byrne, 8 February 1970: PA, and unpublished letter, Les Murray to the Prime Minister, William McMahon, 16 September 1971, Murray Collection MS5332, Box 1, File 1: NLA.
44   Unpublished letter, Les Murray to Mick Byrne, 8 February 1970: PA.
45   Unpublished letter, Les Murray to Mick Byrne, 8 February 1970: PA.
46   Les Murray wrote a detailed account of the Coombs affair to the Prime Minister, William McMahon, on 16 September 1971: Murray Collection MS5332, Box 1, File 1: NLA.

47 Les Murray's unpublished letter to the Prime Minister, William McMahon, 16 September 1971, Murray Collection, MS5332, Box 1, File 1: NLA.
48 Les Murray's unpublished letter to the Prime Minister, William McMahon, 16 September 1971, Murray Collection, MS5332, Box 1, File 1: NLA.
49 Les Murray's unpublished, letter to the Prime Minister, William McMahon, 16 September 1971, Murray Collection MS5332, Box 1, File 1: NLA.
50 Interview with Les Murray, Bunyah, 28 August 1996.
51 'A Question of Influence', Brisbane *Courier-Mail*, 24 August 1996, p. 5.
52 Interview with Valerie Murray, Bunyah, 8 October 1996.
53 Interview with Valerie Murray, Bunyah, 8 October 1996.
54 Unpublished letter, Les Murray to Mick Byrne, 13 August 1970: PA.
55 Unpublished letter, Les Murray to Mick Byrne, 13 August 1970: PA.
56 Unpublished letter, Les Murray to Geoffrey Lehmann, 20 June 1970: GL.
57 Interview with Les Murray and Valerie Murray, Bunyah, 28 August 1996.
58 Unpublished letter, Les Murray to Geoffrey Lehmann, 20 June 1970: GL.
59 Unpublished letter, Les Murray to Mick Byrne, 13 August 1970: PA.
60 Interview with Mick Byrne, Sydney, 15 July 1997.
61 Interview with Les Murray, Bunyah, 28 August 1996.
62 Unpublished letter, Les Murray to Geoffrey Lehmann, 20 June 1970: GL.
63 'Circle City', published in the *Canberra Times*, 13 January 1973, p. 9.
64 Les Murray, unpublished poem, 'Culture-history: Document'; Murray Collection, MS5332, Box 1: NLA.
65 Interview with Les Murray, Bunyah, 28 August 1996.
66 Unpublished letter, Les Murray to Mick Byrne, 13 August 1970: PA.
67 Unpublished letter, Les Murray to Mick Byrne, 8 February 1970: PA.
68 Interview with Valerie Murray, Bunyah, 9 October 1998.
69 Unpublished letter, B. E. Butler to Les Murray, 20 August 1970; Murray Collection, MS5332, Box 1, File 1: NLA.
70 Donald Bruce Dawe (b. 15 February 1930) had a country upbringing in Victoria, left school early, and after a series of part-time jobs of the sort Murray held, went to university late and eventually gained a PhD. He worked as an academic at this time, in Toowoomba.
71 Interview with Bruce Dawe, Sydney, 15 September 1995.
72 Dawe was to remark that they had both written poems about the police, for instance: 'We've both written in our latest books for example poems about the police force ... I think it's interesting that in neither his case nor in mine are they poems that are entirely negative. That is, they don't take the standard left-wing views, the authoritarian figures of the state stuff'. Interview with Bruce Dawe, Sydney, 15 September 1995.
73 Interview with Bruce Dawe, Sydney, 15 September 1995.
74 Unpublished letter, Les Murray to Mick Byrne, 13 August 1970: PA.
75 He wrote that month to Lehmann asking how he could get hold of transcripts of Jimmy Governor's trial: unpublished letter to Lehmann, 3 March 1970: GL. 'The Ballad of Jimmy Governor' was first collected in *Poems Against Economics*.
76 Unpublished letter, Cecil Murray to Les Murray, Sunday 8 [November 1970], Murray Collection, MS5332, Box 1, File 1: NLA.
77 Judith Brett, 'Publishing and Censorship', in *The Penguin New Literary History of Australia*, p. 458.

78. 'Of the 293 writers who responded [to the *Australian Author*] only seven earned more than $7000 per annum, nine between $5000 and $7000, eighteen between $2500 and $5000, and the rest less than $2500'. Judith Brett, 'Publishing and Censorship', in *The Penguin New Literary History of Australia*, p. 458.
79. Interview with Valerie Murray, Bunyah, 8 October 1996.
80. Unrecorded conversation with Les Murray, Sydney, 17 December 1998.
81. Interview with Valerie Murray, Bunyah, 8 October 1996.
82. The purchase documents for the Edgar Street house, 11 March 1971, are in the Murray Collection, MS5332, Box 1, File 1: NLA.
83. Interview with Valerie Murray, Bunyah, 8 October 1996.
84. Interview with Valerie Murray, Bunyah, 8 October 1996.

13 The Test of Faith, 1971–74

1. Unpublished letter, Les Murray to the Prime Minister, William McMahon, 16 September 1971, Murray Collection, MS5332, Box 1, File 1: NLA.
2. Unpublished letter, 'Tony' of Angus & Robertson to Les Murray, 21 January 1972, Murray Collection, MS5332, Box 1, File 2: NLA.
3. It appears on the back cover of *Lunch & Counter Lunch*.
4. Unpublished letter, Les Murray to the Prime Minister, William McMahon, 16 September 1971, Murray Collection, MS5332, Box 1, File 1: NLA.
5. Les Murray's annotations (December 1998) to an earlier draft of this book: PA.
6. Les Murray, 'On Being Subject Matter', in *The Paperbark Tree*, p. 186.
7. Les Murray, 'On Being Subject Matter', in *The Paperbark Tree*, p. 186.
8. Interview with Les Murray, Bunyah, 28 August 1996.
9. Interview with Les Murray, Bunyah, 28 August 1996.
10. Unpublished letter, Les Murray to John Barnie, 9 January 1991: JB.
11. Matthew 19.29.
12. Unpublished letter, Les Murray to John Barnie, 6 August 1981: JB.
13. Treloar, *24 Hours*, vol. 1(10), November 1976, pp. 47–8.
14. Allen Ginsberg, (b. 3 June 1926, d. 5 April 1997), American poet whose long poem *Howl* (1956) is considered by enthusiasts to be one of the most significant products of the Beat movement.
15. Lawrence Monsanto Ferlinghetti (b. 24 March 1919), American poet, was one of the founders of the Beat movement in San Francisco in the mid-1950s. His City Lights bookshop was an early gathering place of the Beats, and the publishing arm of City Lights was the first to print the Beats' books of poetry. Peter Barden would take Les Murray to City Lights on his first visit to San Fransisco.
16. Andrey Andreyevich Voznesensky, (b. 12 May 1933), Soviet poet who was one of the most prominent of the generation of writers that emerged after the Stalinist era.
17. 'Two Festivals', in *The Peasant Mandarin*, p. 251.

18 Interview with Les Murray, Bunyah, 19 December 1994: 'It was a tour of West Australia. The poem's a mixture of that and fantasy. It really came out of a drive from Kalgoorlie to Esperance. So the parts further north, north of Kalgoorlie, are invented. I know so much country like it that I probably got it pretty right'. The poem was first collected in *Lunch & Counter Lunch*.
19 Chronology provided to the author by Les Murray: PA.
20 Carl Harrison-Ford, *New Poetry*, vol. 20(3), June 1972, pp. 40–1.
21 *Canberra Times*, 14 October 1972, p. 10.
22 'The Names of the Humble', first collected in *Poems Against Economics*.
23 The term would be popularised by Michael Pusey of the University of New South Wales, in his book *Economic Rationalism in Canberra: A Nation Changes its Mind*, Cambridge: CUP, 1991.
24 'In Australia They Spare Only the Kulaks', first collected in *Poems Against Economics*.
25 'The Names of the Humble'.
26 In 'Writer and Reader', *Southerly*, vol. 33(2), June 1973, pp. 234–5.
27 In *Poetry Australia*, no. 47, 1973, pp. 71–3.
28 In *Australian Book Review*, December 1972, pp. 42–3.
29 Philip Roberts, *Sydney Morning Herald*, 26 August 1972, p. 20.
30 *Observer*, 5 August 1973, p. 28.
31 'The Coming Republic', *Quadrant*, April 1976, pp. 36–42.

14 The Battle of the Books, 1974–76

1 Les Murray, 'The Suspect Captivity of the Fisher King', the version sent by Les Murray to the author on 19 August 1998: PA.
2 Les Murray, 'Locum at Lyons Road—My Years at *Poetry Australia*', in *Persistence in Folly*, p. 142.
3 I have drawn for this account partly on the excellent article on 'New Australian Poetry' in Wilde, Hooton and Andrews' *The Oxford Companion to Australian Literature*, and on Dennis Haskell's essay 'Modernity's Battle of the Books' in Bennett and Strauss (eds), *The Oxford Literary History of Australia*, partly on interviews with Les Murray, John Tranter, Tom Thompson, Margaret Connolly, Jamie Grant, Robert Gray, Alan Gould, Christopher Koch, Mark O'Connor, Peter Porter and Chris Wallace-Crabbe.
4 John Tranter, quoted in Bennett and Strauss (eds), *The Oxford Literary History of Australia*, p. 268.
5 Les Murray, 'Locum at Lyons Road—My Years at *Poetry Australia*', in *Persistence in Folly*, p. 130.
6 He was to review it in 'More Wow Than Flutter', *Quadrant*, October 1976, pp. 45–51. The piece was republished in *The Peasant Mandarin*.
7 Interview with Les Murray, Bunyah, 23 September 1997.
8 Tom Shapcott, 'John Tranter and Les Murray', *Australian Literary Studies*, vol. 10(3), May 1982, p. 382.
9 Telephone interview with Les Murray, Bunyah, 27 October 1998.
10 Les Murray, 'Locum at Lyons Road—My Years at *Poetry Australia*', in *Persistence in Folly*, pp. 135–6.

11 *honi soit*, 29 September 1960, p. 8.
12 She married Les Murray's former German lecturer Michael Nelson in 1964.
13 Unpublished letter, Les Murray to Penny Nelson, 27 February 1976: PN.
14 Undatable typescript returned with handwritten corrections to Duncan Miller: Murray Collection, MS5332, Box 1, File 1: NLA.
15 Unpublished letter, Gary Catalano to Les Murray, 24 October 1976, Murray Collection, MS5332, Box 1, File 5: NLA.
16 Unpublished letter, B. M. O'Donoghue to Les Murray, 16 July 1976, Murray Collection, MS5332, Box 1, File 6: NLA.
17 Copy of Haskell's poem 'Visiting Friends at Henley', Murray Collection, MS5332, Box 1, File 7: NLA.
18 'I do genuinely appreciate it', Haskell wrote to Les Murray, unpublished letter, 2 June 1978, Murray Collection, MS5332, Box 1, File 7: NLA.
19 Colebatch to Les Murray, undated, Murray Collection, MS5332, Box 1, File 7: NLA.
20 'I only wish other editors took half the trouble you do', Donna Hellier told him, unpublished letter, 14 August 1978, Murray Collection, MS5332, Box 1, File 7: NLA.
21 Interview with Mark O'Connor, Canberra, 3 July 1997.
22 Interview with Mark O'Connor, Canberra, 3 July 1997.
23 Interview with Mark O'Connor, Canberra, 3 July 1997.
24 Interview with Mark O'Connor, Canberra, 3 July 1997.
25 Les Murray, 'Locum at Lyons Road—My Years at *Poetry Australia*', in *Persistence in Folly*, p. 136.
26 Les Murray, 'Locum at Lyons Road—My Years at *Poetry Australia*', in *Persistence in Folly*, p. 136.
27 Les Murray, 'Locum at Lyons Road—My Years at *Poetry Australia*', in *Persistence in Folly*, p. 141.
28 Les Murray, 'Locum at Lyons Road—My Years at *Poetry Australia*', in *Persistence in Folly*, p. 142.
29 Interview with Les Murray, Sydney, 17 November 1997.
30 Les Murray, 'Locum at Lyons Road—My Years at *Poetry Australia*', in *Persistence in Folly*, pp. 139–40.
31 Telephone interview with Les Murray, Bunyah, 27 October 1998.
32 Tranter's first book, *Parallax*, had been published as an issue of the magazine in 1970. Interview with John Tranter, Sydney, 4 September 1997.
33 Les Murray, 'Locum at Lyons Road—My Years at *Poetry Australia*', in *Persistence in Folly*, p. 140.
34 Unpublished letter, Les Murray to Craig Powell, 29 April 1974, Powell Collection, G152, Box 1, Folder 1: ADFA.
35 His first *Sydney Morning Herald* review seems to have been 'Getting to Know the Landscape', a recommendation of George Seddon's *Sense of Place*, 23 June 1973, p. 25. The subject was particularly close to Murray's heart.
36 Tranter, 'Anchored in the local earth', *Australian*, 2 November 1974, p. 19.
37 *Sydney Morning Herald*, 9 November 1974, p. 15.
38 Malouf, *Poetry Australia*, no. 57, December 1975, pp. 70–2.
39 Malouf, *Poetry Australia*, no. 57, December 1975, pp. 70–2.
40 Adelaide *Advertiser*, 7 December 1974, p. 28.
41 Hart, *Southern Review*, vol. 10(1), 1977, pp. 83–5.

42 Unpublished letter, Peter Porter to Les Murray, 18 February 1975, Murray Collection, MS5332, Box 1, File 1: NLA.
43 Robert Gray, *New Poetry*, vol. 23(1), 1975, pp. 77–8.
44 'More Wow Than Flutter', in *The Peasant Mandarin*, pp. 195–6.
45 'More Wow Than Flutter', in *The Peasant Mandarin*, pp. 195–6.
46 Interview with John Tranter, Sydney, 4 September 1997.
47 Tranter's reviews of Les Murray's work repeatedly illustrate the mixture: 'Anchored in the local earth', *Australian*, 2 November 1974, p. 19, and 'A Warrior poet living still on Anzac Cove', *Australian*, 29 January 1977, provide representative examples, as does his review of Les Murray's *Ethnic Radio*, in *24 Hours*, July 1978, pp. 70–1.
48 'Requiem for a Heavyweight', in *Heat*, no. 5, 1997, p. 186. The emphasis is Bolton's.
49 Gray, *Sydney Morning Herald*, 11 September 1976, p. 15.
50 Porter, *Observer Review*, 17 May 1981, p. 29.
51 McDonald, *National Times*, 18–23 October 1976, pp. 64–5.
52 Treloar, *24 Hours*, vol. 1(10), November 1976, pp. 47–8.
53 Unpublished letter, Les Murray to Craig Powell, 1 July 1975, Powell Collection, G152, Box 1, Folder 1: ADFA. Powell was living in Brandon, Manitoba, Canada.
54 This debate opened in *Australian Poems in Perspective* (ed. P. K. Elkin), in which Porter's poem 'On First Looking into Chapman's Hesiod' (which paralleled the themes of Murray's poem 'The Returnees', written at the end of 1974 and first collected in *Ethnic Radio*) was followed by one of Les Murray's finest essays, 'On Sitting Back and Thinking About Porter's Boeotia', reprinted in *The Paperbark Tree*, pp. 56ff.
55 Les Murray, 'The Boeotian Strain', *Kunapipi*, vol. 2(1), 1980, pp. 54–64.
56 Les Murray, 'The Boeotian Strain', *Kunapipi*, vol. 2(1), 1980, p. 55.
57 Les Murray, 'The Boeotian Strain', *Kunapipi*, vol. 2(1), 1980, p. 59.
58 'Red Herrings Inc.', *Australian's Review of Books*, November 1997, p. 23.
59 Beazley was introduced to Les Murray by Bob Ellis, who acted as a speech-writer to Beazley for a time.
60 Bernard Smith made Les Murray's urging that 'Australians must look for convergence rather than cause for division' the basis of his 1980 Boyer Lectures for the ABC.
61 Professor Rhys Jones, in the 1997 Annual Lecture of the Australian Academy of the Humanities, made Les Murray's 'Not indigenous, merely born here' the keynote of his scholarly analysis of Australian archaeology.
62 Unpublished letter, Donald Horne to Les Murray, 27 April 1976, congratulating Les Murray on his republican articles in *Quadrant*, Murray Collection, MS5332, Box 1, File 6: NLA.
63 Interview with Peter Porter, Sydney, 4 March 1995.
64 Unpublished letter, Les Murray to Valerie Murray, 22 August 1974, Murray Collection, MS5332, Box 1, File 1: NLA.
65 Unpublished letter, Les Murray to Valerie Murray, 18 September 1974, Murray Collection, MS5332, Box 1, File 1: NLA.
66 Unpublished letter, L. O. Martin and Edwards, Solicitors, Taree, to Les Murray, 15 November 1974, confirming the purchase, Murray Collection, MS5332, Box 1, File 2: NLA.
67 Unpublished letter, Les Murray to Craig Powell, 13 October 1975, Powell Collection, G152, Box 1, Folder 1: ADFA.
68 Interview with Bruce Clunies Ross, Armidale, 29 September 1997. Clunies Ross's colleague James Stewart first noticed the Gaelic inspiration.

69 'We get along fine now: he agists cattle on this paddock of ours & does odd jobs in return. And we even call the gully that passes thru' from his place to the creek The Water of Leith (q.v. in Edinburgh)': Les Murray's annotations (December 1998) to an earlier draft of this book: PA.
70 Unpublished letter, Con Kiriloff to Les Murray, 21 December 1975, Murray Collection, MS5332, Box 1, File 2: NLA.
71 Unpublished letter, Les Murray to Penny Nelson, 22 May 1975: PN.
72 Interview with Christina Murray, Sydney, 11 July 1997.
73 Les Murray's annotations (December 1998) to an earlier draft of this book: PA.
74 Interview with Jamie Grant, Sydney, 18 April 1995.
75 Les Murray found the Berndt translation in Willard R. Trask's *The Unwritten Song*, vol. 1, pp. 246–54: unpublished letter, Les Murray to Prof. Laurie Hergenham, 7 October 1976, Hergenham Collection, G357, Box 43, Wallet 327: ADFA.
76 Les Murray, 'The Human Hair-Thread', in *Persistence in Folly*, p. 24.
77 Les Murray, 'The Human Hair-Thread', in *Persistence in Folly*, p. 24.
78 Les Murray to Prof. Laurie Hergenham, 7 October 1976, Hergenham Collection, G357, Box 43, Wallet 327: ADFA.
79 Malouf, Lecture to the English Association at the University of Sydney, 25 May 1973: quoted by Les Murray in 'The Human Hair-Thread', in *Persistence in Folly*, p. 27.
80 Les Murray, 'The Human Hair-Thread', in *Persistence in Folly*, p. 27.
81 Unpublished letter, 17 September 1976, Michael Costigan to Les Murray, Murray Collection, MS5332, Box 1, File 2: NLA.

15 Public and Private, 1977–81

1 In Valerie's view, however, 'Les often put on a simple tea when I was working and put away dishes, etc. i.e. some house-work if only to a minimal standard'. Valerie Murray's annotations (December 1998) to an earlier draft of this book: PA.
2 Interview with Christina Murray, Sydney, 11 July 1997.
3 Telephone interview with Valerie Murray, Bunyah, 4 November 1998.
4 Interview with Christina Murray, Sydney, 11 July 1997.
5 Valerie Murray's Journal, entry for 8 March 1989, though she is here recalling the past.
6 Interview with Les Murray, Bunyah, 8 October 1996.
7 Interview with Les Murray, Bunyah, 1 September 1997.
8 Unpublished letter, Christina Murray to the author, 30 October 1997: PA.
9 'Notes on poems in Chapbook', attachment to unpublished letter to John Barnie, 16 November 1981: JB.
10 Unpublished letter to John Barnie, 27 January 1982: JB.
11 Interview with Alan Gould, Sydney, 9 September 1997.
12 Les Murray's annotations (December 1998) to an earlier draft of this book: PA.
13 As Les Murray told the interviewer, 'Desert Island Discs', BBC Radio, 1998.
14 Les Murray, in BBC interview, 'Desert Island Discs', 1998.
15 Unpublished postcard, Les Murray to Geoff Page, 22 December 1993, Page Collection, G258: ADFA.

16 Email, Angela Smith to the writer, 3 March 1998: PA.
17 Unpublished postcard to Philip Hodgins, 9 April 1992, Hodgins Collection, G13, Box 4, Wallet 23: ADFA.
18 *Times Literary Supplement*, 13 February 1981, p. 162.
19 Les Murray's pocket diary for 1981, Murray Collection, MS5332, Box 12, File 86: NLA.
20 Les Murray's annotations (December 1998) to an earlier draft of this book: PA.
21 Les Murray's pocket diary, 30 March 1981, Murray Collection, MS5332, Box 12, File 86: NLA.
22 Les Murray, 'Three Talks', *Australian Literary Studies*, vol. 11(3), May 1984, pp. 322–3.
23 Les Murray's pocket diary, 17 February 1981, Murray Collection, MS5332, Box 12, File 86: NLA.
24 'More than an Obiter Dichter', written in 1998, and to be collected in *Conscious and Verbal*.
25 I am grateful to Dr Sonya Mycak of the University of New South Wales, who supplied me with information on Dennis Lee that I would otherwise have missed.
26 A copy of the Dedication Address was kindly supplied to me by Angela Smith: AS.
27 As soon as he had finished it he sent it to the *Times Literary Supplement*, which published it on 19 June 1981, p. 705.
28 Unpublished letter, Les Murray to John Barnie, 18 May 1984: JB.
29 Les Murray's pocket diary for 1981, Murray Collection, MS5332, Box 12, File 86: NLA. He would publish 'The Steel' in *Meanjin*, vol. 41(1), April 1982, pp. 107–11.
30 Unpublished letter, Les Murray to John Barnie, 7 June 1981: JB.
31 Unpublished letter, Les Murray to John Barnie, 6 August 1981: JB.
32 Unpublished letter, Les Murray to John Barnie, 27 September 1984: JB.
33 Published in Copenhagen in 1982.
34 Interview with Bruce Clunies Ross, Armidale, 29 September 1997.
35 Unpublished letter, Les Murray to John Barnie, 27 September 1984: JB.
36 Interview with Bruce Clunies Ross, Armidale, 29 September 1997.
37 Interview with Bruce Clunies Ross, Armidale, 29 September 1997.
38 Interview with Bruce Clunies Ross, Armidale, 29 September 1997.
39 Les Murray's pocket diary for 1981, Murray Collection, MS5332, Box 12, File 86: NLA.
40 Unpublished letter, Les Murray to John Barnie, 6 August 1981: JB.
41 Unpublished postcard, Les Murray to Anurag Sharma, 27 May 1993: ASh.
42 Les Murray's annotations (December 1998) to an earlier draft of this book: PA.
43 Les Murray's annotations (December 1998) to an earlier draft of this book: PA.
44 Telephone interview with Les Murray, Bunyah, 3 February 1999.
45 Interview with Les Murray, Sydney, 9 September 1997.
46 Interview with Les Murray, 23 September 1997.
47 Interview with Les Murray, Sydney, 9 September 1997.
48 Unpublished letter, Les Murray to Mark O'Connor, 27 September 1977; O'Connor Collection, Box 1, File 1: NLA.
49 Interview with Les Murray, Sydney, 9 September 1997.
50 Unpublished postcard, Les Murray to Chris Wallace-Crabbe: CW-C.
51 SBS television report, 3 November 1998.
52 Interview with Christina Murray, Sydney, 11 July 1997.
53 'The Wedding at Berrico' (written for Christina and James), first collected in *Translations From the Natural World*.

54 Interview with Mark O'Connor, Canberra, 3 July 1997.
55 Unpublished letter, Les Murray to John Barnie, 13 April 1983: JB.
56 Interview with Alan Gould, Sydney, 9 September 1997.
57 Published as *Poetry in Pictures: The Great Barrier Reef*, with photographs by Neville Coleman: Sydney, Hale & Iremonger, 1985.
58 Interview with Alan Gould, Sydney, 9 September 1997.
59 Interview with Alan Gould, Sydney, 9 September 1997.
60 Interview with Alan Gould, Sydney, 9 September 1997.
61 One of Byrne's sons, who repeatedly got into fights, inspired the image of 'the man with beer-glass-cut arms' in Les Murray's poem 'Blowfly Grass': interview with Mick Byrne, Sydney, 15 July 1997.
62 Interview with Jamie Grant, Sydney, 18 April 1995.
63 Unpublished letter, Les Murray to Geoff Page, 16 September 1975, Page Collection, G258, Box 7, Wallet 50: ADFA.
64 Gray did the same to me when I made elaborate arrangements to interview him. On a second visit I found him in, but afterwards discovered that my tape of the interview was blank: it seemed entirely appropriate.
65 Interview with Les Murray, Bunyah, 18 August 1997.
66 Laverty's mother was a Nathan, one of the direct descendants of Isaac Nathan, friend of Byron and musician in the early days of the colony of New South Wales. The Mackerrasses and Nathans had intermarried.
67 Interview with Piers Laverty, Sydney, 20 July 1997.
68 Interview with Piers Laverty, Sydney, 20 July 1997.
69 Laverty's stone-crushing machine, for making glazes, fascinated Les Murray and would appear in the poem 'Blowfly Grass', written in January 1996.
70 Unpublished letter, Les Murray to John Barnie, 13 January 1984: JB.
71 Unpublished letter, Mohammad Tavallaie to Les Murray, 1 August 1993: MT.
72 Unpublished letter, Les Murray to the author, 25 November 1991: PA.
73 Unpublished postcard, Les Murray to Anurag Sharma, 1 January 1993: ASh
74 Unpublished letter, Les Murray to Anurag Sharma, 17 December 1991: ASh.
75 Unpublished letter, Les Murray to Anurag Sharma, 26 August 1991: ASh.
76 Unpublished letter, Les Murray to Philip Hodgins, 13 July 1990, Hodgins Collection, G13, Box 4, Wallet 23: ADFA.
77 Unpublished letter, Christopher Koch to Les Murray, 8 December 1978, Murray Collection, MS5332, Box 10, File 70: NLA.
78 Interview with Les Murray, Sydney, 23 September 1997.
79 Unpublished postcard, Les Murray to Peter Goldsworthy, 20 March 1986, Goldsworthy Collection, G39: ADFA.
80 It was published in *Nation Review* in March 1976.
81 Unpublished reader's report for Angus & Robertson, 6 January 1989, Tom Thompson Collection G9: ADFA.
82 Telephone interview with Les Murray, Bunyah, 3 February 1999.
83 Hart in 'Saturday Extra', *Age*, 17 October 1992, p. 9.
84 Telephone interview with Les Murray, Bunyah, 3 February 1999.

The poet at work, 1994. He has a particular fondness for composing with black Pentel pens.

Murray in Sydney in 1994 in characteristic pose wearing one of his baseball caps. *(Photograph: Graeme McCarter)*

In Mildura, March 1995, for the annual Arts Festival, Murray's favourite and one he tried never to miss. In the foreground, left to right, Robert Gray and Paul Kane; Murray is in the centre of the group behind; on its far right is the poet Philip Hodgins.

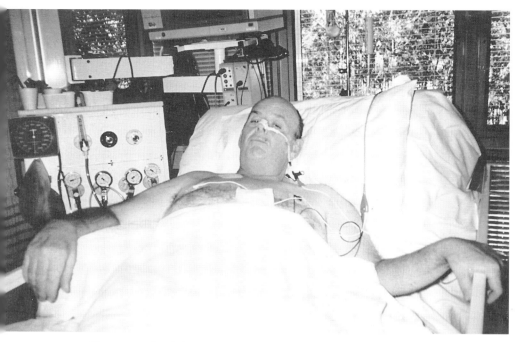

'Conscious and verbal': Murray recovering in the Intensive Care Unit of the John Hunter Hospital, Newcastle, 10 August 1996. (*Photograph: Valerie Murray*)

Bob Ellis, Les Murray and the Labor politician Kim Beazley, Canberra, April 1998, during the making of Ellis's film on Murray, *Bastards from the Bush*.

Peter Porter at the Maryborough Railway Station in 1995, on his way to visit Philip Hodgins shortly before the latter's death. (*Photograph: Peter Rose*)

16 Anguish & Robbery, 1978–92

1. Interview with Penny Nelson, Sydney, 3 April 1995.
2. Interview with Les Murray, Sydney, 7 October 1997.
3. Interview with Les Murray, Sydney, 7 October 1997.
4. Interview with Les Murray, Sydney, 7 October 1997.
5. Les Murray's contract with Angus & Robertson: TT.
6. Interview with Margaret Connolly, Sydney, 18 April 1995.
7. Interview with Margaret Connolly, Sydney, 18 April 1995.
8. Interview with Tom Thompson, Sydney, 6 November 1997.
9. I have suppressed names in these reports at Les Murray's request: his annotations (December 1998) to an earlier draft of this book: PA.
10. In the Tom Thompson Collection, G9: ADFA.
11. In the Tom Thompson Collection, G9: ADFA.
12. In the Tom Thompson Collection, G9: ADFA.
13. In the Tom Thompson Collection, G9: ADFA.
14. In the Tom Thompson Collection, G9: ADFA.
15. Reader's report for Angus & Robertson, 13 October 1989, in the Tom Thompson Collection, G9: ADFA.
16. In the Tom Thompson Collection, G9: ADFA.
17. Reader's report for Angus & Robertson, undated [1987]: TT.
18. Reader's report for Angus & Robertson, 8 March 1991, in the Tom Thompson Collection, G9: ADFA.
19. As Jamie Grant, who briefly ran Isabella Press with him, discovered: interview with Grant, Sydney, 18 April 1995.
20. Name suppressed at Les Murray's suggestion: his annotations (December 1998) to an earlier draft of this book: PA.
21. Interview with Les Murray, Sydney, 7 October 1997.
22. Les Murray's annotations to (December 1998) an earlier draft of this book: PA.
23. Lansdown became a good friend of Les Murray's, who called him 'my devout Baptist mate from Perth', and wrote for him 'The Verb Agreement'.
24. Interview with Les Murray, Sydney, 7 October 1997.
25. Unpublished postcard, Les Murray to Chris Wallace-Crabbe, 28 August 1986: CW-C. Les Murray did later produce a second limerick, extemporised at the wheel while driving with Alan Gould in the Murray valley: 'The spatchcock we ate in Echuca/Dived on my innards like a Stuka/Producing such masses/Of volatile gases/That my arse became a bazooka'. Interview with Les Murray, Sydney, 16 December 1998.
26. Interview with Tom Thompson, Sydney, 6 November 1997.
27. Interview with Les Murray, Sydney, 7 October 1997. Walsh's memory is that he usually, though not always, suppressed Les Murray's name in passing on his opinions: telephone interview with Richard Walsh, Sydney, 4 February 1999.
28. Interview with Tom Thompson, Sydney, 6 November 1997.
29. This contract is dated 3 May 1990, and had been hastily secured for him by Margaret Connolly, acting as Les Murray's agent: TT.
30. Unpublished letter, Tom Thompson to Ken [Bolton], 1 December 1989: KB.

31 Unpublished letter, Ken Bolton to the author, 19 October 1997: PA. Bolton asserted he was specifically told that Murray had criticised his work as 'unChristian', a detail that Tom Thompson did not recall in my interview with him, Sydney, 6 November 1997.
32 Les Murray's annotations (December 1998) to an earlier draft of this book: PA.
33 Unpublished letter, Ken Bolton to Lisa Highton, 28 June 1990: KB.
34 Notably in *Heat*, no. 5, 1997, pp. 184–95. The poem was entitled 'Untimely Meditations'. In an unpublished letter, Ken Bolton to the author, 19 October 1997, he added that he had written his attacks on Les Murray 'I hope to his annoyance'.
35 Les Murray's annotations (December 1998) to an earlier draft of this book: PA.
36 Interview with Tom Thompson, Sydney, 6 November 1997.
37 Unpublished memorandum, Thompson to Ken Bolton, 2 July 1990: TT.
38 Interview with Tom Thompson, Sydney, 6 November 1997.
39 Unpublished letter, Sue Phillips to Lisa Highton, 21 June 1990: TT.
40 Interview with Jamie Grant, Sydney, 18 April 1995.
41 Unpublished memorandum, Thompson to Ken Bolton, 2 July 1990: TT.
42 Interview with Les Murray, Sydney, 7 October 1997.
43 Editor Nikki Christer's unpublished memorandum to Lisa Highton, 15 March 1991, makes it clear that she was in touch with Tranter: TT.
44 Unpublished memorandum, Thompson to Ken Bolton, 6 August 1990: TT. Also unpublished letter, Tom Thompson to Ken Bolton, 1 December 1989: KB.
45 Unpublished memorandum, Nikki Christer to Lisa Highton, 15 March 1991: TT.
46 Unpublished letter, Les Murray to the author, 31 May 1983: PA.
47 Les Murray, on sheet also bearing unpublished reader's report on Alan Gould's *Momentum*, 10 June 1991: TT.
48 Unattributed, undated press clipping: TT.
49 Unpublished postcard, Les Murray to Philip Hodgins, 14 November 1990, Hodgins Collection, G13, Box 4, Wallet 23: ADFA.
50 This is the defectors' list published by John Foulcher in *Island Magazine*, vol. 55, 1992, pp. 69–72.
51 'Dazzling Work from a Poet in Full Flight', *Weekend Australian Magazine*, 5–6 November 1983, p. 19.
52 In Bennett and Strauss (eds), *The Oxford Literary History of Australia*, p. 277.
53 Interview with Jamie Grant, Sydney, 18 April 1995.
54 Interview with Jamie Grant, Sydney, 18 April 1995.
55 Letter of resignation, Tom Thompson to Angus & Robertson, complaining of pressure from Lisa Highton; the accompanying papers record Highton's concern 'that I [Tom Thompson] would be unable to bring in the books required of a developing and growing list because of "bad publicity", which had led to certain un-named people to be [sic] reluctant to work with me': TT.
56 Unpublished letter, Les Murray to Philip Hodgins, 22 August 1993, Hodgins Collection, G13, Box 4, Wallet 23: ADFA.
57 Interview with Michael Duffy, Sydney, 8 September 1998.

17 Stealing the Funeral, 1979–81

1 Unpublished letter, Les Murray to Peter Goldsworthy, 1 June 1980, Goldsworthy Collection, G39, Box 2, Wallet 13: ADFA.

2   Wearne's *The Nightmarkets* would be published in 1986, Scott's *St Clair: Three Narratives* in 1986, and Porter's *Akhenaten* in 1992. Other long verse-novels to follow Les Murray's include David Budbill's *Judevine* (1991), Mark Jarman's *Iris* (1992), Charlotte Mandel's *The Marriage of Jacob* (1991) and Frederick Pollack's *The Adventure* (1986). There is an excellent essay by Thomas Disch, 'Onegin's Children: Poems in the Form of a Novel', in *Parnassus: Poetry Review*, vol. 17(2), and vol. 18(1), 1992–93, pp. 166–85.
3   Unpublished letter to Angela Smith, no date [1983?]: AS.
4   Unpublished letter, Christopher Koch to Les Murray, 26 December 1978, Murray Collection, MS5332, Box 10, Folder 70: NLA
5   These were his experiences during his Writer in Residenceship at the University of New South Wales in April and May 1983.
6   Information from Dr Peter Kuch, University of New South Wales, to whom I am grateful.
7   Exceptions included Geoff Page in the *National Times*, 4–10 May 1980, p. 45, Christopher Koch in *Quadrant*, vol. 24, September 1980, pp. 40–2, Gary Catalano in *Meanjin*, vol. 39(3), October 1980, pp. 351–5, John Barnie in *Kunapipi*, vol. 4(1), 1982, pp. 172–8.
8   Forbes in *New Poetry*, vol. 28(1), May 1980, pp. 60–3.
9   *Sydney Morning Herald*, 15 March 1980, p. 14.
10 Admittedly overseas publication came nearly a decade later, but in Australia Les Murray was no less controversial a figure by then. Laudatory British reviews included those of Neil Corcoran in the *London Review of Books*, 25 January 1990, p. 15, Mick Imlah in *Times Literary Supplement*, 18 May 1990, p. 521, John Saunders in *Strand*, vol. 33(4), Autumn 1992, pp. 94–5; those in the USA included Manly Johnson in *World Literature Today*, vol. 65(1), 1991, pp. 185–6, and an anonymous reviewer in *Publishers Weekly*, 16 August 1991, p. 49, and Michael Heyward in *Book World*, vol. 22, 16 February 1992, p. 11.
11 In the Seedwillow Production film *The Bastards from the Bush*, screened on ABC television, 1 September 1998.
12 Griffiths in telephone interview from Perth, 2 October 1998.
13 Unpublished letter, Les Murray to Penny Nelson, 15 July 1983: PN.
14 Interview with Geoffrey Lehmann, Sydney, 5 September 1998.
15 Interview with Les Murray, Sydney, 18 August 1997.
16 Les Murray's annotations (December 1998) to an earlier draft of this book: PA.
17 Conversation with Gail Pearson, Sydney, 3 February 1999.
18 Interview with Les Murray, 18 November 1997.
19 Telephone interview with Geoffrey Lehmann, Sydney, 4 February 1999.
20 Unpublished letter, Les Murray to Peter Goldsworthy, 1 June 1980, Goldsworthy Collection, G39, Box 2, Wallet 13: ADFA.
21 Les Murray's annotations (December 1998) to an earlier draft of this book: PA. John Sprott Ryan, *The Land of Ulitarra: Early Records of the Aborigines of the Mid-North Coast of New South Wales*.
22 Stephen Morelli's book is *Gumbaynggirr Dreaming, vol. 1, Stories of Uncle Harry Buchanan* translated by the Gumbaynggirr Language and Culture Group, and published by the same Group, in 1988. It contains the original language text and then word by word translation, and also a sense translation. 'In the following two hero ancestors are referred to: Yuludarra who is called Babaga, the Father, and in English "the Lord", and Birrugan who is called Jesus when Harry Buchanan talks about him in English.' *Gumbaynggirr Dreaming*, p. 9.
23 Letter, Judith Wright McKinney to Les Murray, 16 June 1980, Murray Collection, MS5332, Box 10, File 71: NLA.

24 Letter, Judith Wright McKinney to Les Murray, 16 June 1980, Murray Collection, MS5332, Box 10, File 71: NLA.
25 Murray made his recommendation to Whitlam through Dick Hall, Whitlam's private secretary in early 1973: Whitlam seriously considered Wright before instead choosing John Kerr. He should have taken Les Murray's advice. Les Murray tells the story in 'This is Your Sovereign Speaking', *Independent Monthly*, 20 June 1993, p. 20.
26 And still do: at the University of New South Wales in 1998 I was blocked from offering a subject examining representations of Aboriginals in Australian literature, on the grounds that such a subject should be taught by an Aboriginal.
27 Letter, Les Murray to Judith Wright McKinney, 21 July 1980, Murray Collection, MS5332, Box 10, File 71: NLA.
28 Letter, Judith Wright McKinney to Les Murray, 7 August 1980, Murray Collection, MS5332, Box 10, File 71: NLA.
29 Letter, Les Murray to Judith Wright McKinney, 24 September 1980, Murray Collection, MS5332, Box 10, File 71: NLA.
30 Letter, Les Murray to Judith Wright McKinney, 24 September 1980, Murray Collection, MS5332, Box 10, File 71: NLA.
31 Letter, Les Murray to Judith Wright McKinney, 13 January 1981, Murray Collection, MS5332, Box 10, File 71: NLA.
32 Letter, Les Murray to Judith Wright McKinney, 13 January 1981, Murray Collection, MS5332, Box 10, File 71: NLA.
33 Interview with Les Murray, Bunyah, 28 August 1996. On Christmas Day 1995 he had three of his Aboriginal relations at his dinner table: unpublished letter, Les Murray to Angela Smith, 22 March 1996: AS.
34 Unpublished letter, Les Murray to Angela Smith, 17 August 1981: AS.

18 Autism and Isolation, 1981–87

1 Unpublished letter, Les Murray to Angela Smith, 29 September 1981: AS.
2 Unpublished letter, Les Murray to Angela Smith, 29 September 1981: AS.
3 Les Murray's annotations (December 1998) to an early draft of this book: PA.
4 Unpublished letter, Les Murray to John Barnie, 27 January 1982: JB.
5 At least one other artist would do the same: the South African writer Stephen Gray, who met Murray in Sydney in 1982, was fascinated to hear his account of Alexander's condition, and he later met the boy when Gray visited the Murrays. Alexander became the inspiration of Gray's novel *War Child* (Johannesburg: Justified Press, 1991). I am indebted to the playwright Anthony Akerman of Johannesburg for this information.
6 Unpublished letter, Les Murray to John Barnie, 16 November 1981: JB.
7 Unpublished letter, Les Murray to John Barnie, 14 February 1986: JB.
8 Valerie Murray's diary for 2 August 1982: VM.
9 Unpublished postcard, Les Murray to John Barnie, undated [1990?]: JB.
10 Unpublished postcard, Les Murray to John Barnie, 14 February 1989: JB, and unpublished letter, Les Murray to Geoff Page, 25 February 1989, Page Collection G258, Box 7, Wallet 51: ADFA.
11 Interview with Ann Barden, San Francisco, 27 January 1998.

NOTES (CHAPTER 18) 335

12   Unpublished letter, Les Murray to John Barnie, 9 November 1990: JB
13   Unpublished postcard, Les Murray to John Barnie, 16 November 1981: JB.
14   Unpublished letter, Les Murray to John Barnie, 12 May 1986: JB.
15   Unpublished letter, Les Murray to the author, 18 August 1998: PA.
16   Unpublished postcard, Les Murray to Christine Alexander, 18 March 1986: CA.
17   'Extract from a Verse Letter to Dennis Haskell', first collected in *The Daylight Moon*.
18   Eric Rolls's *A Million Wild Acres* (Melbourne: Nelson, 1981), piles up evidence to this effect, drawing many of its examples from Les Murray's own country, and Les Murray himself added to the evidence in his 'Eric Rolls and the Golden Disobedience', in *The Paperbark Tree*, pp. 163ff.
19   Valerie Murray's Journal, entry for 26 June 1992: VM.
20   Unpublished letter, Les Murray to Angela Smith, 24 April 1986: AS.
21   Unpublished letter, Les Murray to John Barnie, 12 May 1986: JB.
22   'I tried A&R as a distributer to UK bookshops & that failed & I did publ. Vernac. Rep. with Canongate in Edinburgh, but it was ignored.' Les Murray's annotations (December 1998) to an earlier draft of this book: PA.
23   Michael Schmidt set up the magazine *PN Review* in Oxford in the 1960s, then moved it to Manchester, establishing there his Carcanet Press, which published poetry and the more demanding sorts of fiction. Himself an author of poems and novels, he taught at the University of Manchester.
24   Walcott in the *New Republic*, 6 February 1989, pp. 25–8.
25   Scupham in *Poetry Review*, vol. 128(1), 1988, p. 8.
26   Stead in *London Review of Books*, vol. 10(4), 18 February 1988, pp. 11–12.
27   Unpublished postcard, Les Murray to John Barnie, 11 December 1987: JB.
28   Unpublished letter, Les Murray to John Barnie, 18 May 1984: JB.
29   Les Murray uses this term to mean 'extremely Australian in tone and consciously super-elegant'.
30   Unpublished letter, Les Murray to John Barnie, 27 September 1984: JB.
31   Unpublished letter, Les Murray to Peter Goldsworthy, 11 May 1987, Goldsworthy Collection, G39: ADFA.
32   Unpublished letter, Les Murray to Angela Smith, 15 December 1984: AS.
33   Chris Wallace-Crabbe in *Australian Book Review*, December/January 1986/87, pp. 12–13. There is broad agreement with his view from Mark Thomas in the *Canberra Times*, 22 February 1986, p. B2.
34   Smith in 'Les Murray's Year', *Quadrant*, vol. 30, April 1986, pp. 83–4.
35   Porter in 'The Map of the Murray', *Scripsi*, vol. 4(2), 1986, pp. 12–18.
36   Buckley in *Age*, 'Saturday Extra', 24 May 1986, p. 14.
37   Rowbotham in the Brisbane *Courier-Mail*, 22 February 1986, p. 6.
38   Unpublished letter, Les Murray, to Ruth Sparrow, 20 March 1987: RS.
39   Les Murray, *Embodiment and Incarnation: Notes on Preparing an Anthology of Religious Verse*, Aquinas Library, Brisbane, Queensland, p. 9.
40   Unpublished postcard, Les Murray to Philip Salom, 22 May 1985, Salom Collection, G150, Box 1, Folder 4: ADFA.
41   Wallace-Crabbe in *Australian Book Review*, December/January 1986/87, pp. 12–13.
42   Unrecorded telephone interview with Chris Wallace-Crabbe, 11 December 1998.
43   In later years he would be sceptical when his cousin Ray Murray, the Free Presbyterian minister, told him that St Paul had written that we are God's poems.

'Never!' snorted Murray: 'I've read the New Testament and that's not in there'. 'Alas', said Ray Murray, 'You read it in English'. In the original Greek, 'creations' are *poemata*, from *poein* to create or make. 'I am grateful to your reverence for this', said Les Murray sincerely. Unpublished letter, Les Murray to the author, 20 December 1998: PA.
44 Les Murray's choice of the best writing of 1993, in *Times Literary Supplement*, 3 December 1993, p. 11.
45 Les Murray wrote 'Oasis City' about the Mildura Literary Festival.
46 Interview with Robert Gray, Sydney, 11 August 1997.
47 Interview with Robert Gray, Sydney, 11 August 1997.
48 Interview with Bob Ellis, 13 July 1997.
49 'Hearing Loss'.
50 Unpublished postcard, Les Murray to Peter Goldsworthy, 4 August 1994: PG.
51 Interview with Jamie Grant, Sydney, 18 April 1995.
52 Unpublished postcard, Les Murray to Geoff Page, 8 February 1987, Page Collection, G258, Box 7, Wallet 51: ADFA.
53 Interview with Les Murray, Bunyah, 28 August 1996.
54 Les Murray, *Killing the Black Dog*, p. 2.

19 The Power of the Dog, 1987–89

1   *London Review of Books*, 29 October 1987. Les Murray published the same poem under the title 'The Liberated Plague' in *Overland*, no. 109, December 1987, p. 19.
2   *London Review of Books*, 10 December 1987, p. 4.
3   *London Review of Books*, 7 January 1988, p. 4.
4   Unpublished postcard to John Barnie, 20 January 1988: JB.
5   John Fletcher in the *London Review of Books*, 4 February 1988, p. 4. Les Murray replied to Fletcher in *London Review of Books*, 18 February 1988, p. 4; Fletcher responded, *London Review of Books*, 31 March 1988, pp. 4–5.
6   *London Review of Books*, 4 February 1988, p. 4.
7   Les Murray, *Killing the Black Dog*, p. 3.
8   Valerie Murray's diary, 5 February 1990: VM.
9   Unpublished letter to John Barnie, 5 June 1990: JB.
10 Interview with Les Murray, Sydney, 9 September 1997.
11 In the Seedwillow Production film *The Bastards from the Bush*, screened on ABC television, 1 September 1998.
12 Interview with Peter and Anne Barden, San Francisco, 27 January 1998.
13 Unpublished letter, Les Murray to John Barnie, 5 March 1993: JB.
14 Interview with Valerie Murray, Bunyah, 8 October 1996.
15 Unpublished letter, Les Murray to Philip Hodgins, 11 January 1988: Hodgins Collection, G13, Box 4, File 23: ADFA.
16 Unpublished letter, Les Murray to the author, 3 August 1988: PA.
17 'The Suspect Captivity of the Fisher King', the version sent by Les Murray to the author on 19 August 1998: PA.
18 Unpublished card, Les Murray to John Barnie, 16 November 1988: JB.

19 *Killing the Black Dog*, p. 8.
20 Interview with Les Murray, Sydney, 19 December 1994.
21 *Killing the Black Dog*, p. 7.
22 Interview with Christina Murray, Sydney, 11 July 1997.
23 *Killing the Black Dog*, p. 14.
24 Unpublished letter, Les Murray to Philip Hodgins, 15 December 1989, Hodgins Collection, Box 4, Wallet 23: ADFA.
25 Interview with Jamie Grant, Sydney, 18 April 1995.
26 *Killing the Black Dog*, p. 10.
27 Interview with Geoffrey Lehmann, Sydney, 5 September 1998.
28 Unpublished postcard, Les Murray to the author, 19 December 1989: PA.

20 Fighting the Black Dog, 1989–92

1 The other was Tom Shapcott.
2 Unpublished letter, Les Murray to Penny Nelson, 1 February 1989: PN.
3 Paul Keating was chosen by Prime Minister Bob Hawke to be federal Treasurer in 1983. He became a stellar performer, making his mark with a blend of earthy attacks on his opponents and high-level explanations and lectures on the more arcane aspects of economics. On Hawke's party room defeat in 1991, Keating, his designated successor, at forty-seven became the youngest prime minister in Australia's history.
4 Unpublished postcard, Les Murray to the author, 13 September 1989: PA.
5 Valerie Murray's Journal, entry for 5 February 1990: VM.
6 Interview with Valerie Murray, Bunyah, 9 October 1998: 'He's been up to 25 stone, at his worst in the late 1980s'.
7 Unpublished letter, Les Murray to Anurag Sharma, 26 September 1994: ASh.
8 Interview with Mark O'Connor, Canberra, 3 July 1997.
9 Unpublished postcard, Les Murray to Philip Hodgins, 20 February 1990, Hodgins Collection, G13, Box 4, Wallet 23: ADFA.
10 Interview with Les Murray, Sydney, 4 August 1997.
11 *Fredy Neptune*, 'The Middle Sea'.
12 Unpublished postcard, Les Murray to Peter Goldsworthy, 29 July 1992: PG.
13 Unpublished postcard, Les Murray to Philip Hodgins, 30 March 1990, Hodgins Collection, G13, Box 4, Wallet 23: ADFA.
14 Unrecorded conversation with Les Murray, Sydney, 17 December 1998.
15 Unpublished letter to John Barnie, 27 September 1990: JB.
16 Unpublished letter to John Barnie, 27 September 1990: JB.
17 Unrecorded telephone conversation with Les Murray, Bunyah, 23 November 1998.
18 Unpublished postcard, Les Murray to Peter Goldsworthy, 31 March 1990: PG.
19 Unpublished postcard, Les Murray to Philip Hodgins, 20 February 1990, Hodgins Collection, Box 4, Wallet 23: ADFA.
20 Unpublished letter, Tranter to Les Murray, 20 October 1990: copy JT.
21 Unpublished postcard, Les Murray to Philip Hodgins, 18 January 1991, Hodgins Collection, G13, Box 4, Wallet 23: ADFA.
22 Unpublished postcard to John Barnie, 5 September 1992: JB.

23 Unpublished letter, Les Murray to Penny Nelson, 23 February 1991: PN.
24 Unpublished letter, Les Murray to Angela Smith, 19 July 1990: AS.
25 Hart, *Overland*, no. 122, 1991, pp. 69–71.
26 Rowe, *Southerly*, vol. 51(2), June 1991, pp. 319–30.
27 Pollnitz, *Age*, 'Saturday Extra', 13 July 1991, p. 8.
28 Unpublished postcard, Les Murray to Penny Nelson, 14 April 1991: PN.
29 Unpublished postcard, Les Murray to Penny Nelson, 14 April 1991: PN.
30 Glyn Maxwell's review, *Poetry Review*, vol. 81, 1992, pp. 26–7.
31 'Books Briefly Noted', *New Yorker*, vol. 69, 24 May 1993, p. 105.
32 Murray came across them in the Swiss-based magazine *2 plus 2*, 1985, though they were originally printed in H. V. Morton's *In Search of Wales* (Methuen, 1932): unpublished letter, Les Murray to John Barnie, 11 September 1985: JB.
33 Interview with Les Murray, Sydney, 2 September 1997.
34 Unpublished letter, Les Murray to Angela Smith, 19 July 1990: AS.
35 'A Dog's Elegy', written in 1998 and to be collected in *Conscious and Verbal*.
36 'The Octave of Elephants'.
37 'Mollusc'.
38 Foulcher, *Island Magazine*, vol. 55, 1992, pp. 69–72.
39 Foulcher, *Island Magazine*, vol. 55, 1992, pp. 69–72.
40 In Bennett and Strauss (eds), *The Oxford Literary History of Australia*, p. 281.
41 Unpublished letter, Les Murray to Greg O'Hara, 28 November 1962: GO'H.
42 Unpublished letter, Les Murray to John Barnie, 18 July 1992: JB.
43 The poem was written in late April, 1996, and first read to a large audience in New York on 9 May 1996. Reading it to a Sydney audience on 19 July 1998, he explained: 'Now this one is based on an Aboriginal legend from up our way. When the Southern Cross was a man he was a great hero, he went about doing good, being kind to people, so he got into a lot of trouble. He was a great warrior too and his enemies planned to destroy him and they were losing badly. But then they remembered that there was one vulnerable spot on him, there [points to base of his own neck above left collar-bone]. If they got two spears into him there he would die. They achieved this. And to bring him back from the dead took the consent of both of his wives, they both had to call him back from the dead. And this poem is based on the moment when the elder wife calls him back from the dead, and the younger one still has to be persuaded, she's not absolutely sure she wants him back from the dead. So they're arguing about it.'
44 Les Murray first published the poem in the *Weekend Australian*, 8–9 August 1992, p. 6.

21 Becoming a Name, 1992–94

1 Les Murray, who saw a draft of Bourke's volume, thought it accurate but dull, and never read the published version.
2 Unpublished postcard, Les Murray to Chris Wallace-Crabbe, 16 November 1994: CW-C.
3 Telephone interview with Chris Pollnitz, Newcastle, 17 February 1993.
4 Unpublished letter, Les Murray to John Foulcher, 5 March 1993, Foulcher Collection, G281, Box 5, Folder 20: ADFA.

5   Telephone interview with Chris Pollnitz, Newcastle, 17 February 1993. According to Pollnitz, the publisher, Oxford University Press, decided to drop the book on the dual grounds that it was offensive to Les Murray, and that the likely market for it had dwindled.
6   Unpublished postcard, Les Murray to Chris Wallace-Crabbe, 8 February 1995: CW-C.
7   Unpublished postcard, Les Murray to Penny Nelson, 15 June 1992: PN.
8   Les Murray's annotations (December 1998) to an earlier draft of this book: PA.
9   It was based on Patricia Wrightson's 1968 novel of the same name.
10 Unpublished letter, Les Murray to Penny Nelson, 24 March 1992: PN.
11 The film was made in 1992: The Ellis character is called Kenneth Elkin, played by Noah Taylor; McAlister is played by Jack Campbell.
12 Unpublished letter, Les Murray to John Barnie, 20 August 1992: JB.
13 Bell's palsy is the most common lesion of the facial nerve. An abrupt weakness of all the facial muscles on one side, it is often accompanied by pain around the ear, unusual loudness of sounds heard in the ear on the same side, and loss of taste on the front of the tongue. Many patients believe that they have had a stroke, a conclusion corrected when it is seen that they cannot close the eye on the affected side.
14 The palsy would recur in 1999, on the left side this time, and caused by an ear infection. Telephone conversation with Les Murray, Bunyah, 9 February 1999.
15 'The Wedding at Berrico', first collected in *Translations From the Natural World*.
16 Les Murray's annotations (December 1998) to an earlier draft of this book: PA.
17 Unpublished postcard, Les Murray to John Barnie, 20 September 1993: JB.
18 Unpublished postcard, Les Murray to John Barnie, 13 November 1993: JB.
19 Interview with Daniel Murray, Sydney, 9 August 1997.
20 Interview with Clare Murray, New York, 10 May 1996.
21 Unpublished postcard, Les Murray to Penny Nelson, 3 November 1992: PN.
22 Unrecorded telephone interview with Chris Wallace-Crabbe, 11 December 1998.
23 Interview with Peter and Ann Barden, San Francisco, 27 January 1998.
24 Interview with Les Murray, Bunyah, 18 August 1997.
25 Les Murray's reasoning was that 'Jesus had forbidden oaths to Christians, and they weren't binding on unbelievers, so that left only a smallish middle range of people who might feel bound by them'. 'This is your Sovereign Speaking', *Independent Monthly*, 20 June 1993, p. 20.
26 'More coffee Senator? Now about this oath . . .', *Manning River Times*, 23 December 1992, p. 1.
27 Australian Broadcasting Corporation television news report, 22 March 1999.
28 *Age*, 6 January 1993, p. 11.
29 *Age*, 6 January 1993, p. 11.
30 Costigan's letter was published in the *Australian*, 20 January 1993, under the heading 'Literature Board Above Politics'. Rodney Hall's article appeared in the *Canberra Times*, 24 January 1993; Murray replied to it on 31 January 1993 in the same paper, p. 22.
31 Tom Thompson in letter sent to the *Age* and the *Sydney Morning Herald*, 18 February 1993: TT. In a subsequent letter, sent to the *Age* on 24 February 1993, he characterised Les Murray's arguments as 'the lowing of disgruntled cows at dusk. Ah, but is it poetry?': TT. Murray, replying, rebutted his arguments, and riposted smoothly, 'Not one of Tom's major efforts, like losing practically all of Angus & Robertson's famous poetry list to Heinemann'. Les Murray's letter in the *Age*, 5 March 1993, p. 12.

32 Peter Craven, *Times Literary Supplement*, 20 August 1993.
33 Les Murray, *Times Literary Supplement*, 10 September 1993.
34 Rodney Hall, *Canberra Times*, 24 January 1993.
35 Les Murray, *Canberra Times*, 31 January 1993, p. 22.
36 This is the figure given by Peter Ryan in the *Age*, 20 February 1993, p. 18.
37 Les Murray (and others such as Mark O'Connor) firmly believed that the phrase was routinely used about him by members of the Literature Board, but other well-placed informants such as Susan Lever deny this, and I have found no written evidence to support his view. Les Murray was not surprised: 'Would they have put that on paper?' he asked rhetorically. Les Murray's annotations (December 1998) to an earlier draft of this book: PA.
38 Interview with Les Murray, Sydney, 7 October 1997.
39 Les Murray, letter to the Editor, *Sydney Morning Herald*, 22 July 1994, p. 12.
40 Les Murray's annotations (December 1998) to an earlier draft of this book: PA.
41 Unrecorded conversation with Valerie Murray, Bunyah, 1993.
42 Interview with Mark O'Connor, Canberra, 3 July 1997.
43 Les Murray published articles on it, in addition to those already noted, in the *Sydney Morning Herald*, 22 February 1993, p. 13; letter in the *Age*, 5 March 1993, p. 12.
44 Interview with Susan Lever (an assessor on the Writing Grants program from 1988), Armidale, 30 September 1997. 'You're also aware that there's such a pressure on you when you're reading his [O'Connor's] work that in a way, if you gave him a grant, you're succumbing to the pressure. He's created a negative position.'
45 Interview with Les Murray, Sydney, 7 October 1997. Sharah secured Literature Board funding in 1993 and 1995: *Index of Literature Board Grants 1973–1996*.
46 Interview with Les Murray, Sydney, 7 October 1997.
47 Unpublished postcard, Les Murray to John Barnie, 20 September 1993: JB.
48 Unpublished postcard, Les Murray to John Barnie, 7 November 1993: JB.
49 Publishing proposal sent to Penny Nelson with letter of 29 September 1993: PN.
50 Les Murray's annotations (December 1998) to an earlier draft of this book: PA.
51 His first article for the *Independent Monthly* was 'This is Your Sovereign Speaking', in June 1993, but the regular articles did not commence until October.
52 'Assault with a Deadly Metaphor', *Independent Monthly*, October 1993.
53 'A Modest Proposal', *Independent Monthly*, November 1993.
54 'Poetic Injustice', *Independent Monthly*, November 1994.
55 Unpublished letter, Les Murray to Angela Smith, 6 March 1994: AS.
56 'Pommy Bastard', in the *Economist*, 21 May 1994, p. 106.
57 *The Times*, 12 and 14 May 1994.
58 Unrecorded conversation with Les Murray, 1994.
59 *Fivefathers* was published by Carcanet Press in Manchester, 1994.
60 Les Murray, 'Poetry Finds a New Voice', *Independent Monthly*, September 1994, p. 78.
61 Les Murray, 'Poetry Finds a New Voice', *Independent Monthly*, September 1994, p. 78.

22 Killing the Black Dog, 1994–96

1 Medical details from Cecil Murray's Death Certificate, 7 February 1995: LM.

2   Transcript of interview with Dr Peter Braude, Physician in General Medicine, Manning Base Hospital, Taree, 12 July 1996: PA.
3   Les Murray's annotations (December 1998) to an earlier draft of this book: PA.
4   Unpublished letter, Les Murray to Angela Smith, 6 March 1994: AS.
5   Les Murray's annotations (December 1998) to an earlier draft of this book: PA.
6   Interview with Christina Murray, Sydney, 11 July 1997.
7   Conversation with Jennifer Strauss, Armidale, 29 September 1997.
8   Unpublished postcard, Les Murray to Philip Hodgins, 12 January 1995, Hodgins Collection, G13, Box 4, Wallet 23: ADFA. Brady and Zwicky, both Western Australian academics, had reviewed his writing in lengthy, thoughtful articles: Brady in 'What Will Suffice', *Helix* nos 21–2, 1985, pp. 112–20, and Zwicky in 'Language or Speech? A Colonial Dilemma', *Overland*, no. 98, 1985, pp. 42–6. Though these reviews were respectful and judicious, Les Murray in his vulnerable state was hurt by them.
9   As Bolton made clear to me: unpublished letter, Ken Bolton to the author, 19 October 1997: PA.
10 Published in *Heat*, no. 5, 1997, pp. 184ff.
11 John Tranter showed the same spirit in an unpublished poem, 'On the Nose', of which he kindly sent me a copy, comparing Murray's writing to the stench of a decomposing hippopotamus: JT. Les Murray's self-portrait, 'Dreambabwe', turns the image to better account.
12 Mead, *Australian Society*, August 1991, pp. 40–2.
13 Gould, *Canberra Times*, 28 September 1991, p. C8.
14 Published by Farrar, Straus & Giroux, 1991.
15 Judith Kitchen, *Georgia Review*, Spring 1992, pp. 150–66.
16 William Logan, *Poetry*, vol. 160(3), June 1992, pp. 162–6.
17 Bruce Clunies Ross, *Poetry Wales*, vol. 29, 1993, pp. 52–5.
18 William Scammell, *Spectator*, vol. 270, 23 January 1993, p. 38.
19 Giles Foden in *Times Literary Supplement*, 29 May 1992, p. 24.
20 Unpublished letter, Les Murray to Peter Goldsworthy, 21 November 1994: PG.
21 'Waking up on Tour', *Bulletin*, 10 January 1995, p. 89.
22 Unpublished letter, Les Murray to Peter Barden, 31 October 1994: PB.
23 Unpublished letter, Les Murray to Peter Barden, 31 October 1994: PB.
24 Unpublished letter, Les Murray to Peter Barden, 31 October 1994: PB.
25 Unpublished letter, Les Murray to Peter Goldsworthy, 21 November 1994: PG.
26 Unpublished card, Les Murray to John Barnie, 7 December 1994: JB.
27 Unpublished card, Les Murray to the author, 8 January 1995: PA.
28 'The Last Hellos', first collected in *Subhuman Redneck Poems*.
29 Unpublished card, Les Murray to Penny Nelson, 13 January 1995: PN.
30 Unpublished card, Les Murray to the author, 8 January 1995: PA.
31 Unpublished letter, Les Murray to Angela Smith, 3 March 1995: AS.
32 Unpublished letter, Les Murray to Bishop John Reid, 19 March 1995: New College Archives.
33 Les Murray's 'Chronology', supplied to the author: PA.
34 Unpublished letter, Les Murray to the author, 8 April 1995: PA.
35 First published in the *Bulletin*, 16 May 1995, p. 80.
36 The Petrarca Preis is funded by *Burda* magazine.
37 Unpublished letter, Valerie Murray to Angela Smith, 15 July 1995: AS.
38 Unpublished letter, Valerie Murray to Angela Smith, 15 July 1995: AS.

39 Unpublished postcard, Les Murray to Peter Barden, 23 July 1995: PB.
40 Les Murray's addition to Valerie Murray's unpublished letter to Angela Smith, 15 July 1995: AS.
41 Interview with Bruce Clunies Ross, Armidale, 29 September 1997.
42 Les Murray's addition to Valerie Murray's unpublished letter to Angela Smith, 15 July 1995: AS.
43 Transcript of interview with Dr Peter Braude, Physician in General Medicine, Manning Base Hospital, Taree, 12 July 1996: PA.
44 Valerie Murray's Journal for 1996: VM.
45 Valerie Murray's Journal for 1996: VM.
46 Valerie Murray's Journal for 1996: VM.
47 Valerie Murray's Journal for 1996: VM.
48 Interview, Les Murray, with Margaret Throsby, ABC Radio, 11 February 1997.
49 Transcript of interview with Dr Peter Saul, Senior Specialist in Intensive Care at John Hunter Hospital, Newcastle, 12 July 1996: PA.
50 Transcript of interview with Dr Peter Saul, Senior Specialist in Intensive Care at John Hunter Hospital, Newcastle, 12 July 1996: PA.
51 Valerie Murray's Journal for 1996: VM. The Catholic Chaplain, Fr Corrigan, hearing that his Anglican colleague had preceded him in administering the sacrament, said half-seriously to Valerie, 'This is the real thing, you know'.
52 Interview with Piers Laverty, Sydney, 20 July 1997.
53 Transcript of interview with Dr Jon Gani, Gastro-intestinal surgeon and Clinical Director of the Division of Surgery at John Hunter Hospital, Newcastle, 12 July 1996: PA.
54 Telephone interview with Les Murray, Bunyah, 26 November 1998.
55 For instance, the *Daily Telegraph*, 18 August 1996, which referred to Les Murray as 'Australia's best-known poet', and quoted Margaret Connolly as saying he would not have survived had he been a heavy drinker.
56 *Killing the Black Dog*, p. 23.
57 Unpublished letter, Les Murray to Angela Smith, undated (first page missing), [?mid-September 1996]: AS.
58 Unpublished postcard, Les Murray to Geoff Page, 1 October 1996, Page Collection, G258: ADFA.
59 The figures are given in 'Return of the Redneck', *Sydney Morning Herald*, 21 September 1996.
60 *Killing the Black Dog*, p. 23.
61 'A Reticence', first collected in *Killing the Black Dog*.

23 Forgiving the Victim, 1996–98

1 Interview with Valerie Murray, Bunyah, 9 October 1998.
2 It had been awarded about 400 000 times by the 1990s: 'A Question of Influence', Brisbane *Courier-Mail*, 24 August 1996, p. 5.
3 'A Question of Influence', Brisbane *Courier-Mail*, 24 August 1996, p. 5.
4 'A Question of Influence', Brisbane *Courier-Mail*, 24 August 1996, p. 5.
5 Conversation with John Paul, Sydney, 9 December 1998. Paul became a Senior Lecturer in Political Science at the University of New South Wales.
6 Conversation with John Paul, Sydney, 9 December 1998.

7   Conversation with John Paul, Sydney, 9 December 1998.
8   Articles on the subject appeared in the *Age*, 25 August 1996, p. 5, the *Sun Herald*, 25 August 1996, pp. 7 & 39, the *Australian*, 26 August 1996 p. 2, *Sydney Morning Herald*, 26 August 1996, pp. 1–2, *West Australian*, 26 August 1996, p. 5, the *Age*, 27 August 1996, p. 13, the *Australian*, 27 August 1996, p. 4, the *Economist*, 15 February 1997, p. 4, etc.
9   'Beazley Says Clark Allegation "Oddball"', *Courier-Mail*, 27 August 1996, p. 2. Bill Hayden commented in 'Trial by Innuendo', *Courier-Mail*, 31 August 1996, p. 24.
10 'Poet Rues the Day he Noticed a Medal Around a Historian's Neck', *Age*, 27 August 1996, p. 5.
11 'Clark Definitely Wore Soviet Medal—Murray', *West Australian*, 26 August 1996, p. 5. Also 'Les Murray's Exit Note', *Courier-Mail*, 29 August 1996, p. 1: 'Unequivocally, the medal I saw Manning Clark wearing in Canberra was the Order of Lenin'.
12 For instance, 'Why did Lenin—a man who seems to have been Christ-like, at least in his compassion—have to die?', *Meeting Soviet Man*, p. 12.
13 'A Question of Influence', Brisbane *Courier-Mail*, 24 August 1996, p. 5.
14 Brian Buckley, *Economist*, 15 February 1997, p. 4.
15 'Redneck in Tooth and Claw', *Australian Book Review*, no. 186, November 1996, pp. 9–10.
16 Unrecorded interview, Les Murray, late November 1996.
17 Interview with Bruce Clunies Ross, Armidale, 29 September 1997.
18 Lowry, *Times Literary Supplement*, 10 January 1997, p. 8.
19 'Redneck in Tooth and Claw', *Australian Book Review*, no. 186, November 1996, p. 9.
20 Sophie Masson in a letter to *Australian Book Review*, no. 187, December 1996.
21 'Deaf Language'.
22 'Requiem for a Heavyweight', *Heat*, no. 5, 1997, pp. 184ff.
23 Michael Fitzgerald, *Time*, 3 February 1997, p. 78.
24 Interview with Michael Duffy, Sydney, 8 September 1998.
25 The opening salvo of this attack took the form of a letter to *Australian Jewish News*, 9 June 1995, from Dr Ben Haneman.
26 Among them was the biographer David Marr, who had lauded the book and its author when he handed Demidenko the Vogel Award, and who savaged her in interviews subsequent to her 'outing': Jost, Totaro and Tyshing, *The Demidenko File*, pp. 1, 240ff.
27 Jost, Totaro and Tyshing, *The Demidenko File*, p. 285.
28 Interview with Les Murray, Sydney, 17 November 1997.
29 Interview with Les Murray, Sydney, 17 November 1997.
30 Riemer is quoted in Jost, Totaro and Tyshing, *The Demidenko File*, pp. 16ff, Singer in *Sydney Morning Herald*, 16 September 1995, p. 33, Kenneally in Jost, Totaro and Tyshing, *The Demidenko File*, pp. 157ff, and Kramer in Jost, Totaro and Tyshing, *The Demidenko File*, pp. 295ff.
31 Les Murray's annotations (December 1998) to an earlier draft of this book: PA.
32 Interview with Les Murray, Sydney, 17 November 1997.
33 Interview with Les Murray, Sydney, 17 November 1997.
34 Robert Manne, 'Bowing Out, With Regret', *Sydney Morning Herald*, 17 November 1997, p. 19.
35 Unpublished postcard, Les Murray to Christine Alexander, 20 February 1997: CA.
36 Unpublished postcard, Les Murray to Geoff Page, 22 May 1997, Page Collection, G285: ADFA.
37 Robert Manne, 'Bowing Out, With Regret', *Sydney Morning Herald*, 17 November 1997, p. 19.

38   The author was present during the telephone interview of an unnamed journalist with Les Murray, Sydney, 17 November 1997.
39   Les Murray's annotations (December 1998) to an earlier draft of this book: PA.
40   Gerard Henderson's column, making this argument, appeared in the *Sydney Morning Herald* at the end of February 1997.
41   *Sydney Morning Herald*, 3 March 1997.
42   'When it couldn't be confirmed by phone that CM had in fact sent this letter in, it didn't go into the Letters column, but SMH liked it so much as a near-successful hoax & a piece of writing that they publ. it whole on their snobby "Stay in Touch" page': Les Murray's annotations (December 1998) to an earlier draft of this book: PA.
43   *Sydney Morning Herald*, 7 June 1997.
44   Telephone interview with Les Murray, Bunyah, 4 September 1998.
45   Telephone interview with Les Murray, Bunyah, 4 September 1998.
46   Written in 1997, published in *Times Literary Supplement*, 13 March 1998, p. 12.
47   'Queen Honours Poet of the Common People', *Sydney Morning Herald*, 2 December 1998, p. 3.

24 Fredy Murray, 1993–

1   Interview with Les Murray, Sydney, 20 March 1995.
2   Interview with Les Murray, Sydney, 2 September 1997.
3   Interview with Les Murray, Sydney, 20 March 1995.
4   Interview with Valerie Murray, Bunyah, 8 October 1996.
5   Unpublished letter, Les Murray to Geoffrey Lehmann, 29 July 1961: GL.
6   One of the children in Alexander Murray's special school was known as 'the headbanger', and had to wear a crash-helmet. A 'squeeze machine', a kind of gentle cattle-crush for the treatment of autistic children, was invented by an American autist, Temple Grandin, who found it gave her great relief.
7   Les Murray mistakenly names him as Atom Ergoyan in the opening pages of *Fredy Neptune*: he corrected the error in his annotations (December 1998) to an earlier draft of this book: PA.
8   Quoted in *Fredy Neptune*, p. 9.
9   Les Murray says so in *Killing the Black Dog*, p. 13,
10 *Hitler's Table Talk, 1941–1944*, translated from the German by N. Cameron and R. H. Stevens, London: Weidenfeld & Nicolson, 1953.
11 Les Murray at the launch of *Fredy Neptune*, Sydney, 19 July 1998.
12 Unpublished letter, Les Murray to Elisabeth and Walter Davis, 22 May 1994: WD.
13 Interview with Les Murray, Sydney, 20 March 1995.
14 The two creators of *Superman*, Jerry Siegel and Joseph Schuster, encounter Fredy Boettcher during his stay in the United States, in Book III of *Fredy Neptune*, and he inspires the comic strip.
15 Unpublished postcard to Geoff Page, 9 August 1993, Page Collection, G258: ADFA.
16 Les Murray at the launch of *Fredy Neptune*, Sydney, 19 July 1998.
17 Unpublished postcard, Les Murray to Philip Hodgins, 15 June 1993, Hodgins Collection, G13, Box 4, Wallet 23: ADFA.

18 Les Murray's annotations (December 1998) to an earlier draft of this book: PA.
19 Les Murray at the launch of *Fredy Neptune*, Sydney, 19 July 1998.
20 Unpublished letter, Les Murray to Penny Nelson, 28 July 1993: PN.
21 Unpublished card, Les Murray to Penny Nelson, 10 August 1993: PN.
22 Unpublished letter, Les Murray to Elisabeth and Walter Davis, 22 May 1994: WD.
23 Unpublished letter, Les Murray to Peter Goldsworthy, 4 August 1994: PG.
24 Interview with Les Murray, 19 December 1994.
25 Interview with Les Murray, Sydney, 20 March 1995.
26 Interview with Les Murray, Sydney, 20 March 1995.
27 Interview with Les Murray, Sydney, 4 August 1997.
28 *Fredy Neptune*, 'Lazarus Unstuck'.
29 Interview with Les Murray, Sydney, 4 August 1997.
30 Interview with Les Murray, Sydney, 4 August 1997.
31 Interview with Les Murray, Sydney, 4 August 1997.
32 Les Murray's annotations (December 1998) to an earlier draft of this book: PA.
33 Interview with Les Murray, Sydney, 23 September 1997.
34 The announcement was made on 2 December 1998, but Les Murray had been approached about it months before in a letter from Ted Hughes, the Poet Laureate, who to Les Murray's great regret died shortly before the official announcement could be made. Murray received the medal at Buckingham Palace in June 1999.

SELECT BIBLIOGRAPHY

Part I
Works by Les A. Murray

Poetry volumes

The Ilex Tree, with Geoffrey Lehmann, Canberra: ANU Press, 1965.
The Weatherboard Cathedral, Sydney: Angus & Robertson, 1969.
Poems Against Economics, Sydney: Angus & Robertson, 1972.
Lunch & Counter Lunch, Sydney: Angus & Robertson, 1974.
Selected Poems: The Vernacular Republic, Sydney: Angus & Robertson, 1976; London: Angus & Robertson, 1976; Sydney: Angus & Robertson, 1979.
Ethnic Radio, Sydney: Angus & Robertson, 1977.
The Boys Who Stole The Funeral, Sydney: Angus & Robertson, 1979, 1980; Manchester: Carcanet, 1989; New York: Farrar, Straus and Giroux, 1991.
The Vernacular Republic: Poems 1961–1981 (enlarged and revised edition of 1976 publication), Sydney: Angus & Robertson, 1982; Edinburgh: Canongate, 1982; New York: Persea Books, 1982; enlarged and revised edition, Sydney: Angus & Robertson, 1988.
Equanimities, Copenhagen: Razorback Press 1982; limited edition, 350 copies.
The People's Otherworld, Sydney: Angus & Robertson, 1983.
Selected Poems, Manchester: Carcanet, 1986.
The Daylight Moon, Sydney: Angus & Robertson, 1987; Manchester: Carcanet, 1988; New York: Persea Books, 1988.
The Idyll Wheel: Cycle of a Year at Bunyah, NSW, April 1986–April 1987, Canberra: Officina Brindabella, 1989, limited edition, 200 copies.
Dog Fox Field, Sydney: Angus & Robertson, 1990; Manchester: Carcanet, 1991; New York: Farrar, Straus and Giroux, 1993.
Collected Poems, Sydney: Angus & Robertson, 1991; Manchester: Carcanet, 1991; London: Minerva, 1992; released as *The Rabbiter's Bounty: Collected Poems*, New York: Farrar, Straus and Giroux, 1991.
Translations From the Natural World, Paddington: Isabella Press, 1992; Manchester: Carcanet, 1993; New York: Farrar, Straus and Giroux, 1994.
Collected Poems, Port Melbourne: William Heinemann Australia, 1994.
Subhuman Redneck Poems, Manchester: Carcanet, 1996; Sydney: Duffy & Snellgrove, 1996.
Fredy Neptune, Sydney: Duffy & Snellgrove, 1998.
Conscious & Verbal, Sydney: Duffy & Snellgrove, 2000.

Poetry in translation

Ein ganz gewöhnlicher Regenbogen, translated by Margitt Lehbert, Munich: Carl Hanser Verlag, 1996.

De slabonenpreek, introduced and translated by Maarten Elzinga, Amsterdam: Meulenhof, 1997.
En helt almindelig Regubue: Digte, translated by Martin Leer, Copenhagen: Gyldendal, 1998.

General prose

The Peasant Mandarin: Prose Pieces, St Lucia: UQP, 1978.
Persistence in Folly: Selected Prose Writings, Sydney: Angus & Robertson, 1984.
The Australian Year: The Chronicle of our Seasons and Celebrations, with photographs by Peter Solness and others, Sydney: Angus & Robertson, 1985.
Blocks and Tackles: Articles and Essays 1982 to 1990, Sydney: Angus & Robertson, 1990.
The Paperbark Tree: Selected Prose, Manchester: Carcanet, 1992; London: Minerva, 1993.
Killing the Black Dog, introduced and edited by Christine Alexander, Annandale: Federation Press, 1996.
A Working Forest, Sydney: Duffy & Snellgrove, 1997.
The Quality of Sprawl: Thoughts about Australia, Sydney: Duffy & Snellgrove, 1999.

Short stories (uncollected)

'Red Cedar', *Hermes*, 1959, pp. 48–9.
'The Withdrawal', *honi soit*, 8 October 1959, p. 6.
'The Crime of Justice', *honi soit*, 21 April 1960, pp. 8–9.
'The End of Summer', *honi soit*, 28 July 1960, p. 6.
'The rights of man', *honi soit*, 29 September 1960, p. 6.
'A dream of death', *honi soit*, 27 March 1962, pp. 8–9.
'The enemy', *honi soit*, 17 April 1962, p. 9.

Individual poems published in journals and edited collections (chronological order of publication)

'Property', *honi soit*, 23 April 1959, p. 6.
'The first time', *Hermes*, 1959, p. 25.
'Evening at Home', *honi soit/Tharunka*, 1 October 1959, p. 8.
'Poem for Poor Dolores', *Hermes*, 1960, p. 28.
'The Winter Rising', *honi soit*, 28 April 1960, p. 6.
'The Materialist Apocalypse', *honi soit*, 30 June 1960, p. 10.
'The Japanese Barge', *Arna*, 1961, p. 30.
'Song of a Successful Chevalier', *Arna*, 1961, p. 50.
'Personality', *Hermes*, Michaelmas Term 1961, p. 9.
'Civil War Incident', *Hermes*, Michaelmas Term 1961, p. 29.
'Veterans', *Southerly*, no. 1, 1961, p. 42.
'The Englishman', *Southerly*, no. 3, 1961, p. 39.
'Eternity', *Arna*, 1962, p. 65.
'A New England Farm—August 1914', *Hermes*, 1962, p. 33.
'Halt and Turn', *Hermes*, 1962, p. 70.

'The Second Innocence', *honi soit*, 3 April 1962, p. 8.
'Court Hearing', *honi soit*, 12 June 1962, p. 8.
'Trapeze', *honi soit*, 10 July 1962, p. 8.
'Suibne Geilt to his wife', *honi soit*, 11 September 1962, p. 7.
'Agitation', *Arna*, 1963, p. 28.
'Minuet', *Hermes*, 1963, p. 35.
'Manoeuvres', *Southerly*, no. 1, 1964, p. 41.
'Beside the Highway', in G. Dutton (ed.), *Modern Australian Writing*, London: Fontana, 1966, pp. 75–6.
'Another Continent', *Quadrant*, May–June 1966, pp. 56–7.
'Shorelines', *Meanjin*, vol. 26(1), 1967, pp. 54–5.
'Tableau with Academic Figures', *Quadrant*, March–April 1967, p. 23.
'If a Pebble Fall', *Southerly*, vol. 28, 1968, p. 273.
'The Borgia Pope Relates a Painful Incident', *Southerly*, vol. 28, 1968, p. 300.
'The Garden Path', *Meanjin*, vol. 28, Autumn 1969, p. 96.
'Visiting Anzac in the Year of Metrication', 'The Powerline Incarnation' and 'The Returnees', *Poetry Australia*, no. 55, June 1975, pp. 29–35.
'The Euchre Game' and 'The New Expatriation', *Times Literary Supplement*, 9 April 1976, p. 429.
'The Canberra Style. A small selection of new poetry', *National Times*, 12–17 April 1976, p. 24.
'Digestif', *New Letters*, vol. 43(1), October 1976, pp. 36–7.
'Laconics: The Forty Acres', *Times Literary Supplement*, 17 December 1976, p. 1594.
Five Gaelic Poems: 'Free Kirk Cemetery, Northern New South Wales', 'A Skirl for Outsets', 'Spiritual Conflict on the Manly Ferry', 'The Gum Forest', 'Elegy for Angus Macdonald of Cnoclinn', *Meanjin*, vol. 36(1), May 1977, pp. 73–80.
'The Figures in Quoniam', *Quadrant*, August 1977, pp. 40–1.
'Prayer Carving For All Souls Day', *Times Literary Supplement*, 19 August 1977, p. 1012.
'Two Poems' ['The Future' and 'A Presentiment'], *New Review*, vol. 4(43), October 1977, pp. 35–6.
'Sonnets from a Novel in Progress', *Poetry Australia*, no. 66, March 1978, pp. 62–6, being a selection from *The Boys Who Stole The Funeral*.
'A New England Farm, August 1914', in Chris Wallace-Crabbe (ed.), *The Golden Apples of the Sun*, Melbourne: Melbourne University Press, 1980, p. 184.
'Telling the cousins', *New Letters*, vol. 46, Spring 1980, p. 21.
'The Doorman', *New Yorker*, 13 October 1980, p. 46.
'The Fishermen at South Head', *Poetry Australia*, no. 74/75, 1980, pp. 23–4.
'Bent Water in the Tasmanian Highlands', *Times Literary Supplement*, 13 February 1981, p. 162.
'Quintets for Robert Morley', *Island*, 6 March 1981, pp. 6–7.
'Anthropomorphics', *Times Literary Supplement*, 3 April 1981, p. 375.
'First Essay on Interest', *Times Literary Supplement*, 19 June 1981, p. 705.
'Flowering Eucalypt in Autumn' and 'Little Boy Impelling a Scooter', *Poetry Australia*, no. 84/85, 1982, pp. 48–9.

'An Immortal', *Times Literary Supplement*, 19 February 1982, p. 117.
'The Steel', *Meanjin*, vol. 41(1), April 1982, pp. 107–11.
'Three Interiors', *Times Literary Supplement*, 1983, p. 1100.
'Time Travel', *Times Literary Supplement*, 25 March 1983, p. 286.
'The Chimes of Niegeschah', *Poetry Australia*, April 1983, pp. 62–3.
'Art History: The Suburb of Surrealls', *Times Literary Supplement*, 27 April 1984, pp. 462–3.
'The Hypogeum', *New Yorker*, vol. 60, 21 May 1984, p. 46.
'The House of Four-X', in Leonie Kramer (ed.), *My Country: Australian Poetry and Short Stories, Two Hundred Years, vol. 2 1930s–1980s*, Sydney: Lansdowne Press, 1985, p. 635.
'The Butter Factory' and 'The Milk Lorry', *Overland*, no. 101, 1985, p. 32.
'Tropical Window', *Poetry Australia*, no. 100, 1985, p. 13.
'Machine Portraits with Pendant Spaceman', *Partisan Review*, vol. 52(3), 1985, pp. 237–41.
'The China Pear Tree', *Australian*, 28–29 September 1985, p. 10.
'The Dream of Wearing Shorts Forever', 'Physiognomy on the Savage Manning River', 'Easter 1984', 'At the Aquatic Carnival', 'The Vol Sprung From Heraldry', 'Tropical Window', 'The Edgeless' and 'The Sleepout', *American Poetry Review*, vol. 15(2), 1986, pp. 23–7.
'Nocturne' and 'The Lake Surnames', *Poetry Australia*, no. 107/108, 1986, pp. 64–5.
'The Emu and the Nobilities of Interest', *New Yorker*, 26 July 1986, pp. 36–7.
'The Megaethon: 1850, 1906–1929', *Atlantic Monthly*, September 1987, pp. 74–5.
'The transposition of Clermont', *Meanjin*, vol. 46(3), September 1987, pp. 326–7.
'The Liberated Plague', *Overland*, no. 109, December 1987, p. 19.
'Mercurial September', *New York Review of Books*, 3 December 1987, p. 25.
'Max Fabre's Yachts', *New York Review of Books*, 3 December 1987, p. 25.
'The Grandmother's Story' and 'At Min-Min Camp', *American Poetry Review*, vol. 17, 1988, p. 39.
'The Inverse Transports', *Meanjin*, vol. 47(4), 1988, pp. 586–7.
'Hearing Impairment', *Prairie Schooner*, vol. 62(4), Winter 1988/89, pp. 89–90.
'The 1812 Overture at Topkapi Saray', *Prairie Schooner*, vol. 62(4), Winter 1988/89, pp. 91–3.
'Araucarie Bidwilli', *Southerly*, vol. 49(3), 1989, p. 302.
'From the Other Hemisphere', *Yale Review*, vol. 78(1), 1989, pp. 32–3.
'The International Terminal', *Yale Review*, vol. 78(1), 1989, pp. 33–4.
'Hastings River Cruise', *Yale Review*, vol. 78(1), 1989, p. 35–6; *Landfall*, vol. 43(1), March 1989, pp. 8–9.
'An Australian History of the Practical Man', 'Accordion Music', The Inverse Transports', 'Experiential', *Descant*, vol. 20(3–4), 1989, pp. 221–6.
'A Torturer's Apprenticeship', *Poetry Review*, vol. 79(4), 1989, p. 27.
'The Cows on Killing Day', *Paris Review*, vol. 31(112), Fall 1989, pp. 183–4.
'Gun-E-Darr', 'The Tube', 'Cave Divers Near Mount Gambier', 'The Emerald Dove', *Paris Review*, vol. 31(112), Fall 1989, pp. 185–9.

'The Assimilation of Background', *New Republic*, 6 February 1989, p. 26.
'Dog Fox Field', *Landfall 169*, vol. 43(1), March 1989, p. 9.
'But Canberra's', 'Mow the parklands', 'Citizens live in peace and honour', 'The Interstate Driver' (titled 'Circle City' when published in *Canberra Times*, 13 January 1973, p. 9), 'As I walked', 'All the rabbits' and 'The Canberra Cop', in Phillip Mackenzie (ed.), *The Poetry of Canberra*, Canberra: Polonius, 1990, pp. 1, 21–2, 31, 48, 53–4.
'High River', *Grand Street*, vol. 9, Summer 1990, pp. 43–50.
'Presence: Translations from the Natural World'—'Eagle Pair', 'Layers of Pregnancy', 'Insect Mating Flight', 'Two Dogs', 'Cockspur Bush', 'Lyre Bird', 'Shoal', 'Prehistory of Air', 'The Gods', 'Cattle Ancestor', 'Mollusc', 'Cattle Egret', 'The Snake's Heat Organ', 'Great Bole', 'Echidna', 'Yard Horse', in *Paris Review*, vol. 32(117), Winter 1990, pp. 208–23.
'Ariel', *Yale Review*, vol. 79(2), Winter 1990, p. 286.
Antarctica', *Yale Review*, vol. 79(2), Winter 1990, pp. 286–7.
'An Era', *Poetry Review*, vol. 80(1), 1990, p. 19.
'Manners of the Supranation', *Times Literary Supplement*, 9–15 March 1990, p. 261.
'The Gaelic Long Tunes', 'The Past Ever Present' and 'Midnight Lake', *Landfall*, vol. 44(2), June 1990, pp. 150–1.
'Crankshaft', *Sydney Review*, October 1991, p. 10.
'The Sports Machine', *Australian*, 19–20 October 1991, review p. 6.
'Where humans can't leave and mustn't complain', *Sydney Morning Herald*, 28 December 1991, p. 31; *Times Literary Supplement*, 7 February 1992, p. 6.
'The Ballad of the Barbed Wire Ocean', *Westerly*, vol. 35(1), 1990, p. 43; *Partisan Review*, vol. 59(1), 1992, pp. 97–8.
'Home Suite', *Times Literary Supplement*, 1991, p. 12; *Westerly*, vol. 36(4), 1991, pp. 70–1; *World Literature Today*, vol. 67(3), Summer 1993, p. 556.
'Green Rose Tan', *Scripsi*, vol. 8(1), 1992, p. 1.
'Poetry and Religion' and 'Incorrigible Grace', *Commonweal*, 22 May 1992, pp. 11–12.
'Extract from a Verse Novel in Progress', *Adelaide Review*, Festival 1992, p. 30.
'The Family Farmers' Victory', *Quadrant*, vol. 36(6), June 1992, pp. 44–5, *World Literature Today*, vol. 67, Summer 1993, p. 555.
'Rock Music', *Times Literary Supplement*, 26 June 1992, p. 11; *Sydney Review*, July 1992, p. 10.
'Late Summer Fires', *Sydney Review*, August 1992, p. 4.
'The Rollover', *Australian*, 8–9 August 1992, review p. 6.
'Corniche', *Adelaide Review*, October 1992, p. 25; *Times Literary Supplement*, 5 February 1993, p. 24.
'Dead Trees in the Dam', *Antipodes*, vol. 6(2), December 1992, p. 123.
'Kimberley Brief', *Partisan Review*, vol. 60(1), 1993, pp. 103–7.
'The Bacchantes' and 'The Water Column', *Poetry Wales*, vol. 29(1), 1993, p. 33.
'A Brief History', *World Literature Today*, vol. 67(3), Summer 1993, p. 553.
'The say-but-the-word centurion attempts a summary', *Adelaide Review*, March 1993, p. 35; *World Literature Today*, vol. 63, Summer 1993, p. 554.

'The Water Column', *Quadrant*, April 1993, p. 25.
'The Contractors', *Quadrant*, May 1993, p. 69.
'Midlife Propeller Blur', *Sydney Review*, June 1993, p. 12; *Adelaide Review*, May 1993, p. 28.
'The Portrait Head', *Bulletin*, 6 July 1993, p. 85.
'Like Wheeling Stacked Water', *Times Literary Supplement*, 20 August 1993, p. 7.
'Suspended Vessels, Alice Springs 1989', *Age*, 4 September 1993, 'Saturday Extra', p. 9.
'The Middle Sea' (Book 1 of a verse novel in progress), *Adelaide Review*, August 1993, 'Supplement' pp. 1–16; *Sydney Review*, 13 October 1993, pp. 1–16 (supplement).
'Barking at the Thunder' (Book 2 of a verse novel in progress), *Adelaide Review*, April 1994, pp. 1–24 (supplement).
'The Somatic Nobility' (Book 3 of a verse novel in progress), *Adelaide Review*, Festival 1996, pp. 1–16 (supplement).
'On the present slaughter of feral animals', *Canberra Times*, 5 December 1993, p. 19.
'Performance', *Ulitarra*, no. 5, 1994, p. 17.
'It allows a portrait in line-scan at fifteen', *Adelaide Review*, Festival 1994, p. 37; *Times Literary Supplement*, 18 March 1994, p. 4.
'Australian Love Poem', *Qudarant*, June 1994, p. 13.
'The Bohemian Occupation', *Times Literary Supplement*, 8 July 1994, p. 18.
'Turning Points', *Age*, 16 July 1994, 'Saturday Extra', p. 5.
'The Shield-Scales of Heraldry', *Times Literary Supplement*, 4 August 1994, p. 13.
'Each Morning Once More Seamless', *Eureka Street*, October 1994, p. 24.
'The Suspension of Knock', *Canberra Times*, 15 October 1994, p. C13.
'Goose Feet on Breakthrough Day', *Adelaide Review*, November 1994, p. 25.
'Contested Landscape At Forsayth', *Times Literary Supplement*, 4 November 1994, p. 6.
'The Sand Coast Sonnets', *Antipodes*, vol. 8(2), December 1994, pp. 127, 129.
'The Year of the Kiln Portraits', *Hobo Poetry Magazine*, vol. 4, December 1994, p. 23.
'Earth Tremor at Night', *Adelaide Review*, January 1995, p. 26.
'Waking up on Tour', *Bulletin*, 10 January 1995, p. 89.
'A Lego of Driving to Sydney', *Sydney Morning Herald*, 29 April 1995, 'Spectrum', p. 12A.
'Tympan Alley', *Bulletin*, 16 May 1995, p. 80, *Times Literary Supplement*, 4 August 1995, p. 25.
'Under the Banana Mountains', *Adelaide Review*, August 1995, p. 22.
'Inside Ayers Rock', *Adelaide Review*, August 1995, p. 22.
'The Ambient', *Adelaide Review*, October 1995, p. 28.
'Burning Want', *Adelaide Review*, October 1995, p. 28.
'The Last Hellos', *Adelaide Review*, October 1995, p. 28; *Independent Monthly*, December 1995/January 1996, p. 78.
'My Ancestress and the Secret Ballot 1848 and 1851', *Bulletin*, 28 November 1995, p. 110; *Times Literary Supplement*, 10 May 1996, p. 15.
'The Trances', *Five Bells*, vol. 3(2), 1996, p. 20.
'The Devil', *Poetry Wales*, vol. 31(4), 1996, pp. 35–6.

'Cotton Flannelette', *Southerly*, Winter 1996, pp. 20–1; *Poetry Wales*, vol. 31(4), 1996, p. 34.
'The Nearly Departed', *Southerly*, vol. 56(2), Winter 1996, p. 21.
'Comete', *Age*, 9 March 1996, 'Saturday Extra', p. 8.
'The Warm Rain', *Independent Monthly*, May 1996, p. 52, *Times Literary Supplement*, 5 July 1996, p. 9.
'Dreambabwe', *Independent Monthly*, May 1996, p. 52.
'Life Cycle of Ideas', *Adelaide Review*, August 1996, p. 23.
'The Devil', *Adelaide Review*, August 1996, p. 23.
'One Kneeling, One Looking Down', *Times Literary Supplement*, 27 December 1996, *Sydney Morning Herald*, 21 September 1996, p. 5.

Poetry in translation (published in journals)

'Gedichte', 'Folklore', 'Bildnis des Künstlers als Neue-Welt-Fahrer', 'Die Saubohnenpredigt', 'Lachlan Macquaries erste Sprache', 'Immigrantenreise', 'Die Eigenschaft des Sprawls', 'Lotosdamm', 'Dichtung und Religion' and 'Die junge Besucherin', *Akzente*, vol. 40, 1993, pp. 27–44, translated from English by Margitt Lehbert.

Articles and other prose (published in journals and edited collections)

'Notes', as guest editor, *Poetry Australia*, no. 8, February 1966, p. 4.
'Les A. Murray', in Thomas W. Shapcott (ed.), *Australian Poetry Now*, Melbourne: Sun Books, 1970, pp. 74–5.
'Preface' in J. Palmer (ed.), *Poems For Senior Students*, Sydney: William Brooks, pp. 197ff.
'Autobiographical notes' and 'Afterword', in Alexander Craig (ed.), *Twelve Poets 1950–1970*, Milton: Jacaranda Press, 1971, pp. 191, 218–20.
'Patronage in Australia: A Critique and Two Proposals', *Australian Quarterly*, vol. 44(3), September 1972, pp. 67–80.
'The Death of a Poet: A Tribute', *Sydney Morning Herald*, 19 January 1974, p. 15.
'The Human-Hair Thread', *Meanjin*, vol. 36, December 1977, pp. 505–71.
'The Coming Republic', *Quadrant*, April 1976, pp. 36–42.
'More Wow Than Flutter', *Quadrant*, October 1976, p. 45–51.
'Clapped in Macedonia', *Quadrant*, April 1977, pp. 16–21.
'Peter Porter: *On first Looking into Chapman's Hesiod*', in P. K. Elkin (ed.), *Australian Poems in Perspective*, St Lucia: UQP, 1978, pp. 171–84.
'Critics Choice', *Sydney Morning Herald*, 16 December 1978, p. 11.
'The Boeotian Strain', *Kunapipi*, vol. 2(1), 1980, pp. 54–64.
'The Bonny Disproportion', *Helix*, no. 5/6, February–August 1980, pp. 113–28.
'Isaac Rosenberg', *Quadrant*, March 1980, pp. 52–5.
'Notes on the Writing of a Novel Sequence', *Australasian Catholic Record*, July 1981, pp. 272–5.
'The city and the harbor, and the Cross', *Mercury*, 27 January 1982, p. 7.

'Eric Rolls and The Golden Disobedience', *Quadrant*, December 1982, pp. 44–53.
'Some Different Commonwealth Games', *Quadrant*, November 1982, pp. 10–13.
'Inside *Poetry Australia*', *Quadrant*, April 1983, pp. 16–24.
'Three Talks: David Malouf, Les Murray and David Rowbotham', *Australian Literary Studies*, vol. 11(3), May 1984, pp. 220–3.
'The worst she can do is tell you she's not interested', 'Farming is a hard door', 'What to do if you're lost in the bush', 'Chicks dig poems. You might want to learn a few', in John Birmingham (ed.), *How To Be a Man*, Sydney: Duffy & Snellgrove, 1985, pp. 35, 63–4, 134–5, 143.
'Eulogy for Douglas Stewart', *Southerly*, vol. 45(2), June 1985, pp. 123–8.
'Les A. Murray', *Australian Literary Studies*, vol. 12(2), October 1985, pp. 268–70.
'Alas No, Kids, I Didn't See A Mountie', *CRNL Reviews Journal*, no. 1, 1987, pp. 90–6.
'Mit den Siedlern Kam die Wildnis', *Merian*, vol. 41(1), 1988, pp. 6–9.
'Editor's Preface', *Poetry Australia*, April 1988, pp. 4–5.
'1950's Flumine Pereant Illae', in *Torch* 1988, The Bicentennial Issue. Also reprints a Les Murray article published in *Torch* in 1955, 'Cadet Entwhistle and the Sergeant'.
'A Global Perspective', *Poetry Book Society Bulletin*, no. 136, Spring 1988, p. 4.
'Poemes and the Mystery of Embodiment', *Meanjin*, 47(3), Spring 1988, pp. 519–33; also *PN Review* 1989, 16 (4[72]), pp. 28–35.
'Wholespeak: Body, Mind and Soul', *Australian*, 22 April 1988, p. 8.
'Prospecting on the Property', *The Macquarie Dictionary Society*, vol. 5(2), December 1988, pp. 2–3.
'Les Murray: *The Daylight Moon*', in G. Turcotte (ed.), *Writers in Action*, Sydney: Currency Press, 1990, pp. 87–112.
'The Suspect Captivity of the Fisher King', *Quadrant*, September 1990, pp. 16–19.
'A Generation of Changes', *Quadrant*, January/February 1991, pp. 37–40.
'My Country Childhood', in *Australian Country Style*, June–July 1991, p. 18.
'Call for Survival and Wage Justice', *Canberra Times*, 31 January 1993, p. 22.
'Wanted: A Regular Crust for Everyone Who Lives by the Pen', *Sydney Morning Herald*, 22 February 1993, p. 13.
'Time's Up for Literature Board', *Age*, 6 January 1993, p. 11.
'This Is Your Sovereign Speaking', *Independent Monthly*, 20 June 1993, p. 20.
'Assault with a Deadly Metaphor', *Independent Monthly*, October 1993, p. 97.
'A Modest Proposal', *Independent Monthly*, November 1993, p. 16.
'Under Sydney's Spell', *Independent Monthly*, December 1993/January 1994, p. 57.
'The Culture of Hell', *Independent Monthly*, February 1994, p. 18.
'The Bushland's Fatal Attraction', *Independent Monthly*, March 1994, p. 20.
'Amazing Grace and Other Stories', *Independent Monthly*, April 1994, p. 67.
'Poetic Injustice', *Independent Monthly*, May 1994, p. 85.
'A Suitable Way of Treatment', *Independent Monthly*, July 1994, p. 48.
'Poetry Finds A New Voice', *Independent Monthly*, September 1994, p. 78.
'The New White Man's Burden', *Independent Monthly*, October 1994, p. 71.

'Poetic Injustice', *Independent Monthly*, November 1994, p. 81.
'The Day the Killing Stopped', *Independent Monthly*, December 1994, p. 46.
'Board Games', *Independent Monthly*, February 1995, p. 87.
'How to Break the Logjam', *Independent Monthly*, March 1995, p. 55.
'Confessions of a Former Scab', *Independent Monthly*, April 1995, p. 70.
'Creative Accounting', *Independent Monthly*, May 1995, p. 35.
'In Defence of Country Folk', *Independent Monthly*, June 1995, p. 55.
'Cultural Cringe', *Rananim*, vol. 3(2), June 1995, p. 21.
'Identity Crises', *Independent Monthly*, July 1995, p. 89.
'Cross-Legged to Europe', *Independent Monthly*, August 1995, p. 82.
'Many Happy Returns', *Independent Monthly*, October 1995, p. 58.
'Ugly Republicans with Plastic Bags over their Heads', *Australian*, 3 October 1995, p. 13.
'Sidelined by the Elite Republican Guard', *Independent Monthly*, November 1995, p. 65.
'Postcard from Canada', *Independent Monthly*, December 1995/January 1996, p. 56.
'The Noblesse Trap: the ills and possibilities of arts patronage' in P. Coleman (ed.), *Double Take*, Melbourne: Mandarin, 1996, pp. 63–99.
'Our Man in Bunyah', *Independent Monthly*, February 1996, p. 43.

Published letters

'One for Wong—Murray in Flurry', *honi soit*, 17 July 1958, p. 2.
'Murray Mad at Society Slackness', *honi soit*, 8 October 1959, p. 2.
'Ideas Party', Letter to the editor, *Bulletin*, 2 December 1972, p. 5.
'Les Murray', Letter to the editor, *Quadrant*, August 1977, pp. 42–4.
'Who's Ignatius, Whose Loyola', Letter to the editor, *Kunapipi*, vol. 1(2), 1979, pp. 149–54.
'Letters to the Winner', *Atlantic Monthly*, vol. 261, January 1988, pp. 76–7.
'Aphrodite Street', Letter to editor, *London Review of Books*, 7 January 1988, p. 4.
'Aphrodite Street', Letter to editor, *London Review of Books*, 18 February 1988, p. 4.
'Royalty Scheme Delivers Equality', *Australian*, 26 January 1993, p. 10.
'A Modest Way of Paying our Writers a Living Wage', *Age*, 5 March 1993, p. 12.
'Literary Funding in Australia', *Times Literary Supplement*, 10 September 1993, p. 15.
'Australia Council Under Fire', *Guide*, vol. 3(4), 1994, pp. 10–11.
'Peeved Poet', *Sydney Morning Herald*, 22 July 1994, p. 12.
'For Helen Darville', *Independent Monthly*, March 1996, p. 8.
'More on Murray, Manning, and Lenin', *Notes and Furphies*, no. 38, April/May 1997, p. 1.

Book reviews

'Getting to Know the Landscape', reviewing *Sense of Place: A Response to an Environment* by George Seddon, *Sydney Morning Herald*, 23 June 1973, p. 25.
'Our Best Customer', reviewing *Japan: Its History and Culture* by Scott Morton, *Sydney Morning Herald*, 25 August 1973, p. 21.

'Of Working People', reviewing *The Principle of Water* by Jon Silkin, *Sydney Morning Herald*, 10 August 1974, p. 15.
'The Paradox of Technology', reviewing *The Earth from Space* by J. Bodechtel and H. G. Glerloff-Emden, trans. Hildegard Mayhew and Lotte Evans, *Sydney Morning Herald*, 31 August 1974, p. 15.
'A World that Has Passed Away', reviewing *W. H. Auden, a tribute*, Stephen Spender (ed.), *Sydney Morning Herald*, 2 August 1975, p. 17.
'Landscape-as-Identity', reviewing *Bindibu Country* by Donald Thompson, *Sydney Morning Herald*, 1 November 1975, p. 17.
'Solitary Soldier', reviewing *No Surrender: My Thirty-Year War*, by Hiroo Onoda, trans. Charles S. Terry, *Sydney Morning Herald*, 8 November 1975, p. 15.
'Poet's Guide', reviewing *A Map of Australian Verse* by James McAuley, *Sydney Morning Herald*, 7 February 1976, p. 17.
'My New Country Enjoys Good Relations with Death', reviewing *Living In A Calm Country* by Peter Porter, *Sydney Morning Herald*, 14 February 1976, p. 15.
'The Great Federal Poetry Takeover Plot', reviewing *Devil's Rock and other Poems 1970–1972* and *Deaths and Pretty Cousins* by David Campbell, and *A Late Picking* by A. D. Hope, *National Times*, 12–17 April 1976, pp 23–4.
'It Started About 6,000 Years Ago', reviewing *The Birth of Writing* by Robert Clairborne, *Sydney Morning Herald*, 4 September 1976, p. 18.
'Tom Keneally Passes the Enjoyability Test', reviewing *Season in Purgatory* by Thomas Keneally, *Bulletin*, 8 January 1977, pp. 54–5.
'Doomster's Day—or How to Avoid the Apocalypse', reviewing *How to Avoid the Future* by Gordon Rattray Taylor, *Sydney Morning Herald*, 14 May 1977, p. 19.
'Poet of Urban Australia', reviewing *Sometimes Gladness: Collected Poems, 1954–1978* by Bruce Dawe, and *The Aviary: Poems (1976–1977)*, by Peter Skrzynecki, *Sydney Morning Herald*, 3 February 1979, p. 19.
'Posterity Now. Present and Future texts for Australian Literature', reviewing *The Oxford History of Australian Literature*, Leonie Kramer (ed.), *Island*, no. 8, November 1981, pp. 6–9.
'A Taste of Poets', reviewing *Counterpoise* by A. Lansdown, *Readings from Ecclesiates* by P. Goldsworthy, *Transplants* and *(W)holes* by C. Macdonald and *Selected Poems 1960–1980* by A. Taylor, in *Sydney Morning Herald*, 6 March 1982, p. 44.
'Porter: An Infinitely More Serious Bertie Wooster', reviewing *Collected Poems* by Peter Porter, *Sydney Morning Herald*, 8 June 1983, p. 37.
'The Scots in Australia', reviewing *The Scots in Australia: A Study of New South Wales, Victorian and Queensland 1788–1900* by Malcolm D. Prentis, in *Quadrant*, September 1984, pp. 71–3.
'A Yawning Cultural Divide is Bridged', reviewing *Feathers and the Horizon* by Anne Fairbairn and Ghazi al-Gosaibi, *Weekend Australian*, 30 September – 1 October 1989, p. 10.
'Innocence Abroad in Richmond', reviewing *A Man of Marbles* by Rod Usher, *Age*, 7 October 1989, 'Saturday Extra', p. 10.

'Wild Colonial Bards', reviewing *The Poets' Discovery: Nineteenth-Century Australia in Verse* by Richard D. Jordan and Peter Pierce (eds), *Sydney Morning Herald*, 2 June 1990, p. 77.

Reviewing *The Irish-Australian Connection/An Caidreamh Gael-Austrálach* by Semus Grimes and Gearóid Ó Tuathaigh (eds), *Australian Studies* (London), no. 4, December 1990, pp. 124–6.

'Clone Me Up, Scotty', reviewing *Honk if you are Jesus* by Peter Goldsworthy, *Sydney Review*, November 1992, p. 16.

'Up On All Fours', reviewing *Up On All Fours* by Philip Hodgins, *Times Literary Supplement*, 3 December 1993, p. 11.

'Understated Mastery', reviewing *Up On All Fours* by Philip Hodgins, *Adelaide Review*, January 1994, pp. 31–2.

'Lylies and Ratbags', reviewing *Modern Australian Usage* by Nicholas Hudson and *Words of the West*, Maureen Brools and Joan Ritchie (eds), in *Times Literary Supplement*, 18 November 1994, p. 8.

'My Dreams, I Only Put Them Down for a Minute', *Age*, 2 December 1995, 'Saturday Extra', p. 9.

Addresses and lectures

'Embodiment and Incarnation: Notes on Preparing an Anthology of Australian Religious Verse', Aquinas Memorial Lecture 1987, delivered at the Court Terrace Restaurant, Law Courts, George St, Brisbane, Queensland, 25 September 1987. Published as Les Murray, *Embodiment and Incarnation: Notes on Preparing an Anthology of Religious Verse*, Aquinas Library, Brisbane, Queensland, p. 9.

'The Gravy in Images', presented at International Liturgy Assembly, Hobart, January 1988. Later published in *Blocks and Tackles* as 'The Trade in Images'.

'Killing the Black Dog'. Lecture delivered at New College, University of New South Wales, 11 November 1996.

Edited volumes

The New Oxford Book of Australian Verse, Melbourne: Oxford University Press, 1986; 2nd edition, 1991; 3rd edition, 1996.

Anthology of Australian Religious Poetry, Melbourne: Collins Dove, 1986, 2nd edition, 1991.

A. B. Paterson: Selected Poems, Australia: Collins/Angus & Robertson, 1992, 1996.

Fivefathers: Five Australian Poets of the Pre-Academic Era, Manchester: Carcanet Press, 1994.

Translations by Les Murray

Introduction to the Principles of Phonological Description, by Trubetzkoy, The Hague: Nijhoff, 1968.

'The Idiot in His Bath' by M. Vasalis, a poem translated from Dutch, in *Quadrant*, June 1990, p. 37.

'Ultima Ratio', translated from the German of Friedrich Georg Jünger, in *Times Literary Supplement*, 21 February 1992, p. 11.

Part II
Writings about Les A. Murray (up to 1997)

Books

Bourke, L., *A Vivid Steady State*, Sydney: New South Wales University Press and New Endeavour Press, 1992.

Gaffney, Carmel (ed.), *Counterbalancing Light: Essays on the Poetry of Les Murray*, Armidale: Kardoorair Press, 1997.

Nelson, P., *Notes on the Poetry of Les A. Murray*, Sydney: Methuen, 1978.

Sharma, A., *A Dimension of the Angel*, Jaipur, India: Bohra Prakshan, 1997.

Major articles

Ailwood, D., 'The Poetry of Les A. Murray', *Southerly*, vol. 31(3), 1971, pp. 188–201.

Almon, B., 'Fullness of Being in Les Murray's "Presence: Translations from the Natural World", *Antipodes*, vol. 8(2), December 1994, pp. 123–26, 128, 130.

Baker, C., 'Les A. Murray', in *Yacker 2: Australian Writers Talk About Their Work*, Sydney: Pan Books, 1987, pp. 218–46.

Barnie, J., ' "The Common Dish" and the Uncommon Poet', *Kunapipi*, vol. 4(1), 1982, pp. 172–8.

——, 'The Naming of Places', *Poetry Wales*, vol. 19, 1983, pp. 33–6.

——, 'The Poetry of Les Murray', *Australian Literary Studies*, May 1985, pp. 22–34.

Beaver, B., 'Younger Poets of Australia', *Hemisphere*, vol. 12(1), November 1968, pp. 13–15.

Bennett, B., 'Versions of the Past in the Poetry of Les Murray and Peter Porter', in K. Singh (ed.), *The Writer's Sense of the Past*, Singapore: Singapore University Press, 1987, pp. 178–88.

——, 'Perceptions of Australia, 1965–1988', *Australian Literary Studies*, vol. 13(4), 1988, pp. 433–53.

——, 'Patriot and expatriate: Les A. Murray and Peter Porter", in Bruce Bennett, *An Australian Compass*, Fremantle: Fremantle Arts Centre Press, 1991, pp. 38–51.

——, 'Living Spaces: Some Australian Houses of Childhood', *Kunapipi*, vol. 16(2), 1994, pp. 35–42.

Billen, A., 'Les miserable', *Observer Life*, 22 June 1997, pp. 6–8.

Blair, R., 'Les Murray Talks', *24 Hours*, vol. 1(10), November 1976, pp. 45–7.

Blight, J., 'An Elder Practising Poet's Point of View—Some Australian Contemporary Poetry', *Southerly*, vol. 34(2), June 1974, pp. 179–95.

Bourke, L., 'Les A. Murray', *Journal of Commonwealth Literature*, vol. 21(1), 1986, pp. 167–87.

——, ' "Digging Under the Horse": Surface as Disguise in the Poetry of Les A. Murray', *Southerly*, vol. 47(1), March 1987, pp. 26–41.

——, ' "The Ballad Trap": Les A. Murray and Pegasus', *Meridian*, May 1987, pp. 31–40.

——, 'The Rapture of Place: From Immanence to Transcendence in the Poetry of Les A. Murray', *Westerly*, March 1988, pp. 41–51.

——, 'Family and the Father in the Poetry of Les A. Murray', *Australian Literary Studies*, vol. 13(3), May 1988, pp. 282–95.
——, 'A Place in History: *The Ash Range*, Landscape and Identity', *Westerly*, Autumn 1993, pp. 17–24.
Brady, V., 'What Will Suffice: Les A. Murray's *The People's Otherworld*', in *Caught in the Draught*, Sydney: Angus & Robertson, 1994, pp. 177–90.
Burns, G., 'Good News from the Vegetable Patch: Les A. Murray's "The Broad Bean Sermon"', *Viewpoints 88: VCE English Literature*, Melbourne, Longman Cheshire, 1988, pp. 72–8.
Capp, F., 'Les Murray—an interview', *Australian Book Review*, April 1985, pp. 12–14.
Carter, D., 'The Death of Satan and the Persistence of Romanticism', in C. Narasimhaiah (ed.), *An Introduction to Australian Literature*, Brisbane: John Wiley & Sons, 1982, pp. 59–82.
Catalano, G., '"Evading the Modernities": The Poetry of Les A. Murray', *Meanjin*, vol. 36, 1977, pp. 67–72.
Chenery, S., 'The Bard of Bunyah', *Australian*, 4–5 May 1991, review pp. 1–2.
Clunies Ross, B., 'The American Model', *Overland*, no. 92, 1983, pp. 46–54.
——, 'Landscape and the Australian Imagination', in P. R. Eaden and F. H. Mares (eds), *Mapped But Not Known*, South Australia: Wakefield Press, 1986, pp. 224–43.
——, 'Les Murray's Vernacular Republic', in Peter Quartermaine (ed.), *Diversity Itself: Essays in Australian Arts and Culture*, Exeter: Exeter University, 1986, pp. 21–37.
——, 'Les Murray and the Poetry of Australia', *The Literature of Region and Nation*, in R. P. Draper (ed.), London: Macmillan, 1989, pp. 206–18.
——, 'A Poetic Novel for the Vernacular Republic: Les Murray's *The Boys Who Stole The Funeral*', in Alan Brissenden (ed.), *Aspects of Australian Fiction*, Perth: University of Western Australia Press, 1990, pp. 173–90.
——, 'Fiction and Poetry: Les Murray's *The Boys Who Stole The Funeral*', in *Studies in Modern Fiction*, University of Copenhagen: Department of English, pp. 101–22.
Coleman, P., 'A Vision Painted on a Wall', *National Library of Australia News*, vol. 3(6), March 1993, pp. 15–17.
Craven, P., 'Bard from Bunyah Makes Bid for Oxford', *Australian*, 4 May 1994, pp. 25, 27.
Crawford, R., 'Les A. Murray Talking with Robert Crawford', *Verse* (Oxford), 1986, pp. 21–32.
——, 'Les Murray: Radical Republican and Religious Conservative', *Cencrastus*, Autumn 1987, pp. 36–41.
——, 'Les Murray: Shaping an Australian Voice', in *Identifying Poets*, Edinburgh: Edinburgh University Press, 1993, pp. 73–101.
——, 'Les A. Murray Talking with Robert Crawford', *Verse* (Oxford), vol. 11(3)/vol. 12(1), 1995, pp. 162–72.
Daniel, M., 'Poetry Is Presence: An Interview with Les Murray', *Commonweal*, 22 May 1992, pp. 9–12.

Davidson, J., 'Les A. Murray', in *Sideways From the Page: the Meanjin interviews*, Melbourne: Fontana Books, 1983, pp. 346–72.

Dawe, B., 'Tributary Streams: Some Sources of Social and Political Concerns in Modern Australian Poetry', *Australian Literary Studies*, vol. 15(3), May 1992, pp. 97–109.

Diwell, S., 'Poetic Touch in Switch of Oz Loyalty Pledge', *Mercury*, 24 December 1992, p. 9.

Dobrez, L., 'The Battle of the Books: Poetics of Praxis vs The Reflective Mode', in *Parnassus Mad Ward*, St Lucia: UQP, 1990, pp. 201–30.

Duffy, M., 'How the Australia Council Is Killing Australian Literature', *Independent Monthly*, June 1995, pp. 73–5.

Elliott, B. (ed.), *The Jindyworobaks*, St. Lucia: UQP, 1979, pp. 283–8, 304–13.

Gaffney, C., 'Les Murray's Otherworld', *Quadrant*, July/August 1984, pp. 55–8.

——, 'Les Murray Again', *Quadrant*, January/February 1988, pp. 66–71.

——, 'This country Is My Mind', *Westerly*, Autumn 1994, pp. 67–79.

Goodwin, K., 'Les Murray: Toward Imminent Days', in P. K. Elkin (ed.), *Australian Poems in Perspective*, St Lucia: UQP, 1978, pp. 185–202.

Gould, A., 'A Verse Novel', *Helix*, no. 21–22, 1985, pp. 120–2.

——, '"With the Distinct Timbre of an Australian Voice"—The Poetry of Les Murray', *Antipodes*, vol. 6(2), December 1992, pp. 121–9.

Gray, R., 'An Interview with Les Murray', *Quadrant*, vol. 20(12), December 1976, pp. 69–72.

Gray, R., and Lehmann, G. (eds), 'Introduction' and 'Les A. Murray', in *The Younger Australian Poets*, Sydney: Hale & Iremonger, 1983, pp. 11–42.

Hart, K., '"Interest" in Les A. Murray', *Australian Literary Studies*, vol. 14(2), October 1989, pp. 147–59.

——, 'After Poetry II: A Quarterly Account of Recent Poetry', *Overland*, no. 125, 1991, pp. 61–7.

——, 'Open, Mixed, and Moving: Recent Australian Poetry', *World Literature Today*, vol. 67(3), Summer 1993, pp. 482–8.

Hauge, I., 'Les A. Murray-Enpresentasjon', *Vinduet*, vol. 45(3), June 1991, pp. 66–9.

Headon, D., 'Naming the Landscape—Les Murray's Literary Language', *Westerly*, no. 1, March 1983, pp. 71–8.

——, 'An Interview with Les Murray', *LINQ (Literature in North Queensland)*, vol. 13(3), 1985, pp. 7–16.

Hergenhan, L., 'War in Post-1960's Fiction: Johnston, Stow, McDonald, Malouf and Les Murray', *Australian Literary Studies*, vol. 12(2), October 1985, pp. 248–60.

Heseltine, H. P., 'Criticism and the Individual Talent', *Meanjin Quarterly*, vol. 31(1), March 1972, pp. 10–24.

Hope, D., 'Murray Goes Back to the Bush to Retrieve Australian Poetry', *Bulletin*, 11 March 1986, pp. 78–80.

Indyk, I., 'The Pastoral Poets', *Australian Literary Studies*, vol. 13(4), 1988, pp. 353–69.

James, C., 'Les is More', in *Snake Charmers in Texas*, London: Jonathon Cape, 1988, pp. 49–57. (Originally published in *New York Review of Books*, 14 April 1983.)

Janakiram, A., 'Les Murray on Poetry: An Interview', *Rajasthan University Studies in English*, vol. 20, 1988, pp. 99–109.

Jennings, K., 'Wrangles, Yawps and Awful Moans', *Vogue Australia*, vol. 31(11), 1987, pp. 74–6.

Jones, D., 'Evoking the Past in Contemporary Australian Poetry', in K. Singh (ed.), *The Writer's Sense of the Past*, Singapore: Singapore University Press, 1987, pp. 198–211.

Kane, P., 'Sydney and the Bush: The Poetry of Les A. Murray', in A. Cromwell (ed.), *From Outback to City: Changing Preoccupations in Australian Literature of the Twentieth Century*, New York: American Association of Australian Literary Studies, 1988, pp. 15–22.

——, 'Les Murray', in Ross L. Ross (ed.), *International Literature in English*, New York and London: Garland Publishing, 1991, pp. 437–46.

——, 'Les Murray and Poetry's Otherworld', in *Australian Poetry: Romanticism and Negativity*, Cambridge: Cambridge University Press, 1996, ch. 11, pp. 185–202.

Kavanagh, P., and Kuch, P., 'An Interview with Les Murray', *Southerly*, vol. 44(4), December 1984, pp. 367–78. Republished as 'Creations From Our Side', in P. Kavanagh and P. Kuch (eds), *Conversations: Interviews with Australian Writers*, Sydney: Angus & Robertson, 1991, pp. 191–214.

Kennedy, L., 'Lunch with Les, Bush Bard', *Canberra Times*, 5 December 1993, p. 19.

Kiley, D., 'The Vernacular Country Club: Traditional Experiment, Experimental Tradition and Les Murray's *The Boys Who Stole The Funeral*', in *Association for the Study of Australia Literature: Sixteenth Annual Conference 3–8 July 1994*, convened by S. Lever and C. Pratt, Canberra: Association for the Study of Australian Literature and ADFA, 1995, pp. 64–70.

Kirkwood, P., 'Two Australian Poets as Theologians', *Compass Theology Review*, vol. 19, Autumn 1985, pp. 31–44.

Kinross Smith, G., '". . . The Frequent Image of Farms"—A Profile of Les Murray', *Westerly*, no. 3, September 1980, pp. 39–52.

Koch, C. J., 'Les Murray's Watershed', *Quadrant*, September 1980, pp. 40–2.

Koval, R., 'Les Murray', *One to One*, ABC Enterprises, 1992, pp. 93–101.

——, 'Extracts From the Poetry Special on Radio National's *Books and Writing*: with Les Murray, Judith Rodriguez and Kevin Hart', *Australian Book Review*, June 1995, pp. 45–7.

Krüger, M., 'Über Les Murray', *Akzente*, August 1995, pp. 320–31.

Leer, M., 'From Linear to Areal: Suggestions Towards a Comparative Literary Geography of Canada and Australia', *Kunapipi*, vol. 12(3), 1990, pp. 75–85.

——, 'Imagined Counterpart: Outlining a Conceptual Literary Geography of Australia', in G. Capone (ed.), *European Perspectives: Contemporary Essays on Australian Literature*, *Australian Literary Studies*, vol. 15(2), 1991, pp. 1–13.

——, '"Countour-line by Countour": Landscape Change as an Index of History in the Poetry of Les Murray', *Australian Literary Studies*, May 1994, pp. 249–61.
Longhurst, G., and Tylman, L., 'A Yarn with Les Murray', *Narcissis*, no. 5, 1992, pp. 12–16.
Lucas, J., 'An English Reading of Les Murray', *Meridian*, vol. 12(1), May 1993, pp. 76–83.
McAuley, J., 'The Sixties and After', in *A Map of Australian Verse*, Melbourne: Oxford University Press, 1975, ch. 14, pp. 297–334.
McDougall, R., 'The Railway in Australian Literature', *Australian-Canadian Studies*, vol. 5(1), 1987, pp. 13–20, republished in *World Literature Written in English*, vol. 28(1), 1988, pp. 75–82.
Macleod, M., 'Soundings in Middle Australia', *Meanjin*, vol. 39(1), 1980, pp. 103–11.
Malouf, D., 'Some Volumes of Selected Poems of the 1970s', *Australian Literary Studies*, vol. 10(3), May 1982, pp. 300–10.
Marsden, P., 'Paradise Mislaid: The Hostile Reception of Les A. Murray's Poem "The Liberated Plague"', in G. Davis and H. Maes-Jelinek (eds), *Crisis and Creativity in the New Literatures in English*, Amsterdam: Rodopi, 1990, pp. 265–89.
Maynard, N., 'Cultural Gerrymander', *Courier-Mail*, 4 February 1993, p. 14.
Neill, R., 'Verses, Curses', *Australian*, 17–18 April 1993, p. 19.
O'Connor, M., 'Australian Poetry—The Achievement of the Last 10 Years', in *Modern Australian Styles*, Foundation for Australian Literary Studies, Monograph no. 8, James Cook University, 1982, pp. 19–38.
Oles, C., 'Les Murray: An Interview by Carole Oles', *American Poetry Review*, vol. 15(2), March–April 1986, pp. 28–36.
Owen, J., 'Speaking Australian', *Poetry Wales*, vol. 24, 1988, pp. 41–5.
Page, G., 'Les Murray's "Otherworld"', *Quadrant*, January/February 1984, pp. 124–6.
Peacock, N., '"Embracing the Vernacular": An interview with Les A. Murray', *Australian and New Zealand Studies in Canada*, no. 7, June 1992, pp. 28–40.
Perrett, B., 'Les A. Murray and the "Aboriginal Way"', *Meridian*, May 1988, pp. 73–9.
Pierce, P., 'Australian Literature Since Patrick White', *World Literature Today*, vol. 67(3), Summer 1993, pp. 515–18.
Pollnitz, C., 'The Bardic Pose: A Survey of Les A. Murray's Poetry', *Southerly*, part 1, vol. 40(4), December 1980, pp. 367–87, part 2, vol. 41(1), March 1981, pp. 52–74, part 3, vol. 41(2), June 1981, pp. 188–210.
Porter, P., 'Country Poetry and Town Poetry: A Debate with Les Murray', *Australian Literary Studies*, vol. 9(1), May 1979, pp. 39–48.
——, 'Les Murray: An Appreciation', *Journal of Commonwealth Literature*, vol. 17(1), 1982, pp. 45–52.
——, 'Barding it up in Bunyah', *Scripsi*, June 1988, pp. 191–6.
——, 'Les Murray Interviewed by Peter Porter', *Australian Studies*, no. 4, December 1990, pp. 77–87.
——, 'Some Outstanding Australian Poets Today', in B. Olinder (ed.), *Breaking Circles*, Gothenburg: Dangaroo Press, 1991, pp. 108–17.

Rothwell, N., 'Poetic Justice', *Australian*, 10–11 May 1997, 'Weekend Magazine', pp. 12–17.
Rowlands, G., 'Behind the Weatherboard Mask', *Nation Review*, 12 October 1978, p. 18.
Semmler, C., 'Australian Poetry of the 1960's: Some Personal Impressions', *Poetry Australia*, no. 35, August 1970, pp. 44–52.
Shapcott, T., 'John Tranter and Les Murray', *Australian Literary Studies*, vol. 10(3), May 1982, pp. 381–8.
Sharkey, M., 'Les Murray's Single-minded Many-sidedness', *Overland*, vol. 82, December 1980, pp. 19–25.
Sharma, A., 'The Image of India in Les Murray's Poetry', *Literary Criterion*, vol. 25(2), 1990, pp. 47–57.
Sharp, I., 'Interview with Les Murray', *Landfall*, vol. 42(2), June 1988, pp. 150–68.
Shoemaker, A., 'The Poetry of Politics: Australian Aboriginal Verse', in *Black Words, White Page*, St Lucia: UQP, 1989, reprint 1992, pp. 179–229.
Singh, L., 'Landscape as Revelation: The Case of Les Murray', *SPAN*, no. 28, April 1989, pp. 90–6.
Smith, V., 'Poetry', in L. Kramer (ed.), *The Oxford History of Australian Literature*, Melbourne: Oxford University Press, 1981, pp. 271–426.
Stilz, G., 'Topographies of the Self: Coming to Terms with the Australian Landscape in Contemporary Australian Poetry', in G. Capone (ed.), *European Perspectives: Contemporary Essays on Australian Literature*, *Australian Literary Studies*, vol. 15(2), 1991, pp. 55–71.
Strauss, J., 'Anthologies and Orthodoxies', *Australian Literary Studies*, vol. 13(1), May 1987, pp. 87–95.
——, 'Elegies for Mothers: Reflections on Gwen Harwood's "Mother Who Gave Me Life" and Les Murray's "Three Poems in Memory of My Mother"', *Westerly*, vol. 34(4), December 1989, pp. 58–63.
——, 'Essayists Not At All Anonymous', *Overland*, no. 123, 1991, pp. 47–50.
Sykes, N., 'Christianity and Writing', *Studio*, Spring 1987, pp. 13–20. Also published in *Ministry*, March 1988.
Tacey, D. J., 'Australia's Otherworld: Aboriginality, Landscape and the Imagination', *Meridian*, vol. 8(1), May 1989, pp. 57–65.
Taylor, A., 'Past Imperfect? The Sense of the Past in Les A. Murray', *Southern Review*, vol. 19(1), 1986, pp. 89–103.
——, 'The Past Imperfect of Les A. Murray', *Reading Australian Poetry*, St Lucia: UQP, 1987, pp. 139–55.
——, 'The Past Imperfect: The Sense of the Past in Les A. Murray', in K. Singh (ed.), *The Writer's Sense of the Past*, Singapore: Singapore University Press, 1987, pp. 189–97.
——, 'A Blameless Boyhood: Australian Poetry About the Great War', *Westerly*, vol. 32(2), June 1987, pp. 55–61.
Throsby, M, 'The Search for "ah!"', *Look and Listen*, August 1984, pp. 68–71.

Tipping, R. K., 'Upon Making a Videotape of Les Murray, in the Series "Writers Talking"', in *Nearer By Far*, St Lucia: UQP, 1986, pp. 132–7.
Trigg, S., 'Les A. Murray, the Boeotian Count', *Scripsi*, vol. 2(4), June 1984, pp. 139–48.
Tulip, J., 'Three Poets—Modern, Australian and Religious', *Journal of Christian Education*, Papers 80, July 1984, pp. 34–48.
——, 'Les Murray in the 1980s: A New Religious Equanimity', *Southerly*, vol. 44(3), September 1984, pp. 281–96.
——, 'Poetry Since 1965', *Australian Literary Studies*, vol. 13(4), 1988, pp. 475–92.
——, 'Les A. Murray's "Haught Pastoral"', *Poetry Australia*, no. 120, 1989, pp. 12–25.
Walcott, D., 'Crocodile Dandy: Les Murray', in *What the Twilight Says*, New York: Farrar Straus & Giroux, 1998, pp. 182–92.
Wallace-Crabbe, C., 'And What About Forms', in *Three Absences in Australian Writing*, Foundation for Australian Literary Studies, Monograph no. 7, James Cook University, 1983, pp. 28–41.
Washington, P., 'Les Murray: The National Aesthetic and the Space of Poetry', in L. McCredden and S. Trigg (eds), *The Space of Poetry*, Melbourne: Melbourne University Literary and Cultural Studies, 1996, pp. 183–94.
Williams, B., 'Blood Histories, Welcoming Surfaces, and Celebratory Chuckles', *Poetry Canada Review*, vol. 7(2), Winter 1985–86, pp. 47–48.
——, '"I am a Characteristic Australian": an interview with Peter Porter', *Australian & New Zealand Studies in Canada*, no. 2, Fall 1989, pp. 65–73.
——, 'An Interview with Les A. Murray', *Westerly*, vol. 37(2), Winter 1992, pp. 45–56.
——, 'Malouf, Martin, Murray', *Nimrod*, vol. 36(2), 1993, pp. 135–42.
Williams, M., 'Looking Sideways: English Studies, Tradition, and Cross-Cultural Comparisons', *SPAN*, no. 28, April 1989, pp. 22–39.
Wilson, B. (Bishop), Gould, A., and Page, G., 'A Wild and Holy Calling', *Eremos Newsletter*, 1987, pp. 3–10.
Woodley, B., 'A Cry from the Bush', *Australian*, 18–19 January 1997, p. 25.
Wright, J. M., 'Lyricism in Contemporary Australian Poetry', *Westerly*, no. 4, December 1974, pp. 35–43.
Zwicky, F., 'Language or Speech? A Colonial Dilemma', *Overland*, no. 98, April 1985, pp. 42–6.
——, 'Nine Radio Commentaries: No. 6', in *The Lyre in the Pawnshop*, Western Australia: University of Western Australia Press, 1986, pp. 277–80.

Minor articles making reference to Les Murray

Anon., 'Poetry Competition', *honi soit*, 3 October 1962, p. 16.
Anon., 'Literary Prize After Lean Times', *Canberra Times*, 28 October 1970, p. 3.
Anon., 'Poet Murray Wins Another Top Award', *Australian*, 4 September 1984, p. 1.
Anon., 'I'm the Regius Professor of Idle Yarning', *Union Recorder*, vol. LXV(6), 1985, pp. 14–15.
Anon., 'Awards', *Quill & Quire*, vol. 51, June 1985, p. 34.

Anon., 'Former *Hermes* editor returns', *Gazette* (University of Sydney), September 1985, p. 11.
Anon., 'All Honourable Men', *Quadrant*, May 1989, p. 5.
Anon., 'Booknotes', *Sydney Morning Herald*, 4 November 1989, p. 84.
Anon., 'Booknotes', *Sydney Morning Herald*, 6 July 1991, p. 41.
Anon., 'Inklings', *Tasmanian Writers Union Newsletter*, vol. 12(1), 1992, pp. 9–10.
Anon., 'Just Les', *Economist*, 5 June 1993, p. 82.
Anon., 'Patronage', *Sydney Morning Herald*, 2 September 1996, editorial column.
Anon., 'Les Is More', *Sydney Morning Herald*, 17 March 1997, p. 24.
Anon., 'Poet Leads Revolt Against the Handling of Arts Grants', *Age*, 6 July 1994, p. 5.
Anon., 'Les Murray's Poetic Licence', *Sydney Morning Herald*, 9 July 1994, p. 32.
Anderson, D., 'Pressing Matters on the Mind', *Sydney Morning Herald*, 17 November 1990, p. 81.
Armitage, C., 'Les Back From the Dead, Lighter in Body and Soul', *Australian*, 21–22 September 1996, p. 3.
Baker, C., 'John Tranter', *Sydney Review*, June 1989, p. 10.
Beaver, B., 'Murray, Les A.', in R. Murphy (ed.), *Contemporary Poets of the English Language*, London: St James Press, 1970, pp. 785–7.
Beeby, R., 'Burly Bard Makes Light of Gold Gong', *Age*, 28 August 1984, p. 1.
Bennie, A., 'Poetry's Redneck Rebel', *Sydney Morning Herald*, 10 September 1994, 'Spectrum', p. 9A.
Bolton, K., 'Triptych: Dream' (poem), in Ken Bolton, *Selected Poems 1975–1990*, Ringwood, Vic: Penguin, 1992, pp. 67–8.
Bone, P., 'Writing and Rewriting From the Right', *Age*, 19 May 1990, 'Saturday Extra', p. 9.
Burchill, G., 'Australia Council on Brink Over Funding of Artists', *Age*, 1 May 1995, p. 16.
Capp, F., 'The Farther Shore', *Age*, 23 October 1993, 'Saturday Extra', p. 8.
Chenery, S., 'Glittering Prizes Lose Their Sparkle', *Australian*, 28–29 July 1989, 'Review', p. 6.
——, 'Murray Not Averse to a Move', *Australian*, 25–26 January 1992, 'Review', p. 6.
Chung, C., 'Poet Calls For New Arts Funding Ways', *Mercury*, 12 April 1995, p. 11.
Collins, K., 'Bush Bard Buffers the City Slings and Arrows', *Courier-Mail*, 23 December 1992, p. 26.
Costigan, M., 'Literature Board Above Constraints of Politics', *Australian*, 20 January 1993, p. 10.
Craven, P., 'Number's Up for Literary Lottery', *Australian*, 3 May 1995, p. 30.
Daly, M., 'Les Murray: A Lot More Than Just Any Old Poet', *Courier-Mail*, 'The Great Weekend', 9 November 1985, p. 8.
Davidson, J., 'The De-Dominionisation of Australia', *Meanjin*, vol. 38(2), July 1979, p. 148.
Devine, F., 'The Wisdom of Citizen Murray', *Sydney Morning Herald*, 31 December 1992, p. 9.

——, 'Suspicious of Rhyme and Rhythm Method', *Australian*, 23 September 1994, p. 13.
Doogue, E., 'Nearer to God With Les', *Age*, 15 November 1986, 'Saturday Extra', p. 11.
Duggan, L., 'Peasant Mandarin' (poem), *Southerly*, vol. 40(2), June 1980, pp. 224–5.
Elliott, B., 'Poetry: Primitive, Paroxysmal, and Even Jindyworobak', *WLWE (World Literature Written in English)*, vol. 17(2), 1978, pp. 467–87.
Ellis. B., 'Those Decadent University Days', *Sydney Morning Herald*, 19 September 1987, pp. 44–5.
Emery, J., 'At Last, Icons Make Way for Real Business', *Advertiser*, 4 March 1994, p. 19.
England, K., 'Writers Week: The Festival Awards', *Advertiser*, 5 March 1988, 'Magazine', p. 7.
Erlich, R., 'Dawe Wins Inaugural Literary Prize', *Age*, 24 March 1997, p. C6.
Fairfax, G., 'Funding Keeps the Arts Alive', *Australian*, 21 January 1993, p. 10.
Faust, B., 'Literature Board: The Inside Story', *Age*, 8 January 1993, p. 11.
Field, A., 'Losing Sight of the Goal', *Courier-Mail*, 5 July 1995, p. 17.
Field, M., 'Literary London', *Australian*, 1–2 December 1991, 'Review', p. 6.
Fitzgerald, M., 'A Sprawling Stillness', *Time*, 3 February 1997, pp. 78–9.
Frizell, H., 'Les Murray Takes Off', *Sydney Morning Herald*, 23 February 1980, p. 17.
Gibson, M., 'Enjoy Your Next Feed, Fellers; It's On Me', *Sydney Morning Herald*, 30 May 1989, p. 15.
Glover, R., 'Defending 'Art' for the Sake of National Pride', *Sydney Morning Herald*, 3 February 1993, p. 11.
Goodwin, K. and Lawson, A., 'Writing the Self' in *Macmillan Anthology of Australian Literature*, Melbourne: Macmillan, 1990, pp. 526–9.
Gould, A., 'Letters to Les Murray' (poem), *Overland*, no. 100, 1985, p. 41.
Halligan, M., 'Literary list' (letter), *Sydney Morning Herald*, 4 March 1993, p. 12.
Hart, K., 'After Poetry 17, A Quarterly Account of Recent Poetry', *Overland*, no. 131, 1993, pp. 42–8.
Hawley, J., 'Loneliness of the Short Term Writer-in-Residence', *Age*, 16 August 1986, 'Saturday Extra', pp. 9, 14.
Hefner, B., 'A Stirring of the Waters over Literature Grants', *Canberra Times*, 17 January 1993, p. 20.
——, 'A New Scheme for Funding Writers', *Canberra Times*, 24 January 1993, p. 22.
Hefner, R., 'Hope "Blows whistle" on Hoax Again', *Canberra Times*, 6 September 1987, 'Extra', p. 7.
——, 'Litbits', *Canberra Times*, 15 April 1990, p. 23.
——, 'Poets Take Aim at Australia Council Again', *Canberra Times*, 10 July 1994, p. 22.
Hickey, B., 'Literatures Black and White', in P. Bertinetti and C. Gorlier (eds), *Australiana: Italia, Europa, Australia: Ieri e Oggi*, Rome: Bulzoni Editore, 1982, pp. 93–7.
Hicks, I., '"Ingenious" Book Wins a Banjo', *Sydney Morning Herald*, 26 June 1993, p. 6.
Holland, M., 'Audio Poetry', *Poetry Review*, vol. 85, 1995, pp. 70–1.
Hugo, G., 'Les, the FX Holden of Aussie Poetry', *Mercury*, 20 May 1989, 'Weekend Review', p. 18.

Hugo, G., 'At Last, the Return of the Reclusive One', *Mercury*, 5 May 1990, p. 21.
Jackson, K., 'Murray's Natural Talent', *Courier-Mail*, 9 June 1993, 'Weekend', p. 2.
Jones, T., 'T. S. Eliot Prize', *Observer Review*, 19 January 1997.
Joseph, J., 'Auntie Seeks Poetic Justice for Favourite', *Times*, 14 May 1994, p. 6.
Kane, P., 'Mildura Writers Festival', *Notes & Furphies*, no. 38, April/May 1997, p. 12.
Kearney, C., 'Les Is More', *Gazette* (University of Sydney), vol. 25(1), April 1997, p. 6.
Layland, P., 'Unhurried Poetry of the Republic: Murray's Vision in the Vernacular', *Canberra Times*, 8 June 1996, p. 3.
Leunig, M., 'Travels With a Poet', *Age*, 22 December 1990, 'Saturday Extra', p. 1.
Liverani, M. R., 'All Ears for the Finest of Poets', *Uniken*, 20 November 1992, p. 4.
Loudon, J., 'Poetry: for Les Murray', *Studio*, no. 46, 1992, pp. 6–7.
Lumen, C., 'An Absolutely Ordinary Rainbow', in Michele Field (ed.), *Oz Shrink Lit*, Ringwood, Vic.: Penguin, 1983, p. 97.
Macklin, R., 'It Won't All Be Smooth Sailing', *Canberra Times*, 13 September 1995, p. 24.
MacLeod, M., 'Finding Echo Point' (poem), *Southerly*, vol. 44(2), June 1984, p. 207.
McGrath, S., 'An Otherworld of Dreaming in Poetry', *Weekend Australian Magazine*, 5–6 November 1983, p. 17.
McNicoll, D., 'Republican Poet Stands Up for the Queen', *Australian*, 3 October 1995, pp. 1, 2.
Mangan, J., 'There's Art In That There Venom', *Age*, 31 August 1995, p. 3.
Mead, P., 'Cultural Pathology: What Ern Malley Means', *Australian Literary Studies*, vol. 17(1), 1995, pp. 83–7.
Metherell, G., 'The Knockabout Intellectual', *Canberra Times*, 6 July 1996, p. C8.
Moffitt, I., 'The Poet of the Republic', *Bulletin*, 5 January 1977, pp. 36–7.
Moorhouse, F., 'The Taxi Driver's Complaint', *Adelaide Review*, May 1996, p. 14.
Morrison, B., 'Man of Might Belongs in Poetry Superleague', *Canberra Times*, 28 April 1990, p. B10.
——, 'The Fat Man in Literature', *Age*, 22 July 1990, 'Agenda', p. 11.
Neilsen, P., 'Les A. Murray and John Tranter Fight It Out At the Sydney Cricket Ground', *Southerly*, vol. 50(3), 1990, pp. 324–5.
Newman, M., 'ARNA: a Review', *honi soit*, 15 June 1961, p. 6.
O'Brien, G., 'Murray Gives the Word On His World', *Sydney Morning Herald*, 8 November 1993, p. 4.
O'Connor, M., 'Rejoinder', *Quadrant*, September 1992, pp. 70–1.
——, 'Professional Jealousy Can Fuel Literary Bias Claims', *Australian*, 26 January 1993, p. 10.
O'Neill, H., 'No-Novel Concept', *Sydney Morning Herald*, 22 May 1990, p. 78.
Porter, J. and Walker, J., 'Difficult Birth for Nation's New Pledge', *Sydney Morning Herald*, 31 December 1992, p. 1.
Pratt, N., 'Showbiz of the Solitary Man', *Australian*, 7 November 1970, p 19.
Reid, B., 'On Line', *Overland*, no. 130, 1993, pp. 20–1.
Riach, A., 'Scottish Studies in Australia: An Interim Report', *Scottish Literary Journal*, vol. 20, 1993, pp. 49–61.

Roberts, B., 'Les Murray' (poem), *Quadrant*, April 1977, p. 21.
Rodriguez, J., 'Murray, Les(lie), A(llan)', *Contemporary Poets*, 1975, pp. 1084–6; 3rd edition, J. Vinson (ed.), New York: St Martin's Press, 1980, pp. 1084–6; 4th edition, J. Vinson and D. L. Kirkpatrick (eds), London and Chicago: St James Press, 1985, pp. 603–4.
Shapcott, T. W., 'Poets Today', *Australian Book Review*, 1970, pp. 277–9.
Smith, H., 'Outstanding Poetry', *Age Monthly Review*, September 1989, pp. 6–8.
Smith, V., 'Experiment and Renewal: A Missing Link in Modern Australian Poetry', *Southerly*, no. 1, March 1987, pp. 3–18.
Stephens, T., 'Surviving Member of the Almost Dead Poets' Society', *Sydney Morning Herald*, 21 September 1996, p. 5.
——, 'Return of the Redneck', *Sydney Morning Herald*, 21 September 1996, p. 3.
Swain, T., 'Dreaming, Whites and the Australian Landscape: Some Popular Misconceptions', *Journal of Religious History*, vol. 15(3), June 1989, pp. 345–50.
Swanson, E., 'Prizewinner's Pride Pricked', *Australian*, 12–13 March 1988, 'Magazine', p. 13.
——, 'Striking a Blow for Knobbly Knees', *Australian*, 18–19 February 1989, 'Weekend', p. 9.
——, 'Forward: Scholarly Aussies', *Australian*, 20–21 May 1989, 'Weekend', p. 10.
——, 'Moving Experiences', *Australian*, 23–24 December 1989, 'Weekend', p. 5.
——, 'Forward', *Australian*, 13–14 April 1991, review p. 6.
——, 'Beating the Pacific Drum', *Australian*, 28–29 April 1991, 'Weekend', p. 6.
Sullivan, J., 'Shelf Life', *Age*, 6 January 1990, 'Saturday Extra', p. 7.
Talbot, D., 'Pledge a Win for Politics Over Poetry', *Age*, 29 December 1992, p. 5.
——, 'Poet Attacks Australia Council's Focus on "Politics over Art"', *Age*, 31 December 1992, p. 5.
——, 'Australia Council Defends Its Record', *Age*, 1 January 1993, p. 6.
Thompson, T., 'Australia Council Deserves Applause', *Age*, 15 February 1993, p. 12.
Tomlinson, C., 'From Gloucestershire: A Letter to Les Murray' (poem), *Quadrant*, vol. 34(9), September 1990, p. 85.
Treloar, C., 'Literary View', *Australian*, 22–23 July 1978, 'Magazine', p. 8.
Urquhart, A., 'Hacking at the Pattern: Post-Romantic Consciousness in the Poetry of John Tranter', *Southerly*, vol. 53(3), September 1993, pp. 12–29.
Van Niekerk, M., 'Writers Weekend', *West Australian*, 4 October 1989, p. 83.
Voumard, S., 'Les Murray Sets Off a Literary Kerfuffle', *Age*, 9 January 1993, pp. 1, 4.
Waldren, M., 'Drawing a Bead On the National Word Festival', *Australian*, 16–17 March 1991, 'Review', p. 6.
——, 'Les Lets Fly in War of Words', *Weekend Australian*, 23–24 January 1993, 'Review', p. 6.
Wallace-Crabbe, C., 'Mixed Motives, Mixed Diction: Recent Australian Poetry', *Journal of Commonwealth Literature*, vol. 19(1), 1984, pp. 2–9.
Williams, B., 'An Interview with Robert Gray', *Southerly*, May 1990, pp. 27–44 (discusses Murray, pp. 34, 37–8).

Wyndham, S., 'New from New York', *Australian*, 21–22 January 1989, 'Weekend', p. 7.
——, 'New from New York', *Australian*, 10–11 November 1990, 'Review', p. 7.

Miscellaneous articles that involve or mention the work of Les Murray

Anon., 'NBC Book Awards 1980', *Australian Book Review*, October 1980, p. 24.
Adamson, R., 'Poetry in Australia', *Weekend Australian Magazine*, 28–29 April 1979, p. 10.
Bourke, L., 'Maori and Aboriginal Literature in Australian and New Zealand Poetry Anthologies: Some Problems and Perspectives', *New Literatures Review*, no. 25, 1993, pp. 23–35.
Brady, V., 'Text but not Textbook; Or Rescuing the Delights of Reading', Agnes Nieuwenhuizen (ed.), *The Written World*, Melbourne: Thorpe, 1994, pp. 69–80.
Buckley, V., 'Identity: Invention or Discovery?', *Quadrant*, August 1980, pp. 12–19.
Carbines, L., 'Winning Author Hauls in a Bounty', *Age*, 13 September 1993, p. 6.
Conrad, P., 'So Men Write Poems in Australia', in *Down Home*, London: Chatto & Windus, 1988, pp. 196–212.
Fairbairn, A., 'Rapotec at Seventy', *Quadrant*, November 1983, pp. 29–35.
Fenton, J., 'Of Rods, Pens and Public Service', *The Times*, 12 May 1994, p. 16.
Fitzgerald, R., 'Liars and Larrikins', *Age*, 19 May 1990, 'Saturday Extra', p. 7.
Griffiths, T., 'History and Natural History: Conservation Movements in Conflict?', *Australian Historical Studies*, vol. 24, 1991, pp. 16–32.
Hart, K., 'After Poetry 13: A Quarterly Account of Recent Poetry', *Overland*, no. 127, 1992, pp. 28–34.
Haskell, D., and Fraser, H. (eds), 'Philip Salom', in *Wordhord*, Fremantle: Fremantle Arts Centre Press, 1989, pp. 152–4.
Hawley, J., 'The Works of Henry Lawson', *Age*, 22 September 1984, 'Saturday Extra', p. 7.
Hellyer, J., 'The Luxury of Dreaming', in D. Brown, H. Ellyard and B. Polkinghorne (eds), *Angry Women*, Sydney: Hale & Iremonger, 1989, pp. 81–7.
Hugo, G., 'Wandering Poet Settles on State's Haunting Landscape', *Mercury*, 1 July 1989, 'Weekend Review', p. 18.
——, 'Humour From the Dark Side is Raymond's Literary Forte', *Mercury*, 3 March 1990, p. 21.
Ikin, V and Dolin, K., 'Australia (with Papua New Guinea)', *Journal of Commonwealth Literature*, vol. 23(2), 1988, pp. 8–35.
Indyk, I., 'Some Versions of Australian Pastoral', *Southerly*, no. 2, June 1988, pp. 115–27.
Jose, N., 'Cultural Identity: "I think I'm Something Else"', *Daedalus*, vol. 114(1), Winter 1985, pp. 311–42.
Kavanagh, P. and Kuch, P., 'Little Harmonic Labyrinths' (interview with Peter Porter), in *Conversations: Interviews with Australian Writers*, Sydney: Angus & Robertson, 1991, pp. 215–30, (originally published in *Southerly*).
Kellas, A., 'An Aussie Poet's Philosophy—It's About Having Fun', *Mercury*, 10 February 1990, p. 18.

Keneally, T., 'The World's Worse End?', *Antipodes*, vol. 2(1), Spring 1988, pp. 5–8. Also published in *Caliban*, no. 14, 1977, pp. 81–9.
Koviloska-Poposka, I., 'Australian Literature and Art in Macedonia', Mirko Jurak (ed.), *Australian Papers: Yugoslavia, Europe and Australia*, Ljubljana, Yugoslavia: Faculty of Arts and Science, Edvard Kardelj University of Ljubljana, 1983, pp. 83–8.
Morgan, P., 'Submerged Cultures in Australia', *Meanjin*, vol. 47(2), 1988, pp. 203–13.
Murdoch, D., 'The Riches of Empire: Postcolonial Literature and Criticism', *Choice*, vol. 32, March 1995, pp. 1059–70.
Murphy, P., 'Scarab as Cypher', *Poetry Australia*, no. 100, 1985, pp. 4–12.
Owen, J., 'Beauty and the Beast', *Island*, no. 58, Autumn 1994, pp. 56–9.
Pierce, P., 'Perceptions of the Enemy in Australian War Literature', *Australian Literary Studies*, vol. 12(2), October 1985, pp. 166–81.
Pollnitz, C., 'Peter Porter: Whether "the World is But a Word" ', *Scripsi*, June 1988, pp. 197–209.
Priessnitz, H., 'Dreams in Austerica: A Preliminary Comparison of the Australian and the American Dream', *Westerly*, vol. 39(3), Spring 1994, pp. 45–64.
Sharkey, M., 'The Breaks' (poem), *Otis Rush*, no. 4, April 1989, p. 1.
Sluga, G., 'Dis/placed', *Meanjin*, vol. 48(1), 1989, pp. 153–60.
Tacey, D., *Edge of the Sacred*, Melbourne: Harper Collins, 1995, references to Murray passim: see index.
Taylor, A., 'War Poetry: Myth as De-formation and Re-formation', *Australian Literary Studies*, vol. 12(2), October 1985, pp. 182–93.
——, 'A Book on Australian Poetry', in *Reading Australian Poetry*, St Lucia: UQP, 1987, pp. 7–21.
Tipping, R., 'Australia's Living History: The Writers', *Book Magazine*, December 1987/January 1988, pp. 2, 3, 5.
Tomlinson, C., 'From Gloucestershire', *Quadrant*, vol. 34(9), September 1990, p. 85.
Totaro, P., 'Saving the Land with Poetry', *Bulletin*, 30 January – 6 February 1990, pp. 188–92.
Turner Hospital, J., 'An Expatiation on Expatriation', *Overland*, no. 114, May 1989, pp. 35–9.
Voumard, S., 'A Night Oodgeroo Would Have Relished', *Sydney Morning Herald*, 18 September 1993, p. 11.
Wallace-Crabbe, C., 'Vincent Buckley and the Poetry of Presence', *Journal of Popular Culture*, vol. 23(2), Fall 1989, pp. 81–91.
——, 'Spaces, Cargoes, Documents, Values and Principles: Some Recent Poetry Anthologies', *Australian Literary Studies*, vol. 15(4), October 1992, pp. 323–7.
Willams, B., 'Interview with Peter Porter', *Westerly*, no. 2, June 1990, pp. 57–73.
Wyndham, S., 'Two Hundred Years On and Still In the Cell', *Australian*, 22–23 October 1988, 'Magazine', p. 10.

Letters published with reference to Les Murray

Crawford, R., 'Australian Poets', *Times Literary Supplement*, 18 December 1987, p. 1403.
Fletcher, J., 'Aphrodite Street', *London Review of Books*, 4 February 1988, p. 4.
——, 'Aphrodite Street', *London Review of Books*, 31 March 1988, p. 4.
Gould, A., untitled, *Australian Book Review*, April 1995, pp. 5–6.
Halligan, M., 'Les Murray's Problems', *Independent Monthly*, March 1995, pp. 22–3.
James, C., 'Australian Poets', *Times Literary Supplement*, 18 December 1987, p. 1403.
Schmidt, M., 'Chair of Poetry', *The Times*, 14 May 1994, p. 19.
Wallace-Crabbe, C., untitled, *Australian Book Review*, April 1995, p. 6.
Wearne, A., 'Aphrodite Street', *London Review of Books*, 10 December 1987, p. 4.

Reviews of Les Murray's volumes

The Ilex Tree

Anon., *Times Literary Supplement*, 15 December 1966, p. 1172.
Anon., *Current Affairs Bulletin*, 26 December 1966, pp. 44–5.
Anon., *Expression*, Autumn 1968, pp. 22–3.
Anderson, D., *Australian Highway*, Winter 1968, p. 15.
Dunlop, R., *Poetry Australia*, vol. 2(10), June 1966, pp. 31–4.
Douglas, D., *Age*, 10 September 1966, p. 23.
Fuller, R., *London Magazine*, January 1967, pp. 86–8.
Hart-Smith, W., *Poetry Magazine*, no. 1, 1966, pp. 28–30.
Haynes, F., *Westerly*, no. 3, December 1966, pp. 90–4.
Lee, S. E., *Southerly*, vol. 26(2), 1966, pp. 129–30.
McCuaig, R., *Canberra Times*, 11 December 1965, p. 11.
Nesbitt, B., *Australian*, 11 June 1966, p. 8.
Reeves, P., *Westerly*, no. 3, December 1966, p. 92.
Smith, V., *Bulletin*, 12 February 1966, p. 48.
Slessor, Kenneth, *Daily Telegraph* (Sydney), 18 December 1965, p. 17.

The Weatherboard Cathedral

Dunlop, R., *Poetry Australia*, February 1970, pp. 51–2.
England, K., Adelaide *Advertiser*, 8 November 1969, p. 14.
Goodwin, K., *Meanjin*, vol. 30(3), September 1971, p. 373.
Hall, R., *Australian*, 24 January 1970, p. 19.
Harrison, K., *WLWE Newsletter*, no. 18, November 1970, pp. 45–6.
Jones, E., *Nation*, 13 December 1969, pp. 22–3.
Kellaway, F., *Overland*, Summer 1970–71, pp. 38–40.
Lehmann, G., *Bulletin*, 7 February 1970, p. 43.
McDonald, R., *Makar*, vol. 5(4), December 1969, pp. 27–31.
Riddell, A., *Sydney Morning Herald*, 22 November 1969, p. 16.
Rowlands, G., *Makar*, vol. 5(4), December 1969, pp. 32–4.
Slessor, K., *The Daily Telegraph* 18 October 1969, p. 17.

Simpson, R. A., *Age*, 6 December 1969, p. 17.
Tulip, J., *Southerly*, no. 2, 1970, pp. 148–51.
Ward, P., *Australian Book Review*, December 1969/January 1970, pp. 60–1.

Poems Against Economics

Curtis, G., *Makar*, vol. 8(2), September 1972, pp. 43–5.
England, K., Adelaide *Advertiser*, 28 October 1972, p. 20.
Harrison-Ford, C., *New Poetry*, June 1972, pp. 40–1.
Keesing, N., *Sydney Morning Herald*, 9 December 1972.
Kynaston, E., *Nation Review*, 5–11 August 1972, p. 1215.
McDonald, R., *Poetry Australia*, no. 47, 1973, pp. 71–3.
Page, G., *Canberra Times*, 14 October 1972, p. 10.
Porter, P., *Observer*, 5 August 1973, p. 28.
Roberts, P., *Sydney Morning Herald*, 26 August 1972, p. 20.
Shapcott, T., *Australian Book Review*, December 1972, pp. 42–3.
Simpson, R. A., *Age*, 14 October 1972, p. 17.
Tulip, J., *Bulletin*, 5 August 1972, pp. 38–9.
——, *Southerly*, vol. 33(2), June 1973, pp. 234–5.

Lunch & Counter Lunch

England, K., Adelaide *Advertiser*, 7 December 1974, p. 28.
Garfitt, R., *Stand*, vol. 17(1), 1975, pp. 67–8.
Gray, R., *New Poetry*, vol. 23(1), 1975, pp. 77–8.
Hart, K., *Southern Review*, vol. 10(1), 1977, pp. 83–5.
Johnston, M., *Sydney Morning Herald*, 9 November 1974, p. 15.
Malouf, D., *Poetry Australia*, no. 57, December 1975, pp. 70–2.
Rappolt, P., *Canberra Times*, 15 November 1974, p. 8.
Samson, C., *Nation Review*, 14–20 February 1975, p. 480.
Simpson, R. A., *Age*, 8 March 1975, p. 16.
Tranter, J., *Australian*, 2 November 1974, p. 19.

Selected Poems: The Vernacular Republic (1976)

Catalano, G., *Meanjin*, vol. 36(1), May 1977, pp. 67–72.
Gould, A., *Nation Review*, 26 November – 2 December 1976, p. 141.
Gray, R., *Sydney Morning Herald*, 11 September 1976, p. 15.
——, *Sydney Morning Herald*, 11 December 1976, p. 13.
Hall, M., in Jan Fox and Brian MacFarlane (eds), *Perspectives 79: HSC English*, Melbourne: Sorrett Publishing, 1978, pp. 70–7.
McDonald, R., *National Times*, 18–23 October 1976, pp. 64–5.
Langford, G, *Sydney Morning Herald*, 11 December 1976, p. 13.
Nelson, P. , *Poetry Australia*, no. 65, October 1977, pp. 74–8.
Pringle, J., *Sydney Morning Herald*, 11 December 1976, p. 13.
Taylor, A., *Makar*, vol. 14(2), June 1980, pp. 53–9.

Tranter, J., *Australian*, 29 January 1977, p. 28.
Treloar, C., *24 Hours*, November 1976, pp. 47–8.

Ethnic Radio

Anon., *Australian Book Review*, no. 5, October 1978, p. 30.
Gould, A., *Nation Review*, 14–20 July 1978, pp. 18–19.
——, *Poetry Australia*, no. 70, 1979, pp. 67–9.
Gray, R., *Sydney Morning Herald*, 16 December 1978, p. 11.
Griffin, J., Adelaide *Advertiser*, 25 February 1978, p. 25.
Hall, R., *Weekend Australian Magazine*, 4–5 March 1978, p. 8.
Lee, S. E., and Pollnitz, C., *Southerly*, vol. 39(4), December 1979, pp. 443–5.
Lindsay, E., *Quadrant*, vol. 70, March 1979, p. 70.
Macainsh, N., *Australian Book Review*, 9 September 1978, pp. 9–10.
O'Connor, M., *Kunapipi*, vol. l(l), 1979, pp. 40–52.
Page, G., *Canberra Times*, 14 October 1978, p. 17.
Porter, P., *Observer Review*, 17 May 1981, p. 29.
Rodriguez, J., *Sydney Morning Herald*, 8 July 1978, p. 19.
Shapcott, T., *Age*, 1 July 1978, p. 23.
Talbot, N., *The Companion to This Place*, vol. 1, 1980, pp. 120–33.
Taylor, A., *Makar*, vol. 14(2), June 1980, pp. 53–9.
Tranter, J., *24 Hours*, July 1978, pp. 70–1.

The Boys Who Stole The Funeral

Barnie, J., *Kunapipi*, vol. 4(1), 1982, pp. 172–8.
Castan, C., in Helen Daniel (comp.), *The Good Reading Guide*, Fitzroy: McPhee Gribble, 1989, p. 213.
Catalano, G., *Meanjin*, vol. 39(3), October 1980, pp. 351–5.
Dunlevy, M., *Canberra Times*, 1 November 1980, p. 14.
Forbes, J., *New Poetry*, vol. 28(1), May 1980, pp. 60–3.
Giles, B., *Australian Book Review*, September 1980, pp. 4–5.
Grant, J., in Helen Daniel (comp.), *The Good Reading Guide*, 1989, pp. 213–14.
Griffin, J., Adelaide *Advertiser*, 3 May 1980, p. 35.
Koch, C., *Quadrant*, vol. 24, September 1980, pp. 40–2.
Page, G., *National Times*, 4–10 May 1980, p. 45.
Porter, P., *Observer Review*, 17 May 1981, p. 29.
Pringle, J. D., *Sydney Morning Herald*, 15 March 1980, p. 14.
Pringle, J., *Sydney Morning Herald*, 20 December 1980, p. 35.
Shapcott, T., *Australian Literary Studies*, vol. 10(3), May 1982, pp. 381–8.
Thomas, K., *Australian*, 12 March 1980, p. 10.
Wallace-Crabbe, C., *Age*, 19 July 1980, p. 23.

The Vernacular Republic Poems 1961–1981

Anon., *Publishers Weekly*, 4 June 1982, pp. 61–2.
Adcock, F., *Times Literary Supplement*, 30 July 1982, p. 830.

Benfey, C., *Parnassus: Poetry in Review*, vol. 11(2), 1983, pp. 236–2.
Crossley-Holland, *Times Educational Supplement*, 6 August 1982, p. 20.
Gibson, M., *Library Journal*, August 1982, p. 1466.
Grant, J., *Age Monthly Review*, vol. 2(4), August 1982, pp. 9–10.
James, C., *New York Review of Books*, 14 April 1983, pp. 31–2.
Kinzie, M., *American Poetry Review*, July–August 1983, pp. 33–4.
Lucas, J., *New Statesman*, 7 May 1982, pp. 20–1.
McClatchy, J., *Poetry*, vol. 143, December 1983, pp. 172–4.
Porter, P., *Observer Review*, 17 May 1981, p. 29.
Stephen, I., *Kunapipi*, vol. 4(2), 1982, pp. 154–5.

Equanimities

Stephen, I., *Kunapipi*, vol. 4(2), 1982, pp. 154–5.

The People's Otherworld

Anderson, D., *National Times*, 23–29 December 1983, p. 28.
Barnie, J., *Kunapipi*, vol. 6(1), 1984, pp. 107–22.
Brady, B., *Helix*, nos. 21–22, 1985, pp. 112–20.
Croft, J., *Australian Book Review*, no. 62, July 1984, pp. 19–20.
Dutton, G., *Bulletin*, 6 December 1983, p. 99.
Duwell, M., *Weekend Australian Magazine*, 5–6 November 1983, p. 19.
Gould, A., *Age*, 3 December 1983, 'Saturday Extra', p. 15.
Haskell, D., *Westerly*, vol. 29(4), 1984, pp. 73–6.
Lehmann, G., *Sydney Morning Herald*, 12 November 1983, p. 41.
Lugg, P., *Canberra Times*, 4 February 1984, p. 14.
Morrison, B., *Times Literary Supplement*, 9 August 1985, p. 873.
——, *Age Monthly Review*, vol. 5(5), 1985, pp. 4–5.
Morse, R., *PN Review*, vol. 44, 1985, p. 68.
O'Donohue, B., *Arts National*, vol. 2(4), 1985, pp. 59, 106.
Porter, P., *Observer*, 2 December 1984, p. 19.
Pybus, R., *Stand*, vol. 26(3), 1985, pp. 62–4.
Rowlands, G., *Ash*, vol. 16 (Winter), 1984, pp. 31–2.
Zwicky, F., *Overland*, no. 98, 1985, pp. 42–6.

Selected Poems

Corcoran, N., *Times Literary Supplement*, 22 August 1986, p. 919.
Dodsworth, M., *Guardian Weekly*, 11 January 1987, p. 21.
Polard, A., *British Book News*, July 1986, p. 429.
Speirs, L., *English Studies*, vol. 68(5), October 1987, p. 453.
Ward, J., *Poetry Review*, vol. 76, October 1986, pp. 48–9.

The Daylight Moon

Anon, *Publishers Weekly*, 11 November 1988, p. 50.
Anon, *Virginia Quarterly Review*, vol. 66(1), Winter 1990, p. 28.

Anon., *Canadian Literature*, no. 129, Summer 1991, p. 251.
Allen, *Library Journal*, 1 February 1989, p. 66.
Beston, J. B., *Choice* (USA), vol. 26(11/12), July/August 1989, p. 1837.
Birkets, S., *Parnassus: Poetry Review*, vol. 15(2), 1989, pp. 31–48.
Buckley, V., *Age*, 2 January 1988, 'Saturday Extra', p. 8.
Calder, R., *Scottish Literary Journal*, Spring 1989, pp. 45–7.
D'Evelyn, T., *Christian Science Monitor*, 14 June 1989, p. 12.
Dodsworth, M., *Guardian*, 13 May 1988, p. 26.
J. E., *Booklist*, 15 December 1988, p. 678.
Grant, J., *Adelaide Review*, January 1988, p. 27.
Guillory, D., *Magill's Literary Annual*, 1990, pp. 157–62.
Imlah, M., *Times Literary Supplement*, 18 May 1990, p. 521.
Jenkins, A., *Observer*, 8 May 1988, p. 42.
Jones, E., *National Times on Sunday*, 27 December 1987, p. 30.
Kane, P., *Antipodes*, vol. 2(1), 1988, p. 67.
Lehmann, G., *Weekend Australian Magazine*, 27–28 February 1988, p. 14.
Lynch, M., *Canberra Times*, 6 February 1988, p. B5.
Macrae, A. D. F., *Australian Studies* (UK), no, 1, June 1988, pp. 100–5.
Narogin, M., *Age Monthly Review*, vol. 8(2), May 1988, pp. 3–4.
Naisby, T. H., *Newcastle Herald*, 29 October 1988, p. 9.
O'Grady, R., *Advertiser Magazine*, 27 February 1988, p. 7.
Porter, P. , *Journal of Commonwealth Literature*, vol. 17(1), 1982, pp. 45–52.
Pybus, R., *Stand*, vol. 31(1), Winter 1989, pp. 75–6.
Russell, K., *Overland*, no. 110, March 1988, pp. 82–3.
Scammell, W., *London Magazine*, August/September 1988, pp. 108–9.
Scupham, P., *Poetry Review*, vol. 128(1), 1988, p. 8.
Shaw, R., *Poetry*, vol. 156(3), 1990, pp. 164–5.
Sheppard, R., *New Statesman*, 13 May 1988, pp. 31–2.
Stead, C. K., *London Review of Books*, vol. 10(4), 18 February 1988, pp. 11–12.
Urquhart, A., *Westerly*, no. 4, December 1988, pp. 89–91.
Vendler, H., *New York Review of Books*, 17 August 1989, pp. 26–30.
Walcott, D., *The New Republic*, 6 February 1989, pp. 25–8.

The Vernacular Republic (1988)

D'Evelyn, T., *Christian Science Monitor*, 14 June 1989, p. 12.
Walcott, D., *The New Republic*, 6 February 1989, pp. 25–8.

The Idyll Wheel: Cycle of a Year at Bunyah

Cam, H., *Sydney Morning Herald*, 29 July 1989, p. 78.
Duwell, M., *Australian*, 19–20 August 1989, 'Weekend', p. 9.
Page, G., *Canberra Times*, 7 October 1989, p. 14.

Dog Fox Field

Anon., *New Yorker*, 26 December 1992, p. 61.
Adcock, F., *Sunday Times*, 10 March 1991, p. 6.
Cam, H., *Sydney Morning Herald*, 27 April 1991, p. 41.
Croft, J., *Australian Book Review*, November 1990, pp. 6–7.
Foulcher, J., *Canberra Times*, 17 November 1990, p. B8.
Guillory, D., *Library Journal*, vol. 118, 1 February 1993, p. 84.
Hart, K., *Overland*, no. 122, 1991, pp. 69–71.
Hodgins, P., *Adelaide Review*, January 1991, pp. 21–2.
Hodgins, P., *Sydney Review*, April 1991, p. 12.
Norfolk, L., *Times Literary Supplement*, 5 July 1991, pp. 21–2.
Pollnitz, C., *Age*, 13 July 1991, 'Saturday Extra', p. 8.
Rowe, N., *Southerly*, vol. 51(2), 1991, pp. 319–30.
Russell, K., *Newcastle Herald*, 26 January 1991, p. 14.
Salusinzsky, I., *Australian*, 9–10 February 1991, 'Review', p. 7.
Seaman, D., *Booklist*, 15 January 1993, p. 873.
Sharma, A., *Antipodes*, vol. 6(2), 1992, pp. 158–9.
Sisson, C., *Spectator*, 2 March 1991, pp. 27–8.
Stead, C., *London Review of Books*, 23 May 1991, pp. 10–11.

Collected Poems

Beake, F., *Stand*, vol. 34(4), Autumn 1993, pp. 79–82.
Clunies Ross, B., *Poetry Wales*, vol. 29, 1993, pp. 52–5.
Foden, G., *Times Literary Supplement*, 29 May 1992, p. 24.
Gould, A., *Canberra Times*, 28 September 1991, p. C8.
Kelly, D., *Oz Muze*, vol. 1(13), October 1991, p. 8.
Mead, P., *Australian Society*, August 1991, pp. 40–2.
Pollnitz, C., *Age*, 13 July 1991, 'Saturday Extra', p. 8.
Symons, J., *London Review of Books*, 12 March 1992, p. 27.

The Rabbiter's Bounty: Collected Poems (USA publication)

Anon., *Virginia Quarterly Review*, vol. 68, Summer 1992, p. 101.
Alexander, M., *Agenda*, vol. 29, 1991, pp. 79–82.
Dooley, D., *Hudson Review*, Autumn 1992, pp. 509–17.
Filkins, P., *New England Review*, vol. 15(3), 1993, pp. 197–207.
Heyward, M., *Book World*, vol. 22, 16 February 1992, p. 11.
Kitchen, J., *Georgia Review*, Spring 1992, pp. 150–66.
Logan, W., *Poetry*, vol. 160(3), June 1992, pp. 162–6.
Maxwell, G., *Poetry Review*, vol. 81, 1992, pp. 26–7.

Translations From The Natural World

Cam, H., *Sydney Morning Herald*, 12 December 1992, p. 48.
Coad, D., *World Literature Today*, vol. 69(1), 1995, pp. 219–20.
Crichton Smith, I., *Scottish Literary Journal*, vol. 20, 1993, pp. 35–7.
Foulcher, J., *Island*, vol. 55, 1992, pp. 69–72.
Gould, A., *Canberra Times*, 5 December 1992, p. C8.
Hart, K., *Age*, 17 October 1992, 'Saturday Extra', p. 9.
Hodgins, P., *Adelaide Review*, October 1992, pp. 32–3.
Hulse, M., *Guardian Weekly*, 23 May 1993, p. 29.
MacKinnon, L., *Times Literary Supplement*, 20 August 1993, p. 6.
Muratori, F., *Library Journal*, vol. 119, January 1994, p. 120.
Pollnitz, C., *Weekend Australian*, 30–31 January 1993, 'Review', p. 4.
Pybus, R., *Stand*, vol. 35(2), Spring 1994, pp. 54–5.
Speirs, L., *English Studies*, vol. 76(2), March 1995, pp. 156–84 ('Review', pp. 174–5).
Thorpe, A., *Observer*, 20 June 1993, p. 61.
Wilmer, C., *Poetry Review*, vol. 83, 1993, pp. 34–5.
Wood, J., *London Review of Books*, 5 August 1993, pp. 13–14.

Collected Poems (1994)

Bradley, J., *Courier-Mail*, 25 February 1995.
Cox, R., *Mercury*, 16 January 1995, p. 26.
Elliott, R., *Canberra Times*, 13 May 1995, p. C13.
Leadbetter, D., *Overland*, vol. 141, 1995, pp. 74–5.
Page, G., *Voices*, Winter 1995, pp. 113–17.
Scammell, W., *Spectator*, 21 November 1992, p. 42.
——, *Spectator*, 23 January 1993, p. 38.
Thorpe, A., *Observer*, 26 July 1992, p. 54.
Wallace-Crabbe, C., *Australian Book Review*, no. 168, February/March 1995, pp. 48–9.

Subhuman Redneck Poems

Anderson, D., *Australian Book Review*, November 1996, pp. 9–10.
Fitzgerald, M., *Time*, 3 February 1997, pp. 78–9.
Lowry, E., *Times Literary Supplement*, 10 January 1997, p. 8.

The Peasant Mandarin

Anon., *Choice*, vol. 16, April 1979, p. 244.
Dutton, G., *Bulletin*, 21 November 1978, p. 68.
Duwell, M., *Australian Literary Studies*, vol. 9, 1979, pp. 259–62.
Edwards, C., *New Poetry*, vol. 27(2), 1979, pp. 4–12.
Garrett, J., *Australian Book Review*, no. 17, December 1979/January 1980, pp. 21–2.
Johnson, M., *World Literature Today*, Winter 1980, p. 174.
Kelly, C., *National Times*, 30 September 1978, p. 37.
Lowe, L., *Campaign*, no. 37, 1978, p. 50.

Monaghan, P., *Helix*, no. 2, 1978, p. 54.
——, *Canberra Times*, 3 February 1979, p. 17.
Myers, D., *International Fiction Review*, vol. 7(1), 1980, pp. 69–70.
Noonan, W., *24 Hours*, November 1978, p. 67.
Richards, M., *Helix*, no. 4, 1979, pp. 73–8.
Tulip, J., *Sydney Morning Herald*, 30 September 1978, p. 17.

Persistence in Folly

Grant, J., *Sydney Morning Herald*, 1 September 1984, p. 41.
McLaren, J., *Australian Book Review*, no. 69, April 1985, p. 14.
Mitchell, A., *Weekend Australian Magazine*, 4–5 August 1984, p. 15.
Morrison, B., *Times Literary Supplement*, 9 August 1985, p. 873.
——, *Age Monthly Review*, September 1985, pp. 4–5.
Morse, R., *PN Review*, vol. 12(5), 1986, pp. 49–50.
Roderick, C., *Courier-Mail*, 'Great Weekend', 15 December 1984, p. 31.
Rodriguez, J., *Meridian*, vol. 4(1), May 1985, pp. 72–5.

The Australian Year: The Chronicle of Our Seasons and Celebrations

Hill, B., *Australian Book Review*, July 1986, pp. 6–7.

Blocks and Tackles

Croft, J., *Australian Book Review*, November 1990, pp. 6–7.
Foulcher, J., *Canberra Times*, 17 November 1990, p. B8.
Hodgins, P., *Adelaide Review*, January 1991, pp. 21–2.
——, *Sydney Review*, April 1991, p. 12.
Jennings, K., *Sydney Morning Herald*, 17 November 1990, p. 81.
Pollnitz, C., *Age*, 13 July 1991, 'Saturday Extra', p. 8.
Rowe, N., *Southerly*, vol. 51(2), 1991, pp. 319–30.
Salusinzsky, I., *Australian*, 9–10 February 1991, 'Review', p. 7.
Sharma, A., *Antipodes*, vol. 7(1), June 1993, p. 65.
Talbot, N., *Newcastle Herald*, 6 April 1991, p. 12.

The Paperbark Tree

Davie, D., *London Review of Books*, 5 November 1992, pp. 26–7.
Fraser, M., *Sydney Morning Herald*, 23 January 1993, p. 38.
Lovely, D., *PN Review*, vol. 19(3), 1993, p. 52.
Scammell, W., *Spectator*, 23 January 1993, p. 38.
Wilmer, C., *Poetry Review*, 1993, pp. 34–5.
Wormald, M., *Times Literary Supplement*, 21 May 1993, p. 27.

The New Oxford Book of Australian Verse

Brissenden, R. F., *Weekend Australian Magazine*, 22–23 February 1986, p. 20.
Buckley, V., *Age*, 24 May 1986, 'Saturday Extra', p. 14.

Conrad, P., *Times Literary Supplement*, 19 December 1986, p. 1421.
Edgar, S., *Island*, no. 28, 1986, pp. 56–9.
Harrington, T., *Overland*, no. 103, July 1986, pp. 28–31.
Heyward, M., *Australian Book Review*, July 1986, pp. 4–5.
Kantaris, S., *Poetry Review*, vol. 77, June 1987, pp. 54–5.
McDuff, D., *Stand*, vol. 34(3), Summer 1993, pp. 24–5.
McKernan, S., *Bulletin*, 11 March 1986, p. 80.
McLeod, A. L., *Choice*, vol. 24, October 1986, p. 309.
Nelson, P., *Australian*, 30 November – 1 December 1991, 'Review', p. 5.
O'Grady, R., Adelaide *Advertiser*, 26 April 1986, p. 21.
Page, G., *Canberra Times*, 8 April 1994 (The Reader), p. 13.
——, *Sydney Morning Herald*, 15 March 1986, p. 45.
Porter, P., *Scripsi*, vol. 4(2), 1986, pp. 12–18.
Rowbotham, D., *Courier Mail*, 'The Great Weekend', 22 February 1986, p. 6.
Smith, V., *Quadrant*, vol. 30, April 1986, pp. 83–4.
Taylor, A., *CRNLE Reviews Journal*, no. 2, 1986, pp. 84–6.
Thomas, M., *Canberra Times*, 22 February 1986, p. B2.
Wallace-Crabbe, C., *Australian Book Review*, December/January 1986/87, pp. 12–13.
Williams, H., *New Statesman*, vol. 113(2919), 6 March 1987, p. 39.

Anthology of Australian Religious Poetry

Ayers, P., *Quadrant*, January/February 1992, pp. 109–10.
Flanagan, M., *Age*, 24 August 1991, 'Saturday Extra', p. 6.
Goodwin, K., *Courier-Mail*, 26 October 1991, 'Weekend', p. 7.
O'Grady, R., *Austlit*, January 1987, p. 20.
Rodriguez, J., *Sydney Morning Herald*, 27 December 1986, p. 28.
Treloar, C., Adelaide *Advertiser*, 7 September 1991, 'Magazine', p. 14.
Van Ikin and Dolin, K., *Journal of Commonwealth Literature*, vol. 23(2), 1988, pp. 15–16.
Wilson, R., *Canberra Times*, 31 August 1991, p. C7.

Selected Poems by A. B. Paterson

Russell, K., *Newcastle Herald*, 21 November 1992, 'Saturday Review', p. 4.

Fivefathers

Jaffa, H., *Antipodes*, vol. 9(2), December 1995, pp. 163–5.
James, C., *Times Literary Supplement*, 5 July 1996, pp. 8–10.
McDuff, D., *Stand*, Spring 1995, pp. 14–15.
McLeod, A., *Choice*, November 1994, p. 462.
Smith, V., *Quadrant*, September 1995, pp. 84–6.

Other works

Connell, W. F. et al., *Australia's First: A History of the University of Sydney 1940–1990*, vol. 2, Sydney: University of Sydney Press and Hale & Iremonger, 1995.

Coombs, Anne, *Sex and Anarchy: The Life and Death of the Sydney Push*, Sydney: Viking Books, 1996.

Dallen, R. A., *The University of Sydney: Its History and Progress Illustrated*, Sydney: Angus & Robertson, 1914.

Fischer, G. L., *The University of Sydney 1950–1975*, Sydney: University of Sydney Press, 1975.

Frost, A. K., *Paterson Easton Family History*, Taree: privately printed, 1985.

Green, J. M., 'Major Themes in the Work of Les A. Murray', thesis, School of English, UNSW, 1989.

James, Clive, *Unreliable Memoirs*, London: Jonathan Cape, 1980.

Jost, John, Totaro, Gianna and Tyshing, Christine, *The Demidenko File*, Ringwood: Penguin Books, 1996.

Morelli, Stephen, *Gumbaynggirr Dreaming vol. 1, Stories of Uncle Harry Buchanan translated by the Gumbaynggirr Language and Culture Group*, Kempsey, NSW: Gumbaynggirr Language and Culture Group, 1988.

Murray, Joan, *The History of the Australian Murrays from Roxburghshire, Scotland*, Wingham: Wingham Chronicle, 1981.

Nelson, Penny, *Penny Dreadful*, Sydney: Random House, 1995.

Otto, Rudolf, *The Idea of the Holy: An Inquiry Into the Non-Rational Factor in the Idea of the Divine and Its Relation to the Rational*, trans. [from the German] J. W. Harvey, Oxford: Oxford University Press, 1936.

Riemer, Andrew P., *Inside Outside*, Sydney: Angus & Robertson, 1992.

——, *Sandstone Gothic*, Sydney: Allen & Unwin, 1998.

Rogers, Bob, with O'Brien, Denis, *Rock 'n' Roll Australia: The Australian Pop Scene 1954–1964*, Sydney: Cassell, 1975.

Rolls, Eric, *A Million Wild Acres: 200 Years of Man and an Australian Forest*, Melbourne: Nelson, 1981.

Ruthven-Murray, Peter, *The Murrays of Rulewater: A Genealogical History of a Border Family*, London: RCS Ltd, 1986.

Ryan, John Sprott, *The Land of Ulitarra: Early Records of the Aborigines of the Mid-North Coast of New South Wales*, Grafton: Mid-North Coast Regional Office, Dept of University Extension, University of New England, 1964.

Sturma, M., *Australian Rock 'n' Roll: The First Wave*, Sydney: Kangaroo Press, 1991.

Trask, Willard R., *The Unwritten Song: Poetry of the Primitive and Traditional Peoples of the World*, New York: Macmillan, 1966.

Turcotte, G. (ed.), *Writers in Action*, Sydney: Currency Press, 1990.

INDEX

Murray's poems, indicated by inverted commas, and his published volumes, italicised, are indexed together with all other references.

Abeles, Sir Peter, 101
'Abomination, The' (poem by Les Murray), 41, 131
'Absolutely Ordinary Rainbow, An' (poem by Les Murray), 74, 91, 146, 209, 244, 260, 287, 308 n22
Ackland, Margaret, 270
Adamson, Robert, 156, 161, 162, 169, 170, 200, 202–3, 204, 231, 256
Adler, Louise, 258
'Agitation', 120
Akerman, Anthony, x, 334 n5
Alexander, Christine, xii, 194, 219, 231, 267, 283
Alexander, Peter, 193–4, 231, 235
Alexander, Rebecca, xii
Alexander, Roland, xii
Allen, Bill, 55
'Amanda's Painting' (poem by Les Murray), xi, 271
Anderson, Don, 278–9
Anderson, John, 97
Angus & Robertson, Les Murray's connections with, 129–30, 146, 197–205, 220, 224, 235, 240
'Another Continent' (poem by Les Murray), 125
Anthology of Australian Religious Poetry (volume edited by Les Murray), 222–3
'Anthropomorphics' (poem by Les Murray), 186
'Aphrodite Street' (poem by Les Murray), 227–8
Arnall, Harry (uncle of Les Murray), 29
Arnall, Isobel, *see* Hickling, Isobel
Arnall, Miriam, *see* Murray, Miriam
Arnall, Tasman, 35, 194
'Aspects of Love and War on the Gloucester Road' (poem by Les Murray), 247
'Assault of the Elements' (poem by Les Murray), 90–1
Atwood, Margaret, 166
Australia Council, Les Murray's links with, 145, 147–8, 178, 257–8
Australian Commonwealth Party (founded by Les Murray), 144–5

'Australian Love Poem' (poem by Les Murray), 262–3
Australian Year, The (prose volume by Les Murray), 221
'Away-Bound Train, The' (poem by Les Murray), 120, 121
Ayres, Marie-Louise, xi

'Ballad of Jimmy Governor, The' (poem by Les Murray), 151, 158
'Ballad of the Barbed Wire Ocean, The' (poem by Les Murray), 29, 242
Banning, Lex, 73–4, 97, 98
Barden, Ann, x, 218, 230
Barden, Peter, x, 81–3, 87, 105, 108, 116, 117, 129, 190, 191, 230, 254–5, 260, 265, 324 n15
Barnie, John, x, 154, 185, 186, 189, 193, 207, 216, 218–19, 229, 233, 241, 244, 247, 253, 258
Bateman, Ros, 85–6, 87, 152
'Bat's Ultrasound' (poem by Les Murray), 243–4
Battersby, Jean, 148
Beaver, Bruce, 161
Beazley, Kim, 172, 327 n59, 343 n9
Bell, John, 62
Bement, Peter, 127, 130
'Bent Water in the Tasmanian Highlands' (poem by Les Murray), 182
Beresford, Bruce, 62
Berndt, Ronald M., 176
'Beside the Highway' (poem by Les Murray), 120
Blocks and Tackles (volume of essays by Les Murray), 172
'Blood' (poem by Les Murray), 131
Boden, Ian, 94
Bolton, Ken, x, 162, 170, 202, 203, 263, 280
'Bottles in the Bombed City' (poem by Les Murray), 274
Bourke, Laurence, 249
Boys Who Stole the Funeral, The (verse novel), 29, 142, 187, 192, 204, 205–14, 287
Brady, Sister Veronica, 263, 314 n39, 341 n8
Braude, Dr Peter, x
Brett, Judith, 323 n77
'Broad Bean Sermon, The' (poem by Les Murray), 28, 167–9, 194
Brodsky, Joseph, 186–7, 264

Buckley, Vincent, 94–5, 186, 222, 223, 250, 314 n39
'Bulahdelah-Taree Holiday Song Cycle, The' (poem by Les Murray), 1–2, 176–8
'Burning Truck, The' (poem by Les Murray), 91, 93, 95, 120, 121
'Burning Want' (poem by Les Murray), 40, 45, 268
Burns, William, 166
Burrell, Bill, x
Butler, Richard, 62
Buzo, Alex, 258
Byrne, Mick, x, 63, 76, 88, 89, 147, 148–9, 190, 310 n43, 330 n61

'Cadet Entwhistle and the Sergeant' (first published short story by Les Murray), 56–7
Cairns, Jim, 144
Calwell, Arthur, 199
Campbell, David, 120, 148, 149, 261
Campbell, Jackie, 87–8
Campbell, Roy, 127
Campion, Edmund: 155
'Canberra Remnant, The' (poem by Les Murray), 118–19
Carcanet Press, Les Murray's association with, 220, 239, 274
'Cardiff Commonwealth Arts Festival Poetry Conference 1965, Recalled, The' (poem by Les Murray), 126
Carmody, John, xi, 301 n6 and n10
Catalano, Gary, 164–5
Chamberlain, Lindy, viii, 52, 282
Christer, Nikki, 203
'Circle City' (poem by Les Murray), 149
'City of Tigers' (poem by Les Murray), 92
Clark, Manning, 148, 276–8, 283, 343 n8 and n11
Clarke, John, 258
Clunies Ross, Anna Maria, 270
Clunies Ross, Bruce, x, 185, 249, 270, 278
Coady, Tony, x, 63, 94–5
Colebatch, Hal, 165, 204, 257, 283
Coleman, Alma, *see* Murray, Alma
Coleman, Dianne, 41–2
Collected Poems (book of poems by Les Murray), 205, 263–4, 271
'Comete' (poem by Les Murray), 279–80
'Commercial Hotel, The' (poem by Les Murray), 132
Commonwealth Literary Fund, Les Murray's links with, 152, 156

Compton, Jennifer, 181
Connolly, Margaret, 191, 197–8, 202, 204, 258, 274
'Conquest, The' (poem by Les Murray), 151
'Coolongolook Timber Mill' (poem by Les Murray), 59
Coombs, Anne, 98
Coombs, H. C., 147–8, 153
'Corniche' (poem by Les Murray), 230
Costigan, Michael, 257
'Cotton Flannellette' (poem by Les Murray), 288
'Cows on Killing Day, The' (poem by Les Murray), 243–4
'Crankshaft' (poem by Les Murray), 247
Craven, Peter, 257
Croft, Julian, 200
'Culture-history, Document' (poem by Les Murray), 150
Cummins, Harry, 199
'Cwdeitar, The' (poem by Les Murray), 189
'Cycling in the Lake Country' (poem by Les Murray), 156, 159, 325 n18

Dalton, Maureen, 105
Darville, Helen ('Helen Demidenko'), viii, 52, 280–3
Davis, Elisabeth (née Knowler), x, 63, 106, 141, 149, 190, 289, 291–2, 306 n7
Davis, Walter, x, 62–3, 71, 105, 106, 141, 149, 190, 289, 291–2, 305–6 n7
Dawe, Bruce, x, 151, 161, 222, 323 n71 and n73
Daylight Moon, The (volume of poems by Les Murray), 204, 220–1, 231, 241
Daylight Moon, The (film by Don Featherstone about Les Murray), 247, 250–1
'Dead Trees in the Dam' (poem by Les Murray), 279
'Deaf Language' (poem by Les Murray), 279
'Deck Chair Story' (poem by Les Murray), 95
Deer, Horace, 12, 21
Demidenko, Helen, *see* Darville, Helen
'Deployment of Fashion, A' (poem by Les Murray), 282
'Devil, The' (poem by Les Murray), 30–1
Di Pieri, Stefano, 224
Disney, Walt, 244
'Distinguo' (poem by Les Murray), 107
Dobson, Rosemary, 165
Dodson, Mick, 284
Dodson, Pat, 284
Dog Fox Field (volume of poems by Les Murray), 241–5

'Dog Fox Field' (poem by Les Murray), 241–2
'Dog's Elegy, A' (poem by Les Murray), 245
'Dolores' (poem by Les Murray), 85
Dransfield, Michael, 161, 162
'Dreambabwe' (poem by Les Murray), 271
'Dream of Wearing Shorts Forever, The' (poem by Les Murray), 185
'Driving Through Sawmill Towns' (poem by Les Murray), 120, 121, 122
Duffy, Michael, x, 205
Duffy & Snellgrove (publishers), Les Murray's links with, 205, 292
Duggan, Laurie, 235
Dunlop, Ronald, 121
Duwell, Martin, 204

'Each Morning Once More Seamless' (poem by Les Murray), 238–9
'Eagle Shooter, The' (poem by Les Murray), 70
'Earth Tremor at Night' (poem by Les Murray), 9
Easton, Robert, 6
'East Sydney' (poem by Les Murray), 72
Ellis, Bob, x, 62, 78–81, 84, 85–6, 89, 103, 104–5, 108, 113, 137, 190, 207, 224, 229–30, 250, 266, 309 n44, 313 n28
Ellis, Jennifer, 250
Elzinga, Maarten, 240
'Emerald Dove, The' (poem by Les Murray), 242
'Employment for the Castes in Abeyance' (poem by Les Murray), 114–15, 316 n43
England, Katherine, 168
'Englishman, The' (poem by Les Murray), 77
Equanimities (chapbook of poems by Les Murray), 185, 241
Ethnic Radio (volume of poems by Les Murray), 204, 241
'Evening Alone at Bunyah' (poem by Les Murray), 12, 127, 146
'Evening at Home' (poem by Les Murray), 78
'Exile Prolonged by Real Reasons' (poem by Les Murray), 61

Fabre, Max, 144
Fairbairn, Geoffrey, 277
Fay, Virginia, xi
Featherstone, Don, 247, 250–1
Fenton, James, 260
Ferlinghetti, Lawrence, 155
Fialla, Oliver, 103
'Fire Autumn, The' (poem by Les Murray), 139
'First Essay on Interest' (poem by Les Murray), 183

FitzGerald, R. D., 161
Fivefathers (volume of Australian poems edited by Les Murray), 260–1
Fletcher, John, 229, 336 n5
Forbes, John, 162, 200, 202, 207
'For Helen Darville' (poem by Les Murray), 281–2
Foulcher, John, 166, 200, 246, 249–50
Frances, Gary, 166
Fredy Neptune (verse novel by Les Murray), 3, 23, 30, 51, 64, 71, 87, 89, 91, 99, 114, 141, 142, 216, 238, 241, 250, 265, 285, 286–94, 344 n14
Freeman, Michael, 29
Fuller, Roy, 121

Gani, Dr Jon, x, 272, 273
Gaudron, Mary, 62
Generation of '68', 162, 167, 169, 170, 172, 195, 200–1, 204, 206, 221, 222, 240, 257, 274
Gibb, Tony, 152
Gilbert, Lionel, x, 44
Gilkerson, James (son-in-law of Les Murray), 252–3, 295
Gilkerson, Grace Eleanor Murray (granddaughter of Les Murray), 295
Ginsberg, Allen, 155
Goldsworthy, Helen, 195
Goldsworthy, Peter, x, 166, 191, 195, 200, 204, 208–9, 225, 240, 265, 292
'Goose to Donkey' (poem by Les Murray), 246
Gorton, John, 144, 149
Gosling, Dr, 272
Gould, Alan, x, 163, 166, 180, 183, 187, 190, 191, 195, 199–200, 202, 204, 221, 264
Graneek, Jack, 112, 113, 129, 315 n27
Grant, Jamie, x, 166, 175, 178, 191, 195, 200, 204–5, 225, 234, 245, 257, 258, 340 n41
Grant, Sandy, 204
Gray, Robert, x, 163, 166, 169, 170, 191, 195, 200, 204, 221–2, 224, 258, 330 n64
Gray, Stephen, x, 334 n5
Green, Judith, x
Greer, Germaine, 62, 66
Greig, Douglas, 43
Greig, Marion, 45
Grieves, Vicki (cousin of Les Murray), 213, 298 n44
Griffis, Leila (née Maurer, cousin of Les Murray), x, 1, 25, quoted 23
Griffiths, Gareth, 127–8, 130, 131, 136, 207
Groves, Lynne, xi

Hall, Dick, 145, 190, 192, 334 n 25
Hall, Rodney, 147, 161, 197, 250, 257
Halligan, Marion, 257
'Halt and Turn' (poem by Les Murray), 109
Hampton, Jennifer, 166
Hanson, Pauline, viii, 52, 282
Harpur, Charles, 185
Harrington, Monsignor, 107
Harris, Ellen (née Hile), x, 23, 25, 26, 36, 37–8, 42, 44
Harrison, Keith, 146
Harrison-Ford, Carl, 162
Hart, Kevin, 163, 166, 168, 180, 187, 193, 195–6, 242
Hartcher, John, 53
Hart-Smith, W., 121
Harwood, Gwen, 201
Haskell, Dennis, 59, 165, 204, 219, 246
Hasluck, Sir Paul, 144
Haynes, Felicity, 121, 122
'Head-Spider, The' (poem by Les Murray), 99
Heaney, Marie, 187
Heaney, Seamus, 187, 264
'Hearing Loss' (poem by Les Murray), 225
Hergenham, Laurie, 177
Heseltine, Harry, 231
Hickling, Isobel (aunt of Les Murray), 32–3, 35
Hickling, Patrick (uncle of Les Murray) 32
Hile, Leo, 111
Hile, Thomas, 42
Hirschfeld, Jonathan, 270
Hodgins, Philip, 193, 200, 204, 205, 223–4, 231, 234, 237–8, 240–1, 263, 291
Hogan, Colin, x
'Holy Show, The' (poem by Les Murray), 26
Hope, A. D., 119–20, 130, 142, 149, 161, 165, 243, 264
Horne, Donald, 172, 231
Horowitz, Frances, 125–6
Horowitz, Michael, 125–6, 127
Howard, John, 256, 284
Howard, Pat, xi
Hubert, Marie-Christine, 240
Hughes, Robert, 62, 65, 66
Hughes, Ted, 166, 186, 188, 244, 245, 345 n34
Humphries, Barry, 222
Hutchison, Ruth, x

Idyll Wheel, The (volume of poems by Les Murray), 220
'If a Pebble Fall' (poem by Les Murray), 133
Ilex Tree, The (volume of poems by Les Murray and Geoffrey Lehmann), 121–2, 125, 129, 145, 146, 147, 187

'Ill Music' (poem by Les Murray), 136
'Immigrant Voyage' (poem by Les Murray), 101
'Impulse Resisted on the Manly Ferry' (poem by Les Murray), 173
'In Australia They Spare Only the Kulaks' (poem by Les Murray), 157
'Incorrigible Grace' (poem by Les Murray), 157
'Incunabular' (poem by Les Murray), 67
Independent Monthly (journal), Les Murray's writing for, 205, 259–60, 341 n57
'Infant Among Cattle' (poem by Les Murray), 24
'Insect Mating Flight' (poem by Les Murray), 246
'International Terminal, The' (poem by Les Murray), 237
'It Allows a Portrait in Line-Scan at Fifteen' (poem by Les Murray), 253–4

James, Clive, x, 3, 62, 66–7, 76, 78, 87, 97, 140, 258, 273–4
'Japanese Barge, The' (poem by Les Murray), 92–3, 120
Jardine, Brian, 116
Jenkins, Brian, 73, 97–8, 119–20
Jenkins, John, 162
Jennings, Kate, 258
Jindyworobak poets, 176, 210
Johnson, Bruce, xi
Johnston, Martin, 162, 168
Jones, Alexander, 190, 306 n24
Jones, Barry, 145
Jones, Libby (née Sweet), x, 65–6, 190, 300 n64
Jones, Rhys, 172
'Juggernaut's Little Scrapbook' (poem by Les Murray), 156

Kane, Paul, 224, 249
Keating, Paul, 236, 337 n3
Kelly, Peter, 276–7
Kenneally, Thomas, 136, 151, 281
Kerr, Sir John, 159, 334 n25
Kessler, Clive, x, 63
Kessler, Naomi, *see* Kronenberg, Naomi
Killing the Black Dog (lecture by Les Murray), 267
King, Elizabeth (cousin of Les Murray), 51
Kirby, Don, 134–5, 136
Kirby, Michael, 62
Kiriloff, Constantine, 112, 113, 114, 115, 130, 175, 316 n43

Knievel, Evel, 149
Knowler, Elisabeth, *see* Davis, Elisabeth
Koch, Christopher, x, 95–6, 123, 153, 190, 207, 258, 312 n93
Kocan, Peter, 199, 203, 204, 257
Kramer, Dame Leonie, 153–4, 281, 283
Kronenberg, Naomi, x, 63–4
Kronenberg, Vernon, 63
Kuhner, Herbert, 166, 195
Kunitz, Stanley, 186

'Laconics: The Forty Acres' (poem by Les Murray), 174–5
Lake, Paul, 166
'Lake Surnames, The' (poem by Les Murray), 20
Lansdown, Andrew, 166, 200, 202, 204
Lantry, Shirley, x
Larkin, Philip, 113, 116, 234
'Last Hellos, The' (poem by Les Murray), 266–7
Latham, Jan, xi
Laverty, Peter, 192
Laverty, Piers, x, 190, 191–2, 265, 273, 284, 330 n66 and n69
Lawrie, Les, x, 53, 55, 57–8
'Lecture Halls of the Fisher King, The' (essay by Les Murray), 231–3
Lee, Dennis, 183, 184
Lee, S. E., 121
Leer, Martin, 240
Lehmann, Geoffrey, x, 62, 65–7, 69, 73, 77, 87, 92, 94, 99, 106, 108, 109, 114, 116, 119–23, 132, 136, 141, 146, 147, 149, 151, 152, 166, 168, 190, 200, 208, 221, 235, 288, 298 n42
Lehmann, Leo, 67, 141
Lehbert, Margitt, 240, 260
Leonard, John, 190
Leunig, Michael, 237
Lever, Susan, x, 340 n41, 340 n48
'Levities of the Short Giant' (poem by Les Murray), 3–4, 270–1
Liddell, Jane, *see* McWhirter, Jane
'Like the Joy at His First Lie' (poem by Les Murray), 241–2
Limerick, Mike, 108
Literature Board/Fund of Australia Council, Les Murray's relations with, 189, 204, 217, 240–1, 256–7, 284, 340 n41
Lobban, Eddie, 1, 38, 296 n1
'Love After Loneliness' (poem by Les Murray), 77, 88, 120
Lowry, Elizabeth, 278
Lunch & Counter Lunch (volume of poems), 167–70, 172–3

MacCallum, Mungo, 62
Mackerras, Colin, 62, 73
MacThómais, Ruaraidh, 166
McAuley, James, 125, 126, 161, 261
McCabe, Colin, 50
McCarter, Graham, 278
McCuaig, Ronald, 121
McDonald, Roger, 159, 163, 170, 221
McGuinness, Judy, 98
McGlashan, Len, 103, 112
McInerney, Ross, 77
McInerney, Sally, 151, 208
McCay, Adam, 255
McKinley, Rose, 270
McKinney, Jack, 122
McLaughlin, Edith, x, 55, 56, 58
McLaughlin, Keith, x, 53, 55, 56, 57, 58
McLennan, Doug, 145
McMahon, Sir William, 148, 153
McMaster, Rhyll, 221
McNamara, Frank the Poet, 222
McNicoll, David, 112, 310 n9
McNicoll, Penny, *see* Nelson, Penny
McWhirter, Jane (née Liddell), x
Magassy, Béla, 150
Malouf, David, 168, 177, 186
Manne, Robert, 240, 258, 280–4
'Manoeuvres' (poem by Les Murray), 121
Marks, Amanda, xi, 271
'Masculeene, Cried the Bulls' (poem by Les Murray), 243
Masson, Sophie, x, 278
Masters, Ian, 105
Matthews, Brian, 172, 231
Maurer, Evelyn (cousin of Les Murray), 25
Maurer, George (cousin of Les Murray), 32, 188
Maurer, Lynette (cousin of Les Murray), 32
Maurer, Myrtle (née Murray, aunt of Les Murray), 25, 46, 288–9
Mead, Philip, 263–4
Meadows, Shari (daughter in law of Les Murray), 253, 295
'MeMeMe' (poem by Les Murray), 245–6
'Memories of the Height-to-Weight Ratio' (poem by Les Murray), 129
'Midsummer Ice' (poem by Les Murray), 184
Miller, Duncan, 164
Miller, Nora, x, 302 n42

Millett, John, 194
'Mirror-Glass Skyscrapers' (poem by Les Murray), 152
Modjeska, Drusilla, 203
Molloy, Mike, 63, 84, 94, 108
'Mollusc' (poem by Les Murray), 246
Montgomery, Barbara, *see* O'Neill, Barbara
Moorhouse, Frank, 231
Morelli, Berta (mother-in-law of Les Murray), 100, 104, 105, 110, 113, 139, 142, 152
Morelli, Cornelia, 102
Morelli, Gino (father-in-law of Les Murray), x, 100–2, 104, 105, 110, 113, 139, 142, 152, 251
Morelli, József, 102, 104
Morelli, Stephen (brother-in-law of Les Murray), 100, 110, 209, 315 n7, 333 n22
Morelli, Valerie, *see* Murray, Valerie
'More than an Obiter Dichter' (poem by Les Murray), 182
Muddle, Bruce, 81–3
Mulhall, John, x, 69–70, 81–3, 108, 190
Murdoch, James, x, 53, 55
Murdoch, Rupert, 197, 201, 204
Murphy, Judy (cousin of Les Murray), 152
Murphy, Richard, 166
Murray, Agnes (great-great-aunt of Les Murray), 6, 7, 10, 12
Murray, Alexander Joseph Cecil (son of Les Murray), 22, 179, 215–16, 217, 218, 230, 241–2, 252, 253–4, 269–70, 288, 295, 334 n5
Murray, Alice (aunt of Les Murray), x, 37
Murray, Alma (née Coleman), x, 23, 29, 41–2, 46
Murray, Archie (uncle of Les Murray), 19
Murray, Cecil Allan (father of Les Murray):
  alcoholism, horror of, 15, 192
  beaten by his father and brother, 13, 15, 41
  beats Les Murray, 25, 27
  birth, 15
  Catholicism, disaffection from, 108, 218
  courtship and marriage, 16–17
  death, 261–7
  evicted from his farm, 2, 111–12, and returns to it, 173
  Forty Acres, living on, 173, 217
  generosity, 68, 80, 110, 192
  grief, 38–9, 43, 183
  health, 218, 261–7
  humour, 16, 20, 69, 70, 105, 175, 218, 265
  imagination and fantasy, love of, 175, 262, 290
  indulgence of his grandchildren, 175, 218
  inhibitions, 37, 40, 90
  literacy, 15
  musical abilities, 16, 218, 278
  panic, tendency to, 37
  poverty, 20–2, 25–6, 34, 70, 111
  pride, 19, 23, 35–7, 111
  provokes Les Murray, 237
  quarrels with Les Murray, 68
  resentment of his father and brothers, 19–20, 111–12, 287
  strength, 15, 24, 69
  timber-cutting, 2, 13, 15
  uncivilization, 38–9, 69, 218
  worries about Les Murray, 58, 61, 68, 70, 94, 97
  women, relations with, 16–17, 41–2, 62, 90, 218, 252
Murray, Charlie (uncle of Les Murray), x, 12, 13, 27, 28, 29, 94, 111
Murray, Christina Miriam (daughter of Les Murray), x, 116–17, 118, 133, 142, 152, 175, 179, 188, 217, 234, 252–3, 254, 262–3, 295, 300 n56
Murray, Clare Luisa (daughter of Les Murray), xii, 179, 217, 252, 255, 268, 273, 295
Murray, Daniel Allan (son of Les Murray), x, 116, 133, 139, 142, 152, 178, 179, 217, 253, 254, 295
Murray, Darryl (cousin of Les Murray), xi, 297 n21
Murray, Emily (née Payne, grandmother of Les Murray), 13, 15, 19, 21, 27
Murray, Eric (uncle of Les Murray), 111, 218, 265
Murray, George (great-great-uncle of Les Murray), 8
Murray, Hannah Rose (grand-daughter of Les Murray), 295
Murray, Hugh (great-great-grandfather of Les Murray), 5–6, 7, 9, 10, 11, 12
Murray, Isabella (great-great-great-grandmother of Les Murray), 1, 5, 7, 8, 10, 17
Murray, Isabella (great-grandmother of Les Murray), 11
Murray, James (great-great-uncle of Les Murray), 6, 174
Murray, Sir James Augustus, 6, 115
Murray, Jane (great-aunt of Les Murray), 29, 37, 66
Murray, Joan, 296 n2

Murray, John (great-great-great-grandfather of Les Murray), 5, 10
Murray, John (great-great-uncle of Les Murray), 8
Murray, John ('Bunyah Johnny', great-grandfather of Les Murray), 7, 10, 11, 12
Murray, John Allan (grandfather of Les Murray), 10, 12–13, 15, 17, 19, 21, 27, 34, 37, 111, 174
Murray, John (cousin of Les Murray), 41
Murray, General Sir John Irvine, 6
Murray, Lavinia (cousin of Les Murray), 247
Murray, Leith (cousin of Les Murray), 111, 174, 328 n69
Murray, Leslie Allan:
    Aborigines, influence of, 1, 9, 11, 14, 16, 38, 64, 67, 83, 114, 136, 144, 147, 151, 158, 172, 176–8, 206–14, 215, 219, 222, 247, 283–4, 293, 334 n26
    academics, dislike of, 76, 132, 153–4, 172, 180, 193
    animals, love of, 27, 59, 97, 132, 244–6, 247, 302 n48
    animals, abuse of, 32, 41, 42, 54, 70, 90
    autism, belief in his own, 25
    baptism, 22, 107
    beatings, 24–5, 116–17, 152, 179–80
    biography, agrees to cooperate on, xi, 285–6
    birth, 18–19, 40
    Bunyah, links with and love of, 1–2, 10, 112, 173–5, 186, 214, 215, 218–19, 247, 274
    Bunyah dialect, use of, 14, 20, 158–9, 290
    Catholicism, influence of, 85, 100–7, 134, 137, 139–40, 218 and passim
    Celtic heritage, 5–15, 30, 127, 132, 133, 136, 137, 174, 182–3
    childhood, 22–33, 175, 220
    children, resentment of, 34–5, 41–2
    children, love of, 179, 215–16, 217, 218, 252–3
    class-consciousness, 21, 64, 72, 155–6, 184, 259–60
    confinement or restriction, hatred of, 24, 27, 117
    conversation, 72–3
    courage, ix, 3
    critical reception of his poems, 121–2, 231
    deafness, 225–6, 252
    dentists, fear of, 72, 128
    dependence on his wife, 234
    depression, 30, 40–3, 80–99, 117, 136, 142, 148–9, 152, 179, 193, 196, 204, 218, 224–37, 259, 265–7, 287 and passim
    dirtiness, 48, 71–2, 84, 303 n7
    driving, love of dangerous, 131, 139, 149, 190, 230, 234
    drugs, use of, 88, 98, 233
    economics, views on, 144, 145, 156, 205, 248
    editing skills, 77, 85, 92–3, 95, 109, 123, 163–7, 198–201, 221–4, 240, 260–1
    essays, Les Murray's, 171–2
    fashion, hatred of, 47–51, 129–30, 171–2, 259–60, 280, 281–3
    feminism, viii, 23, 98, 142, 206–7, 293
    films, love of, 44, 54, 64, 68, 72, 80, 104, 247, 250, 290–1
    flag, desire for a new, 144, 153
    Forty Acres, love of, 2, 173–5, 186, 217, 247, and moves to, 217–18
    friends, Les Murray's wide range of, 191
    general knowledge, 28–9, 55–6, 71, 73, 82, 115, 194
    health, 1–4, 224–5, 229, 251, 262, 339 n13
    honorary degrees, 112, 183
    humble upbringing and poverty, 17, 19–21, 71, 93–4, 113, 122
    humour, 72, 89, 126, 129, 142, 149, 188–9, 191, 263, 274
    intelligence, 25–6, 28, 67–8, 71, 73, 85, 103, 180
    isolation, 25, 34, 44, 47–58
    jobs, dislike of, 110, 112, 117–18, 142, 153
    Judaism, influence of, 63–4, 81, 100, 237–9, 293, 298 n46
    language, love of, 28, 30, 44–5, 55, 134, 238, 290
    languages, knowledge of, 3, 57, 67–8, 73, 76, 82, 86, 89, 94, 104, 112, 114–15, 128, 133, 137, 165, 166, 173, 174, 185, 238, 239–40, 247, 261, 270, 290
    literary influences, 26, 27, 30–1, 32, 46, 56, 58, 73–4, 77, 80, 82, 90, 91, 93, 120, 130, 169, 260–1, 291
    literature, love of, 44, 46, 56, 58, 71, 76
    marriage to Valerie Morelli, 107–8 and passim
    memory, 56, 181–2, 254–5
    Modernism, hatred of, 56, 80, 106–7, 120, 126, 233, 263–4

music, 64, 94, 98, 306 n19
near-death from liver abscess, 1–4, 272–5
numeracy, lack of, 94, 131
paranoia, 230–1, 241, 249–50
physical appearance, 27, 48, 53, 71–3, 79, 180–1
poetic vocation, 2, 26, 30, 31, 38, 59, 65–6, 68, 73–4, 76, 112, 305 n75
poetic theories, 74, 75, 91–2, 106–7, 126, 135, 154, 214, 222, 223–4, 238-9, 287
poet laureate, potential, 188, unofficial, 256
political beliefs, 142–5, 157, 159–60, 239, 256, 257, 259–60, 281–2
political persecution suffered by, viii, ix
postcards, love of, 165–6, 291
private mythology, 40, 54, 289
prizes, grants and honours, 122, 132, 133, 151–2, 154, 155, 156, 159, 172–3, 178, 187–8, 217, 230, 231, 236, 243, 256, 257–9, 260–1, 269–70, 280, 345 n34
precocity, 28–9, 44
prejudiced against intellectuals, 76, 132, 153–4, 172, 180, 193
publishers, Les Murray's, 186–7, 204, 205, 220–1, 245, 263, 292, 335 n22
quarrels with his father, 68, 237
rage, fits of, 25–6, 152
reconciliation of Australian cultures, Les Murray's desire for, 176, 209, 211, 221–2
religious upbringing and spiritual beliefs, 22, 23, 31, 62-3, 75, 91–2, 97, 104, 106, 107, 151, 154–5, 172, 177, 186, 188–9, 222–3, 238, 241, 246, 266, 273, 293, 339 n25
republicanism, 142–4, 159–60, 172, 259–60
reviews, Les Murray as writer of, 167, 169–70, 171, 326 n35
Satan, Les Murray as, 103
schooling, 28–9, 31–3, 43, 46, 47–58, 229–30, 242, 255
sex, terror of, 40, 49, 50, 52, 64, 80, 86, 88, 99
shooting, expertise at, 40–1, 53, 69–70, 219, 302 n39
short stories, Les Murray as writer of, 56–7, 78
shyness, 44, 48, 103, 193
social polish, 194, 255

speech impediment, 48
strength, physical, 3, 43–4, 50, 82, 112, 116, 130, 139, 150, 190, 224–5
sympathy for the underdog, 52, 67, 151, 289
university education, 38, 58, 61–94, 110, 142, 154, 220
untidiness, 44, 53, 71–2, 73, 79–80
walks, love of, 28, 40–1, 59, 82–3, 135–6, 218, 224
war, fascination by, 29–30, 42, 45–6, 53, 55, 66–7, 77, 82, 95, 137, 142
weight, 48, 53, 73, 93, 97, 103, 116, 128, 139, 182, 224, 237, 257, 274
women, relations with, 34–40, 45, 47–58, 54, 80, 84–8, 103, 104, 274
writing, 56–7, 58, 71, 76, 93, 134–5 and passim
writer and reader on university campuses, at literary festivals etc, 142, 155, 173, 180–1, 186, 187, 207, 217, 231, 237, 261, 264–5, 269, 285–6, 314 n4
Murray, Margaret (great-great-grandmother of Les Murray), 5, 7, 10
Murray, Mavis (neighbour of Les Murray), xii, 13, 36, 37
Murray, Miriam Pauline (née Arnall, mother of Les Murray):
  ancestry, 16
  compassion, 23, 27, 34
  competence, 20–4, 116
  coldness, 23, 35, 40, 116
  courtship and marriage, 16–17
  death, 2, 34–8, 41, 183–5, 220, 265, 272, 294
  French, knowledge of, 57
  hardship faced, 18–23
  love of Les Murray, 23, 61
  Newcastle upbringing, 2, 16, 28
  nursing skill, 27
  pregnancy, 18, 34–8
Murray, Nettie (aunt of Les Murray), 262–3
Murray, Oscar (cousin of Les Murray), 42
Murray, Peter Benedict (son of Les Murray), 217, 269–70, 295
Murray, Ray (cousin of Les Murray), 32, 40, 127, 131, 336 n43
Murray, Reg (uncle of Les Murray) 174, 263
Murray, Robert (great-great-uncle of Les Murray), 8
Murray, Sam (uncle of Les Murray), 40, 43
Murray, Stanley (uncle of Les Murray), 13, 15, 17, 19, 42

Murray, Thomas (great-great-uncle of Les Murray), 6
Murray, Valerie, née Morelli (wife of Les Murray):
  appearance, 102, 105–6, 108
  artistic gifts, 103, 241, 268–9
  biography, agrees to cooperate on, xi
  birth, 100
  breadwinner for family, 110, 116, 142, 152–3, 154, 257–8
  character, 102
  courage, ix
  competence, 116, 118, 119, 194
  depression, 148–9
  diary, 179, 217, 229, 236–7
  discipline, 102
  fears death of Les Murray, 2
  health, 252
  languages, knowledge of, 101, 102, 103, 138, 165, 270
  marriage to Les Murray, 107–8
  meets Les Murray, 99, 102–4
  religious belief, 102, 107
  restraining influence on Les Murray, 179, 234–5
  teaching, 110, 116, 142, 147–8, 152–3, 154, 179, 217, 218
  travels, 100–4, 187, 230, 239, 269–70
  upbringing, 100–4
  wisdom, 128, 152, 229
Murray, Veitch (great-great-uncle of Les Murray), 8
Murray, Walter (great-great-uncle of Les Murray), 8
Murray, William (great-great-uncle of Les Murray), 6
'Mr Cuthbert and the Devil' (early short story by Les Murray), 57
'My Ancestress and the Secret Ballot' (poem by Les Murray), 7–8
Mylan, John, 32

'Names of the Humble, The' (poem by Les Murray), 157, 158
Nelson, Annette, x
Nelson, Jeremy, 63
Nelson, Michael, x, 68, 73, 87
Nelson, Penny (née McNicoll), x, 81, 84–5, 87, 90, 91, 94–5, 105–6, 108, 111, 112, 164, 175, 190, 207, 236, 241, 243, 250, 254, 255, 291, 310 n9
'New England Farm, August 1914, A' (poem by Les Murray), 120, 121

'New Moreton Bay, The' (poem by Les Murray), 195
New Oxford Book of Australian Verse (edited by Les Murray), 221
New Poetry (literary journal), Les Murray's links with, 156, 162, 169
Newton, Harry, 87
'Noonday Axeman' (poem by Les Murray), 10–11, 15–16, 120, 121
Norling, Robin, x, 50, 54–5, 56, 147, 284
Nostradamus Kid, The (film by Bob Ellis with character based on Les Murray), 250
'Notes from the House of Mrs Harvey' (poem by Les Murray), 86–7
Nuttall, Jeff, 126

Oakes, Laurie, 62
Oakley, Barry, 108
O'Connor, Mark, x, 165, 180, 186, 189–90, 191, 195, 237, 256, 258, 259, 340 n41, 340 n48
'Octave of Elephants, The' (poem by Les Murray), 246
O'Donoghue, Barry, 165
O'Driscoll, Dennis, 166, 258
O'Hara, Greg, x, 63, 69, 71, 74–5, 89–90, 108, 110, 111, 114, 116, 117, 119, 142–4, 190, 246
O'Hara, Maureen, x
O'Neill, Barbara, 284–5
'One Kneeling, One Looking Down' (poem by Les Murray), 248, 338 n43
Osborne, Alan, 127
Otto, Rudolf, 92
Owen, Jan, 204

Padel, Ruth, 280
Page, Geoff, 157, 163, 181, 191, 200, 204, 221, 225, 274, 283–4
Paperbark Tree, The (volume of essays by Les Murray), 172
'Past Ever Present, The' (poem by Les Murray), 242
Paul, John, x, 276, 277
Pearson, Gail, x
Peasant Mandarin, The (volume of essays by Les Murray), 172
People's Otherworld, The (volume of poems by Les Murray), 184, 187, 204, 241
'Performance' (poem by Les Murray), 181
Perkins, Charles, 148
Persistence in Folly (volume of essays by Les Murray), 172

Perry, Grace, 123, 162–4, 166, 194–5
Phillips, Sue, 201
'Physiognomy on the Savage Manning River' (poem by Les Murray), 8–9
Plomer, William, 126, 166
Poems Against Economics (volume of poems), 153, 156–9
'Poetry and Religion' (poem by Les Murray), 224
Poetry Australia (literary journal), Les Murray's connections with, 123, 162–7, 191, 194–5, 197, 200
Poetry Society, 123, 163
Pollnitz, Christopher, x, 242–3, 249–50, 339 n5
Porter, Dorothy, 206
Porter, Peter, x, 140, 159, 166, 168, 170, 172, 182, 191, 195, 208, 222, 327 n54
Potter, Helen, 270
Powell, Craig, 167, 171
'Prime Numbers' (poem by Les Murray), 285–6
Pringle, John Douglas, 207
'Privacy' (poem by Les Murray), 120
'Property' (poem by Les Murray), 76–7, 120
'Prosper the Commonwealth' (poem by Les Murray), 132
Pryke, Roger, 63

Quadrant (literary journal), Les Murray's links with, 172, 240, 280–4
'Quality of Sprawl, The' (poem by Les Murray), 183

Rabbiter's Bounty, The (American title of Les Murray's *Collected Poems*), 264
Radford, Ann, 87
'Rainwater Tank' (poem by Les Murray), 22
Rankin, Jennifer, 166, 195
'Recourse to the Wilderness' (poem by Les Murray), 96
'Red Cedar' (short story by Les Murray), 78
Redgrove, Peter, 166
Reedy, Jack, 149
Reinhardt, Olaf, x, 76, 87, 102, 113, 116–17, 149, 190, 193, 310 n34
'Requiem for a Revolutionary Army' (poem by Les Murray), 145
'Reticence, A' (poem by Les Murray), 275
Richardson, Dr Michael, 235
Riddell, Alan, 146
Riemer, Andrew, 281
Robinson, Roland, 260

'Rock Music' (poem by Les Murray), 51
'Rollover, The' (poem by Les Murray), 248
'Roman Cage Cups' (poem by Les Murray), 220
Rose, Peter, viii, ix, x
Rowe, Mary, 23
Rowe, Noel, 242
Rowbotham, David, 222
Ryan, Prof. J. S., 209, 210
Ryan, Gig, 162

Saffron, Abe, 79
Salom, Philip, 222
Sambell, John, 46
Sambell, Lily (née Paterson, cousin of Les Murray), xi, quoted 14, 23, 28, 32
'Satis Passio' (poem by Les Murray), 135
Saul, Peter, x, 3
Schmidt, Michael, 220, 274, 335 n23
Scott, John A., 162, 206
Scupham, Peter, 220
'Self-Portrait From a Photograph' (poem by Les Murray), 251–2
'Senryu' (poem by Les Murray), 146
'Session in Camera' (poem by Les Murray), 288
'Seven Cities' (poem by Les Murray), 138
'Seven Points for an Imperilled Star' (poem by Les Murray), 151, 156
Shapcott, Tom, 159, 161, 163, 187, 250
Sharah, Jemal, 258
Sharma, Anurag, x, 193
Sheldon, John, 73
'Shower' (poem by Les Murray), 182
'Sidere Mens Eadem Mutato' (poem sequence by Les Murray), 64, 67, 76, 80, 104
Sigel, Karla, x, 192
Simon, Ella, 247
Simpson, R. A., 146
Singer, Peter, 281
'Singing to the Butcherbirds' (poem by Les Murray), 269
'Sleepout, The' (poem by Les Murray), 20
Slessor, Kenneth, 93, 120, 122–3, 146, 152, 170, 172, 190, 260, 311 n73
Smith, Angela, x, 181–2, 183, 193, 206, 220, 222, 244, 254, 262, 269, 274
Smith, Bernard, 172
Smith, Grahame, 183, 269
Smith, Keith, 123
Smith, Vivien, 121, 222
'Smell of Coal Smoke, The' (poem by Les Murray), 2, 28
'SMLE' (poem by Les Murray), 158–9

Sontag, Susan, 187
Soyinka, Wole, 126, 186
Sparrow, Ruth, x
'Spring Hail' (poem by Les Murray), 59–60, 112, 117, 120
Stead, Karl, 220–1
'Steel, The' (poem by Les Murray), 18, 35–6, 38, 39, 183–4, 224
Stewart, Douglas, 93, 95, 129–30, 190, 311 n74
'Stockman Songs' (poem by Les Murray), 158
Stoneking, Billy Marshall, 201
Strand, Mark, 186
'Strangler Fig' (poem by Les Murray), 246
Strauss, Jennifer, x, 262–3
Strehlow, Theodore George, 222
Subhuman Redneck Poems (volume of poems by Les Murray), 278–80, 293
Suters, Ralph, 50, 284
Sweet, Libby, *see* Jones, Libby
'Sydney and the Bush' (poem by Les Murray), 175

'Tableau in January' (poem by Les Murray), 120
Tate, Senator Michael, 256
Tavallaie, Mohammad, x, 192
Thatcher, Margaret, 183
Thomas, Mark, 335 n33
Thompson, John, 74
Thompson, Tom, 198, 200–5, 257, 340 n35
'Three Interiors' (poem by Les Murray), 138–9
'Three Tries at Englynion' (poem by Les Murray), 131
'Tin Wash Dish, The' (poem by Les Murray), 21, 43, 231, 242
Tjiong, Dr, 225–6
'Torturer's Apprenticeship, A' (poem by Les Murray), 51–2, 53–4, 242
'Towards the Imminent Days' (poem by Les Murray), 151, 315 n15
'Trainee, The' (poem by Les Murray), 78
Translations from the Natural World (volume of poems by Les Murray), 186, 205, 244–7, 258–9, 287
Tranter, John, x, 156, 161, 162, 163, 166–7, 169–70, 200, 203, 204, 221, 231, 240, 241, 250, 256, 340 n51, 341 n11
Treece, Henry, 127
Treloar, Carol, 155, 170
Trocchi, Alexander, 126
Tulip, Jim, 146, 159

Turner, Brian, 258
'Two Dogs' (poem by Les Murray), 245
'Tympan Alley' (poem by Les Murray), 268

Vernacular Republic, The (selection of Les Murray's previously collected poems), 170–1, 204
Viidikas, Vicki, 161
'Vindaloo in Merthyr Tidfyl' (poem by Les Murray), 130
Voznesensky, Andrey, 155

Wagner, Peter, 63, 108, 306 n13
'Waking up on Tour' (poem by Les Murray), 265
Walcott, Derek, 187, 188, 220, 264
'Walk With O'Connor, A' (poem by Les Murray), 133, 135, 146
'Walking to the Cattle-Place' (poem by Les Murray), 156, 157, 193
Wallace, Bob, x, 50, 56
Wallace-Crabbe, Christopher, x, 95, 191, 201, 222, 223, 254, 258, 312 n89, 335 n33
Walsh, Richard, 62, 85, 197, 200, 201
Watkins, Vernon, 126
Wearne, Alan, 206, 228–9
Weatherboard Cathedral, The (volume of poems), 134, 146–7, 197, 241
Webb, Francis, 166, 261
'Wedding at Berrico, The' (poem by Les Murray), 252–3
Weilley, John, 250
Weilley, Susanna, 250
Welton, Kenneth, x, 81–3, 93, 108, 190
'Where Humans Can't Leave and Mustn't Complain' (poem by Les Murray), 252
Wherrett, Richard, 62
White, Patrick, 185
Whitelock, Derek, 122, 130
Whitlam, Gough, 145, 159, 190, 210, 334 n25
'Widower in the Country, The' (poem by Les Murray), 39, 120, 122
'Wilderness, The' (poem by Les Murray), 83
Wilding, Michael, 162
Wilson, Steve, 208
Windsor, Gerard, xi, 231
'Windy Hill' (poem by Les Murray), 134
'Winter Rising, The' (poem by Les Murray), 120
Woolley, Pat, 162

Working Forest, A (volume of essays by Les Murray), 172
Worth family, connection with Les Murray, 16, 213
Wright McKinney, Judith, x, 118, 122, 161, 170, 185, 209–14, 221, 247, 264, 334 n25

Yarjanian, Atom, 288–9
'You Find You Can Leave It All' (poem by Les Murray), 3

Zaunders, Lee, 270, 272
Zwicky, Fay, 231, 263, 341 n8

[Background letter, partially visible:]

...yes, it was my 50th birthday, and
...erly delighted by your kindness in sendin...
...ent. And what a good, honest, sensible...
...you're quite right: I did admire that kni...
...the day you had us over to lunch (the...
...ked that... and I'm
...d for th... in finding
...om and... eat principl...
...in super... you a t...
...t for a... a lump
...d to th...

Than...
a...   ...irthday u...
                                         ...who sen...
he's done...   ...Jamie &...
...ht me...   ...ek, and
t so far...   ...alone pre...
..., outside...   ...is a cool
no way to be confused with friendship. Bu...
...ing to a depressing description Koch gave m...
...writers' 50th birthdays are fêted in European...
...with such vanity: I'm really grateful to hav...
...t all, and with so little mishap ever. The poe...
...of this came from Porcupine Hill, at Gunn...
...s taken to the top of on my long trip ho...
...owne: I send it as a reply to your writing f...

Blood

Pig-crowds in successive, screaming pens
We still to greedy drinking, trough by trough
Tusk-heavy boars, fat mud-beslabbered sows:
Gahn, let him drink you slut, you've had enough

~~Laughing~~ and grave by turns, in milky boots
We stand and yarn, and whet our butcher's knife,
Sling cobs of corn — hey, careful of his nuts!
It's made you cruel, all that gay city life...

In paper spills, we roll coarse, sweet tobacco
That's him down there, the one we'll have to catch
That little Berkshire with the pointy ears.
I call him Georgie. Here, you got a match?

The shadow of a cloud moves down the ridge,
On summer hills, a patch of autumn light
My cousin sheathes in dirt his priestly knife.
They say pigs see the wind. You think that's right?

I couldn't say. It sounds like a good motto.
I know some poets — Yah! get back, you sods.
Let him drink his fill: it's his last feed
He'll get some peaches after. Hell, what odds?

I'm sentimental — 'course, I know you're not.
Beyond the circle of my jabbing stick
Excited mobbing pigs ~~with~~ mindless eyes
Peer at our favourite munching, and the thick